I0834022

Roma parentem,
Roma patrem patriae Ciceronem libera dixit.

JUV. VIII. 243, 244.

M. TULLI CICERONIS

ORATIONES ET EPISTOLÆ SELECTÆ

SELECT ORATIONS AND LETTERS OF CICERO

With an Introduction, Notes, and Vocabulary

BY

FRANCIS W. KELSEY

UNIVERSITY OF MICHIGAN

NINTH EDITION

Wipf & Stock
PUBLISHERS
Eugene, Oregon

Wipf and Stock Publishers
199 W 8th Ave, Suite 3
Eugene, OR 97401

Select Orations and Letters of Cicero
With an Introduction, Notes, and Vocabulary
By Ciceronis, M. Tulli
ISBN 13: 978-1-55635-422-9
ISBN 10: 1-55635-422-3
Publication date 4/20/2007
Previously published by Allyn and Bacon, 1892

PREFACE.

THE orations presented in this edition are arranged in the order which seems most advantageous to the student reading them for the first time; in the Introduction, however, they have been treated in their chronological sequence. In making the selection of letters the political career of Cicero was not specially kept in mind. Only a small proportion of the whole number could find place in a volume of this compass in any case; and so it was thought best to choose letters of more general human interest, which would reveal Cicero the man rather than the politician, at different periods of his life and under different circumstances. The shorter letters in particular may be found suitable for rapid reading, or for sight translation.

The speeches should be interpreted as spoken rather than as written language. In the study of them nothing can take the place of practice in oral delivery, or of the work of the classroom in the rhetorical analysis of sentences, paragraphs, and orations as wholes. At the same time, an oration becomes effective in the degree that it is adapted to the audience and the occasion, — in a word, to its environment; and the interpretation of it will be sound and satisfactory only when the matter, motive, method of presentation, occasion, and surroundings are all clearly understood. In view of this fact it appears unnecessary to offer further justification for the brief discussion, given in the Introduction, of the oration as distinguished from other literary efforts, and of Cicero's life and character, as affecting his oratory; or for the attention paid, in both Introduction and Notes, to the circumstances of delivery and to the subject-matter.

Besides obligation of a more general nature to the critical editions of Cicero's complete works, and to several other of the editions and works mentioned on pp. 356–358, the editor takes pleasure in making acknowledgment of special indebtedness to the editions of the orations by Richter and Eberhard, Halm and Laubmann, and Reid's *Pro Archia;* and to those of the letters by Tyrrell, Boot, and Schütz. He is also under obligations to Professor John C. Rolfe and Dr. W. K. Clement for help on the proofs; and to Assistant Professor Carl W. Belser for assistance in preparing the Vocabulary.

FRANCIS W. KELSEY.

ANN ARBOR, MICHIGAN,
August 15, 1892.

NOTE TO THIRD EDITION.

For the references to Professor Bennett's Latin Grammar given in this edition the editor is indebted to Mr. Anthony Pratt.

F. W. K.

June 15, 1895.

CONTENTS.

ILLUSTRATIONS AND MAPS.

INTRODUCTION.

I. MARCUS TULLIUS CICERO.

i. LIFE OF CICERO.

THE Cicero family was of plebeian stock. From time immemorial it had been settled near Arpinum, an ancient town in the Volscian territory, about sixty miles southeast of Rome. Arpinum had been conquered by the Romans B. C. 305; its inhabitants received the full rights of Roman citizenship B. C. 188. The ancestral estate of the Ciceros lay in the valley of the Liris, near its junction with the Fibrenus, just below the hill on which the city stood. Here MARCUS TULLIUS CICERO was born, January 3, B. C. 106. His grandfather had been prominent in the local affairs of Arpinum; his father was a member of the equestrian order, and enjoyed the friendship of prominent men at Rome,—being withal a man of literary tastes. So when Marcus and his younger brother Quintus were old enough to profit by the educational advantages of the metropolis, their father bought a house in Rome and removed thither.

For a time at least, the brothers studied under teachers recommended by the orator Crassus.[1] Among the intimate advisers of Marcus was the gifted Archias, who aroused in him a decided bent for poetry. In his sixteenth year, B. C. 91,

[1] See Vocabulary, under *Crassus* (1).

Marcus assumed the *toga virilis*,[1] and became a constant attendant at the Forum; for at this time the Forum was an important means of liberal education. Here were the Rostra, from which orators addressed the people; the courts, where the most distinguished men of the time could be seen and heard; places of business, also, where the financial interests of the Roman world centred. In the Forum, too, one might hear the latest news from all quarters, and meet representatives of every nation; and young Cicero was no idle listener. Having been commended by his father to Q. Mucius Scaevola, one of the most learned jurists of the time, he accompanied Scaevola on all occasions, thus accumulating a store of wisdom and experience of incalculable value. At the same time he pursued regular studies with the greatest industry.

In 89 B. C. these pursuits were interrupted for a time by a campaign under the father of Pompey, who was successfully prosecuting the Social War. But on his return to Rome Cicero laid aside all hope of distinction in a military career, and for six years devoted himself to the study of logic, rhetoric, philosophy, and declamation, under the most eminent instructors. One of them — Diodotus the Stoic — afterwards lived in his house and died there. Every day, Cicero informs us, he practised speaking, — sometimes in Latin, oftener in Greek. He also made translations from Greek authors, wrote verses, and composed a treatise on rhetoric. Absorbed in these studies, he passed unscathed through the terrible period of strife between Sulla and the party of Marius.

At the age of twenty-five Cicero entered the courts as a pleader. The most noteworthy of his earlier efforts at the bar is the speech in defence of Sextus Roscius, who had been falsely accused of parricide by Chrysogonus, an influential

[1] See Note to p. 77, l. 30, *praetexta*.

freedman of Sulla. The older lawyers feared to undertake the case; and it required more than ordinary courage to run the risk of incurring the enmity of Sulla, who was then supreme. But the young orator maintained his side with tact as well as vehemence, and came off victorious.

The strain of professional life soon began to wear upon his health. Desirous of a change, in 79 B. C. he went to Athens, where he attended lectures on rhetoric and philosophy. Afterwards he travelled in Asia Minor, and spent some time at Rhodes with Molo, the famous rhetorician, under whom he had previously studied at Rome. After an absence of two years he returned home, not only recovered in health but greatly improved in his style of speaking. His abilities as a pleader quickly gained for him a wide reputation.

Having now reached the age at which Roman citizens were permitted to enter upon the course of advancement in the public offices, Cicero presented himself as a candidate for the quaestorship, and was elected with flattering evidences of his popularity. The year of office (B. C. 75) he spent in Sicily, as quaestor to the praetor Sextus Peducaeus. He discharged the duties assigned him with strict justice and impartiality, — virtues most rare among Roman provincial officers of that period.

Five years later he was called upon to plead the cause of the Sicilians against Verres, who had been governor of the island in the years 73–71, and had robbed, scourged, and in other ways maltreated the inhabitants with unprecedented brutality. Many of the most prominent men at Rome found it for their interest to sustain Verres, who was defended by Hortensius, at that time the most famous pleader in the law-courts. Every obstacle that bribery or influence could raise was thrown in the way of the prosecution. But with indomitable persistency, Cicero surmounted every difficulty. He collected evidence, and opened the case. Before the evidence was all presented, Hortensius abandoned his client, and Verres fled from Rome, preferring voluntary exile to certain condemnation.

Cicero now rose rapidly to the zenith of his popularity and influence. In 69 B.C. he was aedile. It was customary for aediles to celebrate the public games with lavish expenditure of their own money as a bid for popular favor. Cicero, not possessing the means to rival the display of wealthier predecessors, conducted the celebrations without extravagance, but with so good taste that he lost nothing in general estimation. Striking proof of his standing with the people appeared at the time of his election to the office of praetor, B.C. 67.[1]

The year of his praetorship — 66 — was marked by extraordinary activity. His office required him to serve as the highest magistrate for the administration of justice in civil matters, and also to preside at the trial of such criminal cases as might be assigned him. Nevertheless, as the Roman custom permitted, he kept up his practice at the bar, and successfully conducted the defence of Cluentius, who had been accused of poisoning, with one of the most adroit and effective pleas ever made. This year, also, he mounted the Rostra for the first time, and addressed the people in behalf of the bill of Manilius. The significance of this event was not limited to the fact that it was his first appearance as a political speaker. His attitude regarding the measure proposed sorely offended the aristocratic and senatorial party, with whose principles he was really more in sympathy than with those of the opposition; but it secured for him the friendship of Pompey, who might at any time prove to be

[1] See p. 116, ll. 16–19, and Notes.

the successor of Sulla as master of Rome, and it won the enthusiastic support of the populace, with whom Pompey was then the hero of the hour.

On the expiration of his term as praetor, Cicero declined the governorship of a province, which naturally fell to his lot, and directed all his energies toward securing the consulship, the last and highest of the offices in the order of civil preferment. He had six competitors, among whom were Gaius Antonius,[1] an uncle of Mark Antony, and Catiline. These two united to secure the office. They received the powerful support of Marcus Crassus,[2] who had great influence on account of his wealth, and of Julius Caesar, who was coming to the front as a political organizer. Nevertheless, Cicero was elected by an overwhelming majority. Antonius was chosen as his colleague, having received a few more votes than Catiline. The new consuls entered upon their official duties January 1, B.C. 63.

The consulship of Cicero and Antonius was one of the most memorable in the annals of Rome. At the outset an important question of public policy demanded attention. In the December of the preceding year, one of the tribunes of the people, P. Servilius Rullus, had proposed an extravagant scheme for the purchase of lands in Italy for apportionment among the poorer citizens. Cicero's attitude toward the measure in any case could not fail to be one of extreme delicacy. If he opposed it he would jeopardize his standing with the popular party, to which in so great measure he owed his elevation to power; but if he favored it he would alienate the party of the Senate, with whose leaders he appeared now to have come to an understanding. Yet his position was such that he must commit himself to one side or the other. He

[1] See Note to p. 94, l. 34, *collēgae*.
[2] See Vocab. under *Crassus* (3).

spoke against the bill, first in the Senate, afterwards before the people, but with so great tact and persuasiveness that he seems to have suffered no loss of influence. A short time afterwards his power over the masses was shown by the ease with which he quelled a popular movement against L. Roscius Otho, who had incurred the displeasure of the populace by means of a measure providing separate reserved seats at public spectacles for members of the equestrian order.

While consul he defended Gaius Rabirius, one of the few surviving senators who had been present at the murder of Saturninus, thirty-seven years before, and who was now, for political effect, charged with the crime. He also spoke in opposition to a bill proposing the restoration of political rights to the children of those proscribed by Sulla, on the ground that the harmony of the commonwealth would thereby be endangered. But during the latter part of the year all other interests were lost sight of in the excitement attending the discovery of the Catilinarian conspiracy, which for a time threatened to overwhelm the existing order of things in riot and bloodshed. The prompt and efficient action of Cicero averted the catastrophe. He well deserved the honors which were heaped upon him as savior of the State.

After his consulship Cicero again declined the government of a province. Since the expiration of his term as quaestor he had been entitled to a seat in the Senate, in which he now became an active member, at the same time continuing his practice as an advocate. Among other noteworthy cases, in 62 B. C. he defended P. Cornelius Sulla, who had been accused of complicity in the Catilinarian conspiracy, and made his memorable plea for the poet Archias.

In the same year the mysteries of Bona Dea,[1] from which men were rigorously excluded, were celebrated at the house

[1] See Vocab.

of Julius Caesar, then pontifex maximus. P. Clodius Pulcher, a dissolute young patrician, disguised himself as a female musician, and thus gained admission. He was discovered, but made his escape. The offence, on account of its impiety, was brought before the Senate. It was referred to the board of pontifices, who decided that sacrilege had been committed. At the trial which followed, Clodius tried to prove that he was away from the city on the day of the festival; but Cicero testified to having been with him in Rome only three hours before the discovery at Caesar's house. By means of the most shameful bribery and intimidation, Clodius secured an acquittal, and was afterward bitterly attacked by Cicero in the Senate. He thenceforth became an avowed enemy of the orator, all the more dangerous because utterly lacking in principle. Furthermore, Pompey, who had returned from the East loaded with spoils, was led to give up in large measure the advantage he had gained over the other public men, and was drawn into the coalition known as the first triumvirate. As the triumvirs proposed to keep the control of public affairs in their own hands, it was clear that Cicero, through his influence, might work mischief to their plans. Pompey was well disposed toward him; but Caesar, the ruling spirit of the coalition, finally resolved to humiliate the orator, and found in Clodius a suitable instrument.

With Caesar's help Clodius secured an adoption into a plebeian family, that he might become eligible to the office of tribune; and was chosen to this magistracy for the year 58. Early in the year he brought forward a bill to the effect that any one who should be found to have put Roman citizens to death without a trial should be interdicted from the use of fire and water.[1] This was aimed at Cicero, and had refer-

[1] That is, *ut ei aquā et igni interdiceretur,* — the usual formula of banishment

ence to the execution of the Catilinarian conspirators. If he had ignored the attack, assuming his own innocence as a matter of course, he might perhaps have gained the advantage. But instead, thoroughly frightened, he put on mourning, and appeared in public as a suppliant. Many citizens, particularly of the equestrian order, put on mourning also, as a mark of their support. For a time the hostile movement was checked; but the persistency of the tribune availed more than the passing sympathy of the populace. Foreseeing the success of Clodius, in the latter part of March Cicero fled from Rome. He went first to Vibo,[1] then by way of Tarentum to Brundisium, whence he proceeded through Greece to Thessalonica, — a voluntary exile. Immediately after his departure a formal decree of banishment was passed, forbidding him to live within four hundred miles of the city. It was enacted also that any person who should take measures to secure his recall should be pronounced a public enemy.

The spirit of the orator was completely broken. For a time he lost all courage, all hope.[2] Yet within three months after he had gone his friends began to agitate the subject of his return. The consuls and tribunes of the year 57 were well disposed toward him. The triumvirs had accomplished their purposes, and viewed with disapprobation the increasing turbulence of Clodius, whose armed band engaged in frequent riots in the city. Caesar was now in Gaul; but Pompey joined the movement in Cicero's favor. At length the Senate sanctioned a proposal that voters from all parts of Italy should be invited to come to Rome, and unite in passing a bill for his recall. The proposed measure was submitted to the comitia centuriata on the 4th of August, and carried by a large majority. Cicero had come back as far as Dyrrachium

[1] See Vocab. [2] See Ep. VII, VIII., IX.

the previous November. On the very day of the assembly he crossed over to Brundisium, where his daughter met him. He proceeded with her slowly to Rome, being received with congratulations and distinguished honors in the towns along the way. At Rome he was welcomed with extravagant demonstrations of joy. His house on the Palatine and his villas were ordered rebuilt at public expense.

Yet the city was no longer to him what it had been. The triumvirs were all-powerful. They did not deem it necessary to take Cicero into their confidence, and he dared not offer any opposition. In all outward appearances he was friendly to them. He felt obliged to yield to their wishes on many occasions. In their interest, as he himself informs us,[1] he even defended men to whom he had previously been unfriendly. Intervals of leisure in his professional work he devoted to writing. In 53 B. C. he was chosen augur.

On Jan. 20, B. C. 52, the collision between the armed bands of Clodius and Milo occurred at Bovillae, resulting in the death of the former. Cicero undertook the defence of Milo. At the trial, in April, the adherents of Clodius created great disturbance, and Pompey filled the Forum with soldiers. Cicero was afraid to deliver his speech, but afterward wrote it out and sent it to Milo, who had gone into exile at Massilia. In the same year a law was passed that a consul or praetor should not be eligible to the governorship of a province until five years after the expiration of his term of office. In the mean time provinces were to be assigned to ex-consuls and ex-praetors who had not yet had such an appointment. To Cicero was allotted the province of Cilicia, with the surrounding region.

He entered upon his duties in Cilicia on the last day of July,

[1] Cf. Ep. *ad Fam.* VII. I., *ad Att.* IV., V., VI.

B.C. 51. He administered the affairs of the province with great uprightness, but found the position, as he had expected, not at all to his liking. With the help of his brother Quintus, an experienced officer, he subdued certain mountain tribes along the Syrian frontier, and was weak enough to desire a triumph. As soon as the year of his appointment had expired he set out for Rome, reaching the city on the fourth of January, B.C. 49.

In the beginning of the year 49 hostilities commenced between Caesar and Pompey. Cicero, having vainly attempted to bring about a reconciliation between them, hesitated with which to cast in his lot. He finally decided to join the side of Pompey. In June he passed over to Greece, and appears to have been with Pompey till the battle of Pharsalus, which was fought on the 9th of August, B.C. 48. In November he returned to Brundisium. Here he remained unmolested till the following August, when he received a letter from Caesar which relieved him of all apprehensions regarding his personal safety. He now devoted himself to the composition of treatises on subjects connected with rhetoric and philosophy, dividing his time between his different villas.

In 46 he divorced his wife Terentia, whom he had married about the year 79. She appears to have been a high-spirited woman, having withal a large property, regarding the management of which she and her husband did not agree. Being financially embarrassed, he married Publilia, a wealthy young lady, for whom he had been acting as guardian; but this marriage was soon dissolved. The most crushing blow to his domestic happiness was the death, early in B.C. 45, of his daughter Tullia,[1] to whom he had been devotedly attached. For a time he retired to his secluded

[1] See Vocab.

villa at Astura, and gave himself up to grief.[1] Her death left a deep impress upon his writings, which were now more than ever undertaken as a means of consolation.

Cicero was fully in sympathy with the assassination of Caesar (March 15, B. C. 44).[2] In the reaction against the conspirators he thought it unsafe for him to remain in Italy, and started for Greece. As the ship touched at Regium he learned that there was a prospect of reconciliation between Antony and the party of the Senate, and returned to Rome. All hope of a peaceful solution of the existing complications was soon lost. Antony left the city, where Octavianus gradually acquired control. Cicero was once more in a position of influence, the favorite of the people. He assailed Antony before the Senate and from the Rostra, in the so-called Philippic orations.[3] But the coalition of Antony with Lepidus, and of these two later with Octavianus, was fatal to all hopes of the supporters of constitutional liberty. In the latter part of November, B. C. 43, the new triumvirs made out their proscription list. On it were placed the names of seventeen men who were to be put out of the way at once. That of Cicero was among them. The news reached him at Tusculum. He fled to Antium and took ship. Adverse winds prevented escape. He landed at Formiae and remained in his villa there, resolved to meet his fate. When the soldiers of the triumvirs came (Dec. 7), his slaves placed him in a litter and started with him through the woods to the seashore, a mile away. They were overtaken, and prepared for defence. Cicero bade them be quiet, and put his head forth from the litter. The executioners struck off both his head and his hands, took them to Rome, and, by order of Antony, nailed them to the Rostra, — the scene of so many of his triumphs.

[1] See Ep. XXXIV–XXXVII. [2] See Ep. XL. [3] See pp. 51, 52.

ii. Cicero as an Orator.

No just view of Cicero as an orator can be obtained without some knowledge of the nature of oratory, its place in ancient life, and its history up to his time.

Oratory may be defined as the art of persuasion by means of speech. It aims not simply to convince, but to lead to a decision, — to move to action. It is thus distinguished, not only from poetry, the purpose of which primarily is to please, but also from ordinary prose, of which the main function is to make clear to another the thought that one wishes to convey. The oration forms a distinct literary species, with its own traditions, its own laws of structure, and principles of composition.

In the life of Greece and Rome oratory played a much more important part than in that of modern times. In antiquity those who possessed the rights of citizenship, the voters, lived in cities. The land was tilled ordinarily by slaves or subjects, and there was no large farming class, as there is in our country, in possession of the elective franchise, and liable to hold the balance of power between political parties. The number of voters in ancient States formed a small minority of the whole population. Civic life was concentrated. An orator, speaking in the central part of a city, might gather the whole body of citizens within the sound of his voice. In those States where a democratic form of government prevailed, oratory naturally reached its highest perfection; for in the ancient democracies, unlike those of the modern era, questions were submitted, not to representatives of the people, but directly to the people themselves, with whom lay the decision of the most important matters. The easiest way to reach and mould opinion was through public address. This function of oratory has now been almost wholly superseded by the newspaper and the political pamphlet. Wide opportunity for public speaking was afforded also by the larger governmental bodies, as the Council at Athens and the Senate at Rome. Finally, the constitution of the tribunals, referring the decision of cases generally to a much greater number of individuals than the modern courts, was favorable to the development of oratory.

The practice of oratory at an early date in Greece is clearly indicated by the Homeric poems; but to Athens belongs the glory of having first produced great orators. Among the leaders in the earlier period of her history at least two, Themistocles and Pericles, were hardly less famous for their eloquence than for their statesmanship. But the treatment of oratory as an art, under the name of rhetoric, began in Sicily in the first half of the fifth century B. C., when the expulsion of the tyrants from Agrigentum and Syracuse, and the establishment of democracies, created a demand for instruction in this subject. Gorgias, the greatest of the Sicilian teachers of oratory, gave instruction at Athens in the latter part of the same century, emphasizing the poetic coloring of eloquence, while the work of the sophists in the same period tended to point out distinctions in the meanings of words, and directed attention to grammatical usage. The golden age of Athenian oratory lasted from the end of the fifth to the latter part of the fourth century B. C. Among the numerous orators of this period later criticism reckoned ten as pre-eminent: Aeschines, Andocides, Antiphon, Deinarchus, Demosthenes, Hyperides, Isaeus, Isocrates, Lycurgus, and Lysias. Demosthenes was recognized both by his own and by succeeding ages as the greatest of them all. After his death, B. C. 322, with the extinction of Greek liberties, Athenian eloquence rapidly declined. A new type of oratory came into vogue soon afterwards in the Greek cities of the western part of Asia Minor, —

known as the Asiatic style. It was more ornate and artificial than that of Athens, which by way of distinction was known as the Attic style.

At Rome public speaking was extensively practised from an early time. The flourishing period of Roman oratory lay between the end of the second Punic war and the establishment of the Empire. This period of almost two hundred years may be conveniently viewed in three epochs. In the first, the most prominent figure was that of Cato the Censor, whose unpolished but effective oratory reflected his uncompromising sturdiness of character. Among the younger contemporaries of Cato was Gaius Laelius, whose speaking showed more refinement. At this time Greek culture was exerting more and more influence upon Roman life, but in oratory apparently there was no study of Greek models. The second epoch extends from the time of the Gracchi to that of the eminent orators Marcus Antonius, grandfather of Mark Antony, and L. Licinius Crassus, who died B. C. 91. The Greek orators were now studied, and Greek teachers of rhetoric were freely employed; but there was as yet little open acknowledgment of indebtedness to them. The two eminent names of the third period are Cicero and Hortensius. In oratory, as in other fields of literature and art, Greek models were now supreme, being taken as standards of excellence. The question was no longer whether Greece should be the instructor of Rome in eloquence; it was rather, which style of Greek oratory should be followed, the Attic or the Asiatic. This question each Roman settled for himself, some going so far as to confine their study to a single Greek orator as model. Greek teachers of rhetoric abounded everywhere. Hortensius preferred the florid exuberance of the Asiatic style; Cicero's taste inclined rather to the compact simplicity of the Attic, to which, however, influenced no doubt by Asiatic models,

A Roman Orator. From an ancient statue.

in his own speaking he added a richer and more rounded expression.

In Cicero's time the theory of oratory had long since been worked out with so great completeness that modern literary criticism has added nothing of importance to it. The matter of oratory was reckoned of three kinds: *demonstrative*, employed in praising or censuring some one; *deliberative*, used with reference to some measure, or proposal, either in the way of advocacy or of opposition; and *juridical*, employed in the courts, in accusation or defence. Five qualities were considered essential to an orator. These were: *invention*, the power to gather facts and arguments; *disposition*, the ability to arrange matter in the proper or most effective order; *expression*, a choice of words suitable to the thought; *memory*, a firm grasp of matter, words, and arrangement; and *delivery*, a perfect command of the voice, features, and gesticulation. A typical oration was said to comprise six parts, as follows: —

I. INTRODUCTION (*exordium*), designed to win the favorable attention of the audience; often considered of two kinds: —
  - *a.* The Opening (*principium*), preliminary remarks.
  - *b.* The Ingratiating (*insinuatio*), intended by a skilful use of language to remove prejudices and put the audience into a receptive mood.

II. STATEMENT OF THE CASE (*narratio*), a summary of the facts leading up to the point at issue.

III. DIVISION (*partitio*, or *divisio*), indicating the treatment of the theme proposed, or the point to be proved.

IV. PROOF, or affirmative argument (*confirmatio*), setting forth the arguments on the speaker's side of the case.

V. REBUTTAL (*refutatio*, or *reprehensio*), refuting the arguments of the opposite side.

VI. PERORATION, or CONCLUSION (*peroratio*, or *conclusio*), bringing the address to an impressive close; frequently divided into three parts: —

a. Summary (*enumeratio*), a brief recapitulation of the speaker's points.
b. Outburst (*indignatio*), a burst of anger, designed to excite the indignation of the audience against the opposite side.
c. Appeal (*conquestio*), an appeal to the sympathies of the audience.

According to modern ideas of literary analysis, these six divisions may generally be more conveniently grouped in three, thus: —

I. INTRODUCTION: —
Exordium.
Narratio.
Partitio.

II. DISCUSSION: —
Confirmatio.
Refutatio.

III. CONCLUSION: —
Peroratio or conclusio.

This arrangement will be followed in presenting the outline of the eight orations in this edition.

Careful rules were laid down by rhetoricians for the handling of each of the divisions. We are not to suppose that orators held rigidly to the outline given; yet it was regarded as the norm, or type, from which wide deviation was exceptional. The subjects most likely to lead away from it were those which inspired invective. Thus, the orations against Catiline show marked divergence from the typical structure. On the other hand, speeches of a more quiet tone, like that for Pompey's commission, and the majority of those made at the bar, were in this respect more nearly regular.

Cicero possessed all the qualities characteristic of a true orator. He was endowed with great activity and versatility of mind, breadth of view, ready sympathy, and intense feelings, — with a marvellous command of language, nice sense of literary form, and excellent memory; with attractive face and figure, great vivacity of manner, and keen power of repartee. From early youth he cultivated his natural gifts with unflagging industry; fired with the ambition to become the leading public speaker of his day, he set before himself the highest ideals. He realized his ambition; and the verdict of the ages has placed his name, with that of Demosthenes, high above all other ancient orators. His orations lack the conciseness and nervous force, the unabating earnestness of the Greek orator; but in richness and fulness of expression, in beauty of language, he is superior. His words gush forth like a torrent. He is broader in the range of thought and feeling to which he appeals. He is equally at home in the dignified tone suitable to the tragic, and in the stinging jest; in savage invective, and in the graceful language of compliment. Yet no comparison between the two men would be fair which did not take into account the difference in the character of the audiences before which they spoke. The polished, critical, cool-headed Athenian could best be influenced through the reason; the less critical Roman could be more easily swayed by an appeal to the feelings. Cicero was a consummate master of the art of putting things, of saying what he had to say in a way to carry the greatest weight. His points follow one another so naturally that one almost forgets that there is another side of the case. What the other side was, in most instances we do not clearly know; but Cicero always makes his own appear plausible.

On the whole, Demosthenes was stronger in thought, Cicero in literary form. But here, where the greatest power of the Roman orator lay, was also his greatest weakness; for now and then copiousness and charm of expression conceal a paucity of ideas. We are also at times conscious of a lack of sharpness in the statement of points. Yet the orations to-day, though in an ancient and difficult tongue, though read and not heard, continue to please and move us as they have pleased and moved men for two thousand years. How much more must they have stirred those to whom they were addressed!

It has been the fashion in some quarters to style Cicero a declaimer, — to assign the oration for the poet Archias, for example, to the province of declamation rather than of true oratory. All such disparagement rests upon a misapprehension. If the aim of an oration is to persuade, it should be judged according to the effect produced at the time of delivery, as well as by the effect upon the reader. No other Roman ever moved an audience as Cicero did. Witness his speech for Roscius Otho, which transformed a hostile mob, against their will, into an assemblage of well-disposed citizens. He was equally successful as a pleader; his contemporaries declared, says Quintilian, that he reigned in the law courts. For these reasons alone, apart from the overwhelming verdict of posterity regarding the power of his speeches, he would worthily be ranked as the greatest of Roman orators, one of the greatest of the world.

iii. Cicero as a Writer.

At Rome, both in his lifetime and afterward, Cicero was noted hardly less as a writer than as an orator. In his youth he devoted himself to the study of rhetoric and philosophy as a means of training for public speaking; and he retained an interest in both branches, but more particularly in the latter, which appeared to deepen as years passed by. Moments that could be spared from his many engagements were given to reading and to the society of the learned. When driven from his customary pursuits by untoward circumstances, he found diversion and consolation in literary composition. Most of his works were written in the two seasons of enforced retirement from political affairs, — the first after his return from exile, B. C. 57, and the second between his reconciliation with Caesar, B. C. 47, and the autumn after the dictator's death, B. C. 44.

Not including orations, poems, or correspondence, Cicero left not far from thirty different works. Some of them were brief; the rest were in two or more books. Fifteen of these works are still extant, and others are known from considerable sections which have been preserved; a few have entirely perished. His extant writings on rhetorical and philosophical subjects fill five octavo volumes. Those of the former class comprise several treatises dealing with the theory of oratory, and a sketch of the history of oratory down to Cicero's own time. His philosophical works treat a great variety of topics in morals, theology, and political philosophy. His poems consisted in part of translations from the Greek, in part of verses upon Roman themes. Two at least were autobiographical; their titles were, 'On the Events of my Consulship,' and 'On my Times.' Only a few hundred lines of the poems are extant, most of which are from his translation of Aratus. His correspondence was collected and published after his death. The portion extant fills two octavo volumes, and comprises eight hundred and sixty-four letters, of which ninety, however, are addressed to Cicero.

As a poet Cicero was not successful. His verses were metrically correct, but lacked poetic inspiration. His prose writings, however, are characterized by a finish and charm that have called forth universal admiration. His services to the Latin language and literature cannot be overestimated. Previous to his time Latin prose had been crude, awkward, and labored; he developed a flowing and graceful style, which set before later writers a model of refined yet forceful expression. Very little had been written in Latin on the subject of philosophy; so he formed the design of presenting to his countrymen the gist of the Greek speculation in their own tongue. He was admirably fitted for this task by his extended intercourse with teachers of philosophy, his wide reading in the subject, and his own philosophical position, which was eclectic and negative, rather than dogmatic, so that he was able to present the views of the different schools on the whole fairly. He followed Greek models closely, and made few original contributions to the matter which he borrowed. But he coined new Latin terms, introduced illustrations of his own, and gave to the often dry and technical discussions of the Greeks a living and attractive form. In a word, he popularized philosophy, and his writings in this field are of all the greater value now because in many cases the Greek originals have perished. Most of his works, after the example of the Greeks, were cast in the form of a dialogue. The philosophical vocabulary which he developed prepared the way not only for later Pagan writers, but also for a Latin literature of Christian theology. The orderly development of thought, the graceful transitions, the happy perspective observed in the elaboration of points, the balance, yet variety, in the structure of sentences, the harmonious arrangement of words, the faultless phrasing, — these are some of the qualities that have caused several of his works to be accepted as literary masterpieces of the first rank. As a stylist Cicero has had no superior and few equals.

The tone of the correspondence is naturally less formal than that of the treatises. When chatting with intimate friends, as

Atticus, he is frank and artless, — too much so for his reputation; he is more reserved when writing to others. His letters reflect the mood of the moment, — now sparkling with humor, or overflowing with pleasantries; now burdened with trouble, or altogether in despair. Nowhere else do we find so vivid a picture of Roman life in his time; nowhere else, perhaps, except in the autobiography of Benvenuto Cellini, do we have the inmost privacy of a strong mind so unreservedly revealed. The style is matchless for simplicity, clearness, and grace. If the world to-day were to be forced to choose whether it would more willingly part with Cicero's orations, his prose works, or his correspondence, it is doubtful which would be given up with the greatest regret.

iv. Cicero as a Man.

The character of Cicero presents a singular combination of opposite qualities. Modern writers, who have studiously examined the facts of his career, have held the most diverse opinions concerning it. Middleton, for example, finds Cicero almost faultless, and dwells upon his noble qualities in many pages of undiscriminating praise; Mommsen, being unable to glorify Caesar and Cicero at the same time, loses no opportunity to belittle the orator as he lavishes unstinted commendation upon the dictator. It is clear that views so extreme cannot both be just. In all such matters men's opinions are in large measure determined by their point of view. Mommsen fastens his eye upon the constitutional development of Rome, and sees in every change of the later republican period a nearer approach to the inevitable end, — imperialism. With him Caesar is the incarnation of the imperialistic principle, and the upholders of the earlier constitutional usages are short-sighted supporters of a hopeless cause.

To a man holding this view, the orator's power as a speaker and influence as a writer appear of little moment. On the other hand, the biographers of Cicero have generally read into his life the lofty ideals of his moral treatises, and have either ignored or tried to explain away his many inconsistencies. A fairer view may be gained by emphasizing neither aspect of his character unduly, but by subjecting his political activities, his moral ideals, and his daily life to the same impartial scrutiny.

The sources of our knowledge of Cicero are threefold: first, the references in contemporary writers, — chiefly Caesar and Sallust, both of whom were more or less unfriendly to him on political grounds; secondly, his own works; and thirdly, the statements of later Greek and Roman writers, — mainly, Appian, Dion Cassius, Plutarch, Suetonius, and Florus. By far the greater number of facts about him are gleaned from his own writings, particularly the letters. It is safe to say that if his correspondence had not been preserved, his name would have been spared most of the unfriendly criticism that has gathered about it. He was indiscreet enough to think on paper; his passing fancies or suggestions, to most of which he may have given no second thought, are to-day before us, subject to cool critical analysis and comparison. It is said that no man is a hero to his valet. What impulsive person, whose eventful life had brought him into contact with many public men in a trying period, would not shrink from having his most private correspondence given to the world? What man, whose inmost heart should be so revealed, would not be convicted of numberless foibles, weaknesses, inconsistencies? Such are the frailties of human nature; a most unhappy illustration may be found in the Carlyle correspondence, recently published. The letters of Cicero charm and enlighten us, yet show us many things unworthy of a great man; but, after all, deeds are greater than thoughts, more than words. Granted that a high-minded man, whose prominent position brought him many enemies and numberless trials, may have shown himself, in the privacy of friendly intercourse, at times weak and inconsistent with his professed ideals, — should that make us blind to his nobler traits, or to the greatness of his life-work for humanity?

The age of Cicero abounded in eminent men who from childhood had had the advantages of wealth and family prestige in their favor. Cicero entered the lists a 'new man,' without great wealth, without a long line of distinguished ancestry to bring him favorable recognition, apparently without anything in his favor, excepting a limited acquaintance with public men, a fair education, and an ambition to make the most of himself. He practised law, and generally won his cases. He came forward as a candidate, and received from the people unprecedented favor, for a man without powerful connections, in the rapid promotion to public offices. He accomplished all these things by the sheer force of personal effort, in that period of Roman history when the influence of military leaders was rapidly becoming paramount. Surely this betokens no ordinary power.

The natural gifts of Cicero fitted him to be an orator and writer rather than a statesman. His nice sense of balance, and his philosophical habit of looking at all sides of a case, sometimes made it impossible for him to decide quickly where a prompt decision was necessary. His mind was rather of the contemplative than the executive type. His tastes drew him toward the ideal; but an irresistible impulse drove him into practical affairs. He did not escape the contagious passion for political power characteristic of his generation; yet he lacked the steadiness of view, the singleness of aim, the persistency — perhaps also the courage — needful for one who would be more than temporarily great as a political leader. He was possessed also of a naïve and thoroughly good-natured egotism, which asserted itself on all occasions. Yet in an age of bribery, he was never convicted of giving or receiving a bribe. In a period of mad dissipation and debauchery, he remained untainted with vice, and in his affection for his daughter has left us one of the most beautiful pictures of ancient home-life. At a time of broils and violence, he was a man of peace, hating strife, — a man of honor in all the relations of life. That was no unfitting tribute paid him by the historian Livy:[1] 'Sixty-three years he lived, so that his death, except that it was violent, cannot be considered untimely. . . . After both his faults and his virtues have been taken into account, he remains a great, spirited, and distinguished man, to whose praises only the eloquence of a Cicero could do justice.'

V. The Portraits of Cicero.

The name of Cicero has been given to many busts that have come down from antiquity. The great majority of them, however, have no claim to be considered genuine. One famous bust, at Madrid, is marked with the name of Cicero in an inscription undoubtedly ancient; but the head is modern. Of the busts in Italian museums which probably give a true likeness of the orator, three are worthy of mention. One is at Florence, in the Uffizi Gallery. The other two are at Rome, one in the Vatican collection, the other in the Capitoline Museum. The frontispiece of this volume is from the one last mentioned. The expansive forehead, the sensitive mouth, and the open, thoughtful face not free from lines of care, correspond closely with the characteristics of Cicero revealed in his works.

[1] Sen. Suas. vii.

II. THE ORATIONS OF CICERO.

i. General View of the Orations.

Cicero left more than a hundred speeches. Of these, fifty-seven are still extant. Fragments of twenty others remain, and the titles of thirty more are known. The themes and general character of the extant orations may be learned from the following summary: —

1. *Speeches in Legal Cases.*

a. In civil cases.

For Quinctius, delivered B. C. 81; in connection with a suit for debt.

For Roscius the Comedian, 76; in a case concerning payment of damages for the death of a slave.

For Tullius, 72 or 71; in a suit for damages on account of the destruction of property.

For Caecina, 69; in a suit concerning an inheritance.

b. In criminal cases.

For Roscius of Ameria, B. C. 80. See pp. 2, 3.

Against Caecilius, 70; a prelude to the action against Verres.

Against Verres, 70; six speeches in all, of which only the first was actually delivered. See pp. 3, 4.

For Fonteius, 69; against a charge of provincial extortion.

For Cluentius, 66. See p. 4.

For Rabirius, 63. See p. 6.

For Murena, 63; against a charge of corrupt canvassing for votes.

For Cornelius Sulla, 62. See p. 6.

For Archias, 62. See p. 45.

For Valerius Flaccus, 59; against a charge of provincial extortion.

For Sestius, 56; against a charge of violence.

Against Vatinius, 56; for the impeachment of a witness for the prosecution of Sestius.

For Caelius, 56; in a suit arising from an intrigue.

For Cornelius Balbus, 56; against the charge of having illegally assumed the rights of citizenship.

For Plancius, 54; against a charge of bribery.

For Rabirius Postumus, 54; against a charge of extortion.

For Milo, 52. See p. 9.

For Marcellus, 46. See p. 49.

For Ligarius, 46; in favor of a former partisan of Pompey, then in exile.

For Deiotarus, King of Galatia, 45; against a charge of complicity in a plot to murder Caesar.

2. *Political Speeches.*

On Pompey's Commission, 66. See p. 27.

On the Agrarian measure of Rullus, 63; three speeches, the first addressed to the Senate, the second and third to the people. There was a fourth speech, now lost. See pp. 5, 6.

Against Catiline, 63; four speeches. See p. 36.

After Return from Exile, four speeches: the first giving thanks to the Senate, 57; the second thanking the people, 57; the third, 'On his House,' showing that his house on the Palatine, destroyed by Clodius, should be restored at public expense, 57; the fourth, 'On the Answers of the Soothsayers,' against objections to the rebuilding of his house on a site that had been consecrated, 56.

On the Consular Provinces, 56; urging the prolongation of Caesar's command in Gaul; before the Senate.

Against Piso, 55; an abusive attack upon a personal enemy; before the Senate.

Against Antony, 44–43; fourteen orations. See p. 51.

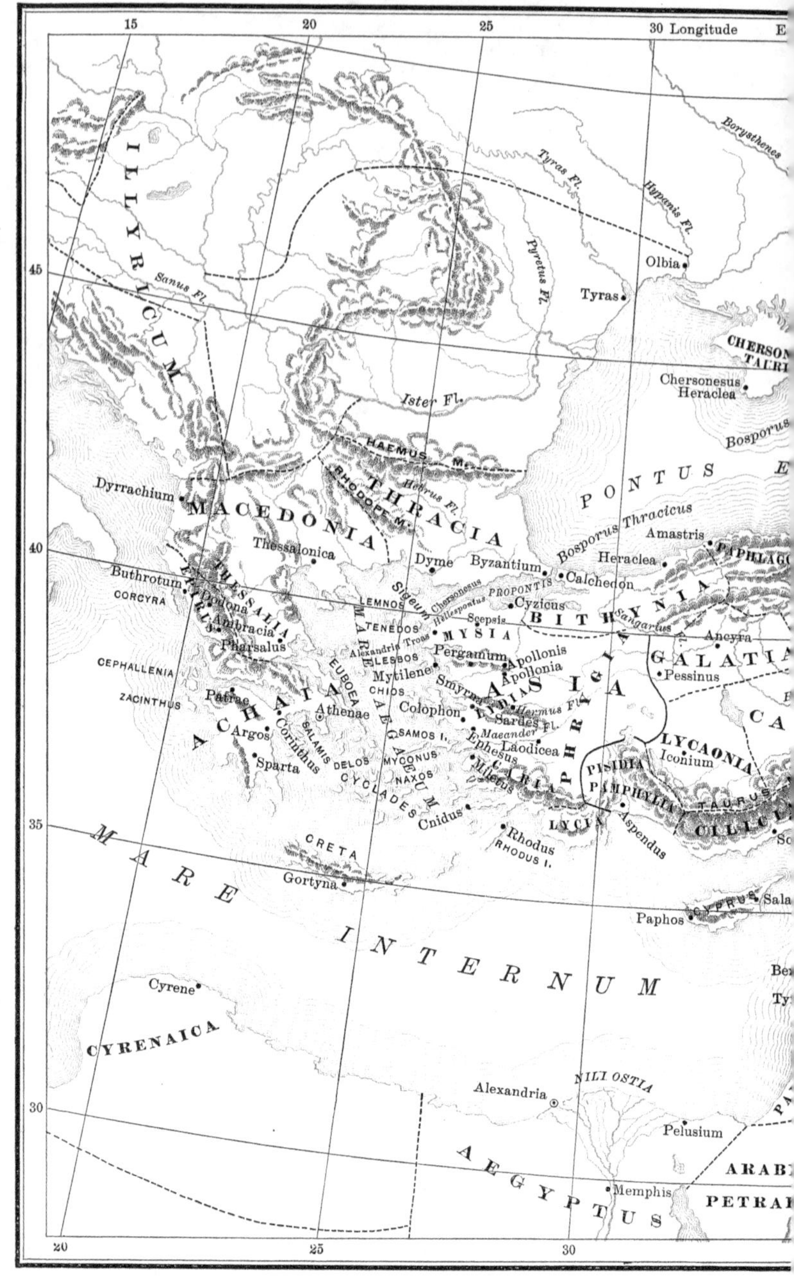

30 Longitude
ILLYRICUM
MACEDONIA
THRACIA
PONTUS
BITHYNIA
GALATIA
ASIA
PHRYGIA
LYCAONIA
PISIDIA
PAMPHYLIA
LYCIA
CARIA
LYDIA
MYSIA
ACHAIA
THESSALIA
EPIRUS
CYRENAICA
AEGYPTUS
MARE INTERNUM
MARE AEGAEUM
Ister Fl.
Tyras Fl.
Hypanis Fl.
Borysthenes
Pyretus Fl.
Sanus Fl.
Hebrus Fl.
Hermus Fl.
Maeander Fl.
Sangarius
HAEMUS M.
RHODOPE M.
TAURUS
Bosporus Thracicus
PROPONTIS
Hellespontus
Chersonesus
Olbia
Tyras
Chersonesus
Heraclea
Dyrrachium
Thessalonica
Dyme
Byzantium
Calchedon
Heraclea
Amastris
Cyzicus
Scepsis
Sigeum
Buthrotum
Dodona
Ambracia
Pharsalus
CORCYRA
CEPHALLENIA
ZACINTHUS
Patrae
Corinthus
Argos
Sparta
Athenae
SALAMIS
EUBOEA
LEMNOS
TENEDOS
Alexandria Troas
LESBOS
Mytilene
CHIOS
Pergamum
Apollonis
Apollonia
Smyrna
Colophon
Sardes
SAMOS I.
Ephesus
Laodicea
Miletus
DELOS
MYCONUS
NAXOS
CYCLADES
Cnidus
Rhodus
RHODUS I.
Ancyra
Pessinus
Iconium
Aspendus
CRETA
Gortyna
Paphos
CYPRUS
Cyrene
Alexandria
NILI OSTIA
Pelusium
Memphis
ARABIA
PETRAEA
15
20
25
30
45
40
35
30
20
25
30

Greenwich
40
45
50
55
45
40
35
30
Tanais Fl.
Phanagoria
Hypanis Fl.
MARE CASPIUM
CAUCASUS M.
COLCHIS
Dioscurias
Phasis Fl.
Amisus
Trapezus
Cabira
Comana
Cyrus Fl.
Artaxata
ARMENIA MINOR
Niphates M.
ARMENIA
Araxes Fl.
Euphrates Fl.
TAURUS M.
MEDIA
ATROPATENE
MEDIA
MAIOR
Tigranocerta
MESOPOTAMIA
Carrhae
Chaboras Fl.
ASSYRIA
Lycus Fl.
Caprus Fl.
Tigris Fl.
Antiochia
SYRIA
Damascus
REGNUM PARTHORUM
Euphrates Fl.
Seleucia
Babylon
Hierosolyma
SINUS PERSICUS
ASIA CITERIOR
M. TULLI CICERONIS TEMPORE
MILIA PASSUUM
0 50 100 200 300 400 500
MILIARIA ANGLICA
0 100 200 300 400 500
40
45
50

ii. The Speech on Pompey's Commission.

I. OCCASION AND CIRCUMSTANCES OF DELIVERY.

The country of Pontus lay in the eastern part of Asia Minor, south of the Black Sea. It was bounded on the west by Paphlagonia and Galatia, on the south by Cappadocia and Lesser Armenia, and on the east by Greater Armenia and Colchis. When Xenophon the Athenian passed through this region, in 400 B. C., it was inhabited by a number of barbarous tribes, which were in nominal subjection to Persia. In less than a century afterwards it was the seat of an independent monarchy, whose reigning house traced its descent back to a former Persian governor. In the earlier part of the second century B. C. Pharnaces I. brought the adjoining portions of Paphlagonia under his rule; and Sinope, a colony of the Greek city Miletus, became the place of royal residence. The last and greatest of the kings of Pontus was Mithridates VI., who came to the throne about 120 B. C., and proved to be a formidable antagonist of Rome. The reverses suffered by the Romans at his hands led Manilius to bring forward a bill granting Pompey extraordinary powers. This was the immediate occasion of Cicero's famous speech 'For the Bill of Manilius,' or 'On Pompey's Commission,' which, however, cannot be understood without a more detailed examination of the circumstances leading up to it.

Mithridates VI. is one of the most striking characters of ancient history. Possessed of a large and powerful frame, he was endowed also with a mind of great strength and alertness, indomitable courage, and a consuming ambition. He could converse in twenty-five languages, so that he needed no interpreter in dealing with the different peoples under his sway.

He delighted to fill his palaces with statuary, pictures, and the surroundings of culture, yet in his relations with rivals and subjects he was a typical Oriental despot, — jealous, cruel, and implacable. He would put to death even the members of his own family for slight reasons; to protect himself against secret enemies, it is said that he commenced early in life to take poisons in small quantities, that his system might become inured to them. As a general, if he may not be compared with Alexander and Caesar, he may at any rate be mentioned along with the great Oriental conquerors, — Tiglath-Pileser, Cyrus, and Darius; for with the troops at his command, numerous indeed, but of poor fighting quality, he was able to destroy several Roman armies, and to fight against Rome for almost thirty years. As a hater of the Romans he was second only to Hannibal.

Mithridates commenced to reign when very young. After he had established himself firmly upon the throne, he entered upon a career of conquest. He annexed Lesser Armenia and Colchis, and crossed the Caucasus range. Having been requested by the Greek cities of Olbia and Chersonesus to chastise the marauding tribes north of the Euxine Sea, he sent his generals over the country as far as the Tyras River (now *Dniester*), and made the whole subject to himself. But on the west side of his kingdom opportunity for extension was checked by the bounds of the Roman province of Asia. This at first comprised the portion of Asia Minor west of Bithynia, Phrygia, and Lycia, which had been bequeathed to the Roman people by Attalus III., the last king of Pergamus, in B. C. 133. The states lying between Pontus and the province, particularly Bithynia, Paphlagonia, and Cappadocia, were nominally independent, but were on good terms with the Romans, and really under a Roman protectorate.

A collision between the two aggressive powers — Rome, ever

impatient of rivals, and Mithridates, fired with the spirit of conquest — was inevitable; but the first provocation came from the Romans. Early in the reign of Mithridates they took from him Phrygia, which had been under the rule of his father. Biding his time, he increased his resources as rapidly as possible, and formed an alliance with Tigranes, king of Armenia, to whom he gave a daughter in marriage. He made various attempts to get control of Cappadocia, and would have been successful had not the Roman Senate — in 92 B. C. — placed the Cappadocian Ariobarzanes on the throne. The Romans also obliged him to evacuate Paphlagonia, which, he claimed, belonged to him by inheritance. Not yet willing openly to break with Rome, he instigated Tigranes to drive Ariobarzanes out of Cappadocia. About the same time he was instrumental in bringing about the expulsion of Nicomedes III. from Bithynia, supporting against the lawful king a claimant of the throne friendly to himself. Both the exiled princes appealed to Rome. She reinstated them without a protest from Mithridates, who had apparently supposed that the disturbances of the Social War would make the Romans forgetful of their interests in the East. Nicomedes, at the instigation of the Roman embassador, now assumed the offensive, and invaded Pontus.

Mithridates sent to Rome to demand satisfaction, but received none. He at once prepared for hostilities. Thus began the first Mithridatic war, which lasted from 88 to 84 B. C. Mustering an army of 250,000 infantry and 40,000 cavalry, in one season, B. C. 88, he overran Bithynia, Cappadocia, and the greater part of the Roman province of Asia. He defeated the Romans at every point, and gained control of all the western part of Asia Minor, with the exception of a few cities. He poured molten gold down the throat of the Roman governor, M'. Aquillius, in mockery of the man's avarice. He made Pergamus the place of royal residence. From Ephesus he sent forth a decree that on a given day all the Italians in the cities of Asia Minor, without distinction of rank, sex, or age, should be put to death. The command was carried out to the letter. In one day 80,000 Italians, some say 150,000, perished. In the rest of the war Mithridates was less fortunate. He sent two armies to Greece, which were defeated by Sulla in 86 and in 85 B. C. In 85 also his forces were beaten on their own ground by Fimbria, who had succeeded Flaccus as the representative of the Marian party in the East. A peace was concluded with Sulla in 84. According to the terms of it, Mithridates was to pay an indemnity of three thousand talents ($3,500,000), furnish the Romans with eighty galleys, and give up all the territory he had conquered west of Pontus.

In the second Mithridatic war (83–81 B. C.), Murena, the successor of Sulla in command, was the aggressor. He was soon defeated by Mithridates, who again seized upon Cappadocia. Sulla, then supreme at Rome, commanded Murena to cease from hostilities, whereupon Mithridates withdrew from Cappadocia.

It was clear that no peace beween Mithridates and the Romans could be more than a truce, to be broken whenever either of the contracting parties might find it advantageous to assume the offensive. In 75 Nicomedes died, leaving Bithynia by will to the Roman people, who immediately took possession of it. Early in 74 Mithridates commenced war, and prosecuted it vigorously. At the lowest estimate his army comprised 120,000 infantry, of which at least a part was armed and trained according to the Roman system; 16,000 cavalry, and a hundred scythe-bearing chariots. At first successful, he defeated a Roman army under Cotta, and besieged Chalcedon; but Lucullus soon forced him to raise the siege. His powerful fleet was in part defeated by the Romans, in part shattered by a storm in the Euxine Sea

His great army melted away in successive engagements. The following year Lucullus advanced into Pontus, and in 72 encamped near the king at Cabira. Mithridates, being hard pressed, gave orders to break camp and retreat. A panic ensued; the Romans took advantage of the situation and cut his army to pieces. The king would himself have fallen into their hands had his pursuers not stopped to plunder a mule laden with gold. Thus escaping, he sent a eunuch to put to death his wives and sisters, that they might not be captured, and fled to Armenia.

Tigranes gave orders that his father-in-law be received with becoming dignity; yet for a year and a half, wishing to avoid cause of rupture with Rome, he refused to admit the king of Pontus to his presence. At length, offended by the haughty demand of the Romans that he surrender Mithridates, he made common cause with the deposed monarch. The kings both raised armies; but in 69 B. C., before their forces had united, Tigranes engaged in battle with Lucullus at Tigranocerta, and suffered a disastrous defeat. Lucullus now pressed on into the interior of Armenia, towards Artaxata; but mutiny among his troops prevented further advance, and he led them into Mesopotamia. Mithridates quickly gathered another army, and returned to Pontus. Here he gained a victory over Fabius, the Roman lieutenant, and obtained possession of the greater part of the country. In 67 he dealt the Romans a crushing blow in the defeat of the forces under Triarius. Seven thousand Romans fell, including many officers; their camp was taken, and only the fact that Mithridates was wounded saved the rest from destruction. Lucullus was almost powerless on account of the disaffection of his troops. At the end of the year 67 Mithridates was once more in power over Pontus and the adjoining regions; he was in alliance with Tigranes, and liable at any moment to make a descent on the province of Asia.

But the war with Mithridates and Tigranes was not the only cause of disturbance in Roman foreign relations at this time. For some years pirates had gradually become more and more numerous and powerful in all parts of the Mediterranean. They rendered navigation perilous. They cut off the supplies of grain which Rome was wont to receive by sea. They made raids upon cities along the coast, and even carried men of distinction away from Italy to be held for ransom. The evil had grown to such intolerable proportions that in 67 B. C. A. Gabinius proposed a bill giving Pompey absolute jurisdiction for three years over all the Mediterranean coast for fifty miles inland. The bill was passed, though contrary to precedent both in the powers it conferred and in the manner of conferring them; for the people in passing the measure assumed a function supposed to belong to the Senate. But Pompey more than sustained the reputation he already enjoyed as a commander. In three months he cleared the sea of pirates from the Pillars of Hercules to the Hellespont. While Mithridates was making fruitless the victories of Lucullus, Pompey was capturing the strongholds of the pirates in Cilicia, which was immediately organized into a Roman province.

Under these circumstances, early in 66 B. C., Manilius proposed to the people that the government of Bithynia, which had been given to the incompetent Glabrio, as well as of Cilicia and Asia, and the absolute command of the war with Mithridates, be intrusted to Pompey. The bill was opposed by the leaders of the aristocratic party, particularly Catulus and Hortensius, on constitutional grounds. Cicero's speech was addressed to the people, and served to intensify the popular feeling in favor of Pompey. It is not difficult to see what motives probably influenced him in thus breaking with the party whose principles he favored. The aristocrats were indeed glad to have Cicero on their side; but in the interest of patrician traditions they would never countenance the election of a 'new man' to the consulship, which was the goal of the orator's ambition. It appeared necessary for him to win the favor of the people; in what way could he do this better than by praising the people's hero? he might at the same time also assure himself of that hero's favor.

The speech for the bill of Manilius, or 'On Pompey's Commission,' as it is more commonly called, shows rather the adroitness of the special pleader than the depth of a true statesman. It belongs to the *deliberative* class, though the part referring to Pompey is properly *demonstrative*. From whatever point it is viewed, it is a masterly effort. The orderly and effective arrangement of the matter is matched by the rich, yet forceful and pleasing, manner of expression.

Whether the objections to Manilius's proposal were valid or not, it was carried. By the end of 66 Pompey had forced Mithridates to take refuge in Dioscurias, a Greek city on the northeast side of the Euxine Sea, and had made terms with Tigranes. The king of Pontus raised another army; but becoming involved in disaffection and treachery, he put an end to his own life in the year 63. Part of his kingdom was annexed to the province of Bithynia; the rest, left for over a century under native princes, in 63 A.D. became a Roman province under the name of Pontus Polemoniacus.

2. OUTLINE OF THE SPEECH ON POMPEY'S COMMISSION.

INTRODUCTION.

Exordium. Reasons for not having come forward previously as a public speaker. Your favor, my practice in speaking, and the happy nature of the theme, the singular merit of Gnaeus Pompey, make it a duty and a pleasure to speak on this occasion. CHAP. I.

Narratio. A war, destructive to our revenues, fraught with danger to our allies, is being waged against us by two very powerful kings. The voice of all demands the appointment of a certain commander. II., first paragraph.

Partitio. What ought to be done? Three points are to be considered: the character of the war, the greatness of the war, and the choice of a commander. II., second paragraph.

DISCUSSION.

Confirmatio. A. The character of the war. II., last paragraph. The war is of a kind that involves:—

1. The reputation of the Roman people, who have suffered at the hands of Mithridates more flagrant causes of grievance than those for which our ancestors inflicted summary vengeance. III., IV., V., first paragraph.

2. The safety of our allies, who are threatened by the enemy, and are pleading for the appointment of Pompey. V., last part.

3. Our most important revenues, which are imperilled, not simply by war, but by the mere rumor of war. VI.

4. The property of many Roman citizens engaged in business in Asia, whom expediency and humanity alike require us to protect. VII.

B. The greatness of the war: so urgent as to demand active measures, yet not so formidable that there need be apprehension regarding the final issue. VIII., first paragraph.

1. The efforts of Lucullus against the enemy were at first successful. VIII., second paragraph.

2. But reverses followed, and the war is now more urgent than ever. IX.

C. The choice of a commander.

A. Affirmative argument: Pompey the best man.

1. He possesses all the requisite qualifications, namely:—

a. Mastery of the art of war. X.

b. Traits characteristic of a great general and of a great man:—

On the one hand, power of persistent effort, bravery, activity, rapidity of movement, forethought. XI., XII.

On the other, incorruptibility, self-restraint, good-faith, courtesy, talent, humaneness. XIII., XIV.

c. Standing, witnessed by the general demand for his services, the influence of his name, the confidence reposed in him by our enemies. XV., XVI., first paragraph.

d. Good luck. XVI., latter part.

2. He is more favorably situated than any one else for prosecuting the war. XVII., first paragraph.

Refutatio. B. Refutation. Objections to the choice of Pompey considered.

1. Answer to particular objections:

a. To that of Hortensius, that absolute authority ought not to be vested in one person; met by reference to the success of the war against the pirates. Brief answer also to an objection raised against the lieutenancy of Gabinius. XVII., last part; XVIII., XIX.

b. To those of Catulus, based upon the risk of placing all hope in one person, and upon respect for precedent; shown to be without just grounds, by the citation of examples from the cases of others and of Pompey himself. XX., XXI.

2. Answer to the objections in general:

a. The influence of opponents of high standing ought not to outweigh the true interests of the Roman people. XXII., first paragraph.

b. This war demands a peculiar combination of military power and irreproachable character, such as only Pompey possesses. XXII., last part; XXIII., first part.

c. The standing of the opponents of this measure is offset by that of the eminent men who favor it. XXIII., last paragraph.

CONCLUSION.

Peroratio. The orator urges Manilius to stand firm, relying upon the support of the people; calls the gods to witness to the purity of his motives in advocating the measure; assures the people of his loyalty to the interests of the State and to their own wishes. XXIV.

iii. THE SPEECHES AGAINST CATILINE.

1. OCCASION AND CIRCUMSTANCES OF DELIVERY.

LUCIUS SERGIUS CATILINA was born about 108 B.C. He was descended from an old patrician family which had lost its prestige and was in straitened circumstances. From early youth he indulged in all forms of vice with seeming recklessness; yet he was a man of great courage, strong personal magnetism, and unusual abilities as a leader. During the reign of terror under Sulla he distinguished himself, as a partisan of the dictator, by the number of his victims and his remorseless cruelty. Nevertheless he gained the office of praetor for the year 68 B.C., and served as governor of Africa in 67. The following year he returned to Rome to present himself as a candidate for the consulship for 65; but he had scarcely entered the city when he was charged with provincial extortion, and thus disqualified for the proposed candidacy.

The consuls-elect for 65, P. Autronius Paetus and P. Cornelius Sulla, soon after their election (July, 66) were impeached for bribery, their office being conferred on L. Aurelius Cotta and L. Manlius Torquatus. Autronius, Catiline, and Cn. Calpurnius Piso now formed a plot to murder the new consuls on the day of their entry into office (Jan. 1, B.C. 65), and seize the authority. As the arrangements were then not complete, the execution of the project was deferred till the 5th of the following February, and it was extended to compass the destruction of many of the leading men of the State. On the appointed day, however, Catiline gave the signal for attack before the armed helpers had assembled in sufficient numbers, and the plot miscarried. This is known as the first conspiracy of Catiline; the details of it are obscure and uncertain.

Nothing daunted, Catiline presented himself as a candidate for the consulship for the year 63, having meanwhile freed himself from the charges against him by wholesale bribery. He set before his associates a program which included the division of the offices of State among themselves, the cancellation of all debts, and the murdering of the wealthiest citizens, with the confiscation of their property. As he failed to receive an election,[1] he now rapidly furthered his preparations for a revolution by force of arms. He borrowed great sums of money on his own credit and that of his friends, collected military stores, and gave to C. Manlius, who had been an officer under Sulla, a commission to enroll and train an army. The centre of operations was the neighborhood of Faesulae (now *Fiesole*), a few miles north of the city of Florence. As Pompey was in the East, Italy contained no Roman army and no great general, and the time seemed favorable for a sudden stroke.

In the midst of these preparations, early in 63, Catiline offered himself as a candidate for the consulship for 62. His plan was, if elected, to put Cicero out of the way; then, as consul-elect, to enter into coalition with the consul Antonius, who to some extent at least was committed to his plans, and thus gain the supreme power. It happened that one of the conspirators, Q. Curius, had made a confidant of Fulvia, a high-born but dissolute woman, in regard to the projects of Catiline; she, becoming disturbed at the prospect of a revo-

[1] See p. 5.

lution which threatened the security of all, had allowed information regarding the matter to reach the ears of Cicero, and afterwards entered into communication with him. Through her influence, and the offer of large rewards, Cicero succeeded in inducing Curius to act as a secret agent, or detective, and to report every movement of the conspirators at once to himself. As the time for the consular election (July) drew near, he threw out hints about the danger to be apprehended from Catiline, and secured a postponement that there might be opportunity for investigation. He detached his colleague, Antonius, from the revolutionary party by the promise of the governorship of the rich province of Macedonia, after the expiration of the consular term. When the election was finally held (the date is uncertain), Catiline was again rejected, and a plot he had formed for the murder of several magistrates was rendered incapable of execution by the elaborate preparations of Cicero.

Driven now to desperation, Catiline fixed upon Oct. 27 (B. C. 63) as the date for raising the standard of open rebellion, and the following day for the massacre of his opponents and the pillaging of Rome. But on Oct. 21 Cicero attacked him openly in the Senate, which, immediately afterwards passed a decree vesting supreme authority in the consuls for the protection of the State. Some days later word came that Manlius had actually taken up arms on the 27th, as expected, and that slaves were arming in Capua and in Apulia. Thereupon the Senate authorized the drafting of troops, and ordered all precautions for the defence of the city. Catiline was charged with sedition by a young patrician, L. Aemilius Paulus; protesting his innocence, he offered to place himself in free custody.[1]

On the night of Nov. 6 he met his followers at the house

[1] See N. to p. 69, l. 5.

of Marcus Laeca, where arrangements were perfected for the firing and plundering of Rome. He said that Cicero stood in the way of accomplishing his designs; whereupon L. Vargunteius, a senator, and C. Cornelius, a knight, volunteered to murder the consul at daybreak in his own house. A report of the meeting was brought to Cicero in the night; when the would-be assassins went to call on him in the morning, they found the house closed against them. On the 8th of November Cicero called a meeting of the Senate in the temple of Jupiter Stator; finding Catiline present, he assailed the arch-conspirator in the bitter invective known as the FIRST ORATION against Catiline. Catiline attempted to justify himself, emphasizing the public services and respectability of his family; but being greeted with cries of "enemy" and "traitor" he left the Senate. The same night he set out for Etruria, causing the report to be circulated that he was gcing to live in exile at Marseilles.

On the following day (Nov. 9) Cicero addressed thc people from the Rostra in the SECOND ORATION, congratulating them on the departure of Catiline, and endeavoring to frighten the remaining conspirators into leaving the city. But though Lentulus, Cethegus, and their associates kept actively at work in Rome, three weeks passed before the consul could secure evidence against them sufficient to warrant making any arrests. The 19th of December was the date finally set for murdering the officers of State and plundering the city. Meanwhile news came that Catiline had assumed command of the insurgent forces at Faesulae. The Senate promptly pronounced both him and Manlius public enemies, and sent the consul Antonius against them with an army.

A delegation from the Allobroges happened to be in Rome at this time, seeking relief from certain abuses. Having received no satisfaction from the Senate, they readily listened to a proposal to interest their people in the conspiracy. Impressed with the seriousness of the matter, however, they laid it before their patron, Q. Fabius Sanga, who immediately reported the facts to Cicero. The consul saw here a golden opportunity for obtaining the evidence he so much needed. Acting in accordance with his instructions, the deputies of the Allobroges professed the warmest interest in the conspiracy, and asked for written pledges to take to their people. These were freely given. They promised furthermore that on their way back to Gaul they would turn aside to confer with Catiline in Etruria; and Lentulus designated a certain T. Volturcius to accompany them, with a letter and messages for Catiline. Late in the night of December 2 the deputies, accompanied by Volturcius, set out from Rome. At the Mulvian bridge, two miles north of the city, they were stopped by two praetors and a company of soldiers sent to intercept them in accordance with a previous understanding with Cicero. After a show of resistance, they yielded up the documents which they had received from the conspirators, and returned to Rome. Early in the morning (Dec. 3), before news of the affair had spread, Cicero sent for Lentulus, Cethegus, Statilius, and Gabinius, and brought them before the Senate, which met in the temple of Concord, in the Forum. Here Volturcius, having turned State's evidence, gave important testimony; the letters delivered to the deputies of the Allobroges, after the seals had been acknowledged by the writers, were read, and the guilt of the conspirators was conclusively established. The meeting of the Senate lasted till late in the day. At the close Cicero appeared before the people and delivered the THIRD ORATION, which gave an account of the day's proceedings and, like the second, answered the purpose of an official bulletin of information.

The day after the arrest of the conspirators, the report was spread abroad that an attempt would be made to rescue them by force; but stringent measures prevented any outbreak. The next day (Dec. 5) the Senate met to decide what should be done with the prisoners. Silanus, the consul-elect, declared himself in favor of putting them to death, and was supported in this by the other senators present till the question came to Julius Caesar. He proposed that the conspirators in custody be distributed under life-sentence among the municipal towns. As the Senate now wavered in opinion, Cicero arose and delivered the FOURTH ORATION, in which, after reviewing the propositions of both Silanus and Caesar, he clearly revealed his own feeling in favor of the extreme penalty. The decisive turn to the debate, however, was given by Marcus Cato, who spoke so earnestly in favor of the immediate execution of the prisoners that he carried the great majority of the Senate with him. That evening Lentulus, Cethegus, Gabinius, Statilius, and Ceparius, who had been captured just outside the city, were strangled[1] in the Tullianum, a loathsome subterranean dungeon on the slope of the Capitoline Hill, northwest of the Forum. Early in January (62) the forces of Catiline, comprising not far from 5,000 men, were annihilated near Pistoria (modern *Pistoja*), about twenty miles northwest of Florence, and he himself, while fighting with the courage of despair, was slain.

The Catilinarian orations were written out after their delivery, and no doubt carefully revised before publication. The genuineness of the speeches as they stand has been questioned, but without good reason. As might be expected from the nature of the theme and the occasion, their structure is less symmetrical than that of Cicero's more carefully prepared addresses. The following outlines may be of assistance in following the thought.

[1] On the constitutionality of this act, see N. to p. 108, l. 3.

2. Outline of the First Oration against Catiline.

Introduction.

Exordium. Abrupt outburst against Catiline's effrontery, and the degeneracy of the time. CHAP. I., ll. 1–18.

Narratio. Precedent and authority warrant putting Catiline to death. The danger is great, but he is foiled. I., l. 19 to end; II.

Discussion.

Confirmatio. A. *Addressed to Catiline.*

1. Your plans are clearly revealed to us. III., IV.
2. It is best for you to leave Rome and take your followers with you; for
   a. Your plots against my life have failed. V.
   b. Here you are hated and feared on account of your crimes, as shown to-day in the Senate. VI., VII.
   c. No good man will be security for you. VIII., to l. 22.
   d. The Senate wants you to go. VIII., l. 22 to end.
   e. You are altogether hopeless; the life of a freebooter will suit you. IX., X.

B. *Addressed to the Senate.*

1. Why do I not have Catiline put to death, as precedent and public interest demand? Because it is better for him to leave Rome and so lure forth his associates. XI., XII.
2. We are at a climax of wickedness; but I pledge the victory of the good. XIII., to l. 27.

Conclusion.

Conclusio. Final exhortation to Catiline to depart. Prayer to Jupiter Stator for protection. XIII., end.

3. Outline of the Second Oration.

Introduction.

Exordium. Congratulations on Catiline's departure. CHAP. I., ll. 1–8.

Narratio. He is conquered and undone. I., l. 9 to end.

Partitio. It was better to drive him forth than to put him to death, on account of his associates. II.

DISCUSSION.

Confirmatio. 1. Catiline's associates, hopelessly depraved, should leave the city. III., IV., V.

2. Catiline himself, reprobate that he is, has not been driven into exile, but has joined Manlius. VI., VII.

3. Catiline's forces are recruited from six classes, each of which needs a special warning:

a. Rich but extravagant men, in financial embarrassment. VIII.

b. Bankrupts, desirous of power. IX., to l. 21.

c. Veterans of Sulla, who long for a renewal of the seasons of violence. IX., l. 22 to end.

d. Hopeless but restless debtors. X., to l. 20.

e. Professional criminals. X., ll. 21–25.

f. Profligates. X., l. 26 to end.

4. Such forces bear no comparison with ours. XI.

CONCLUSION.

Conclusio. The orator reminds the citizens of their duty, and assures them of safety, warns the conspirators (XII.); promises a complete but bloodless victory, with the help of the gods. XIII.

4. OUTLINE OF THE THIRD ORATION.

INTRODUCTION.

Exordium et Narratio. The State, your lives, this city have narrowly escaped destruction. CHAP. I., ll. 1–20.

Partitio. I shall explain how the conspiracy has been traced out and checked. I., l. 21 to end of paragraph.

DISCUSSION.

Confirmatio. 1. My efforts to secure evidence for conviction were crowned with success through the interception of the deputies of the Allobroges and the arrest of leading conspirators. I., end; II., III.

2. This evidence was to-day presented to the Senate:

a. The testimony of Volturcius, and of the Gauls. IV.

b. Reading of the letters, — their seals acknowledged by the prisoners. V.

c. Action of the Senate after hearing the evidence; rewards to officers, decrees against nine conspirators, appointment of special thanksgiving. VI.

3. The conspiracy is now checked once for all. VII.

4. This result has been achieved through the immediate help of the gods. VIII., IX.

5. The present disturbance differs from all preceding disturbances in this State in its deadly character, and in the fact that it has been put down without bloodshed. X.

CONCLUSION.

Conclusio. For my services I ask only the undying recollection of this day, and your protection, present and future. Guard your homes; I will guard the city. XI., XII.

5. OUTLINE OF THE FOURTH ORATION.

INTRODUCTION.

Exordium. My own safety; its relation to the safety of all. CHAP. I.; II., to l. 31.

Narratio. The present state of the conspiracy. II., end; III. to l. 26.

Partitio. The question of penalty before the Senate. III., l. 27 to end.

DISCUSSION.

Confirmatio. 1. The two proposals regarding punishment, the one of Silanus, that the conspirators be put to death; the other of Caesar, that they be guarded under life-sentence in the municipalities. IV.

2. The character of Caesar's proposal. V., to l. 34.

Refutatio. 3. Caesar's objections to the proposal of Silanus met: —

a. The conspirators should be treated as enemies, not as citizens. V., end.

b. Apparent cruelty may in reality be kindness and mercy. VI.

4. Well-considered and decisive action demanded,

a. On account of the patriotic feeling of all classes. VII., VIII.

b. On account of the magnitude and sacredness of the interests at stake. IX.

5. Digression on the orator's peril, and services. X., XI., first part.

CONCLUSION.

Conclusio. Vote as the importance of the case demands; at no matter how great cost to myself, I will carry out your decision. XI., last paragraph.

6. Chronology of the Speeches against Catiline.

	A. U. C. 691 = B. C. 63.
Assembly for the Election of Consuls for 62	Sept.? Sept.?
Cicero lays information about the conspiracy before the Senate, which confers extraordinary authority on the consuls	a. d. XII. Kal. Nov. = Oct. 21.
Manlius takes up arms at Faesulae	a. d. VI. Kal. Nov. = Oct. 27.
Day set by Catiline for the massacre of the nobles	a. d. V. Kal. Nov. = Oct. 28.
Unsuccessful attempt on Praeneste . . .	Kal. Nov. = Nov. 1.
Meeting of the conspirators at Laeca's, night of	a. d. VIII. Id. Nov. = Nov. 6.
Miscarrying of the plan to murder Cicero, morning of	a. d. VII. Id. Nov. = Nov. 7.
First Oration, before the Senate	a. d. VI. Id. Nov. = Nov. 8.
The following night Catiline left Rome.	
Second Oration, to the people . .	a. d. V. Id. Nov. = Nov. 9.
Antonius sent north with an army . . .	about the middle of Nov.
Interception of the deputies of the Allobroges, night of	a. d. IV. Non. Dec. = Dec. 2.
Arrest of conspirators; laying of evidence before the Senate; Third Oration, to the people	a. d. III. Non. Dec. = Dec. 3.
Rumors of a proposed attempt to rescue the conspirators	pr. Non. Dec. = Dec. 4.
Trial of the conspirators before the Senate; Fourth Oration	Non. Dec. = Dec. 5
The following night the five conspirators in custody were executed.	
Catiline falls in battle, beginning of	A. U. C. 692 = B. C. 62.

iv. The Oration for Archias.

I. OCCASION AND CIRCUMSTANCES OF DELIVERY.

The poet Archias was a Greek by nationality, born at Antioch, then the chief city of Syria, about 119 B. C. He received what was considered a liberal education, and early developed a remarkable facility in poetic composition. He was especially gifted as an improviser, being able to compose and recite verses offhand with great skill. As the unsettled state of affairs in his native city gave little encouragement to the arts, while yet a youth he started out to visit the Greek towns in Asia Minor and Greece. Everywhere his talents received enthusiastic recognition. After a time he crossed over to Southern Italy, where public honors were conferred upon him by the citizens of Tarentum, Regium, Neapolis, and perhaps Locri.

In 102 B.C. Archias came to Rome. Here he was soon on terms of intimacy with many prominent men; for the educated Romans of this period as a rule cultivated a taste for Greek literature. But his chief patrons were the Luculli.[1] After he had been at Rome for some time he accompanied M. Lucullus on a journey to Sicily; on the way back he was honored with the citizenship of Heraclea. In 89 B.C. a law (*Lex Plautia Papiria*) was passed which conferred Roman citizenship on the citizens of such Italian towns as possessed formal treaty relations with Rome. In order to become Roman citizens under this act, the inhabitants of the favored cities must be able to fulfil two conditions: they must possess a settled place of residence in Italy, and within sixty days must give their names to one of the Roman praetors holding office at the time. Archias complied with these conditions, and for twenty-seven years his standing as a Roman citizen was unquestioned.

At this time a common way of annoying public men was to attack their friends. Lucius Lucullus, who had taken Archias with him on his Asiatic campaigns, was still a man of influence, but had bitter enemies. It was apparently rather to vex him

[1] See Vocab.

than to disturb Archias that in 62 B.C. a man named Gratius attempted to invalidate the poet's claim of Roman citizenship. Cicero undertook the defence of the case partly no doubt to accommodate Lucullus, partly to discharge an obligation he felt under to Archias. At the trial Quintus Cicero, the orator's brother, presided, being praetor. The case for the prosecution was extremely weak. It rested mainly on the assumption that the poet's citizenship of Heraclea could not be established, because the records of that city had perished; and on the fact that his name did not appear on the lists of the Roman census, where it would naturally be registered. But the orator brought forward witnesses whose testimony took the place of the missing records of Heraclea, and easily explained the omission of the poet's name from the census lists. The argument for the defence was irrefutable.

As a piece of legal argument, the speech for Archias is less to the point than would be tolerated in a plea before a modern court. Very likely when Cicero wrote it out for publication he cut down the technical portion, dealing with the facts, eliminating such details as would detract from the interest of the reader, but did not reduce the more attractive matter of the latter part, concerning the relation of literary pursuits to the public welfare, and the services of Archias in extending the glory of Rome. A Roman court allowed the presentation of a wider range of matter in sustaining a point than would now be considered in place; and certainly the orator strengthened his case by showing that the interests of his client were in a measure the interests of the State, whose duty it should always be to favor those who promote literature. The singular charm of this oration lies in its expression of universal sentiment regarding literature, particularly poetry, in a well-nigh faultless style, which at times approaches the manner of the essay. Its genuineness has been attacked, but without success; nothing could be more Ciceronian.

2. Outline of the Oration for Archias.

Introduction.

Exordium. Obligation of the orator to undertake the defence of Archias. The character of the case, requiring treatment out of the ordinary. CHAP. I.; II., first part.

Partitio. It will be proved that Archias is a Roman citizen; that if he were not, he ought to be. II., end.

Narratio. Birth, fame, travels of Archias; his reception at Rome; his enrolment as a citizen at Heraclea, then at Rome. III.; IV., first part.

Discussion.

A. *Proof that Archias is a Roman citizen.*

Confirmatio. 1. Proof of enrolment as a citizen at Heraclea by witnesses. IV., middle.

2. Proof of residence and registration at Rome by the concentration of his interests there, by the presence of his name on a praetor's register, and by the recognition of his standing as a citizen in various transactions. IV., end; V.

B. *Proof that Archias ought in any case to be a Roman citizen.*

1. The promotion of literature a matter of general interest: —

a. Indebtedness of the orator to literature for both ideals and inspiration. VI.

Refutatio. *b*. Refutation of the objection that there have been great men who were not versed in letters. VII., first part.

c. Universal appreciation of literature. VII., latter part; VIII., first part.

2. The special claims of Archias as a poet: —

a. Veneration due to poetic genius. VIII., latter part.

b. His treatment of national themes. IX., first part.

c. Precedents from the cases of Ennius and Theophanes. IX., end; X.

d. Fame an incentive and reward of deeds; future services of Archias in magnifying the Roman name. XI.; XII., first part.

Conclusion.

Conclusio. *a*. Summary of evidence. XII., middle.

b. Appeal for a sympathetic consideration of the case. XII., latter part.

V. The Address of Thanks for the Pardon of Marcellus.

1. OCCASION AND CIRCUMSTANCES OF DELIVERY.

Marcus Claudius Marcellus belonged to the most distinguished of the plebeian branches of the great Claudian gens. Nothing is known of his early life except that from boyhood he was a warm friend of Cicero. He was curule aedile in 56 B.C., and consul in 51. During his consulship, being an ardent partisan of Pompey, he manifested the most bitter hatred toward Caesar. The latter had recently settled a colony at Comum, in Cisalpine Gaul, conferring special privileges upon the inhabitants; Marcellus caused a prominent native of the place to be publicly flogged at Rome, simply in order to bring Caesar's authority into contempt. As the relations between Pompey and Caesar became more and more strained, Marcellus was less vehement, and tried to delay the inevitable outbreak of hostilities; failing in this attempt, he lent a half-hearted support to the side of Pompey, whom he joined in Epirus. After the battle of Pharsalus he retired to Mytilene and devoted himself to his favorite studies, oratory and philosophy, remaining there in voluntary exile.

After Caesar had gained the supreme power, his leniency toward his former enemies was a matter of surprise to all. In accordance with his usual policy he paid no attention to Marcellus, who resisted the urgent advice of Cicero to ask the dictator's pardon. Meanwhile Marcellus's friends were active in his behalf. At length in the summer of 46, at a meeting of the Senate, Gaius Marcellus, a brother of Marcus, threw himself at Caesar's feet and implored the forgiveness of the exile, being joined in his supplication by many of the senators. Caesar, having commented on the hatred Marcellus had borne him, and on the danger to himself in freely allowing his enemies to return, declared that he would leave the decision of the matter to the Senate, which was apparently unanimous in the desire to have Marcellus restored to civil rights. Cicero was touched by the magnanimity of the dictator, and also thought he saw in this deference to the opinion of the Senate an entering wedge to the restoration of the authority of that body, and promise of a return to the old constitutional forms. Inspired by the occasion, he arose and expressed the feeling of the moment in an impassioned address of thanks to Caesar, the speech known by the inaccurate title of *Pro Marcello*. Though Marcellus appeared indifferent regarding the opportunity to return to Rome, he soon after set out for Italy. Stopping at the Piraeus on the way, he was murdered there, doubtless in consequence of a private feud.

Since the time of F. A. Wolf, who in 1802 published an elaborate argument against the Ciceronian authorship of the *Pro Marcello*, the genuineness of this speech has been much discussed. Recent criticism has restored it to Cicero, to whom it undoubtedly belongs. It appears, however, to have been published immediately after its delivery, perhaps from short-hand notes, without the careful revision which Cicero usually gave to his speeches. It possesses a peculiar interest for the modern reader on account of the temporary reconciliation of the orator with the dictator which it pictures, even though the enthusiasm of the moment led to an overstatement of Caesar's virtues. Yet such exaggeration, considering the circumstances and the temperament of the speaker, is far from unnatural; and in fact lends a poetic coloring to the style.

2. Outline of the Marcellus.

Introduction.

Exordium. The unprecedented clemency of Caesar, shown by the pardon of Marcellus, forces me to speak. CHAP. I.

Discussion.

A. *The deeds of Caesar.*

Confirmatio. 1. Great beyond description are Caesar's deeds, especially in war. II.

2. But greater is his clemency. III., IV.

3. The pardon of Marcellus augurs well for the peace and welfare of the State. V., VI.

B. *Caesar's danger.*

1. Danger to Caesar is peril to the State. VII.

2. His work is not finished so long as so much remains to be done, not only for the present but also for the future. VIII., IX.

5. Caesar's safety is our safety. X.

Conclusion.

Conclusio. For this gracious pardon we all return our heartfelt thanks. XI.

vi. The Fourth Speech against Antony.

1. Occasion and circumstances of delivery.

In the year 44 B. C. Julius Caesar was consul for the fifth time, with Marcus Antonius (known as Mark Antony, or Antony) as colleague. After the assassination of Caesar (15 March), Antony made a compact with Lepidus, Master of the Horse, and with his help soon gained control of affairs. Those who were prominently connected with the murder of Caesar withdrew from the city. At this time Octavius (afterwards called Octavianus), Caesar's heir, was in Epirus, completing his education by a season in the army. In May he returned to Rome, where, by skilfully taking advantage of every opportunity to advance his own interests, he soon became exceedingly popular.

As soon as it became clear that the attempt to restore the old constitution had failed, Cicero retired to his villas and employed his time in writing works on philosophy. At the end of July, feeling insecure, he went to Sicily, whence on Aug. 2 he set sail for Greece. Being driven back by adverse winds to Leucopetra (south of Regium), he heard that there was a possibility of an agreement between Antony and Brutus and Cassius. Changing his plan he started for Rome, and reached the city on Aug. 31, only to find that all hope of a reconciliation was now gone, and that Antony had summoned a meeting of the Senate for the following day. Cicero, making a pretence of illness, did not attend this meeting, and in his absence was violently attacked by Antony who, as consul, presided. Now that Cicero was on the ground, a collision with Antony was inevitable. The other consul, Dolabella, who had been elected to fill out the unexpired term of Caesar, was friendly to the party of Brutus. On Sept. 2 he presided at a meeting of the Senate in the Temple of Concord, at which Cicero appeared, and replied to Antony's attack in a speech which, though moderate in tone, was nevertheless decided. This was followed in the last weeks of 44 and the earlier part of 43 by other speeches against Antony. Fourteen of these are extant; they are called Philippics, from their similarity to the celebrated Philippics of Demosthenes, directed against Philip of Macedon.

In the latter part of November (44) two legions, the Fourth and the Martian, deserted Antony and went over to Octavianus, whereupon Antony left Rome, to prevent further defections. On the 20th of December, though both consuls were absent from the city, a meeting of the Senate was called to transact important business; Cicero arose and in a vehement speech (the Third Philippic), advocated the passing of a vote of thanks to the two legions that had left Antony, and proposing to make void the recent changes Antony had made in the assignment of the provinces. Both motions passed. At the close of the meeting Cicero informed the people, in the FOURTH PHILIPPIC, of the action of the Senate and its significance.

The Fourth Philippic was probably given to the world without revision. It is, however, full of interest as a specimen of refined invective, and of considerable historical value as a contemporary document for a period whose political movements are complicated and obscure. Its genuineness has been questioned, but without result.

2. Outline of the Fourth Speech against Antony.

Introduction.

Exordium. The presence of the citizens in so great numbers inspires the greatest activity and hope for our State. CHAP. I., beginning.

Narratio et Partitio. There is all the greater reason for hope in the fact that Antony has been judged an enemy, and that the citizens have warmly approved the decision. I., middle.

Discussion.

Confirmatio. A. *Antony has been judged an enemy.*

1. The action of the Senate in honoring Octavianus, the opponent of Antony. I., latter part; II., first part.
2. The approved action of the legions in deserting Antony. II., latter part; III., first part.
3. The action of D. Brutus in resisting him, and the general approval of that course. III., latter part; IV., first part.
4. By reason of these things Antony is considered consul only by the desperate, who have hope of booty; and even the gods are on our side. IV., latter part.

B. *The citizens should remain steadfast in their judgment of Antony as an enemy.*

1. No terms of peace with Antony are possible. V., first part.
2. The valor and military precedents of the Roman people admit no halfway measures. V., latter part; VI., first part.

Conclusion.

Conclusio. The Roman people are engaged in a deadly struggle. Antony must be put down as Catiline was. So far as in me lies, I shall not be found wanting. VI., latter part.

III. THE LETTERS OF CICERO.

i. Private Correspondence among the Romans.

As the relations of Rome with the rest of the ancient world became more and more intimate, and men passed easily from the City to the provinces, while the provincials flocked to Rome, letter-writing increased proportionately in extent and importance. In Cicero's time the Roman of standing frequently carried on a voluminous correspondence. There was, however, no postal system like that of to-day; and letters were carried to their destination, if not at too great distance, by special messengers. Letters to persons in distant parts were sent by sea-captains, by the carriers of despatches for certain classes of government officers (particularly the collectors of revenue), and in general by any one going that way who could be induced to take charge of them. Communications of a confidential nature were often written in cipher, of which the correspondent had previously been furnished the key, and were sometimes sent in duplicate by different conveyances. In good weather letters conveyed by land probably went at the rate of fifty miles a day; but it took three weeks to send from Rome to Athens.

The form of letters varied at different periods and according to circumstances. In the earlier days writing-tablets (*tabulae*, or *pugillares*) were exclusively employed. These consisted of two or more thin slips of wood or ivory, usually oblong, and fastened at the back with wires so that they would open as our books. The average size was probably not much smaller than this page. The inside pages or leaves were provided with a slight raised rim about the margin, so that the enclosed surfaces, which were coated with a thin layer of wax, would not rub. On these surfaces the writing was done with the pointed end of a *stilus* of metal or bone; the other end of the stilus was flattened, so that it could be used to rub the wax back over a word or line in which there was an error. The wax was usually black, and the writing showed the color of the underlying wood or ivory, which was white, or at least of a light tint. Tablets of two leaves (that is, with two outside pages and two pages prepared for writing) were called *diptycha;* of three leaves, with four pages for writing, *triptycha;* there were even *pentaptycha*, of five leaves, in which there were eight pages that could be written on. When the letter was finished, strong thread was passed through one or more perforations in the margin or even at the centre, then wound closely around the tablets and tied. Over the knot the seal of the sender was stamped in wax or in fine clay. As the handwriting within was often that of an amanuensis, who in most cases was a slave, the seal was of very great importance as a means of identification. For this reason when a letter was opened the thread was cut in such a way as to leave the seal undisturbed. These writing-tablets were so convenient that they continued in use to modern times. At Florence there is a waxen tablet of the year 1301.

In the time of Cicero writing-tablets were used for short letters; but longer communications were often written with a reed pen and ink upon paper prepared from the papyrus. Usually before they were written on, but sometimes afterwards, the pages of paper were pasted together at the sides, forming a long sheet, or roll. The writing was in columns, which were parallel to the ends of the sheet, so that the lines ran in the direction of the length. The letter thus prepared was carefully rolled up, in much the same manner as books (*libri*) were at that time, and was then tied about the middle, a seal being placed over the knot.

At the head of a letter stood the name of the sender in the nominative case, with the name of the person to whom it was addressed in the dative, usually accompanied also by the abbreviation S. D. (= *salutem dicit*, 'sends greeting'), or S. P. D., S. PLUR. D. (= *salutem plurimam dicit*, 'sends most cordial greeting'). In more formal correspondence pains was taken to give forenames and titles. At the beginning of the letter, S. V. B. E. V. (= *si vales, bene est; valeo*), or a similar formula was often placed. The close was frequently abrupt; sometimes *vale* or a like expression was added, with the date; the place of writing was given in the ablative. The outside address was of the simplest character, containing the name of the person to whom the letter was sent, in the dative case.

ii. Cicero's Correspondence.

Cicero did not publish his letters. They were given to the world probably by Tiro (see Vocab., and p. 19), arranged in several collections. Those extant comprise only a portion of the number once known. Mention is made of a collection of the letters to Caesar, which must have contained at least three books; and there were similar collections of the letters to Pompey, in at least four books, to M. Brutus, in nine books, and to Octavianus, in three; there was also a collection of letters to Hirtius. Of the letters which have been preserved, the first was written in the year 68 B. C.; the latest in 43, some months before Cicero's death. They vary in length from a few lines to several pages. They are grouped as follows: —

'To his Friends' (*ad Familiares*, abbreviated *ad Fam.*); XVI. books. The title is inaccurate, because some of the letters were written to persons not included within the orator's circle of friends, and also because a number of them are not from Cicero, but addressed to him.

'To his brother Quintus' (*ad Quintum Fratrem*, *ad Q. Fr.*); III. books. The first letter is a rather formal discussion of the duties of a provincial magistrate, in sixteen chapters.

'To Atticus' (*ad Atticum*, *ad Att.*); XVI. books.

'To Marcus Brutus' (*ad M. Brutum*, *ad Brut.*); II. books At least two of the letters to Brutus appear to be forgeries.

The literary value of the letters, and their bearing on our knowledge of Cicero, have been alluded to in another connection (see pp. 20–22). Among noteworthy characteristics of the style are, the common yet delicate use of colloquial expressions, and the employment of language akin to that of comedy; the frequent introduction of Greek words and phrases, just as we often give a turn to a sentence with French or German; the coining of new words on the spur of the moment to suit a passing need; and the free use of superlatives and diminutives. As might be expected of a correspondent at once so sensitive, sympathetic, and vivacious as Cicero, the letters are varied with an ever-surprising richness of feeling and thought; and the variety of the matter is hardly greater than that of the manner of expression. They are pervaded by a breezy freshness that makes the surroundings and emotions of the writer as real to us as our own experiences. Hence it must always be that the more they are read the more they will be appreciated. But they are not simply entertaining or of general human interest; the light they throw on the inner political movements and social life of the time gives them a value as historical documents second to that of no other writings of the period.

IV. THE ROMAN GOVERNMENT IN CICERO'S TIME.

The speeches and letters of Cicero are full of references to the organization and administration of the Roman state in his time. The following outline may be found helpful in grouping the scattered information which the reader of them will naturally acquire. It applies to the constitution after the time of Sulla. For the literature of the subject see the editor's "Fifty Topics in Roman Antiquities," pp. 35–37, 17, 18.

- CITIZENS
  - *Who they were*
    - Free inhabitants of Rome.
    - Free inhabitants of Italy, who must go to Rome if they wished to vote.
  - *Division:* — 35 tribes, each tribe subdivided into 5 classes, each class into 2 centuries, = 350 centuries.
  - *Registration:* — In the lists of the censors, by whom a citizen was assigned to his tribe, class, and century.

- ASSEMBLIES . .
  - *Of the People* .
    - *Comitia Centuriata*, an assembly by centuries, to elect consuls, praetors, censors.
    - *Comitia Tributa*, an assembly by tribes, to elect the lesser magistrates and enact laws, known as *plebiscita*.
  - *Of Counsellors designated by appointment:* — *Senatus*, containing about 600 members; charged with legislation upon foreign affairs, and matters of religion and finance.

- OFFICERS
  - *Magistrates*
    - Ordinary
      - 2 Consuls
      - 8 Praetors (16 under Caesar)
      - 2 Censors
      - 10 Tribunes
      - 4 Aediles (6 under Caesar)
      - 20 Quaestors (40 under Caesar)
    - Extraordinary
      - Dictator
      - Magister Equitum
      - Interrex
  - *Subordinate Officials*
    - Secretaries — *scribae*
    - Criers — *praecones*
    - Lictors — *lictores*
    - Summoners — *viatores*

- STATE PRIESTS
  - *The Great Collegia*
    - 15 Pontifices (16 under Caesar), including the Pontifex Maximus
    - 15 Augurs (16 under Caesar)
    - 15 Quindecimviri sacris faciundis; in charge of the Sibylline books
    - 7 Epulones (10 under Caesar); provided the banquets for the gods
  - *Special Priesthoods*
    - 15 Flamens; most important, those of Jupiter, Mars, Quirinus
    - 6 Vestal Virgins; in charge of the fire of Vesta
    - Rex Sacrorum; charged with certain rites and ceremonies
  - *The Lesser Collegia*
    - Fetiales; performed rites in connection with the making of treaties and declaration of war
    - Salii; guardians of the sacred shields
    - Luperci; conducted the rites of the *Lupercalia*
    - Fratres Arvales; priests of Dea Dia

- LEGAL JURISDICTION
  - *In Civil Procedure*
    - For cases between citizens, Praetor Urbanus
    - For cases one or both parties to which were foreigners, Praetor Peregrinus
    - For cases touching the treasury, the Censors
    - For cases arising in the markets, the Aediles
  - *In Criminal Procedure*
    - For certain crimes against religion, Pontifex Maximus
    - For other crimes, permanent juries or courts — *quaestiones perpetuae* — at least eight in number; of which six were presided over by praetors, the rest by foremen (*iudices quaestionis*)

- PROVINCIAL ADMINISTRATION.
  - *Provinces* (64–30 B. C.)
    - *Western:* — Sicily, Sardinia (with Corsica), Hither Spain, Further Spain, Illyricum, Africa, Narbonese Gaul, Cisalpine Gaul
    - *Eastern:* — Achaia, Macedonia, Asia, Bithynia, Cyrene (with Crete), Cilicia, Syria
  - *Provincial Officers*
    - Governor — either an ex-consul or an ex-praetor
    - Quaestor — in charge of finances
    - Subordinate officers — lieutenants (*legati*), etc.

M. TULLI CICERONIS

IN L. CATILINAM ORATIO PRIMA

HABITA IN SENATU

I. Quō ūsque tandem abūtēre, Catilīna, patientiā nostrā? Quam diū etiam furor iste tuus nōs ēlūdet? Quem ad fīnem sēsē effrēnāta iactābit audācia? Nihilne tē nocturnum praesidium Palātī, nihil urbis vigiliae, nihil timor populī, nihil concursus bonōrum omnium, nihil hīc mūnītissimus habendī senātūs locus, nihil hōrum ōra vultūsque mōvērunt? Patēre tua cōnsilia nōn sentīs? Cōnstrīctam iam omnium hōrum scientiā tenērī coniūrātiōnem tuam nōn vidēs? Quid proximā, quid superiōre nocte ēgeris, ubi fueris, quōs convocāveris, quid cōnsilī cēperis, quem nostrum ignōrāre arbitrāris?

Ō tempora, Ō mōrēs! Senātus haec intellegit, cōnsul videt; hīc tamen vīvit. Vīvit? Immō vērō etiam in senātum venit, fit pūblicī cōnsilī particeps, notat et dēsīgnat oculīs ad caedem ūnum quemque nostrum. Nōs autem, fortēs virī, satis facere reī pūblicae vidēmur, sī istīus furōrem ac tēla vītēmus.

Ad mortem tē, Catilīna, dūcī iussū cōnsulis iam prīdem oportēbat, in tē cōnferrī pestem, quam tū in nōs māchināris. An vērō vir amplissimus, P. Scīpiō, pontifex māximus, Ti. Gracchum mediocriter labefactantem statum reī pūblicae prīvātus interfēcit; Catilīnam, orbem terrae caede atque incendiīs vāstāre cupientem, nōs cōnsulēs perferēmus? Nam illa nimis antīqua praetereō, quod C. Servīlius Ahāla Sp. Maelium, novīs rēbus studentem, manū suā occīdit. Fuit, fuit ista quondam in hāc rē pūblicā virtūs, ut virī fortēs ācriōribus suppliciīs cīvem perniciōsum quam acerbissimum hostem coërcērent. Habēmus senātūs cōnsultum in tē, Catilīna, vehemēns et grave, nōn deest reī pūblicae cōnsilium neque auctōritās hūius ōrdinis; nōs, nōs, dīcō apertē, cōnsulēs dēsumus.

II. Dēcrēvit quondam senātus, ut L. Opīmius cōnsul vidēret, nē quid rēs pūblica dētrīmentī caperet. Nox nūlla intercessit: interfectus est propter quāsdam sēditiōnum suspīciōnēs C. Gracchus, clārissimō patre, avō, māiōribus; occīsus est cum līberīs M. Fulvius cōnsulāris. Similī senātūs cōnsultō C. Mariō et L. Valeriō cōnsulibus est permissa rēs pūblica; num ūnum diem posteā L. Sāturnīnum tribūnum plēbis et C. Servīlium praetōrem mors ac reī pūblicae poena remorāta est? At nōs vīcēsimum iam diem patimur hebēscere aciem hōrum auctōritātis. Habēmus enim hūiusce modī senātūs cōnsultum, vērum inclūsum in tabulīs, tamquam in vāgīnā reconditum, quō ex senātūs cōnsultō cōnfestim tē interfectum esse, Catilīna, convenit. Vīvis, et vīvis nōn ad dēpōnendam, sed ad cōnfīrmandam audāciam.

Cupiō, patrēs cōnscrīptī, mē esse clēmentem, cupiō in tantīs reī pūblicae perīculīs mē nōn dissolūtum vidērī, sed iam mē ipse inertiae nēquitiaeque condemnō. Castra sunt in Italiā contrā populum Rōmānum in Etrūriae faucibus collocāta, crēscit in diēs singulōs hostium numerus; eōrum autem castrōrum imperātōrem ducemque hostium intrā moenia atque adeō in senātū vidēmus intestīnam aliquam cotīdiē perniciem reī pūblicae mōlientem.

Sī tē iam, Catilīna, comprehendī, sī interficī iusserō, crēdō, erit verendum mihi, nē nōn potius hōc omnēs bonī sērius ā mē quam quisquam crūdēlius factum esse dīcat. Vērum ego hōc, quod iam prīdem factum esse oportuit, certā dē causā nōndum addūcor ut faciam. Tum dēnique interficiēre, cum iam nēmō tam improbus, tam perditus, tam tuī similis invenīrī poterit, quī id nōn iūre factum esse fateātur. Quam diū quisquam erit, quī tē dēfendere audeat, vīvēs; sed vīvēs ita, ut vīvis, multīs meīs et fīrmīs praesidiīs oppressus, nē commovēre tē contrā rem pūblicam possīs. Multōrum tē etiam oculī et aurēs nōn sentientem, sīcut adhūc fēcērunt, speculābuntur atque cūstōdient.

III. Etenim quid est, Catilīna, quod iam amplius exspectēs, sī neque nox tenebrīs obscūrāre coetūs nefāriōs nec prīvāta domus parietibus continēre vōcēs coniūrātiōnis tuae potest, sī illūstrantur, sī ērumpunt omnia? Mūtā iam istam mentem, mihi crēde; oblīvīscere caedis atque incendiōrum. Tenēris undique. Lūce sunt clāriōra nōbīs tua cōnsilia omnia; quae iam mēcum licet recognōscās. Meministīne mē ante diem XII Kalendās Novembrēs dīcere in senātū, fore in armīs certō diē, quī diēs futūrus esset ante diem VI Kalendās Novembrēs, C. Mānlium, audāciae satellitem atque administrum tuae? Num mē fefellit, Catilīna, nōn modo rēs tanta, tam atrōx tamque incrēdibilis, vērum, id quod multō magis est admīrandum, diēs?

Dīxī ego īdem in senātū, caedem tē optimātium contulisse in ante diem V Kalendās Novembrēs, tum cum multī prīncipēs cīvitātis Rōmā nōn tam suī cōnservandī quam tuōrum cōnsiliōrum reprimendōrum causā profūgērunt. Num īnfitiārī potes tē illō ipsō diē meīs praesidiīs, meā dīligentiā circumclūsum commovēre tē contrā rem pūblicam nōn potuisse, cum tū discessū cēterōrum nostrā tamen, quī remānsissēmus, caede tē contentum esse dīcēbās? Quid? cum tū tē Praeneste Kalendīs ipsīs Novembribus occupātūrum nocturnō impetū esse cōnfīderēs, sēnsistīne illam colōniam meō iussū meīs praesidiīs, cūstōdiīs, vigiliīs esse mūnītam? Nihil agis, nihil mōlīris, nihil cōgitās, quod nōn ego nōn modo audiam, sed etiam videam plānēque sentiam.

IV. Recognōsce tandem mēcum noctem illam superiōrem; iam intellegēs multō mē vigilāre ācrius ad salūtem quam tē ad perniciem reī pūblicae. Dīcō tē priōre nocte vēnisse inter falcāriōs—nōn agam obscūrē—in M. Laecae domum; convēnisse eōdem complūrēs ēiusdem āmentiae scelerisque sociōs. Num negāre audēs? Quid tacēs? Convincam, sī negās; videō enim esse hīc in senātū quōsdam, quī tēcum ūnā fuērunt.

Ō dī immortālēs! Ubinam gentium sumus? In quā urbe vīvimus? Quam rem pūblicam habēmus? Hīc, hīc sunt in nostrō numerō, patrēs cōnscrīptī, in hōc orbis terrae sānctissimō gravissimōque cōnsiliō, quī dē nostrō omnium interitū, quī dē hūius urbis atque adeō dē orbis terrārum exitiō cōgitent! Hōs ego videō et dē rē pūblicā sententiam rogō et, quōs ferrō trucīdārī oportēbat, eōs nōndum vōce vulnerō!

Fuistī igitur apud Laecam illā nocte, Catilīna; distribuistī partēs Italiae; statuistī, quō quemque proficīscī placēret; dēlēgistī, quōs Rōmae relinquerēs, quōs tēcum ēdūcerēs; discrīpsistī urbis partēs ad incendia; cōnfīrmāstī tē ipsum iam esse exitūrum; dīxistī paulum tibi esse etiam nunc morae, quod ego vīverem. Repertī sunt duo equitēs Rōmānī, quī tē istā cūrā līberārent et sēsē illā ipsā nocte paulō ante lūcem mē in meō lectulō interfectūrōs esse pollicērentur. Haec ego omnia, vixdum etiam coetū vestrō dīmissō, comperī. Domum meam māiōribus praesidiīs mūnīvī atque fīrmāvī; exclūsī eōs, quōs tū ad mē salūtātum māne mīserās, cum illī ipsī vēnissent, quōs ego iam multīs ac summīs virīs ad mē id temporis ventūrōs esse praedīxeram.

V. Quae cum ita sint, Catilīna, perge, quō coepistī. Ēgredere aliquandō ex urbe; patent portae, proficīscere. Nimium diū tē imperātōrem tua illa Mānliāna castra dēsīderant. Ēdūc tēcum etiam omnēs tuōs; sī minus, quam plūrimōs; pūrgā urbem. Māgnō mē metū līberābis, dum modo inter mē atque tē mūrus intersit. Nōbīscum versārī iam diūtius nōn potes; nōn feram, nōn patiar, nōn sinam. Māgna dīs immortālibus habenda est atque huic ipsī Iovī Statōrī, antīquissimō cūstōdī hūius urbis, grātia, quod hanc tam taetram, tam horribilem tamque īnfestam reī pūblicae pestem totiēns iam effūgimus. Nōn est saepius in ūnō homine summa salūs perīclitanda reī pūblicae.

Quam diū mihi, cōnsulī dēsīgnātō, Catilīna, īnsidiātus es, nōn pūblicō mē praesidiō, sed prīvātā dīligentiā dēfendī. Cum proximīs comitiīs cōnsulāribus mē cōnsulem in campō et competītōrēs tuōs interficere voluistī, compressī cōnātūs tuōs nefāriōs amīcōrum praesidiō et cōpiīs, nūllō tumultū pūblicē concitātō; dēnique, quotiēnscumque mē petistī, per mē tibi obstitī, quamquam vidēbam perniciem meam cum māgnā calamitāte reī pūblicae esse coniūnctam.

Nunc iam apertē rem pūblicam ūniversam petis; templa deōrum immortālium, tēcta urbis, vītam omnium cīvium, Italiam tōtam ad exitium et vāstitātem vocās.

Quā rē, quoniam id, quod est prīmum, et quod hūius imperī disciplīnaeque māiōrum proprium est, facere nōndum audeō, faciam id, quod est ad sevēritātem lēnius et ad commūnem salūtem ūtilius. Nam sī tē interficī iusserō, residēbit in rē pūblicā reliqua coniūrātōrum manus; sīn tū, quod tē iam dūdum hortor, exieris, exhauriētur ex urbe tuōrum comitum māgna et perniciōsa sentīna reī pūblicae. Quid est, Catilīna? Num dubitās id mē imperante facere, quod iam tuā sponte faciēbās? Exīre ex urbe iubet cōnsul hostem. Interrogās mē, num in exsilium? Nōn iubeō, sed, sī mē cōnsulis, suādeō.

VI. Quid est enim, Catilīna, quod tē iam in hāc urbe dēlectāre possit? in quā nēmō est extrā istam coniūrātiōnem perditōrum hominum, quī tē nōn metuat; nēmō, quī nōn ōderit. Quae nota domesticae turpitūdinis nōn inūsta vītae tuae est? Quod prīvātārum rērum dēdecus nōn haeret in fāmā? Quae libīdō ab oculīs, quod facinus ā manibus umquam tuīs, quod flāgitium ā tōtō corpore āfuit? Cui tū adulēscentulō, quem corruptēlārum illecebrīs inrētissēs, nōn aut ad audāciam ferrum aut ad libīdinem facem praetulistī?

Quid vērō? nūper, cum morte superiōris uxōris novīs nūptiīs domum vacuēfēcissēs, nōnne etiam aliō incrēdibilī scelere hōc scelus cumulāstī? quod ego praetermittō et facile patior silērī, nē in hāc cīvitāte tantī facinoris immānitās aut exstitisse aut nōn vindicāta esse videātur. Praetermittō ruīnās fortūnārum tuārum, quās omnēs impendēre tibi proximīs Īdibus sentiēs; ad illa veniō, quae nōn ad prīvātam ignōminiam vitiōrum tuōrum, nōn ad domesticam tuam difficultātem ac turpitūdinem, sed ad summam rem pūblicam atque ad omnium nostrum vītam salūtemque pertinent.

Potestne tibi haec lūx, Catilīna, aut hūius caelī spīritus esse iūcundus, cum sciās esse hōrum nēminem, quī nesciat, tē prīdiē Kalendās Iānuāriās Lepidō et Tullō cōnsulibus stetisse in comitiō cum tēlō, manum cōnsulum et prīncipum cīvitātis interficiendōrum causā parāvisse, scelerī ac furōrī tuō nōn mentem aliquam aut timōrem tuum, sed fortūnam populī Rōmānī obstitisse?

Ac iam illa omittō — neque enim sunt aut obscūra aut nōn multa commissa posteā; quotiēns tū mē dēsīgnātum, quotiēns cōnsulem interficere cōnātus es! Quot ego tuās petītiōnēs ita coniectās, ut vītārī posse nōn vidērentur, parvā quādam dēclīnātiōne et, ut āiunt, corpore effūgī! Nihil adsequeris, neque tamen cōnārī ac velle dēsistis. Quotiēns tibi iam extorta est sīca ista dē manibus! Quotiēns excidit cāsū aliquō et ēlāpsa est! Quae quidem quibus abs tē initiāta sacrīs ac dēvōta sit, nesciō, quod eam necesse putās esse in cōnsulis corpore dēfīgere.

VII. Nunc vērō quae tua est ista vīta? Sīc enim iam tēcum loquar, nōn ut odiō permōtus esse videar, quō dēbeō, sed ut misericordiā, quae tibi nūlla dēbētur. Vēnistī paulō ante in senātum. Quis tē ex hāc tantā frequentiā, tot ex tuīs amīcīs ac necessāriīs salūtāvit? Sī hōc post hominum memoriam contigit nēminī, vōcis exspectās contumēliam, cum sīs gravissimō iūdiciō taciturnitātis oppressus?

Quid, quod adventū tuō ista subsellia vacuēfacta sunt, quod omnēs cōnsulārēs, quī tibi persaepe ad caedem cōnstitūtī fuērunt, simul atque adsēdistī, partem istam subselliōrum nūdam atque inānem relīquērunt, quō tandem animō tibi ferendum putās? Servī mē hercule meī sī mē istō pactō metuerent, ut tē metuunt omnēs cīvēs tuī, domum meam relinquendam putārem; tū tibi urbem nōn arbitrāris? et, sī mē meīs cīvibus iniūriā suspectum tam graviter atque offēnsum vidērem, carēre mē aspectū cīvium, quam īnfēstīs omnium oculīs cōnspicī māllem; tū, cum cōnscientiā scelerum tuōrum agnōscās odium omnium iūstum et iam diū tibi dēbitum, dubitās, quōrum mentēs sēnsūsque vulnerās, eōrum aspectum praesentiamque vītāre? Sī tē parentēs timērent atque ōdissent tuī neque eōs ūllā ratiōne plācāre possēs, tū, opīnor, ab eōrum oculīs aliquō concēderēs. Nunc tē patria, quae commūnis est parēns omnium nostrum, ōdit ac metuit et iam diū nihil tē iūdicat nisi dē parricīdiō suō cōgitāre; hūius tū neque auctōritātem verēbere, nec iūdicium sequēre, nec vim pertimēscēs?

Quae tēcum, Catilīna, sīc agit et quōdam modō tacita loquitur:

"Nūllum iam aliquot annīs facinus exstitit nisi per tē, nūllum flāgitium sine tē; tibi ūnī multōrum cīvium necēs, tibi vexātiō dīreptiōque sociōrum impūnīta fuit ac lībera; tū nōn sōlum ad neglegendās lēgēs et quaestiōnēs, vērum etiam ad ēvertendās perfringendāsque valuistī. Superiōra illa, quamquam ferenda nōn fuērunt, tamen, ut potuī, tulī; nunc vērō mē tōtam esse in metū propter ūnum tē, quicquid increpuerit, Catilīnam timērī, nūllum vidērī contrā mē cōnsilium inīrī posse, quod ā tuō scelere abhorreat, nōn est ferendum. Quam ob rem discēde atque hunc mihi timōrem ēripe; sī est vērus, nē opprimar, sīn falsus, ut tandem aliquandō timēre dēsinam."

VIII. Haec sī tēcum, ut dīxī, patria loquātur, nōnne impetrāre dēbeat, etiam sī vim adhibēre nōn possit?

Quid, quod tū tē ipse in cūstōdiam dedistī, quod vītandae suspīciōnis causā ad M'. Lepidum tē habitāre velle dīxistī? Ā quō nōn receptus etiam ad mē venīre ausus es atque, ut domī meae tē adservārem, rogāstī. Cum ā mē quoque id respōnsum tulissēs, mē nūllō modō posse īsdem parietibus tūtō esse tēcum, quī māgnō in perīculō essem, quod īsdem moenibus continērēmur, ad Q. Metellum praetōrem vēnistī. Ā quō repudiātus ad sodālem tuum, virum optimum, M. Metellum, dēmigrāstī; quem tū vidēlicet et ad cūstōdiendum dīligentissimum et ad suspicandum sagācissimum et ad vindicandum fortissimum fore putāstī. Sed quam longē vidētur ā carcere atque ā vinculīs abesse dēbēre, quī sē ipse iam dīgnum cūstōdiā iūdicārit! Quae cum ita sint, Catilīna, dubitās, sī ēmorī aequō animō nōn potes, abīre in aliquās terrās et vītam istam, multīs suppliciīs iūstīs dēbitīsque ēreptam, fugae sōlitūdinīque mandāre?

"Refer," inquis, "ad senātum;" id enim postulās et, sī hīc ōrdō placēre dēcrēverit tē īre in exsilium, obtemperātūrum tē esse dīcis. Nōn referam, id quod abhorret ā meīs mōribus; et tamen faciam, ut intellegās, quid hī dē tē sentiant. *Ēgredere ex urbe, Catilīna, līberā rem pūblicam metū; in exsilium, sī hanc vōcem exspectās, proficīscere.* Quid est, Catilīna? ecquid attendis, ecquid animadvertis hōrum silentium? Patiuntur, tacent. Quid exspectās auctōritātem loquentium, quōrum voluntātem tacitōrum perspicis? At sī hōc idem huic adulēscentī optimō, P. Sēstiō, sī fortissimō virō, M. Mārcellō, dīxissem, iam mihi cōnsulī hōc ipsō in templō iūre optimō senātus vim et manūs intulisset.

Dē tē autem, Catilīna, cum quiēscunt, probant; cum patiuntur, dēcernunt; cum tacent, clāmant; neque hī sōlum, quōrum tibi auctōritās est vidēlicet cāra, vīta vīlissima, sed etiam illī equitēs Rōmānī, honestissimī atque optimī virī, cēterīque fortissimī cīvēs, quī circumstant senātum, quōrum tū et frequentiam vidēre et studia perspicere et vōcēs paulō ante exaudīre potuistī. Quōrum ego vix abs tē iam diū manūs ac tēla contineō, eōsdem facile addūcam, ut tē haec, quae vāstāre iam prīdem studēs, relinquentem ūsque ad portās prōsequantur.

IX. Quamquam quid loquor? Tē ut ūlla rēs frangat? tū ut umquam tē corrigās? tū ut ūllam fugam meditēre? tū ut exsilium cōgitēs? Utinam tibi istam mentem dī immortālēs duint! Tametsī videō sī meā vōce perterritus īre in exsilium animum indūxeris, quanta tempestās invidiae nōbīs, sī minus in praesēns tempus, recentī memoriā scelerum tuōrum, at in posteritātem impendeat. Sed est tantī, dum modo ista sit prīvāta calamitās et ā reī pūblicae perīculīs sēiungātur. Sed tū ut vitiīs tuīs commoveāre, ut lēgum poenās pertimēscās, ut temporibus reī pūblicae cēdās, nōn est postulandum. Neque enim is es, Catilīna, ut tē aut pudor umquam ā turpitūdine aut metus ā perīculō aut ratiō ā furōre revocārit.

Quam ob rem, ut saepe iam dīxī, proficīscere, ac, sī mihi inimīcō, ut praedicās, tuō cōnflāre vīs invidiam, rēctā perge in exsilium. Vix feram sermōnēs hominum, sī id fēceris; vix mōlem istīus invidiae, sī in exsilium iussū cōnsulis ieris, sustinēbō. Sīn autem servīre meae laudī et glōriae māvīs, ēgredere cum importūnā scelerātōrum manū, cōnfer tē ad

Mānlium, concitā perditōs cīvēs, sēcerne tē ā bonīs, īnfer patriae bellum, exsultā impiō lātrōciniō, ut ā mē nōn ēiectus ad aliēnōs, sed invītātus ad tuōs īsse videāris.

Quamquam quid ego tē invītem, ā quō iam sciam esse praemissōs, quī tibi ad Forum Aurēlium praestōlārentur, armātī? cui iam sciam pactam et cōnstitūtam cum Mānliō diem? ā quō etiam aquilam illam argenteam, quam tibi ac tuīs omnibus cōnfīdō perniciōsam ac fūnestam futūram, cui domī tuae sacrārium scelerum tuōrum cōnstitūtum fuit, sciam esse praemissam? Tū ut illā carēre diūtius possīs, quam venerārī ad caedem proficīscēns solēbās, ā cūius altāribus saepe istam impiam dexteram ad necem cīvium trānstulistī?

X. Ībis tandem aliquandō, quō tē iam prīdem ista tua cupiditās effrēnāta ac furiōsa rapiēbat; neque enim tibi haec rēs adfert dolōrem, sed quandam incrēdibilem voluptātem. Ad hanc tē āmentiam nātūra peperit, voluntās exercuit, fortūna servāvit. Numquam tū nōn modo ōtium, sed nē bellum quidem nisi nefārium concupistī. Nactus es ex perditīs atque ab omnī nōn modo fortūnā, vērum etiam spē dērelīctīs cōnflātam improbōrum manum. Hīc tū quā laetitiā perfruēre! quibus gaudiīs exsultābis! quantā in voluptāte bacchābere, cum in tantō numerō tuōrum neque audiēs virum bonum quemquam neque vidēbis!

Ad hūius vītae studium meditātī illī sunt, quī feruntur, labōrēs tuī, iacēre humī nōn sōlum ad obsidendum stuprum, vērum etiam ad facinus obeundum, vigilāre nōn sōlum īnsidiantem somnō marītōrum, vērum etiam bonīs ōtiōsōrum. Habēs, ubi ostentēs tuam illam praeclāram patientiam famis, frīgoris, inopiae rērum omnium, quibus tē brevī tempore cōnfectum esse sentiēs. Tantum prōfēcī tum, cum tē ā cōnsulātū reppulī, ut exsul potius temptāre quam cōnsul vexāre rem pūblicam possēs, atque ut id, quod esset ā tē scelerātē susceptum, lātrōcinium potius quam bellum nōminārētur.

XI. Nunc, ut ā mē, patrēs cōnscrīptī, quandam prope iūstam patriae querimōniam dētester ac dēprecer, percipite, quaesō, dīligenter, quae dīcam, et ea penitus animīs vestrīs mentibusque mandāte. Etenim, sī mēcum patria, quae mihi vītā meā multō est cārior, sī cūncta Italia, sī omnis rēs pūblica loquātur:

"M. Tullī, quid agis? Tūne eum, quem esse hostem comperistī, quem ducem bellī futūrum vidēs, quem exspectārī imperātōrem in castrīs hostium sentīs, auctōrem sceleris, prīncipem coniūrātiōnis, ēvocātōrem servōrum et cīvium perditōrum, exīre patiēre, ut abs tē nōn ēmissus ex urbe, sed immissus in urbem esse videātur? Nōnne hunc in vincula dūcī, nōn ad mortem rapī, nōn summō suppliciō mactārī imperābis?

"Quid tandem tē impedit? Mōsne māiōrum? At persaepe etiam prīvātī in hāc rē pūblicā perniciōsōs cīvēs morte multārunt. An lēgēs, quae dē cīvium Rōmānōrum suppliciō rogātae sunt? At numquam in hāc urbe, quī ā rē pūblicā dēfēcērunt, cīvium iūra tenuērunt. An invidiam posteritātis timēs? Praeclāram vērō populō Rōmānō refers grātiam, quī tē, hominem per tē cognitum, nūllā commendātiōne māiōrum tam mātūrē ad summum imperium per omnēs honōrum gradūs extulit, sī propter invidiae aut alicūius perīculī metum salūtem cīvium tuōrum neglegis. Sed, sī quis est invidiae metus, num est vehementius sevēritātis ac fortitūdinis invidia quam inertiae ac nēquitiae pertimēscenda? An, cum bellō vāstābitur

Italia, vexābuntur urbēs, tēcta ārdēbunt, tum tē nōn exīstimās invidiae incendiō cōnflagrātūrum?"

XII. Hīs ego sānctissimīs reī pūblicae vōcibus et eōrum hominum, quī hōc idem sentiunt, mentibus pauca respondēbō. Ego, sī hōc optimum factū iūdicārem, patrēs cōnscrīptī, Catilīnam morte multārī, ūnīus ūsūram hōrae gladiātōrī istī ad vīvendum nōn dedissem. Etenim, sī summī virī et clārissimī cīvēs Sāturnīnī et Gracchōrum et Flaccī et superiōrum complūrium sanguine nōn modo sē nōn contāminārunt, sed etiam honestārunt, certē verendum mihi nōn erat, nē quid hōc parricīdā cīvium interfectō invidiae mihi in posteritātem redundāret. Quod sī ea mihi māximē impendēret, tamen hōc animō semper fuī, ut invidiam virtūte partam glōriam, nōn invidiam putārem.

Quamquam nōn nūllī sunt in hōc ōrdine, quī aut ea, quae imminent, nōn videant aut ea, quae vident, dissimulent; quī spem Catilīnae mollibus sententiīs aluērunt coniūrātiōnemque nāscentem nōn crēdendō corrōborāvērunt; quōrum auctōritātem secūtī multī nōn sōlum improbī, vērum etiam imperītī, sī in hunc animadvertissem, crūdēliter et rēgiē factum esse dīcerent. Nunc intellegō, sī iste, quō intendit, in Mānliāna castra pervēnerit, nēminem tam stultum fore, quī nōn videat coniūrātiōnem esse factam, nēminem tam improbum, quī nōn fateātur. Hōc autem ūnō interfectō intellegō hanc reī pūblicae pestem paulisper reprimī, nōn in perpetuum comprimī posse. Quod sī sē ēiēcerit sēcumque suōs ēdūxerit et eōdem cēterōs undique collēctōs naufragōs aggregārit, exstinguētur atque dēlēbitur nōn modo haec tam adulta reī pūblicae pestis, vērum etiam stirps ac sēmen malōrum omnium.

XIII. Etenim iam diū, patrēs cōnscrīptī, in hīs perīculīs coniūrātiōnis īnsidiīsque versāmur, sed nesciō quō pactō omnium scelerum ac veteris furōris et audāciae mātūritās in nostrī cōnsulātūs tempus ērūpit. Quod sī ex tantō lātrōciniō iste ūnus tollētur, vidēbimur fortasse ad breve quoddam tempus cūrā et metū esse relevātī, perīculum autem residēbit et erit inclūsum penitus in vēnīs atque in vīsceribus reī pūblicae. Ut saepe hominēs aegrī morbō gravī, cum aestū febrīque iactantur, sī aquam gelidam bibērunt, prīmō relevārī videntur, deinde multō gravius vehementiusque adflīctantur, sīc hīc morbus, quī est in rē pūblicā, relevātus istīus poenā, vehementius reliquīs vīvīs ingravēscet.

Quā rē sēcēdant improbī, sēcernant sē ā bonīs, ūnum in locum congregentur, mūrō dēnique, id quod saepe iam dīxī, sēcernantur ā nōbīs; dēsinant īnsidiārī domī suae cōnsulī, circumstāre tribūnal praetōris urbānī, obsidēre cum gladiīs cūriam, malleolōs et facēs ad īnflammandam urbem comparāre; sit dēnique īnscrīptum in fronte ūnīus cūiusque, quid dē rē pūblicā sentiat. Polliceor hōc vōbīs, patrēs cōnscrīptī, tantam in nōbīs cōnsulibus fore dīligentiam, tantam in vōbīs auctōritātem, tantam in equitibus Rōmānīs virtūtem, tantam in omnibus bonīs cōnsēnsiōnem, ut Catilīnae profectiōne omnia patefacta, illūstrāta, oppressa, vindicāta esse videātis.

Hīsce ōminibus, Catilīna, cum summā reī pūblicae salūte, cum tuā peste ac perniciē cumque eōrum exitiō, quī sē tēcum omnī scelere parricīdiōque iūnxērunt, proficīscere ad impium bellum ac nefārium.

Tū, Iuppiter, quī eīsdem quibus haec urbs auspiciīs ā Rōmulō es cōnstitūtus, quem Statōrem hūius urbis atque imperī vērē nōmināmus, hunc et hūius sociōs ā tuīs cēterīsque templīs, ā tēctīs urbis ac moenibus, ā vītā fortūnīsque cīvium arcēbis, et hominēs bonōrum inimīcōs, hostēs patriae, lātrōnēs Italiae, scelerum foedere inter sē ac nefāriā societāte coniūnctōs, aeternīs suppliciīs vīvōs mortuōsque mactābis.

M. TULLI CICERONIS

IN L. CATILINAM ORATIO SECUNDA

HABITA AD POPULUM.

I. Tandem aliquandō, Quirītēs, L. Catilīnam, furentem audāciā, scelus anhēlantem, pestem patriae nefāriē mōlientem, vōbīs atque huic urbī ferrō flammāque minitantem, ex urbe vel ēiēcimus vel ēmīsimus vel ipsum ēgredientem verbīs prōsecūtī sumus. Abiit, excessit, ēvāsit, ērūpit. Nūlla iam perniciēs ā mōnstrō illō atque prōdigiō moenibus ipsīs intrā moenia comparābitur.

Atque hunc quidem ūnum hūius bellī domesticī ducem sine contrōversiā vīcimus. Nōn enim iam inter latera nostra sīca illa versābitur; nōn in campō, nōn in forō, nōn in cūriā, nōn dēnique intrā domesticōs parietēs pertimēscēmus. Locō ille mōtus est, cum est ex urbe dēpulsus. Palam iam cum hoste nūllō impediente bellum gerēmus. Sine dubiō perdidimus hominem māgnificēque vīcimus, cum illum ex occultīs īnsidiīs in apertum lātrōcinium coniēcimus. Quod vērō nōn cruentum mūcrōnem, ut voluit, extulit, quod vīvīs nōbīs ēgressus est, quod eī ferrum ē manibus extorsimus, quod incolumēs cīvēs, quod stantem urbem relīquit, quantō tandem illum maerōre esse adflīctum et prōflīgātum putātis? Iacet ille nunc

THE ROMAN FORUM AND CAPITOLINE HILL IN CICERO'S TIME.

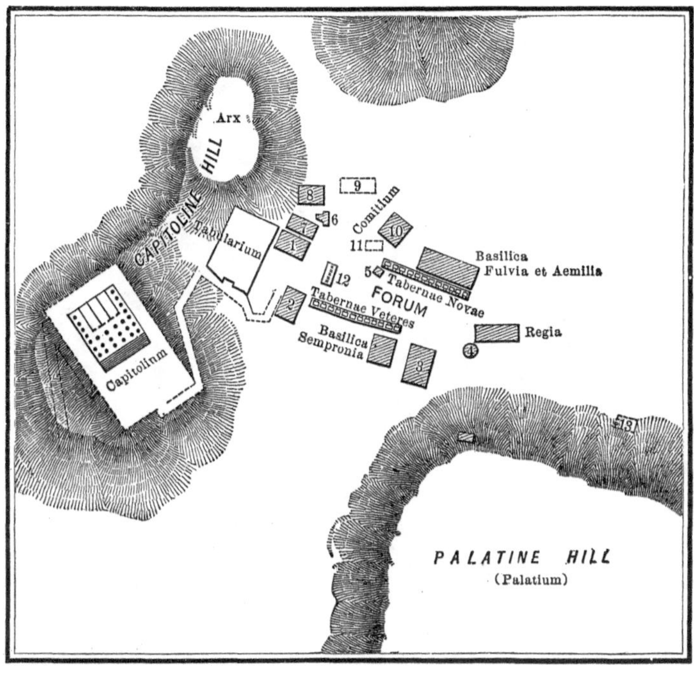

1. Temple of Concord.
2. Temple of Saturn.
3. Temple of Castor.
4. Temple of Vesta.
5. Probable location of the Temple of Janus.
6. Prison — Carcer.
7. Probable location of the Basilica Opimia.
8. Probable location of the Basilica Porcia.
9. Probable location of the Curia Hostilia.
10. Curia Julia.
11. Probable location of the Rostra before 44 B.C.
12. Rostra, after 44 B.C.
13. Probable location of the Temple of Jupiter Stator.

Cicero's house stood on the northern part of the Palatine Hill overlooking the Forum.

prōstrātus, Quirītēs, et sē perculsum atque abiectum esse sentit et retorquet oculōs profectō saepe ad hanc urbem, quam ē suīs faucibus ēreptam esse lūget; quae quidem mihi laetārī vidētur, quod tantam pestem ēvomuerit forāsque prōiēcerit.

II. Ac sī quis est tālis, quālēs esse omnēs oportēbat, quī in hōc ipsō, in quō exsultat et triumphat ōrātiō mea, mē vehementer accūset, quod tam capitālem hostem nōn comprehenderim potius quam ēmīserim, nōn est ista mea culpa, Quirītēs, sed temporum. Interfectum esse L. Catilīnam et gravissimō suppliciō adfectum iam prīdem oportēbat, idque ā mē et mōs māiōrum et hūius imperī sevēritās et rēs pūblica postulābat. Sed quam multōs fuisse putātis, quī, quae ego dēferrem, nōn crēderent? quam multōs, quī etiam dēfenderent?

Ac, sī illō sublātō dēpellī ā vōbīs omne perīculum iūdicārem, iam prīdem ego L. Catilīnam nōn modo invidiae meae, vērum etiam vītae perīculō sustulissem. Sed cum vidērem, nē vōbīs quidem omnibus rē etiam tum probātā, sī illum, ut erat meritus, morte multāssem, fore ut ēius sociōs invidiā oppressus persequī nōn possem, rem hūc dēdūxī, ut tum palam pūgnāre possētis, cum hostem apertē vidērētis.

Quem quidem ego hostem, Quirītēs, quam vehementer forīs esse timendum putem, licet hinc intellegātis, quod etiam illud molestē ferō, quod ex urbe parum comitātus exierit. Utinam ille omnēs sēcum suās cōpiās ēdūxisset! Tongilium mihi ēdūxit, quem amāre in praetextā coeperat, Pūblicium et Minucium, quōrum aes aliēnum, contrāctum in popīnā, nūllum reī pūblicae mōtum adferre poterat; relīquit quōs virōs! quantō aere aliēnō! quam valentēs! quam nōbilēs!

III. Itaque ego illum exercitum prae Gallicānīs legiōnibus et hōc dīlēctū, quem in agrō Pīcēnō et Gallicō Q. Metellus habuit, et hīs cōpiīs, quae ā nōbīs cotīdiē comparantur, māgnō opere contemnō, collēctum ex senibus dēspērātīs, ex agrestī lūxuriā, ex rūsticīs dēcoctōribus, ex eīs, quī vadimōnia dēserere quam illum exercitum māluērunt; quibus ego nōn modo sī aciem exercitūs nostrī, vērum etiam sī ēdictum praetōris ostenderō, concident. Hōs, quōs videō volitāre in forō, quōs stāre ad cūriam, quōs etiam in senātum venīre, quī nitent unguentīs, quī fulgent purpurā, māllem sēcum mīlitēs ēdūxisset; quī sī hīc permanent, mementōte nōn tam exercitum illum esse nōbīs quam hōs, quī exercitum dēseruērunt, pertimēscendōs.

Atque hōc etiam sunt timendī magis, quod, quid cōgitent, mē scīre sentiunt, neque tamen permoventur. Videō, cui sit Āpūlia attribūta, quis habeat Etrūriam, quis agrum Pīcēnum, quis Gallicum, quis sibi hās urbānās īnsidiās caedis atque incendiōrum dēpoposcerit. Omnia superiōris noctis cōnsilia ad mē perlāta esse sentiunt; patefēcī in senātū hesternō diē; Catilīna ipse pertimuit, profūgit; hī quid exspectant? Nē illī vehementer errant, sī illam meam prīstinam lēnitātem perpetuam spērant futūram.

IV. Quod exspectāvī, iam sum adsecūtus, ut vōs omnēs factam esse apertē coniūrātiōnem contrā rem pūblicam vidērētis; nisi vērō sī quis est, quī Catilīnae similīs cum Catilīnā sentīre nōn putet. Nōn est iam lēnitātī locus; sevēritātem rēs ipsa flāgitat. Ūnum etiam nunc concēdam: exeant, proficīscantur, nē patiantur dēsīderiō suī Catilīnam miserum tābēscere. Dēmōnstrābō iter, Aurēliā viā profectus est; sī accelerāre volent, ad vesperam cōnsequentur.

Ō fortūnātam rem pūblicam, sī quidem hanc sentīnam urbis ēiēcerit! Ūnō mē hercule Catilīnā exhaustō, levāta mihi et recreāta rēs pūblica vidētur. Quid enim malī aut sceleris fingī aut cōgitārī potest, quod nōn ille concēperit? Quis tōtā Italiā venēficus, quis gladiātor, quis lātrō, quis sīcārius, quis parricīda, quis testāmentōrum subiector, quis circumscrīptor, quis gāneō, quis nepōs, quis adulter, quae mulier īnfāmis, quis corruptor iuventūtis, quis corruptus, quis perditus invenīrī potest, quī sē cum Catilīnā nōn familiārissimē vīxisse fateātur? Quae caedēs per hōsce annōs sine illō facta est? quod nefārium stuprum nōn per illum?

Iam vērō quae tanta umquam in ūllō homine iuventūtis illecebra fuit, quanta in illō? quī aliōs ipse amābat turpissimē, aliōrum amōrī flāgitiōsissimē serviēbat, aliīs frūctum libīdinum, aliīs mortem parentum nōn modo impellendō, vērum etiam adiuvandō, pollicēbātur. Nunc vērō quam subitō nōn sōlum ex urbe, vērum etiam ex agrīs ingentem numerum perditōrum hominum collēgerat! Nēmō nōn modo Rōmae, sed nē ūllō quidem in angulō tōtīus Italiae oppressus aere aliēnō fuit, quem nōn ad hōc incrēdibile sceleris foedus ascīverit.

V. Atque ut ēius dīversa studia in dissimilī ratiōne perspicere possītis, nēmō est in lūdō gladiātōriō paulō ad facinus audācior, quī sē nōn intimum Catilīnae esse fateātur; nēmō est in scaenā levior et nēquior, quī sē nōn ēiusdem prope sodālem fuisse commemoret. Atque īdem tamen, stuprōrum et scelerum exercitātiōne adsuēfactus, frīgore et fame et sitī et vigiliīs perferendīs fortis ab istīs praedicābātur, cum industriae subsidia atque īnstrūmenta virtūtis in libīdine audāciāque cōnsūmeret.

Hunc vērō sī secūtī erunt suī comitēs, sī ex urbe exierint dēspērātōrum hominum flāgitiōsī gregēs, Ō nōs beātōs, Ō rem pūblicam fortūnātam, Ō praeclāram laudem cōnsulātūs meī! Nōn enim iam sunt mediocrēs hominum libīdinēs, nōn hūmānae ac tolerandae audāciae; nihil cōgitant nisi caedem, nisi incendia, nisi rapīnās. Patrimōnia sua profūdērunt, fortūnās suās obligāvērunt; rēs eōs iam prīdem, fidēs nūper dēficere coepit; eadem tamen illa, quae erat in abundantiā, libīdō manet. Quod sī in vīnō et āleā cōmissātiōnēs sōlum et scorta quaererent, essent illī quidem dēspērandī, sed tamen essent ferendī; hōc vērō quis ferre possit, inertēs hominēs fortissimīs virīs īnsidiārī, stultissimōs prūdentissimīs, ēbriōsōs sōbriīs, dormientēs vigilantibus? quī mihi accubantēs in convīviīs, complexī mulierēs impudīcās, vīnō languidī, cōnfertī cibō, sertīs redimītī, unguentīs oblitī, dēbilitātī stuprīs, ērūctant sermōnibus suīs caedem bonōrum atque urbis incendia.

Quibus ego cōnfīdō impendēre fātum aliquod, et poenam iam diū improbitātī, nēquitiae, scelerī, libīdinī dēbitam aut īnstāre iam plānē aut certē appropinquāre. Quōs sī meus cōnsulātus, quoniam sānāre nōn potest, sustulerit, nōn breve nesciō quod tempus, sed multa saecula prōpāgārit reī pūblicae. Nūlla est enim nātiō, quam pertimēscāmus; nūllus rēx, quī bellum populō Rōmānō facere possit. Omnia sunt externa ūnīus virtūte terrā marīque pācāta; domesticum bellum manet, intus īnsidiae sunt, intus inclūsum perīculum est, intus est hostis. Cum lūxuriā nōbīs, cum āmentiā, cum scelere certandum est.

Huic ego mē bellō ducem profiteor, Quirītēs; suscipiō inimīcitiās hominum perditōrum. Quae sānārī poterunt, quācumque ratiōne sānābō; quae resecanda erunt, nōn patiar ad perniciem cīvitātis manēre. Proinde aut exeant aut quiēscant aut, sī et in urbe et in eādem mente permanent, ea, quae merentur, exspectent.

VI. At etiam sunt, quī dīcant, Quirītēs, ā mē in exsilium ēiectum esse Catilīnam. Quod ego sī verbō adsequī possem, istōs ipsōs ēicerem, quī haec loquuntur. Homō enim vidēlicet timidus aut etiam permodestus vōcem cōnsulis ferre nōn potuit; simul atque īre in exsilium iussus est, pāruit, īvit.

Quid? ut hesternō diē, Quirītēs, cum domī meae paene interfectus essem, senātum in aedem Iovis Statōris convocāvī, rem omnem ad patrēs cōnscrīptōs dētulī: quō cum Catilīna vēnisset, quis eum senātor appellāvit? quis salūtāvit? quis dēnique ita aspexit ut perditum cīvem, ac nōn potius ut importūnissimum hostem? Quīn etiam prīncipēs ēius ōrdinis partem illam subselliōrum, ad quam ille accesserat, nūdam atque inānem relīquērunt.

Hīc ego vehemēns ille cōnsul, quī verbō cīvēs in exsilium ēiciō, quaesīvī ā Catilīnā, in nocturnō conventū apud M. Laecam fuisset necne. Cum ille, homō audācissimus, cōnscientiā convictus prīmō reticuisset, patefēcī cētera; quid eā nocte ēgisset, quid in proximam cōnstituisset, quem ad modum esset eī ratiō tōtīus bellī dēscrīpta, ēdocuī. Cum haesitāret, cum tenērētur, quaesīvī, quid dubitāret proficīscī eō, quō iam prīdem parāret, cum arma, cum secūrēs, cum fascēs, cum tubās, cum sīgna mīlitāria, cum aquilam illam argenteam, cui ille etiam sacrārium domī suae fēcerat, scīrem esse praemissam. In exsilium ēiciēbam, quem iam ingressum esse in bellum vidēbam? Etenim, crēdō, Mānlius iste centuriō, quī in agrō Faesulānō castra posuit, bellum populō Rōmānō suō nōmine indīxit, et illa castra nunc nōn Catilīnam ducem exspectant, et ille ēiectus in exsilium sē Massiliam, ut āiunt, nōn in haec castra cōnferet.

VII. Ō condiciōnem miseram nōn modo administrandae, vērum etiam cōnservandae reī pūblicae! Nunc sī L. Catilīna cōnsiliīs, labōribus, perīculīs meīs circumclūsus ac dēbilitātus subitō pertimuerit, sententiam mūtāverit, dēseruerit suōs, cōnsilium bellī faciendī abiēcerit, ex hōc cursū sceleris ac bellī iter ad fugam atque in exsilium converterit, nōn ille ā mē spoliātus armīs audāciae, nōn obstupefactus ac perterritus meā dīligentiā, nōn dē spē cōnātūque dēpulsus, sed indemnātus, innocēns, in exsilium ēiectus ā cōnsule vī et minīs esse dīcētur; et erunt, quī illum, sī hōc fēcerit, nōn improbum, sed miserum, mē nōn dīligentissimum cōnsulem, sed crūdēlissimum tyrannum exīstimārī velint!

Est mihi tantī, Quirītēs, hūius invidiae falsae atque inīquae tempestātem subīre, dum modo ā vōbīs hūius horribilis bellī ac nefāriī perīculum dēpellātur. Dīcātur sānē ēiectus esse ā mē, dum modo eat in exsilium. Sed, mihi crēdite, nōn est itūrus. Numquam ego ab dīs immortālibus optābō, Quirītēs, invidiae meae levandae causā, ut L. Catilīnam dūcere exercitum hostium atque in armīs volitāre audiātis; sed trīduō tamen audiētis; multōque magis illud timeō, nē mihi sit invidiōsum aliquandō, quod illum ēmīserim potius quam quod ēiēcerim. Sed cum sint hominēs, quī illum, cum profectus sit, ēiectum esse dīcant, īdem, sī interfectus esset, quid dīcerent?

Quamquam istī, quī Catilīnam Massiliam īre dictitant, nōn tam hōc queruntur quam verentur. Nēmō est istōrum tam misericors, quī illum nōn ad Mānlium quam ad Massiliēnsēs īre mālit. Ille autem, sī mē hercule hōc, quod agit, numquam anteā cōgitāsset, tamen lātrōcinantem sē interficī māllet quam exsulem vīvere. Nunc vērō, cum eī nihil adhūc praeter ipsīus voluntātem cōgitātiōnemque acciderit, nisi quod vīvīs nōbīs Rōmā profectus est, optēmus potius, ut eat in exsilium, quam querāmur.

VIII. Sed cūr tam diū dē ūnō hoste loquimur, et dē hoste, quī iam fatētur sē esse hostem, et quem, quia, quod semper voluī, mūrus interest, nōn timeō; dē eīs, quī dissimulant, quī Rōmae remanent, quī nōbīscum sunt, nihil dīcimus? Quōs quidem ego, sī ūllō modō fierī possit, nōn tam ulcīscī studeō quam sānāre sibi ipsōs, plācāre reī pūblicae, neque, id quā rē fierī nōn possit, sī mē audīre volent, intellegō. Expōnam enim vōbīs, Quirītēs, ex quibus generibus hominum istae cōpiae comparentur; deinde singulīs medicīnam cōnsilī atque ōrātiōnis meae, sī quam poterō, adferam.

Ūnum genus est eōrum, quī māgnō in aere aliēnō māiōrēs etiam possessiōnēs habent, quārum amōre adductī dissolvī nūllō modō possunt. Hōrum hominum speciēs est honestissima; sunt enim locuplētēs; voluntās vērō et causa impudentissima. Tū agrīs, tū aedificiīs, tū argentō, tū familiā, tū rēbus omnibus ōrnātus et cōpiōsus sīs, et dubitēs dē possessiōne dētrahere, adquīrere ad fidem? Quid enim exspectās? Bellum? Quid ergō? in vāstātiōne omnium tuās possessiōnēs sacrōsānctās futūrās putās? An tabulās novās? Errant, quī istās ā Catilīnā exspectant; meō beneficiō tabulae novae prōferentur, vērum auctiōnāriae; neque enim istī, quī possessiōnēs habent, aliā ratiōne ūllā salvī esse possunt. Quod sī mātūrius facere voluissent, neque, id quod stultissimum est, certāre cum ūsūrīs frūctibus praediōrum, et locuplētiōribus hīs et meliōribus cīvibus ūterēmur. Sed hōsce hominēs minimē putō pertimēscendōs, quod aut dēdūcī dē sententiā possunt aut, sī permanēbunt, magis mihi videntur vōta factūrī contrā rem pūblicam quam arma lātūrī.

IX. Alterum genus est eōrum, quī, quamquam premuntur aere aliēnō, dominātiōnem tamen exspectant, rērum potīrī volunt, honōrēs, quōs quiētā rē pūblicā dēspērant, perturbātā sē cōnsequī posse arbitrantur. Quibus hōc praecipiendum vidētur, ūnum scilicet et idem quod reliquīs omnibus, ut dēspērent sē id, quod cōnantur, cōnsequī posse; prīmum omnium mē ipsum vigilāre, adesse, prōvidēre reī pūblicae; deinde māgnōs animōs esse in bonīs virīs, māgnam concordiam in māximā multitūdine, māgnās praetereā cōpiās mīlitum; deōs dēnique immortālēs huic invictō populō, clārissimō imperiō, pulcherrimae urbī contrā tantam vim sceleris praesentīs auxilium esse lātūrōs. Quod sī iam sint id, quod summō furōre cupiunt, adeptī, num illī in cinere urbis et in sanguine cīvium, quae mente cōnscelerātā ac nefāriā concupīvērunt, sē cōnsulēs ac dictātōrēs aut etiam rēgēs spērant futūrōs? Nōn vident id sē cupere, quod sī adeptī sint, fugitīvō alicui aut gladiātōrī concēdī sit necesse?

Tertium genus est aetāte iam adfectum, sed tamen exercitātiōne rōbustum; quō ex genere iste est Mānlius, cui nunc Catilīna succēdit. Hī sunt hōmines ex eīs colōniīs, quās Sulla cōnstituit; quās ego ūniversās cīvium esse optimōrum et fortissimōrum virōrum sentiō, sed tamen eī sunt colōnī, quī sē in īnspērātīs ac repentīnīs pecūniīs sūmptuōsius insolentiusque iactārunt. Hī dum aedificant tamquam beātī, dum praediīs lēctīs, familiīs māgnīs, convīviīs apparātīs dēlectantur, in tantum aes aliēnum incidērunt, ut, sī salvī esse velint, Sulla sit eīs ab īnferīs excitandus; quī etiam nōn nūllōs agrestēs, hominēs tenuēs atque egentēs, in eandem illam spem rapīnārum veterum impulērunt.

Quōs ego utrōsque in eōdem genere praedātōrum dīreptōrumque pōnō; sed eōs hōc moneō, dēsinant furere ac prōscrīptiōnēs et dictātūrās cōgitāre. Tantus enim illōrum temporum dolor inūstus est cīvitātī, ut iam ista nōn modo hominēs, sed nē pecudēs quidem mihi passūrae esse videantur.

X. Quārtum genus est sānē varium et mixtum et turbulentum; quī iam prīdem premuntur, quī numquam ēmergunt, quī partim inertiā, partim male gerendō negōtiō, partim etiam sūmptibus in vetere aere aliēnō vacillant; quī vadimōniīs, iūdiciīs, prōscrīptiōne bonōrum dēfatīgātī, permultī et ex urbe et ex agrīs sē in illa castra cōnferre dīcuntur. Hōsce ego nōn tam mīlitēs ācrēs quam īnfitiātōrēs lentōs esse arbitror. Quī hominēs prīmum, sī stāre nōn possunt, corruant; sed ita, ut nōn modo cīvitās, sed nē vīcīnī quidem proximī sentiant. Nam illud nōn intellegō, quam ob rem, sī vīvere honestē nōn possunt, perīre turpiter velint, aut cūr minōre dolōre peritūrōs sē cum multīs, quam sī sōlī pereant, arbitrentur.

Quīntum genus est parricīdārum, sīcāriōrum, dēnique omnium facinerōsōrum. Quōs ego ā Catilīnā nōn revocō; nam neque ab eō dīvellī possunt et pereant sānē in lātrōciniō, quoniam sunt ita multī, ut eōs carcer capere nōn possit.

Postrēmum autem genus est nōn sōlum numerō, vērum etiam genere ipsō atque vītā, quod proprium Catilīnae est, dē ēius dīlēctū, immō vērō dē complexū ēius ac sinū; quōs pexō capillō, nitidōs, aut imberbēs aut bene barbātōs vidētis, manicātīs et tālāribus tunicīs, vēlīs amictōs, nōn togīs; quōrum omnis industria vītae et vigilandī labor in antelūcānīs cēnīs exprōmitur. In hīs gregibus omnēs āleātōrēs, omnēs adulterī, omnēs impūrī impudīcīque versantur. Hī puerī tam lepidī ac dēlicātī nōn sōlum amāre et amārī, neque saltāre et cantāre, sed etiam sīcās vibrāre et spargere venēna didicērunt. Quī nisi exeunt, nisi pereunt, etiam sī Catilīna perierit, scītōte hōc in rē pūblica sēminārium Catilīnārum futūrum. Vērum tamen quid sibi istī miserī volunt? Num suās sēcum mulierculās sunt in castra ductūrī? Quem ad modum autem illīs carēre poterunt, hīs praesertim iam noctibus? Quō autem pactō illī Appennīnum atque illās pruīnās ac nivēs perferent? nisi idcircō sē facilius hiemem tolerātūrōs putant, quod nūdī in convīviīs saltāre didicērunt.

XI. Ō bellum māgnō opere pertimēscendum, cum hanc sit habitūrus Catilīna scortōrum cohortem praetōriam! Īnstruite nunc, Quirītēs, contrā hās tam praeclārās Catilīnae cōpiās vestra praesidia vestrōsque exercitūs.

Et prīmum gladiātōrī illī cōnfectō et sauciō cōnsulēs imperātōrēsque vestrōs oppōnite; deinde contrā illam naufragōrum ēiectam ac dēbilitātam manum, flōrem tōtīus Italiae ac rōbur ēdūcite. Iam vērō urbēs colōniārum ac mūnicipiōrum respondēbunt Catilīnae tumulīs silvestribus. Neque ego cēterās cōpiās, ōrnāmenta, praesidia vestra cum illīus lātrōnis inopiā atque egestāte cōnferre dēbeō.

Sed sī omissīs hīs rēbus, quibus nōs suppeditāmur, eget ille, senātū, equitibus Rōmānīs, urbe, aerāriō, vectīgālibus, cūnctā Italiā, prōvinciīs omnibus, exterīs nātiōnibus, sī hīs rēbus omissīs causās ipsās, quae inter sē cōnflīgunt, contendere velīmus, ex eō ipsō, quam valdē illī iaceant, intellegere possumus. Ex hāc enim parte pudor pūgnat, illinc petulantia; hinc pudīcitia, illinc stuprum; hinc fidēs, illinc fraudātiō; hinc pietās, illinc scelus; hinc cōnstantia, illinc furor; hinc honestās, illinc turpitūdō; hinc continentia, illinc libīdō; dēnique aequitās, temperantia, fortitūdō, prūdentia, virtūtēs omnēs certant cum inīquitāte, lūxuriā, ignāviā, temeritāte, cum vitiīs omnibus; postrēmō cōpia cum egestāte, bona ratiō cum perditā, mēns sāna cum āmentiā, bona dēnique spēs cum omnium rērum dēspērātiōne cōnflīgit. In ēius modī certāmine ac proeliō nōnne, etiam sī hominum studia dēficiant, dī ipsī immortālēs cōgant ab hīs praeclārissimīs virtūtibus tot et tanta vitia superārī?

XII. Quae cum ita sint, Quirītēs, vōs, quem ad modum iam anteā dīxī, vestra tēcta vigiliīs cūstōdiīsque dēfendite; mihi, ut urbī sine vestrō mōtū ac sine ūllō tumultū satis esset praesidī, cōnsultum atque prōvīsum est. Colōnī omnēs mūnicipēsque vestrī, certiōrēs ā mē factī dē hāc nocturnā excursiōne Catilīnae, facile urbēs suās fīnēsque dēfendent. Gladiātōrēs, quam sibi ille manum certissimam fore putāvit, — quamquam animō meliōre sunt quam pars patriciōrum — potestāte tamen nostrā continēbuntur. Q. Metellus, quem ego hōc prōspiciēns in agrum Gallicum Pīcēnumque praemīsī, aut opprimet hominem aut ēius omnēs mōtūs cōnātūsque prohibēbit. Reliquīs autem dē rēbus cōnstituendīs, mātūrandīs, agendīs iam ad senātum referēmus, quem vocārī vidētis.

Nunc illōs, quī in urbe remānsērunt, atque adeō quī contrā urbis salūtem omniumque vestrum in urbe ā Catilīnā relīctī sunt, quamquam sunt hostēs, tamen, quia sunt cīvēs, monitōs etiam atque etiam volō. Mea lēnitās adhūc sī cui solūtior vīsa est, hōc exspectāvit, ut id, quod latēbat, ērumperet. Quod reliquum est, iam nōn possum oblīvīscī, meam hanc esse patriam, mē hōrum esse cōnsulem, mihi aut cum hīs vīvendum aut prō hīs esse moriendum. Nūllus est portīs cūstōs, nūllus īnsidiātor viae; sī quī exīre volunt, cōnīvēre possum; quī vērō sē in urbe commōverit, cūius ego nōn modo factum, sed inceptum ūllum cōnātumve contrā patriam dēprehenderō, sentiet in hāc urbe esse cōnsulēs vigilantēs, esse ēgregiōs magistrātūs, esse fortem senātum, esse arma, esse carcerem quem vindicem nefāriōrum ac manifēstōrum scelerum māiōrēs nostrī esse voluērunt.

XIII. Atque haec omnia sīc agentur, Quirītēs, ut māximae rēs minimō mōtū, perīcula summa nūllō tumultū, bellum intestīnum ac domesticum post hominum memoriam crūdēlissimum et māximum mē ūnō togātō duce et imperātōre sedētur. Quod ego sīc administrābō, Quirītēs, ut, sī ūllō modō fierī poterit, nē improbus quidem quisquam in hāc urbe poenam suī sceleris sufferat. Sed sī vīs manifēstae audāciae, sī impendēns patriae perīculum mē necessāriō dē hāc animī lēnitāte dēdūxerit, illud profectō perficiam, quod in tantō et tam īnsidiōsō bellō vix optandum vidētur, ut neque bonus quisquam intereat paucōrumque poenā vōs omnēs salvī esse possītis.

Quae quidem ego neque meā prūdentiā neque hūmānīs cōnsiliīs frētus polliceor vōbīs, Quirītēs, sed multīs et nōn dubiīs deōrum immortālium sīgnificātiōnibus, quibus ego ducibus in hanc spem sententiamque sum ingressus; quī iam nōn procul, ut quondam solēbant, ab externō hoste atque longinquō, sed hīc praesentēs suō nūmine atque auxiliō sua templa atque urbis tēcta dēfendunt. Quōs vōs, Quirītēs, precārī, venerārī, implōrāre dēbētis, ut quam urbem pulcherrimam flōrentissimamque esse voluērunt, hanc omnibus hostium cōpiīs terrā marīque superātīs ā perditissimōrum cīvium nefāriō scelere dēfendant.

M. TULLI CICERONIS

IN L. CATILINAM ORATIO TERTIA

HABITA AD POPULUM.

I. Rem pūblicam, Quirītēs, vītamque omnium vestrum, bona, fortūnās, coniugēs līberōsque vestrōs atque hōc domicilium clārissimī imperī, fortūnātissimam pulcherrimamque urbem, hodiernō diē deōrum immortālium summō ergā vōs amōre, labōribus, cōnsiliīs, perīculīs meīs ē flammā atque ferrō ac paene ex faucibus fātī ēreptam et vōbīs cōnservātam ac restitūtam vidētis.

Et sī nōn minus nōbīs iūcundī atque illūstrēs sunt eī diēs, quibus cōnservāmur, quam illī, quibus nāscimur, quod salūtis certa laetitia est, nāscendī incerta condiciō, et quod sine sēnsū nāscimur, cum voluptāte servāmur, profectō, quoniam illum, quī hanc urbem condidit, ad deōs immortālēs benevolentiā fāmāque sustulimus, esse apud vōs posterōsque vestrōs in honōre dēbēbit is, quī eandem hanc urbem conditam amplificātamque servāvit. Nam tōtī urbī, templīs, dēlūbrīs, tēctīs ac moenibus subiectōs prope iam īgnēs circumdatōsque restīnximus, īdemque gladiōs in rem pūblicam dēstrīctōs rettūdimus mūcrōnēsque eōrum ā iugulīs vestrīs dēiēcimus. Quae quoniam in senātū illūstrāta, patefacta, comperta sunt per mē, vōbīs iam expōnam breviter, Quirītēs, ut, et quanta et quā ratiōne invēstīgāta et comprehēnsa sint, vōs, quī et ignōrātis et exspectātis, scīre possītis.

Prīncipiō, ut Catilīna paucīs ante diēbus ērūpit ex urbe, cum sceleris suī sociōs, hūiusce nefāriī bellī ācerrimōs ducēs, Rōmae relīquisset, semper vigilāvī et prōvīdī, Quirītēs, quem ad modum in tantīs et tam absconditīs īnsidiīs salvī esse possēmus.

II. Nam tum, cum ex urbe Catilīnam ēiciēbam — nōn enim iam vereor hūius verbī invidiam, cum illa magis sit timenda, quod vīvus exierit — sed tum, cum illum exterminārī volēbam, aut reliquam coniūrātōrum manum simul exitūram aut eōs, quī restitissent, īnfīrmōs sine illō ac dēbilēs fore putābam. Atque ego, ut vīdī, quōs māximō furōre et scelere esse īnflammātōs sciēbam, eōs nōbīscum esse et Rōmae remānsisse, in eō omnēs diēs noctēsque cōnsūmpsī, ut, quid agerent, quid mōlīrentur, sentīrem ac vidērem, ut, quoniam auribus vestrīs propter incrēdibilem māgnitūdinem sceleris minōrem fidem faceret ōrātiō mea, rem ita comprehenderem, ut tum dēmum animīs salūtī vestrae prōvidērētis, cum oculīs maleficium ipsum vidērētis.

Itaque, ut comperī lēgātōs Allobrogum bellī Trānsalpīnī et tumultūs Gallicī excitandī causā ā P. Lentulō esse sollicitātōs, eōsque in Galliam ad suōs cīvēs eōdemque itinere cum litterīs mandātīsque ad Catilīnam esse missōs, comitemque eīs adiūnctum esse T. Volturcium, atque huic ad Catilīnam esse datās litterās, facultātem mihi oblātam putāvī, ut, quod erat difficillimum, quodque ego semper optābam ab dīs immortālibus, ut tōta rēs nōn sōlum ā mē, sed etiam ā senātū et ā vōbīs manifēstō dēprehenderētur.

Itaque hesternō diē L. Flaccum et C. Pomptīnum praetōrēs, fortissimōs atque amantissimōs reī pūblicae

FROM AN ENGRAVING IN THE PIRANESI COLLECTION.

virōs, ad mē vocāvī; rem exposuī; quid fierī placēret, ostendī. Illī autem, quī omnia dē rē pūblicā praeclāra atque ēgregia sentīrent, sine recūsātiōne ac sine ūllā morā negōtium suscēpērunt et, cum advesperāsceret, occultē ad pontem Mulvium pervēnērunt atque ibi in proximīs vīllīs ita bipertītō fuērunt, ut Tiberis inter eōs et pōns interesset. Eōdem autem et ipsī sine cūiusquam suspīciōne multōs fortēs virōs ēdūxerant, et ego ex praefectūrā Reātīnā complūrēs dēlēctōs adulēscentēs, quōrum operā ūtor adsiduē in rē pūblicā, praesidiō cum gladiīs mīseram.

Interim tertiā ferē vigiliā exāctā, cum iam pontem Mulvium māgnō comitātū lēgātī Allobrogum ingredī inciperent ūnāque Volturcius, fit in eōs impetus; ēdūcuntur et ab illīs gladiī et ā nostrīs. Rēs praetōribus erat nōta sōlīs, ignōrābātur ā cēterīs.

III. Tum interventū Pomptīnī atque Flaccī pūgna sēdātur. Litterae, quaecumque erant in eō comitātū, integrīs sīgnīs praetōribus trāduntur; ipsī comprehēnsī ad mē, cum iam dīlūcēsceret, dēdūcuntur. Atque hōrum omnium scelerum improbissimum māchinātōrem, Cimbrum Gabīnium, statim ad mē, nihil dum suspicantem, vocāvī; deinde item arcessītus est L. Statilius et post eum C. Cethēgus; tardissimē autem Lentulus vēnit, crēdō, quod in litterīs dandīs praeter cōnsuētūdinem proximā nocte vigilārat.

Cum summīs et clārissimīs hūius cīvitātis virīs, quī audītā rē frequentēs ad mē māne convēnerant, litterās ā mē prius aperīrī quam ad senātum dēferrī placēret, nē, sī nihil esset inventum, temere ā mē tantus tumultus iniectus cīvitātī vidērētur, negāvī mē esse factūrum, ut dē perīculō pūblicō nōn ad cōnsilium pūblicum rem integram dēferrem. Etenim, Quirītēs, sī ea, quae erant ad mē dēlāta, reperta nōn essent, tamen ego nōn arbitrābar in tantīs reī pūblicae perīculīs esse mihi nimiam dīligentiam pertimēscendam.

Senātum frequentem celeriter, ut vīdistis, coēgī. Atque intereā statim admonitū Allobrogum C. Sulpicium praetōrem, fortem virum, mīsī, quī ex aedibus Cethēgī, sī quid tēlōrum esset, efferret; ex quibus ille māximum sīcārum numerum et gladiōrum extulit.

IV. Intrōdūxī Volturcium sine Gallīs; fidem pūblicam iussū senātūs dedī; hortātus sum, ut ea, quae scīret, sine timōre indicāret. Tum ille dīxit, cum vix sē ex māgnō timōre recreāsset, ā P. Lentulō sē habēre ad Catilīnam mandāta et litterās, ut servōrum praesidiō ūterētur, ut ad urbem quam prīmum cum exercitū accēderet; id autem eō cōnsiliō, ut, cum urbem ex omnibus partibus, quem ad modum dēscrīptum distribūtumque erat, incendissent caedemque īnfīnītam cīvium fēcissent, praestō esset ille, quī et fugientēs exciperet et sē cum hīs urbānīs ducibus coniungeret.

Intrōductī autem Gallī iūs iūrandum sibi et litterās ab Lentulō, Cethēgō, Statiliō ad suam gentem data esse dīxērunt, atque ita sibi ab hīs et ā L. Cassiō esse praescrīptum, ut equitātum in Italiam quam prīmum mitterent; pedestrēs sibi cōpiās nōn dēfutūrās; Lentulum autem sibi cōnfīrmāsse ex fātīs Sibyllīnīs haruspicumque respōnsīs, sē esse tertium illum Cornēlium, ad quem rēgnum hūius urbis atque imperium pervenīre esset necesse; Cinnam ante sē et Sullam fuisse; eundemque dīxisse fātālem hunc annum esse ad interitum hūius urbis atque imperī, quī esset annus decimus post virginum absolūtiōnem, post Capitōlī autem incēnsiōnem vīcēsimus. Hanc autem Cethēgō cum cēterīs contrōversiam fuisse dīxērunt, quod Lentulō et aliīs Sāturnālibus caedem fierī atque urbem incendī placēret, Cethēgō nimium id longum vidērētur.

V. Ac nē longum sit, Quirītēs, tabellās prōferrī iussimus, quae ā quōque dīcēbantur datae. Prīmum ostendimus Cethēgō sīgnum; cognōvit. Nōs līnum incīdimus, lēgimus. Erat scrīptum ipsīus manū Allobrogum senātuī et populō, sēsē, quae eōrum lēgātīs cōnfīrmāsset, factūrum esse; ōrāre, ut item illī facerent, quae sibi eōrum lēgātī recēpissent. Tum Cethēgus, quī paulō ante aliquid tamen dē gladiīs ac sīcīs, quae apud ipsum erant dēprehēnsa, respondisset dīxissetque sē semper bonōrum ferrāmentōrum studiōsum fuisse, recitātīs litterīs dēbilitātus atque abiectus cōnscientiā repente conticuit.

Intrōductus est Statilius; cognōvit et sīgnum et manum suam. Recitātae sunt tabellae in eandem ferē sententiam; cōnfessus est.

Tum ostendī tabellās Lentulō et quaesīvī, cognōsceretne sīgnum. Adnuit. *Est vērō*, inquam, *nōtum quidem sīgnum, imāgō avī tuī, clārissimī virī, quī amāvit ūnicē patriam et cīvēs suōs; quae quidem tē ā tantō scelere etiam mūta revocāre dēbuit.* Leguntur eādem ratiōne ad senātum Allobrogum populumque litterae. Sī quid dē hīs rēbus dīcere vellet, fēcī potestātem. Atque ille prīmō quidem negāvit; post autem aliquantō, tōtō iam indiciō expositō atque ēditō, surrēxit; quaesīvit ā Gallīs, quid sibi esset cum eīs, quam ob rem domum suam vēnissent, itemque ā Volturciō. Quī cum illī breviter cōnstanterque respondissent, per quem ad eum quotiēnsque vēnissent, quaesissentque ab eō, nihilne sēcum esset dē fātīs Sibyllīnīs locūtus, tum ille subitō scelere dēmēns, quanta cōnscientiae vīs esset, ostendit. Nam, cum id posset īnfitiārī, repente praeter opīniōnem omnium cōnfessus est. Ita eum nōn modo ingenium illud et dīcendī exercitātiō, quā semper valuit, sed etiam propter vim sceleris manifēstī atque dēprehēnsī impudentia, quā superābat omnēs, improbitāsque dēfēcit.

Volturcius vērō subitō litterās prōferrī atque aperīrī iubet, quās sibi ā Lentulō ad Catilīnam datās esse dīcēbat. Atque ibi vehementissimē perturbātus Lentulus tamen et sīgnum et manum suam cognōvit. Erant autem sine nōmine, sed ita:

Quis sim, sciēs ex eō, quem ad tē mīsī. Cūrā, ut vir sīs, et cōgitā, quem in locum sīs prōgressus. Vidē, quid tibi iam sit necesse, et cūrā, ut omnium tibi auxilia adiungās, etiam īnfimōrum.

Gabīnius deinde intrōductus cum prīmō impudenter respondēre coepisset, ad extrēmum nihil ex eīs, quae Gallī īnsimulābant, negāvit.

Ac mihi quidem, Quirītēs, cum illa certissima visa sunt argumenta atque indicia sceleris, tabellae, sīgna, manūs, dēnique ūnīus cūiusque cōnfessiō, tum multō certiōra illa, color, oculī, vultūs, taciturnitās. Sīc enim obstipuerant, sīc terram intuēbantur, sīc fūrtim nōn numquam inter sēsē aspiciēbant, ut nōn iam ab aliīs indicārī, sed indicāre sē ipsī vidērentur.

VI. Indiciīs expositīs atque ēditīs, Quirītēs, senātum cōnsuluī, dē summā rē pūblicā quid fierī placēret. Dictae sunt ā prīncipibus ācerrimae ac fortissimae sententiae, quās senātus sine ūllā varietāte est secūtus. Et quoniam nōndum est perscrīptum senātūs cōnsultum, ex memoriā vōbīs, Quirītēs, quid senātus cēnsuerit, expōnam.

Prīmum mihi grātiae verbīs amplissimīs aguntur, quod virtūte, cōnsiliō, prōvidentiā meā rēs pūblica māximīs perīculīs sit līberāta. Deinde L. Flaccus et C. Pomptīnus praetōrēs, quod eōrum operā fortī fidēlīque ūsus essem, meritō ac iūre laudantur. Atque etiam virō fortī, collēgae meō, laus impertītur, quod eōs, quī hūius coniūrātiōnis participēs fuissent, ā suīs et ā reī pūblicae cōnsiliīs remōvisset.

Atque ita cēnsuērunt, ut P. Lentulus, cum sē praetūrā abdicāsset, in cūstōdiam trāderētur; itemque utī C. Cethēgus, L. Statilius, P. Gabīnius, quī omnēs praesentēs erant, in cūstōdiam trāderentur; atque idem hōc dēcrētum est in L. Cassium, quī sibi prōcūrātiōnem incendendae urbis dēpoposcerat; in M. Cēpārium, cui ad sollicitandōs pāstōrēs Āpūliam attribūtam esse erat indicātum; in P. Furium, quī est ex eīs colōnīs, quōs Faesulās L. Sulla dēdūxit: in Q. Annium Chīlōnem, quī ūnā cum hōc Furiō semper erat in hāc Allobrogum sollicitātiōne versātus; in P. Umbrēnum, lībertīnum hominem, ā quō prīmum Gallōs ad Gabīnium perductōs esse cōnstābat. Atque eā lēnitāte senātus est ūsus, Quirītēs, ut ex tantā coniūrātiōne tantāque hāc multitūdine domesticōrum hostium novem hominum perditissimōrum poenā rē pūblicā cōnservātā reliquōrum mentēs sānārī posse arbitrārētur.

Atque etiam supplicātiō dīs immortālibus prō singulārī eōrum meritō meō nōmine dēcrēta est, quod mihi prīmum post hanc urbem conditam togātō contigit, et hīs dēcrēta verbīs est, *quod urbem incendiīs, caede cīvēs, Italiam bellō līberāssem.* Quae supplicātiō sī cum cēterīs supplicātiōnibus cōnferātur, hōc interest, quod cēterae bene gestā, haec ūna cōnservātā rē pūblicā cōnstitūta est.

Atque illud, quod faciendum prīmum fuit, factum atque trānsāctum est. Nam P. Lentulus, quamquam patefactīs indiciīs, cōnfessiōnibus suīs, iūdiciō senātūs nōn modo praetōris iūs, vērum etiam cīvis āmīserat, tamen magistrātū sē abdicāvit, ut, quae religiō C. Mariō, clārissimō virō, nōn fuerat, quō minus

C. Glauciam, dē quō nihil nōminātim erat dēcrētum, praetōrem occīderet, eā nōs religiōne in prīvātō P. Lentulō pūniendō līberārēmur.

VII. Nunc quoniam, Quirītēs, cōnscelerātissimī perīculōsissimīque bellī nefāriōs ducēs captōs iam et comprehēnsōs tenētis, exīstimāre dēbētis omnēs Catilīnae cōpiās, omnēs spēs atque opēs hīs dēpulsīs urbis perīculīs concidisse. Quem quidem ego cum ex urbe pellēbam, hōc prōvidēbam animō, Quirītēs, remōtō Catilīnā nōn mihi esse P. Lentulī somnum nec L. Cassī adipēs nec C. Cethēgī furiōsam temeritātem pertimēscendam.

Ille erat ūnus timendus ex istīs omnibus, sed tam diū, dum urbis moenibus continēbātur. Omnia nōrat, omnium aditūs tenēbat; appellāre, temptāre, sollicitāre poterat, audēbat. Erat eī cōnsilium ad facinus aptum, cōnsiliō autem neque manus neque lingua deerat. Iam ad certās rēs cōnficiendās certōs hominēs dēlēctōs ac dēscrīptōs habēbat. Neque vērō, cum aliquid mandārat, cōnfectum putābat; nihil erat, quod nōn ipse obīret, occurreret, vigilāret, labōrāret; frīgus, sitim, famem ferre poterat.

Hunc ego hominem tam ācrem, tam audācem, tam parātum, tam callidum, tam in scelere vigilantem, tam in perditīs rēbus dīligentem nisi ex domesticīs īnsidiīs in castrēnse lātrōcinium compulissem — dīcam id, quod sentiō, Quirītēs, — nōn facile hanc tantam mōlem malī ā cervīcibus vestrīs dēpulissem. Nōn ille nōbīs Sāturnālia cōnstituisset neque tantō ante exitī ac fātī diem reī pūblicae dēnūntiāvisset neque commīsisset, ut sīgnum, ut litterae suae testēs manifēstī sceleris dēprehenderentur. Quae nunc illō absente sīc gesta sunt, ut nūllum in prīvātā domō fūrtum umquam sit tam palam inventum, quam haec tanta in rē pūblicā coniūrātiō manifēstō inventa atque dēprehēnsa est. Quod sī Catilīna in urbe ad hanc diem remānsisset, quamquam, quoad fuit, omnibus ēius cōnsiliīs occurrī atque obstitī, tamen, ut levissimē dīcam, dīmicandum nōbīs cum illō fuisset neque nōs umquam, cum ille in urbe hostis esset, tantīs perīculīs rem pūblicam tantā pāce, tantō ōtiō, tantō silentiō līberāssēmus.

VIII. Quamquam haec omnia, Quirītēs, ita sunt ā mē administrāta, ut deōrum immortālium nūtū atque cōnsiliō et gesta et prōvīsa esse videantur. Idque cum coniectūrā cōnsequī possumus, quod vix vidētur hūmānī cōnsilī tantārum rērum gubernātiō esse potuisse, tum vērō ita praesentēs hīs temporibus opem et auxilium nōbīs tulērunt, ut eōs paene oculīs vidēre possēmus. Nam ut illa omittam, vīsās nocturnō tempore ab occidente facēs ārdōremque caelī, ut fulminum iactūs, ut terrae mōtūs relinquam; ut omittam cētera, quae tam multa nōbīs cōnsulibus facta sunt, ut haec, quae nunc fīunt, canere dī immortālēs vidērentur, hōc certē, quod sum dictūrus, neque praetermittendum neque relinquendum est.

Nam profectō memoriā tenētis Cottā et Torquātō cōnsulibus complūrēs in Capitōliō rēs dē caelō esse percussās, cum et simulācra deōrum dēpulsa sunt et statuae veterum hominum dēiectae et lēgum aera līquefacta et tāctus etiam ille, quī hanc urbem condidit, Rōmulus, quem inaurātum in Capitōliō, parvum atque lactentem, ūberibus lupīnīs inhiantem, fuisse meministis. Quō quidem tempore cum haruspicēs ex tōtā Etrūriā convēnissent, caedēs atque incendia et lēgum interitum et bellum cīvīle ac domesticum et tōtīus urbis atque imperī occāsum appropinquāre dīxērunt, nisi dī immortālēs omnī ratiōne plācātī suō nūmine prope fāta ipsa flexissent.

Itaque illōrum respōnsīs tum et lūdī per decem diēs factī sunt, neque rēs ūlla, quae ad plācandōs deōs pertinēret, praetermissa est. Īdemque iussērunt simulācrum Iovis facere māius et in excelsō collocāre et contrā, atque anteā fuerat, ad orientem convertere; ac sē spērāre dīxērunt, sī illud sīgnum, quod vidētis, sōlis ortum et forum cūriamque cōnspiceret, fore ut ea cōnsilia, quae clam essent inita contrā salūtem urbis atque imperī, illūstrārentur, ut ā senātū populōque Rōmānō perspicī possent. Atque illud sīgnum collocandum cōnsulēs illī locāvērunt; sed tanta fuit operis tarditās, ut neque superiōribus cōnsulibus neque nōbīs ante hodiernum diem collocārētur.

IX. Hīc quis potest esse, Quirītēs, tam āversus ā vērō, tam praeceps, tam mente captus, quī neget haec omnia, quae vidēmus, praecipuēque hanc urbem deōrum immortālium nūtū ac potestāte administrārī? Etenim, cum esset ita respōnsum, caedēs, incendia, interitum reī pūblicae comparārī, et ea per cīvēs, quae tum propter māgnitūdinem scelerum nōn nūllīs incrēdibilia vidēbantur, ea nōn modo cōgitāta ā nefāriīs cīvibus, vērum etiam suscepta esse sēnsistis. Illud vērō nōnne ita praesēns est, ut nūtū Iovis optimī māximī factum esse videātur, ut, cum hodiernō diē māne per forum meō iussū et coniūrātī et eōrum indicēs in aedem Concordiae dūcerentur, eō ipsō tempore sīgnum statuerētur? Quō collocātō atque ad vōs senātumque conversō omnia, quae erant cōgitāta contrā salūtem omnium, illūstrāta et patefacta vīdistis.

Quō etiam māiōre sunt istī odiō suppliciōque dīgnī, quī nōn sōlum vestrīs domiciliīs atque tēctīs, sed etiam deōrum templīs atque dēlūbrīs sunt fūnestōs ac nefāriōs īgnēs īnferre cōnātī. Quibus ego sī mē restitisse dīcam, nimium mihi sūmam et nōn sim ferendus; ille,

ille Iuppiter restitit; ille Capitōlium, ille haec templa, ille cūnctam urbem, ille vōs omnēs salvōs esse voluit. Dīs ego immortālibus ducibus hanc mentem, Quirītēs, voluntātemque suscēpī, atque ad haec tanta indicia pervēnī.

Iam vērō ab Lentulō cēterīsque domesticīs hostibus tam dēmenter tantae rēs crēditae et ignōtīs et barbarīs numquam essent profectō, nisi ab dīs immortālibus huic tantae audāciae cōnsilium esset ēreptum. Quid vērō? ut hominēs Gallī ex cīvitāte male pācātā, quae gēns ūna restat, quae bellum populō Rōmānō facere et posse et nōn nōlle videātur, spem imperī ac rērum māximārum ultrō sibi ā patriciīs hominibus oblātam neglegerent vestramque salūtem suīs opibus antepōnerent, id nōn dīvīnitus esse factum putātis, praesertim quī nōs nōn pūgnandō, sed tacendō superāre potuerint?

X. Quam ob rem, Quirītēs, quoniam ad omnia pulvīnāria supplicātiō dēcrēta est, celebrātōte illōs diēs cum coniugibus ac līberīs vestrīs. Nam multī saepe honōrēs dīs immortālibus iūstī habitī sunt ac dēbitī, sed profectō iūstiōrēs numquam. Ēreptī enim estis ex crūdēlissimō ac miserrimō interitū; sine caede, sine sanguine, sine exercitū, sine dīmicātiōne; togātī mē ūnō togātō duce et imperātōre vīcistis.

Etenim recordāminī, Quirītēs, omnēs cīvīlēs dissēnsiōnēs, nōn sōlum eās, quās audīstis, sed eās, quās vōsmet ipsī meministis atque vīdistis. L. Sulla P. Sulpicium oppressit; C. Marium, cūstōdem hūius urbis, multōsque fortēs virōs partim ēiēcit ex cīvitāte, partim interēmit. Cn. Octāvius cōnsul armīs expulit ex urbe collēgam; omnis hīc locus acervīs corporum et cīvium sanguine redundāvit. Superāvit posteā Cinna cum Mariō; tum vērō, clārissimīs virīs interfectīs lūmina cīvitātis exstīncta sunt. Ultus est hūius victōriae crūdēlitātem posteā Sulla; nē dīcī quidem opus est, quantā dēminūtiōne cīvium et quantā calamitāte reī pūblicae. Dissēnsit M. Lepidus ā clārissimō et fortissimō virō, Q. Catulō; attulit nōn tam ipsīus interitus reī pūblicae lūctum quam cēterōrum.

Atque illae tamen omnēs dissēnsiōnēs erant ēius modī, quae nōn ad dēlendam, sed ad commūtandam rem pūblicam pertinērent. Nōn illī nūllam esse rem pūblicam, sed in eā, quae esset, sē esse prīncipēs, neque hanc urbem cōnflagrāre, sed sē in hāc urbe flōrēre voluērunt. Atque illae tamen omnēs dissēnsiōnēs, quārum nūlla exitium reī pūblicae quaesīvit, ēius modī fuērunt, ut nōn reconciliātiōne concordiae, sed interneciōne cīvium dīiūdicātae sint. In hōc autem ūnō post hominum memoriam māximō crūdēlissimōque bellō, quāle bellum nūlla umquam barbaria cum suā gente gessit, quō in bellō lēx haec fuit ā Lentulō, Catilīnā, Cethēgō, Cassiō cōnstitūta, ut omnēs, quī salvā urbe salvī esse possent, in hostium numerō dūcerentur, ita mē gessī, Quirītēs, ut salvī omnēs cōnservārēminī, et, cum hostēs vestrī tantum cīvium superfutūrum putāssent, quantum īnfīnītae caedī restitisset, tantum autem urbis, quantum flamma obīre nōn potuisset, et urbem et cīvēs integrōs incolumēsque servāvī.

XI. Quibus prō tantīs rēbus, Quirītēs, nūllum ego ā vōbīs praemium virtūtis, nūllum īnsīgne honōris, nūllum monumentum laudis postulō praeterquam hūius diēī memoriam sempiternam. In animīs ego vestrīs omnēs triumphōs meōs, omnia ōrnāmenta honōris, monumenta glōriae, laudis īnsīgnia condī et collocārī volō. Nihil mē mūtum potest dēlectāre, nihil tacitum, nihil dēnique ēius modī, quod etiam minus dīgnī adsequī possint. Memoriā vestrā, Quirītēs, nostrae rēs alentur, sermōnibus crēscent, litterārum monumentīs inveterāscent et corrōborābuntur; eandemque diem intellegō, quam spērō aeternam fore, prōpāgātam esse et ad salūtem urbis et ad memoriam cōnsulātūs meī, ūnōque tempore in hāc rē pūblicā duōs cīvēs exstitisse, quōrum alter fīnēs vestrī imperī nōn terrae, sed caelī regiōnibus termināret, alter ēiusdem imperī domicilium sēdēsque servāret.

XII. Sed quoniam eārum rērum, quās ego gessī, nōn eadem est fortūna atque condiciō quae illōrum, quī externa bella gessērunt, quod mihi cum eīs vīvendum est, quōs vīcī ac subēgī, illī hostēs aut interfectōs aut oppressōs relīquērunt, vestrum est, Quirītēs, sī cēterīs facta sua rēctē prōsunt, mihi mea nē quandō obsint, prōvidēre. Mentēs enim hominum audācissimōrum scelerātae ac nefāriae nē vōbīs nocēre possent, ego prōvīdī; nē mihi noceant, vestrum est prōvidēre. Quamquam, Quirītēs, mihi quidem ipsī nihil ab istīs iam nocērī potest. Māgnum enim est in bonīs praesidium, quod mihi in perpetuum comparātum est, māgna in rē pūblicā dīgnitās, quae mē semper tacita dēfendet, māgna vīs cōnscientiae, quam quī neglegunt, cum mē violāre volent, sē ipsī indicābunt.

Est enim in nōbīs is animus, Quirītēs, ut nōn modo nūllīus audāciae cēdāmus, sed etiam omnēs improbōs ultrō semper lacessāmus. Quod sī omnis impetus domesticōrum hostium, dēpulsus ā vōbīs, sē in mē ūnum convertit, vōbīs erit videndum, Quirītēs, quā condiciōne posthāc eōs esse velītis, quī sē prō salūte vestrā obtulerint invidiae perīculīsque omnibus; mihi quidem ipsī quid est, quod iam ad vītae frūctum possit adquīrī, cum praesertim neque in honōre vestrō neque in glōriā virtūtis quicquam videam altius, quō mihi libeat ascendere? Illud profectō perficiam, Quirītēs, ut ea, quae gessī in cōnsulātū, prīvātus tuear atque ōrnem, ut, sī qua est invidia in cōnservandā rē pūblicā suscepta, laedat invidōs, mihi valeat ad glōriam.

Dēnique ita mē in rē pūblicā trāctābō, ut meminerim semper, quae gesserim, cūremque, ut ea virtūte, nōn cāsū gesta esse videantur. Vōs, Quirītēs, quoniam iam est nox, venerātī Iovem illum, cūstōdem hūius urbis ac vestrum, in vestra tēcta discēdite et ea, quamquam iam est perīculum dēpulsum, tamen aequē ac priōre nocte cūstōdiīs vigiliīsque dēfendite. Id nē vōbīs diūtius faciendum sit, atque ut in perpetuā pāce esse possītis, prōvidēbō.

M. TULLI CICERONIS

IN L. CATILINAM ORATIO QUARTA

HABITA IN SENATU.

I. Videō, patrēs cōnscrīptī, in mē omnium vestrum ōra atque oculōs esse conversōs; videō vōs nōn sōlum dē vestrō ac reī pūblicae, vērum etiam, sī id dēpulsum sit, dē meō perīculō esse sollicitōs. Est mihi iūcunda in malīs et grāta in dolōre vestra ergā mē voluntās, sed eam, per deōs immortālēs, dēpōnite atque oblītī salūtis meae dē vōbīs ac dē vestrīs līberīs cōgitāte. Mihi sī haec condiciō cōnsulātūs data est, ut omnēs acerbitātēs, omnēs dolōrēs cruciātūsque perferrem, feram nōn sōlum fortiter, vērum etiam libenter, dum modo meīs labōribus vōbīs populōque Rōmānō dīgnitās salūsque pariātur.

Ego sum ille cōnsul, patrēs cōnscrīptī, cui nōn forum, in quō omnis aequitās continētur, nōn campus, cōnsulāribus auspiciīs cōnsecrātus, nōn cūria, summum auxilium omnium gentium, nōn domus, commūne perfugium, nōn lectus ad quiētem datus, nōn dēnique haec sēdēs honōris umquam vacua mortis perīculō atque īnsidiīs fuit.

Ego multa tacuī, multa pertulī, multa concessī, multa meō quōdam dolōre in vestrō timōre sānāvī. Nunc sī hunc exitum cōnsulātūs meī dī immortālēs esse voluērunt, ut vōs populumque Rōmānum ex caede miserrimā, coniugēs līberōsque vestrōs vīrginēsque Vestālēs ex acerbissimā vexātiōne, templa atque dēlūbra, hanc pulcherrimam patriam omnium nostrum ex foedissimā flammā, tōtam Italiam ex bellō et vāstitāte ēriperem, quaecumque mihi ūnī prōpōnētur fortūna, subeātur. Etenim, sī P. Lentulus suum nōmen inductus ā vātibus fātāle ad perniciem reī pūblicae fore putāvit, cūr ego nōn laeter meum cōnsulātum ad salūtem populī Rōmānī prope fātālem exstitisse?

II. Quā rē, patrēs cōnscrīptī, cōnsulite vōbīs, prōspicite patriae, cōnservāte vōs, coniugēs, līberōs fortūnāsque vestrās, populī Rōmānī nōmen salūtemque dēfendite; mihi parcere ac dē mē cōgitāre dēsinite. Nam prīmum dēbeō spērāre, omnēs deōs, quī huic urbī praesident, prō eō mihi, ac mereor, relātūrōs esse grātiam; deinde, sī quid obtigerit, aequō animō parātōque moriar. Nam neque turpis mors fortī virō potest accidere neque immātūra cōnsulārī nec misera sapientī.

Nec tamen ego sum ille ferreus, quī frātris cārissimī atque amantissimī praesentis maerōre nōn movear hōrumque omnium lacrimīs, ā quibus mē circumsessum vidētis. Neque meam mentem nōn domum saepe revocat exanimāta uxor et abiecta metū fīlia et parvulus fīlius, quem mihi vidētur amplectī rēs pūblica tamquam obsidem cōnsulātūs meī, neque ille, quī exspectāns hūius exitum diēī stat in cōnspectū meō, gener. Moveor hīs rēbus omnibus, sed in eam partem, utī salvī sint vōbīscum omnēs, etiam sī mē vīs aliqua oppresserit, potius quam et illī et nōs ūnā reī pūblicae peste pereāmus.

Quā rē, patrēs cōnscrīptī, incumbite ad salūtem reī pūblicae, circumspicite omnēs procellās, quae impendent, nisi prōvidētis. Nōn Ti. Gracchus, quod iterum tribūnus plēbis fierī voluit, nōn C. Gracchus, quod agrāriōs concitāre cōnātus est, nōn L. Sāturnīnus, quod C. Memmium occīdit, in discrīmen aliquod atque in vestrae sevēritātis iūdicium addūcitur; tenentur eī, quī ad urbis incendium, ad vestram omnium caedem, ad Catilīnam accipiendum Rōmae restitērunt; tenentur litterae, sīgna, manūs, dēnique ūnīus cūiusque cōnfessiō; sollicitantur Allobrogēs, servitia excitantur, Catilīna arcessitur; id est initum cōnsilium, ut interfectīs omnibus nēmō nē ad dēplōrandum quidem populī Rōmānī nōmen atque ad lāmentandam tantī imperī calamitātem relinquātur.

III. Haec omnia indicēs dētulērunt, reī cōnfessī sunt, vōs multīs iam iūdiciīs iūdicāvistis, prīmum quod mihi grātiās ēgistis singulāribus verbīs et meā virtūte atque dīligentiā perditōrum hominum coniūrātiōnem patefactam esse dēcrēvistis; deinde quod P. Lentulum sē abdicāre praetūrā coēgistis; tum quod eum et cēterōs, dē quibus iūdicāstis, in cūstōdiam dandōs cēnsuistis, māximēque quod meō nōmine supplicātiōnem dēcrēvistis, quī honōs togātō habitus ante mē est nēminī; postrēmō hesternō diē praemia lēgātīs Allobrogum Titōque Volturciō dedistis amplissima. Quae sunt omnia ēius modī, ut eī, quī in cūstōdiam nōminātim datī sunt, sine ūllā dubitātiōne ā vōbīs damnātī esse videantur.

Sed ego īnstituī referre ad vōs, patrēs cōnscrīptī, tamquam integrum, et dē factō quid iūdicētis, et dē poenā quid cēnseātis. Illa praedīcam, quae sunt cōnsulis. Ego māgnum in rē pūblicā versārī furōrem et nova quaedam miscērī et concitārī mala iam prīdem vidēbam; sed hanc tantam, tam exitiōsam habērī coniūrātiōnem ā cīvibus numquam putāvī. Nunc quicquid est, quōcumque vestrae mentēs inclīnant atque sententiae, statuendum vōbīs ante noctem est. Quantum facinus ad vōs dēlātum sit, vidētis. Huic sī paucōs putātis adfīnēs esse, vehementer errātis. Lātius opīniōne dissēminātum est hōc malum; mānāvit nōn sōlum per Italiam, vērum etiam trānscendit Alpēs et obscūrē serpēns multās iam prōvinciās occupāvit. Id opprimī sustentandō aut prōlātandō nūllō pactō potest; quācumque ratiōne placet, celeriter vōbīs vindicandum est.

IV. Videō duās adhūc esse sententiās; ūnam D. Sīlānī, quī cēnset eōs, quī haec dēlēre cōnātī sunt, morte esse multandōs; alteram C. Caesaris, quī mortis poenam removet, cēterōrum suppliciōrum omnēs acerbitātēs amplectitur. Uterque et prō suā dīgnitāte et prō rērum māgnitūdine in summā sevēritāte versātur.

Alter eōs, quī nōs omnēs vītā prīvāre cōnātī sunt, quī dēlēre imperium, quī populī Rōmānī nōmen exstinguere, pūnctum temporis fruī vītā et hōc commūnī spīritū nōn putat oportēre, atque hōc genus poenae saepe in improbōs cīvēs in hāc rē pūblicā esse ūsūrpātum recordātur.

Alter intellegit mortem ab dīs immortālibus nōn esse supplicī causā cōnstitūtam, sed aut necessitātem nātūrae aut labōrum ac miseriārum quiētem. Itaque eam sapientēs numquam invītī, fortēs saepe etiam libenter oppetīvērunt. Vincula vērō, et ea sempiterna, certē ad singulārem poenam nefāriī sceleris inventa sunt. Mūnicipiīs dispertīrī iubet. Habēre vidētur ista rēs inīquitātem, sī imperāre velīs, difficultātem, sī rogāre. Dēcernātur tamen, sī placet. Ego enim suscipiam et, ut spērō, reperiam, quī id, quod salūtis omnium causā statueritis, nōn putent esse suae dīgnitātis recūsāre. Adiungit gravem poenam mūnicipiīs, sī quis eōrum vincula rūperit;

horribilēs cūstōdiās circumdat et dīgnās scelere hominum perditōrum; sancit, nē quis eōrum poenam, quōs condemnat, aut per senātum aut per populum levāre possit; ēripit etiam spem, quae sōla hominēs in miseriīs cōnsōlārī solet. Bona praetereā pūblicārī iubet; vītam sōlam relinquit nefāriīs hominibus; quam sī ēripuisset, multōs ūnā dolōrēs animī atque corporis et omnēs scelerum poenās adēmisset. Itaque ut aliqua in vītā formīdō improbīs esset posita, apud īnferōs ēius modī quaedam illī antīquī supplicia impiīs cōnstitūta esse voluērunt, quod vidēlicet intellegēbant hīs remōtīs nōn esse mortem ipsam pertimēscendam.

V. Nunc, patrēs cōnscrīptī, ego meā videō quid intersit. Sī eritis secūtī sententiam C. Caesaris, quoniam hanc is in rē pūblicā viam, quae populāris habētur, secūtus est, fortasse minus erunt hōc auctōre et cognitōre hūiusce sententiae mihi populārēs impetūs pertimēscendī; sīn illam alteram, nesciō an amplius mihi negōtī contrahātur. Sed tamen meōrum perīculōrum ratiōnēs ūtilitās reī pūblicae vincat.

Habēmus enim ā Caesare, sīcut ipsīus dīgnitās et māiōrum ēius amplitūdō postulābat, sententiam tamquam obsidem perpetuae in rem pūblicam voluntātis. Intellēctum est, quid interesset inter levitātem cōntiōnātōrum et animum vērē populārem, salūtī populī cōnsulentem. Videō dē istīs, quī sē populārēs haberī volunt, abesse nōn nēminem, nē dē capite vidēlicet cīvium Rōmānōrum sententiam ferat; at is et nūdius tertius in cūstōdiam cīvēs Rōmānōs dedit et supplicātiōnem mihi dēcrēvit et indicēs hesternō diē māximīs praemiīs adfēcit. Iam hōc nēminī dubium est, quī reō cūstōdiam, quaesitōrī grātulātiōnem, indicī praemium dēcrēvit, quid dē tōtā rē et causā iūdicārit.

At vērō C. Caesar intellegit lēgem Semprōniam esse dē cīvibus Rōmānīs cōnstitūtam; quī autem reī pūblicae sit hostis, eum cīvem esse nūllō modō posse; dēnique ipsum lātōrem Semprōniae lēgis iniussū populī poenās reī pūblicae dēpendisse. Īdem ipsum Lentulum, largītōrem et prōdigum, nōn putat, cum dē perniciē populī Rōmānī, exitiō hūius urbis tam acerbē, tam crūdēliter cōgitārit, etiam appellārī posse populārem. Itaque homō mītissimus atque lēnissimus nōn dubitat P. Lentulum aeternīs tenebrīs vinculīsque mandāre et sancit in posterum, nē quis hūius suppliciō levandō sē iactāre et in perniciem populī Rōmānī posthāc populāris esse possit. Adiungit etiam pūblicātiōnem bonōrum, ut omnēs animī cruciātūs et corporis etiam egestās ac mendīcitās cōnsequātur.

VI. Quam ob rem, sīve hōc statueritis, dederitis mihi comitem ad cōntiōnem populō cārum atque iūcundum, sīve Sīlānī sententiam sequī malueritis, facile mē atque vōs ā crūdēlitātis vituperātiōne populus Rōmānus exsolvet, atque obtinēbō eam multō lēniōrem fuisse. Quamquam, patrēs cōnscrīptī, quae potest esse in tantī sceleris immānitāte pūniendā crūdēlitās? Ego enim dē meō sēnsū iūdicō. Nam ita mihi salvā rē pūblicā vōbīscum perfruī liceat, ut ego, quod in hāc causā vehementior sum, nōn ātrōcitāte animī moveor—quis enim est mē mītior?—sed singulārī quādam hūmānitāte et misericordiā.

Videor enim mihi vidēre hanc urbem, lūcem orbis terrārum atque arcem omnium gentium, subitō ūnō incendiō concidentem; cernō animō sepultā in patriā miserōs atque īnsepultōs acervōs cīvium; versātur mihi ante oculōs aspectus Cethēgī et furor in vestrā caede bacchantis. Cum vērō mihi prōposuī rēgnantem Lentulum, sīcut ipse sē ex fātīs spērāsse cōnfessus est, purpurātum esse huic Gabīnium, cum exercitū vēnisse Catilīnam, tum lāmentātiōnem mātrum familiās, tum fugam virginum atque puerōrum ac vexātiōnem virginum Vestālium perhorrēscō, et, quia mihi vehementer haec videntur misera atque miseranda, idcircō in eōs, quī ea perficere voluērunt, mē sevērum vehementemque praebeō. Etenim quaerō, sī quis pater familiās, līberīs suīs ā servō interfectīs, uxōre occīsā, īncēnsā domō, supplicium dē servō nōn quam acerbissimum sūmpserit, utrum is clēmēns ac misericors, an inhūmānissimus et crūdēlissimus esse videātur. Mihi vērō importūnus ac ferreus, quī nōn dolōre et cruciātū nocentis suum dolōrem cruciātumque lēnierit.

Sīc nōs in hīs hominibus, quī nōs, quī coniugēs, quī līberōs nostrōs trucīdāre voluērunt, quī singulās ūnīus cūiusque nostrum domōs et hōc ūniversum reī pūblicae domicilium dēlēre cōnātī sunt, quī id egērunt, ut gentem Allobrogum in vēstīgiīs hūius urbis atque in cinere dēflagrātī imperī collocārent, sī vehementissimī fuerimus, misericordēs habēbimur; sīn remissiōrēs esse voluerimus, summae nōbīs crūdēlitātis in patriae cīviumque perniciē fāma subeunda est. Nisi vērō cuipiam L. Caesar, vir fortissimus et amantissimus reī pūblicae, crūdēlior nūdius tertius vīsus est, cum sorōris suae, fēminae lēctissimae, virum praesentem et audientem vītā prīvandum esse dīxit, cum avum suum iussū cōnsulis interfectum fīliumque ēius impūberem, lēgātum ā patre missum, in carcere necātum esse dīxit. Quōrum quod simile factum, quod initum dēlendae reī pūblicae cōnsilium?

Largītiōnis voluntās tum in rē pūblicā versāta est et partium quaedam contentiō. Atque eō tempore hūius avus Lentulī, vir clārissimus, armātus Gracchum est persecūtus. Ille etiam grave tum vulnus accēpit, nē quid dē summā rē pūblicā dēminuerētur; hīc ad ēvertenda reī pūblicae fundāmenta Gallōs arcessit, servitia concitat, Catilīnam vocat, attribuit nōs trucīdandōs Cethēgō et cēterōs cīvēs interficiendōs Gabīniō, urbem īnflammandam Cassiō, tōtam Italiam vāstandam dīripiendamque Catilīnae. Vereāminī, cēnseō, nē in hōc scelere tam immānī ac nefandō nimis aliquid sevērē statuisse videāminī; multō magis est verendum, nē remissiōne poenae crūdēlēs in patriam, quam nē sevēritāte animadversiōnis nimis vehementēs in acerbissimōs hostēs fuisse videāmur.

VII. Sed ea, quae exaudiō, patrēs cōnscrīptī, dissimulāre nōn possum. Iaciuntur enim vōcēs, quae perveniunt ad aurēs meās, eōrum, quī verērī videntur, ut habeam satis praesidī ad ea, quae vōs statueritis hodiernō diē, trānsigunda. Omnia et prōvīsa et parāta et cōnstitūta sunt, patrēs cōnscrīptī, cum meā summā cūrā atque dīligentiā, tum etiam multō māiōre populī Rōmānī ad summum imperium retinendum et ad commūnēs fortūnās cōnservandās voluntāte. Omnēs adsunt omnium ōrdinum hominēs, omnium dēnique aetātum; plēnum est forum, plēna templa circum forum, plēnī omnēs aditūs hūius templī ac locī. Causa est enim post urbem conditam haec inventa sōla, in quā omnēs sentīrent ūnum atque idem, praeter eōs, quī cum sibi vidērent esse pereundum, cum omnibus potius quam sōlī perīre voluērunt. Hōsce ego hominēs excipiō et sēcernō libenter; neque in improbōrum cīvium, sed in acerbissimōrum hostium numerō habendōs putō. Cēterī vērō, dī immortālēs! quā frequentiā, quō studiō, quā virtūte ad commūnem salūtem dīgnitātemque cōnsentiunt!

Quid ego hīc equitēs Rōmānōs commemorem? quī

vōbīs ita summam ōrdinis cōnsilīque concēdunt, ut vōbīscum dē amōre reī pūblicae certent; quōs ex multōrum annōrum dissēnsiōne hūius ōrdinis ad societātem concordiamque revocātōs hodiernus diēs vōbīscum atque haec causa coniungit. Quam sī coniunctiōnem, cōnfīrmātam in cōnsulātū meō, perpetuam in rē pūblicā tenuerimus, cōnfīrmō vōbīs nūllum posthāc malum cīvīle ac domesticum ad ūllam reī pūblicae partem esse ventūrum.

Parī studiō dēfendundae reī pūblicae convēnisse videō tribūnōs aerāriōs, fortissimōs virōs; scrībās item ūniversōs, quōs cum cāsū hīc diēs ad aerārium frequentāsset, videō ab exspectātiōne sortis ad salūtem commūnem esse conversōs.

Omnis ingenuōrum adest multitūdō, etiam tenuissimōrum. Quis est enim, cui nōn haec templa, aspectus urbis, possessiō lībertātis, lūx dēnique haec ipsa et hōc commūne patriae solum cum sit cārum, tum vērō dulce atque iūcundum?

VIII. Operae pretium est, patrēs cōnscrīptī, lībertīnōrum hominum studia cognōscere, quī suā virtūte fortūnam hūius cīvitātis cōnsecūtī, hanc suam esse patriam iūdicant, quam quīdam hīc nātī, et summō nātī locō, nōn patriam suam, sed urbem hostium esse iūdicāvērunt.

Sed quid ego hōsce hominēs ōrdinēsque commemorō, quōs prīvātae fortūnae, quōs commūnis rēs pūblica, quōs dēnique lībertās, ea quae dulcissima est, ad salūtem patriae dēfendendam excitāvit? Servus est nēmō, quī modo tolerābilī condiciōne sit servitūtis, quī nōn audāciam cīvium perhorrēscat, quī nōn haec stāre cupiat, quī nōn quantum audet et quantum potest, cōnferat ad commūnem salūtem, voluntātis.

Quā rē sī quem vestrum forte commovet hōc, quod audītum est, lēnōnem quendam Lentulī concursāre circum tabernās, pretiō spērāre sollicitāre posse animōs egentium atque imperītōrum, est id quidem coeptum atque temptātum, sed nūllī sunt inventī tam aut fortūnā miserī aut voluntāte perditī, quī nōn illum ipsum sellae atque operis et quaestūs cotīdiānī locum, quī nōn cubīle ac lectulum suum, quī dēnique nōn cursum hunc ōtiōsum vītae suae salvum esse velint. Multō vērō māxima pars eōrum, quī in tabernīs sunt, immō vērō — id enim potius est dīcendum — genûs hōc ūniversum amantissimum est ōtī. Etenim omne īnstrūmentum, omnis opera atque quaestus frequentiā cīvium sustentātur, alitur ōtiō; quōrum sī quaestus occlūsīs tabernīs minuī solet, quid tandem incēnsīs futūrum fuit?

IX. Quae cum ita sint, patrēs cōnscrīptī, vōbīs populī Rōmānī praesidia nōn dēsunt; vōs nē populō Rōmānō deesse videāminī, prōvidēte. Habētis cōnsulem ex plūrimīs perīculīs et īnsidiīs atque ex mediā morte nōn ad vītam suam, sed ad salūtem vestram reservātum. Omnēs ōrdinēs ad cōnservandam rem pūblicam mente, voluntāte, studiō, virtūte, vōce cōnsentiunt. Obsessa facibus et tēlīs impiae coniūrātiōnis vōbīs supplex manūs tendit patria commūnis, vōbīs sē, vōbīs vītam omnium cīvium, vōbīs arcem et Capitōlium, vōbīs ārās Penātium, vōbīs illum īgnem Vestae sempiternum, vōbīs omnium deōrum templa atque dēlūbra, vōbīs mūrōs atque urbis tēcta commendat.

Praetereā dē vestrā vītā, dē coniugum vestrārum atque līberōrum animā, dē fortūnīs omnium, dē sēdibus, dē focīs vestrīs hodiernō diē vōbīs iūdicandum est. Habētis ducem memorem vestrī, oblītum suī, quae nōn semper facultās datur; habētis omnēs ōrdinēs, omnēs hominēs, ūniversum populum Rōmānum, id quod in cīvīlī causā hodiernō diē prīmum vidēmus, ūnum atque idem sentientem. Cōgitāte, quantīs labōribus fundātum imperium, quantā virtūte stabilītam lībertātem, quantā deōrum benīgnitāte auctās exaggerātāsque fortūnās ūna nox paene dēlērit. Id nē umquam posthāc nōn modo nōn cōnficī, sed nē cōgitārī quidem possit ā cīvibus, hodiernō diē prōvidendum est. Atque haec, nōn ut vōs, quī mihi studiō paene praecurritis, excitārem, locūtus sum, sed ut mea vōx, quae dēbet esse in rē pūblicā prīnceps, officiō fūncta cōnsulārī vidērētur.

X. Nunc, ante quam ad sententiam redeō dē mē pauca dīcam. Ego, quanta manus est coniūrātōrum, quam vidētis esse permāgnam, tantam mē inimīcōrum multitūdinem suscēpisse videō; sed eam esse iūdicō turpem et īnfīrmam et abiectam. Quod sī aliquandō alicūius furōre et scelere concitāta manus ista plūs valuerit quam vestra ac reī pūblicae dīgnitās, mē tamen meōrum factōrum atque cōnsiliōrum numquam, patrēs cōnscrīptī, paenitēbit. Etenim mors, quam illī fortasse minitantur, omnibus est parāta; vītae tantam laudem, quantā vōs mē vestrīs dēcrētīs honestāstis, nēmō est adsecūtus. Cēterīs enim bene gestā, mihi ūnī cōnservātā rē pūblicā grātulātiōnem dēcrēvistis.

Sit Scīpiō clārus ille, cūius cōnsiliō atque virtūte Hannibal in Āfricam redīre atque Italiā dēcēdere coāctus est; ōrnētur alter eximiā laude Āfricānus, quī duās urbēs huic imperiō īnfestissimās, Karthāginem Numantiamque, dēlēvit; habeātur vir ēgregius Paulus ille, cūius currum rēx potentissimus quondam et nōbilissimus Persēs honestāvit; sit aeternā glōriā

Marius, quī bis Italiam obsidiōne et metū servitūtis līberāvit; antepōnātur omnibus Pompēius, cūius rēs gestae atque virtūtēs īsdem quibus sōlis cursus regiōnibus ac terminīs continentur: erit profectō inter hōrum laudēs aliquid locī nostrae glōriae, nisi forte māius est patefacere nōbīs prōvinciās, quō exīre possīmus, quam cūrāre, ut etiam illī, quī absunt, habeant, quō victōrēs revertantur.

Quamquam est ūnō locō condiciō melior externae victōriae quam domesticae, quod hostēs aliēnigenae aut oppressī serviunt aut receptī in amīcitiam beneficiō sē obligātōs putant; quī autem ex numerō cīvium, dēmentiā aliquā dēprāvātī, hostēs patriae semel esse coepērunt, eōs cum ā perniciē reī pūblicae reppuleris, nec vī coërcēre nec beneficiō plācāre possīs. Quā rē mihi cum perditīs cīvibus aeternum bellum susceptum esse videō. Id ego vestrō bonōrumque omnium auxiliō memoriāque tantōrum perīculōrum, quae nōn modo in hōc populō, quī servātus est, sed in omnium gentium sermōnibus ac mentibus semper haerēbit, ā mē atque ā meīs facile prōpulsārī posse cōnfīdō. Neque ūlla profectō tanta vīs reperiētur, quae coniūnctiōnem vestram equitumque Rōmānōrum et tantam cōnspīrātiōnem bonōrum omnium cōnfringere et labefactāre possit.

XI. Quae cum ita sint, prō imperiō, prō exercitū, prō prōvinciā, quam neglēxī, prō triumphō cēterīsque laudis īnsīgnibus, quae sunt ā mē propter urbis vestraeque salūtis cūstōdiam repudiāta, prō clientēlīs hospitiīsque prōvinciālibus, quae tamen urbānīs opibus nōn minōre labōre tueor quam comparō, prō hīs igitur omnibus rēbus, prō meīs in vōs singulāribus studiīs prōque hāc, quam perspicitis, ad cōnservandam rem pūblicam dīligentiā, nihil ā vōbīs nisi hūius temporis tōtīusque meī cōnsulātūs memoriam postulō; quae dum erit in vestrīs fīxa mentibus, tūtissimō mē mūrō saeptum esse arbitrābor. Quod sī meam spem vīs improbōrum fefellerit atque superāverit, commendō vōbīs parvum meum fīlium, cui profectō satis erit praesidī nōn sōlum ad salūtem, vērum etiam ad dīgnitātem, sī ēius, quī haec omnia suō sōlīus perīculō cōnservārit, illum fīlium esse memineritis.

Quāpropter dē summā salūte vestrā populīque Rōmānī, dē vestrīs coniugibus ac līberīs, dē ārīs ac focīs, dē fānīs atque templīs, dē tōtīus urbis tēctīs ac sēdibus, dē imperiō ac lībertāte, dē salūte Italiae, dē ūniversā rē pūblicā dēcernite dīligenter, ut īnstituistis, ac fortiter. Habētis eum cōnsulem, quī et pārēre vestrīs dēcrētīs nōn dubitet et ea, quae statueritis, quoad vīvet, dēfendere et per sē ipsum praestāre possit.

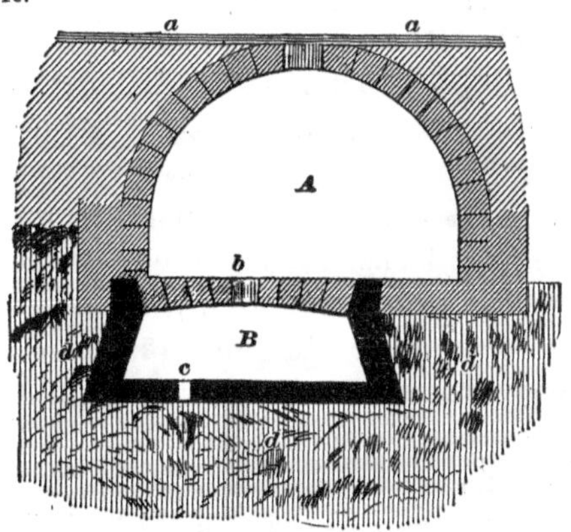

CARCER — MAMERTINE PRISON.

A. Upper Dungeon.
B. Lower Dungeon — *Tullianum*.
a a. Lower floor of present church above.
b. Hole through which the condemned were let down into the *Tullianum*.
c. Spring of clear water.
d d. Solid rock.

M. TULLI CICERONIS

DE IMPERIO GNAEI POMPEI ORATIO

AD QUIRITES.

I. Quamquam mihi semper frequēns cōnspectus vester multō iūcundissimus, hīc autem locus ad agendum amplissimus, ad dīcendum ōrnātissimus est vīsus, Quirītēs, tamen hōc aditū laudis, quī semper optimō cuique māximē patuit, nōn mea mē voluntās adhūc, sed vītae meae ratiōnēs ab ineunte aetāte susceptae prohibuērunt. Nam cum anteā per aetātem nōndum hūius auctōritātem locī attingere audērem statueremque nihil hūc nisi perfectum ingeniō, ēlabōrātum industriā adferrī oportēre, omne meum tempus amīcōrum temporibus trānsmittendum putāvī.

Ita neque hīc locus vacuus umquam fuit ab eīs, quī vestram causam dēfenderent, et meus labor, in prīvātōrum perīculīs castē integrēque versātus, ex vestrō iūdiciō frūctum est amplissimum cōnsecūtus. Nam cum propter dīlātiōnem comitiōrum ter praetor prīmus centuriīs cūnctīs renūntiātus sum, facile intellēxī, Quirītēs, et quid dē mē iūdicārētis et quid aliīs praescrīberētis.

Nunc, cum et auctōritātis in mē tantum sit, quantum vōs honōribus mandandīs esse voluistis, et ad agendum facultātis tantum, quantum hominī vigilantī ex forēnsī ūsū prope cotīdiāna dīcendī exercitātiō potuit adferre, certē et, sī quid auctōritātis in mē est, apud eōs ūtar, quī eam mihi dedērunt, et, sī quid in dīcendō cōnsequī possum, eīs ostendam potissimum, quī eī quoque reī frūctum suō iūdiciō tribuendum esse dūxērunt. Atque illud in prīmīs mihi laetandum iūre esse videō, quod in hāc īnsolitā mihi ex hōc locō ratiōne dīcendī causa tālis oblāta est, in quā ōrātiō deesse nēminī possit. Dīcendum est enim dē Cn. Pompēī singulārī eximiāque virtūte; hūius autem ōrātiōnis difficilius est exitum quam prīncipium invenīre. Ita mihi nōn tam cōpia quam modus in dīcendō quaerendus est.

II. Atque ut inde ōrātiō mea proficīscātur, unde haec omnis causa dūcitur, bellum grave et perīculōsum vestrīs vectīgālibus ac sociīs ā duōbus potentissimīs rēgibus īnfertur, Mithridāte et Tigrāne, quōrum alter relīctus, alter lacessītus occāsiōnem sibi ad occupandam Asiam oblātam esse arbitrātur. Equitibus Rōmānīs, honestissimīs virīs, adferuntur ex Asiā cotīdiē litterae, quōrum māgnae rēs aguntur in vestrīs vectīgālibus exercendīs occupātae; quī ad mē prō necessitūdine, quae mihi est cum illō ōrdine, causam reī pūblicae perīculaque rērum suārum dētulērunt: Bīthȳniae, quae nunc vestra prōvincia est, vīcōs exūstōs esse complūrēs; rēgnum Ariobarzānis, quod fīnītimum est vestrīs vectīgālibus, tōtum esse in hostium potestāte; L. Lūcullum māgnīs rēbus gestīs ab eō bellō discēdere; huic quī successerit, nōn satis esse parātum ad tantum bellum administrandum; ūnum ab omnibus sociīs et cīvibus ad id bellum imperātōrem dēposcī atque expetī, eundem hunc ūnum ab hostibus metuī, praetereā nēminem.

Causa quae sit, vidētis; nunc, quid agendum sit,

cōnsīderāte. Prīmum mihi vidētur dē genere bellī, deinde dē māgnitūdine, tum dē imperātōre dēligendō esse dīcendum.

Genus est enim bellī ēius modī, quod māximē vestrōs animōs excitāre atque īnflammāre ad persequendī studium dēbeat; in quō agitur populī Rōmānī glōria, quae vōbīs ā māiōribus cum māgna in omnibus rēbus, tum summa in rē mīlitārī trādita est; agitur salūs sociōrum atque amīcōrum, prō quā multa māiōrēs vestrī māgna et gravia bella gessērunt; aguntur certissima populī Rōmānī vectīgālia et māxima, quibus āmissīs et pācis ōrnāmenta et subsidia bellī requīrētis; aguntur bona multōrum cīvium, quibus est ā vōbīs et ipsōrum et reī pūblicae causā cōnsulendum.

III. Et quoniam semper appetentēs glōriae praeter cēterās gentēs atque avidī laudis fuistis, dēlenda est vōbīs illa macula Mithridāticō bellō superiōre concepta, quae penitus iam īnsēdit ac nimis inveterāvit in populī Rōmānī nōmine, quod is, quī ūnō diē tōtā in Asiā, tot in cīvitātibus, ūnō nūntiō atque ūnā sīgnificātiōne litterārum cīvēs Rōmānōs necandōs trucīdandōsque dēnotāvit, nōn modo adhūc poenam nūllam suō dīgnam scelere suscēpit, sed ab illō tempore annum iam tertium et vīcēsimum rēgnat, et ita rēgnat, ut sē nōn Pontī neque Cappadociae latebrīs occultāre velit, sed ēmergere ex patriō rēgnō atque in vestrīs vectīgālibus, hōc est, in Asiae lūce, versārī.

Etenim adhūc ita nostrī cum illō rēge contendērunt imperātōrēs, ut ab illō īnsīgnia victōriae, nōn victōriam reportārent. Triumphāvit L. Sulla, triumphāvit L. Mūrēna dē Mithridāte, duo fortissimī virī et summī imperātōrēs, sed ita triumphārunt, ut ille pulsus superātusque rēgnāret. Vērum tamen illīs imperātōribus laus est tribuenda, quod ēgērunt, venia danda, quod relīquērunt, proptereā quod ab eō bellō Sullam in Italiam rēs pūblica, Mūrēnam Sulla revocāvit.

IV. Mithridātēs autem omne reliquum tempus nōn ad oblīviōnem veteris bellī, sed ad comparātiōnem novī contulit; quī cum māximās aedificāsset ōrnāssetque classēs exercitūsque permāgnōs, quibuscumque ex gentibus potuisset, comparāsset et sē Bosporānīs, fīnitimīs suīs, bellum īnferre simulāret, ūsque in Hispāniam lēgātōs ac litterās mīsit ad eōs ducēs, quibuscum tum bellum gerēbāmus, ut, cum duōbus in locīs disiūnctissimīs māximēque dīversīs ūnō cōnsiliō ā bīnīs hostium cōpiīs bellum terrā marīque gererētur, vōs ancipitī contentiōne districtī dē imperiō dīmicārētis.

Sed tamen alterius partis perīculum, Sertōriānae atque Hispāniēnsis, quae multō plūs fīrmāmentī ac rōboris habēbat, Cn. Pompēī dīvīnō cōnsiliō ac singulārī virtūte dēpulsum est; in alterā parte ita rēs ā L. Lūcullō, summō virō, est administrāta, ut initia illa rērum gestārum māgna atque praeclāra nōn fēlīcitātī ēius, sed virtūtī, haec autem extrēma, quae nūper accidērunt, nōn culpae, sed fortūnae tribuenda esse videantur. Sed dē Lūcullō dīcam aliō locō, et ita dīcam, Quirītēs, ut neque vēra laus eī dētrācta ōrātiōne meā neque falsa adfīcta esse videātur; dē vestrī imperī dīgnitāte atque glōriā, quoniam is est exorsus ōrātiōnis meae, vidēte quem vōbīs animum suscipiendum putētis.

V. Māiōrēs nostrī saepe mercātōribus aut nāviculāriīs nostrīs iniūriōsius trāctātīs bella gessērunt; vōs, tot mīlibus cīvium Rōmānōrum ūnō nūntiō atque ūnō tempore necātīs, quō tandem animō esse dēbētis? Lēgātī quod erant appellātī superbius, Corinthum patrēs vestrī, tōtīus Graeciae lūmen, exstīnctum esse voluērunt; vōs eum rēgem inultum esse patiēminī, quī lēgātum populī Rōmānī cōnsulārem vinculīs ac verberibus atque omnī suppliciō excruciātum necāvit? Illī lībertātem cīvium Rōmānōrum imminūtam nōn tulērunt: vōs vītam ēreptam neglegētis? Iūs lēgātiōnis verbō violātum illī persecūtī sunt; vōs lēgātum omnī suppliciō interfectum relinquētis? Vidēte, nē, ut illīs pulcherrimum fuit tantam vōbīs imperī glōriam trādere, sīc vōbīs turpissimum sit id, quod accēpistis, tuērī et cōnservāre nōn posse.

Quid? quod salūs sociōrum summum in perīculum ac discrīmen vocātur, quō tandem animō ferre dēbētis? Rēgnō est expulsus Ariobarzānēs rēx, socius populī Rōmānī atque amīcus; imminent duo rēgēs tōtī Asiae nōn sōlum vōbīs inimīcissimī, sed etiam vestrīs sociīs atque amīcīs; cīvitātēs autem omnēs cūnctā Asiā atque Graeciā vestrum auxilium exspectāre propter perīculī māgnitūdinem cōguntur; imperātōrem ā vōbīs certum dēposcere, cum praesertim vōs alium mīseritis, neque audent neque sē id facere sine summō perīculō posse arbitrantur. Vident et sentiunt hōc idem, quod vōs, ūnum virum esse, in quō summa sint omnia, et eum propter esse, quō etiam carent aegrius; cūius adventū ipsō atque nōmine, tametsī ille ad maritimum bellum vēnerit, tamen impetūs hostium repressōs esse intellegunt ac retardātōs.

Hī vōs, quoniam līberē loquī nōn licet, tacitē rogant, ut sē quoque, sīcut cēterārum prōvinciārum sociōs, dīgnōs exīstimētis, quōrum salūtem tālī virō commendētis, atque hōc etiam magis, quod cēterōs in prōvinciam ēius modī hominēs cum imperiō mittimus, ut, etiam sī ab hoste dēfendant, tamen ipsōrum adventūs in urbēs sociōrum nōn multum ab hostīlī expūgnātiōne differant; hunc audiēbant anteā, nunc praesentem vident tantā temperantiā, tantā mānsuētūdine, tantā hūmānitāte, ut eī beātissimī esse videantur, apud quōs ille diūtissimē commorātur.

VI. Quā rē, sī propter sociōs, nūllā ipsī iniūriā lacessītī, māiōrēs nostrī cum Antiochō, cum Philippō, cum Aetōlīs, cum Poenīs bella gessērunt, quantō vōs studiō convenit, iniūriīs prōvocātōs, sociōrum salūtem ūnā cum imperī vestrī dīgnitāte dēfendere, praesertim cum dē māximīs vestrīs vectīgālibus agātur? Nam cēterārum prōvinciārum vectīgālia, Quirītēs, tanta sunt, ut eīs ad ipsās prōvinciās tūtandās vix contentī esse possīmus; Asia vērō tam opīma est ac fertilis, ut et ūbertāte agrōrum et varietāte frūctuum et māgnitūdine pāstiōnis et multitūdine eārum rērum, quae exportentur, facile omnibus terrīs antecellat.

Itaque haec vōbīs prōvincia, Quirītēs, sī et bellī ūtilitātem et pācis dīgnitātem retinēre vultis, nōn modo ā calamitāte, sed etiam ā metū calamitātis est dēfendenda. Nam in cēterīs rēbus cum venit calamitās, tum dētrīmentum accipitur; at in vectīgālibus nōn sōlum adventus malī, sed etiam metus ipse adfert calamitātem. Nam cum hostium cōpiae nōn longē absunt, etiam sī inruptiō nūlla facta est, tamen pecuāria relinquitur, agrī cultūra dēseritur, mercātōrum nāvigātiō conquiēscit. Ita neque ex portū neque ex decumīs neque ex scrīptūrā vectīgal cōnservārī potest; quā rē saepe tōtīus annī frūctus ūnō rūmōre perīculī atque ūnō bellī terrōre āmittitur.

Quō tandem igitur animō esse exīstimātis aut eōs, quī vectīgālia nōbīs pēnsitant, aut eōs, quī exercent atque exigunt, cum duo rēgēs cum māximīs cōpiīs propter adsint? cum ūna excursiō equitātūs perbrevī tempore tōtīus annī vectīgal auferre possit? cum pūblicānī familiās māximās, quās in saltibus habent, quās in agrīs, quās in portubus atque cūstōdiīs, māgnō perīculō sē habēre arbitrentur? Putātisne vōs illīs rēbūs fruī posse, nisi eōs, quī vōbīs frūctuī sunt, cōnservāritis nōn sōlum, ut ante dīxī, calamitāte, sed etiam calamitātis formīdine līberātōs?

VII. Ac nē illud quidem vōbīs neglegendum est, quod mihi ego extrēmum prōposueram, cum essem dē bellī genere dictūrus, quod ad multōrum bona cīvium Rōmānōrum pertinet; quōrum vōbīs prō vestrā sapientiā, Quirītēs, habenda est ratiō dīligenter. Nam et pūblicānī, hominēs honestissimī atque ōrnātissimī, suās ratiōnēs et cōpiās in illam prōvinciam contulērunt, quōrum ipsōrum per sē rēs et fortūnae vōbīs cūrae esse dēbent. Etenim, sī vectīgālia nervōs esse reī pūblicae semper dūximus, eum certē ōrdinem, quī exercet illa, fīrmāmentum cēterōrum ōrdinum rēctē esse dīcēmus. Deinde ex cēterīs ōrdinibus hominēs gnāvī atque industriī partim ipsī in Asiā negōtiantur, quibus vōs absentibus cōnsulere dēbētis, partim eōrum in eā prōvinciā pecūniās māgnās collocātās habent.

Est igitur hūmānitātis vestrae māgnum numerum eōrum cīvium calamitāte prohibēre, sapientiae vidēre multōrum cīvium calamitātem ā rē pūblicā sēiūnctam esse nōn posse. Etenim prīmum illud parvī rēfert, nōs pūblica hīs omissīs vectīgālia posteā victōriā recuperāre; neque enim īsdem redimendī facultās erit propter calamitātem neque aliīs voluntās propter timōrem. Deinde, quod nōs eadem Asia atque īdem iste Mithridātēs initiō bellī Asiāticī docuit, id quidem certē calamitāte doctī memoriā retinēre dēbēmus. Nam tum, cum in Asiā rēs māgnās permultī āmīserant, scīmus Rōmae solūtiōne impedītā fidem concidisse. Nōn enim possunt ūnā in cīvitāte multī rem ac fortūnās āmittere, ut nōn plūrēs sēcum in eandem trahant calamitātem.

Ā quō perīculō prohibēte rem pūblicam et mihi crēdite, id quod ipsī vidētis, haec fidēs atque haec ratiō pecūniārum, quae Rōmae, quae in forō versātur, implicāta est cum illīs pecūniīs Asiāticīs et cohaeret; ruere illa nōn possunt, ut haec nōn eōdem labefacta mōtū concidant. Quā rē vidēte, num dubitandum vōbīs sit omnī studiō ad id bellum incumbere, in quō glōria nōminis vestrī, salūs sociōrum, vectīgālia māxima, fortūnae plūrimōrum cīvium coniūnctae cum rē pūblicā dēfendantur.

VIII. Quoniam dē genere bellī dīxī, nunc dē māgnitūdine pauca dīcam. Potest enim hōc dīcī, bellī genus esse ita necessārium, ut sit gerendum, nōn esse ita māgnum, ut sit pertimēscendum. In quō māximē labōrandum est, nē forte ea vōbīs, quae dīligentissimē prōvidenda sunt, contemnenda esse videantur.

Atque ut omnēs intellegant mē L. Lūcullō tantum impertīre laudis, quantum fortī virō et sapientī hominī et māgnō imperātōrī dēbeātur, dīcō ēius adventū māximās Mithridātī cōpiās omnibus rēbus ōrnātās atque īnstrūctās fuisse, urbemque Asiae clārissimam nōbīsque amīcissimam, Cyzicēnōrum, obsessam esse ab ipsō rēge māximā multitūdine et oppūgnātam vehementissimē; quam L. Lūcullus virtūte, adsiduitāte, cōnsiliō, summīs obsidiōnis perīculīs līberāvit; ab eōdem imperātōre classem māgnam et ōrnātam, quae ducibus Sertōriānīs ad Italiam studiō atque odiō īnflammāta raperētur, superātam esse atque dēpressam; māgnās hostium praetereā cōpiās multīs proeliīs esse dēlētās patefactumque nostrīs legiōnibus esse Pontum, quī anteā populō Rōmānō ex omnī aditū clausus fuisset; Sinōpēn atque Amīsum, quibus in oppidīs erant domicilia rēgis, omnibus rēbus ōrnātās ac refertās, cēterāsque urbēs Pontī et Cappadociae permultās ūnō aditū adventūque esse captās; rēgem spoliātum rēgnō patriō atque avītō ad aliōs sē rēgēs atque ad aliās gentēs supplicem contulisse; atque haec omnia salvīs populī Rōmānī sociīs atque integrīs vectīgālibus esse gesta. Satis opīnor haec esse laudis, atque ita, Quirītēs, ut hōc vōs intellegātis, ā nūllō istōrum, quī huic obtrectant lēgī atque causae, L. Lūcullum similiter ex hōc locō esse laudātum.

IX. Requīrētur fortasse nunc, quem ad modum, cum haec ita sint, reliquum possit māgnum esse bellum. Cognōscite, Quirītēs; nōn enim hōc sine causā quaerī vidētur.

Prīmum ex suō rēgnō sīc Mithridātēs profūgit, ut ex eōdem Pontō Mēdēa illa quondam profūgisse dīcitur, quam praedicant in fugā frātris suī membra in eīs locīs, quā sē parēns persequerētur, dissipāvisse, ut eōrum collēctiō dispersa maerorque patrius celeritātem persequendī retardāret. Sīc Mithridātēs fugiēns māximam vim aurī atque argentī pulcherrimārumque rērum omnium, quās et ā māiōribus accēperat et ipse bellō superiōre ex tōtā Asiā dīreptās in suum rēgnum congesserat, in Pontō omnem relīquit. Haec dum nostrī colligunt omnia dīligentius, rēx ipse ē manibus effūgit. Ita illum in persequendī studiō maeror, hōs laetitia tardāvit.

Hunc in illō timōre et fugā Tigrānēs, rēx Armenius, excēpit diffīdentemque rēbus suīs cōnfīrmāvit et adflīctum ērēxit perditumque recreāvit. Cūius in rēgnum posteā quam L. Lūcullus cum exercitū vēnit, plūrēs etiam gentēs contrā imperātōrem nostrum concitātae sunt. Erat enim metus iniectus eīs nātiōnibus, quās numquam populus Rōmānus neque lacessendās bellō neque temptandās putāvit; erat etiam alia gravis atque vehemēns opīniō, quae animōs gentium barbarārum pervāserat, fānī locuplētissimī et religiōsissimī dīripiendī causā in eās ōrās nostrum esse exercitum adductum. Ita nātiōnēs multae atque māgnae novō quōdam terrōre ac metū concitābantur.

Noster autem exercitus, tametsī urbem ex Tigrānis rēgnō cēperat et proeliīs ūsus erat secundīs, tamen nimiā longinquitāte locōrum ac dēsīderiō suōrum commovēbātur. Hīc iam plūra nōn dīcam; fuit enim illud extrēmum, ut ex eīs locīs ā mīlitibus nostrīs reditus magis mātūrus quam prōcessiō longior quaererētur. Mithridātēs autem et suam manum iam cōnfīrmārat, et māgnīs adventīciīs auxiliīs multōrum rēgum et nātiōnum iuvābātur. Nam hōc ferē sīc fierī solēre accēpimus, ut rēgum adflīctae fortūnae facile multōrum opēs adliciant ad misericordiam, māximēque eōrum, quī aut rēgēs sunt aut vīvunt in rēgnō, ut eīs nōmen rēgāle māgnum et sānctum esse videātur. Itaque tantum victus efficere potuit, quantum incolumis numquam est ausus optāre. Nam, cum sē in rēgnum suum recēpisset, nōn fuit eō contentus, quod eī praeter spem acciderat, ut illam, posteā quam pulsus erat, terram umquam attingeret, sed in exercitum nostrum clārum atque victōrem impetum fēcit.

Sinite hōc locō, Quirītēs, sīcut poētae solent, quī rēs Rōmānās scrībunt, praeterīre mē nostram calamitātem, quae tanta fuit, ut eam ad aurēs imperātōris nōn ex proeliō nūntius, sed ex sermōne rūmor adferret. Hīc in illō ipsō malō gravissimāque bellī offēnsiōne L. Lūcullus, quī tamen aliquā ex parte eīs incommodīs mederī fortasse potuisset, vestrō iussū coāctus, quī imperī diuturnitātī modum statuendum vetere exemplō putāvistis, partem mīlitum, quī iam stīpendiīs cōnfectī erant, dīmīsit, partem M'. Glabriōnī trādidit.

Multa praetereō cōnsultō; sed ea vōs coniectūrā perspicite, quantum illud bellum factum putētis, quod coniungant rēgēs potentissimī, renovent agitātae nātiōnēs, suscipiant integrae gentēs, novus imperātor noster accipiat vetere exercitū pulsō.

X. Satis mihi multa verba fēcisse videor, quā rē esset hōc bellum genere ipsō necessārium, māgnitūdine perīculōsum; restat, ut dē imperātōre ad id bellum dēligendō ac tantīs rēbus praeficiendō dīcendum esse videātur. Utinam, Quirītēs, virōrum fortium atque innocentium cōpiam tantam habērētis, ut haec vōbīs dēlīberātiō difficilis esset, quemnam potissimum tantīs rēbus ac tantō bellō praeficiendum putārētis! Nunc vērō cum sit ūnus Cn. Pompēius, quī nōn modo eōrum hominum, quī nunc sunt, glōriam, sed etiam antīquitātis memoriam virtūte superārit, quae rēs est, quae cūiusquam animum in hāc causā dubium facere possit? Ego enim sīc exīstimō, in summō imperātōre quattuor hās rēs inesse oportēre, scientiam reī mīlitāris, virtūtem, auctōritātem, fēlīcitātem.

Quis igitur hōc homine scientior umquam aut fuit aut esse dēbuit? quī ē lūdō atque pueritiae disciplīnīs,

Statue at Rome, formerly thought to be of Pompey.

bellō māximō atque ācerrimīs hostibus, ad patris exercitum atque in mīlitiae disciplīnam profectus est; quī extrēmā pueritiā mīles in exercitū fuit summī imperātōris, ineunte adulēscentiā māximī ipse exercitūs imperātor; quī saepius cum hoste cōnflīxit, quam quisquam cum inimīcō concertāvit, plūra bella gessit quam cēterī lēgērunt, plūrēs prōvinciās cōnfēcit quam aliī concupīvērunt; cūius adulēscentia ad scientiam reī mīlitāris nōn aliēnīs praeceptīs, sed suīs imperiīs, nōn offēnsiōnibus bellī, sed victōriīs, nōn stīpendiīs, sed triumphīs est ērudīta.

Quod dēnique genus esse bellī potest, in quō illum nōn exercuerit fortūna reī pūblicae? Cīvīle, Āfricānum, Trānsalpīnum, Hispāniēnse, servīle, nāvāle bellum, varia et dīversa genera et bellōrum et hostium, nōn sōlum gesta ab hōc ūnō, sed etiam cōnfecta, nūllam rem esse dēclārant in ūsū positam mīlitārī, quae hūius virī scientiam fugere possit.

XI. Iam vērō virtūtī Cn. Pompēī quae potest ōrātiō pār invenīrī? Quid est, quod quisquam aut illō dīgnum aut vōbīs novum aut cuiquam inaudītum possit adferre? Neque enim illae sunt sōlae virtūtēs imperātōriae, quae vulgō exīstimantur, labor in negōtiīs, fortitūdō in perīculīs, industria in agendō, celeritās in cōnficiendō, cōnsilium in prōvidendō; quae tanta sunt in hōc ūnō, quanta in omnibus reliquīs imperātōribus, quōs aut vīdimus aut audīvimus, nōn fuērunt.

Testis est Italia, quam ille ipse victor L. Sulla hūius virtūte et subsidiō cōnfessus est līberātam; testis est Sicilia, quam multīs undique cīnctam perīculīs nōn terrōre bellī, sed cōnsilī celeritāte explicāvit; testis est Āfrica, quae māgnīs oppressa hostium cōpiīs eōrum ipsōrum sanguine redundāvit;

testis est Gallia, per quam legiōnibus nostrīs iter in Hispāniam Gallōrum interneciōne patefactum est; testis est Hispānia, quae saepissimē plūrimōs hostēs ab hōc superātōs prōstrātōsque cōnspexit; testis est iterum et saepius Italia, quae cum servīlī bellō taetrō perīculōsōque premerētur, ab hōc auxilium absente expetīvit, quod bellum exspectātiōne ēius attenuātum atque imminūtum est, adventū sublātum ac sepultum; testēs nunc vērō iam omnēs sunt ōrae atque omnēs exterae gentēs ac nātiōnēs, dēnique maria omnia cum ūniversa, tum in singulīs ōrīs omnēs sinūs atque portūs.

Quis enim tōtō marī locus per hōs annōs aut tam fīrmum habuit praesidium, ut tūtus esset, aut tam fuit abditus, ut latēret? Quis nāvigāvit, quī nōn sē aut mortis aut servitūtis perīculō committeret, cum aut hieme aut refertō praedōnum marī nāvigāret? Hōc tantum bellum, tam turpe, tam vetus, tam lātē dīvīsum atque dispersum quis umquam arbitrārētur aut ab omnibus imperātōribus ūnō annō aut omnibus annīs ab ūnō imperātōre cōnficī posse? Quam prōvinciam tenuistis ā praedōnibus līberam per hōsce annōs? Quod vectīgal vōbīs tūtum fuit? Quem socium dēfendistis? Cui praesidiō classibus vestrīs fuistis? Quam multās exīstimātis īnsulās esse dēsertās, quam multās aut metū relīctās aut ā praedōnibus captās urbēs esse sociōrum?

XII. Sed quid ego longinqua commemorō? Fuit hōc quondam, fuit proprium populī Rōmānī, longē ā domō bellāre et prōpūgnāculīs imperī sociōrum fortūnās, nōn sua tēcta dēfendere. Sociīs ego nostrīs mare per hōs annōs clausum fuisse dīcam, cum exercitūs vestrī numquam ā Brundisiō nisi hieme summā trānsmīserint? Quī ad vōs ab exterīs nātiōnibus venīrent, captōs querar, cum lēgātī populī Rōmānī redēmptī sint? Mercātōribus tūtum mare nōn fuisse dīcam, cum duodecim secūrēs in praedōnum potestātem pervēnerint? Cnidum aut Colophōnem aut Samum, nōbilissimās urbēs, innumerābilēsque aliās captās esse commemorem, cum vestrōs portūs atque eōs portūs, quibus vītam ac spīritum dūcitis, in praedōnum fuisse potestāte sciātis?

An vērō ignōrātis portum Cāiētae celeberrimum ac plēnissimum nāvium īnspectante praetōre ā praedōnibus esse dīreptum, ex Mīsēnō autem ēius ipsīus līberōs, quī cum praedōnibus anteā ibi bellum gesserat, ā praedōnibus esse sublātōs? Nam quid ego Ōstiēnse incommodum atque illam lābem atque ignōminiam reī pūblicae querar, cum prope īnspectantibus vōbīs classis ea, cui cōnsul populī Rōmānī praepositus esset, ā praedōnibus capta atque oppressa est? Prō dī immortālēs! tantamne ūnīus hominis incrēdibilis ac dīvīna virtūs tam brevī tempore lūcem adferre reī pūblicae potuit, ut vōs, quī modo ante ōstium Tiberīnum classem hostium vidēbātis, eī nunc nūllam intrā Ōceanī ōstium praedōnum nāvem esse audiātis?

Atque haec quā celeritāte gesta sint, quamquam vidētis, tamen ā mē in dīcendō praetereunda nōn sunt. Quis enim umquam aut obeundī negōtī aut cōnsequendī quaestūs studiō tam brevī tempore tot loca adīre, tantōs cursūs cōnficere potuit, quam celeriter Cn. Pompēiō duce tantī bellī impetus nāvigāvit? Quī nōndum tempestīvō ad nāvigandum marī Siciliam adiit, Āfricam explōrāvit, in Sardiniam cum classe vēnit atque haec tria frūmentāria subsidia reī pūblicae fīrmissimīs praesidiīs classibusque mūnīvit.

Inde cum sē in Italiam recēpisset, duābus Hispāniīs et Galliā Trānsalpīnā praesidiīs ac nāvibus cōnfīrmātā, missīs item in ōram Īllyricī maris et in Achāiam omnemque Graeciam nāvibus Italiae duo maria māximīs classibus fīrmissimīsque praesidiīs adōrnāvit, ipse autem, ut Brundisiō profectus est, ūndēquīnquāgēsimō diē tōtam ad imperium populī Rōmānī Ciliciam adiūnxit; omnēs, quī ubīque praedōnēs fuērunt, partim captī interfectīque sunt, partim ūniūs hūius sē imperiō ac potestātī dēdidērunt. Īdem Crētēnsibus, cum ad eum ūsque in Pamphȳliam lēgātōs dēprecātōrēsque mīsissent, spem dēditiōnis nōn adēmit obsidēsque imperāvit. Ita tantum bellum, tam diūturnum, tam longē lātēque dispersum, quō bellō omnēs gentēs ac nātiōnēs premēbantur, Cn. Pompēius extrēmā hieme apparāvit, ineunte vēre suscēpit, mediā aestāte cōnfēcit.

XIII. Est haec dīvīna atque incrēdibilis virtūs imperātōris. Quid cēterae, quās paulō ante commemorāre coeperam, quantae atque quam multae sunt! Nōn enim bellandī virtūs sōlum in summō ac perfectō imperātōre quaerenda est, sed multae sunt artēs eximiae hūius administrae comitēsque virtūtis. Ac prīmum quantā innocentiā dēbent esse imperātōrēs, quantā deinde in omnibus rēbus temperantiā, quantā fidē, quantā facilitāte, quantō ingeniō, quantā hūmānitāte! Quae breviter quālia sint in Cn. Pompēiō cōnsīderēmus. Summa enim omnia sunt, Quirītēs, sed ea magis ex aliōrum contentiōne quam ipsa per sēsē cognōscī atque intellegī possunt.

Quem enim imperātōrem possumus ūllō in numerō putāre, cūius in exercitū centuriātūs vēneant atque vēnierint? Quid hunc hominem māgnum aut amplum dē rē pūblicā cōgitāre, quī pecūniam ex aerāriō dēprōmptam ad bellum administrandum aut propter cupiditātem prōvinciae magistrātibus dīvīserit aut propter avāritiam Rōmae in quaestū relīquerit? Vestra admurmurātiō facit, Quirītēs, ut agnōscere videāminī, quī haec fēcerint; ego autem nōminō nēminem; quā rē īrāscī mihi nēmō poterit, nisi quī ante dē sē voluerit cōnfitērī.

Itaque propter hanc avāritiam imperātōrum quantās calamitātēs, quōcumque ventum sit, nostrī exercitūs ferant, quis ignōrat? Itinera, quae per hōsce annōs in Italiā per agrōs atque oppida cīvium Rōmānōrum nostrī imperātōrēs fēcerint, recordāminī; tum facilius statuētis, quid apud exterās nātiōnēs fierī exīstimētis. Utrum plūrēs arbitrāminī per hōsce annōs mīlitum vestrōrum armīs hostium urbēs an hībernīs sociōrum cīvitātēs esse dēlētās?

Neque enim potest exercitum is continēre imperātor, quī sē ipse nōn continet, neque sevērus esse in iūdicandō, quī aliōs in sē sevērōs esse iūdicēs nōn vult. Hīc mīrāmur hunc hominem tantum excellere cēterīs, cūius legiōnēs sīc in Asiam pervēnerint, ut nōn modo manus tantī exercitūs, sed nē vēstīgium quidem cuiquam pācātō nocuisse dīcātur? Iam vērō quem ad modum mīlitēs hībernent, cotīdiē sermōnēs ac litterae perferuntur; nōn modo ut sūmptum faciat in mīlitem, nēminī vīs adfertur, sed nē cupientī quidem cuiquam permittitur. Hiemis enim, nōn avāritiae perfugium māiōrēs nostrī in sociōrum atque amīcōrum tēctīs esse voluērunt.

XIV. Age vērō, cēterīs in rēbus quā sit temperantiā, cōnsīderāte. Unde illam tantam celeritātem et tam incrēdibilem cursum inventum putātis? Nōn enim illum eximia vīs rēmigum aut ars inaudīta quaedam gubernandī aut ventī aliquī novī tam celeriter in ultimās terrās pertulērunt, sed eae rēs, quae cēterōs remorārī solent, nōn retardārunt; nōn avāritia ab īnstitūtō cursū ad praedam aliquam dēvocāvit, nōn libīdō ad voluptātem, nōn amoenitās ad dēlectātiōnem, nōn nōbilitās urbis ad cognitiōnem, nōn dēnique labor ipse ad quiētem; postrēmō sīgna et tabulās cēteraque ōrnāmenta Graecōrum oppidōrum, quae cēterī tollenda arbitrantur, ea sibi ille nē vīsenda quidem exīstimāvit.

Itaque omnēs nunc in eīs locīs Cn. Pompēium sīcut aliquem nōn ex hāc urbe missum, sed dē caelō dēlāpsum intuentur; nunc dēnique incipiunt crēdere, fuisse hominēs Rōmānōs hāc quondam continentiā, quod iam nātiōnibus exterīs incrēdibile ac falsō memoriae prōditum vidēbātur; nunc imperī vestrī splendor illīs gentibus lūcem adferre coepit; nunc intellegunt nōn sine causā māiōrēs suōs tum, cum eā temperantiā magistrātūs habēbāmus, servīre populō Rōmānō quam imperāre aliīs māluisse. Iam vērō ita facilēs aditūs ad eum prīvātōrum, ita līberae querimōniae dē aliōrum iniūriīs esse dīcuntur, ut is, quī dīgnitāte prīncipibus excellit, facilitāte īnfimīs pār esse videātur.

Iam quantum cōnsiliō, quantum dīcendī gravitāte et cōpiā valeat, in quō ipsō inest quaedam dīgnitās imperātōria, vōs, Quirītēs, hōc ipsō ex locō saepe cognōvistis. Fidem vērō ēius quantam inter sociōs exīstimārī putātis, quam hostēs omnēs omnium generum sānctissimam iūdicārint? Hūmānitāte iam tantā est, ut difficile dictū sit, utrum hostēs magis virtūtem ēius pūgnantēs timuerint an mānsuētūdinem victī dīlēxerint. Et quisquam dubitābit, quīn huic hōc tantum bellum trānsmittendum sit, quī ad omnia nostrae memoriae bella cōnficienda dīvīnō quōdam cōnsiliō nātus esse videātur?

XV. Et quoniam auctōritās quoque in bellīs administrandīs multum atque in imperiō mīlitārī valet, certē nēminī dubium est, quīn eā rē īdem ille imperātor plūrimum possit. Vehementer autem pertinēre ad bella administranda, quid hostēs, quid sociī dē imperātōribus nostrīs exīstiment, quis ignōrat, cum sciāmus hominēs, in tantīs rēbus ut aut contemnant aut metuant aut ōderint aut ament, opīniōne nōn minus et fāmā quam aliquā ratiōne certā commovērī?

Quod igitur nōmen umquam in orbe terrārum clārius fuit? cūius rēs gestae parēs? Dē quō homine vōs, id quod māximē facit auctōritātem, tanta et tam praeclāra iūdicia fēcistis? An vērō ūllam ūsquam esse ōram tam dēsertam putātis, quō nōn illīus diēī fāma pervāserit, cum ūniversus populus Rōmānus refertō forō complētīsque omnibus templīs, ex quibus hīc locus cōnspicī potest, ūnum sibi ad commūne omnium gentium bellum Cn. Pompēium imperātōrem dēpoposcit?

Itaque, ut plūra nōn dīcam neque aliōrum exemplīs cōnfīrmem, quantum auctōritās valeat in bellō, ab eōdem Cn. Pompēiō omnium rērum ēgregiārum exempla sūmantur; quī quō diē ā vōbīs maritimō bellō praepositus est imperātor, tanta repente vīlitās annōnae ex summā inopiā et cāritāte reī frūmentāriae cōnsecūta est ūnīus hominis spē ac nōmine, quantam vix ex summā ūbertāte agrōrum diūturna pāx efficere potuisset.

Iam acceptā in Pontō calamitāte ex eō proeliō, dē quō vōs paulō ante invītus admonuī, cum sociī pertimuissent, hostium opēs animīque crēvissent, satis fīrmum praesidium prōvincia nōn habēret, āmīsissētis Asiam, Quirītēs, nisi ad ipsum discrīmen ēius temporis dīvīnitus Cn. Pompēium ad eās regiōnēs fortūna populī Rōmānī attulisset. Hūius adventus et Mithridātem īnsolitā īnflammātum victōriā continuit et Tigrānem māgnīs cōpiīs minitantem Asiae retardāvit. Et quisquam dubitābit, quid virtūte perfectūrus sit, quī tantum auctōritāte perfēcerit? aut quam facile imperiō atque exercitū sociōs et vectīgālia cōnservātūrus sit, quī ipsō nōmine ac rūmōre dēfenderit?

XVI. Age vērō illa rēs quantam dēclārat ēiusdem hominis apud hostēs populī Rōmānī auctōritātem, quod ex locīs tam longinquīs tamque dīversīs tam brevī tempore omnēs huic sē ūnī dēdidērunt! quod Crētēnsium lēgātī, cum in eōrum īnsulā noster imperātor exercitusque esset, ad Cn. Pompēium in ultimās prope terrās vēnērunt eīque sē omnēs Crētēnsium cīvitātēs dēdere velle dīxērunt! Quid? Īdem iste Mithridātēs nōnne ad eundem Cn. Pompēium lēgātum ūsque in Hispāniam mīsit? eum, quem Pompēius lēgātum semper iūdicāvit, eī, quibus erat molestum ad eum potissimum esse missum, speculātōrem quam lēgātum iūdicārī maluērunt. Potestis igitur iam cōnstituere, Quirītēs, hanc auctōritātem, multīs posteā rēbus gestīs māgnīsque vestrīs iūdiciīs amplificātam, quantum apud illōs rēgēs, quantum apud exterās nātiōnēs valitūram esse exīstimētis.

Reliquum est, ut dē fēlīcitāte, quam praestāre dē sē ipsō nēmō potest, meminisse et commemorāre dē alterō possumus, sīcut aequum est hominēs dē potestāte deōrum, timidē et pauca dīcāmus. Ego enim sīc exīstimō, Māximō, Mārcellō, Scīpiōnī, Mariō et cēterīs māgnīs imperātōribus nōn sōlum propter virtūtem, sed etiam propter fortūnam saepius imperia mandāta atque exercitūs esse commissōs. Fuit enim profectō quibusdam summīs virīs quaedam ad amplitūdinem et ad glōriam et ad rēs māgnās bene gerendās dīvīnitus adiūncta fortūna. Dē hūius autem hominis fēlīcitāte, dē quō nunc agimus, hāc ūtar moderātiōne dīcendī, nōn ut in illīus potestāte fortūnam positam esse dīcam, sed ut praeterita meminisse, reliqua spērāre videāmur, nē aut invīsa dīs immortālibus ōrātiō nostra aut ingrāta esse videātur.

Itaque nōn sum praedicātūrus, quantās ille rēs domī mīlitiae, terrā marīque, quantāque fēlīcitāte gesserit; ut ēius semper voluntātibus nōn modo cīvēs adsēnserint, sociī obtemperārint, hostēs oboedierint, sed etiam ventī tempestātēsque obsecundārint: hōc brevissimē dīcam, nēminem umquam tam impudentem fuisse, quī ab dīs immortālibus tot et tantās rēs tacitus audēret optāre, quot et quantās dī immortālēs ad Cn. Pompēium dētulērunt. Quod ut illī proprium ac perpetuum sit, Quirītēs, cum commūnis salūtis atque imperī, tum ipsīus hominis causā, sīcutī facitis, velle et optāre dēbētis.

Quā rē cum et bellum sit ita necessārium, ut neglegī nōn possit, ita māgnum, ut accūrātissimē sit administrandum, et cum eī imperātōrem praeficere possītis, in quō sit eximia bellī scientia, singulāris virtūs, clārissima auctōritās, ēgregia fortūna, dubitātis, Quirītēs, quīn hōc tantum bonī, quod vōbīs ab dīs immortālibus oblātum et datum est, in rem pūblicam cōnservandam atque amplificandam cōnferātis?

XVII. Quod sī Rōmae Cn. Pompēius prīvātus

esset hōc tempore, tamen ad tantum bellum is erat dēligendus atque mittendus; nunc, cum ad cēterās summās ūtilitātēs haec quoque opportūnitās adiungātur, ut in eīs ipsīs locīs adsit, ut habeat exercitum, ut ab eīs, quī habent, accipere statim possit, quid exspectāmus? aut cūr nōn ducibus dīs immortālibus eīdem, cui cētera summā cum salūte reī pūblicae commissa sunt, hōc quoque bellum rēgium committāmus?

At enim vir clārissimus, amantissimus reī pūblicae, vestrīs beneficiīs amplissimīs adfectus, Q. Catulus, itemque summīs ōrnāmentīs honōris, fortūnae, virtūtis, ingenī praeditus, Q. Hortēnsius, ab hāc ratiōne dissentiunt. Quōrum ego auctōritātem apud vōs multīs locīs plūrimum valuisse et valēre oportēre cōnfiteor; sed in hāc causā, tametsī cognōscētis auctōritātēs contrāriās virōrum fortissimōrum et clārissimōrum, tamen omissīs auctōritātibus ipsā rē ac ratiōne exquīrere possumus vēritātem, atque hōc facilius, quod ea omnia, quae ā mē adhūc dicta sunt, eīdem istī vēra esse concēdunt, et necessārium bellum esse et māgnum et in ūnō Cn. Pompēiō summa esse omnia.

Quid igitur ait Hortēnsius? Sī ūnī omnia tribuenda sint, dīgnissimum esse Pompēium, sed ad ūnum tamen omnia dēferrī nōn oportēre. Obsolēvit iam ista ōrātiō, rē multō magis quam verbīs refūtāta. Nam tū īdem, Q. Hortēnsī, multa prō tuā summā cōpiā ac singulārī facultāte dīcendī et in senātū contrā virum fortem, A. Gabīnium, graviter ōrnātēque dīxistī, cum is dē ūnō imperātōre contrā praedōnēs cōnstituendō lēgem prōmulgāsset, et ex hōc ipsō locō permulta item contrā eam lēgem verba fēcistī. Quid? tum, per deōs immortālēs! sī plūs apud populum Rōmānum auctōritās tua quam ipsīus populī Rōmānī salūs et vēra causa valuisset, hodiē hanc glōriam atque hōc orbis terrae imperium tenērēmus? An tibi tum imperium hōc esse vidēbātur, cum populī Rōmānī lēgātī, quaestōrēs praetōrēsque capiēbantur, cum ex omnibus prōvinciīs commeātū et prīvātō et pūblicō prohibēbāmur, cum ita clausa nōbīs erant maria omnia, ut neque prīvātam rem trānsmarīnam neque pūblicam iam obīre possēmus?

XVIII. Quae cīvitās anteā umquam fuit, nōn dīcō Athēniēnsium, quae satis lātē quondam mare tenuisse dīcitur, nōn Karthāginiēnsium, quī permultum classe ac maritimīs rēbus valuērunt, nōn Rhodiōrum, quōrum ūsque ad nostram memoriam disciplīna nāvālis et glōria remānsit; quae cīvitās, inquam, anteā tam tenuis, quae tam parva īnsula fuit, quae nōn portūs suōs et agrōs et aliquam partem regiōnis atque ōrae maritimae per sē ipsa dēfenderet? At hercule aliquot annōs continuōs ante lēgem Gabīniam ille populus Rōmānus, cūius ūsque ad nostram memoriam nōmen invictum in nāvālibus pūgnīs permānserit, māgnā ac multō māximā parte nōn modo ūtilitātis, sed dīgnitātis atque imperī caruit; nōs, quōrum māiōrēs Antiochum rēgem classe Persemque superārunt omnibusque nāvālibus pūgnīs Karthāginiēnsēs, hominēs in maritimīs rēbus exercitātissimōs parātissimōsque, vīcērunt, eī nūllō in locō iam praedōnibus parēs esse poterāmus; nōs, quī anteā nōn modo Italiam tūtam habēbāmus, sed omnēs sociōs in ultimīs ōrīs auctōritāte nostrī imperī salvōs praestāre poterāmus, tum, cum īnsula Dēlos, tam procul ā nōbīs in Aegaeō marī posita, quō omnēs undique cum mercibus atque oneribus commeābant, referta dīvitiīs, parva, sinē mūrō nihil timēbat, eīdem nōn modo prōvinciīs atque ōrīs Italiae maritimīs ac portubus nostrīs, sed etiam Appiā iam viā carēbāmus; et eīs temporibus nōn pudēbat magistrātūs populī Rōmānī in hunc ipsum locum ēscendere, cum eum nōbīs māiōrēs nostrī exuviīs nauticīs et classium spoliīs ōrnātum relīquissent!

XIX. Bonō tē animō tum, Q. Hortēnsī, populus Rōmānus et cēterōs, quī erant in eādem sententiā, dīcere exīstimāvit ea, quae sentiēbātis; sed tamen in salūte commūnī īdem populus Rōmānus dolōrī suō māluit quam auctōritātī vestrae obtemperāre. Itaque ūna lēx, ūnus vir, ūnus annus nōn modo nōs illā miseriā ac turpitūdine līberāvit, sed etiam effēcit, ut aliquandō vērē vidērēmur omnibus gentibus ac nātiōnibus terrā marīque imperāre.

Quō mihi etiam indīgnius vidētur obtrectātum esse adhūc, Gabīniō dīcam anne Pompēiō, an utrīque, id quod est vērius, nē lēgārētur A. Gabīnius Cn. Pompēiō expetentī ac postulantī. Utrum ille, quī postulat ad tantum bellum lēgātum, quem velit, idōneus nōn est, quī impetret, cum cēterī ad expīlandōs sociōs dīripiendāsque prōvinciās, quōs voluērunt, lēgātōs ēdūxerint, an ipse, cūius lēge salūs ac dīgnitās populō Rōmānō atque omnibus gentibus cōnstitūta est, expers esse dēbet glōriae ēius imperātōris atque ēius exercitūs, quī cōnsiliō ipsīus ac perīculō est cōnstitūtus? An C. Falcidius, Q. Metellus, Q. Caelius Latīniēnsis, Cn. Lentulus, quōs omnēs honōris causā nōminō, cum tribūnī plēbī fuissent, annō proximō lēgātī esse potuērunt; in ūnō Gabīniō sunt tam dīligentēs, quī in hōc bellō, quod lēge Gabīniā geritur, in hōc imperātōre atque exercitū, quem per vōs ipse cōnstituit, etiam praecipuō iūre esse dēbēret?

Dē quō lēgandō cōnsulēs spērō ad senātum relātūrōs. Quī sī dubitābunt aut gravābuntur, ego mē profiteor relātūrum; neque mē impediet cūiusquam inimīcum ēdictum, quō minus vōbīs frētus vestrum iūs beneficiumque dēfendam, neque praeter intercessiōnem quicquam audiam, dē quā, ut arbitror, istī ipsī, quī minantur, etiam atque etiam, quid liceat, cōnsīderābunt. Meā quidem sententiā, Quirītēs, ūnus A. Gabīnius bellī maritimī rērumque gestārum Cn. Pompēiō socius ascrībitur, propterea quod alter ūnī illud bellum suscipiendum vestrīs suffrāgiīs dētulit, alter dēlātum susceptumque cōnfēcit.

XX. Reliquum est, ut dē Q. Catulī auctōritāte et sententiā dīcendum esse videātur. Quī cum ex vōbīs quaereret, sī in ūnō Cn. Pompēiō omnia pōnerētis, sī quid eō factum esset, in quō spem essētis habitūrī, cēpit māgnum suae virtūtis frūctum ac dīgnitātis, cum omnēs ūnā prope vōce in eō ipsō vōs spem habitūrōs esse dīxistis. Etenim tālis est vir, ut nūlla rēs tanta sit ac tam difficilis, quam ille nōn et cōnsiliō regere et integritāte tuērī et virtūte cōnficere possit. Sed in hōc ipsō ab eō vehementissimē dissentiō, quod, quō minus certa est hominum ac minus diūturna vīta, hōc magis rēs pūblica, dum per deōs immortālēs licet, fruī dēbet summī virī vītā atque virtūte.

At enim "nē quid novī fīat contrā exempla atque īnstitūta māiōrum." Nōn dīcam hōc locō, māiōrēs nostrōs semper in pāce cōnsuētūdinī, in bellō ūtilitātī pāruisse, semper ad novōs cāsūs temporum novōrum cōnsiliōrum ratiōnēs accommodāsse; nōn dīcam, duo bella māxima, Pūnicum atque Hispāniēnse, ab ūnō imperātōre esse cōnfecta duāsque urbēs potentissimās, quae huic imperiō māximē minitābantur, Karthāginem atque Numantiam, ab eōdem Scīpiōne esse dēlētās; nōn commemorābō, nūper ita vōbīs patribusque vestrīs esse vīsum, ut in ūnō C. Mariō spēs imperī pōnerētur, ut īdem cum Iugurthā, īdem cum Cimbrīs, īdem cum Teutonīs bellum administrāret; in ipsō Cn. Pompēiō, in quō novī cōnstituī nihil vult Q. Catulus, quam multa sint nova summā Q. Catulī voluntāte cōnstitūta, recordāminī.

XXI. Quid tam novum quam adulēscentulum prīvātum exercitum difficilī reī pūblicae tempore cōnficere? Cōnfēcit. Huic praeesse? Praefuit. Rem optimē ductū suō gerere? Gessit.

Quid tam praeter cōnsuētūdinem quam hominī peradulēscentī, cūius aetās ā senātōriō gradū longē abesset, imperium atque exercitum darī, Siciliam permittī atque Āfricam bellumque in eā prōvinciā administrandum? Fuit in hīs prōvinciīs singulārī innocentiā, gravitāte, virtūte, bellum in Āfricā māximum cōnfēcit, victōrem exercitum dēportāvit.

Quid vērō tam inaudītum quam equitem Rōmānum triumphāre? At eam quoque rem populus Rōmānus nōn modo vīdit, sed omnium etiam studiō vīsendam et concelebrandam putāvit.

Quid tam inūsitātum, quam ut, cum duo cōnsulēs clārissimī fortissimīque essent, eques Rōmānus ad bellum māximum formīdolōsissimumque prō cōnsule mitterētur? Missus est. Quō quidem tempore cum esset nōn nēmō in senātū, quī dīceret nōn oportēre mittī hominem prīvātum prō cōnsule, L. Philippus dīxisse dīcitur nōn sē illum suā sententiā prō cōnsule, sed prō cōnsulibus mittere. Tanta in eō reī pūblicae bene gerendae spēs cōnstituēbātur, ut duōrum cōnsulum mūnus ūnīus adulēscentis virtūtī committerētur.

Quid tam singulāre, quam ut ex senātūs cōnsultō lēgibus solūtus cōnsul ante fieret, quam ūllum alium magistrātum per lēgēs capere licuisset? Quid tam incrēdibile, quam ut iterum eques Rōmānus ex senātūs cōnsultō triumphāret? Quae in omnibus hominibus nova post hominum memoriam cōnstitūta sunt, ea tam multa nōn sunt quam haec, quae in hōc ūnō homine vidēmus. Atque haec tot exempla, tanta ac tam nova, profecta sunt in eundem hominem ā Q. Catulī atque ā cēterōrum ēiusdem dīgnitātis amplissimōrum hominum auctōritāte.

XXII. Quā rē videant, nē sit perinīquum et nōn ferendum, illōrum auctōritātem dē Cn. Pompēī dīgnitāte ā vōbīs comprobātam semper esse, vestrum ab illīs dē eōdem homine iūdicium populīque Rōmānī auctōritātem improbārī, praesertim cum iam suō iūre populus Rōmānus in hōc homine suam auctōritātem vel contrā omnēs, quī dissentiunt, possit dēfendere, propterea quod īsdem istīs reclāmantibus vōs ūnum illum ex omnibus dēlēgistis, quem bellō praedōnum praepōnerētis. Hōc sī vōs temere fēcistis et reī pūblicae parum cōnsuluistis, rēctē istī studia vestra suīs cōnsiliīs regere cōnantur; sīn autem vōs plūs tum in rē pūblicā vīdistis, vōs eīs repūgnantibus per vōsmet ipsōs dīgnitātem huic imperiō, salūtem orbī terrārum attulistis, aliquandō istī prīncipēs et sibi et cēterīs populī Rōmānī ūniversī auctōritātī pārendum esse fateantur.

Atque in hōc bellō Asiāticō et rēgiō nōn sōlum mīlitāris illa virtūs, quae est in Cn. Pompēiō singulāris, sed aliae quoque virtūtēs animī māgnae et multae requīruntur. Difficile est in Asiā, Ciliciā, Syriā, rēgnīsque interiōrum nātiōnum ita versārī nostrum imperātōrem, ut nihil aliud nisi dē hoste ac dē laude cōgitet. Deinde etiam sī quī sunt pudōre ac temperantiā moderātiōrēs, tamen eōs esse tālēs propter multitūdinem cupidōrum hominum nēmō arbitrātur. Difficile est dictū, Quirītēs, quantō in odiō sīmus apud exterās nātiōnēs propter eōrum, quōs ad eās per hōs annōs cum imperiō mīsimus, libīdinēs et iniūriās. Quod enim fānum putātis in illīs terrīs nostrīs magistrātibus religiōsum, quam cīvitātem sānctam, quam domum satis clausam ac mūnītam fuisse? Urbēs iam locuplētēs et cōpiōsae requīruntur, quibus causa bellī propter dīripiendī cupiditātem īnferātur.

Libenter haec cōram cum Q. Catulō et Q. Hortēnsiō, summīs et clārissimīs virīs, disputārem; nōvērunt enim sociōrum vulnera, vident eōrum calamitātēs, querimōniās audiunt. Prō sociīs vōs contrā hostēs exercitum mittere putātis, an hostium simulātiōne contrā sociōs atque amīcōs? Quae cīvitās est in Asiā, quae nōn modo imperātōris aut lēgātī, sed ūnīus tribūnī mīlitum animōs ac spīritūs capere possit?

XXIII. Quā rē, etiam sī quem habētis, quī collātīs sīgnīs exercitūs rēgiōs superāre posse videātur, tamen, nisi erit īdem, quī sē ā pecūniīs sociōrum, quī ab eōrum coniugibus ac līberīs, quī ab ōrnāmentīs fānōrum atque oppidōrum, quī ab aurō gazāque rēgiā manūs, oculōs, animum cohibēre possit, nōn erit idōneus, quī ad bellum Asiāticum rēgiumque mittātur. Ecquam putātis cīvitātem pācātam fuisse, quae locuplēs sit? ecquam esse locuplētem, quae istīs pācāta esse videātur?

Ōra maritima, Quirītēs, Cn. Pompēium nōn sōlum propter reī mīlitāris glōriam, sed etiam propter animī continentiam requīsīvit. Vidēbat enim imperātōrēs locuplētārī quotannīs pecūniā pūblicā praeter paucōs, neque eōs quicquam aliud adsequī classium nōmine, nisi ut dētrīmentīs accipiendīs māiōre adficī turpitūdine vidērēmur. Nunc quā cupiditāte hominēs in prōvinciās, quibus iactūrīs et quibus condiciōnibus proficīscantur, ignōrant vidēlicet istī, quī ad ūnum dēferenda omnia esse nōn arbitrantur: quasi vērō Cn. Pompēium nōn cum suīs virtūtibus, tum etiam aliēnīs vitiīs māgnum esse videāmus. Quā rē nōlīte dubitāre, quīn huic ūnī crēdātis omnia, quī inter tot annōs ūnus inventus sit, quem sociī in urbēs suās cum exercitū vēnisse gaudeant.

Quod sī auctōritātibus hanc causam, Quirītēs, cōnfīrmandam putātis, est vōbīs auctor vir bellōrum omnium māximārumque rērum perītissimus, P. Servīlius, cūius tantae rēs gestae terrā marīque exstitērunt, ut, cum dē bellō dēlīberētis, auctor vōbīs gravior esse nēmō dēbeat; est C. Cūriō, summīs vestrīs beneficiīs māximīsque rēbus gestīs, summō ingeniō et prūdentiā praeditus; est Cn. Lentulus, in quō omnēs prō amplissimīs vestrīs honōribus summum cōnsilium, summam gravitātem esse cognōvistis; est C. Cassius, integritāte, virtūte, cōnstantiā singulārī. Quā rē vidēte, ut hōrum auctōritātibus illōrum ōrātiōnī, quī dissentiunt, respondēre posse videāmur.

XXIV. Quae cum ita sint, C. Mānīlī, prīmum istam tuam et lēgem et voluntātem et sententiam laudō vehementissimēque comprobō; deinde tē hortor, ut auctōre populō Rōmānō maneās in sententiā nēve cūiusquam vim aut minās pertimēscās. Prīmum in tē satis esse animī persevērantiaeque arbitror; deinde, cum tantam multitūdinem cum tantō studiō adesse videāmus, quantam iterum nunc in eōdem homine praeficiendō vidēmus, quid est, quod aut dē rē aut dē perficiendī facultāte dubitēmus?

Ego autem, quicquid est in mē studī, cōnsilī, labōris, ingenī, quicquid hōc beneficiō populī Rōmānī atque hāc potestāte praetōriā, quicquid auctōritāte, fidē, cōnstantiā possum, id omne ad hanc rem cōnficiendam tibi et populō Rōmānō polliceor ac dēferō; testorque omnēs deōs, et eōs māximē, quī huic locō templōque praesident, quī omnium mentēs eōrum, quī ad rem pūblicam adeunt, māximē perspiciunt, mē hōc neque rogātū facere cūiusquam, neque quō Cn. Pompēī gratiam mihi per hanc causam conciliārī putem, neque quō mihi ex cūiusquam amplitūdine aut praesidia perīculīs aut adiūmenta honōribus quaeram, proptereā quod perīcula facile, ut hominem praestāre oportet, innocentiā tēctī repellēmus, honōrem autem neque ab ūnō neque ex hōc locō, sed eādem illā nostrā labōriōsissimā ratiōne vītae, sī vestra voluntās feret, cōnsequēmur.

Quam ob rem, quicquid in hāc causā mihi susceptum est, Quirītēs, id ego omne mē reī pūblicae causā suscēpisse cōnfīrmō, tantumque abest, ut aliquam mihi bonam grātiam quaesisse videar, ut multās mē etiam simultātēs partim obscūrās, partim apertās intellegam, mihi nōn necessāriās, vōbīs nōn inūtilēs suscēpisse. Sed ego mē hōc honōre praeditum, tantīs vestrīs beneficiīs affectum statuī, Quirītēs, vestram voluntātem et reī pūblicae dīgnitātem et salūtem prōvinciārum atque sociōrum meīs omnibus commodīs et ratiōnibus praeferre oportēre.

M. TULLI CICERONIS

PRO A. LICINIO ARCHIA POËTA ORATIO.

I. Sī quid est in mē ingenī, iūdicēs, quod sentiō quam sit exiguum, aut sī qua exercitātiō dīcendī, in quā mē nōn īnfitior mediocriter esse versātum, aut sī hūiusce reī ratiō aliqua ab optimārum artium studiīs ac disciplīnā profecta, ā quā ego nūllum cōnfiteor aetātis meae tempus abhorruisse, eārum rērum omnium vel in prīmīs hīc A. Licinius frūctum ā mē repetere prope suō iūre dēbet. Nam, quoad longissimē potest mēns mea respicere spatium praeteritī temporis et pueritiae memoriam recordārī ultimam, inde ūsque repetēns hunc videō mihi prīncipem et ad suscipiendam et ad ingrediendam rationem hōrum studiōrum exstitisse.

Quod sī haec vōx hūius hortātū praeceptīsque cōnfōrmāta nōn nūllīs aliquandō salūtī fuit, ā quō id accēpimus, quō cēterīs opitulārī et aliōs servāre possumus, huic profectō ipsī, quantum est situm in nōbīs, et opem et salūtem ferre dēbēmus. Ac nē quis ā nōbīs hōc ita dīcī forte mīrētur, quod alia quaedam in hōc facultās sit ingenī neque haec dīcendī ratiō aut disciplīna, nē nōs quidem huic ūnī studiō penitus umquam dēditī fuimus. Etenim omnēs artēs, quae ad hūmānitātem pertinent, habent quoddam commūne vinculum et quasi cognātiōne quādam inter sē continentur.

II. Sed nē cui vestrum mīrum esse videātur, mē in quaestiōne lēgitimā et in iūdiciō pūblicō, cum rēs agātur apud praetōrem populī Rōmānī, rēctissimum virum, et apud sevērissimōs iūdicēs, tantō conventū hominum ac frequentiā, hōc ūtī genere dīcendī, quod nōn modo ā cōnsuētūdine iūdiciōrum, vērum etiam ā forēnsī sermōne abhorreat, quaesō ā vōbīs, ut in hāc causā mihi dētis hanc veniam, accommodātam huic reō, vōbīs, quem ad modum spērō, nōn molestam, ut mē prō summō poētā atque ērudītissimō homine dīcentem, hōc concursū hominum litterātissimōrum, hāc vestrā hūmānitāte, hōc dēnique praetōre exercente iūdicium, patiāminī dē studiīs hūmānitātis ac litterārum paulō loquī līberius et in ēius modī persōnā, quae propter ōtium ac studium minimē in iūdiciīs perīculīsque trāctāta est, ūtī prope novō quōdam et inūsitātō genere dīcendī. Quod sī mihi ā vōbīs tribuī concēdīque sentiam, perficiam profectō, ut hunc A. Licinium nōn modo nōn sēgregandum, cum sit cīvis, ā numerō cīvium, vērum etiam, sī nōn esset, putētis ascīscendum fuisse.

III. Nam, ut prīmum ex puerīs excessit Archiās atque ab eīs artibus, quibus aetās puerīlis ad hūmānitātem īnfōrmārī solet, sē ad scrībendī studium contulit, prīmum Antiochīae — nam ibi nātus est locō nōbilī — celebrī quondam urbe et cōpiōsā atque ērudītissimīs hominibus līberālissimīsque studiīs adfluentī, celeriter antecellere omnibus ingenī glōriā contigit. Post in cēterīs Asiae partibus cūnctāque Graeciā sīc ēius adventūs celebrābantur, ut fāmam ingenī exspectātiō hominis, exspectātiōnem ipsīus adventus admīrātiōque superāret.

Erat Italia tum plēna Graecārum artium ac disciplīnārum, studiaque haec et in Latiō vehementius tum colēbantur quam nunc eīsdem in oppidīs, et hīc Rōmae propter tranquillitātem reī pūblicae nōn neglegēbantur. Itaque hunc et Tarentīnī et Rēgīnī et Neāpolitānī cīvitāte cēterīsque praemiīs dōnārunt, et omnēs, quī aliquid dē ingeniīs poterant iūdicāre, cognitiōne atque hospitiō dīgnum exīstimārunt. Hāc tantā celebritāte fāmae cum esset iam absentibus nōtus, Rōmam vēnit Mariō cōnsule et Catulō. Nactus est prīmum cōnsulēs eōs, quōrum alter rēs ad scrībendum māximās, alter cum rēs gestās tum etiam studium atque aurēs adhibēre posset.

Statim Lūcullī, cum praetextātus etiam tum Archiās esset, eum domum suam recēpērunt. Et erat hōc nōn sōlum ingenī ac litterārum, vērum etiam nātūrae atque virtūtis, ut domus, quae hūius adulēscentiae prīma fāvit, eadem esset familiārissima senectūtī. Erat temporibus illīs iūcundus Q. Metellō illī Numidicō et ēius Piō fīliō, audiēbātur ā M. Aemiliō, vīvēbat cum Q. Catulō et patre et fīliō, ā L. Crassō colēbātur; Lūcullōs vērō et Drūsum et Octāviōs et Catōnem et tōtam Hortēnsiōrum domum dēvinctam cōnsuētūdine cum tenēret, adficiēbātur summō honōre, quod eum nōn sōlum colēbant, quī aliquid percipere atque audīre studēbant, vērum etiam sī quī forte simulābant.

IV. Interim satis longō intervāllō, cum esset cum M. Lūcullō in Siciliam profectus et cum ex eā prōvinciā cum eōdem Lūcullō dēcēderet, vēnit Hēraclīam. Quae cum esset cīvitās aequissimō iūre ac foedere, ascrībī sē in eam cīvitātem voluit, idque, cum ipse per sē dīgnus putārētur, tum auctōritāte et grātiā Lūcullī ab Hēracliēnsibus impetrāvit. Data est cīvitās Silvānī lēge et Carbōnis: Sī QUĪ FOEDERĀTĪS CĪVITĀTIBUS ASCRĪPTĪ FUISSENT, SĪ TUM, CUM LĒX FERĒBĀTUR, IN ITALIĀ DOMICILIUM HABUISSENT ET SĪ SEXĀGINTĀ DIĒBUS APUD PRAETŌREM ESSENT PROFESSĪ. Cum hīc domicilium Rōmae multōs iam annōs habēret, professus est apud praetōrem Q. Metellum, familiārissimum suum.

Sī nihil aliud nisi dē cīvitāte ac lēge dīcimus, nihil dīcō amplius; causa dicta est. Quid enim hōrum īnfīrmārī, Grātī, potest? Hēraclīaene esse eum ascrīptum negābis? Adest vir summā auctōritāte et religiōne et fidē, M. Lūcullus; quī sē nōn opīnārī, sed scīre, nōn audīvisse, sed vīdisse, nōn interfuisse, sed ēgisse dīcit. Adsunt Hēracliēnsēs lēgātī, nōbilissimī hominēs, hūius iūdicī causā cum mandātīs et cum pūblicō testimōniō, quī hunc ascrīptum Hēracliēnsem dīcunt.

Hīc tū tabulās dēsīderās Hēracliēnsium pūblicās, quās Italicō bellō incēnsō tabulāriō interīsse scīmus omnēs? Est rīdiculum ad ea, quae habēmus, nihil dīcere, quaerere, quae habēre nōn possumus, et dē hominum memoriā tacēre, litterārum memoriam flāgitāre; et, cum habeās amplissimī virī religiōnem, integerrimī mūnicipī iūs iūrandum fidemque, ea, quae dēprāvārī nūllō modō possunt, repudiāre; tabulās, quās īdem dīcis solēre corrumpī, dēsīderāre.

An domicilium Rōmae nōn habuit is, quī tot annīs ante cīvitātem datam sēdem omnium rērum ac fortūnārum suārum Rōmae collocāvit? An nōn est professus? Immō vērō eīs tabulīs professus, quae sōlae ex illā professiōne collēgiōque praetōrum obtinent pūblicārum tabulārum auctōritātem.

V. Nam, cum Appī tabulae neglegentius adservātae dīcerentur, Gabīnī, quam diū incolumis fuit, levitās, post damnātiōnem calamitās omnem tabulārum fidem resīgnāsset, Metellus, homō sānctissimus modestissimusque omnium, tantā dīligentiā fuit, ut ad L. Lentulum praetōrem et ad iūdicēs vēnerit et ūnīus nōminis litūrā sē commōtum esse dīxerit. Hīs igitur in tabulīs nūllam litūram in nōmine A. Licinī vidētis. Quae cum ita sint, quid est, quod dē ēius cīvitāte dubitētis, praesertim cum aliīs quoque in cīvitātibus fuerit ascrīptus? Etenim, cum mediocribus multīs et aut nūllā aut humilī aliquā arte praeditīs grātuītō cīvitātem in Graeciā hominēs impertiēbant, Rēgīnōs crēdō aut Locrēnsēs aut Neāpolitānōs aut Tarentīnōs, quod scaenicīs artificibus largīrī solēbant, id huic summā ingenī praeditō glōriā nōluisse!

Quid? cum cēterī nōn modo post cīvitātem datam, sed etiam post lēgem Pāpiam aliquō modō in eōrum mūnicipiōrum tabulās inrēpsērunt; hīc, quī nē ūtitur quidem illīs, in quibus est scrīptus, quod semper sē Hēraclīēnsem esse voluit, rēiciētur? Cēnsūs nostrōs requīris. Scīlicet; est enim obscūrum proximīs cēnsōribus hunc cum clārissimō imperātōre, L. Lūcullō, apud exercitum fuisse, superiōribus cum eōdem quaestōre fuisse in Asiā, prīmīs, Iūliō et Crassō, nūllam populī partem esse cēnsam. Sed, quoniam cēnsus nōn iūs cīvitātis cōnfīrmat ac tantum modo indicat eum, quī sit cēnsus, sē iam tum gessisse prō cīve, eīs temporibus is, quem tū crīmināris nē ipsīus quidem iūdiciō in cīvium Rōmānōrum iūre esse versātum, et testāmentum saepe fēcit nostrīs lēgibus et adiit hērēditātēs cīvium Rōmānōrum et in beneficiīs ad aerārium dēlātus est ā L. Lūcullō prō cōnsule. Quaere argumenta, sī quae potes;

numquam enim hīc neque suō neque amīcōrum iūdiciō revincētur.

VI. Quaerēs ā nōbīs, Grātī, cur tantō opere hōc homine dēlectēmur. Quia suppeditat nōbīs, ubi et animus ex hōc forēnsī strepitū reficiātur et aurēs conviciō dēfessae conquiēscant. An tū exīstimās aut suppetere nōbīs posse, quod cotīdiē dīcāmus in tantā varietāte rērum, nisi animōs nostrōs doctrīnā excolāmus, aut ferre animōs tantam posse contentiōnem, nisi eōs doctrīnā eādem relaxēmus? Ego vērō fateor mē hīs studiīs esse dēditum. Cēterōs pudeat, sī quī ita sē litterīs abdidērunt, ut nihil possint ex eīs neque ad commūnem adferre frūctum neque in aspectum lūcemque prōferre; mē autem quid pudeat, quī tot annōs ita vīvō, iūdicēs, ut ā nūllīus umquam mē tempore aut commodō aut ōtium meum abstrāxerit aut voluptās āvocārit aut dēnique somnus retardārit?

Quā rē quis tandem mē reprehendat, aut quis mihi iūre suscēnseat, sī quantum cēterīs ad suās rēs obeundās, quantum ad fēstōs diēs lūdōrum celebrandōs, quantum ad aliās voluptātēs et ad ipsam requiem animī et corporis concēditur temporum, quantum aliī tribuunt tempestīvīs convīviīs, quantum dēnique alveolō, quantum pilae, tantum mihi egomet ad haec studia recolenda sūmpserō? Atque hōc ideō mihi concēdendum est magis, quod ex hīs studiīs haec quoque crēscit ōrātiō et facultās, quae quantacumque in mē est, numquam amīcōrum perīculīs dēfuit. Quae sī cui levior vidētur, illa quidem certē, quae summa sunt, ex quō fonte hauriam, sentiō.

Nam, nisi multōrum praeceptīs multīsque litterīs mihi ab adulēscentiā suāsissem, nihil esse in vītā māgnō opere expetendum nisi laudem atque honestātem, in eā autem persequendā omnēs cruciātūs corporis, omnia perīcula mortis atque exsilī parvī esse dūcenda, numquam mē prō salūte vestrā in tot ac tantās dīmicātiōnēs atque in hōs prōflīgātōrum hominum cotīdiānōs impetūs obiēcissem. Sed plēnī omnēs sunt librī, plēnae sapientium vōcēs, plēna exemplōrum vetustās; quae iacērent in tenebrīs omnia, nisi litterārum lūmen accēderet. Quam multās nōbīs imāginēs nōn sōlum ad intuendum, vērum etiam ad imitandum fortissimōrum virōrum expressās scrīptōrēs et Graecī et Latīnī relīquērunt! Quās ego mihi semper in administrandā rē pūblicā prōpōnēns animum et mentem meam ipsā cōgitātiōne hominum excellentium cōnfōrmābam.

VII. Quaeret quispiam: "Quid? illī ipsī summī virī, quōrum virtūtēs litterīs prōditae sunt, istāne doctrīnā, quam tū effers laudibus, ērudītī fuērunt?"

Difficile est hōc dē omnibus cōnfīrmāre, sed tamen est certum, quid respondeam. Ego multōs hominēs excellentī animō ac virtūte fuisse sine doctrīnā, et nātūrae ipsīus habitū prope dīvīnō per sē ipsōs et moderātōs et gravēs exstitisse fateor; etiam illud adiungō, saepius ad laudem atque virtūtem nātūram sine doctrīnā quam sine nātūrā valuisse doctrīnam. Atque īdem ego contendō, cum ad nātūram eximiam et illūstrem accesserit ratiō quaedam cōnfōrmātiōque doctrīnae, tum illud nesciō quid praeclārum ac singulāre solēre exsistere. Ex hōc esse hunc numerō, quem patrēs nostrī vīdērunt, dīvīnum hominem, Āfricānum, ex hōc C. Laelium, L. Furium, moderātissimōs hominēs et continentissimōs, ex hōc fortissimum virum et illīs temporibus doctissimum, M. Catōnem, illum senem; quī profectō, sī nihil ad percipiendam colendamque virtūtem litterīs adiuvārentur, numquam sē ad eārum studium contulissent.

Quod sī nōn hīc tantus frūctus ostenderētur, et sī ex hīs studiīs dēlectātiō sōla peterētur, tamen, ut opīnor, hanc animī remissiōnem hūmānissimam ac līberālissimam iūdicārētis. Nam cēterae neque temporum sunt neque aetātum omnium neque locōrum; at haec studia adulēscentiam alunt, senectūtem oblectant, secundās rēs ōrnant, adversīs perfugium ac sōlācium praebent, dēlectant domī, nōn impediunt forīs, pernoctant nōbīscum, peregrīnantur, rūsticantur.

VIII. Quod sī ipsī haec neque attingere neque sēnsū nostrō gustāre possēmus, tamen ea mīrārī dēbērēmus, etiam cum in aliīs vidērēmus. Quis nostrum tam animō agrestī ac dūrō fuit, ut Rōscī morte nūper nōn commovērētur? quī cum esset senex mortuus, tamen propter excellentem artem ac venustātem vidēbātur omnīnō morī nōn dēbuisse. Ergo ille corporis mōtū tantum amōrem sibi conciliārat ā nōbīs omnibus; nōs animōrum incrēdibilēs mōtūs celeritātemque ingeniōrum neglegēmus?

Quotiēns ego hunc Archiam vīdī, iūdicēs, — ūtār enim vestrā benīgnitāte, quoniam mē in hōc novō genere dīcendī tam dīligenter attenditis, — quotiēns ego hunc vīdī, cum litteram scrīpsisset nūllam, māgnum numerum optimōrum versuum dē eīs ipsīs rēbus, quae tum agerentur, dīcere ex tempore! quotiēns revocātum eandem rem dīcere commūtātīs verbīs atque sententiīs! Quae vērō accūrātē cōgitātēque scrīpsisset, ea sīc vīdī probārī, ut ad veterum scrīptōrum laudem pervenīret. Hunc ego nōn dīligam, nōn admīrer, nōn omnī ratiōne dēfendendum putem? Atque sīc ā summīs hominibus ērudītissimīsque accēpimus, cēterārum rērum studia ex doctrīnā et praeceptīs et arte cōnstāre; poētam nātūrā ipsā valēre et mentis vīribus excitārī et quasi dīvīnō quōdam spīritū īnflārī. Quā rē suō iūre noster ille Ennius "sānctōs" appellat poētās, quod quasi deōrum aliquō dōnō atque mūnere commendātī nōbīs esse videantur.

Sit igitur, iūdicēs, sānctum apud vōs, hūmānissimōs hominēs, hōc poētae nōmen, quod nūlla umquam barbaria violāvit. Saxa et sōlitūdinēs vōcī respondent, bēstiae saepe immānēs cantū flectuntur atque cōnsistunt; nōs īnstitūtī rēbus optimīs nōn poētārum vōce moveāmur? Homērum Colophōniī cīvem esse dīcunt suum, Chiī suum vindicant, Salamīniī repetunt, Smyrnaeī vērō suum esse cōnfīrmant, itaque etiam dēlūbrum ēius in oppidō dēdicāvērunt; permultī aliī praetereā pūgnant inter sē atque contendunt.

IX. Ergo illī aliēnum, quia poēta fuit, post mortem etiam expetunt; nōs hunc vīvum, quī et voluntāte et lēgibus noster est, repudiābimus, praesertim cum omne olim studium atque omne ingenium contulerit Archiās ad populī Rōmānī glōriam laudemque celebrandam? Nam et Cimbricās rēs adulēscēns attigit et ipsī illī C. Mariō, quī dūrior ad haec studia vidēbātur, iūcundus fuit. Neque enim quisquam est tam āversus ā Mūsīs, quī nōn mandārī versibus aeternum suōrum labōrum facile praecōnium patiātur. Themistoclem illum, summum Athēnīs virum, dīxisse āiunt, cum ex eō quaererētur, quod acroāma aut cūius vōcem libentissimē audīret: Ēius, ā quō sua virtūs optimē praedicārētur. Itaque ille Marius item eximiē L. Plōtium dīlēxit, cūius ingeniō putābat ea, quae gesserat, posse celebrārī.

Mithridāticum vērō bellum, māgnum atque difficile et in multā varietāte terrā marīque versātum, tōtum ab hōc expressum est; quī librī nōn modo L. Lūcullum, fortissimum et clārissimum virum, vērum etiam populī Rōmānī nōmen illūstrant. Populus enim Rōmānus aperuit Lūcullō imperante Pontum, et rēgiīs quondam opibus et ipsā nātūrā et regiōne vāllātum; populī Rōmānī exercitus eōdem duce nōn māximā manū innumerābilēs Armeniōrum cōpiās fūdit; populī Rōmānī laus est, urbem amīcissimam Cȳzicēnōrum ēiusdem cōnsiliō ex omnī impetū rēgiō atque ē tōtīus bellī ōre ac faucibus ēreptam esse atque servātam; nostra semper ferētur et praedicābitur L. Lūcullō dīmicante, cum interfectīs ducibus dēpressa hostium classis est, incrēdibilis apud Tenedum pūgna illa nāvālis, nostra sunt tropaea, nostra monumenta, nostrī triumphī. Quae quōrum ingeniīs efferuntur, ab eīs populī Rōmānī fāma celebrātur.

Cārus fuit Āfricānō superiōrī noster Ennius, itaque etiam in sepulcrō Scīpiōnum putātur is esse cōnstitūtus ex marmore; at eīs laudibus certē nōn sōlum ipse, quī laudātur, sed etiam populī Rōmānī nōmen ōrnātur. In caelum hūius proavus Catō tollitur; māgnus honōs populī Rōmānī rēbus adiungitur. Omnēs dēnique illī Māximī, Mārcellī, Fulviī nōn sine commūnī omnium nostrum laude decorantur.

X. Ergō illum, quī haec fēcerat, Rudīnum hominem, māiōrēs nostrī in cīvitātem recēpērunt; nōs hunc Hēraclīēnsem, multīs cīvitātibus expetītum, in hāc autem lēgibus cōnstitūtum, dē nostrā cīvitāte ēiciēmus?

Nam, sī quis minōrem glōriae frūctum putat ex Graecīs versibus percipī quam ex Latīnīs, vehementer errat, propterea quod Graeca leguntur in omnibus ferē gentibus, Latīna suīs fīnibus, exiguīs sānē, continentur. Quā rē, sī rēs eae, quās gessimus, orbis terrae regiōnibus dēfīniuntur, cupere dēbēmus, quō manuum nostrārum tēla pervēnerint, eōdem glōriam fāmamque penetrāre, quod cum ipsīs populīs, dē quōrum rēbus scrībitur, haec ampla sunt, tum eīs certē, quī dē vītā glōriae causā dīmicant, hōc māximum et perīculōrum incitāmentum est et labōrum.

Quam multōs scrīptōrēs rērum suārum māgnus ille Alexander sēcum habuisse dīcitur! Atque is tamen, cum in Sīgēō ad Achillis tumulum astitisset, "Ō fortūnāte," inquit, "adulēscēns, quī tuae virtūtis Homērum praecōnem invēneris!" Et vērē. Nam, nisi Īlias illa exstitisset, īdem tumulus, quī corpus ēius contēxerat, nōmen etiam obruisset.

Quid? noster hīc Māgnus, quī cum virtūte fortūnam adaequāvit, nōnne Theophanem Mytilēnaeum, scrīptōrem rērum suārum, in cōntiōne mīlitum cīvitāte dōnāvit, et nostrī illī fortēs virī, sed rūsticī ac mīlitēs, dulcēdine quādam glōriae commōtī, quasi participēs ēiusdem laudis, māgnō illud clāmōre approbāvērunt? Itaque, crēdō, sī cīvis Rōmānus Archiās lēgibus nōn esset, ut ab aliquō imperātōre cīvitāte dōnārētur, perficere nōn potuit. Sulla cum Hispānōs et Gallōs dōnāret, crēdō, hunc petentem repudiāsset; quem nōs in cōntiōne vīdimus, cum eī libellum malus poēta dē populō subiēcisset, quod epigramma in eum fēcisset, tantum modo alternīs versibus longiusculīs, statim ex eīs rēbus, quās tum vēndēbat, iubēre eī praemium tribuī, sed eā condiciōne, nē quid posteā scrīberet. Quī sēdulitātem malī poētae dūxerit aliquō tamen praemiō dīgnam, hūius ingenium et virtūtem in scrībendō et cōpiam nōn expetisset? Quid? ā Q. Metellō Piō, familiārissimō suō, quī cīvitāte multōs dōnāvit, neque per sē neque per Lūcullōs impetrāvisset? quī praesertim ūsque eō dē suīs rēbus scrībī cuperet, ut etiam Cordubae nātīs poētīs, pingue quiddam sonantibus atque peregrīnum, tamen aurēs suās dederet.

XI. Neque enim est hōc dissimulandum, quod obscūrārī nōn potest, sed prae nōbīs ferendum: trahimur omnēs studiō laudis, et optimus quisque māximē glōriā dūcitur. Ipsī illī philosophī etiam in eīs libellīs, quōs dē contemnendā glōriā scrībunt, nōmen suum īnscrībunt; in eō ipsō, in quō praedicātiōnem nōbilitātemque dēspiciunt, praedicārī dē sē ac nōminārī volunt. Decimus quidem Brūtus, summus vir et imperātor, Accī, amīcissimī suī, carminibus templōrum ac monumentōrum aditūs exōrnāvit suōrum. Iam vērō ille, quī cum Aetōlīs Enniō comite bellāvit, Fulvius, nōn dubitāvit Mārtis manubiās Mūsīs cōnsecrāre. Quā rē, in quā urbe imperātōrēs prope armātī poētārum nōmen et Mūsārum dēlūbra coluērunt, in eā nōn dēbent togātī iūdicēs ā Mūsārum honōre et ā poētārum salūte abhorrēre.

Atque ut id libentius faciātis, iam mē vōbīs, iūdicēs, indicābō et dē meō quōdam amōre glōriae nimis ācrī fortasse, vērum tamen honestō, vōbīs cōnfitēbor. Nam, quās rēs nōs in cōnsulātū nostrō vōbīscum simul prō salūte hūius imperī et prō vītā cīvium prōque ūniversā rē pūblicā gessimus, attigit hīc versibus atque incohāvit. Quibus audītīs, quod mihi māgna rēs et iūcunda vīsa est, hunc ad perficiendum adhortātus sum.

Nūllam enim virtūs aliam mercēdem labōrum perīculōrumque dēsīderat praeter hanc laudis et glōriae;

quā quidem dētrāctā, iūdicēs, quid est, quod in hōc tam exiguō vītae curriculō tantīs nōs in labōribus exerceāmus?

Certē, sī nihil animus praesentīret in posterum, et sī, quibus regiōnibus vītae spatium circumscrīptum est, eīsdem omnēs cōgitātiōnēs termināret suās, nec tantīs sē labōribus frangeret neque tot cūrīs vigiliīsque angerētur nec totiēns dē ipsā vītā dīmicāret. Nunc īnsidet quaedam in optimō quōque virtūs, quae noctēs ac diēs animum glōriae stimulīs concitat atque admonet, nōn cum vītae tempore esse dīmittendam commemorātiōnem nōminis nostrī, sed cum omnī posteritāte adaequandam.

XII. An vērō tam parvī animī videāmur esse omnēs, quī in rē pūblicā atque in hīs vītae perīculīs labōribusque versāmur, ut, cum ūsque ad extrēmum spatium nūllum tranquillum atque ōtiōsum spīritum dūxerimus, nōbīscum simul moritūra omnia arbitrēmur? An statuās et imāginēs, nōn animōrum simulācra, sed corporum, studiōsē multī summī hominēs relīquērunt; cōnsiliōrum relinquere ac virtūtum nostrārum effigiem nōnne multō mālle dēbēmus, summīs ingeniīs expressam et polītam? Ego vērō omnia, quae gerēbam, iam tum in gerendō spargere mē ac dissēmināre arbitrābar in orbis terrae memoriam sempiternam. Haec vērō sīve ā meō sēnsū post mortem āfutūra est, sīve, ut sapientissimī hominēs putāvērunt, ad aliquam animī meī partem pertinēbit, nunc quidem certē cōgitātiōne quādam spēque dēlector.

Quā rē cōnservāte, iūdicēs, hominem pudōre eō, quem amīcōrum vidētis comprobārī cum dīgnitāte tum etiam vetustāte, ingeniō autem tantō, quantum id convenit exīstimārī, quod summōrum hominum ingeniīs expetītum esse videātis, causā vērō ēius modī, quae beneficiō lēgis, auctōritāte mūnicipī, testimōniō Lūcullī, tabulīs Metellī comprobētur. Quae cum ita sint, petimus ā vōbīs, iūdicēs, sī qua nōn modo hūmāna, verum etiam dīvīna in tantīs ingeniīs commendātiō dēbet esse, ut eum, quī vōs, quī vestrōs imperātōrēs, quī populī Rōmānī rēs gestās semper ōrnāvit, quī etiam hīs recentibus nostrīs vestrīsque domesticīs perīculīs aeternum sē testimōnium laudis datūrum esse profitētur, estque ex eō numerō, quī semper apud omnēs sānctī sunt habitī itaque dictī, sīc in vestram accipiātis fidem, ut hūmānitāte vestrā levātus potius quam acerbitāte violātus esse videātur.

Quae dē causā prō meā cōnsuētūdine breviter simpliciterque dīxī, iūdicēs, ea cōnfīdō probāta esse omnibus; quae autem remōta ā meā iūdiciālīque cōnsuētūdine et dē hominis ingeniō et commūniter dē ipsīus studiō locūtus sum, ea, iūdicēs, ā vōbīs spērō esse in bonam partem accepta; ab eō, quī iūdicium exercet, certō sciō.

M. TULLI CICERONIS

PRO M. MARCELLO ORATIO.

I. Diūturnī silentī, patrēs cōnscrīptī, quō eram hīs temporibus ūsus, nōn timōre aliquō, sed partim dolōre, partim verēcundiā, fīnem hodiernus diēs attulit, īdemque initium, quae vellem quaeque sentīrem, meō prīstinō mōre dīcendī. Tantam enim mānsuētūdinem, tam inūsitātam inaudītamque clēmentiam, tantum in summā potestāte rērum omnium modum, tam dēnique incrēdibilem sapientiam ac paene dīvīnam tacitus praeterīre nūllō modō possum. M. enim Mārcellō vōbīs, patrēs cōnscrīptī, reīque pūblicae redditō, nōn illīus sōlum, sed etiam meam vōcem et auctōritātem et vōbīs et reī pūblicae cōnservātam ac restitūtam putō. Dolēbam enim, patrēs cōnscrīptī, et vehementer angēbar virum tālem, cum in eādem causā, in quā ego, fuisset, nōn in eādem esse fortūnā, nec mihi persuādēre poteram nec fās esse dūcēbam versārī mē in nostrō vetere curriculō illō aemulō atque imitātōre studiōrum ac labōrum meōrum quasi quōdam sociō ā mē et comite distrāctō.

Ergō et mihi meae prīstinae vītae cōnsuētūdinem, C. Caesar, interclūsam aperuistī et hīs omnibus ad bene dē omnī rē pūblicā spērandum quasi sīgnum aliquod sustulistī. Intellēctum est enim mihi quidem in multīs et māximē in mē ipsō, sed paulō ante in omnibus, cum M. Mārcellum senātuī reīque pūblicae concessistī, commemorātīs praesertim offēnsiōnibus, tē auctōritātem hūius ōrdinis dīgnitātemque reī pūblicae tuīs vel dolōribus vel suspīciōnibus anteferre. Ille quidem frūctum omnis ante āctae vītae hodiernō diē māximum cēpit, cum summō cōnsēnsū senātūs, tum iūdiciō tuō gravissimō et māximō. Ex quō profectō intellegis, quanta in datō beneficiō sit laus, cum in acceptō sit tanta glōria. Est vērō fortūnātus ille cūius ex salūte nōn minor paene ad omnēs, quam ad ipsum ventūra sit, laetitia pervēnerit; quod quidem eī meritō atque optimō iūre contigit. Quis enim est illō aut nōbilitāte aut probitāte aut optimārum artium studiō aut innocentiā aut ūllō laudis genere praestantior?

II. Nūllīus tantum flūmen est ingenī, nūllīus dīcendī aut scrībendī tanta vīs, tanta cōpia, quae nōn dīcam exōrnāre, sed ēnarrāre, C. Caesar, rēs tuās gestās possit. Tamen adfīrmō, et hōc pāce dīcam tuā, nūllam in hīs esse laudem ampliōrem quam eam, quam hodiernō diē cōnsecūtus es. Soleō saepe ante oculōs pōnere idque libenter crēbrīs ūsūrpāre sermōnibus, omnēs nostrōrum imperātōrum, omnēs exterārum gentium potentissimōrumque populōrum, omnēs clārissimōrum rēgum rēs gestās cum tuīs nec contentiōnum māgnitūdine nec numerō proeliōrum nec varietāte regiōnum nec celeritāte cōnficiendī nec dissimilitūdine bellōrum posse cōnferrī, nec vērō disiūnctissimās terrās citius passibus cūiusquam potuisse peragrārī, quam tuīs nōn dīcam cursibus, sed victōriīs lūstrātae sunt.

Quae quidem ego nisi ita māgna esse fatear, ut ea vix cūiusquam mēns aut cōgitātiō capere possit, āmēns sim; sed tamen sunt alia māiōra. Nam bellicās laudēs solent quīdam extenuāre verbīs eāsque dētrahere ducibus, commūnicāre cum multīs, nē propriae sint

Truly a wonderful man was Caius Julius Caesar!
Better be first, he said, in a little Iberian village,
Than be second in Rome;—and I think he was right when
he said it.

LONGFELLOW: The Courtship of Miles Standish.

imperātōrum. Et certē in armīs mīlitum virtūs, locōrum opportūnitās, auxilia sociōrum, classēs, commeātūs multum iuvant, māximam vērō partem quasi suō iūre Fortūna sibi vindicat et, quicquid prōsperē gestum est, id paene omne dūcit suum. At vērō hūius glōriae, C. Caesar, quam es paulō ante adeptus, socium habēs nēminem; tōtum hōc, quantumcumque est, quod certē māximum est, tōtum est, inquam, tuum. Nihil sibi ex istā laude centuriō, nihil praefectus, nihil cohors, nihil turma dēcerpit; quīn etiam illa ipsa rērum hūmānārum domina, Fortūna, in istīus societātem glōriae sē nōn offert; tibi cēdit, tuam esse tōtam et propriam fatētur. Numquam enim temeritās cum sapientiā commiscētur, neque ad cōnsilium cāsus admittitur.

III. Domuistī gentēs immānitāte barbarās, multitūdine innumerābilēs, locīs īnfīnītās, omnī cōpiārum genere abundantēs; sed tamen ea vīcistī, quae et nātūram et condiciōnem, ut vincī possent, habēbant. Nūlla est enim tanta vīs, quae nōn ferrō et vīribus dēbilitārī frangīque possit. Animum vincere, īrācundiam cohibēre, victōriam temperāre, adversārium nōbilitāte, ingeniō, virtūte praestantem nōn modo extollere iacentem, sed etiam amplificāre ēius prīstinam dīgnitātem, haec quī facit, nōn ego eum cum summīs virīs comparō, sed simillimum deō iūdicō.

Itaque, C. Caesar, bellicae tuae laudēs celebrābuntur illae quidem nōn sōlum nostrīs, sed paene omnium gentium litterīs atque linguīs, nec ūlla umquam aetās dē tuīs laudibus conticēscet; sed tamen ēius modī rēs nesciō quō modō, etiam cum leguntur, obstrepī clāmōre mīlitum videntur et tubārum sonō. At vērō cum aliquid clēmenter, mānsuētē, iūstē, moderātē, sapienter factum, in īrācundiā praesertim, quae est inimīca cōnsiliō, et in victōriā, quae nātūrā īnsolēns et superba est, audīmus aut legimus, quō studiō incendimur, nōn modo in gestīs rēbus, sed etiam in fīctīs, ut eōs saepe, quōs numquam vīdimus, dīligāmus! Tē vērō, quem praesentem intuēmur, cūius mentem sēnsūsque et ōs cernimus, ut, quicquid bellī fortūna reliquum reī pūblicae fēcerit, id esse salvum velīs, quibus laudibus efferēmus? quibus studiīs prōsequēmur? quā benevolentiā complectēmur? Parietēs mē dīus Fidius, ut mihi vidētur, hūius cūriae tibi grātiās agere gestiunt, quod brevī tempore futūra sit illa auctōritās in hīs māiōrum suōrum et suīs sēdibus.

IV. Equidem cum C. Mārcellī, virī optimī et commemorābilī pietāte praeditī, lacrimās modo vōbīscum vidērem, omnium Mārcellōrum meum pectus memoria offūdit, quibus tū etiam mortuīs M. Mārcellō cōnservātō dīgnitātem suam reddidistī nōbilissimamque familiam iam ad paucōs redāctam paene ab interitū vindicāstī. Hunc tū igitur diem tuīs māximīs et innumerābilibus grātulātiōnibus iūre antepōnēs.

Haec enim rēs ūnīus est propria C. Caesaris; cēterae duce tē gestae māgnae illae quidem, sed tamen multō māgnōque comitātū. Hūius autem reī tū īdem es et dux et comes; quae quidem tanta est, ut tropaeīs et monumentīs tuīs adlātūra fīnem sit aetās—nihil est enim opere et manū factum, quod nōn aliquandō cōnficiat et cōnsūmat vetustās—at haec tua iūstitia et lēnitās animī flōrēscit cotīdiē magis, ita ut, quantum tuīs operibus diūturnitās dētrahet, tantum adferat laudibus. Et cēterōs quidem omnēs victōrēs bellōrum cīvīlium iam ante aequitāte et misericordiā vīcerās: hodiernō vērō diē tē ipsum vīcistī. Vereor, ut hōc, quod dīcam, perinde intellegī possit audītum, atque ipse cōgitāns sentiō; ipsam victōriam vīcisse vidēris, cum ea, quae illa erat adepta, victīs remīsistī. Nam cum ipsīus victōriae condiciōne omnēs victī occidissēmus, clēmentiae tuae iūdiciō cōnservātī sumus. Rēctē igitur ūnus invictus es, ā quō etiam ipsīus victōriae condiciō vīsque dēvicta est.

V. Atque hōc C. Caesaris iūdicium, patrēs cōnscrīptī, quam lātē pateat, attendite. Omnēs enim, quī ad illa arma fātō sumus nesciō quō reī pūblicae miserō fūnestōque compulsī, etsī aliquā culpā tenēmur errōris hūmānī, scelere certē līberātī sumus. Nam, cum M. Mārcellum dēprecantibus vōbīs reī pūblicae cōnservāvit, mē et mihi et item reī pūblicae nūllō dēprecante, reliquōs amplissimōs virōs et sibi ipsōs et patriae reddidit, quōrum et frequentiam et dīgnitātem hōc ipsō in cōnsessū vidētis, nōn ille hostēs indūxit in cūriam, sed iūdicāvit ā plērīsque ignōrātiōne potius et falsō atque inānī metū quam cupiditāte aut crūdēlitāte bellum esse susceptum.

Quō quidem in bellō semper dē pāce audiendum putāvī semperque doluī nōn modo pācem, sed etiam ōrātiōnem cīvium pācem flāgitantium repudiārī. Neque enim ego illa nec ūlla umquam secūtus sum arma cīvīlia, semperque mea cōnsilia pācis et togae socia, nōn bellī atque armōrum fuērunt. Hominem sum secūtus prīvātō cōnsiliō, nōn pūblicō, tantumque apud mē grātī animī fidēlis memoria valuit, ut nūllā nōn modo cupiditāte, sed nē spē quidem prūdēns et sciēns tamquam ad interitum ruerem voluntārium. Quod quidem meum cōnsilium minimē obscūrum fuit. Nam et in hōc ōrdine integrā rē multa dē pāce dīxī et in ipsō bellō eadem etiam cum capitis meī perīculō sēnsī. Ex quō nēmō iam erit tam iniūstus exīstimātor rērum, quī dubitet, quae Caesaris dē bellō voluntās fuerit, cum pācis auctōrēs cōnservandōs statim cēnsuērit, cēterīs fuerit īrātior. Atque id minus mīrum fortasse tum, cum esset incertus exitus et anceps fortūna bellī; quī vērō victor pācis auctōrēs dīligit, is profectō dēclārat sē māluisse nōn dīmicāre quam vincere.

VI. Atque hūius quidem reī M. Mārcellō sum testis. Nostrī enim sēnsūs ut in pāce semper, sīc tum etiam in bellō congruēbant. Quotiēns ego eum et quantō cum dolōre vīdī, cum īnsolentiam certōrum hominum, tum etiam ipsīus victōriae ferōcitātem extimēscentem! Quō grātior tua līberālitās, C. Caesar, nōbīs, quī illa vīdimus, dēbet esse. Nōn enim iam causae sunt inter sē, sed victōriae comparandae. Vīdimus tuam victōriam proeliōrum exitū terminātam; gladium vāgīnā vacuum in urbe nōn vīdimus. Quōs āmīsimus cīvēs, eōs Mārtis vīs perculit, nōn īra victōriae, ut dubitāre dēbeat nēmō, quīn multōs, sī fierī posset, C. Caesar ab īnferīs excitāret, quoniam ex eādem aciē cōnservat, quōs potest.

Alterius vērō partis nihil amplius dīcam quam, id quod omnēs verēbāmur, nimis īrācundam futūram fuisse victōriam. Quīdam enim nōn modo armātīs, sed interdum etiam ōtiōsīs minābantur nec, quid quisque sēnsisset, sed ubi fuisset, cōgitandum esse dīcēbant, ut mihi quidem videantur dī immortālēs, etiam sī poenās ā populō Rōmānō ob aliquod dēlīctum expetīvērunt, quī cīvīle bellum tantum et tam lūctuōsum excitāvērunt, vel plācātī iam vel satiātī aliquandō omnem spem salūtis ad clēmentiam victōris et sapientiam contulisse.

Quā rē gaudē tuō istō tam excellentī bonō, et fruere cum fortūnā et glōriā, tum etiam nātūrā et mōribus tuīs; ex quō quidem māximus est frūctus iūcunditāsque sapientī. Cētera cum tua recordābere, etsī persaepe virtūtī, tamen plērumque fēlīcitātī tuae grātulābere; dē nōbīs, quōs in rē pūblicā tēcum simul esse voluistī quotiēns cōgitābis, totiēns dē māximīs tuīs beneficiīs, totiēns dē incrēdibilī līberālitāte, totiēns dē singulārī sapientiā tuā cōgitābis; quae nōn modo summa bona, sed nīmīrum audēbō vel sōla dīcere. Tantus est enim splendor in laude vērā, tanta in māgnitūdine animī et cōnsilī dīgnitās, ut haec ā Virtūte dōnāta, cētera ā Fortūnā commodāta esse videantur. Nōlī igitur in cōnservandīs bonīs virīs dēfatīgārī, nōn cupiditāte praesertim aliquā aut prāvitāte lāpsīs, sed opīniōne officī stultā fortasse, certē nōn improbā, et speciē quādam reī pūblicae. Nōn enim tua ūlla culpa est, sī tē aliquī timuērunt, contrāque summa laus, quod minimē timendum fuisse sēnsērunt.

VII. Nunc veniō ad gravissimam querellam et atrōcissimam suspīciōnem tuam, quae nōn tibi ipsī magis quam cum omnibus cīvibus, tum māximē nōbīs, quī ā tē cōnservātī sumus, prōvidenda est; quam etsī spērō falsam esse, tamen numquam extenuābō verbīs. Tua enim cautiō nostra cautiō est, ut, sī in alterutrō peccandum sit, mālim vidērī nimis timidus quam parum prūdēns. Sed quisnam est iste tam dēmēns? dē tuīsne — tametsī quī magis sunt tuī, quam quibus tū salūtem īnspērantibus reddidistī? — an ex hōc numerō, quī ūnā tēcum fuērunt? Nōn est crēdibilis tantus in ūllō furor, ut, quō duce omnia summa sit adeptus, hūius vītam nōn antepōnat suae. An, sī nihil tuī cōgitant sceleris, cavendum est, nē quid inimīcī? Quī? omnēs enim, quī fuērunt, aut suā pertināciā vītam āmīsērunt aut tuā misericordiā retinuērunt, ut aut nūllī supersint dē inimīcīs aut, quī fuērunt, sint amīcissimī.

Sed tamen cum in animīs hominum tantae latebrae sint et tantī recessūs, augeāmus sānē suspīciōnem tuam; simul enim augēbimus dīligentiam. Nam quis est omnium tam ignārus rērum, tam rudis in rē pūblicā, tam nihil umquam nec dē suā nec dē commūnī salūte cōgitāns, quī nōn intellegat tuā salūte continērī suam et ex ūnīus tuā vītā pendēre omnium? Equidem dē tē diēs noctēsque, ut dēbeō, cōgitāns cāsūs dumtaxat hūmānōs et incertōs ēventūs valētūdinis et nātūrae commūnis fragilitātem extimēscō, doleōque, cum rēs pūblica immortālis esse dēbeat, eam in ūnīus mortālis animā cōnsistere. Sī vērō ad hūmānōs cāsūs incertōsque mōtūs valētūdinis sceleris etiam accēdit īnsidiārumque cōnsēnsiō, quem deum, sī cupiat, posse opitulārī reī pūblicae crēdāmus?

VIII. Omnia sunt excitanda tibi, C. Caesar, ūnī, quae iacēre sentīs, bellī ipsīus impetū, quod necesse fuit, perculsa atque prōstrāta; cōnstituenda iūdicia, revocanda fidēs, comprimendae libīdinēs, prōpāganda subolēs, omnia, quae dīlāpsa iam diffluxērunt, sevērīs lēgibus vincienda sunt. Non fuit recūsandum in tantō cīvīlī bellō, tantō animōrum ārdōre et armōrum, quīn quassāta rēs pūblica, quīcumque bellī ēventus fuisset, multa perderet et ōrnāmenta dīgnitātis et praesidia stabilitātis suae, multaque uterque dux faceret armātus, quae īdem togātus fierī prohibuisset. Quae quidem tibi nunc omnia bellī vulnera sānanda sunt, quibus praeter tē mederī nēmō potest.

Itaque illam tuam praeclārissimam et sapientissimam vōcem invītus audīvī: "Satis diū vel nātūrae vīxī vel glōriae." Satis, sī ita vīs, fortasse nātūrae, addō etiam, sī placet, glōriae; at, quod māximum est, patriae certē parum. Quā rē omitte istam, quaesō, doctōrum hominum in contemnendā morte prūdentiam; nōlī nostrō perīculō esse sapiēns. Saepe enim vēnit ad aurēs meās, tē idem istud nimis crēbrō dīcere, tibi satis tē vīxisse. Crēdō; sed tum id audīrem, sī tibi sōlī vīverēs aut sī tibi etiam sōlī nātus essēs. Omnium salūtem cīvium cūnctamque rem pūblicam rēs tuae gestae complexae sunt; tantum abes ā perfectiōne māximōrum operum, ut fundāmenta nōndum, quae cōgitās, iēceris. Hīc tū modum vītae tuae nōn salūte reī pūblicae, sed aequitāte animī dēfīniēs? Quid, sī istud nē glōriae tuae quidem satis est? cūius tē esse avidissimum, quamvīs sīs sapiēns, nōn negābis.

"Parumne igitur," inquiēs, "māgna relinquēmus?" Immō vērō aliīs quamvīs multīs satis, tibi ūnī parum. Quicquid est enim, quamvīs amplum sit, id est parum tum, cum est aliquid amplius. Quod sī rērum tuārum immortālium, C. Caesar, hīc exitus futūrus fuit, ut dēvictīs adversāriīs rem pūblicam in eō statū relinquerēs, in quō nunc est, vidē, quaesō, nē tua dīvīna virtūs admīrātiōnis plūs sit habitūra quam glōriae, sī quidem glōria est illūstris ac pervagāta māgnōrum vel in suōs cīvēs vel in patriam vel in omne genus hominum fāma meritōrum.

IX. Haec igitur tibi reliqua pars est; hīc restat āctus, in hōc ēlabōrandum est, ut rem pūblicam cōnstituās, eāque tū in prīmīs summā tranquillitāte et ōtiō perfruāre; tum tē, sī volēs, cum et patriae, quod dēbēs, solveris et nātūram ipsam explēveris satietāte vīvendī, satis diū vīxisse dīcitō. Quid enim est omnīnō hōc ipsum diū, in quō est aliquid extrēmum? Quod cum vēnit, omnis voluptās praeterita prō nihilō est, quia posteā nūlla est futūra. Quamquam iste tuus animus numquam hīs angustiīs, quās nātūra nōbīs ad vīvendum dedit, contentus fuit, semper immortālitātis amōre flagrāvit.

Nec vērō haec tua vīta dūcenda est, quae corpore

et spīritū continētur; illa, inquam, illa vīta est tua, quae vigēbit memoriā saeculōrum omnium, quam posteritās alet, quam ipsa aeternitās semper tuēbitur. Huic tū īnserviās, huic tē ostentēs oportet, quae quidem, quae mīrētur, iam prīdem multa habet; nunc etiam, quae laudet, exspectat. Obstipēscent posterī certē imperia, prōvinciās, Rhēnum, Ōceanum, Nīlum, pūgnās innumerābilēs, incrēdibilēs victōriās, monumenta, mūnera, triumphōs audientēs et legentēs tuōs. Sed nisi haec urbs stabilīta tuīs cōnsiliīs et īnstitūtīs erit, vagābitur modo tuum nōmen longē atque lātē, sēdem stabilem et domicilium certum nōn habēbit.

Erit inter eōs etiam, quī nāscentur, sīcut inter nōs fuit, māgna dissēnsiō, cum aliī laudibus ad caelum rēs tuās gestās efferent, aliī fortasse aliquid requīrent, idque vel māximum, nisi bellī cīvīlis incendium salūte patriae restīnxeris, ut illud fātī fuisse videātur, hōc cōnsilī. Servī igitur eīs etiam iūdicibus, quī multīs post saeculīs dē tē iūdicābunt, et quidem haud sciō an incorruptius quam nōs; nam et sine amōre et sine cupiditāte et rūrsus sine odiō et sine invidiā iūdicābunt. Id autem etiam sī tum ad tē, ut quīdam falsō putant, nōn pertinēbit, nunc certē pertinet esse tē tālem, ut tuās laudēs obscūrātūra nūlla umquam sit oblīviō.

X. Dīversae voluntātēs cīvium fuērunt distrāctaeque sententiae. Nōn enim cōnsiliīs sōlum et studiīs, sed armīs etiam et castrīs dissidēbāmus; erat enim obscūritās quaedam, erat certāmen inter clārissimōs ducēs; multī dubitābant, quid optimum esset, multī, quid sibi expedīret, multī, quid decēret, nōn nūllī etiam, quid licēret. Perfūncta rēs pūblica est hōc miserō fātālīque bellō; vīcit is, quī nōn fortūnā īnflammāret odium suum, sed bonitāte lēnīret, neque omnēs, quibus īrātus esset, eōsdem etiam exsiliō aut morte dīgnōs iūdicāret. Arma ab aliīs posita, ab aliīs ērepta sunt. Ingrātus est iniūstusque cīvis; quī armōrum perīculō līberātus animum tamen retinet armātum, ut etiam ille melior sit, quī in aciē cecidit, quī in causā animam prōfūdit. Quae enim pertinācia quibusdam, eadem aliīs cōnstantia vidērī potest.

Sed iam omnis frācta dissēnsiō est armīs, exstīncta aequitāte victōris; restat, ut omnēs ūnum velint, quī modo habent aliquid nōn sōlum sapientiae, sed etiam sānitātis. Nisi tē, C. Caesar, salvō et in istā sententiā, quā cum anteā, tum hodiē vel māximē ūsus es, manente salvī esse nōn possumus. Quā rē omnēs tē, quī haec salva esse volumus, et hortāmur et obsecrāmus, ut vītae tuae et salūtī cōnsulās, omnēsque tibi, — ut prō aliīs etiam loquar, quod dē mē ipse sentiō, — quoniam subesse aliquid putās, quod cavendum sit, nōn modo excubiās et cūstōdiās, sed etiam laterum nostrōrum oppositūs et corporum pollicēmur.

XI. Sed ut, unde est orsa, in eōdem terminētur ōrātiō, māximās tibi omnēs grātiās agimus, C. Caesar, māiōrēs etiam habēmus. Nam omnēs idem sentiunt, quod ex omnium precibus et lacrimīs sentīre potuistī. Sed quia nōn est omnibus stantibus necesse dīcere, ā mē certē dīcī volunt, cui necesse est quōdam modō; et, quod fierī decet M. Mārcellō ā tē huic ōrdinī populōque Rōmānō et reī pūblicae redditō, fierī id intellegō. Nam laetārī omnēs nōn dē ūnīus sōlum, sed dē commūnī salūte sentiō.

Quod autem summae benevolentiae est, quae mea ergā illum omnibus semper nōta fuit, ut vix C. Mārcellō, optimō et amantissimō frātrī, praeter eum quidem cēderem nēminī, cum id sollicitūdine, cūrā, labōre tam diū praestiterim, quam diū est dē illīus salūte dubitātum, certē hōc tempore māgnīs cūrīs, molestiīs, dolōribus līberātus praestāre dēbeō. Itaque, C. Caesar, sīc tibi grātiās agō, ut omnibus mē rēbus ā tē nōn cōnservātō sōlum, sed etiam ōrnātō, tamen ad tua in mē ūnum innumerābilia merita, quod fierī iam posse nōn arbitrābar, māximus hōc tuō factō cumulus accesserit.

M. TULLI CICERONIS

IN M. ANTONIUM ORATIO PHILIPPICA QUARTA.

I. Frequentia vestrum incrēdibilis, Quirītēs, cōntiōque tanta, quantam meminisse nōn videor, et alacritātem mihi summam dēfendendae reī pūblicae adfert et spem recuperandae. Quamquam animus mihi quidem numquam dēfuit, tempora dēfuērunt, quae simul ac prīmum aliquid lūcis ostendere vīsa sunt, prīnceps vestrae lībertātis dēfendendae fuī. Quod sī id ante facere cōnātus essem, nunc facere nōn possem. Hodiernō enim diē, Quirītēs, nē mediocrem rem āctam arbitrēminī, fundāmenta iacta sunt reliquārum āctiōnum. Nam est hostis ā senātū nōndum verbō appellātus, sed rē iam iūdicātus Antōnius. Nunc vērō multō sum ērēctior, quod vōs quoque illum hostem esse tantō cōnsēnsū tantōque clāmōre approbāvistis. Neque enim, Quirītēs, fierī potest, ut nōn aut eī sint impiī, quī contrā cōnsulem exercitūs comparāvērunt, aut ille hostis, contrā quem iūre arma sūmpta sunt.

Hanc igitur dubitātiōnem, quamquam nūlla erat, tamen nē qua posset esse, senātus hodiernō diē sustulit. C. Caesar, quī rem pūblicam lībertātemque vestram suō studiō, cōnsiliō, patrimōniō dēnique tūtātus est et tūtātur, māximīs senātūs laudibus ōrnātus est. Laudō, laudō vōs, Quirītēs, quod grātissimīs animīs prōsequiminī nōmen clārissimī adulēscentis vel puerī potius — sunt enim facta ēius immortālitātis, nōmen aetātis. Multa meminī, multa audīvī, multa lēgī, Quirītēs; nihil ex omnium saeculōrum memoriā tāle cognōvī, — quī, cum servitūte premerēmur, in diēs malum crēsceret, praesidī nihil habērēmus, capitālem et pestiferum ā Brundisiō tum M. Antōnī reditum timērēmus, hōc īnspērātum omnibus cōnsilium, incognitum certē cēperit, ut exercitum invictum ex paternīs mīlitibus cōnficeret Antōnīque furōrem crūdēlissimīs cōnsiliīs incitātum ā perniciē reī pūblicae āverteret.

II. Quis est enim, quī hōc nōn intellegat, nisi Caesar exercitum parāvisset, nōn sine exitiō nostrō futūrum Antōnī reditum fuisse? Ita enim sē recipiēbat ārdēns odiō vestrī, cruentus sanguine cīvium Rōmānōrum, quōs Suessae, quōs Brundisī occīderat, ut nihil nisi dē perniciē populī Rōmānī cōgitāret. Quod autem praesidium erat salūtis lībertātisque vestrae, sī C. Caesaris fortissimōrum suī patris mīlitum exercitus nōn fuisset? Cūius dē laudibus et honōribus, quī eī prō dīvīnīs et immortālibus meritīs dīvīnī immortālēsque dēbentur, mihi senātus adsēnsus paulō ante dēcrēvit, ut prīmō quōque tempore referrētur.

Quō dēcrētō quis nōn perspicit hostem esse Antōnium iūdicātum? Quem enim possumus appellāre eum, contrā quem quī exercitūs dūcunt, eīs senātus arbitrātur singulārēs exquīrendōs honōrēs? Quid? legiō Mārtia, quae mihi vidētur dīvīnitus ab eō deō trāxisse nōmen, ā quō populum Rōmānum generātum accēpimus, nōn ipsa suīs dēcrētīs prius quam senātus hostem iūdicāvit Antōnium? Nam sī ille nōn hostis, hōs, quī cōnsulem relīquērunt, hostēs necesse est iūdicēmus. Praeclārē et locō, Quirītēs, reclāmātiōne vestrā factum pulcherrimum Mārtiālium comprobāvistis; quī sē ad senātūs auctōritātem, ad lībertātem vestram, ad ūniversam rem pūblicam contulērunt, hostem illum et lātrōnem et parricīdam patriae relīquērunt. Nec sōlum id animōsē et fortiter, sed cōnsīderātē etiam sapienterque fēcērunt; Albae cōnstitērunt, in urbe opportūnā, mūnītā, propinquā, fortissimōrum virōrum, fidēlissimōrum cīvium atque optimōrum. Hūius Mārtiae legiōnis legiō quārta imitāta virtūtem, duce L. Egnātulēiō, quem senātus meritō paulō ante laudāvit, C. Caesaris exercitum persecūta est.

III. Quae exspectās, M. Antōnī, iūdicia graviōra? Caesar fertur in caelum, quī contrā tē exercitum comparāvit; laudantur exquīsītissimīs verbīs legiōnēs, quae tē relīquērunt, quae ā tē arcessītae sunt, quae essent, sī tē cōnsulem quam hostem māluissēs, tuae; quārum legiōnum fortissimum vērissimumque iūdicium cōnfīrmat senātus, comprobat ūniversus populus Rōmānus, nisi forte vōs, Quirītēs, cōnsulem, nōn hostem iūdicātis Antōnium.

Sīc arbitrābar, Quirītēs, vōs iūdicāre, ut ostenditis. Quid? mūnicipia, colōniās, praefectūrās num aliter iūdicāre cēnsētis? Omnēs mortālēs ūnā mente cōnsentiunt, omnia arma eōrum, quī haec salva velint, contrā illam pestem esse capienda. Quid? D. Brūtī iūdicium, Quirītēs, quod ex hodiernō ēius ēdictō perspicere potuistis, num cui tandem contemnendum vidētur? Rēctē et vērē negātis, Quirītēs. Est enim quasi deōrum immortālium beneficiō et mūnere datum reī pūblicae Brūtōrum genus et nōmen ad lībertātem populī Rōmānī vel cōnstituendam vel recipiendam. Quid igitur D. Brūtus dē M. Antōniō iūdicāvit? Exclūdit prōvinciā, exercitū obsistit, Galliam tōtam hortātur ad bellum, ipsam suā sponte suōque iūdiciō excitātam. Sī cōnsul Antōnius, Brūtus hostis; sī cōnservātor reī pūblicae Brūtus, hostis Antōnius. Num igitur, utrum hōrum sit, dubitāre possumus?

IV. Atque ut vōs ūnā mente ūnāque vōce dubitāre vōs negātis, sīc modo dēcrēvit senātus, D. Brūtum optimē dē rē pūblicā merērī, cum senātūs auctōritātem populīque Rōmānī lībertātem imperiumque dēfenderet. Ā quō dēfenderet? Nempe ab hoste; quae est enim alia laudanda dēfēnsiō? Deinceps laudātur prōvincia Gallia meritōque ōrnātur verbīs amplissimīs ab senātū, quod resistat Antōniō. Quem sī cōnsulem illa prōvincia putāret neque eum reciperet, māgnō scelere sē astringeret; omnēs enim in cōnsulis iūre et imperiō dēbent esse prōvinciae. Negat hōc D. Brūtus imperātor, cōnsul dēsīgnātus, nātus reī pūblicae cīvis; negat Gallia, negat cūncta Italia, negat senātus, negātis vōs.

Quis illum igitur cōnsulem nisi lātrōnēs putant? Quamquam nē eī quidem ipsī, quod loquuntur, id sentiunt, nec ab iūdiciō omnium mortālium, quamvīs impiī nefāriīque sint, sīcut sunt, dissentīre possunt. Sed spēs rapiendī atque praedandī occaecat animōs eōrum, quōs nōn bonōrum dōnātiō, nōn agrōrum adsīgnātiō, nōn illa īnfīnīta hasta satiāvit; quī sibi urbem, quī bona et fortūnās cīvium ad praedam prōposuērunt; quī, dum hīc sit, quod rapiant, quod auferant, nihil sibi dēfutūrum arbitrantur; quibus M. Antōnius — ō dī immortālēs, āvertite et dētestāminī, quaesō, hōc ōmen! — urbem sē dīvīsūrum esse prōmīsit.

Ita vērō, Quirītēs, ut precāminī, ēveniat, atque hūius āmentiae poena in ipsum familiamque ēius recidat! Quod ita futūrum esse cōnfīdō. Iam enim nōn sōlum hominēs, sed etiam deōs immortālēs ad rem pūblicam cōnservandam arbitror cōnsēnsisse. Sīve enim prōdigiīs atque portentīs dī immortālēs nōbīs futūra prae-dīcunt, ita sunt apertē prōnūntiāta, ut et illī poena et nōbīs lībertās appropinquet, sīve tantus cōnsēnsus omnium sine impulsū deōrum esse nōn potuit, quid est, quod dē voluntāte caelestium dubitāre possīmus?

V. Reliquum est, Quirītēs, ut vōs in istā sententiā, quam prae vōbīs fertis, persevērētis. Faciam igitur, ut imperātōrēs instrūctā aciē solent, quamquam parātissimōs mīlitēs ad proeliandum videant, ut eōs tamen adhortentur, sīc ego vōs ārdentēs et ērēctōs ad lībertātem recuperandam cohortābor.

Nōn est vōbīs, Quirītēs, cum eō hoste certāmen, cum quō aliqua pācis condiciō esse possit. Neque enim ille servitūtem vestram ut anteā, sed iam īrātus sanguinem concupīscit. Nūllus eī lūdus vidētur esse iūcundior quam cruor, quam caedēs, quam ante oculōs trucīdātiō cīvium. Nōn est vōbīs rēs, Quirītēs, cum scelerātō homine atque nefāriō, sed cum immānī taetrāque bēluā, quae quoniam in foveam incidit, obruātur. Sī enim illim ēmerserit, nūllīus supplicī crūdēlitās erit recūsanda. Sed tenētur, premitur, urgētur nunc eīs cōpiīs, quās iam habēmus, mox eīs, quās paucīs diēbus novī cōnsulēs comparābunt. Incumbite in causam, Quirītēs, ut facitis. Numquam māior cōnsēnsus vester in ūllā causā fuit, numquam tam vehementer cum senātū cōnsociātī fuistis. Nec mīrum; agitur enim, nōn quā condiciōne victūrī, sed victūrīne sīmus an cum suppliciō ignōminiāque peritūrī.

Quamquam mortem quidem nātūra omnibus prōposuit, crūdēlitātem mortis et dēdecus virtūs prōpulsāre solet, quae propria est Rōmānī generis et sēminis. Hanc retinēte, quaesō, quam vōbīs tamquam hērēditātem māiōrēs vestrī relīquērunt. Nam cum alia omnia falsa, incerta sint, cadūca, mōbilia, virtūs est ūna altissimīs dēfīxa rādīcibus; quae numquam vī ūllā labefactārī potest, numquam dēmovērī locō. Hāc virtūte māiōrēs vestrī prīmum ūniversam Italiam dēvīcērunt, deinde Karthāginem excidērunt, Numantiam ēvertērunt, potentissimōs rēgēs, bellicōsissimās gentēs in diciōnem hūius imperī redēgērunt.

VI. Ac māiōribus quidem vestrīs, Quirītēs, cum eō hoste rēs erat, quī habēret rem pūblicam, cūriam, aerārium, cōnsēnsum et concordiam cīvium, ratiōnem aliquam, sī ita rēs tulisset, pācis et foederis; hīc vester hostis vestram rem pūblicam oppūgnat, ipse habet nūllam; senātum, id est orbis terrae cōnsilium, dēlēre gestit, ipse cōnsilium pūblicum nūllum habet; aerārium vestrum exhausit, suum nōn habet. Nam concordiam cīvium quī habēre potest, nūllam cum habet cīvitātem? pācis vērō quae potest esse cum eō ratiō, in quō est incrēdibilis crūdēlitās, fidēs nūlla?

Est igitur, Quirītēs, populō Rōmānō, victōrī omnium gentium, omne certāmen cum percussōre, cum lātrōne, cum Spartacō. Nam quod sē similem esse Catilīnae glōriārī solet, scelere pār est illī, industriā īnferior. Ille cum exercitum nūllum habuisset, repente cōnflāvit; hīc eum exercitum, quem accēpit, āmīsit. Ut igitur Catilīnam dīligentiā meā, senātūs auctōritāte, vestrō studiō et virtūte frēgistis, sīc Antōnī nefārium lātrōcinium vestrā cum senātū concordiā tantā, quanta numquam fuit, fēlīcitāte et virtūte exercituum ducumque vestrōrum brevī tempore oppressum audiētis. Equidem quantum cūrā, labōre, vigiliīs, auctōritāte, cōnsiliō ēnītī atque efficere poterō, nihil praetermittam, quod ad lībertātem vestram pertinēre arbitrābor; neque enim id prō vestrīs amplissimīs in mē beneficiīs sine scelere facere possum. Hodiernō autem diē prīmum referente virō fortissimō vōbīsque amīcissimō, hōc M. Servīliō, collēgīsque ēius, ōrnātissimīs virīs, optimīs cīvibus, longō intervāllō mē auctōre et prīncipe ad spem lībertātis exārsimus.

M. TULLI CICERONIS

EPISTOLAE SELECTAE.

I.

Scripta est epistola Romae A. U. C. 686.

CICERO ATTICO SAL.

Apud mātrem rēctē est, eaque nōbīs cūrae est. L. Cīnciō HS. XXCD. cōnstituī mē cūrātūrum Īdibus Febr. Tū velim ea, quae nōbīs ēmisse tē et parāsse scrībis, dēs operam ut quam prīmum habeāmus, et velim cōgitēs, id quod mihi pollicitus es, quem ad modum bibliothēcam nōbīs cōnficere possīs; omnem spem dēlectātiōnis nostrae, quam, cum in ōtium vēnerimus, habēre volumus, in tuā hūmānitāte positam habēmus.

II.

Scr. Romae A. U. C. 692.

M. TULLIUS M. F. CICERO S. D. CN. POMPEIO CN. F. MAGNO IMPERATORI.

S. T. E. Q. V. B. E. Ex litterīs tuīs, quās pūblicē mīsistī, cēpī ūnā cum omnibus incrēdibilem voluptātem; tantam enim spem ōtī ostendistī, quantam ego semper omnibus tē ūnō frētus pollicēbar. Sed hōc scītō, tuōs veterēs hostēs, novōs amīcōs, vehementer litterīs perculsōs atque ex māgnā spē dēturbātōs iacēre.

Ad mē autem litterās, quās mīsistī, quamquam exiguam sīgnificātiōnem tuae ergā mē voluntātis habēbant, tamen mihi scītō iūcundās fuisse; nūllā enim rē tam laetārī soleō quam meōrum officiōrum cōnscientiā, quibus sī quandō nōn mūtuē respondētur, apud mē plūs officī residēre facillimē patior. Illud nōn dubitō, quīn, sī tē mea summa ergā tē studia parum mihi adiūnxerint, rēs pūblica nōs inter nōs conciliātūra coniūnctūraque sit.

Ac, nē ignōrēs, quid ego in tuīs litterīs dēsīderārim, scrībam apertē, sīcut et mea nātūra et nostra amīcitia postulat. Rēs eās gessī, quārum aliquam in tuīs litterīs et nostrae necessitūdinis et reī pūblicae causā grātulātiōnem exspectāvī; quam ego abs tē praetermissam esse arbitror, quod verērēre, nē cūius animum offenderēs. Sed scītō ea, quae nōs prō salūte patriae gessimus, orbis terrae iūdiciō ac testimōniō comprobārī; quae, cum vēneris, tantō cōnsiliō tantāque animī māgnitūdine ā mē gesta esse cognōscēs, ut tibi multō māiōrī, quam Āfricānus fuit, mē nōn multō minōrem quam Laelium facile et in rē pūblicā et in amīcitiā adiūnctum esse patiāre.

III.

Scr. in Tusculano mense Martio A. U. C. 695.

CICERO ATTICO SAL.

Fēcistī mihi pergrātum, quod Serāpiōnis librum ad mē mīsistī, ex quō quidem ego — quod inter nōs liceat dīcere — mīllēsimam partem vix intellegō. Prō eō tibi praesentem pecūniam solvī imperāvī, nē tū expēnsum mūneribus ferrēs. At, quoniam nummōrum mentiō facta est, amābō tē, cūrā, ut cum Titiniō, quōquō modō poteris, trānsigās; sī in eō, quod ostenderat, nōn stat, mihi māximē placet ea, quae male ēmpta sunt, reddī, sī voluntāte Pompōniae fierī poterit; sī nē id quidem, nummī potius addantur, quam ūllus sit scrūpulus. Valdē hōc velim, ante, quam proficīscāre, amanter, ut solēs, dīligenterque cōnficiās.

Clōdius ergō, ut ais, ad Tigrānem? velim Syrpiae condiciōne, sed facile patior; accommodātius enim nōbīs erit ad līberam lēgātiōnem tempus illud, cum et Quīntus noster iam, ut spērāmus, in ōtiō cōnsēderit, et, iste sacerdōs Bonae Deae cūius modī futūrus sit, scierimus. Intereā quidem cum Mūsīs nōs dēlectābimus animō aequō, immō vērō etiam gaudentī ac libentī; neque mihi umquam veniet in mentem Crassō invidēre neque paenitēre, quod ā mē ipse nōn dēscīverim.

Dē geōgraphiā, dabō operam, ut tibi satis faciam; sed nihil certī polliceor. Māgnum opus est, sed tamen, ut iubēs, cūrābō, ut hūius peregrīnātiōnis aliquod tibi opus exstet. Tū quicquid indagāris dē rē pūblicā et māximē, quōs cōnsulēs futūrōs putēs, facitō ut sciam. Tametsī nimis sum cūriōsus; statuī enim nihil iam dē rē pūblicā cōgitāre.

Terentiae saltum perspeximus. Quid quaeris? praeter quercum Dōdōnaeam nihil dēsīderāmus, quō minus Ēpīrum ipsam possīdēre videāmur.

Nōs circiter Kal. aut in Formiānō erimus aut in Pompēiānō. Tū, sī in Formiānō nōn erimus, sī nōs amās, in Pompēiānum venītō; id et nōbīs erit periūcundum et tibi nōn sānē dēvium.

Dē mūrō imperāvī Philotīmō, nē impedīret, quō minus id fieret, quod tibi vidērētur; tū cēnseō tamen adhibeās Vettium. Hīs temporibus, tam dubiā vītā optimī cūiusque, māgnī aestimō ūnīus aestātis frūctum palaestrae Palātīnae, sed ita tamen, ut nihil minus velim, quam Pompōniam et puerum versārī in timōre ruīnae.

IV.

Scr. in Formiano mense Aprili A. U. C. 695

CICERO ATTICO SAL.

Facinus indīgnum! epistolam *αὐθωρεὶ* tibi ā Tribus Tabernīs rescrīptam ad tuās suāvissimās epistolās nēminem reddidisse! At scītō eum fasciculum, quō illam coniēceram, domum eō ipsō diē lātum esse, quō ego dederam, et ad mē in Formiānum relātum esse; itaque tibi tuam epistolam iussī referrī, ex quā intellegerēs, quam mihi tum illae grātae fuissent.

Rōmae quod scrībis silērī, ita putābam; at hercule in agrīs nōn silētur, nec iam ipsī agrī rēgnum vestrum ferre possunt. Sī vērō in hanc *Τηλέπυλον* vēneris *Λαιστρυγονίην* — Formiās dīcō, — quī fremitūs hominum! quam īrātī animī! quantō in odiō noster amīcus Māgnus! cūius cognōmen ūnā cum Crassī Dīvitis cognōmine cōnsenēscit. Crēdās mihi velim: nēminem adhūc offendī, quī haec tam lentē, quam ego ferō, ferret.

Quā rē, mihi crēde, *φιλοσοφῶμεν*: iūrātus tibi possum dīcere nihil esse tantī. Tū sī ad Sicyōniōs litterās habēs, advolā in Formiānum, unde nōs prīdiē Nōnās Māiās cōgitāmus.

V.

Scr. ab Appi Foro mense Aprili A. U. C. 695.

CICERO ATTICO SAL.

Volō amēs meam cōnstantiam. Lūdōs Antī spectāre nōn placet. Est enim *ὑποσόλοικον*, cum velim vītāre omnium dēliciārum suspīciōnem, repente *ἀνα-*

φαίνεσθαι nōn sōlum dēlicātē, sed etiam ineptē peregrīnantem. Quā rē ūsque ad Nōnās Māiās tē in Formiānō exspectābō. Nunc fac, ut sciam, quō diē tē vīsūrī sīmus. Ab Appī Forō, hōrā quartā. Dederam aliam paulō ante ā Tribus Tabernīs.

VI.

Scr. Romae mense Sextili A. U. C. 695.

CICERO ATTICO SAL.

Numquam ante arbitror tē epistolam meam lēgisse, nisi meā manū scrīptam. Ex eō colligere poteris, quantā occupātiōne distinear; nam, cum vacuī temporis nihil habērem et cum recreandae vōculae causā necesse esset mihi ambulāre, haec dictāvī ambulāns. Prīmum igitur illud tē scīre volō, Sampsiceramum, nostrum amīcum, vehementer suī statūs paenitēre restituīque in eum locum cupere, ex quō dēcidit, dolōremque suum impertīre nōbīs et medicīnam interdum apertē quaerere, quam ego possum invenīre nūllam; deinde omnēs illīus partis auctōrēs ac sociōs nūllō adversāriō cōnsenēscere; cōnsēnsiōnem ūniversōrum nec voluntātis nec sermōnis māiōrem umquam fuisse.

Nōs autem — nam id tē scīre cupere certō sciō — pūblicīs cōnsiliīs nūllīs intersumus tōtōsque nōs ad forēnsem operam labōremque contulimus; ex quō, quod facile intellegī possit, in multā commemorātiōne eārum rērum, quās gessimus, dēsīderiōque versāmur. Sed βοώπιδος nostrae cōnsanguineus nōn mediocrēs terrōrēs iacit atque dēnūntiat, et Sampsiceramō negat, cēterīs prae sē fert et ostentat. Quam ob rem, sī mē amās tantum, quantum profectō amās, sī dormīs, expergīscere; sī stās, ingredere; sī ingrederis, curre; sī curris, advolā. Crēdibile nōn est, quantum ego in cōnsiliīs et prūdentiā tuā, quodque māximum est, quantum in amōre et fidē pōnam.

Māgnitūdō reī longam ōrātiōnem fortasse dēsīderat, coniūnctiō vērō nostrōrum animōrum brevitāte contenta est. Permāgnī nostrā interest tē, sī comitiīs nōn potueris, at dēclārātō illō esse Rōmae. Cūrā, ut valeās.

VII.

Scr. in itinere mense Aprili A. U. C. 696.

CICERO ATTICO SAL.

Utinam illum diem videam, cum tibi agam grātiās, quod mē vīvere coēgistī! Adhūc quidem valdē mē paenitet. Sed tē ōrō, ut ad mē Vibōnem statim veniās, quō ego multīs dē causīs convertī iter meum. Sed eō sī vēneris, dē tōtō itinere ac fugā meā cōnsilium capere poterō. Sī id nōn fēceris, mīrābor, sed cōnfīdō tē esse factūrum.

VIII.

Scr. Brundisi prid. Kalendas Maias A. U. C. 696.

TULLIUS S. D. TERENTIAE ET TULLIAE ET CICERONI SUIS.

Ego minus saepe dō ad vōs litterās, quam possum, propterеā quod cum omnia mihi tempora sunt misera, tum vērō, cum aut scrībō ad vōs aut vestrās legō, cōnficior lacrimīs sīc, ut ferre nōn possim. Quod utinam minus vītae cupidī fuissēmus! certē nihil aut nōn multum in vītā malī vīdissēmus.

Quod sī nōs ad aliquam alicūius commodī aliquandō recuperandī spem fortūna reservāvit, minus est errātum ā nōbīs; sīn haec mala fīxa sunt, ego vērō tē quam prīmum, mea vīta, cupiō vidēre et in tuō complexū ēmorī, quoniam neque dī, quōs tū castissimē coluistī, neque hominēs, quibus ego semper servīvī, nōbīs grātiam rettulērunt.

Nōs Brundisī apud M. Laenium Flaccum diēs XIII. fuimus, virum optimum, quī perīculum fortūnārum et capitis suī prae meā salūte neglēxit neque lēgis improbissimae poenā dēductus est, quō minus hospitī et amīcitiae iūs officiumque praestāret. Huic utinam aliquandō grātiam referre possīmus! habēbimus quidem semper. Brundisiō profectī sumus prīd. K. Māi.; per Macedoniam Cȳzicum petēbāmus.

Ō mē perditum! Ō adflīctum! Quid nunc rogem tē, ut veniās, mulierem aegram, et corpore et animō cōnfectam? Nōn rogem? Sine tē igitur sim? Opīnor, sīc agam: sī est spēs nostrī reditūs, eam cōnfīrmēs et rem adiuvēs; sīn, ut ego metuō, trānsāctum est, quōquō modō potes ad mē fac veniās. Ūnum hōc scītō: sī tē habēbō, nōn mihi vidēbor plānē perīsse. Sed quid Tulliolā meā fīet? iam id vōs vidēte; mihi deest cōnsilium. Sed certē, quōquō modō sē rēs habēbit, illīus misellae et mātrimōniō et fāmae serviendum est. Quid? Cicerō meus quid aget? iste vērō sit in sinū semper et complexū meō. Nōn queō plūra iam scrībere; impedit maeror. Tū quid ēgeris, nesciō; utrum aliquid teneās an, quod metuō, plānē sīs spoliāta. Pīsōnem, ut scrībis, spērō fore semper nostrum.

Dē familiā līberātā nihil est, quod tē moveat: prīmum tuīs ita prōmissum est, tē factūram esse, ut quisque esset meritus; est autem in officiō adhūc Orpheus, praetereā māgnō opere nēmō. Cēterōrum servōrum ea causa est, ut, sī rēs ā nōbīs abīsset, lībertī nostrī essent, sī obtinēre potuissent, sīn ad nōs pertinēret, servīrent, praeterquam oppidō paucī.

Sed haec minōra sunt. Tū quod mē hortāris, ut animō sim māgnō et spem habeam recuperandae salūtis, id velim sit ēius modī, ut rēctē spērāre possīmus. Nunc, miser quandō tuās iam litterās accipiam? quis ad mē perferet? quās ego exspectāssem Brundisī, sī esset licitum per nautās, quī tempestātem praetermittere nōluērunt. Quod reliquum est, sustentā tē, mea Terentia, ut potes. Honestissimē vīximus, flōruimus. Nōn vitium nostrum, sed virtūs nostra nōs adflīxit. Peccātum est nūllum, nisi quod nōn ūnā animam cum ōrnāmentīs āmīsimus. Sed, sī hōc fuit līberīs nostrīs grātius, nōs vīvere, cētera, quamquam ferenda nōn sunt, ferāmus. Atquī ego, quī tē cōnfīrmō, ipse mē nōn possum.

Clōdium Philhetaerum, quod valētūdine oculōrum impediēbātur, hominem fidēlem, remīsī. Sallustius officiō vincit omnēs. Pescennius est perbenevolus nōbīs, quem semper spērō tuī fore observantem. Sicca dīxerat sē mēcum fore, sed Brundisiō discessit.

Cūrā, quoad potes, ut valeās et sīc exīstimēs, mē vehementius tuā miseriā quam meā commovērī. Mea Terentia, fīdissima atque optima uxor, et mea cārissima fīliola, et spēs reliqua nostra, Cicerō, valēte. Pr. K. Māi. Brundisiō.

IX.

Scr. Dyrrhachi a. d. VI. Kal. Decembres A. U. C. 696.

TULLIUS TERENTIAE SUAE, TULLIOLAE SUAE, CICERONI SUO SALUTEM DICIT.

Et litterīs multōrum et sermōne omnium perfertur ad mē, incrēdibilem tuam virtūtem et fortitūdinem esse tēque nec animī neque corporis labōribus dēfatīgārī. Mē miserum! tē istā virtūte, fidē, probitāte, hūmānitāte in tantās aerumnās propter mē incidisse! Tulliolamque nostram, ex quō patre tantās voluptātēs capiēbat, ex eō tantōs percipere lūctūs! Nam quid ego dē Cicerōne dīcam? quī cum prīmum sapere coepit, acerbissimōs dolōrēs miseriāsque percēpit.

Quae sī, tū ut scrībis, fātō facta putārem, ferrem paulō facilius; sed omnia sunt meā culpā commissa, quī ab eīs mē amārī putābam, quī invidēbant, eōs nōn sequēbar, quī petēbant. Quod sī nostrīs cōnsiliīs ūsī essēmus neque apud nōs tantum valuisset sermō aut stultōrum amīcōrum aut improbōrum, beātissimī vīverēmus. Nunc, quoniam spērāre nōs amīcī iubent, dabō operam, nē mea valētūdō tuō labōrī dēsit. Rēs quanta sit, intellegō, quantōque fuerit facilius manēre domī quam redīre. Sed tamen, sī omnēs tribūnōs pl. habēmus, sī Lentulum tam studiōsum, quam vidētur, sī vērō etiam Pompēium et Caesarem, nōn est dēspērandum.

Dē familiā, quō modō placuisse scrībis amīcīs, faciēmus. Dē locō, nunc quidem iam abiit pestilentia, sed, quam diū fuit, mē nōn attigit. Plancius, homō officiōsissimus, mē cupit esse sēcum et adhūc retinet. Ego volēbam locō magis dēsertō esse in Ēpīrō, quō neque Hispō venīret nec mīlitēs, sed adhūc Plancius mē retinet; spērat posse fierī, ut mēcum in Italiam dēcēdat. Quem ego diem sī vīderō et sī in vestrum complexum vēnerō ac sī et vōs et mē ipsum recuperārō, satis māgnum mihi frūctum vidēbor percēpisse et vestrae pietātis et meae.

Pīsōnis hūmānitās, virtūs, amor in omnēs nōs tantus est, ut nihil suprā possit. Utinam ea rēs eī voluptātī sit! glōriae quidem videō fore. Dē Q.

frātre nihil ego tē accūsāvī, sed vōs, cum praesertim tam paucī sītis, voluī esse quam coniūnctissimōs. Quibus mē voluistī agere grātiās, ēgī et mē ā tē certiōrem factum esse scrīpsī.

Quod ad mē, mea Terentia, scrībis tē vīcum vēnditūram, quid, obsecrō tē — mē miserum! — quid futūrum est? Et, sī nōs premet eadem fortūna, quid puerō miserō fīet? Nōn queō reliqua scrībere — tanta vīs lacrimārum est — neque tē in eundem flētum addūcam. Tantum scrībō: sī erunt in officiō amīcī, pecūnia nōn deerit; sī nōn erunt, tū efficere tuā pecūniā nōn poteris. Per fortūnās miserās nostrās, vidē, nē puerum perditum perdāmus. Cui sī aliquid erit, nē egeat, mediocrī virtūte opus est et mediocrī fortūnā, ut cētera cōnsequātur.

Fac valeās et ad mē tabellāriōs mittās, ut sciam, quid agātur et vōs quid agātis. Mihi omnīnō iam brevis exspectātiō est. Tulliolae et Cicerōnī salūtem dīc. Valēte. D. a. d. VI. K. Decemb. Dyrrhachī.

Dyrrhachium vēnī, quod et lībera cīvitās est et in mē officiōsa et proxima Italiae; sed, sī offendet mē locī celebritās, aliō mē cōnferam; ad tē scrībam.

X.

Scr. Dyrrhachi mense Ianuario A. U. C. 697.

CICERO ATTICO SAL.

Litterae mihi ā Q. frātre cum senātūs cōnsultō, quod dē mē est factum, allātae sunt. Mihi in animō est lēgum lātiōnem exspectāre; et, sī obtrectābitur, ūtar auctōritāte senātūs et potius vītā quam patriā carēbō. Tū, quaesō, festīnā ad nōs venīre.

XI.

Scr. Dyrrhachi exeunte mense Ianuario A. U. C. 697.

CICERO ATTICO SAL.

Ex tuīs litterīs et ex rē ipsā nōs funditus perīsse videō. Tē ōrō, ut, quibus in rēbus tuī meī indigēbunt, nostrīs miseriīs nē dēsīs. Ego tē, ut scrībis, cito vidēbō.

XII.

Scr. in Cumano X. Kalendas Maias A. U. C. 699.

CICERO ATTICO SAL.

Puteolīs māgnus est rumor Ptolemaeum esse in rēgnō. Sī quid habēs certius, velim scīre. Ego hīc pāscor bibliothēcā Faustī: fortasse tū putārās, hīs rēbus Puteolānīs et Lucrīnēnsibus. Nē ista quidem dēsunt. Sed mē hercule ut ā cēterīs oblectātiōnibus dēseror voluptātum propter rem pūblicam, sīc litterīs sustentor et recreor malōque in illā tuā sēdēculā, quam habēs sub imāgine Aristotelis, sedēre quam in istōrum sellā cūrūlī, tēcumque apud tē ambulāre quam cum eō, quōcum videō esse ambulandum. Sed dē illā ambulātiōne fors vīderit aut sī quī est, quī cūret, deus.

Nostram ambulātiōnem et Lacōnicum eaque, quae Cȳrēa sint, velim, cum poteris, invīsās et urgeās Philotīmum, ut properet, ut possim tibi aliquid in eō genere respondēre. Pompēius in Cūmānum Parīlibus vēnit. Mīsit ad mē statim, quī salūtem nūntiāret. Ad eum postrīdiē māne vādēbam, cum haec scrīpsī.

XIII.

Scr. Romae mense Maio A. U. C. 700.

CICERO TREBATIO.

Ego tē commendāre nōn dēsistō; sed, quid prōficiam, ex tē scīre cupiō. Spem māximam habeō in Balbō, ad quem dē tē dīligentissimē et saepissimē scrībō. Illud soleō mīrārī, nōn mē totiēns accipere tuās litterās, quotiēns ā Quīntō mihi frātre adferuntur.

In Britanniā nihil esse audiō neque aurī neque argentī. Id sī ita est, essedum aliquod capiās, suādeō, et ad nōs quam prīmum recurrās. Sīn autem sine Britanniā tamen adsequī, quod volumus, possumus, perfice, ut sīs in familiāribus Caesaris. Multum tē in eō frāter adiuvābit meus, multum Balbus, sed, mihi crēde, tuus pudor et labor plūrimum. Imperātōrem līberālissimum, aetātem opportūnissimam, commendātiōnem certē singulārem habēs, ut tibi ūnum timendum sit, nē ipse tibi dēfuisse videāre.

XIV.

Scr. Romae A. U. C. 701.

M. CICERO S. D. C. CURIONI.

Gravī teste prīvātus sum amōris summī ergā tē meī, patre tuō, clārissimō virō; quī cum suīs laudibus, tum vērō tē fīliō superāsset omnium fortūnam, sī eī contigisset, ut tē ante vidēret, quam ā vītā discēderet. Sed spērō nostram amīcitiam nōn egēre testibus. Tibi patrimōnium deī fortūnent! Mē certē habēbis, cui et cārus aequē sīs et iūcundus, ac fuistī patrī.

XV.

Scr. anno incerto.

CICERO SILIO SAL.

Quid ego tibi commendem eum, quem tū ipse dīligis? Sed tamen, ut scīrēs eum ā mē nōn dīligī sōlum, vērum etiam amārī, ob eam rem tibi haec scrībō. Omnium tuōrum officiōrum, quae et multa et māgna sunt, mihi grātissimum fuerit, sī ita trāctāris Egnātium, ut sentiat et sē ā mē et mē ā tē amārī; hōc tē vehementer etiam atque etiam rogō. Illa nostra scīlicet cecidērunt. Ūtāmur igitur vulgārī cōnsōlātiōne: "Quid, sī hōc melius?" Sed haec cōram; tū fac, quod facis, ut mē amēs tēque amārī ā mē sciās.

XVI.

Scr. Ephesi VII. Kal. Sextiles A. U. C. 703.

CICERO ATTICO SAL.

Ephesum vēnimus a. d. XI. Kal. Sextīlēs sexāgēsimō et quīngentēsimō post pūgnam Bovīllānam. Nāvigāvimus sine timōre et sine nauseā, sed tardius propter aphractōrum Rhodiōrum imbēcillitātem. Dē concursū lēgātiōnum, prīvātōrum, et dē incrēdibilī multitūdine, quae mihi iam Samī, sed mīrābilem in modum Ephesī praestō fuit, aut audīsse tē putō, aut "Quid ad mē attinet?" Vērum tamen.

Decumānī, quasi vēnissem cum imperiō, Graecī quasi Ephesiō praetōrī sē alacrēs obtulērunt; ex quō tē intellegere certō sciō multōrum annōrum ostentātiōnēs meās nunc in discrīmen esse adductās. Sed, ut spērō, ūtēmur eā palaestrā, quam ā tē didicimus, omnibusque satis faciēmus, et eō facilius, quod in nostrā prōvinciā cōnfectae sunt pactiōnēs. Sed haec hāctenus, praesertim cum cēnantī mihi nūntiārit Cestius sē dē nocte proficīscī.

Tua negōtiola Ephesī cūrae mihi fuērunt, Thermōque, tametsī ante adventum meum līberālissimē erat pollicitus tuīs omnibus, tamen Philogenem et Sēium trādidī, Apollōnidēnsem Xenōnem commendāvī; omnīnō omnia sē factūrum recēpit. Ego praetereā ratiōnem Philogenī permūtātiōnis ēius, quam tēcum fēcī, ēdidī. Ergō haec quoque hāctenus.

Redeō ad urbāna. Per fortūnās! quoniam Rōmae manēs, prīmum illud praefulcī atque praemūnī, quaesō, ut sīmus annuī, nē intercalētur quidem; deinde exhaurī mea mandāta, māximēque, sī quid potest, dē illō dōmesticō scrūpulō, quem nōn ignōrās, dein dē Caesare, cūius in cupiditātem tē auctōre incubuī, nec mē piget; et, sī intellegis, quam meum sit scīre et cūrāre, quid in rē pūblicā fīat — fīat autem? immō vērō etiam quid futūrum sit, perscrībe ad mē omnia, sed dīligentissimē, in prīmīsque, ecquid iūdiciōrum status aut factōrum aut futūrōrum etiam labōret. Dē aquā, sī cūrae est, sī quid Philippus aget, animadvertēs.

XVII.

Scr. in provincia mense Februario A. U. C. 704.

M. CICERO C. TITIO L. F. RUFO PR. URB. SAL.

L. Custidius est tribūlis et mūniceps et familiāris meus. Is causam habet, quam causam ad tē dēferet. Commendō tibi hominem, sīcut tua fidēs et meus pudor postulat, tantum, ut facilēs ad tē aditūs habeat, quae aequa postulābit, ut libente tē impetret sentiatque meam sibi amīcitiam, etiam cum longissimē absim, prōdesse, in prīmīs apud tē.

XVIII.

Scr. in provincia pridie Nonas Apriles A. U. C. 704.

M. CICERO IMP. S. D. M. CAELIO AEDILI CUR.

Putārāsne umquam accidere posse, ut mihi verba deessent, neque sōlum ista vestra ōrātōria, sed haec etiam levia nostrātia? Dēsunt autem propter hanc causam, quod mīrificē sum sollicitus, quidnam dē prōvinciīs dēcernātur. Mīrum mē dēsīderium tenet urbis, incrēdibile meōrum atque in prīmīs tuī, satietās autem prōvinciae, vel quia vidēmur eam fāmam cōnsecūtī, ut nōn tam accessiō quaerenda quam fortūna metuenda sit, vel quia tōtum negōtium nōn est dīgnum vīribus nostrīs, quī māiōra onera in rē pūblicā sustinēre et possīmus et soleāmus, vel quia bellī māgnī timor impendet, quod vidēmur effugere, sī ad cōnstitūtam diem dēcēdēmus.

Dē panthērīs, per eōs, quī vēnārī solent, agitur mandātū meō dīligenter; sed mīra paucitās est et eās, quae sunt, valdē āiunt querī, quod nihil cuiquam īnsidiārum in meā prōvinciā nisi sibi fīat; itaque cōnstituisse dīcuntur in Cāriam ex nostrā prōvinciā dēcēdere. Sed tamen sēdulō fit, et in prīmīs ā Patiscō. Quicquid erit, tibi erit, sed, quid esset, plānē nesciēbāmus.

Mihi mē hercule māgnae cūrae est aedīlitās tua. Ipse diēs mē admonēbat; scrīpsī enim haec ipsīs Megalēnsibus. Tū velim ad mē dē omnī reī pūblicae statū quam dīligentissimē perscrībās; ea enim certissima putābō, quae ex tē cognōrō.

XIX.

Scr. Ephesi Kalendis Octobribus A. U. C. 704.

CICERO ATTICO SAL.

Cum īnstituissem ad tē scrībere calamumque sūmpsissem, Batōnius ē nāvī rēctā ad mē vēnit domum Ephesī et epistolam tuam reddidit prīdiē Kal. Octobrēs.

Laetātus sum fēlīcitāte nāvigātiōnis tuae, opportūnitāte Piliae, etiam hercule sermōne ēiusdem dē coniugiō Tulliae meae. Batōnius autem mīrōs terrōrēs ad mē attulit Caesariānōs, cum Lepta etiam plūra locūtus est, spērō falsa, sed certē horribilia, Caesarem exercitum nūllō modō dīmissūrum, cum illō praetōrēs dēsīgnātōs, Cassium tribūnum pl., Lentulum cōnsulem facere, Pompēiō in animō esse urbem relinquere. Sed heus tū, num quid molestē fers dē illō, quī sē solet anteferre patruō sorōris tuae fīlī? at ā quibus victus?

Sed ad rem. Nōs etēsiae vehementissimē tardārunt; dētrāxit xx. ipsōs diēs etiam aphractus Rhodiōrum. Kal. Octobr. Ephesō cōnscendentēs hanc epistolam dedimus L. Tarquitiō, simul ē portū ēgredientī, sed expedītius nāvigantī; nōs Rhodiōrum aphractīs cēterīsque longīs nāvibus tranquillitātēs aucupātūrī erāmus. Ita tamen properābāmus, ut nōn posset magis.

Dē raudusculō Puteolānō, grātum. Nunc velim dispiciās rēs Rōmānās, videās, quid nōbīs dē triumphō cōgitandum putēs, ad quem amīcī mē vocant. Ego, nisi Bibulus, quī, dum ūnus hostis in Syriā fuit, pedem portā nōn plūs extulit quam domō suā, adnīterētur dē triumphō, aequō animō essem; nunc vērō *αἰσχρὸν σιωπᾶν*. Sed explōrā rem tōtam, ut, quō diē congressī erimus, cōnsilium capere possīmus. Sat multa, quī et properārem et eī litterās darem, quī aut mēcum aut paulō ante ventūrus esset.

Cicerō tibi plūrimam salūtem dīcit; tū dīcēs utrīusque nostrum verbīs et Piliae tuae et filiae.

XX

Scr. Corcyrae XV. Kal. Decembres A. U. C. 704.

TULLIUS ET CICERO S. D. TIRONI SUO.

Septimum iam diem Corcȳrae tenēbāmur; Quīntus autem pater et fīlius Būthrōtī. Sollicitī erāmus dē tuā valētūdine mīrum in modum, nec mīrābāmur nihil ā tē litterārum; eīs enim ventīs istim nāvigātur, quī sī essent, nōs Corcȳrae nōn sedērēmus. Cūrā igitur tē et cōnfīrmā et, cum commodē et per valētūdinem et per annī tempus nāvigāre poteris, ad nōs amantissimōs tuī venī. Nēmō nōs amat, quī tē nōn dīligat; cārus omnibus exspectātusque veniēs. Cūrā ut valeās. Etiam atque etiam, Tīrō noster, valē. XV. Kal. Corcȳrā.

XXI.

Scr. A. U. C. 704?

TULLIUS TERENTIAE SUAE S. D.

S. V. B. E. V. Sī quid habērem, quod ad tē scrīberem, facerem id et plūribus verbīs et saepius; nunc, quae sint negōtia, vidēs. Ego autem quō modō sim adfectus, ex Leptā et Trebātiō poteris cognōscere. Tū fac, ut tuam et Tulliae valētūdinem cūrēs. Valē.

XXII.

Scr. Formiis IX. Kal. Februarias A. U. C. 705.

TULLIUS TERENTIAE SUAE ET PATER SUAVISSIMAE FILIAE, CICERO MATRI ET SORORI S. D. PLUR.

Cōnsīderandum vōbīs etiam atque etiam, animae meae, dīligenter putō, quid faciātis, Rōmaene sītis an mēcum in aliquō tūtō locō; id nōn sōlum meum cōnsilium est, sed etiam vestrum. Mihi veniunt in mentem haec: Rōmae vōs esse tūtō posse per Dolābellam, eamque rem posse nōbīs adiūmentō esse, sī quae vīs aut sī quae rapīnae fierī coeperint; sed rūrsus illud mē movet, quod videō omnēs bonōs abesse Rōmā et eōs mulierēs suās sēcum habēre. Haec autem regiō, in quā ego sum, nostrōrum est cum oppidōrum, tum etiam praediōrum, ut et multum esse mēcum et, cum abieritis, commodē in nostrīs praediīs esse possītis.

Mihi plānē nōn satis cōnstat adhūc, utrum sit melius. Vōs vidēte, quid aliae faciant istō locō fēminae, et nē, cum velītis, exīre nōn liceat. Id velim dīligenter etiam atque etiam vōbīscum et cum amīcīs cōnsīderētis. Domus ut prōpūgnācula et praesidium habeat, Philotīmō dīcētis. Et velim tabellāriōs īnstituātis certōs, ut cotīdiē aliquās ā vōbīs litterās accipiam; māximē autem date operam, ut valeātis, sī nōs vultis valēre. VIIII. Kal. Formiīs.

XXIII.

Scr. A. U. C. 706.

TULLIUS TERENTIAE SUAE S. D.

S. V. B. E. V. Dā operam, ut convalēscās; quod opus erit, ut rēs tempusque postulat, prōvideās atque administrēs et ad mē dē omnibus rēbus quam saepissimē litterās mittās. Valē.

XXIV.

Scr. Brundisi XVII. Kal. Quinctil. A. U. C. 707.

TULLIUS S. D. TERENTIAE SUAE.

S. V. B. E. V. Tullia nostra vēnit ad mē pr. Īdūs Iūn.; cūius summā virtūte et singulārī hūmānitāte graviōre etiam sum dolōre adfectus nostrā factum esse neglegentiā, ut longē aliā in fortūnā esset, atque ēius pietās ac dīgnitās postulābat. Nōbīs erat in animō Cicerōnem ad Caesarem mittere et cum eō Cn. Sallustium; sī profectus erit, faciam tē certiōrem. Valētūdinem tuam cūrā dīligenter. Valē. XVII. K. Quīnctīlēs.

XXV.

Scr. Brundisi VII. Idus Quinctiles A. U. C. 707.

TULLIUS S. D. TERENTIAE SUAE.

Quid fierī placēret, scrīpsī ad Pompōnium sērius, quam oportuit; cum eō sī locūta eris, intellegēs, quid fierī velim. Apertius scrībī, quoniam ad illum scrīpseram, necesse nōn fuit. Dē eā rē et dē cēterīs rēbus quam prīmum velim nōbīs litterās mittās. Valētūdinem tuam cūrā dīligenter. Valē. VII. Īdūs Quīnctīlēs.

XXVI.

Scr. Brundisi III. Idus Sextiles A. U. C. 707.

TULLIUS TERENTIAE SUAE S. D.

S. V. B. E. V. Nōs neque dē Caesaris adventū neque dē litterīs, quās Philotīmus habēre dīcitur, quicquam adhūc certī habēmus. Sī quid erit certī, faciam tē statim certiōrem. Valētūdinem tuam fac ut cūrēs. Valē. III. Īdūs Sextīlēs.

XXVII.

Scr. Brundisi prid. Idus Sextiles A. U. C. 707.

TULLIUS TERENTIAE SUAE S. D.

S. V. B. E. V. Redditae mihi tandem sunt ā Caesare litterae satis līberālēs, et ipse opīniōne celerius ventūrus esse dīcitur; cui utrum obviam prōcēdam, an hīc eum exspectem, cum cōnstituerō, faciam tē certiōrem. Tabellāriōs mihi velim quam prīmum remittās. Valētūdinem tuam cūrā dīligenter. Valē. D. pr. Īd. Sext.

XXVIII.

Scr. Brundisi Kalendis Septembribus A. U. C. 707.

TULLIUS S. D. TERENTIAE SUAE.

S. V. B. E. V. Nōs cotīdiē tabellāriōs nostrōs exspectāmus, quī sī vēnerint, fortasse erimus certiōrēs, quid nōbīs faciendum sit, faciēmusque tē statim certiōrem. Valētūdinem tuam cūrā dīligenter. Valē. K. Septemb.

XXIX.

Scr. in Cumano A. U. C. 708.

M. CICERO S. D. M. MARIO.

A. d. VIIII. Kal. in Cūmānum vēnī cum Lībōne tuō vel nostrō potius; in Pompēiānum statim cōgitō, sed faciam ante tē certiōrem. Tē cum semper valēre cupiō, tum certē, dum hīc sumus; vidēs enim, quantō post ūnā futūrī sīmus. Quā rē, sī quod cōnstitūtum cum podagrā habēs, fac, ut in alium diem differās. Cūrā igitur, ut valeās, et mē hōc bīduō aut trīduō exspectā.

XXX.

Scr. in Cumano A. U. C. 708.

CICERO PAETO.

Herī vēnī in Cūmānum; crās ad tē fortasse, sed, cum certum sciam, faciam tē paulō ante certiōrem. Etsī M. Caepārius, cum mihi in silvā Gallīnāriā obviam vēnisset quaesissemque, quid agerēs, dīxit tē in lectō esse, quod ex pedibus labōrārēs. Tulī scīlicet molestē, ut dēbuī, sed tamen cōnstituī ad tē venīre, ut et vidērem tē et vīserem et cēnārem etiam; nōn enim arbitror coquum etiam tē arthrīticum habēre. Exspectā igitur hospitem cum minimē edācem, tum inimīcum cēnīs sūmptuōsīs.

XXXI.

Scr. in Antiati mense Septembri A. U. C. 708.

CICERO ATTICO SAL.

Male, mē hercule, dē Athamante; tuus autem dolor hūmānus is quidem, sed māgnō opere moderandus. Cōnsōlātiōnum autem multae viae, sed illa rēctissima; impetret ratiō, quod diēs impetrātūra est. Alexin vērō cūrēmus, imāginem Tīrōnis, quem aegrum Rōmam remīsī, et, sī quid habet collis ἐπιδήμιον, ad mē cum Tīsamenō trānsferāmus; tōta domus vacat superior, ut scīs. Hōc putō valdē ad rem pertinēre.

XXXII.

Scr. Romae A. U. C. 708.

CICERO SERVIO SAL.

Asclāpōne Patrēnsī, medicō, ūtor familiāriter ēiusque cum cōnsuētūdō mihi iūcunda fuit, tum ars etiam, quam sum expertus in valētūdine meōrum; in quā mihi cum ipsā scientiā, tum etiam fidēlitāte benevolentiāque satis fēcit. Hunc igitur tibi commendō et ā tē petō, ut dēs operam, ut intellegat dīligenter mē scrīpsisse dē sēsē meamque commendātiōnem ūsuī māgnō sibi fuisse; erit id mihi vehementer grātum.

XXXIII.

Scr. Romae ineunte anno A. U. C. 709.

M. CICERO S. D. C. CASSIO.

Longior epistola fuisset, nisi eō ipsō tempore petīta esset ā mē, cum iam īrētur ad tē; longior autem, sī φλύαρον aliquem habuissem; nam σπουδάζειν sine perīculō vix possumus. "Rīdēre igitur," inquiēs, "possumus." Nōn, mē hercule, facillimē; vērum tamen aliam aberrātiōnem ā molestiīs nūllam habēmus. "Ubi igitur," inquiēs, "philosophia?" Tua quidem in culīnā, mea in palaestrā est. Pudet enim servīre; itaque faciō mē aliās rēs agere, nē convīcium Platōnis audiam.

Dē Hispāniā nihil adhūc certī, nihil omnīnō novī. Tē abesse meā causā molestē ferō, tuā gaudeō. Sed flāgitat tabellārius; valēbis igitur mēque, ut ā puerō fēcistī, amābis.

XXXIV.

Scr. Asturae mense Martio A. U. C. 709.

CICERO ATTICO SAL.

Apud Appulēium, quoniam in perpetuum nōn placet, in diēs ut excūser, vidēbis. In hāc sōlitūdine careō omnium colloquiō, cumque māne mē in silvam abstrūsī dēnsam et asperam, nōn exeō inde ante vesperum; secundum tē nihil est mihi amīcius sōlitūdine. In eā mihi omnis sermō est cum litterīs; eum tamen interpellat flētus, cui repūgnō, quoad possum, sed adhūc parēs nōn sumus. Brūtō, ut suādēs, rescrībam; eās litterās crās habēbis. Cum erit cui dēs, dabis.

XXXV.

Scr. Asturae mense Martio A. U. C. 709.

CICERO ATTICO SAL.

Tē tuīs negōtiīs relīctīs nōlō ad mē venīre. Ego potius accēdam, sī diūtius impediēre; etsī nē discessissem quidem ē cōnspectū tuō, nisi mē plānē nihil ūlla rēs adiuvāret. Quod sī esset aliquod levāmen, id esset in tē ūnō, et, cum prīmum ab aliquō poterit esse, ā tē erit; nunc tamen ipsum sine tē esse nōn possum. Sed nec tuae domī probābātur nec meae poteram, nec, sī propius essem ūspiam, tēcum tamen essem; idem enim tē impedīret, quō minus mēcum essēs, quod nunc etiam impedit. Mihi adhūc nihil aptius fuit hāc sōlitūdine, quam vereor nē Philippus tollat; herī enim vesperī vēnerat. Mē scrīptiō et litterae nōn lēniunt, sed obturbant.

XXXVI.

Scr. Asturae mense Martio A. U. C. 709.

CICERO ATTICO SAL.

Dum recordātiōnēs fugiō, quae quasi morsū quōdam dolōrem efficiunt, refugiō ad tē admonendum; quod velim mihi ignōscās, cuicuimodī est. Etenim habeō nōn nūllōs ex eīs, quōs nunc lēctitō, auctōrēs, quī dīcant fierī id oportēre, quod saepe tēcum ēgī et quod ā tē approbārī volō: dē fānō illō dīcō, dē quō tantum, quantum mē amās, velim cōgitēs. Equidem neque dē genere dubitō — placet enim mihi Cluātī, — neque dē rē — statūtum est enim, — dē locō nōn numquam. Velim igitur cōgitēs.

Ego, quantum hīs temporibus tam ērudītīs fierī potuerit, profectō illam cōnsecrābō omnī genere monumentōrum ab omnium ingeniīs sūmptōrum et Graecōrum et Latīnōrum, quae rēs forsitan sit refricātūra vulnus meum; sed iam quasi vōtō quōdam et prōmissō mē tenērī putō, longumque illud tempus, cum nōn erō, magis mē movet quam hōc exiguum, quod mihi tamen nimium longum vidētur; habeō enim nihil, temptātīs rēbus omnibus, in quō adquiēscam. Nam, dum illud trāctābam, dē quō ad tē ante scrīpsī, quasi fovēbam dolōrēs meōs; nunc omnia respuō, nec quicquam habeō tolerābilius quam sōlitūdinem, quam, quod eram veritus, nōn obturbāvit Philippus; nam, ut herī mē salūtāvit, statim Rōmam profectus est.

Epistolam, quam ad Brūtum, ut tibi placuerat, scrīpsī, mīsī ad tē. Cūrābis cum tuā perferendam; ēius tamen mīsī ad tē exemplum, ut, sī minus placēret, nē mitterēs.

Domestica quod āis ōrdine administrārī, scrībēs, quae sint ea; quaedam enim exspectō. Coccēius vidē nē frūstrētur; nam, Lībō quod pollicētur, ut Erōs scrībit, nōn incertum putō. Dē sorte meā Sulpiciō cōnfīdō et Egnātiō scīlicet. Dē Appulēiō quid est quod labōrēs, cum sit excūsātiō facilis?

Tibi ad mē venīre, ut ostendis, vidē nē nōn sit facile; est enim longum iter, discēdentemque tē, quod celeriter tibi erit fortasse faciendum, nōn sine māgnō dolōre dīmittam. Sed omnia, ut volēs; ego enim, quidquid fēceris, id cum rēctē, tum etiam meā causā factum putābō.

XXXVII.

Scr. Asturae exeunte mense Aprili A. U. C. 709.

CICERO ATTICO SAL.

Fānum fierī volō, neque hōc mihi ēripī potest. Sepulcrī similitūdinem effugere nōn tam propter poenam lēgis studeō, quam ut māximē adsequar *ἀποθέωσιν*. Quod poteram, sī in ipsā vīllā facerem, sed, ut saepe locūtī sumus, commūtātiōnēs dominōrum reformīdō; in agrō ubicumque fēcerō, mihi videor adsequī posse, ut posteritās habeat religiōnem. Hae meae tibi ineptiae — fateor enim — ferendae sunt; nōn habeō, nē mē quidem ipsum, quīcum tam audācter commūnicem quam tēcum. Sīn tibi rēs, sī locus, sī īnstitūtum placet, lege, quaesō, lēgem mihique eam mitte; sī quid in mentem veniet, quō modō eam effugere possīmus, ūtēmur.

Ad Brūtum sī quid scrībēs, nisi aliēnum putābis, obiūrgātō eum, quod in Cūmānō esse nōluerit propter eam causam, quam tibi dīxit; cōgitantī enim mihi nihil tam vidētur potuisse facere rūsticē. Et, sī tibi placēbit sīc agere dē fānō, ut coepimus, velim cohortēre et exacuās Cluātium; nam, etiam sī aliō locō placēbit, illīus nōbīs operā cōnsiliōque ūtendum putō. Tū ad vīllam fortasse crās.

XXXVIII.

Scr. anno incerto.

CICERO TREBATIO SAL.

Illūserās herī inter scyphōs, quod dīxeram contrōversiam esse, possetne hērēs, quod fūrtum anteā factum esset, fūrtī rēctē agere. Itaque, etsī domum bene pōtus sērōque redieram, tamen id caput, ubi haec contrōversia est, notāvī et dēscrīptum tibi mīsī, ut scīrēs id, quod tū nēminem sēnsisse dīcēbās, Sex. Aelium, M'. Mānīlium, M. Brūtum sēnsisse; ego tamen Scaevolae et Testae adsentior.

XXXIX.

Scr. in Tusculano mense Maio A. U. C. 709.

CICERO ATTICO SAL.

Domī tē libenter esse facile crēdō; sed velim scīre, quid tibi restet aut iamne cōnfēceris. Ego tē in Tusculānō exspectō, eōque magis, quod Tīrōnī statim tē ventūrum scrīpsistī et addidistī tē putāre opus esse. Sentiēbam omnīnō, quantum mihi praesēns prōdessēs, sed multō magis post discessum tuum sentiō; quam ob rem, ut ante ad tē scrīpsī, aut ego ad tē tōtus aut tū ad mē, quod licēbit.

XL.

Scr. A. U. C. 710.

CICERO BASILO SAL.

Tibi grātulor, mihi gaudeō. Tē amō, tua tueor. Ā tē amārī et, quid agās quidque agātur, certior fierī volō.

XLI.

Scr. in Tusculano exeunte mense Iunio A. U. C. 710.

CICERO ATTICO SAL.

Mīrificē torqueor, sine dolōre tamen; sed permulta mihi dē nostrō itinere in utramque partem occurrunt. "Quō ūsque?" inquiēs. Quoad erit integrum; erit autem ūsque, dum ad nāvem. Pānsa sī rescrīpserit, et meam tibi et illīus epistolam mittam. Sīlium exspectābam, cui hypomnēma compositum est. Sī quid novī. Ego litterās mīsī ad Brūtum, cūius dē itinere etiam ex tē velim, sī quid sciēs, cognōscere.

XLII.

Scr. in Tusculano a. d. III. Kalendas Quinctiles A. U. C. 710.

CICERO ATTICO SAL.

Dē meō itinere variae sēntentiae, multī enim ad mē; sed tū incumbe, quaesō, in eam cūram: māgna rēs est. An probās, sī ad Kal. Iān. cōgitāmus? meus animus est aequus, ita tamen, sī nihil offēnsiōnis sit. Velim etiam scīre, quō diē ōlim piāculum, mystēria scīlicet. Utut est rēs, cāsus cōnsilium nostrī itineris iūdicābit. Dubitēmus igitur; est enim hīberna nāvigātiō odiōsa, eōque ex tē quaesieram mystēriōrum diem. Brūtum, ut scrībis, vīsum īrī ā mē putō. Ego hinc volō pr. Kal.

XLIII.

Scr. in Arpinati a. d. V. Nonas Quinctiles A. U. C. 710.

CICERO ATTICO SAL.

Ego, ut ad tē prīdiē scrīpseram, Nōnīs cōnstitueram venīre in Puteolānum; ibi igitur cotīdiē tuās litterās exspectābō, et māximē dē lūdīs, dē quibus etiam ad Brūtum tibi scrībendum est, cūius epistolae, quam interpretārī ipse vix poteram, exemplum prīdiē tibi mīseram. Atticae meae velim mē ita excūsēs, ut omnem culpam in tē trānsferās et eī tamen cōnfīrmēs mē minimē tōtum amōrem eō mēcum abstulisse.

XLIV.

Scr. in Puteolano prid. Nonas Novembres A. U. C. 710.

CICERO ATTICO SAL.

Bīnae ūnō diē mihi litterae ab Octāviānō; nunc quidem, ut Rōmam statim veniam, velle sē rem agere per senātum. Cui ego nōn posse senātum ante K. Iānuār., quod quidem ita crēdō. Ille autem addit, "cōnsiliō tuō." Quid multa? Ille urget, ego autem *σκήπτομαι*. Nōn cōnfīdō aetātī; ignōrō, quō animō; nihil sine Pānsā tuō volō.

Vereor, nē valeat Antōnius, nec ā marī discēdere libet, et metuō, nē quae *ἀριστεία* mē absente. Varrōnī quidem displicet cōnsilium puerī, mihi nōn. Sī fīrmās cōpiās habet, Brūtum habēre potest, et rem gerit palam; centuriat Capuae, dīnumerat. Iam iamque videō bellum. Ad haec rescrībe. Tabellārium meum Kalend. Rōmā profectum sine tuīs litterīs mīror.

XLV.

Scr. Romae III. Nonas Maias A. U. C. 711.

CICERO PLANCO SAL.

Ō grātam fāmam bīduō ante victōriam dē subsidiō tuō, dē studiō, dē celeritāte, dē cōpiīs! Atque etiam hostibus fūsīs spēs omnis est in tē. Fūgisse enim ex proeliō Mutinēnsī dīcuntur nōtissimī lātrōnum ducēs. Est autem nōn minus grātum extrēma dēlēre quam prīma dēpellere.

Equidem exspectābam iam tuās litterās, idque cum multīs, spērābamque etiam Lepidum reī pūblicae temporibus admonitum tēcum et reī pūblicae esse factūrum. In illam igitur cūram incumbe, mī Plance, ut nē quae scintilla taeterrimī bellī relinquātur. Quod sī erit factum, et rem pūblicam dīvīnō beneficiō adfēceris et ipse aeternam glōriam cōnsequēre. D. III. Nōn. Māi.

XLVI.

Scr. Romae XIIII. Kal. Quinctiles A. U. C. 711.

M. CICERO S. D. D. BRUTO.

Exspectantī mihi tuās cotīdiē litterās Lupus noster subitō dēnūntiāvit, ut ad tē scrīberem, sī quid vellem. Ego autem, etsī, quid scrīberem, nōn habēbam — ācta enim ad tē mittī sciēbam, inānem autem sermōnem litterārum tibi iniūcundum esse audiēbam — brevitātem secūtus sum tē magistrō.

Scītō igitur in tē et in collēgā spem omnem esse. Dē Brūtō autem nihil adhūc certī; quem ego, quem ad modum praecipis, prīvātīs litterīs ad bellum commūne vocāre nōn dēsinō. Quī utinam iam adesset! Intestīnum urbis malum, quod est nōn mediocre, minus timērēmus. Sed quid agō? Nōn imitor λακωνισμὸν tuum; altera iam pagella prōcēdit. Vince et valē. XIIII. K. Quīnctīl.

NOTES.

THE FIRST ORATION AGAINST CATILINE.

M. TULLI CICERONIS: see p. 1. B. 373; A. 80, *a*; H. 649, and 649, 1.[1] For *Tulli* instead of *Tullii*, see B. 25, 1; A. 40, *b*; H. 51, 5.

IN L. CATILINAM: this title, though used of the four Catilinarian speeches, is, strictly speaking, applicable only to the first; cf.[2] the outlines on pp. 42–44. Cicero himself, in naming his ten 'consular' orations, characterizes those against Catiline as follows (ad Att. II. i. 3): *septima* (*oratio*, the first Catilinarian), *qua Catilinam emisi; octava, quam habui ad populum postridie quam Catilina profugit; nona in contione, quo die Allobroges indicarunt*; *decima in senatu, Nonis Decembribus.*

HABITA: 'delivered;' an idiomatic use of *habere*, like that of the German *halten* in *rede halten.* IN SENATU: for the place and circumstances of delivery, see p. 39, and below, ll. 4–7.

INTRODUCTION.

Page 61. Chapter I. 1. Quo usque: strengthened by *tandem*, 'How long, pray;' introduces an abrupt, indignant question,

[1] B. = Bennett's Latin Grammar, A. = Allen and Greenough's, H. = Harkness's. References like this, p. 65, 7 (page 65, line 7) are to the pages of this book. Translations of Latin words or phrases are put in single quotation marks.

[2] Cf. (*confer*) = "compare;" sc. (*scilicet*) = "supply," or "understood;" N. = "note;" R. = "remark;" Vocab. = "Vocabulary," at the end of the book; dir. disc. = "direct discourse;" indir. disc. = "indirect discourse" (*oratio obliqua*); constr. = "construction;" l. = "line;" lit. = "literally;" dep. = "depends" or "dependent;" trans. = "translate" or "translation;" pred. = "predicate."

For other abbreviations see the list preceding the vocabulary.

suggested by the appearance of Catiline in the Senate. Sallust (Cat. xx. 9), puts a similar expression into the mouth of Catiline; *quae* (= 'and this state of affairs') *quo usque tandem patiemini, o fortissumi viri?* **abutere**: *abūtēre*, not *abūtĕre*. **patientia**: B. 218, 1; A. 249; H. 421, I. **2. etiam**: temporal, 'still.' **furor iste tuus**: 'that frenzy of yours.' Why is *iste* used? Cf. B. 246, 4; A. 102, *c*; H. 450, 1, N. **eludet**: here in the sense of 'make sport of.' **3. Quem ad finem**: i. e. how far, how long. **effrenata**: suggests what comparison?

4. Nihil: adverbial acc., taking the place of an emphatic *non*. B. 176, 3; A. 240, *a*, N.; H. 378, 2. The rhetorical force is heightened by the repetition of *nihil* with each item mentioned. **praesidium Palati**: the situation, shape, and elevation of the Palatine hill made it one of the strongest military positions in Rome. At a very early period it was surrounded by a massive wall, extensive portions of which still remained in Cicero's time. Consequently in times of special danger it was occupied by a garrison. Cf. Middleton's "Remains of Ancient Rome," Vol. I., Chap. IV. **5. vigiliae**: the Senate had ordered that watchmen be placed on guard throughout the city, under the charge of the lesser magistrates (aediles, tribunes, and quaestors). See Sall. Cat. XXX. 7, and XXXI. 1–3, where the 'terror' of the Roman populace is vividly described. **bonorum**: i. e. *bonorum civium*, = 'of the patriotic,' who had assembled in great numbers before the temple where the Senate was in session. **6. hic . . . locus**: the temple of Jupiter Stator (cf. p. 74, 32–34 and N.), on the Palatine, where the Senate had met, for the sake of security, rather than in the Senate-house (see Vocab. under *curia*, 1), or in one of the temples about the Forum. Cicero had taken the precaution to protect the temple with a company of armed knights. See Plan facing p. 76. **7. horum**: the senators; spoken with a gesture. **ora vultusque**: = 'the expression on the faces' (see p. 81, 13–18, particularly the sentence *quis denique . . . hostem*); hendiadys, for which see B. 374, 4; A. 385; H. 636, III., 2.

8. Constrictam — teneri: 'is held and bound fast,' as a captive wild beast closely fettered. B. 336, 3; A. 292, R.; H. 549, 5. **10. proxima** [nocte]: Nov. 7. **superiore nocte**: Nov. 6; see p. 45, and cf. N. to p. 81, 10. **quos**: for a list of the principal conspirators see Sall. Cat. XVII. 3–4. **11. quem**: introduces a dir. question; the other interrogatives in this sentence are indir.

13. tempora: B. 183; A. 240, *d*; H. 381. **14. consul**: sing. as referring to the office rather than to the consuls as individuals; so in l. 19 also. **Vivit?** = '"Lives" did I say?' the argument is strengthened by first questioning, then supplementing, the previous statement, — a figure called by the grammarians *correctio*. **15. publici consili particeps**: in accordance with the Roman custom, after his praetorship Catiline had been given a seat in the Senate. **16. notat et designat**: 'singles out and marks.' **unum quemque nostrum**: i. e. 'us one by one,' individually. Why not *nostri?* B. 242, 2; A. 194, *b*; H. 446, N. 3. **17. fortes viri**: ironical. **satis facere rei publicae videmur** [nobis]: trans. 'we think we are doing our duty by the state;' *satis facere videmur* is stronger than *satis faciamus*, which would have been more in accordance with the ordinary construction. **18. istius**: 'of that (wretch).'

19. te duci — iam pridem oportebat: 'you ought long ago to have been led.' **iussu consulis**: i. e. in accordance with the authority vested in the consuls by the Senate's decree of Oct. 21; see p. 38. Whether this authority was sufficient to warrant putting a Roman citizen to death without a formal trial is yet an open question; see p. 108, l. 3, and N. **20. conferri**: sc. *iam pridem oportebat*. **21. An**: introduces a rhetorical double question, in which (see Quintil. VIII. iv. 13) not only wholes but even parts are forcefully contrasted. In translating, the first member may be made subordinate and introduced by 'If' or 'While;' or the expression may be varied, thus: 'What? did not Publius Scipio . . ., and shall we . . .?' **P. Scipio**: see Vocab. under Scipio, (3), and Mommsen's "History of Rome," Vol. III. **22. pontifex maximus — privatus**: the office of supreme pontiff, although one of great dignity and influence, was not reckoned among the magistracies; cf. p. 59. **mediocriter labefactantem**: 'though only in slight measure disturbing;' strongly contrasted with *orbem . . . cupientem*.

Page 62. 3. consules: contrasted with *privatus*, l. 1. **illa nimis antiqua**: 'those (precedents) as too remote;' only one is given B. 246, 2; A. 102, *b*; H. 450, 3. **4. quod . . . occidit**:

in apposition with *illa*. B. 299, 1, *a*; A. 333, and N.; H. 540, IV. N. **C. Servilius Ahala**: master of the horse under the dictator Cincinnatus. **5. Fuit, fuit**: repetition for emphasis; so in l. 11, *nos*, *nos*. **6. ista**: here almost = *talis*. **8. senatus consultum**: the decree (*ultimum decretum*) of Oct. 21; see p. 38. **10. rei publicae**: dat. with *deest*. The thought is: the Senate has given the emergency due deliberation, and has conferred the proper authority upon the consuls; not the deliberative but the executive branch of the government is at fault. By thus complimenting the Senate and transferring the blame to his colleague and himself, the orator clearly strengthens his case with the senators. **11. desumus**: i. e. *rei publicae desumus*.

II. 12. Decrevit, etc.: having alluded to remote precedents, the orator passes to those nearer his own time. Those cited present a sharp contrast with the dilatoriness of the consuls in dealing with Catiline, and suggest immediate and decisive action. The intent of the speaker here is evidently not so much to convince the Senate as to frighten Catiline into leaving the City. **L. Opimius . . . caperet**: the language of the decree is of interest (see Cic. Phil. VIII. iv. 14): *quod L. Opimius consul verba fecit de re publica, de ea re censuerunt, uti L. Opimius consul rem publicam defenderet.* The other consul, Q. Fabius Maximus, was in the southern part of Transalpine Gaul at the time. **13. quid detrimenti**: 'any harm.' B. 201, 2; A. 216, *a*, 3; H. 397, 3. **14. propter . . . suspiciones**: a form of expression purposely mild, to heighten the contrast. **15. clarissimo**, etc.: = 'though a son, grandson and descendant of very famous men.' B. 224; A. 251; H. 419, II. The mother of the Gracchi was the noble Cornelia, daughter of the elder Scipio Africanus; their father, Tiberius Sempronius Gracchus, was twice consul, and twice honored with a triumph; and among their ancestors of the same name was that Tiberius Gracchus who in 214 B. C. got together an army composed largely of slaves and conquered Hanno near Beneventum. **16. liberis**: two sons; cf. p. 109, 28–30, and N. **M. Fulvius**: see Vocab. under *Flaccus*, (1).

17. L. Valerio: dat. See Vocab. under *Flaccus*, (2). **20. C. Servilium**: see Vocab. under *Glaucia*. **ac**: introduces an explanation of *mors*, 'and (that) as state's penalty.' **21. remorata est**: the force of *remorari* here, as often, is 'to keep' one 'waiting.' The thought is simply, *eodem die interfecti sunt.* **vicesimum**: in round numbers; how many days since Oct. 21? **22. horum**: spoken with a gesture; but the reference is not so much to the authority of the Senate as to that which the Senate had vested in the consuls. **23. in tabulis**: 'in the archives,' among the records of the proceedings of the Senate. **24. tamquam**, etc.: carries out the comparison suggested by *aciem*, l. 22. **26. convenit**: milder than *oportuit*; 'you might well have been put to death.' **et**: put rhetorically for *et quidem*. **ad . . . audaciam**: in what ways may purpose be expressed in Latin?

28. Cupio . . . cupio . . . videri: rhetorical expression for *cupio me esse clementem neque tamen dissolutum videri.* B. 331, IV., *a*; H. 535, II. **patres conscripti**: the senators as individuals were called *senatores*; sitting as a body they were always addressed as *patres conscripti.* The origin and primitive force of the latter title are not clearly understood. The prevalent view is, that *patres*, 'fathers,' or 'chiefs,' was the term of address used in the beginning, when the Senate as a council of advisers consisted exclusively of patricians; and that *conscripti*, 'elect,' or 'chosen,' refers to the plebeian members admitted afterwards. On the other hand, it has been maintained that the phrase contains no reminiscence of an original social distinction, but means simply 'assembled fathers.'

29. dissolutum: stronger than *neglegens.* **30. inertiae nequitiaeque**: 'of inactivity and lack of energy.' B. 208, 2, *a*; A. 220; H. 409, II. **31. in Italia**: not in the provinces, but near home, where rebellion would least be expected. **32. in Etruriae faucibus**: at Faesulae, a convenient centre for military operations because it commanded one of the main routes into Cisalpine Gaul. It was also a good rallying-point for the old soldiers of Sulla, being one of Sulla's colonies; cf. p. 95, 11. **in dies**: see IDIOMS.

Page 63. **1. adeo**: 'actually.' **2. rei publicae**: *not* gen. **3. iam**: 'at once.' **4. credo**: ironical, 'I suppose,' or 'of course.' **ne non . . . hoc**: i. e, *ne non omnes boni hoc a me serius factum esse dicant potius quam*, etc. The force of *erit verendum* is really made negative by the ironical turn, as if the orator had said *non verendum erit.* From the influence of this negation the subordinate negative clause *ne non . . .* (*dicant*) acquires an affirmative force; 'I shall not have to fear that . . . will not say' = 'I shall have to fear that . . . will say.' B. 296, 2, *a*; A. 331, *f*; H. 498, III., N. I. **5. boni**: cf. p. 61, 5, and N. **serius, crudelius**: B. 240, 1; A. 93, *a*; H. 444, 1. **quisquam**: usually found in negative sentences; here = 'any one at all,' implying that there may be one or two such, but not more. **6. quod . . . oportuit**: cf. p. 61, 19 and N. **8. interficiere**: the consul avoids the expression *te interficiam*, which might have been expected from the preceding argument. **9. tui**: why not dat.? B. 204, 3; A. 234, *d*, 2; H. 391, II., 4, (2). **12. ita ut**: 'just as.' **13. oppressus**: 'overpowered.' **14. Multorum**: emphatic.

Discussion.

A. *Addressed to Catiline.* III.–X.

III. 18. exspectes: B. 283, 2; A. 320, *a*; H. 503, I. **19. parietibus**: how different from *murus*, *moenia*? **continere**: i. e. *intus servare*. **21. crede**: see p. 363. **22. caedis**: B. 206, 2; A. 219; H. 406, II. **Teneris**: i. e. *Deprehensus es*. **24. licet recognoscas**: 'you may recall;' concessive expression instead of the impf. **ante diem** XII, etc.: = *ante diem duodecimum*; trans. as if *die duodecimo ante Kalendas Novembres*, i. e. Oct. 21. B. 371, 372; A. 259, *e*, and 376, *a*; H. 642–644. **26. ante diem** VI: cf. pp. 38, 45. **27. satellitem**: implies a lower kind of service than *administrum*. **28. fefellit**: see IDIOMS.

34. sui conservandi [causa]: 'in order to save themselves;' idiomatic use of the gerundive with *sui*. B. 339, 5; A. 298, *a*, and N.; H. 542, I., N. I.

Page 64. 2. profugerunt: why not subj.? B. 288, 1, *A*; A. 325, and N.; H. 517, 2. **3. die**: cf. p. 45. **5. nostra caede**: trans. as if *caede nostri*. B. 251, 2; A. 197, *f*; H. 445, 6. **remansissemus**: what form in dir. disc.? **6. Quid**: acc.; idiomatic use, originating in some such expression as *Quid dicam de hoc?* Its force here is that of our 'again,' 'furthermore.' **7. Praeneste**: from its location, its situation upon an eminence, and its strong fortifications, Praeneste was an advantageous centre for military operations. In early times it had been an important member of the Latin League. When it became a Roman colony is not known; probably in the time of Sulla. **10. Nihil . . . cogitas:** climax, with anaphora. B. 350, 11, *b*; A. 344, *f*; H. 636, III. 3.

IV. 13. noctem superiorem — priore nocte (l. 16): = 'night before last,' the night of Nov. 6. **14. ad**: 'with a view to,' 'with reference to.' **15. Dico**: emphatic, directing attention to the speaker's intimate knowledge of all the plans and acts of the conspirators; cf. p. 38. **16. inter falcarios**: 'on Scythe-makers' Street,' or 'in the Scythe-makers' Quarter;' condensed expression to indicate the location of Laeca's house. **non agam obscure**: i. e. *aperte dicam*, mentioning the name. **18. complures — socios**: cf. Sall. Cat. XXVII. 3–4: *intempesta nocte* ('in the dead of night') *coniurationis principes convocat per M. Porcium Laecam*, etc. **19. Quid taces**: spoken after a brief pause, — doubtless a moment of singular impressiveness. **20. in senatu**: defines and strengthens *hic.*

22. O di, etc.: outburst against the treason of Catiline's sympathizers in the Senate, suggested by the thought of the preceding sentence. **Ubinam gentium**: see IDIOMS. B. 201, 3; A. 216, *a*, 4; H. 397, 4. **24. Hic, hic**: cf. p. 62, 5, and N. **25. sanctissimo**: *sanctus*, as often, 'worthy of reverence,' 'worthy of respect.' **26. qui**: '(men) who.' **nostro omnium**: trans. as if *nostri omnium.* B. 243, 2, 3, *a*; A. 217, *a*, N.; H. 396, III., N. 2. **28. de re publica sententiam rogo**: with *hos*, in the phrase of our parliamentary law, = 'I put the question to them on (matters affecting) the public welfare.' As consul Cicero presided at meetings of the Senate appointed by him, and called upon the senators in turn for their votes upon each question. A senator might respond either with his vote simply or with a speech explaining or defending his position (*sententia*). **29. voce vulnero**: i. e. I do not call them by name.

31. Fuisti igitur: the orator returns from his digression (ll. 22–30) to the topic in hand; *igitur* refers back to l. 18, *Num negare audes? Quid taces?* implying that Catiline's silence indicates his assent. **32. quo**: 'to which part,' 'to which division.' **statuisti**: refers to the process of deliberation, while *placeret* (*tibi*) suggests the decision.

Page 65. 1. ad incendia: modern anarchists have an advantage over the ancient in that they understand the use of violent explosives. Had Catiline and his followers been familiar with dynamite, — the last resort of the coward and the desperado, — the conspiracy might not so easily have been suppressed. **confirmasti**: B. 116, 1; A. 128, *a*; H. 235. **2. paulum . . . morae**: in dir. disc., *est mihi etiam nunc paulum morae* (idiomatically, 'I am even now suffering a little delay'); hence in the indir. form we find *nunc* instead of *tum*, which might have been expected from the tense of *dixisti*. **3. viverem**: why not indic.? **duo equites**: according to Sallust (Cat. XXVIII. 1), C. Cornelius, a knight, and L. Vargunteius, a senator. **4. cura**: B. 214, 1, *a*; A. 243; H. 414, I. **liberarent**: subj. of characteristic, with *qui* = *tales, ut*. **illa . . . lucem**: i. e. early in the morning of Nov. 7; see N. to p. 81, 10.

5. lectulo: the diminutive, suggestive of home-life and retirement, heightens the impression of wickedness associated with the intended crime. **9. salutatum**: 'in order to pay their respects.' B. 340, 1; A. 302; H. 546. Roman gentlemen received their clients and friends early in the morning; the earlier the visit, the greater the respect implied. **cum**: 'since.' **10. iam**: 'already,' i. e. after the meeting at Laeca's and before the early morning call of the would-be assassins. By means of his numerous slaves and special guards (cf. p. 91, 8–11), Cicero was able to keep in constant communication with his friends and supporters, day and night. **id temporis**: see IDIOMS. B. 185, 2; A. 216, *a*, 3 and 240, *b*; H. 378, 2.

V. 12. Quae . . . sint: see IDIOMS. B. 286, 2; 251, 6; A. 201, *e*; H. 453. For the outline of the following argument, see p. 42. **13. aliquando**: for *tandem aliquando*. **14. Manliana castra**: the camp at Faesulae. B. 354, 4; A. 214, *a*, 2; H. 395, N. 2. **15. Educ**, etc.: i. e. *Educ etiam omnes tuos* ('your associates') *tecum, si fieri potest; si minus* (trans. as if *si non*), *at tamen educ quam plurimos*. **16. quam plurimos**: see IDIOMS. **18. intersit**: B. 310, II.; A. 314; H. 513, I. **versari**: here 'abide.' **19. non . . . sinam**: cf. p. 64, 10 and N. **Magna**: i. e. *magna gratia habenda est dis immortalibus*, etc. B. 348, 349; A. 344, *e*; H. 561, III. **20. huic ipsi Iovi Statori**: with a gesture toward the statue of the divinity in whose temple they were. **21. antiquissimo custodi**: see N. to p. 74, 32. **23. pestem**: abstract for concrete. **24. in uno homine**: i. e. *in te uno*, as shown by what follows; the existence of the state ought not too often to be endangered by the conduct of one man.

26. mihi, consuli designato: i. e. during the latter part of the year 64. That Cicero was Catiline's main object of attack is evident from the statement of Sallust, Cat. XXVI. 1. **27. privata diligentia**: (*Cicero*) *circum se praesidia amicorum atque clientium occulte habebat.* Sall. Cat. XXVI. 4. **28. proximis comitiis**: held for the election of consuls for the year 62; see pp. 37, 38. **29. in campo**: i. e. *in campo Martio*, where the *comitia centuriata* (see. p. 59) were held. **competitores tuos**: D. Junius Silanus and L. Licinius Murena, who received the election, and Servius Sulpicius. **31. nullo tumultu publice concitato**: i. e. without calling out the troops, = 'without any official summons to arms.' **32. me**: for *me unum.* **per me**: i. e. *meis copiis*, instead of *publicis copiis.* **33. perniciem meam . . . coniunctam**: i. e. *si perirem*, *etiam rem publicam magna calamitate adfectum iri.* **34. rei publicae**: kind of gen.?

Page 66. **5. Qua re**: 'And for this reason,' = 'Wherefore.' **id**: the putting of Catiline to death. **primum**: 'the first thing' to be done, as we say. **6. huius imperi**: i. e. *nostri imperi*, the power given to the consuls by the Senate's decree of Oct. 21; see p. 62, 8–11. B. 204, 2; A. 218; H. 399. **disciplinae maiorum proprium**: shown by the precedents cited, p. 62. **7. ad**: 'with respect to.'

10. quod: for *id* (referring to the clause *sin tu exieris*) *quod;* trans. *quod . . . hortor* idiomatically, 'as I have long been urging you.' B. 178, *d*; A. 238, *b*; H. 371, II. **12. sentina rei publicae**: treated as expressing one concept, hence followed by the gen. (*tuorum*) *comitum*, = 'consisting of your associates.' Cf. Sall. Cat. XXXVII. 5: *Omnes, quos flagitium aut facinus domo expulerat, ei Romam sicut in sentinam confluxerant*, where *sentina* by metonymy is used of the receptacle (= 'cess-pool') rather than the 'sewage.' **Quid est**: like our 'How now?' 'How is that?' **13. me imperante**: see IDIOMS. **14. faciebas**: 'you were trying to do.' B. 260, 3; A. 277, *c*; H. 469, II, 1. **consul hostem**: more dignified and more forcible than *ego te.* **15. num**: 'still, not;' fuller, 'you don't mean into exile, do you?'

VI. 17. Quid est enim: rhetorical question, much more effective than the simple form of statement, *Nihil est enim.* The very thought of his career of crime, and the fear and hatred with which he is regarded, ought to make Catiline flee the city. **19. coniurationem**: concrete, 'sworn band.' **20. domesticae**: arising from his family relations (see l. 28 et seq.), while *privatarum rerum* (l. 21) refers to his private life in general, as distinguished from his public career. **21. inusta**: 'branded upon,' as on the forehead of a runaway slave. **23. facinus**: 'wicked deed' affecting others, while *flagitium* is a 'burning shame' touching more directly the agent himself. **26. facem praetulisti**: as slaves were wont to do for their masters when going about the streets by night. The fascinating but baneful influence which Catiline gained over the young is described by Sallust, Cat. XIV. 5–7.

28. Quid vero: introduces still stronger evidence of Catiline's wickedness. **morte**: for *nece*. This murder is mentioned nowhere else. **29. alio scelere**: i. e. the murder of a son by the first marriage, from fear that he might become a source of annoyance to the new wife, whose name was Aurelia Orestilla. **30. quod**: 'but this.' B. 251, 6; A. 201, *e*; H. 453. **32. non vindicata esse**: = 'to have been left unpunished;' sc. *si exstiterit*. B. 328, 2; A. 271, *c*; H. 536, 2, (1), N. According to Roman criminal procedure (cf. p. 60) a court would take cognizance of a crime only when some one formally directed attention to it by lodging a complaint. In this instance the fact that no one could be found who would bring so atrocious and well-known a crime to the notice of the authorities — the orator implies — bore witness to the shameful degeneracy of the times.

34. omnis: acc. with *quas*; trans. as if *omnium fortunarum*, 'the complete downfall of all your fortunes, which.' **proximis Idibus**: the Ides and Kalends (to a less extent the Nones also) were the customary times for the computation of interest and the payment of debts. Cicero hints that Catiline, hopelessly in debt (cf. p. 37), is nearing a financial crisis, and will realize the failure of all his schemes when the next day of settlement comes, as his creditors are losing confidence in him.

Page 67. 3. difficultatem: financial 'straits.' **summam**: see IDIOMS.

7. cum: 'seeing that.' B. 286, 2; A. 326; H. 517. **horum**: **cf. p. 61, 7, and N. 8. pridie Kalendas Ianuarias**: i. e. the last day of Dec. B. C. 66; on the following day it was proposed to murder the in-coming consuls, Cotta and Torquatus; see p. 36.

B. 144, 1, 2; A. 261, *a*; H. 437, 1. **10. manum . . . paravisse**: in preparation for the attempt on Feb. 5, B. C. 65. **12. mentem aliquam**: 'any reflection,' 'any (change of) purpose.' **fortunam**: Catiline accidentally gave the signal prematurely; see p. 37.

14. illa: 'those (earlier attempts).' **neque . . . postea**: = *nam et nota sunt et multa alia postea a te commissa sunt;* the negative force of *neque* affects the whole sentence, while that of *non* is confined to *multa*. **17. petitiones ita coniectas**: 'thrusts so directed;' this phrase, as that in the next line, is borrowed from the speech of fencers or gladiators. **ut . . . viderentur**: render idiomatically, 'that it did not seem possible to avoid them.' How lit.? In cases like this the Latin prefers the personal construction, the English the impersonal. B. 332, *b*; A. 330, *b*; H. 534, N. 1. **18. declinatione et corpore**: hendiadys; 'by a mere twist of the body.'

19. neque tamen: trans. as if *et tamen . . . non*. **20. tibi**: B. 188, 2, *d*; A. 229; H. 385, 2. **21. excidit**: i. e. *e manibus tuis*. **22. Quae . . . defigere**: i. e. *Et quidem quibus sacris ea (sica) abs te initiata ac devota sit, quod* ('for the reason that') *putas necesse esse eam in corpore consulis defigere, nescio* ('I'm sure I don't know,' i. e. 'I don't care to say'). A weapon with which a violent deed had been committed was often consecrated to a divinity.

SICA.

VII. 26. odio: 'enmity.' **permotus esse**: why not *permoveri?* **27. quae tibi nulla debetur**: idiomatically, 'which you do not at all deserve;' *nulla* is much stronger here than *non*. Cf. B. 239; A. 191; H. 443. **30. contigit**: used generally of favorable occurrences. **31. vocis, taciturnitatis**: explanatory genitives.

33. Quid, quod: 'What of this, that;' cf. N. to p. 64, 6. **quod . . . sunt**: explained by the following clause. **34. tibi**: trans. as if *abs te*. Cf. N. to p. 159, 23. B. 189, 2; A. 232, *a*; H. 388, 1.

Page 68. 1. constituti fuerunt: more forcible than *constituti sunt*, as implying that Catiline's attempts are all and altogether in the past. **3. quo animo**: see IDIOMS. **4. isto pacto, ut**: 'in such a way, as,' = 'as.' **5. omnes cives**: Cicero does not regard the followers of Catiline as citizens. **domum . . . arbitraris**: i. e. *domum meam mihi relinquendam esse putarem; tu tibi urbem relinquendam esse non arbitraris?* Notice the conditional statements in this paragraph, which lead up to a climax ('slaves' — 'citizens' — 'parents'), and present the orator's thought far more effectively than the simple direct assertion of the same points.

7. iniuria: 'undeservedly.' **suspectum**: here an adj., but trans. 'an object of suspicion.' **9. omnium**: we should say 'by all.' **cum**: cf. p. 67, 7 and N. **10. odium**: sc. *esse.* **14. tui**: B. 348, 349; A. 344, *e*; H. 561, III. **16. Nunc**: = νῦν δέ, 'But as it is.' **17. nihil . . . cogitare**: *te cogitare nihil* (for *de nulla re*) *nisi de,* etc. **18. parricidio**: for *exitio,* or *interitu,* carrying out the personification of *patria* as *communis parens.* **huius**; 'her.' **19. iudicium sequere**: i. e. *iudicio, quod de te facit, obtemperabis.*

21. Quae: 'Now she.' **22. tacita**: '(though) silent;' oxymoron in *tacita loquitur,* the force of which is somewhat lessened by *quodam modo,* 'in a way.' B. 375, 2; H. 637, XI. 6.

23. annis: abl. as indicating the period in which (*not* through which) the statement in *exstitit* was true. **per te**: why not *abs te?* **25. neces**: in connection with the proscriptions of Sulla; see p. 36. The pl. of *nex* is rare. **sociorum**: i. e. *provincialium.* Previous to 89 B. C. only the inhabitants of the Italian cities in league with Rome were called *socii;* but as these were then admitted to the Roman citizenship (p. 148, 1–5), the term was afterwards extended to the natives of the provinces. The reference here is to Catiline's governorship in Africa, which was characterized by rapacity and brutality. **27. quaestiones**: 'judicial investigations.' Catiline had been accused of provincial extortion, but had purchased an acquittal.

28. ferenda: see IDIOMS. **30. totam**: i. e. not now merely in regard to individuals or provinces, but as a whole. **quicquid increpuerit**: = 'at every sound;' how lit.? **31. videri**: we should say 'apparently.' **32. quod a tuo scelere**: trans. as if *a quo tuum scelus.*

Page 69. VIII. 3. loquatur, debeat: the condition is in fact impossible; but consistently with the personification of *patria* it is conceived as possible, and hence put in the pres. subj. **4. possit**: concessive. B. 309, 2, *a*; A. 313, *c*; H. 515, II.

5. Quid, quod: cf. p. 67, 33, and N. **in custodiam**: i. e. *in custodiam liberam*. In cases where a Roman citizen was charged with a crime against the state, if a person of rank he was not imprisoned but put under surveillance, either in his own house or in the house of some magistrate who became responsible for his appearance when wanted for trial. In this instance Catiline had been accused of inciting to riot (sedition) by Lucius Paulus; see p. 38. Nothing better illustrates the audacity of the man than the attempt to get Lepidus, Metellus, and even Cicero, to take charge of him. Owing to the rapid culmination of events the trial did not take place.

6. ad: in the sense of *apud*. **8. domi**: B. 232, 2; A. 258, *d*; H. 426, 2. **10. nullo modo**: 'by no means.' **parietibus**: abl. of means, but trans. with 'within.' **12. contineremur**: why not indic.? **13. virum optimum**: bitter irony. **14. videlicet**: sarcastic. **17. carcere, vinculis**: contrasted with *custodia* in the sense of *custodia libera*. **19. iudicarit**: B. 283; A. 320, *a*; H. 503, I. Full form? **Quae . . . sint**: see IDIOMS. **20. aequo animo**: 'with resignation.' You deserve physical death, by your own hand or by that of the executioner; if you cannot be brought to this, at least favor us with your political death by going into exile.

23. Refer: sc. *rem*, 'the matter.' See IDIOMS. **postulas**: perhaps referring to previous utterances of Catiline. **25. referam**: i. e. *rem ad senatum*. **id . . . moribus**: = 'a course inconsistent with my character' as a mild man opposed to severe measures. As a matter of fact, however, the right to pronounce a sentence of exile belonged to the courts alone, and was outside the jurisdiction of the Senate.

27. hi: cf. *horum*, p. 61, 7, and N. **Egredere . . . proficiscere**: probably spoken with deliberation and great distinctness. **29. Quid est**: spoken after a pause, giving opportunity for dissent; cf. p. 66, 12, and N. There were friends of Catiline present (see p. 73, 17 et seq.), but after the orator's vigorous reference to them (p. 64, 20–30) they did not dare to come to the rescue of their leader. **31. auctoritatem**: 'the express request.' **34. M. Marcello**: see Vocab. under *Marcellus* (2), and pp. 49, 50.

Page 70. 1. hoc ipso in templo: heightens the rhetorical effect; a temple was considered a place of refuge, its sacredness being a protection against violence. **vim et manus**: = 'violent hands;' hendiadys.

3. cum quiescunt, probant: = 'by their stillness, they approve;' coincident action, hence indic. with *cum*. Notice the oxymoron and climax in the three *cum*-clauses. **4. neque hi solum**: trans. as if *et non solum hi*. **5. auctoritas**, etc.: refers back to p. 69, 24. **6. illi**: with a gesture; the knights were gathered in front of the temple, in view of the speaker. Cf. N. to p. 61, 6. **7. ceteri cives**: below the rank of senator and knight. **9. paulo ante**: i. e. as Catiline was entering the temple to meet with the Senate. **exaudire**: here 'plainly hear,' 'hear distinctly.'

11. haec: i. e. the city Rome and the Roman power; doubtless spoken with a wide gesture. **12. iam pridem**: see IDIOMS. **13. ad portas**: it was customary for the friends and relatives of those who were going into exile to escort them as far as the city gate; Catiline will have a large escort of those eager to see him depart, who will also protect him.

IX. 14. Quamquam: 'And yet.' **Te ut**, etc.: idiomatic, 'You — anything break your resolution? You — ever reform yourself?' B. 277, *a*; A. 332, *c*; H. 486, II. N. **17. duint**: = *dent;* archaic form, apparently from stem *du-*, with subj. ending same as in *velint*, *possint;* appropriate in prayers and wishes, just as our so-called "solemn" style, as in English, "Thy Kingdom *come*, Thy will *be done*." B. 116, 4, *d*; 279; A. 128, *e*, 2, and 267, *b*; H. 240, 3, and 483, I. **18. animum**: see IDIOMS. **19. nobis**: refers to Cicero alone, as shown by the use of *mea* in l. 18. B. 187, II., *a*; A. 98, *b*; H. 446, N. 2. **21. in posteritatem**: = *in posterum tempus*. That Cicero's fear was not groundless, his subsequent persecution and sufferings plainly enough showed. See pp. 7–9. **est tanti**: 'it is worth while,' i. e. *invidiam istam mihi impendere*. B. 203, 3; A. 252, *a*; H. 404, 405. **22. privata**: 'personal,' not extending beyond the person of the speaker. **24. temporibus**: 'to the exigencies,' — that Catiline subordinate his personal convenience to the good of the state. **26. is**: 'such a man.'

29. inimico, ut praedicas: Catiline interpreted the acts of the consul as those of a 'personal enemy.' Cf. N. to p. 65, 26. **30. Vix feram**: see IDIOMS.

Page 71. 2. latrocinio: 'brigandage,' as against law and order; called *impio* because against the Fatherland — *communis parens*. **3. ad alienos**: sc. *isse*.

5. Quamquam: as p. 70, 14. **quid**: adverbial acc., = 'why.' **invitem**: B. 277, and *a*; A. 268; H. 486, II. **6. esse praemissos**: '(men) have been sent forward,' in the night of Nov. 7. **qui . . . praestolarentur**: trans. by 'to' with the infin. **8. aquilam illam argenteam**: in Marius's time a silver eagle with outstretched wings was adopted as the ensign of the legion; later eagles were sometimes of gold. The one mentioned here had been carried in the army of Marius, in the campaign against the Cimbri (Sall. Cat. LIX. 3).

10. cui: refers to *aquilam*. **sacrarium**: the eagle of a legion was considered sacred, and intimately associated with the fortunes of the host. When in camp it was kept in a consecrated place near the commander's tent. So Catiline is here represented as having the eagle in a 'sanctuary' or 'shrine' in his house, and as making it an object of veneration. **11. scelerum tuorum**: characterizes *sacrarium*; freely, 'sacred to your crimes.' **12. tu — possis**; cf. p. 70, 14, and N.

X. 18. haec res: departure to join Manlius in war against the state. **20. voluntas**: 'inclination.' **fortuna servavit**: Catiline had thus far escaped punishment for his misdeeds. **21. non modo**: trans. as if *non modo non*. In expressions like this the Latin omits the negative after *modo*, because a negative is understood with the verb (in this case *concupisti*) from the following clause; but as English idiom requires the verb in the first clause, the negative must be supplied in translating. B. 343, 2, *a*; A. 149, *e*; H. 552, 2. **22. nefarium**: i. e. *civile*. **ex perditis**: i. e. *ex* (*hominibus*) *perditis atque derelictis non modo ab omni fortuna verum etiam* (*ab omni*) *spe*. B. 216, 1; H. 415, I. 2.

28. huius vitae: the life of a bandit. **meditati sunt**: here passive. **29. feruntur**: here = *praedicantur*, 'are (so much) talked about,' 'are matter of current report.' **labores**: 'exertions.' **iacēre, vigilare**: in apposition with *labores*. **30. obsidendum**: here = *speculandum*. **32. otiosorum**: peaceably disposed citizens, who would go to bed with no thought of danger from burglars or brigands. **Habes, ubi ostentes**: 'You have an opportunity to display;' *ubi* with the sense of (*locum*) *in quo* is used with the subj. of characteristic.

Page 72. **2. a consulatu reppuli**: at the last consular election; cf. p. 65, 28–30, and N. **exsul, consul**: play upon words; so below (l. 18), *emissus, immissus.* **5. latrocinium**: cf. p. 71, 2, and N.

B. *Addressed to the Senate.* XI.–XIII., l. 27.

XI. 7 detester ac deprecer: 'I may beg to avert and plead against.' The following justification of the orator's course is a kind of *refutatio;* it seems too elaborate to have been altogether extempore, and was very likely inserted, or at least expanded, when the speech was revised. **11. est**: why not *sit?* Cf. B. 324, 1; A. 342, *a*, N.; H. 529, II., N. 1 (2). **12. loquatur**: the apodosis is omitted, on account of the length of the address which follows; for the mood, cf. p. 69, 3, and N. Notice the climax in *patria — cuncta Italia — omnis res publica.*

13. Tunc . . . patiere: cf. B. 351, 5; A. 346, *a*, *b*; H. 573. **16. evocatorem servorum**: according to Sallust (Cat. LVI. 5), Catiline refused the help of slaves, thinking that it would be to his disadvantage if he should appear to have made common cause with them; yet Lentulus urged their employment, and there were uprisings of slaves at Capua and in Apulia at this time. **19. vincla**: See Vocab. under *vinculum.*

22. persaepe . . . multarunt: rhetorical exaggeration; the orator has cited only one case of the kind (p. 61, 21 et seq.). **23. leges**: the laws guarding the right of appeal to the people from the decision of a magistrate. The earliest was one of the Valerian Laws (508 B. C.), which enacted: *ne quis magistratus civem Romanum adversus provocationem* ('against an appeal' to the people assembled in *comitia*) *necaret neve verberaret.* There was also a *Lex Porcia* (probably of 197 B. C.), which seems to have made it possible for a Roman citizen to save himself from the death penalty, or from scourging, by voluntarily going into exile; and the right of appeal, in accordance with which a Roman could not be put to death or flogged without the assent of the people, was reaffirmed by one of the laws proposed by Gaius Gracchus, B. C. 123. Cicero's position is, that citizens who have taken up arms against the state have forfeited their civil rights, and are no longer entitled to the protection afforded by the laws. On this question, see N. to p. 108, 3.

27. refers: see IDIOMS. **28. hominem . . . maiorum**: Cicero was a *novus homo*. **commendatione**: B. 224; A. 251; H. 419, II. **29. tam mature — extulit**: Cicero was elected to each office *suō annō*, i. e. in each case as soon as he had reached the age required by law. Usually 'new men' were not able to secure the consulship till some years after they had reached the legal age. **30. honorum**: = 'of public office.' **33. severitatis**: 'arising from strictness.' **inertiae**: cf. p. 62, 30, and N.

Page 73. XII. 3. vocibus: 'utterances,' as contrasted with the 'thoughts' (*mentibus*) of those who keep their opinions to themselves. **4. idem**: B. 176, 2, *a*; A. 238, *b*; H. 378, 2. **5. factu**: B. 340, 2; A. 303, R.; H. 547. **iudicarem**: why not plup.? **6. Catilinam multari**: in apposition with *hoc*. **8. summi viri**: magistrates, as L. Opimius; while *clarissimi cives* refers to private citizens, as P. Scipio (p. 61, l. 21 et seq.). **9. Flacci**: M. Fulvius Flaccus; see p. 62, 16. **12. quid invidiae**: here 'any enmity.' **13. in posteritatem**: cf. p. 70, 21, and N. **redundaret**: 'should overwhelm me,' as a flood which has burst over the banks of a stream. **Quod**: 'But.' B. 185, 2; 251, 6; A. 240, *b*; H. 453, 6.

17. Quamquam: 'But;' introduces a more immediate reason for apprehension than that mentioned above. **non nulli**: = 'some.' **hoc ordine**: = *senatu*. **qui**: why with subj., while *quae — quae* (l. 18) are with the indic.? **19. sententiis**: 'expressions of opinion.' **21. multi**: i. e. *multi alii*, *extra hunc ordinem*. **22. improbi**: i. e. *ei qui ea, quae vident, dissimulant;* while *imperiti* refers to those *qui ea, quae imminent, non vident*. **23. regie**: = τυραννικῶς, *tyrannice*, i. e. more after the manner of a tyrant than of a Roman magistrate. **factum esse**: '(the deed) had been done.' **dicerent**: notice the force of the impf., 'would be saying.' **30. eiecerit**: i. e. *ex urbe*. **31. naufragos**: implies financial wreck; while *perditus* usually refers to moral ruin.

Page 74. XIII. 2. nescio quo pacto: = *nescio quo modo*, 'somehow.' B. 253, 6; A. 334, *e*; H. 529, 5, 3). **5. latrocinio**: concrete, 'band of brigands.' **8. venis atque visceribus**: a parallel to our "flesh and blood." **9. Ut**, etc.: B. 351, 5; A. 346, *b*; H. 573, and N. 3. **10. aestu febrique**: = 'in the burning heat of fever.' What figure? **13. rele-**

vatus: = *si relevatus erit.* B. 305, 1; A. 310, *a*; H. 507, 3, N. 7.

17. insidiari . . . consuli: see p. 65, 2–11. **18. circumstare tribunal**: for the purpose of intimidation, thus interfering with the administration of justice. The tribunal of the 'city praetor' (cf. p. 60) was in the Comitium. **19. cum gladiis**: for *armati.* **curiam**: the curia Hostilia, where the Senate usually met; see Vocab. under *curia* (1). **malleolos**: 'fire-darts,' used principally in siege operations. They were shaped like a mallet, the head being filled with tow and pitch, which were ignited before the missile was thrown. **25. omnibus bonis**: 'all patriotic citizens,' exclusive of the senators and knights just mentioned. **27. videatis**: 'you shall see.' Why is the pres. subj. in Latin often used with reference to future time?

CONCLUSION.

28. Hisce ominibus: 'With these prophetic words.' **cum . . . exitio**: in our idiom, 'to the highest welfare of the state, to the plague and destruction of yourself,' etc. **31. impium**: cf. p. 71, l. 2, and N.

32. Tu, Iuppiter: the orator addresses the statue of Jupiter Stator in the temple, and through it the divinity represented by it. **eisdem quibus auspiciis**: = *eisdem auspiciis quibus.* The statement is not literally true; for though there was a tradition that Romulus in a battle with the Sabines vowed a temple to Jupiter Stator on this site, the temple was not actually built till 294 B. C. (Liv. I. XII. 5, X. XXXVII. 15). **33. Statorem**: here 'Establisher,' 'Protector;' in the vow as given by Livy, the word means rather 'stayer of flight.'

Page 75. 5. aeternis suppliciis: cf. p. 107, 8–13, and N.

THE SECOND ORATION AGAINST CATILINE.

Page 76. IN L. CATILINAM: see N. on p. 209. In some of the oldest MSS. the following argument of this oration is found: *Superiore libro* (here = *oratione*) *Catilina circumventus eloquentia Ciceronis spontaneum elegit exsilium, unde oratori maxima venisse videbatur invidia. Sed postero die timore dissimulato processit ad populum fingens se timere quod emiserit Catilinam, ut minus sit invidiosum, quod eum in exsilium expulerit. Prooemium sumptum ab exsultatione dicentis verbis paene triumphantibus, qui sine damno rei publicae superare bellum potuerit.*

HABITA AD POPULUM: speeches addressed 'to the people' were delivered from the Rostra, an elevated speaker's platform, to the front of which were fastened the bronze beaks of the ships captured in the famous sea-fight off Antium, in 338 B. C.; hence the name. The original location of the Rostra was in the Comitium, at the edge of the Forum; see Plan opposite p. 76. The speaker faced the people assembled in the Forum; directly behind them were the Old Shops (*Tabernae Veteres*), low stores or booths along the southwestern side. If he glanced to the left he saw the Temple of Castor and Pollux and perhaps the round Temple of Vesta, behind which rose the northern slope of the Palatine Hill; if he turned toward the right, his eye fell on the Temple of Saturn, or the Temple of Concord, or, high above these, the southern part of the Capitoline Hill crowned with the splendid and imposing Temple of Jupiter Optimus Maximus. From the Old Rostra were delivered many of the greatest speeches of ancient Rome; among them that of Cicero for the Bill of Manilius, and the Second and Third against Catiline.

In 44 B. C. Julius Caesar removed the Rostra to the upper end of the Forum (see Plan), bringing thither the beaks and many statues that had adorned the old Rostra. The foundations of this later structure have been discovered. It was about seventy feet long and ten feet high. On the front apparently were thirty-nine beaks, arranged in two tiers. This speaker's platform also witnessed stirring scenes. Here Julius Caesar refused the crown offered him by Antony; here also his bleeding form was exposed to public gaze, and Antony's funeral address stirred the populace to fury. Here Cicero delivered several of the Philippics; and to the Rostra above the beaks his head and hands were nailed (Plut. Cic. XLIX.); cf. p. 11. and Middleton's "Remains of Ancient Rome," Vol. I., chapters VI., VII.; also, Hülsen's "Forum Romanum" (Rome, 1893).

INTRODUCTION. I., II.

I. **1. Tandem aliquando**: 'Now at last.' For the circumstances of delivery, and an outline of the argument, see pp. 39, 42, 43. **Quirites**: not *Romani*, because addressed as voters rather than as soldiers. **2. scelus anhelantem**: cf. Acts ix. 1, 'breathing out threatenings and slaughter.' **4. vel . . . vel . . . vel**: gives the hearers a choice among three alternatives; apparently the orator did not dare to say outright that he had driven Catiline forth (cf. p. 90, 9–14). This whole chapter, as Halm justly remarks, appears to our modern taste somewhat inflated, from the accumulation of synonyms and striking expressions; but it must be remembered that the speech was addressed to the people, with whom this style of speaking was more effective, and more in place, than it would have been in the Senate.

5. ipsum egredientem: trans. as if *eum sua sponte egredientem.* **verbis prosecuti sumus**: just as we accompany departing friends with "Bon voyage!" "Good luck to you!" and similar expressions; ironical, but cf. p. 70, 13 and N. **Abiit . . . erupit**: difference in meaning between these four words? **6. monstro**: suggests something unnatural, a physical or moral 'monstrosity;' while *prodigio* implies influence of the supernatural, something uncanny or of ill omen, a 'portent.' **7. moenibus ipsis**: i. e. *urbi ipsi et eius aedificiis.*

10. controversia: see IDIOMS. **11. latera**: we should say 'breast;' cf. p. 67, 20–24. **versabitur**: 'will ply its task.' **in campo**: cf. p. 65, 28–32 and N. **12. in curia . . . parietes**: cf. p. 74, 17–20, and 69, 9–12. **13. Loco motus est**:

'was forced from his vantage-ground,' an expression drawn from the language of wrestlers and gladiators.

14. nullo: see IDIOMS. **16. hominem**: 'the fellow;' used instead of *illum* or *eum*, with implied contempt. **cum**: 'in that.' **occultis**: introduced in contrast with *apertum* (l. 17); for *insidiis* itself involves the idea of concealment. **17. latrocinium**: cf. p. 71, 2 and N. **18. extulit**: i. e. *ex urbe.* **19. vivis nobis**: 'while we were (yet) living.' Why abl.? **22. Iacet**: as a gladiator who has lost in his fight and been struck down.

Page 77. 2. retorquet . . . faucibus: as some monstrous and blood-thirsty wild beast, cheated of its prey. **4. quidem**: adversative; with *quae*, 'but it.'

II. 7. in hoc ipso: 'in this very matter;' explained by *quod . . . emiserim.* **9. comprehenderim**: B. 286, 1; A. 341, *d*; H. 516, II. **10. non . . . culpa**: in full, *istius rei culpa non est mea culpa.* **sed temporum**: 'but (that) of circumstances.' **11. Interfectum esse**: cf. p. 61, 19 and N. **13. huius imperi**: cf. p. 66, 6, and N. **14. res publica**: for *salus rei publicae*, 'the welfare of the state.' **fuisse**: i. e. among the senators; cf. p. 73, 17 et seq. **16. defenderent**: 'tried to justify (it).'

17. Ac: = 'And yet,' in spite of the scepticism and opposition in the Senate. **illo sublato**: 'by putting him out of the way.' B. 227, 2; A. 255, 5, N.; H. 431, 2. **18. iudicarem . . . sustulissem**: cf. p. 73, 5–8, and N. **19. invidiae meae periculo**: i. e. *periculo ut in invidiam venirem;* trans. 'at the risk of personal enmity.' **20. ne . . . probata**: = 'as the matter had not yet been made clear to all even of your number,' not to mention the senators who professed ignorance or openly sympathized with Catiline (*quam multos*, ll. 14, 16). **22. fore ut — possem**: a round-about form of expression, made necessary by the lack of a fut. infin. (participle) of *posse;* in dir. disc., *si multavero, non potero.* B. 319; 270, 3; A. 337; H. 527, I. **23. huc**: 'to this point;' cf. p. 76, 15–17.

25. Quem . . . putem: trans. as if *Et quam vehementer illum quidem hostem*, etc. The irony increases in intensity to the end of the chapter. **26. hinc, quod**: 'from this, that.' **28. comitatus**: here pass.; with *parum*, = 'with too small a retinue;' *nocte intempesta* (cf. N. to p. 64, 18) *cum paucis in*

Manliana castra profectus est (Sall. Cat. XXXII. 1). **exierit**: why not same mood as *fero* (l. 27)?

29. Tongilium, Publicium, Minucium: mentioned apparently as typical reprobates of the Catilinarian contingent. **mihi**: ethical dat.; 'He has taken forth my Tongilius,' 'He has, I see, taken Tongilius out.' B. 188, 2, *b*; A. 236; H. 389. **30. in praetexta**: =*praetextatum*, i. e. 'when a youth.' The toga of the ordinary Roman citizen was white, retaining the color of the undyed wool; but sons of freeborn parents were allowed to wear a toga with a red border (see Vocab. under *purpura*), until they became of age. The plain garment (in this connection called *toga virilis*) was placed upon the youth, with appropriate ceremonies, at the Feast of the Liberalia (March 17), when he was between fourteen and sixteen years old. **31. popina**: a low place where wines and articles of food were sold; frequented largely by slaves. **33. aere**: why abl.?

DISCUSSION. III.–XI.

Page 78. III. 1. illum exercitum: of Catiline; explained by *collectum* (l. 4) et seq. **Gallicanis legionibus**: the regular troops stationed in Cisalpine Gaul, which could easily be brought down to Faesulae from the north; cf. N. to p. 62, 32. **2. dilectu**: a fresh 'levy' of soldiers drafted in the coast regions east of Faesulae; also within easy reach. **3. Gallico** [agro]: 'the Gallic country,' so called because formerly settled by the Senones, a Gallic tribe. It lay south of the Rubicon (hence in Italy, not in Cisalpine Gaul), and extended along the coast as far south as Picenum, including the cities Ariminum, Pisaurum, Fanum, and Sena Gallica. **Q. Metellus**: he had been sent north to draft troops immediately after the senate learned of the operations of Manlius at Faesulae. Cf. Vocab., *Metellus*, (4).

5. senibus desperatis: veterans from the army of Sulla; *non nullos ex Sullanis coloniis, quibus lubido atque luxuria ex magnis rapinis nihil reliqui fecerat* (Sall. Cat. XXVIII. 4). Cf. p. 84, 22, et seq. **agresti luxuria**: abstract for concrete. **6. decoctoribus**: the Romans viewed extravagance in living, and resulting bankruptcy, with the sternest disapproval. **vadimonia deserere**: 'to forsake their legal obligations; i. e.

having given security to appear in court when summoned, they preferred to run away and let judgment go against them by default, which in this case would be satisfied by the confiscation and sale of any property they might leave behind. **7. quibus si**: = *hi, si eis.*

9. edictum praetoris: particularly that part in which the penalties for forsaking one's legal obligations were given. Each praetor, on entering upon the duties of his office, issued a 'proclamation' of the principles and penalties in accordance with which — apart from the established rules of the Civil Law — he purposed to administer justice during his term. Cf. p. 60. **concident**: 'they will fall powerless,' very like our colloquial expression, "fall all in a heap." **Hos**: 'these' conspirators who dare yet to remain in the city; in sharp contrast with the wretches just characterized.

11. unguentis: fragrant oils, which were thoroughly rubbed into the skin after a bath. **12. purpura**: not on the *toga*, but on the under-garment, the *tunica*, on which senators and knights were allowed to have one or two perpendicular brilliant red stripes. The stripe distinguishing the senator was broad (*latus clavus*); those of the knight were narrow (*angustus clavus*), a stripe running down from each shoulder on the front, and probably also on the back, of the tunic. **milites**: 'as soldiers;' most editions read *suos milites*, 'his own force,' i. e. 'his body-guard.' **eduxisset**: B. 296, 1, *a*; A. 331, *f*, R.; H. 499, 2. **13. qui si**: 'but if they.'

17. neque tamen: trans. as if *et tamen non;* their audacious confidence implies that there must be behind them some secret and dangerous force. **18. Apulia**, et seq.: cf. p. 64, 32, et seq., and Sall. Cat. XXVII. 1: *Septimium quendam Camertem in agrum Picenum, C. Iulium in Apuliam* (*Catilina*) *dimisit, praeterea alium alio, quem ubique opportunum sibi fore credebat.* **19. Gallicum** [agrum]: cf. l. 2 above, and N. **20. urbanas**: = *in urbe.* **caedis**: trans. with 'for.' **21. superioris noctis**: cf. p. 64, 13, et seq. If the chronology given on p. 45 is correct (cf. p. 81, 10, and N.), the expression here is inexact, as two nights had passed since the meeting at Laeca's. **24. Ne**: here *not* negative.

IV. 28. nisi si: 'unless perhaps,' *nisi* having an adverbial force. B. 306, 5; A. 315, *a*, 2; H. 507, 3, N. 4. **29. simi-**

lis: acc.; '(men) like Catiline.' **32. miserum**: 'wretchedly,' 'in wretchedness.' B. 239; A. 191; H. 443. **33. via**: B. 218, 9; A. 258, *g*; H. 420, 1, 3). The report was circulated that Catiline was going to Marseilles, into exile. **34. volent**: fut., where our idiom requires the pres.

Page 79. 1. rem publicam: why acc.? **sentinam**: cf. p. 66, 10–12, and N. **2. exhausto**: carries out the idea of *sentinam*. **5. Italia**: B. 228, 1, *b*; A. 258, *f*, 2; H. 425, 2. **7. circumscriptor**: 'confidence-man,' who makes it his business to defraud the inexperienced, particularly the young. **10. perditus**: here a subst., 'reprobate.'

15. iuventutis illecebra: cf. p. 66, 26, and N., and Cic. *pro Caelio*, V. 12, et seq. **17. fructum**: 'gratification.' **18. impellendo, adiuvando**: almost = *impellens, adiuvans*. **21. non modo**: i. e. *non modo non fuit*; cf. p. 71, 21, and N.

V. 25. Atque . . . possitis: introductory purpose clause, loosely connected with the main idea. B. 282, 4; A. 317, 3, *c*; H. 499, 2, N. **diversa . . . ratione**: 'different pursuits in an altogether different sphere (of life).' **26. ludo gladiatorio**: in the gladiatorial schools, or barracks, captives, slaves, and condemned malefactors forced to serve as gladiators, received a merciless training. **27. audacior**: i. e. than his fellows. **intimum**: 'bosom-friend,' while *sodalis* (l. 29) is a 'fraternity friend,' or 'society brother,' as we say, — one bound by the same vows to mutual obligations. **28. levior, nequior**: i. e. than the average. Actors in Rome were generally slaves or freedmen, their occupation being considered degrading. **21. frigore . . . perferendis**: the gerundive construction used as abl. of specification instead of dat. with *adsuefactus* (= 'hardened'). **32. cum**: 'although.' **33. instrumenta virtutis**: i. e. the mental qualities and physical traits which render the practice of virtue possible.

Page 80. 1. Hunc, et seq.: stands as a climax to p. 79, 1–3. **sui**: instead of *eius*. Cf. B. 244, II., 4; A. 196, *c*. **4. laudem consulatus mei**: cf. p. 74, 1–4. **5. mediocres**: i. e. *quae modum* ('limit') *quendam habeant*. **lubidines, audaciae**: 'lust for pleasures,' 'deeds of boldness.' B. 55, 4, *c*; A. 75, *c*; H. 130, 2. **humanae**: 'consistent with human nature.'

8. fortunas: refers particularly to landed property. **res**: i. e. *res familiaris*, 'means,' 'property,' as contrasted with *fides*, 'credit.' **9. nuper**: after Catiline's last candidacy for the consulship, the failure of which had frustrated their plans and hopes, and caused their creditors to become impatient. Cf. p. 66, 34, and N. **11. alea**: gambling was one of the most prevalent and pernicious vices of Roman life. **comissationes**: a Roman banquet was followed by a drinking-bout. This was sometimes held in a different place from that in which the dinner was served, and the merry revellers would proceed thither through the streets with torches and music.

13. inertes: referring to their dislike of exertion. **15. dormientis**: with the force of an adjective, 'the sleepy.' **mihi**: cf. p. 77, 29, and N. **17. sertis**: of ivy or myrtle, entwined with roses or other flowers; worn not only because agreeable, but also because such 'garlands' were thought to ward off or delay intoxication. **unguentis**: see N. to p. 78, 11. **obliti**: not *oblītī*.

20. Quibus: B. 251, 6; A. 201, *e*; H. 453. **24. breve nescio quod**: i. e. *breve quoddam*. B. 253, 6; A. 334, *e*; H. 455, 2. **25. propagarit rei publicae**: 'it will have secured to the state the continuance of,' i. e. 'it will have prolonged the existence of the state for;' the ordinary form of expression would have been, *non in breve nescio quod tempus, sed in multa saecula propagarit rem publicam*. **28. unius**: i. e. of Pompey, who was now at the zenith of his fame, having finished the wars with Sertorius, with the Pirates, and with Mithridates. Cf. p. 127, 13–15, and notes. **29. intus . . . hostis**: climax, anaphora, asyndeton, as also in *Cum . . . est*.

32. suscipio inimicitias: cf. p. 70, 21, and N. **34. quacumque ratione**: sc. *potero*, or *sanari poterunt*.

Page 81. **3. permanent**: taken literally with *urbe*, figuratively with *mente*, as when we say, "He missed his train and his opportunity;" trans. by two verbs.

VI. 4. At: often used to introduce an objection which the speaker wishes to meet. Chapters VI. and VII. are a kind of *refutatio* (cf. p. 15). **5. Quod**: cf. p. 73, 13, and N. **verbo**: 'by a word (merely)' 'by a (single) word.' **7. Homo**: cf. p. 76, 16, and N.; notice the irony of the sentence, which sounds as if the orator were quoting or parodying a statement of one of Catiline's defenders. **9. paruit, ivit**: the rhetorical effect is heightened by the asyndeton. B. 346; A. 346, *c*; H. 636, I. 1.

10. hesterno die: if the attempt on Cicero's life was made on the morning of Nov. 7, and this speech was delivered on Nov. 9, *hesterno die* can be taken only with the principal clause, *senatum . . . convocavi*, not with *cum . . . interfectus essem*. To many this interpretation has seemed somewhat forced; and it has also been thought strange that the orator was able to get word of the proposed murder to so many friends in the brief interval between the midnight gathering at Laeca's and daybreak of the following morning (see p. 65, 10, and N.). On the supposition that *hesterno die* is to be taken with *cum . . . interfectus essem*, two explanations have been offered. The first is, that the First Oration was delivered on the 7th of November, and the Second on the 8th. Much may be said in favor of this view from other evidence, and until recently it has been held by a good many scholars. The other explanation, proposed by Mommsen (Hermes, Vol. I., p. 435), is, that while Cornelius and Vargunteius offered and expected to kill the consul on the morning after the meeting, it was so late when the assembly at Laeca's broke up that they were obliged to postpone their action for twenty-four hours. To this the reply may be made, that Cicero's own words seem decisive for the morning after the meeting, and that the two men assigned to the deed, knowing Catiline's impatience (p. 65, 2, 3), would no doubt have excused themselves, if the meeting continued too long, in order to make the attempt as they had promised. On the whole, — though there are many points of obscurity and difficulty, — the chronology given on p. 45 seems best to represent the course of events, and is that accepted by the majority of scholars; cf. Stern, "Catilina," pp. 166–174; but particularly John in "Philologus" for 1888 (Vol. XLVI., p. 650, et seq.). The clause *cum . . . interfectus essem* may be taken as parenthetical, and unemphatic.

11. aedem Iovis Statoris: see p. 61, 6, and N. **13. Quo . . . reliquerunt**: cf. p. 67, 28, et seq. **14. ita, ut**: in our idiom, 'as;' here = 'merely as.'

20. quaesivi, et seq.: see Or. I., chap. IV. **21. necne**: B. 300, 4, *a*; A. 211, *a*; H. 529, 3, 2). **22. conscientia**: 'by his guilty knowledge,' 'by his sense of guilt.' **24. in proximam** [noctem]: the night of Nov. 7. We are not told what Catiline's plans for that night (cf. p. 61, 10) were; but probably if the attempt on Cicero's life had been successful, it would have been immediately followed by similar deeds of violence already planned and only awaiting a favorable opportunity. **25. ratio totius belli**: 'the plan of the entire campaign.'

26. quaesivi: cf. p. 65, 12–25; p. 71, 5–15. **27. pararet**: i. e. *proficisci.* **secures, fasces**: ensigns of magisterial authority, the assumption of which by Catiline was unlawful, even though he had been entitled to the use of them when a praetor; *cum fascibus atque aliis imperi insignibus in castra ad Manlium contendit* (Sall. Cat. XXXVI. 1). **28. aquilam, sacrarium**: see p. 71, 8–10, and notes. **30. eiciebam**: why not *eieci?* **32. credo**: cf. p. 63, 4, and N. **in agro Faesulano**: cf. p. 62, 32, and N. **33. suo**: with emphasis; 'on *his own* account.'

Page 82. 2. haec castra: not *illa castra*, as in the preceding clause, because contrasted with the more distant Massilia.

VII. 3. condicionem: here 'lot,' 'task,' 'vocation,' referring to the peculiar difficulties surrounding the office of consul. **6. debilitatus**: 'crippled.' **12. vi et minis**: 'by threats of violence;' hendiadys. **15. tyrannum**: cf. p. 73, 23, and N.

16. Est mihi: see IDIOMS, and N. to p. 70, 21. **falsae**: 'misdirected,' as based upon ungrounded charges. **18. depellatur**: cf. p. 70, 23. **20. non est iturus**: 'he does not intend to go;' more forcible than *non ibit.* **24. illud**: in our idiom 'this,' as referring to what follows. B. 246, 2; A. 102, *b*; H. 450, 3.

29. Quamquam: 'And yet.' **31. tam misericors**: Catiline's true friends ought to rejoice to hear that he has gone to Marseilles and avoided war with the state, thus to escape sure destruction; but in fact those who are posing as his friends are merely his associates in crime, who would be grievously disappointed if he did not go to Faesulae; for that would mean the frustrating of all their evil plans and hopes. **33. me**: B. 183; A. 240, *d*, N. 2; H. 381, and p. 152, foot-note 4. **34. latrocinantem**: i. e. 'in the midst of brigandage.'

Page 83. 1. Nunc: 'But as it is.' **2. nisi quod**: introduces an exception; 'except that.' H. 555, III. 1. **3. vivis nobis**: cf. p. 76, 19, and N. **4. quam queramur**: we certainly have no reason to complain that he has left us, no matter with what aim in view. B. 284, 4; A. 332, *b*; H. 502, 2.

VIII. 5. sed: the orator passes from Catiline's case to that of his associates. **7. quod**: cf. p. 66, 10, and N. **murus**: why not *paries?* cf. p. 69, 9–13. **8. de eis**: in contrast with the absent Catiline. **qui dissimulant**: i. e. *se hostes esse*. **10. ulcisci**: here = *punire*, *persequi*. **11. sanare sibi ipsos**: 'to restore (them) to themselves,' i. e. 'to restore them to their right minds;' like our colloquial phrase, 'to bring him to his senses.'

13. ex . . . comparentur: the following characterizations (cf. p. 43) seem to have been introduced for two reasons: to disabuse the people of any ungrounded apprehensions regarding the extent and strength of the conspiracy, and to overawe the conspirators themselves by revealing an intimate acquaintance with the character and condition of their constituency.

17. in: '(although) in.' **18. possessiones**: particularly lands and buildings. **19. dissolvi**: = 'to clear themselves,' by selling out and paying up their indebtedness. **20. species**: 'outward appearance.' **voluntas, causa**: 'inclination' or 'intentions,' 'attitude' toward the government. **21. Tu**, etc.: addressed to an imaginary representative of this class, 'You — to be abundantly supplied . . . and (yet) to hesitate . . .' Cf. p. 70, 14, and N. **22. argento**: 'with silver ware,' 'with plate,' chased and ornamented with artistic designs. Much beautiful silver ware of the Roman period has been discovered. **familia**: 'establishment,' comprising slaves and freedmen, particularly the former.

24. adquirere ad fidem: i. e. by the cancellation of indebtedness, on the principle that a man's credit is better if he have even a small property free from debt than if he have a great estate mortgaged to nearly or quite its full value. **26. sacrosanctas**: i. e. exempt from the general destruction. **tabulas novas**: 'new accounts,' following the repudiation of all outstanding debts. This was an important part of Catiline's program: *Tum Catilina polliceri tabulas novas, proscriptionem locupletium, magistratus, sacerdotia, rapinas, alia omnia, quae bellum atque lubido victorum fert* (Sall. Cat. XXI. 2).

27. meo beneficio: = 'thanks to me.' **28. auctionariae**: '(those) of the auctioneers;' the consul will interfere, and will clear off these debts by confiscating the mortgaged property and selling it at auction. It seems that Cicero when consul actually made an attempt to improve the general credit by drastic measures of some sort; see Cic. de Off. II. XXIV. 84; cf. pro Sulla, XX. 56. **30. salvi**: financially 'sound.' **32. fructibus praediorum**: 'by the income of their estates;' as this was less than the interest they had to pay, the contest between income and outgo was a losing one. **his — uteremur**: 'we should find them' (or 'in them'). **33. minime**: as compared with the following classes.

Page 84. IX. **3. premuntur aere alieno**: i. e. are hopelessly in debt, not having property to offset their indebtedness, and thus being worse off than those in the first class. **5. rerum**: B. 212, 2; 218, 1, *a*; A. 223, *a*; H. 410, V. 3. **honores**: 'the public offices.' **6. perturbata**: sc. *eā*. **7. unum et idem**: much stronger than *idem* alone. **scilicet**: 'that is to say,' 'as I hardly need say.' **8. quod reliquis omnibus**: sc. *praecipiendum videtur.*

9. primum: adj. or adv.? **me . . . laturos**: gives the ground for *ut desperent;* '(from the thought) that I,' etc. **11. animos**: 'spirit.' **15. praesentis**: 'with immediate presence.' Cf. p. 88, 28. **16. Quod si — adepti sint**: 'But supposing they have once obtained.' **21. fugitivo alicui**: 'to some runaway (slave);' an allusion not only to the fact of human experience that if free reign be given to violence the most violent and lawless will prevail, but also to the terrible experiences of the wars with Spartacus and the slaves. Cf. p. 72, 16, and N. **21. concedi**: see IDIOMS.

22. Tertium genus: cf. p. 43, and Sall. Cat. XVI. 4: *Plerique Sullani milites, largius suo usi, rapinarum et victoriae veteris memores, civile bellum exoptabant.* **25. eis coloniis**: Sulla rewarded 120,000 of his troops (so Appian, Bel. Civ. I. 104) with lands, dispossessing the previous owners. A large number of these 'colonies' were planted in Etruria, the inhabitants of which had been staunch supporters of the party of Marius. **universas**: 'on the whole,' 'in general;' the orator softens his sweeping statement in order not to give offence.

29. beati: 'well off,' 'well-to-do.' To a soldier who had been serving for about six cents a day the possession of even a small landed property naturally seemed great wealth. **30. apparatis**: 'splendid,' in the decoration and furniture of the dining-room, as well as in the table service and viands. **31. in tantum aes**: see IDIOMS under *aes*. **salvi**: as p. 83, 30.

33. agrestis: in many cases no doubt the previous possessors of the farms taken by Sulla's soldiers; cf. Sall. Cat. XXVIII. 4: *Interea Manlius in Etruria plebem sollicitare, egestate simul ac dolore iniuriae novarum rerum cupidam, quod Sullae dominatione agros bonaque omnia amiserat.*

Page 85. **1. Quos,** etc.: 'Now I put both of these classes in the same category.' **2. eos hoc**: see p. 361. B. 178, *d*; A. 238, *b*; H. 374, 2, and 371, II. **4. illorum temporum**: of the dictatorship and proscriptions of Sulla. **5. non modo**: cf. p. 71, 21, and N. **6. videantur**: for trans. cf. p. 67, 17, and N.

X. 8. qui: i. e. *eorum qui.* **premuntur**: i. e. *aere alieno;* cf. p. 84, 3, and N. **9. emergunt**: 'get their heads above water,' as we say. **11. iudiciis**: by *vadimoniis* (cf. p. 78, 6 and N.), *iudiciis*, and *proscriptione bonorum*, the three steps in an action for debt are indicated: (*a*) The summons, in response to which the debtor must give 'bail' to present himself at the specified time for trial. (*b*) The 'trial,' followed by a sentence. (*c*) The execution, which comprised a taking possession of the property and the sale of it at auction, in case the judgment was not satisfied in full within a certain fixed period. **16. non modo civitas**: i. e. *non sentiat.* **20. soli**: 'by themselves.'

24. pereant: '(I pray) they may perish.' **25. carcer**: see N. to p. 88, 7.

26. est: sc. *postremum*, in the sense of both 'last' and 'lowest.' **27. proprium Catilinae . . . sinu**: = 'Catiline's own, of his special choice, — no, rather his dearest bosom friends.' **29. imberbis**: i. e. with smooth, womanish faces. **30. bene barbatos**: a sign of dissolute life; for in this period it was not customary to let the beard grow except in times of mourning. **manicatis . . . tunicis**: at this time it was considered in good taste to wear the tunic sleeveless and extending just below the knees; sleeved tunics were looked upon as a badge of effeminacy. **31. velis**: 'with sails,' spoken contemptuously of the breadth of the fop's toga. **33. gregibus**: scornfully, 'gangs.'

Page 86. **1. neque**: 'and not (only).' **2. spargere venena**: i. e. in wine or other drinks. **6. mulierculas**: dim. here to express contempt.

XI. **16. praesidia**: 'garrisons' of troops stationed in the cities for defence, as distinguished from *exercitus*, the 'hosts' under training in the field.

18. confecto et saucio: cf. p. 76, 22 et seq. **20. naufragorum**: see N. to p. 73, 31. **eiectam**: carrying out the idea of *naufragorum*, 'stranded.' **21. coloniarum, municipiorum:** partitive gen., dividing the concept *urbes*, both of these classes of towns possessing fortifications. **22. respondebunt**: in ordinary prose *pares erunt.* **23. tumulis silvestribus**: the natural resort of brigands. **24. inopia, egestate**: Catiline had two legions, but according to Sallust (Cat. LVI. 3) only about one-fourth of his men were properly armed.

29. causas: the parties and the principles. **30. contendere**: here = *conferre.* **31. intellegere possumus**: instead of *intellegamus.* **Ex hac parte**: 'on this side.' **34. pietas**: i. e. *erga patriam.*

Page 87. **1. honestas**: *not* 'honesty.' **2. aequitas . . . prudentia**: the four so-called cardinal virtues of Plato and the Stoics were 'justice' (δικαιοσύνη, = *iustitia*, represented here by *aequitas*), 'self-mastery' (σωφροσύνη, = *temperantia*), 'courage' (ἀνδρεία, = *fortitudo*), and 'wisdom' (φρόνησις, = *prudentia*). **3. omnes**: in our idiom 'all (other).' **5. bona ratio**: in a political sense, 'an upright principle;' conservatism against anarchy. **6. cum omnium rerum desperatione**: = 'with utter despair.'

CONCLUSION. XII., XIII.

XII. **12. dixi**: omitted by some editors, because the speech as it now stands contains no other passage corresponding with this. **13. mihi — consultum atque provisum est**: = 'on me rests the responsibility, which has been fully met, of seeing to it that,' etc. **urbi**, etc.: see IDIOMS. **14. sine ullo tumultu**: cf. p. 65, 31, and N. **16. hac nocturna excursione**: see N. to p. 77, 28. **17. Gladiatores**: a particular source of fear to the Romans after the war with Spartacus. In this instance the Senate had made special provision for keeping the gladiators under control; see Sall. Cat. XXX. 7.

19. quamquam . . . patriciorum: a side-thrust at Catiline's adherents among the aristocracy. **20. Q. Metellus**, et seq.: see p. 78, 1–4, and notes. **22. hominem**: cf. p. 76, 16, and N.

25. vocari: i. e. *per praecones* (cf. p. 59); apparently a meeting of the Senate followed soon after the close of this speech.

28. hostes: see N. to p. 108, 3. **30. hoc exspectavit**: 'it has held this in view.' **31. Quod reliquum**: see IDIOMS.

Page 88. 1. portis: in our idiom, 'at the gates.' **2. qui**: 'if any one.' **3. cuius**: almost = *si illius*. **7. carcerem**: now known as the Mamertine Prison; properly called 'an avenger,' because never used as a place of confinement for life sentences, but only for the detention of prisoners who gave no bail pending trial, or for the execution of those condemned. In the lower Dungeon, or *Tullianum*, many notable men perished; among them Jugurtha, and the Gallic general Vercingetorix. See illustration on p. 115, and N. to p. 115, 15.

XIII. 10. nullo tumultu: cf. p. 65, 31, and N. **13. togato**: i. e. as a civil magistrate; in war the *sagum* for the soldier and the *paludamentum* for the commander took the place of the *toga*. Cicero prided himself on the fact that his victory over Catiline was won without an appeal to the military. **20. neque — -que**: rare for *neque — et*; 'on the one hand not — and on the other hand.'

24. significationibus: explained p. 97, 15, et seq. **26. ut quondam**: as at the battle of Lake Regillus, the legend of which is given, in a spirited form, in Macaulay's "Lays of Ancient Rome." **28. suo numine**: 'with their divine will.'

THE THIRD ORATION AGAINST CATILINE.

Page 89. IN L. CATILINAM: see N. on p. 209. HABITA AD POPULUM: see N. on p. 227.

INTRODUCTION. I. to p. 90, 3.

I. 1. Quirites: see N. to p. 76, 1. For the date and circumstances of delivery, and an outline of the matter, see pp. 39, 40, 43, 45. **3. imperi**: B. 25, 2; A. 40, *b*; H. 51, 5. **6. flamma atque ferro**: cf. p. 76, 3. Which did Cicero consider worse, *flamma* or *ferrum?* B. 341, 1, *c*; A. 156, *a* (*atque*): H. 554, I., 2. **7. ex faucibus fati**: like our expression, 'from the jaws of death.' **8. restitutam videtis**: sc. *esse*. The news of the arrest at the Mulvian bridge had spread like wildfire, so that many already knew something at least of what the orator was about to say to them.

11. nascendi condicio: '(our) lot at birth,' the position or surroundings into which we are born. **13. illum**: the belief in the deification of Romulus, under the name Quirinus, was kept alive by an annual festival, the Quirinalia. This was held on the 17th of February, in commemoration of the day on which he was said to have been taken up into heaven. **14. benevolentia famaque**: 'with affection and praise.' **17. delubris**: the lesser sanctuaries. **20. rettudimus**: 'we have struck back.' **21. Quae quoniam**: = 'And since all this.' **22. per me**: '(and that too) through my agency.' A. 246, *b*; H. 415, I., 1, N. 1.

Page 90. 1. quanta: = *quantae res*. **3. exspectatis**: the people had a right to look to the consul for an official report.

DISCUSSION. I. (p. 90, 4) –X.

4. ut: here 'ever since.' **paucis ante diebus**: in fact almost four weeks before; for Catiline left Rome on the night of Nov. 8 (cf. p. 45). The orator makes as little as possible of the interval, in order not to direct attention to the fact that during so long a time nothing was accomplished in the way of checking the conspiracy. **erupit**: cf. p. 76, 5–6. **5. sceleris sui socios**: their nefarious plans for the destruction of the city are given by Sallust, Cat. XLIII.

II. 9. eiciebam: why impf.? **10. non . . . invidiam**: cf. p. 71, 4, et seq., and N. to p. 76, 4. **12. exterminari**: *not* . . . 'exterminated.' **13. eos . . . putabam**: cf. p. 87, 26, et seq. **20. fidem faceret**: see IDIOMS. **rem ita comprehenderem**: 'I might get the matter so in my grasp;' the consul bent all his energies toward securing tangible and convicting evidence.

23. ut comperi: through Quintus Fabius Sanga; see pp. 39, 40. **24. tumultus**: when applied to political matters, used only of disturbances in Italy and Cisalpine Gaul; cf. Cicero's explanation (Phil. VIII. i. 3): *Quid est enim aliud tumultus nisi perturbatio tanta, ut maior timor oriatur? . . . Itaque maiores nostri tumultum Italicum, quod erat domesticus* (hence liable to cause a panic on account of its nearness), *tumultum Gallicum, quod erat Italiae finitimus, praeterea nullum nominabant.*

25. eodem itinere: their road lay through Etruria. **26. ad**: '(addressed) to.' **28. facultatem oblatam**: see IDIOMS.

33. hesterno die: Dec. 2. **L. Flaccum**: see Vocab. under *Flaccum* (3). **34. amantissimos**: see IDIOMS.

Page 91. 1. rem: 'the plan' for intercepting the deputies of the Allobroges. **placeret**: see IDIOMS. **2. qui . . . sentirent**: in our idiom, 'being men of sound and excellent political sentiments in all respects;' subj. on account of the causal force of *qui*. **5. pontem Mulvium**: the foundations at least still remain in the *Ponte Molle*, two Roman miles north of Rome; see Illustration facing p. 90. Across this bridge ran the *Via Flaminia*, one of the most important of the roads leading to the north of Italy; and here Constantine defeated Maxentius in the memorable battle of 312 A. D.

9. ex praefectura Reatina: Cicero was patron of Reate, i. e. he was the legal representative of the inhabitants of Reate at Rome; he could therefore count on their loyalty to him. **10. in re publica**: i. e. 'for public business.'

12. tertia fere vigilia exacta: about 3 A. M.; the night was divided up into four watches of equal length. See IDIOMS.

13. magno comitatu: B. 222, 1; A. 248, *a*, N.; H. 419, III., 1, 1). **15. Res praetoribus . . . solis**: the soldiers with the praetors did not know for what purpose they had been sent out; and the deputies of the Allobroges, though they no doubt understood in a general way that they would be asked to give up the documents received from the conspirators, had apparently not been informed when or how the demand would be made upon them, so that the attack at first surprised them. Cf. Sall. Cat. XLV.

III. **17. Tum interventu,** et seq.: i. e. the praetors explained that they represented the consul, to whom the documents were to be delivered. Sallust says that the Gauls, as soon as they understood matters, placed themselves in charge of the praetors; but that Volturcius made a valiant resistance until he saw that he was deserted by the rest, whereupon he surrendered, begging that his life be spared. **19. integris signis**: 'with the seals unbroken;' see p. 55. **ipsi**: the Gallic deputies and Volturcius. **20. cum iam dilucesceret**: early in the morning of Dec. 3.

23. vocavi: as chief executive the consul had the right to summon citizens into his presence, and even to have them brought by force if they offered resistance. In this case the deputies and the conspirators were no doubt kept at the orator's house, which stood on the northwest slope of the Palatine hill, until they were taken before the Senate; cf. Plan facing p. 76. **25. credo**: scornful, alluding to the 'sleepiness' of Lentulus (see p. 96, 10); the letter (see p. 94, 8–11), in the preparation of which he is represented as having "burned the midnight oil," contains less than forty words! **26. vigilarat**: 'he had been up late.'

27. viris: many of them had no doubt been sent for by the consul himself, to be his witnesses and advisers. **28. frequentes**: 'in great numbers.' **29. quam deferri**: *quam deferrem* or *quam deferrentur* might have been expected. Cf. A. 336, *c*, N. 2. **30. nihil**: i. e. nothing incriminating. **temere**: 'rashly,' without sufficient reason. **31. esse facturum, ut — deferrem**: periphrasis, more emphatic than the simple *delaturum esse;* with *negavi* (= *dixi non*), 'I said that in a matter fraught with danger to the state I could not but lay the facts unprejudiced before the state's council.' Cf. B. 297, 1; A. 332, *e*; H. 498, II., N. 2. **33. si**: = *etiam si*, 'even if.'

Page 92. 3. **frequentem**: 'with full attendance.' The Senate met in the Temple of Concord, in the Forum; see Plan facing p. 76. **coegi**: the term regularly used of convening the Senate. 6. **quid**; see IDIOMS.

IV. 8. **Introduxi**: i. e. before the Senate. **fidem publicam dedi**: 'I gave him a pledge in the name of the state,' i. e. a pledge of pardon if he would turn state's evidence; followed by *iussu senatus* because the Senate alone had authority to grant or promise amnesty. 12. **ad**: as p. 90, 26. **ut**: '(to the effect) that.'

14. **id**: i. e. *ut id faceret.* **ex**: in our idiom, 'in.' 15. **omnibus partibus**: according to Sallust (Cat. XLIII. 2) the city was to be fired in twelve places at once, under the direction of Statilius and Gabinius; but Plutarch (Cic. XVIII.) says in a hundred places. **quem . . . erat**: parenthetical explanation of the speaker; hence with the indic. Cf. p. 64, 34. 16. **caedem infinitam**: cf. Plut. Cic. XVIII.: 'There was nothing small or mean about the designs of Lentulus; for he had resolved to kill the entire Senate, and as many of the other citizens as he could.' 17. **ille**: Catiline.

21. **dixerunt**: followed by indirect discourse in two degrees of subordination, — as a wheel within a wheel, — thus: (1) by *esse praescriptum*, which in turn is followed by *pedestres . . . defuturas* in indir. disc. subordinate to itself; (2) by *Lentulum . . . confirmasse*, similarly followed by *se . . . fuisse;* (3) by *eundem dixisse*, to which *annum . . . vicesimus* is subordinate. The reflexive in each case refers to the chief agent or subject of the clause to which its own clause is subordinate; thus *sibi* (l. 21) refers to *Galli* (l. 19), but *sibi* (l. 23) to *his et L. Cassio* (l. 21).

24. **ex fatis Sibyllinis**: = 'from the Sibylline prophecies.' The original Sibylline Books, purchased by King Tarquin, perished when the Temple of Jupiter on the Capitoline hill was burned, in 83 B. C. After that a new collection of Sibylline prophecies was made with great care at the different places where oracles were given through sibyls, and placed in the new Temple (cf. N. to l. 30). Here they were guarded by a special college of priests, the Quindecimviri, who consulted them, however, only upon request of the Senate. In addition to these, there appear to have been smaller private collections, of a simi-

lar character; and to one of these latter, in the possession of some family of the Cornelian gens, Lentulus probably referred.

27. necesse: see IDIOMS. **28. fatalem annum**: really no more 'decreed by fate' than that year in the famous prophecy of Mother Shipton, —

> "The world unto an end shall come
> In eighteen hundred and eighty-one."

30. virginum: for *virginum Vestalium*. The trial of a Vestal on the charge of breaking her vows was considered in a high degree portentous, even though her innocence might be proved and the trial followed by acquittal. **Capitoli incensionem**: in 83 B. C.; immediately afterwards Sulla commenced to rebuild the temple on a much grander scale, but the edifice was not completed till some years later, by Quintus Lutatius Catulus. According to Sallust, the soothsayers were quoted as affirming that the twentieth year after the burning of the Capitol would be one of bloody civil war.

33. Saturnalibus: Dec. 19, the chief day of the festival; a favorable time for a bold stroke, on account of the cessation of business and the merriment and freedom of restraint characteristic of the festival of Saturn, during which the Romans "kept open house" to friends and clients. **34. nimium longum**: 'too far off,' 'too remote (a date).'

Page 93. V. 1. ne longum: see IDIOMS. **tabellas**: containing the *litterae* of p. 92, 19. **2. datae**: sc. *esse*. Cf. B. 332, *c*; 328, 2; A. 271, *c*; H. 536, 2, 1), N. **3. cognovit**: 'he acknowledged (it)' as his own. For the seal, the thread, and other matters connected with the form of the letters, see pp. 54–57. Cicero had done well to leave the letters untouched until they could be opened in the presence of the Senate. **7. sibi — recepissent**: 'had undertaken for him,' i. e. had promised him.

8. aliquid: see IDIOMS. Kind of acc.? **tamen**: 'nevertheless,' though appearances were all against him. **quae**: why neuter? B. 250, 2; A. 198, *a*; H. 445, 3, N. 1. **10. bonorum ferramentorum studiosum**: 'a fancier of good tools;' avoiding the use of *telorum* and implying that he was a collector, a *connoisseur*, of steel implements in general. **11. conscientia**: as p. 81, 22.

14. in eandem sententiam: i. e. *scriptae*. See IDIOMS.

18. avi tui: see Vocab. under *Lentulus* (1). It was customary to place upon seals the likenesses of distinguished ancestors. **20. etiam muta**: 'even though speechless;' with *revocare*, oxymoron. **eadem ratione**: 'of the same tenor,' 'to the same effect.' **21. Si**: 'In case.' **23. negavit**: 'said, No,' i. e. that he did not care to say anything.

24. exposito atque edito: in our court phrase, 'given and taken down,' i. e. taken down in writing by the senators who were keeping the record. **25. quid,** etc.: see IDIOMS. **27. per quem**: i. e. *a quo perducti*, referring to Umbrenus. **30. scelere demens**: i. e. *conscientia sceleris demens factus*. **33. exercitatio**: 'readiness.' Of the oratory of this Lentulus Cicero elsewhere says (Brut. LXVI. 235): 'His slowness of thought and delivery was lost sight of by reason of the impressiveness of his person, his gesticulation alike skilful and full of grace, and the sweetness and power of his voice.'

Page 94. 1. superabat: 'endeavored to surpass.' B. 260, 3; A. 277, *c*; H. 469, II., I.

7. sine nomine: without address or signature, we should say. **sed ita**: 'but as follows,' the contents indicating the personality of sender and receiver. The same letter is thus given by Sallust (Cat. XLIV. 5; text of Eussner):

Qui sim, ex eo, quem ad te misi, cognosces. Fac cogites, in quanta calamitate sis, et memineris te virum esse. Consideres, quid tuae rationes postulent. Auxilium petas ab omnibus, etiam ab infimis.

This version of the letter differs from that given by Cicero only in greater refinement of expression. The latter shows traces of the haste in which the letter was no doubt written, and may be accepted as unquestionably the original form.

11. infimorum: = *servorum*; cf. p. 92, 12, and N. to p. 72, 16.

12. cum primo: 'although at first.' **13. ex eis**: B. 201, I, *a*; A. 216, *c*; H. 397, 3, N. 3.

15. certissima: force of the superlative? Cf. *certiora* in l. 18.

VI. 22. expositis atque editis: cf. p. 93, 24, and N. Why is *Indiciis* pl.? **23. de summa re publica**: i. e. *de salute rei publicae*. **24. Dictae . . . sententiae**: on the method of procedure, see N. to p. 64, 28. **a principibus**: 'by the leaders' of the Senate, comprising the consuls-elect, who voted first; after them the ex-consuls voted.

29. gratiae: see p. 362. **verbis**: see IDIOMS. **30. quod**: 'because (as they said).' B. 285; 286, 1; A. 341, *d*; H. 516, II. **virtute**: 'by my resolution.' **32. opera**: we say 'services.' **34. collegae meo**: in the consulship; i. e. Gaius Antonius Hybrida, who had been a supporter of Catiline until Cicero won him over; cf. p. 38.

Page 95. 1. eos . . . removisset: i. e. he had refused to have anything more to do with them, either as a public officer or as an individual.

3. cum . . . abdicasset: no action could be brought against a Roman magistrate so long as he remained in office, his person and office being considered inviolable (*sacrosanctus*). **4. in custodiam**: see N. to p. 69, 5. **7. L. Cassium**: Cassius, Furius, Annius Chilo, and Umbrenus escaped; Ceparius had left the city, but was arrested and brought back. **11. colonis**: see N. to p. 84, 25. **18. novem hominum**: of these only five actually suffered the penalty imposed; see N. to p. 115, 15.

21. supplicatio: here refers to a period of public thanksgiving, in this case probably of five days' duration. The chief religious observance on such occasions was the banquet for the gods (*lectisternium*). Couches, on which images of the gods reclined, were placed in front of the temples and shrines, and offerings of food and wine were set before them.

22. meo nomine: = *honoris mei causa*, 'in my honor.' **quod**: '(an experience) which.' **23. primum**: 'for the first time.' **togato**: cf. p. 88, 13, and N.; in previous cases a thanksgiving had been appointed only in recognition of military successes. **24. quod**: cf. p. 94, 30, and N. **25. Italiam bello**: rhetorical exaggeration. **Quae si**: 'And if this.' **26. hoc interest**: 'there is this difference;' more forcible than *hoc interesse videatur*, the indic. implying that the difference certainly exists, whether the comparison be made or not. **27. ceterae bene gesta**: i. e. *ceterae supplicationes bene gesta re publica constitutae sunt.*

29. factum atque transactum est: originally a legal formula. **33. magistratu se abdicavit**: of course under compulsion; but the form of voluntary resignation must be kept up (cf. l. 4, above). Plutarch says (Cic. XIX.): 'Lentulus, having been convicted, resigned his office (for he happened to be praetor), and laying aside his purple-bordered toga in the Senate, assumed a garb in keeping with his misfortune.' The last clause may mean that he put on the white toga of the ordinary citizen (see N. to p. 77, 30), but more likely that he secured one of dark color, as the Romans were wont to do, as a sign of mourning in times of trouble. **ut,** et seq.: 'that we might be free from religious scruple, . . . though such scruples had not prevented Gaius Marius from,' etc.; referring to the sacredness of the person of a magistrate. Marius, however, was only indirectly responsible for the death of Glaucia, who was pelted to death by a mob.

Page 96. **1. nihil**: see IDIOMS.

VII. 10. somnum, adipes: cf. N. to p. 91, 25. Shakespeare (following a hint of Plutarch's) represents Caesar as saying:

> "Let me have men about me that are fat,
> Sleek-headed men, and such as sleep o' nights:
> Yond' Cassius has a lean and hungry look;
> He thinks too much: such men are dangerous."

11. C. Cethegi furiosam temeritatem: according to Sallust (Cat. XLIII. 3), 'Cethegus kept making complaint about the inactivity of his associates. He said that they were losing great opportunities by their hesitation and procrastination; that at such a critical time they needed action, not deliberation; and that if he could get a few to help him, even if the rest should hang back, he would make an attack on the Senate.'

13. tam diu, dum: '(only) so long as.' B. 293, II.; A. 276, *e*, N. **14. omnium aditus tenebat**: 'he understood how to get at every one.' **15. consilium,** etc.: he could not only plan crime, but also carry out his wicked plans. **18. certas, certos**: 'particular,' 'special.' **19. descriptos**: 'assigned' to the part they were to take, 'detailed.' **20. quod**: properly with *obiret* only; 'which he did not undertake, did not meet; on which he did not bestow watchfulness, effort.'

24. paratum: 'ready (to strike).' **25. in perditis**: see IDIOMS. **28. Saturnalia**: see p. 92, 33, and N. It yet lacked more than two weeks to the Saturnalia; Catiline would have set the day of destruction earlier. **30. neque commisisset**: 'and would not have made the mistake of allowing his seal . . . to be secured as,' etc.; i. e. if he had remained in the city.

Page 97. VIII. 4. **ut levissime**: IDIOMS. B. 282, 4; H. 499, 2, N. 8. **Quamquam**: 'And yet.' 10. **cum**: 'not only.' 11. **vix videtur . . . esse potuisse**: 'it seems hardly possible that human wisdom can have directed matters of so great moment.' Cf. N. to p. 67, 17. B. 203, 5; A. 214, *c*; H. 402. 13. **praesentes**: cf. p. 84, 15, and N. 15. **illa**: those that had been noticed some time previously; contrasted with *haec* in l. 18. How far Cicero himself believed in portents is doubtful; but, as other Roman statesmen, he was ready to make the most of them in dealing with a superstitious populace. These unusual phenomena were treated at length in his poem 'On his Consulship;' cf. his De Div., I., XI., XII., XIII., and Plin. Nat. Hist., II., § 137. **omittam — omittam**: an example of *praeteritio*; cf. p. 135, 13, and N. **ab occidente**: a quarter of ill omen. See IDIOMS.

16. **faces**, etc.: cf. Dio Cass., XXXVII., XXV., 2 (referring to this time): 'Many thunderbolts fell from a cloudless sky, and the earth shook violently; spectral forms also were seen in many places, and torches shot up into the sky above the sunset.' For the portents preceding the murder of Caesar, see the editor's "Selections from Ovid," pp. 156, 157, and notes. 17. **quae tam multa**: either 'so many of which,' or 'which in so great number.' B. 201, 1, *b*; A. 216, *e*; H. 397, 2, N. 21. **relinquendum**: 'left out of consideration;' how different from *praetermittendum*?

22. **Cotta et Torquato consulibus**: the year 65 B. C. 23. **de caelo**: see IDIOMS. 24. **depulsa**: from their pedestals. 25. **veterum hominum**: 'of men of the olden time;' in and about the Capitol stood a host of statues. **aera**: 'the bronzes,' i. e. bronze pillars or tablets; see Dio Cass., XXXVII., IX.: 'The writing of the pillars, on which the laws were graven, ran together and became illegible.' Such copies of laws were set up in and around temples; but this passage does not refer to the Laws of the Twelve Tables, which were placed in the Forum, in the earlier period at least on the Rostra.

28. **fuisse**: i. e. it was at that time on the Capitoline hill, but has since been removed. A bronze group similar to that here described (the twins Romulus and Remus being modern) is now in a museum on the Capitoline hill at Rome. The wolf, undoubtedly of very ancient workmanship, is perhaps the same

as that referred to here, for it shows a fracture which may not unlikely have been caused by lightning. **32. nisi**: i. e. and would be upon us 'unless.'

Page 98. 1. responsis: why abl.? **ludi**: all the Roman public games (including the various spectacles of the circus, amphitheatre, and theatre) were religious in their origin. **4. facere**: the subject-acc., referring to those seeking advice, is omitted. **in excelso**: 'on a high (pedestal);' cf. Cic. de Div., I., XII., 20, 21. **5. contra, atque antea fuerat**: 'opposite to what it had previously been.' According to the ancient Roman custom, the worshipper faced the east, so that statues of divinities would naturally look toward the west, unless there were some reason to the contrary.

6. illud signum, quod videtis: spoken with a gesture on the right toward the height of the Capitoline hill, where the new statue on its column was plainly visible from the Rostra and the Forum; see N. to *Habita ad Populum*, on p. 227, and Plan facing p. 76. **10. collocandum locaverunt**: 'let the contract for erecting.' The charge of such contracts properly belonged to the censors; but the censors for B. C. 65, Quintus Lutatius Catulus and Marcus Licinius Crassus, disagreed and resigned, so that the function in this case devolved upon the consuls. **12. superioribus consulibus**: i. e. consuls for the two preceding years. The consuls for 64 were Lucius Julius Caesar and Gaius Figulus. **nobis**: sc. *consulibus*; see IDIOMS.

IX. 14. aversus, mente captus: see IDIOMS. **15. qui neget**: 'as to say that — not.' **haec omnia**: the visible universe; spoken with a wide gesture. **19. et ea**: 'and that too.' B. 247, 4; A. 195, *c*; H. 451, 2. **quae**: '(prophecies) which.' **23. praesens**: 'immediate,' 'evident.' **24. per forum**: as Cicero's house was on the Palatine hill and the conspirators had come to him there (see p. 91, 23, and N.), he was obliged to conduct them through the Forum in order to reach the Temple of Concord, where the Senate met; see Plan facing p. 76.

30. Quo: 'And on this account.' **34. ille**: with a gesture on the right toward the statue, the divinity being associated with the image; cf. p. 74, 32, and N. Notice the forceful anaphora, with asyndeta and climax.

Page 99. **1. haec templa**: about the Forum; spoken with a gesture. **3. hanc mentem voluntatemque**: 'this purpose and determination.'

9. audaciae: why dat.? **consilium esset ereptum**: on the theory of the proverb, *quos deus perdere vult, dementat.* **10. homines Galli**: 'men from Gaul;' more forcible than *Galli* alone, suggesting the bravery and fickleness of the Gallic character. **quae gens una**: 'the only people which.' **12. non nolle**: 'to be not indisposed;' in 66 B. C. Piso had put down an uprising among the Allobroges: but in 61 they rebelled again. **13. ultro**: 'without their seeking (it).' **16. qui — potuerint**: 'as they had it in their power.'

X. 18. ad omnia pulvinaria: i. e. *omnibus dis quorum pulvinaria Romae erant*, referring to the *lectisternium;* see N. to p. 95, 21. **25. togato**: cf. p. 88, 9–13, and N.

27. sed eas, et seq.: for the events referred to in this paragraph (all of which had happened within the quarter of a century preceding B. C. 63), consult the Vocab. under each name, and the Roman histories. **29. custodem huius urbis**: so characterized from his victories over the Teutons and Cimbri. **30. collegam**: Cornelius Cinna. **hic locus**: the Forum. **32. redundavit**: construed by zeugma with *acervis;* trans. with *acervis*, 'was choked;' with *sanguine*, 'overflowed.' **34. lumina civitatis**: members of the aristocratic party, as the consuls Gnaeus Octavius and Lucius Merula, Quintus Catulus, the orator Marcus Antonius, the Pontifex Quintus Scaevola, and others.

Page 100. **1. Ultus est . . . Sulla**: in 82 B. C. **2. quanta deminutione civium**: according to Mommsen ("History of Rome," Vol. III., p. 423), the proscription lists of Sulla contained the names of at least 4,700 citizens, including 40 senators and 1,600 knights. **6. ceterorum**: i. e. who perished with him.

8. quae: = *ut eae.* **16. uno**: strengthens the superlative. **post**: see IDIOMS. **17. quale bellum, quo in bello**: 'a war such as,' 'a war in which.' **barbaria**: abstract for concrete, = 'horde of savages.' **20. salvi**: i. e. financially 'safe,' who had property enough to make it worth while to murder them; different force in *salva* and in *salvi* of l. 21. **22. tantum civium**: '(only) so many citizens.' B. 201, 2; A. 216, *a*, 3; H.

397, 3, N. 5. **23. quantum . . . restitisset**: 'as had remained over from unlimited slaughter;' i. e. 'as had escaped unchecked bloodshed.'

CONCLUSION. XI.

XI. 27. Quibus pro tantis rebus: 'Now in return for these so great services (of mine).' **33. Nihil mutum**: as a statue.

Page 101. 2. res: 'achievements.' **4. diem**: 'period;' *in eandemque diem propagatam esse et salutem urbis et memoriam consulatus mei* might have been expected. Cicero believed that the memory of his consulship would endure as long as Rome's sovereignty, which would last forever. Cf. Bryce's "Holy Roman Empire." **7. alter . . . terminaret**: Pompey; rhetorical exaggeration, yet not without some basis; for Pompey had fought with Sertorius in the extreme west, and with Mithridates in the extreme east.

XII. 11. condicio: 'lot.' **quae illorum**: 'as of those.' **14. vestrum est**: 'it is your (duty).' **15. recte**: = *merito*, '(and) deservedly.' **20. nihil**: see IDIOMS. B. 187, II., *b*; A. 230; H. 384, 5. **23. tacita**: 'though silent,' i. e. by silent influence. **conscientiae**: 'of inner knowledge' that Cicero had really saved the state. **24. quam . . . indicabunt**: i. e. *si qui, ea* (*conscientia*) *neglecta, me violare volent, se ipsi indicabunt* ('they will betray themselves' by their very appearance).

27. nullius: for the gen. of *nemo*. **28. Quod si**, et seq.: cf. p. 70, 19–21, and N. **33. fructum**: 'gains.' **34. in honore vestro**: i. e. 'in the honors you have it in your power to bestow.'

Page 102. 1. virtutis: 'won by valor.' Kind of gen.? **quicquam altius**: 'any greater height.' **4. ornem**: 'make even more splendid.' **ut**: final.

7. me tractabo: = *versabor*, 'I shall conduct myself.' **10. est nox**: the meeting of the Senate preceding this address lasted till late in the day. **illum**: cf. p. 98, 34, and N. **12. aeque ac**: 'just the same as.' **priore nocte**: after the second oration; cf. p. 87, 11–13. **15. providebo**: a hint at the fate of the conspirators in custody.

THE FOURTH ORATION AGAINST CATILINE.

Page 103. IN L. CATILINAM: see N. on p. 209.

HABITA IN SENATU: Dec. 5, B. C. 63, the Senate being assembled in the Temple of Concord; cf. Plan facing p. 76.

INTRODUCTION. I.–III.

I. 1. Video — in me, etc.: for the circumstances of delivery, and an outline of the thought, see pp. 41, 44. At what point in the debate Cicero spoke is not clear; but evidently the discussion regarding the punishment of the conspirators was becoming involved with the question of his own safety. That the debate should for the moment take this direction is not strange, for the consul was yet the hope of all patriots in the contest with the conspiracy, which had been shown to be so dangerous; while in view of the desperate character of the leaders, and his efforts to bring them to justice, every one knew that he would be the first object of attack. At this point, when the senators were looking toward him to divine his feeling in the matter, the orator took advantage of his position as presiding officer (see p. 113, 12–13) to urge them to make all personal considerations secondary to the true interests of the state, and presented clearly the two views before the house regarding the disposition of the conspirators, delicately but distinctly revealing his own preference for the extreme penalty. The exordium, which under other circumstances might have appeared unwarrantably egotistical, is thus seen to be entirely in keeping with the occasion, whether it was spoken as it stands, or the present form is a fuller statement of what was said at the time.

5. in dolore: i. e. *animi.* **voluntas**: ='kindly regard;' it is not their good-will but their anxiety for his welfare that the orator begs them to lay one side.

14. aequitas: for *iustitia;* cf. p. 87, 2, and N. **continetur**: 'is centred;' the law courts were about the Forum. **15. auspiciis**: abl.; an election of consuls was held only after certain auspices, taken in the Campus Martius, had been declared favorable. **curia**: there is no record of any attempt on the orator's life in the Senate-house; but cf. p. 74, 19. **16. auxilium omnium gentium**: refers to the Senate's adjustment of foreign relations; cf. p. 58. **17. commune perfugium**: suggestive of that maxim of English law, "Every man's house is his castle." **datus**: to be taken closely with *lectus*.

18. haec sedes honoris: the curule chair, the official seat of the higher Roman magistrates. It had a square seat, with no back or arms, and was so made that it would fold up as a camp-stool. This arrangement appears to have been originally a matter of convenience, that the chair might readily be moved about, implying magisterial jurisdiction wherever it was placed; possibly in the earliest times it was carried in the chariot with the magistrate (hence *curulis*, from *currus*, 'carriage-chair'). See Illustration.

20. multa tacui: a hint at the revelations he might have made — had he thought it expedient — involving prominent men in the conspiracy; such, perhaps, as Caesar and Crassus. **21. meo . . . timore**: i. e. yours the fear merely, but mine the pain ('with some pain to myself').

Page 104. **2. virgines Vestales**: cf. N. to p. 92, 30. **4. delubra**: cf. p. 89, 17, and N. **5. totam Italiam**: cf. p. 95, 25, and N. **8. fatale**, etc.: see p. 92, 23–31. **10. prope**: 'I might almost say,' 'as it were;' softens *fatalem exstitisse*, which otherwise would have seemed arrogant. Notice the chiasmus in *fatale ad perniciem — ad salutem fatalem*. B. 350, 11, *c*; A. 344, *f*; H. 562.

II. **11. consulite**: cf. IDIOMS. **16. praesident**: in the sense of *tuentur*. **pro eo, ac**: see IDIOMS. **17. si quid obtigerit**: euphemistic, as shown by *moriar*. **19. consulari**: 'to him who has been consul,' because he has reached the highest goal of human ambition, the highest honor men can bestow. **sapienti**: 'to the philosopher;' cf. p. 106, 25. The ancient systems of philosophy, but more particularly the Stoic and the Epicurean, inculcated disregard of death.

20. ille ferreus: 'a man so made of iron,' 'a man so devoid of feeling.' **fratris**: now praetor-elect; see Vocab. under *Cicero* (2). **21 horum omnium**: senators, the orator's special friends, who were disturbed at the thought of danger to him. The Greeks and the Romans gave vent to their feelings much more freely than would be considered in good form among us. **24. exanimata**: from anxiety. **uxor, filia, filius**: see Vocab. under *Terentia*, *Tullia*, and *Cicero* (3); Marcus, the son, was now only two years old. **26. ille — gener**: see Vocab., under *Piso*. As Piso was not yet admitted to the Senate, he stood with the throng before the open door of the temple. **28. in eam partem**: = '(only) to this determination.' **30. quam**: for *quam ut*. B. 284, 4; A. 332, *b*; H. 502, 2. **una**: = *communi*. **31. peste**: instrumental abl., where we should use 'in.'

32. incumbite: nautical term; cf. *procellas*, l. 33. **34. Non Ti. Gracchus**: 'Not a Tiberius Gracchus,' or 'No Tiberius Gracchus.' **iterum**: in the time of the Gracchi it was not lawful to hold the office of tribune of the people for two years in succession.

Page 105. **2. agrarios**: those who favored a more equable division and management of the public lands. **5. vestram omnium**: trans. as if *vestri omnium*. Why? **6. Romae restiterunt**: i. e. instead of going forth with Catiline. **7. litterae, signa, manus**: i. e. the letters with each one's seal and hand-writing; see p. 93, 1 et seq. **8. servitia**: abstract for concrete, = *servi*; see p. 94, 9-11. **9. id est**: sums up; 'in short, the design was formed, that.' **10. nemo ne — quidem**: B. 347, 2; A. 209, *a*, 1; H. 553, 2. **12. relinquatur**: present because *consilium* (l. 9), summing up the preceding present tenses, looks toward the future; our idiom here requires the impf.

III. 14. multis . . . iudicavistis: 'you have already, by many (previous) decisions, settled;' a very clever turn, implying that the Senate had already committed itself regarding the guilt of the conspirators and its own jurisdiction in the case. **15. gratias . . . decrevistis**: see p. 94, 29–31. **17. P. Lentulum . . . coëgistis**: see p. 95, 33, and N. **19. in custodiam**: see p. 95, 3–15. **20. meo nomine**: see p. 95, 21–25, and N.

22. praemia — amplissima: what these were is not known; probably they were gifts of money. Reason for the position of *amplissima?* **24. nominatim dati sunt**: i. e. each prisoner was placed in charge of a different person; see N. to p. 69, 5. According to Sallust (Cat. XLVII. 4), Lentulus was turned over to the aedile P. Lentulus Spinther, Cethegus to Quintus Cornificius, Statilius to Gaius Caesar, Gabinius to Marcus Crassus, and Ceparius, after he was caught, to the senator Gnaeus Terentius.

27. instituі: here = *coepi.* **referre**: object? **28. tamquam integrum**: 'as still an open question,' notwithstanding the fact that you have virtually passed a sentence of condemnation already. **30. consulis**: as chief executive of the state and presiding officer of the Senate; cf. N. to p. 61, 14. **31. misceri**: idiomatically, 'were brewing.' **32 haberi**: stronger than *factam esse; habere* is used of holding meetings of political bodies, as the Senate. **33. putavi**: forcible; so we sometimes say, 'I never thought it of him,' when we mean 'I never would have thought it of him.'

Page 106. 1. statuendum . . . est: 'you must reach a decision before nightfall;' because a decree of the Senate passed after sunset was not valid, and because the emergency was such as to admit of no postponement of action. **3. vehementer**: see IDIOMS. **4. Latius**: see IDIOMS. **6. multas provincias occupavit**: rhetorical exaggeration; yet Catiline had reckoned on receiving armies from Spain and Mauretania (Sall. Cat. XXI. 3).

DISCUSSION. IV.–XI., l. 9.

IV. 10. duas sententias: cf. pp. 41, 44. **D. Silani**: as consul-elect he was the first one called on to give his opinion and vote. Cf. N. to p. 94, 24. **11. haec**: cf. p. 70, 11, and N. **12. C. Caesaris**: he was now praetor-elect, and therefore one of the first to be called on after the consuls-elect and ex-consuls. His speech is given at length by Sallust, Cat. LI. **13. removet**: brief for *removendum esse censet.* **15. in — versatur**: 'insists upon.'

24. laborum ac miseriarum: like our phrase, 'toils and troubles.' Caesar's argument is, that life sentence is a severer punishment than the death penalty; he thinks that death ends all. Sallust reports his words thus (Cat. LI. 20): *De poena possum equidem dicere — id quod res habet — in luctu atque* *miseriis mortem aerumnarum requiem, non cruciatum esse; eam cuncta mortalium mala dissolvere; ultra neque curae neque gaudio locum esse.*

25. inviti: trans. by an adv. B. 239; A. 191; H. 443. **26. Vincula**: in a general sense. **et ea**: cf. 98, 19, and N. **27. singularem poenam**: as in the case of a certain Vettienus, who had cut off the fingers of his left hand in order to make himself unfit for military service; he was condemned to imprisonment for life, with the confiscation of his property. Still, sentence to perpetual imprisonment or death was much rarer in Rome than with us, for the reason that citizens could escape sentence by going into exile. Cf. N. to p. 72, 23.

28. dispertiri: sc. *eos*, the conspirators. **29. iniquitatem**: 'unfairness,' because imposing a heavy and unnecessary burden on the municipalities; 'difficulty,' because if not obliged to receive the charge they would be disinclined voluntarily to accept it. **30. placet**: see IDIOMS. **33. Adiungit**: sc. *Caesar*.

Page 107. 1. custodias: 'prison regulations.' **7. quam si**: 'but if — this.' **9. in vita**: i. e. while yet on earth. **10. illi antiqui**: 'those men of the olden time,' particularly the poets, as Homer. **11. voluerunt**: 'wished' to have it believed, = 'made out;' the language implies that Cicero himself did not believe in future punishment. The orator is now addressing the Senate, the members of which in the main were sceptical in regard to the teachings of the national religion; when talking to the people his attitude toward current beliefs is different. See p. 75, 5; cf. N. to p. 97, 15.

V. 14. Nunc: = 'Under these conditions.' **intersit**: cf. IDIOMS. B. 210; 211, 1, *a*, 3, *c*; A. 222, *a*; H. 408, 1, 2. **18. populares impetus**: 'attacks of the people.' Caesar was allied with the popular or democratic party, which was constantly making efforts to break the power of the Senate and the aristocracy. **19. illam alteram**: of Silanus. **nescio an**: here = 'probably.' **amplius negoti**: 'a larger measure of difficulty.' **20. Sed tamen**: 'But (even if this be the case), nevertheless.'

22. enim: 'then;' the orator enters upon a closer examination of Caesar's proposition. **23. maiorum**: referring not only to the prominence of the Caesar family for a century previous to this time, but also to the alleged descent of the *Iulii* from *Iulus*, Aeneas's son. **24. obsidem**: 'pledge.' **25. In-**

tellectum est, quid interesset: 'we understood (when Caesar spoke) what a difference there is.'

28. **non neminem**: = 'more than one.' **de capite**: 'regarding the life;' they absented themselves with the pretext that only the people assembled in the comitia had the right to pass a sentence of death upon a Roman citizen, and that the Senate in dealing with the conspirators was going beyond its jurisdiction. 29. **is**: refers to *non nemo*; 'but those men.' **nudius tertius**: i. e. at the meeting of the Senate on Dec. 3; there these pretended friends of the people joined with the rest of the Senate in acts which virtually condemned the conspirators (cf. p. 105, 25), thus tacitly admitting the jurisdiction of the Senate in the case. To judge from this the decrees of the Senate on Dec. 3 must have been carried unanimously.

32. **adfecit**: cf. p. 361. **hoc**, etc.: *hoc, quid* (*ille*), *qui . . . decrevit, de tota re et causa* ('the whole matter of fact and question at issue'), *iudicarit, nemini dubium est.* 33. **quaesitori**: refers to Cicero as having conducted the investigation; the term is technically applied to the presiding officer of a *quaestio*, or court for criminal cases. **gratulationem**: here = *supplicationem.*

Page 108. 1. **At**: introduces the orator's reply to Caesar's argument. **intellegit**: as shown by Caesar's not refusing to vote on the matters before the Senate, Dec. 3; by voting then, as Cicero clearly enough indicates, he admitted the jurisdiction of the Senate in dealing with the conspirators as 'enemies,' not as 'citizens.' **legem Semproniam**: proposed by Gaius Sempronius Gracchus B. C. 123, enacting *ne de capite civium Romanorum iniussu populi iudicaretur*; see N. to p. 72, 23. Cicero cites this enactment particularly because he wishes to point his argument with an allusion to the death of Gracchus without a trial by the people or an appeal, as showing that immediately after the passage of the law it was so construed that those considered enemies of their country were not protected by it.

3. **hostis, eum civem nullo modo**: i. e. granted that a Roman citizen can only be tried before a regular court, and cannot be put to death without an opportunity to appeal his case to the Roman people gathered in assembly (see N. to p. 72, 23); yet if he makes an attempt against his country, by that

very act he becomes a 'public enemy,' is no longer entitled to the protection afforded by laws guarding the rights of citizens, and as an enemy may properly be tried and sentenced by the Senate. To us the argument here seems like begging the question. For, first of all, the question whether a man is a 'public enemy' or not is one of fact, which can properly be determined only after due deliberation by a judicial body having jurisdiction in such matters; and at Rome there were two courts for two different kinds of crimes against the state, the *quaestio perpetua* for cases of treason (*de maiestate*), and that for cases of violence or riot (*de vi*). But even in cases of treason the precedents at least of the earlier time guarded sacredly the right of appeal to the people. Certainly according to the letter of the Roman constitution, the Senate had not the jurisdiction to try and condemn the conspirators, at any rate without an opportunity to appeal from its decision.

Again, in the first oration Cicero had earnestly maintained the position that the supreme power vested in the consuls by the Senate (*ultimum decretum*) was sufficient to warrant putting a disturber of the peace to death at once, without the formality of a trial or appeal; but when the Catilinarian conspirators were actually in his power, he shifted the responsibility by referring their fate to the Senate. As a matter of fact this right of the consul, when invested with the supreme power, had been conceded by the aristocracy, but never admitted by the popular party; only this year the aged Rabirius had been called to account for his part in the killing of Saturninus (see p. 6).

But if there was no warrant on strictly constitutional grounds for the attitude of the consul or of the Senate in this case, and for the execution of the conspirators without a formal trial, on other grounds there was justification most ample. Throughout the speeches the orator is constantly reminding his hearers of the peril which is threatening the state, the city Rome, their own lives. Human society as an organism, as represented by states and communities, has a right to protect itself to maintain its own existence. At Rome the constitution had literally broken down; it had shown itself incapable of adjustment to the wide expansion of political boundaries and to the rapid development of new conditions in the last centuries of the republic. This plot of Catiline was anarchistic, contemplating not merely a redistribution of political emoluments, but the overthrow of existing institutions amid riot and bloodshed. Where the orator urges the public safety as ground for decisive action against the enemies of society, his argument must stand as long as society itself shall endure; it is just as applicable now as it was then. If it is ever justifiable for a governmental body to violate the letter of a constitution in obedience to the higher law of the self-preservation of society itself, the Roman Senate was fully justified in taking cognizance of the case of the Catilinarian conspirators, and dealing with them summarily.

8. popularem: 'a friend of the people.' **13. publicationem bonorum**: confiscation of property usually accompanied severe sentences; still Caesar's attitude in this matter is difficult to understand. He probably believed that the Senate had no right to condemn the conspirators; yet his motion itself recognized the Senate's jurisdiction. It may be that he proposed the life sentence simply to save the lives of the prisoners temporarily, trusting to the future to restore either their freedom or their property, or both, if after sufficient time the sentence seemed too severe.

VI. 17. comitem: Caesar, who, if his motion prevailed, would according to custom accompany the consul when formal announcement of it should be made to the people. **20. eam**: i. e. *Silani sententiam.* **24. ita — ut**: 'so may it be my lot to enjoy . . . as.'

28. Videor, etc.: a striking example of vision, a figure known to the Roman rhetoricians as *subiectio in oculos.* **30. sepulta in patria**: we should say, 'on the grave of my country.' **31. miseros, insepultos**: trans. as if with *civium.* **acervos**: i. e. *acervos corporum.* **32. aspectus**: 'the (ferocious) appearance.' **33. regnantem**: more graphic than *regnare.* Cf. B. 337, 3, *a*; A. 292, *e*; H. 335, I., 4. **34. fatis**: cf. p. 92, 24, and N.

Page 109. 1. purpuratum: suggesting oriental luxury and despotism; for in the eastern monarchies the ministers and courtiers nearest the king were dressed in royal purple. **3. familias**: B. 21, 2, *a*; A. 36, *b*; H. 49, I. **9. supplicium**: see IDIOMS. **11. an**: for *an potius.* **12. qui**: = *si is.* B. 312, 2; A. 316; H. 507, III., 2. Owing to the immense numbers of slaves owned by the Romans, recourse was had to the severest measures to keep them submissive. If a master was killed by a slave, all the slaves under his roof at the time were put to death, on the pretext that they ought to have prevented the crime.

15. in: 'in the case of.' **19. vestigiis**: 'remains.' **23. fama**: in the sense of *infamia*. **24. Nisi vero**: introduces an exception ironically. B. 306, 5; A. 315, *b*. **L. Caesar**: see Vocab. under *Caesar* (2). He made these remarks probably at the meeting of the Senate, Dec. 3, when called upon to give his vote. **26. virum**: 'husband;' the conspirator Lentulus, who had married Lucius Caesar's sister Julia.

28. avum: M. Fulvius Flaccus, put to death by the consul Opimius; see p. 62, 16. Lucius Caesar introduced this precedent from his family history in order to justify the severity of his judgment on Lentulus. **29. legatum**: the boy, eighteen years of age, had been sent by his father to treat with Opimius, who would listen to no offer of reconciliation. As he was sent a second time, Opimius placed him in custody, and then suddenly directing a vigorous attack slew among others both the father and the elder brother. Afterwards the younger son was killed in prison. **30. Quorum**: = *Atque horum*. **simile**: i. e. to what the Catilinarian conspirators proposed; sc. *fuit*.

32. versata est: 'prevailed,' 'was prevalent.' **34. avus**: see Vocab. under *Lentulus* (1); cf. p. 93, 18.

Page 110. **2. quid . . . deminueretur**: = 'that the welfare of the state might not suffer in any degree.' **hic**: i. e. *hic Lentulus;* but *hic* does not imply that Lentulus was now present. Probably the conspirators were kept closely guarded during this meeting of the Senate, in the various houses to which they had been assigned. **4. servitia**: cf. p. 105, 8, and N., and N. to p. 72, 16. **7. Vereamini, censeo**: 'Of course you may well be afraid;' ironical; potential subj.

VII. 13. ea, quae exaudio: refers to whispered remarks among the senators, as shown by what follows. **15. vereri — ut**: cf. *est verendum, ne* (l. 10); difference in force? **17. transigunda**: B. 116, 2; A. 12, *d*, end; H. 239. **Omnia . . . sunt**: strong guards had been placed about the Forum and the adjacent parts. **19. multo maiore — voluntate**: why separated? B. 350, 11, *a*; A. 344, *e*; H. 561, III. **20. summum imperium**: '(their) full sovereignty,' threatened by Catiline; perhaps also a hint at the designs of Lentulus. **23. circum forum**: attributive to *templa.* **24. huius templi ac loci**: the temple of Concord; redundant expression.

25. Causa — haec — sola: reason for position? **post**: see IDIOMS. **26. omnes**: *omnes cives*, several classes of whom are mentioned below. **28. soli**: cf. p. 85, 20, and N.

34. Quid — commemorem: notice the difference between this and *quid — commemoro* (p. 111, 26).

Page 111. 1. ita — ut: = 'only so far that.' **summam ordinis consilique**: 'the first place in rank and counsel.' **2. de**: we should say 'in.'

3. huius ordinis: = 'with this body,' the Senate. The strife between the Senate and the body of knights arose over the right to sit as jurors for criminal trials, in the *quaestiones perpetuae* (cf. p. 60). Originally this right belonged exclusively to members of the Senate; but most of the greater trials arose from the misgovernment of provinces, and as the governors in all cases were senators, miscarriage of justice was alarmingly frequent. To remedy this evil, Gaius Gracchus in 122 B. C. had a law passed which took away from the senators the right to serve in such trials, and conferred it upon the knights exclusively. This arrangement proved to be hardly better than the other; for the knights, as the capitalist body, controlled the farming of revenues, having their financial agents (*publicani*) in every province; and they were influenced in their judgment of questions of misgovernment very largely by the consideration whether the governor on trial had been favorable or unfavorable to the men of their class engaged in collecting the revenue in the territory under his administration. Sulla restored the earlier arrangement; but the feeling between the orders was more bitter than ever. Finally in 70 B. C. the *Lex Aurelia* brought about at least a surface reconciliation, by providing for a division of judicial functions equally among the Senate, the body of knights, and the paymasters (*tribuni aerarii*), a class recognized now for the first time.

3. societatem concordiamque: 'harmonious fellowship;' hendiadys. **4. revocatos**: by the *Lex Aurelia*, passed seven years before; but previous to this day no emergency had arisen of such a character as to bring this harmony to the surface and make it manifest to all.

11. tribunos aerarios: the position and functions of these officials are not clearly understood, apart from the fact that they were plebeians, and that in earlier times at least they were especially concerned with the collecting and disbursement of moneys for military purposes. **scribas**: sc. *publicos*. As at Rome the principal officers of government changed every year, the permanent 'clerks' or 'secretaries' naturally came to be indispensable by reason of their experience, and reached a degree of importance entitling them to recognition as a distinct class. The most prominent among them were those under the quaestors (*scribae quaestorii*); for the management of the public finances in large measure rested in their hands.

12. quos casu, etc.: on the nones of December the new quaestors came to the Treasury (in the Temple of Saturn, near the Temple of Concord; see Plan facing p. 76), in order to settle by lot in what provinces they would spend their year of office. The clerks gathered at the same place to determine (probably also by lot) under what quaestors they were to serve. **13. frequentasset**: 'had gathered in throngs;' plup. on account of *esse conversos*.

15. ingenuorum: 'free-born citizens,' as contrasted with those that had come up from slavery, the 'freedmen' (*libertini*); cf. l. 20.

VIII. 20. Operae: see IDIOMS. **21. sua virtute**: i. e. by their exertions they had obtained their liberty and secured the boon of citizenship. Cf. p. 58, and Acts xxii. 27, 28.

26. commemoro; why not *commemorem?* **29. Servus est nemo**: more emphatic than *nullus servus est*. **30. qui modo — sit**: 'provided only he be,' or 'none at least who is;' close limitation of *servus nemo*, while the following relative clauses deal with broader characteristics. **32. haec**: cf. p. 70, 11, and N. **non quantum,** etc.: i. e. *non tantum voluntatis conferat, quantum conferre audet;* referring to slaves of the conspirators. Reason for the position of *voluntatis?*

Page 112. 2. lenonem: a term of contempt. **3. pretio**: 'for money.' Why abl.? **7. illum — locum**: referring particularly to the Forum, on two sides of which at this time there were rows of shops (*tabernae*); see Plan. **8. lectulum**: cf. p. 65, 5, and N. **9. otiosum**: 'quiet,' 'peaceful,' as undisturbed by war's alarms. **13. instrumentum**: 'appliance (of industry).' **14. frequentia civium sustentatur, alitur otio**: what is this arrangement of words called? B. 350, 11, *c*; A. 344, *f*; H. 562. **16. quid,** etc.: more forcible than *quid tandem fuisset, si incensae essent?* B. 305, 1; A. 310; H. 507, III., 3, N. 7.

IX. 20. ex media morte: see IDIOMS. **27. arcem**: on the northern summit of the Capitoline hill, while the *Capitolium* occupied the southern; these elevations were separated at the middle of the hill by a depression. **aras Penatium**: i. e. *aras Penatium publicorum*, in the Temple of Vesta. **28. illum**: with a gesture toward the small round Temple of Vesta, over the centre of whose conical roof perhaps a thread of smoke was seen curling upwards; cf. Plan facing p. 76. Notice the rhetorical effect of the anaphora and asyndeta.

32. omnium: sc. *vestri.* **33. hodierno die**: see p. 106, 1, and N.

Page 113. 1. quae — facultas: 'an advantage which.' **habetis**: 'you have (on your side).' **3. in civili causa**: 'in a political issue.' **4. quantis . . . delerit**: condensed for *quantis laboribus fundatum sit imperium* ('the sovereignty' of our state), *quanta virtute stabilita sit libertas, . . . quae una nox paene delerit.* Why subj.?

7. una nox: the night of the arrest of the Allobroges, as indicated by a passage in the oration for Flaccus (XL. 102): *O nox illa, quae paene aeternas huic urbi tenebras attulisti, cum Galli ad bellum, Catilina ad urbem, coniurati ad ferrum et flammam vocabantur;* some, however, think that the night of the meeting at Laeca's, or that of the 19th of December, is referred to. **8. non modo non**: the second *non* is omitted in some of the MSS., and may possibly have been inserted by some copyist. Cf. p. 71, 21, and N. **13. officio consulari**: cf. N. to p. 103, 1.

X. 14. ad sententiam: sc. *rogandam;* cf. N. to p. 64, 28. **20. dignitas**: here = *auctoritas.* **22. paenitebit**: cf. Vocab. **mors, quam — minitantur**: so modern anarchists are constantly threatening death to those who enforce the laws. **26. gratulationem**: = *supplicationem.* Cf. p. 95, 21–28, and N.

28. ille: force? B. 246, 3; A. 102, *b*; H. 450, 4. **29. in Africam redire, Italia decedere**: hysteron proteron. B. 374, 7; A. 385; H. 636, V., 2. **30. Africanus**: see Vocab. under *Scipio* (2). **33. quondam**: belongs with the superlatives.

Page 114. **1. bis**: by conquering the Teutones at Aquae Sextiae in 102 B. C., the Cimbri at Vercellae in 101. **3. isdem . . . continentur**: cf. p. 101, 7–9, and N. **5. nisi forte**: like *nisi vero* (cf. p. 109, 24), used to introduce an exception ironically. B. 306, 5; A. 315, *b*; H. 507, III., 3, N. I. **8. habeant, quo**: i. e. *habeant locum, quo.*

9. uno loco: 'in one respect.' **14. cum**: = 'although,' 'even though;' here, as not infrequently, with the indefinite second person singular. **16. possis**: 'you cannot hope to be able.' Why subj.? **23. coniunctionem . . . Romanorum**: so soon as the common danger was past, the old strife between the two orders broke out again; cf. N. to p. 111, 3.

XI. 26. pro: 'in place of.' **imperio**: the military command associated with the governorship of a province. **exercitu**: which he might have as provincial governor. **27. provincia**: the provinces set aside for the consuls of 63 on the expiration of their term of office were Cisalpine Gaul and Macedonia, of which the latter fell by lot to Cicero, the former to Antonius. But the orator made an exchange, in order to give Macedonia, which of the two was far preferable, to his colleague (see p. 38); and afterwards gave up Cisalpine Gaul also, in order to remain at Rome. **triumpho**: which might be secured by an aggressive governorship.

29. clientelis: provincial communities often retained a governor after his term as their legal and business representative at Rome, — a relation considered both honorable and lucrative for the Roman. **30. quae**: 'relations which.' **urbanis opibus**: 'by my influence in the city.' **31. tueor**: refers to the old, *comparo* to the new, relations. **pro**: here 'in return for.'

Page 115. **1. memoriam**: cf. p. 100, 27, et seq. **4. meam . . . superaverit**: 'is destined to frustrate my hopes and to prevail.' **5. filium**: see p. 104, 24, and N. **8. suo solius periculo**: 'with danger to himself alone.' B. 243, 3, *a*; H 398, 3.

CONCLUSION.

15. qui . . . possit: Cicero was as good as his word. After the speech of Marcus Cato (Sall. Cat., LII.; cf. p. 41), the Senate voted for the execution of the conspirators. The consul thought it best to carry out the decree before nightfall, as the darkness might encourage an attempt at rescue (cf. Sall. Cat., LV.). Having distributed an armed force about the central parts of the city, he himself conducted Lentulus to the Mamertine Prison; the other conspirators were brought thither by the praetors. 'In the prison,' says Sallust, 'there is a place called the *Tullianum* (see Illustration on p. 115), about twelve feet below the surface of the ground. It is built with strong walls, and above it there is a room constructed with stone vaulting; but it is a disgusting and horrible place, on account of the filth, the darkness, and the stench. After Lentulus had been let down into this dungeon, the executioners broke his neck with a noose; so that patrician, of the most noble line of the Cornelii, a man who had exercised the consular authority at Rome, met an end suited to his character and his deeds. Cethegus, Statilius, Gabinius, and Ceparius suffered the same penalty.' When they were all dead, it is said that Cicero, who had waited at the door of the prison, proclaimed the outcome to the silent and expectant crowd that filled the Forum, with the single word *Vixerunt*, 'They are no more.' (Plut. Cic. 22, "Ἔζησαν" εἶπεν.)

THE SPEECH ON POMPEY'S COMMISSION.

Page 116. IMPERIO: here referring to a military command of a special character (see p. 32); ='Commission.' In the best MSS. the title is given as *de imperio Cn. Pompei;* in some others, as *pro lege Manilia.*

INTRODUCTION. I.–II. (p. 118, l. 3).

Exordium (see p. 34).

I. **1. frequens conspectus vester**: refers to the sea of upturned faces over which the orator looked as he came forward on the Rostra; 'your assembled presence,' 'your thronging presence.' For the occasion and circumstances of delivery, see p. 27 et seq. **2. hic locus**: see N. to *Habita ad Populum*, on p. 227. **ad agendum**: i. e. *ad agendum cum populo*, 'for addressing the people,' an expression used only of a magistrate, and applicable to Cicero, as praetor; but *ad dicendum* (sc. *apud populum*), 'for public speaking,' has reference to any one not a magistrate who may have been permitted to speak from the Rostra. The same distinction is carried out in the adjectives; for what was 'most dignified' for a magistrate was 'most honorable,' 'most full of honor' for a private citizen.

4. aditu laudis: 'pathway to fame.' Kind of gen.? **5. optimo cuique**: 'to all the best' in a political sense; outside of the magistrates only the most eminent men of the state were allowed to speak from the Rostra. B. 252, 5, *c*; A. 93, *c*; H. 458, 1. **mea me**: cf. p. 159, 20, and N. **6. rationes**: ='plan.' **ab ineunte aetate**: refers to the beginning of life as a citizen, when the boy put on the *toga virilis* (see N. to p. 77, 30); ='from my entrance upon civil life,' 'when I became of age.' **7. per aetatem**: 'by reason of my years.' **8. huius auctoritatem loci**: ='this place of dignity.' B. 350, 11, *a*;

9. perfectum ingenio: i. e. finished with maturity of intellectual powers; referring to the thought, while *elaboratum* has reference to the form. **11 temporibus** : 'demands.'

12. Ita: belongs with the clause *meus labor . . . consecutus.* In trans. make the first clause subordinate; 'So while this place, . . . my efforts,' etc. The co-ordinate construction was preferred by the orator for the sake of the rhetorical antithesis. **13. vestram causam**: i. e. *causam rei publicae.* **14. periculis**: often used of criminal trials; here a synonym of *temporibus* above. **caste integreque**: 'irreproachably,' as not having accepted presents contrary to the Cincian Law, passed in 204 B. C., which made it unlawful for an advocate to receive fees; 'and incorruptibly,' as never having taken a bribe to handle his side of the case poorly so as to allow an opponent to win the suit over his client.

16. dilationem comitiorum: many circumstances were considered of enough significance to warrant the interruption and postponement of an election. Such were the occurrence of lightning, thunder, or rain, which were supposed to indicate the disapproval of the gods; the setting of the sun before the voting was all done; and the outbreak of a disturbance in the city. The reasons for a postponement in this case are not known.

17. primus — renuntiatus sum: 'I had been the first to be announced.' There were eight praetorships to be filled (cf. p. 59). Cicero each time received the first choice of all the centuries; but on the first two occasions the comitia were adjourned before the other seven praetors had all been elected, and the election had to be held over again as if nothing had been done. **18. quid aliis praescriberetis**: i. e. *ut ipsi quoque caste integreque in aliorum periculis versarentur.*

20. auctoritatis: 'personal influence.' **21. honoribus mandandis**: 'by entrusting official positions' to me. **22. vigilanti**: 'energetic;' so we speak of a 'wide-awake' man.

Page 117. **1. forensi**: = 'in the courts;' cf. p. 103, 14, and N. **3. utar**: 'I shall make use (of it).' **4. in dicendo**: = 'as an orator.' **5. ei rei**: 'that accomplishment.' **fructum**: in the way of a longer opportunity to speak, and that too with the prestige of an official position. **6. Atque**: 'And further.' **7. in . . . dicendi**: = 'while I have not had practice in speaking from this place.' **9. oratio**: 'speech,' 'language.' **10. Cn.**: Why not *Gn.?* A. 6; H. 2, 3. **11. virtute**: i. e. *virtute imperatoria*, 'military character,' the combination of qualities found in a perfect general. **orationis**: here 'matter.'

Narratio.

II. 14. Atque: 'And so.' The *narratio* is brief, because the people were already familiar with the facts. **inde — unde . . . ducitur**: 'with that in which this entire state of affairs originates.' **16. vectigalibus**: 'payers of tribute,' 'tributaries,' the inhabitants of the provinces Asia and Bithynia; while *sociis* includes not only the provincials (see N. to p. 68, 25), but also the rulers and inhabitants of associated states, as Cappadocia and Galatia. **17. Mithridate**: the original form of the word was Mithradates. **18. relictus**: 'let slip' by Lucullus before Cabira; see p. 31. **lacessitus**: 'provoked' by the haughty demand of the Roman ambassador Appius Claudius for the surrender of Mithridates; for the excuse which Tigranes made see Memnon, XLVI.

20. Equitibus: the capitalists; cf. N. to p. 111, 3. **21. Asia**: the Roman province, comprising Mysia, Lydia, Caria, Lycia, and Phrygia; see Map. **magnae . . . occupatae**: 'great fortunes are at stake, invested in farming your revenues;' see N. to p. 122, 2. **23. necessitudine**, etc.: Cicero's family belonged to the order of knights; see p. 1.

25. Bithyniae . . . neminem: in indir. disc. as representing the contents of the letters. **nunc**: Bithynia had been left by will to the Roman people by Nicomedes III. in 75 B. C., and organized as a province the following year. **26. regnum Ariobarzanis**: Cappadocia. **27. vestris vectigalibus**: 'the lands tributary to you,' 'your tithe-yielding lands,' the taxes being put by metonymy for the regions in which they were raised.

29. ab eo bello: we should say 'from the seat of war.' **huic qui successerit**: Glabrio. **30. non esse paratum**: sc. *eum;* a hint at the notorious incompetency of Glabrio. **31. unum**: i. e. Pompey. **civibus**: Roman citizens in Asia Minor, as indicated by the position after *sociis*.

Partitio.

34. Causa, et seq.: a short but clear and appropriate transition to the treatment of the subject. A statement of the theme, as that in *quid agendum sit, considerate*, was called by the rhetoricians *propositio*.

DISCUSSION.

A. The Character of the War. II. (p. 118, l. 4) -VII.

Page 118. **4. quod**: grammatically refers back to *genus*, logically to *belli;* in our idiom, 'The war is of such a character (i. e. being defensive) that it ought.' **5. ad persequendi studium**: = *ad id (bellum) studiose persequendum*. **6. agitur**: 'is at stake.' In the enumeration with *agitur*, *aguntur* (notice the forceful anaphora), an outline of the subsequent argument of this division is given; first come the considerations involving the national honor, then those based upon expediency. **9. amicorum**: the title 'friend of the Roman People' was often conferred upon allied princes. **11. certissima**: the wealth and fertility of the province Asia were proverbial; cf. p. 121, 17 et seq. **12. pacis ornamenta, subsidia belli**: chiastic order. The former refers particularly to the sums lavished on the erection of temples and public buildings, and on the maintenance of public worship. **14. a vobis**: not dat., to avoid confusion with the dat. *quibus;* 'for whose interests you must make provision.'

III. **16. Et**: 'And (indeed),' 'And (to be sure).' **praeter ceteras**: in our idiom, 'above all other.' **18. bello superiore**: 88–84 B. C.; no account is made of the second Mithridatic war, 83–81; cf. pp. 29, 30. **19. insedit**: 'has sunk in.' **21. tota in Asia**: used instead of *tota Asia*, so as to correspond with *tot in civitatibus*. Cf. B. 228, 1, *b*; A. 258, *f*, 2; H. 425, 2. **22. una significatione litterarum**: = 'by a single written order,' explaining *nuntio;* like our phrase, 'by a stroke of the pen.' So Ahasuerus (Xerxes) sent forth an order to destroy all the Jews (Esther iii. 12–15). **24. suscepit**: 'has suffered.' **26. et ita**: = 'yes, and so.' **28. patrio regno**: cf. p. 27. **vectigalibus**: cf. 117, 27, and N. **29. in Asiae luce**: =

'in the front of Asia,' 'in the face of Asia,' the populous and highly civilized regions along the Aegean Sea; contrasted with *Ponti neque Cappadociae latebris.*

31. insignia victoriae: for *triumphos;* preferred for the sake of contrast with *victoriam.* **32. L. Sulla**: his triumph was in 81 and lasted two days, presenting a magnificent display of spoils and captives; that of Murena — more a mockery than a triumph — was celebrated in the following year. **34. ita**: i. e. in such a limited way — after the manner of "the play of Hamlet with Hamlet left out."

Page 119. 1. ille . . . regnaret: '(though) routed and vanquished, he (yet) remained king.' **2. quod egerunt**: 'in that they were energetic,' 'in that they did something;' implied reflection upon Glabrio, who is doing nothing. **3. reliquerunt**: 'left (something) undone.' **4. res publica**: 'the (condition of) public affairs,' 'the public interest.'

IV. 7. ad oblivionem veteris belli: i. e. *ad oblivionem veteris belli faciendam sibi et populo Romano.* **10. Bosporanis**: peoples along the Cimmerian Bosporus (*Bosporus Cimmericus*), in the modern Crimea; see Map. **12. legatos ac litteras**: a kind of hendiadys; we should say, 'envoys with letters.' **duces**: Sertorius and his associates. This alliance was brought about by two renegade Romans, Lucius Magius and Lucius Fannius. Sertorius sent Roman officers to train the forces of Mithridates; the latter agreed to send ships and men to Sertorius (see p. 124, 2-4). **14. disiunctissimus**: 'very widely separated,' while *maxime diversis* means 'most unlike,' referring to the differences in climate and surroundings. **15. binis**: why not *duo?* Cf. B. 81, 4, *b*; A. 95, *b*; H. 174, 2, 3). **16. ancipiti**: 'on two sides.' **de imperio**: 'for empire,' 'for sovereignty.'

19. quae . . . habebat: spoken out of compliment to Pompey. **firmamenti**: 'support,' referring to external resources, as contrasted with *roboris*, 'strength,' internal power. **21. virtute**: cf. p. 117, 11, and N. **res — est administrata**: for *bellum est administratum.* **22. initia . . . videantur**: = 'it appears that those great and brilliant successes at the beginning must have been due, not to good fortune, but to generalship,' etc. Cf. N. to p. 67, 17. **24. extrema . . . fortunae**: see p. 31; the defeat of Triarius took place in the absence of

Lucullus. **27. ut — videatur**: 'that it will be seen that.' Why not fut.? **30. exorsus**: 'first part;' more general than *exordium*. **31. putetis**: Cicero often introduces a word meaning 'think,' 'consider,' in cases like this, in order to soften the expression. Trans. freely, 'in your view,' as if *quem . . . suscipiendum* followed immediately after *videte*.

V. 33. nostris: 'of ours.' **iniuriosius**: '(only) somewhat unfairly;' perhaps the orator has in mind the wars against the piratical peoples of Illyria. Cf. Cic. in Verr. V. LVIII. 149: *Quot bella maiores nostros et quanta suscepisse arbitramini, quod cives Romani iniuria adfecti, quod navicularii retenti, quod mercatores spoliati dicerentur?*

Page 120. 2. appellati superbius: at a meeting of the Achaean League, at Corinth. Cicero for obvious reasons adopts the mildest form of the tradition regarding the treatment of the ambassadors; according to one account they were hooted out of the meeting, and in another mention is made of violence.

3. totius Graeciae lumen: there is a similar expression in a fugitive Greek verse, Κόρινθος ἄστρον οὐκ ἄσημον Ἑλλάδος, 'Corinth, of Greece the undimmed star.' So Milton (Par. Regained, IV. 240) speaks of

"Athens, the eye of Greece, mother of arts."

exstinctum: not *exstinctam*, on account of the influence of the nearer appositive *lumen*. B. 254, 3, *a*; A. 204, *b*; H. 462, N. 2.

5. legatum consularem: Manius Aquillius, who had been consul in 101 B.C. with Marius; see p. 29. **6. omni supplicio**: 'with every kind of torture.' **excruciatum necavit**: trans. as if *excruciavit et necavit*. B. 336, 3; A. 292, R.; H. 549, 5. **8. vitam ereptam**: 'the taking of life,' i.e. *civibus Romanis*. B. 337, 5; A. 292, *a*; H. 549, 5, N. 2. **9. verbo**: 'by a word (merely).' **10. relinquetis**: for *inultum esse patiemini*. Of the sacredness of the right of embassy Cicero elsewhere says (de Har. Res. XVI. 34): *Sic enim sentio, ius legatorum, cum hominum praesidio munitum sit, tum etiam divino iure esse vallatum.*

14. Quid, quod: cf. p. 67, 33, and N. **summum periculum ac discrimen**: rhetorical amplification, as if we should say 'the greatest and extreme danger.' **15. animo**: see IDIOMS. **16. Ariobarzanes**: see pp. 29, 30. **17. ami-**

cus: see N. to p. 118, 9. **duo reges**: see p. 117, 15-19. **20. cuncta Asia**: without *in*, after the analogy of *tota Asia*; cf. p. 118, 21, and N. **24. id facere**, etc.: Glabrio or Lucullus might make life a burden for them if they should present such a request.

25. quod vos: i. e. *videtis et sentitis.* **26. summa sint omnia**: 'all qualities exist in the highest degree.' **propter**: 'close at hand,' in Cilicia, settling the affairs of that region after the campaign against the pirates. **27. quo**: 'wherefore.' **carent aegrius**: we might say, 'feel all the worse' not to have his help. **ipso**: = 'merely.' **28. maritimum bellum**: see p. 32. **29. impetus hostium repressos**: it was thought that Mithridates refrained from following up his victory over Triarius and pushing again to the west of Asia on account of the nearness of Pompey, who might come up from the south coast and attack him in the rear.

33. dignos, et seq.: 'to consider them worthy of having their welfare entrusted to such a man.' B. 282, 3; A. 320, *f*; H. 503, II. 2. **34. hoc**: why abl.? **ceteros**: here = 'in other cases.'

Page 121. **2. defendant**: sc. *eam* (i. e. *provinciam*). **3. adventus**: pl. because more than one instance is thought of. **4. hostili expugnatione**: almost = *hostium expugnatione*; see p. 131, 9, et seq. **5. praesentem**: cf. p. 120, 26, and N. **8. commoratur**: the indic. shows that here the orator is presenting the thought as his own, rather than that of the provincials.

VI. **9. propter socios**: unhappily in ancient as in modern times, the rights of allies only too often have been made merely a pretext to crush a weaker or rival power. **10. cum Antiocho**: on behalf of the kings Attalus and Eumenes of Pergamus, and the Rhodians; 192-188 B. C. **cum Philippo**: at the request of Athens; 201–196 B. C. **11. cum Aetolis**: they had become involved in the war with Antiochus, 191. **cum Poenis**: in the First Punic war, at the request of the Mamertini, in Messana; in the Second, for Saguntum; and in the Third, for Massinissa. The orator presents instances of wars for allies first with two kings, then with two peoples, making no account of the chronological order.

14. de . . . agatur: trans. as if *maxima vestra vectigalia* *aguntur;* cf. p. 118, 11. **16. tanta:** *tantula,* i. e. '(only) great enough.' **ad — tutandas:** i. e. to provide for the troops stationed in those provinces. **17. Asia:** Sicily and Asia were the most fertile among all the Roman provinces. **18. ubertate,** etc.: an enumeration of the three great sources of revenue, — produce of the soil, pasturage, and exports and imports. **19. fructuum:** 'of products,' including not only the different varieties of grain, but also vegetables, as peas and beans, and olive-oil and wine. **20. quae exportentur:** yielding *portoria;* cf. l. 31, below.

22. et belli utilitatem et pacis dignitatem: rhetorical expression for *eas res* (i. e. *vectigalia*) *quibus et belli utilitas et pacis dignitas continentur;* cf. p. 118, 12, and N. **25. venit:** i. e. *vēnit.* **26. in:** 'in the case of.' **31. ex portu:** corresponds to *mercatorum navigatio.* Customs duties (*portoria*) were collected at the harbors. **32. decumis:** 'tithes,' i. e. a tenth of all the produce of the soil. **ex scriptura:** 'from (pasturage) registration.' The herdsmen and shepherds were obliged to state in writing to the tax-collectors the number of animals they purposed to keep in the pastures during the season; the lists thus obtained were made the basis of taxation for this source of revenue.

Page 122. 2. qui — pensitant: the natives; Roman citizens at this time paid no taxes anywhere. **qui exercent:** 'who farm (them).' The revenues of a province at this time were sold to the highest bidder, that is to the corporation or individual who would agree to collect and pay over the largest sum to the state treasury each year for a specified term, keeping all that might be collected over and above that sum for profit. Revenue farmers were required to give ample security, and were bound by rigorous contracts. In the case of Asia and the other large provinces, the amounts involved were so enormous that the revenues were farmed by great stock companies, which kept their headquarters at Rome, where all payments were made into the treasury, but had stockholders or other representatives at every place in the territory in which they made collections. Ordinarily each company undertook to handle but one kind of revenue. So wealthy and powerful were these revenue corporations, which were composed of members of the equestrian order, the knights, that in a measure they took the place of government banking institutions. **3. exigunt**: '(who) collect (them);' refers particularly to the members of the corporation on the ground, who in the actual collecting were assisted by paid agents and slaves.

6. familias: 'troops of helpers,' mainly slaves. **in saltibus**: 'on the pasture lands,' collecting taxes on flocks and herds. **7. portubus**: cf. B. 49, 3; A. 70, *d*; H. 117, 1, 2). **custodiis**: '(at the) stations,' guarding frontiers and coasts to prevent smuggling. **8. magno periculo**: '(only) at great risk.' **Putatisne**: might *Num putatis* have been expected? **9. vobis fructui**: = 'a source of income to you.'

VII. 12. Ac ne illud quidem: 'And that too — not.' **13. cum essem — dicturus**: 'as I set out to speak.' **14. ad — pertinet**: 'it (i. e. *bellum*) affects.' **17. et**: expects a corresponding *et*, the place of which is taken by *deinde* in l. 23. **18. ornatissimi**: from a financial point of view. **rationes et copias**: 'enterprises and capital.' **19. ipsorum per se**: 'in and of themselves' as a class, leaving other interests out of consideration.

21. nervos rei publicae: like our 'sinews of war.' **22. eum ordinem**: i. e. *publicanorum*. **firmamentum**, etc.: i. e. because holding the purse-strings; see N. to l. 2, above. **23. ceterorum ordinum**: comprising (*a*) the senatorial order; (*b*) those members of the equestrian order not members of the revenue corporations, i. e. *ordo equestris* so far as this was not included in the *ordo* (*publicanorum*) of l. 22; and (*c*) the third estate, or commons, — all those not belonging to the senatorial or equestrian orders.

25. ipsi: 'in person,' referring to the men of the commons who were in the provinces, especially as traders. **absentibus**: 'in their absence' from Italy; cf. p. 58 under "citizens." **26. Consulere**: cf. p. 361. **partim eorum**: '(while) part of them.' (B. 201, 2; A. 216, *a*, 4; H. 397, 4), i. e. *ex ceteris ordinibus*, having especial reference to members of the Senate. It was considered inconsistent with the standing of senators to engage openly in commercial enterprises; hence they often made investments as silent partners with those engaged in business in the provinces. **27. pecunias**: 'sums of money;' hence *magnas* instead of *multas*. **collocatas habent**: 'have placed' in a financial sense, 'have invested.' B. 337, 6; A. 292, *c*; H. 388, 1, N.

28. Est: subject? **30. a re publica**: i. e. *a calamitate rei publicae.* **31. parvi refert**: in reply to a possible objection, = 'there is little in the consideration that.' B. 203, 3; A. 252, *a*; H. 404. **32. his**: sc. *vectigalibus.* **33. isdem**, etc.: the present revenue farmers, ruined, will not have the 'means,' others will not dare, to undertake the farming of revenues in these regions hereafter. **redimendi**: sc. *vectigalia;* the regular term used of bidding off the right to collect the revenues of a particular province or district.

Page 123. **2. iste**: the orator views Mithridates as if he were an opponent present before them. **3. certe**: with *docti*, 'at any rate made wiser.' **4. res**: 'property.' **5. solutione impedita**: 'by the stopping of payments' from the province. **6. fidem**: 'credit.' **7. ut**, etc.: trans. by 'without' and a participial construction. Is the economic principle stated a sound one?

10. haec ratio pecuniarum: 'this system of finance.' **11. in foro**: the shops of the money changers and money lenders (*tabernae argentariae*) were about the Forum. **12. implicata est cum — et cohaeret**: 'is involved and intimately connected with.' **13. illa**: 'those (interests).' **14. eodem motu**: 'by the same shock.' **Qua re videte**: introduces the summing up of the first division of the speech. **15. studio**: 'earnestness.' **17. fortunae — coniunctae cum re publica**: 'interests involved with those of the state.'

B. The Greatness of the War. VIII.–IX.

VIII. **20. enim**: 'Now really.' **22. ita magnum**: used instead of *tantum*, to correspond with *ita necessarium.* **In quo**: 'And in this regard.'

26. L. Lucullo, et seq.: the laudation of Lucullus is introduced opportunely at this point. The orator thereby forestalls the possible charge of slighting the services of this general, arouses the interest of his audience by suggesting the inquiry how, if Lucullus accomplished so much, the war can now be so urgent, and prepares the way for the commendation of Pompey, who is to be made out so much greater.

28. dico: emphatic, 'I affirm.' **eius adventu**: 'at (the time of) his arrival.' **27. Mithridati**: B. 188, 1, N.; A. 235, *a*; H. 384, 4, N. 2. **copias**: see p. 30. **30. instructas fuisse**

— **obsessam esse**: in dir. disc., *instructae erant — obsidebatur.* Why? **urbem**, et seq.: after withdrawing from Chalcedon (see p. 30) Mithridates besieged Cyzicus, which held out against him with great obstinacy. After a time Lucullus cut off his supplies and forced him to give up the siege and retreat.

Page 124. 1. liberavit: parenthetical statement, hence not *liberatam esse.* **classem**: consisting of fifty ships and conveying ten thousand men; it was defeated near the island of Lemnos in the Aegean Sea. See N. to p. 154, 15. **2. studio**: 'with party feeling.' **3. raperetur**: 'was being hurried along;' appropriately spoken of a fleet of war-ships driven by oars. **6. Pontum**: see p. 27 and Map. **qui**: concessive, = *cum is.* **7. ex omni aditu**: i. e. *ex omni parte, ubi aditus est.* Cf. p. 154, 5, et seq. **8. domicilia regis**: i. e. βασίλεια, 'royal residences.' **10. permultas**: 'in very great number.' **uno aditu**: rhetorical exaggeration; several of the cities offered vigorous resistance, and were finally taken only after a siege.

12. alios reges: Tigranes, king of Armenia; Machares, a son of Mithridates, who ruled the regions about the Cimmerian Bosporus; and Arsaces, king of the Parthians. **13. salvis**: in a financial sense, as often; freely, 'without taxing the allies of the Roman people, and without drawing on your revenues,' the booty amounting to more than enough to pay the expenses of the war. **15. atque ita**: 'and of such a degree.' **16. huic obtrectant legi**: 'oppose this bill,' on the ground that Lucullus is able to bring the war to a successful termination.

IX. 19. Requiretur fortasse: anticipating a possible objection; having given Lucullus so high praise, the orator proceeds to show why he is no longer able to cope with Mithridates.

24. Ponto: used in a broad sense, also with anachronism; for the myth of Medea was associated with Colchis, which was east of Pontus proper, and could be reckoned with it only as forming a part of the kingdom of Mithridates, — that, too, long after the time to which the myth belonged. **illa**: trans. 'the famous.' B. 246, 3; A. 102, *b*; H. 450, 4. **25. quam**, etc.: as Medea was fleeing with Jason — the story ran — and wished to impede the pursuit of her father Aeëtes, she hacked to pieces her small brother Absyrtus and scattered the fragments of his body along the way. **27. eorum collectio dispersa**: i. e.

collectio eorum dispersorum ('in different places'). **31. bello . . . congesserat**: see p. 29. **direptas**: trans. as if *diripuerat et.* B. 336, 3; A. 292, R.; H. 549, 5. **33. omnia**: reason for position? **diligentius**: put mildly for *avide.* **34. illum**: Aeëtes. **35. hos**: the soldiers of Lucullus.

Page 125. **2. excepit**: not immediately; see p. 31. **rebus**: dat. after *diffidentem.* **3. recreavit**: as we say, 'put new life into him.' **Cuius in regnum — venit**: in 69 B. C.; see p. 31. **5. gentes**: peoples along the Caspian Sea and southwards to the Persian Gulf; cf. Plut. Lucullus, XXVI.

7. quas . . . putavit: implying criticism of Lucullus. Though there had been no lack of pretexts for interference, the Roman Senate had refrained from becoming involved in hostilities with Tigranes and other rulers in the interior. **8. lacessendas bello**: = 'provoked by (active) hostilities,' while *temptandas*, 'exasperated,' refers to the taxing of patience with unreasonable demands and petty meanness. **9. gravis atque vehemens opinio**: 'a deep-seated and fanatical conviction.' **10. fani**: what temple is referred to is not known; according to Mommsen (Vol. IV., p. 89), probably "the temple of the Persian Nanaea or Anaitis in Elymais or the modern Luristan, the most celebrated and the richest shrine in the whole region of the Euphrates."

15. urbem: Tigranocerta; see Map. **ex regno**: instead of *regni;* lends prominence to the fact that but one city was taken, and indirectly detracts from the credit of Lucullus. **16. proeliis**: see IDIOMS. **17. tamen . . . commovebatur**: a euphemistic way of alluding to the mutiny, which was the real cause of the retreat. For the facts cf. p. 31. **18. Hic**: 'On this point.' **19. illud extremum**: 'the final outcome.' **25. fortunae**: pl. because referring to more than one instance. **multorum opes**: i. e. *multos potentes;* we should say 'many men of resources.' **30. regnum suum**: Pontus. **31. eo**: explained by the clause *ut . . . attingeret.*

Page 126. **1. poëtae**: as perhaps Naevius, who wrote a history of the First Punic War in Saturnian metre; or Ennius (see Vocab.) in his *Annales.* **2. calamitatem**: euphemistic for *cladem*, referring to the defeat of Triarius in 67 B. C. **4. non ex proelio nuntius**: i. e. Lucullus first learned of the defeat from the natives, before messengers from Triarius reached him. Some understand the passage to imply that not a Roman of that corps was left alive to tell the tale; this would be rhetorical exaggeration, for Triarius escaped, as well as a small portion of his troops.

5. in illo ipso malo: i. e. in that disaster as it stood, = 'immediately upon that disaster.' **6. tamen**: 'nevertheless,' in spite of the seriousness of the defeat. **aliqua ex parte**: 'in some measure.' **7. potuisset**: i. e. if he had retained the command. Why subj.? **vestro — qui**: cf. *nostra — qui*, p. 64, 5 and N. **9. vetere exemplo**: 'in accordance with ancient precedent.' Lucullus had held command in Asia since 74; but the limitation of the period of military commissions was being observed now less strictly than ever before. The real reason for the recall of Lucullus lay in the number and activity of his personal enemies. **10. qui**: '(those) who.' Lucullus remained in charge of a part of his troops till Pompey assumed command of the war against Mithridates.

12. ea: i. e. *quae praetereo;* explained by *quantum . . . pulso.* **13. quantum**: i. e. *quam magnum et quam periculosum.* **putetis**: 'you are to consider;' cf. N. to p. 119, 31. **14. coniungant**: = 'unite in waging.' Reason for the order of words in this and the following clauses? **15. integrae**: with which the Romans have not yet waged war. **novus**: hence inexperienced; a hint at Glabrio. **16. noster**: 'of ours,' 'sent by us.'

C. The Choice of a Commander. X.–XXIII.

A. *Affirmative Argument* (see p. 35).

X. 17. Satis . . . videor: 'I think I have said enough (to show);' followed by a summary of the preceding parts. **18. esset**: trans. as if present; why not *sit?* B. 268, 2; A. 287, *i*; H. 495, I. **19. restat ut — dicendum esse videatur**: = 'there remains only the apparent necessity of speaking,' 'I have yet to speak only of;' *restat ut*, like *reliquum est ut*, is used to introduce the last point in a series; here, the last of the three main divisions of the speech. **21. videatur**: used, like *putetis* (cf. p. 119, 31, and N.) to lend an air of modesty to the expression and round out the sentence.

22. innocentium: opposed to *avarorum*; see p. 130, 24 et seq. **haberetis**: why not *habeatis?* B. 279, 2; A. 267, and *b*; H. 483, 1, 2. **23. potissimum**: = 'above all others.' **25. unus**: '(only) one.' **26. sunt**: why not *sint?* **27. antiquitatis**: abstract for concrete; 'the man of the past cherished in memory.' **virtute**: cf. p. 117, 11 and N. **30. summo**: 'of the first rank.' **res**: 'qualities.' **31. scientiam rei militaris**: 'mastery of the art of war.' An enumeration such as the following was called by the rhetoricians a thesis. **virtutem**: here 'power as a general.'

33. scientior: sc. *rei militaris*. **34. pueritiae disciplinis**: 'the training of childhood.'

Page 127. **1. bello maximo**: the Social War. In 89 B. C. Pompey's father, then consul, took Asculum and conquered the people of Picenum. The next year as proconsul he reduced the Vestinians and Paelignians. In 87, at the request of the Senate, he went to Rome to prevent Cinna from entering the city; and at this time young Pompey rendered him important service in repressing mutiny and thwarting plots to take his life. **4. ineunte**: see IDIOMS. In 83 B. C., as Sulla came back from the East, Pompey raised three legions in the Picene country, where his father had great estates, and set out to join that champion of the aristocracy. On the way he gained three victories over detachments of the Marian party. When he finally joined Sulla, greeting his commander with the salutation "Imperator," the latter, pleased with his troops and his victories, hailed him "Imperator" in return.

5. hoste, inimico: distinction? **7. confecit**: 'has completely reduced.' **9. alienis . . . triumphis**: an elaborate but forceful climax of antitheses.

13. Civile [bellum]: between Marius and Sulla; reference in particular to Pompey's brief and victorious campaign in 82 B. C. against Carbo in Sicily, and that in 77 against M. Aemilius Lepidus, who endeavored to overthrow the constitution as established by Sulla, but was driven out of Italy, then out of Cisalpine Gaul. **Africanum**: this campaign, also in 82 B. C., was against Gnaeus Domitius Ahenobarbus, of the Marian party, and Hiarbas, king of Numidia, who had entered into an alliance with him. With six legions Pompey destroyed the forces of both commanders at Utica, and captured their camp. Domitius was killed. Hiarbas escaped to his own kingdom, where he was shortly afterwards murdered, being succeeded by Hiempsal.

14. Transalpinum: a series of engagements with tribes of Transalpine Gaul that had been induced by emissaries of Sertorius to oppose Pompey on his march to Spain, in 76 B. C. **Hispaniense**: with Sertorius and the remnants of the Sertorian party in Spain; this war came to an end shortly after the death of Sertorius in 72 B. C. Between *Hispaniense* and *servile* the MSS. insert *mixtum ex civitatibus atque ex bellicosissimis nationibus*. The thought of the inserted clause is not inappropriate in the connection; yet it is not good Latin, and interrupts the movement of the sentence, so that it may safely be rejected as not Ciceronian, at least in its present form. **servile**: on his way from Spain in 71, Pompey accidentally fell in with a troop of five thousand slaves from the army of Spartacus, and easily defeated and slew them. They had escaped the fate of their associates in the battle with Crassus in Lucania, and were trying to cut their way through into Gaul. Elated with the victory, Pompey sent word to the Senate that Crassus had beaten the slaves in battle, but that he had plucked up the war by the roots. **navale**: with the pirates; see p. 32, and chap. XII.

15. varia . . . hostium: i. e. 'different kinds of wars with enemies in far different places.' **17. nullam . . . militari**: 'that there is no point arising in military experience.'

XI. 19. virtuti: here 'character,' as the sum of the traits mentioned below. **22. illae sunt**, etc.: *illae virtutes imperatoriae* ('qualities befitting a commander'), *quae vulgo existimantur* ('are generally so regarded'), *non sunt solae virtutes imperatoriae*. The 'other qualities' are not discussed till chap. XIII. (p. 130, 19 et seq.).

23. labor in negotiis: i. e. 'power of application in matters of routine.' **24. industria in agendo**: 'energy in action.' **25. consilium in providendo**: 'resource in calculation.' **26. quae**: 'and these qualities.'

29. Italia, etc.: see N. to l. 4, above. The orator touches lightly on this point; for Pompey's service under Sulla was against the leaders of that party to representatives of which he was speaking. **31. Sicilia — Africa**: see N. to l. 13, above.

Page 128. 1. Gallia — Hispania — Italia: see N. to p. 127, 14. **7. absente**: in Spain. Crassus requested the Senate to recall Pompey from Spain and Marcus Lucullus from Thrace to help in putting down the war with Spartacus, then made haste to finish the war himself in order to get the full credit **9. iam**: 'further.' **11. universa**: 'throughout their extent.'

13. Quis locus, etc.: the boldness and success of the pirates at the time referred to almost transcend belief. In the words of Mommsen (Vol. IV., p. 99): "Almost under the eyes of the fleet of Lucullus, the pirate Athenodorus surprised in 685 (= 69 B. C.) the island of Delos, destroyed its far-famed shrines and temples, and carried off the whole population into slavery. The island Lipara, near Sicily, paid to the pirates a fixed tribute annually to remain exempt from like attacks. Another pirate chief, Heracleon, destroyed in 682 (72 B. C.) the squadron equipped in Sicily against him, and ventured with no more than four open boats to sail into the open harbor of Syracuse. . . . But even the sacred soil of Italy was no longer respected by the shameless transgressors: from Croton they carried off with them the temple treasures of the Lacinian Hera; they landed in Brundisium, Misenum, and Caieta, in the Etruscan ports, and even in Ostia itself; they seized the most eminent Roman officers as captives, among others the admiral of the Cilician army, and two praetors with their whole retinue, with the dreaded *fasces* themselves and all the insignia of their dignity; . . . they destroyed in the port of Ostia the Roman war fleet equipped against them and commanded by a consul. The Latin husbandman, the traveller on the Appian highway, the genteel visitor at the terrestrial paradise of Baiae, were no longer secure of their property or their life for a single moment; all traffic and all intercourse were suspended; the most dreadful scarcity prevailed in Italy, and especially in the capital, which subsisted on transmarine grain."

17. hieme: i. e. exposed to winter storms; yet even these (cf. Dio Cass., XXXVI., IV.) were not a protection against the freebooters. Navigation on the Mediterranean ordinarily ceased from about the middle of November to the earlier part of March; cf. Acts xxvii. 9, 12. **referto**: followed by the gen. after the analogy of *plenus*. Cf. B. 204, 1; A. 218, *a*; H. 399, I., 3. **20. omnibus imperatoribus**: i. e. living at that time. Notice the chiastic order in *ab omnibus uno anno — omnibus annis ab uno imperatore*. **omnibus annis**: i. e. of his life.

XII. 28. Fuit: not *erat*, as implying that what has been no longer is; cf. p. 62, 5 and N. **29. proprium**: 'characteristic.' **30. propugnaculis**: armies and fleets. **32. dicam**: why subj.? **33. vestri**: emphatic, 'your own.' According to Plutarch (Pomp. xxiv.), the pirates had more than a thousand ships, and had captured over four hundred towns. **hieme**: see IDIOMS.

Page 129. 1. venirent: to Rome, as ambassadors. **2. redempti sint**: 'were ransomed.' There is a story that a certain Roman ambassador was ransomed by his wife; as no other instance of the kind has come down to us, possibly the pl. here is rhetorical. **3. duodecim secures**: i. e. two praetors; for outside of Rome a praetor was allowed to have six lictors. Cf. Plut. Pomp. XXIV.: 'On one occasion (the pirates) seized two praetors, Sextilius and Bellinus, in their purple-bordered robes of office, together with their attendants and lictors, and carried them all off.'

4. Cnidum, etc.: all formerly great commercial centres. See Map. **7. eos portus, quibus**, etc.: Caieta, Misenum, Ostia. Owing to the decline of Italian farming and the enormous increase of population at Rome, the city depended for its subsistence on the supplies of grain which were imported from Sicily, Sardinia, Egypt, and Africa, through the harbors nearest the city. If the importation of grain was interfered with, there was immediate alarm; if it was stopped, distress was soon felt.

9. An vero ignoratis: in ordinary prose, *Nam profecto non ignoratis*. **celeberrimum**: 'much frequented.' **10. inspectante praetore**: 'under the eyes of the praetor' who, presumably, had been sent to protect the harbor. **12. liberos**: rhetorical pl.; the daughter of Marcus Antonius the orator was taken, and was 'ransomed for a great sum of money' (Plut. Pomp. xxiv.). For the efforts of this Antonius against the pirates in 102 B.C., see Mommsen, Vol. III., p. 171; for those of his son, see N. to p. 143, 2.

15. cum: i. e. *quae tum accepta est, cum*. **prope inspectantibus vobis**: Ostia, at the mouth of the Tiber, was only sixteen miles from Rome; yet there the pirates sailed into the harbor 'and burned the ships and plundered everything' (Dio Cass. XXXVI. v.). **16. consul**: his name, omitted by Cicero no doubt to spare the disgrace, is not known. **20. lucem**: i. e. hope of safety. **adferre**: 'shed.' **22. ei**: saves the repetition of *vos;* in our idiom, = 'even you.' How lit.? **Oceani ostium**: i. e. *fretum Gaditanum*, the Straits of Gibraltar; contrasted — also with chiastic arrangement — with *ostium Tiberinum*. The contrast was more forceful to the ancient than to the modern mind, because of the primitive but current conception of the ocean as a stream flowing about the earth.

24. Atque: 'And then.' **25. praetereunda non sunt**: for *praetereundum non est;* attracted to agree with *haec*, which belongs with *gesta sint*. **27. tam brevi tempore**: repeated in *celeriter;* for *tam brevi tempore quam celeriter* is simply a fuller expression for *tam celeriter quam*, making prominent the great rapidity of movement. **29. tanti belli impetus**: i. e. 'an attacking fleet of so great force;' a striking metaphor, perhaps chosen to provide a subject parallel with *quis;* in simple prose, *quam Cn. Pompeius dux cum tanta classe tanto impetu navigavit*. **31. adiit, exploravit, venit**: simultaneously, through his lieutenants. **32. frumentaria subsidia**: see N. to l. 7, above.

Page 130. 1. duabus Hispaniis: *Citeriore et Ulteriore;* cf. p. 60. **2. Gallia Transalpina**: i. e. *Gallia Narbonensis*, along the southern coast. **4. Achaiam**: when coupled with *Graecia* refers to the Peloponnesus only; the province of *Achaia* was not organized till many years after the subjugation of Greece, in 146 B. C. **Italiae duo maria**: the Tuscan and the Adriatic. **6. ut**: 'after.' **8. Ciliciam**: the stronghold of piracy. **10. imperio ac potestati**: i. e. they not only surrendered, but surrendered unconditionally. According to Strabo (XIV. III. par. 665), Pompey burned more than thirteen hundred ships of the pirates (cf. N. to p. 128, 33), 'and utterly destroyed their settlements. Of those who survived the battles he carried some off to Soli (in Cilicia; see Map), to which he gave the name Pompeiopolis, and others to Dyme (in Thrace), which was losing its population, but is now a Roman colony.'

11. Cretensibus, etc.: the task of subduing the Cretans had been assigned in 68 B. C. to Quintus Metellus, who was carrying it out with the greatest cruelty. Nominally Crete came under the provisions of the Gabinian bill; and Pompey, in the face of all requirements of military courtesy, encouraged the inhabitants to make terms with him, from whom they would no doubt receive better treatment than from Metellus. The latter, however, strenuously resisted this interference with his prerogatives, and Pompey wisely let the matter drop. **usque in Pamphyliam**: strong expression, appropriate for one going from Rome; but it was only a short distance from Crete to Pamphylia. Cicero's hearers were not well posted on nice points in the geography of the Orient. **12. legatos deprecatoresque**: i. e. *legatos ad deprecandum.* **13. non ademit**; 'he did not withhold.' **-que**: = 'but.' **15. quo bello**: 'a war in which.'

XIII. 18. Est haec: 'Such is.' **19. Quid**: = 'But further.' **quas paulo ante**, etc.: implied rather than mentioned, p. 127, 22–23. **21. bellandi virtus**: not merely 'fighting quality,' as shown by what follows; rather 'military character.' **23. artes**: not 'arts;' used as a synonym of *virtutes.* **huius . . . virtutis**: = 'which attend and wait upon this trait;' cf. p. 35, *b.* **27. Quae**: 'Now — these.' Why neut.? **28. Summa**, etc.: cf. p. 120, 26, and N. **29. aliorum**: 'with others,' we should say.

32. ullo in numero: i. e. *imperatorum;* = 'of any standing.' **34. Quid**, etc.: sc. *putare possumus;* 'What exalted or worthy thought for the welfare of the state can we suppose that this man has, who.' B. 176, 2; A. 238, *b*; H. 371, II. (2). It is not known to whom reference is made.

Page 131. 3. cupiditatem provinciae: i. e. *cupiditatem provinciae retinendae;* the commander mentioned by way of illustration was supposed to be already in charge. **4. in quaestu**: i. e. on interest. So Cicero charges Piso (in Pis. XXXV. 86), among other dishonorable transactions, with having placed 18,000,000 sesterces (more than $725,000) of government money at interest in Rome. **5. facit**: 'shows.' **7. nisi qui**: 'unless (some one) who;' on the principle expressed in our proverb, "Whom the cap fits, let him put it on."

11. ferant: 'bring' with them. **12. civium Romanorum**: free inhabitants of Italy who had become Roman citizens after 89 B. C.; cf. p. 148, 1–5 and N. **13. fecerint**: why not *fecerunt?* **15. plures**, etc.: *plures urbes hostium armis militum vestrorum esse deletas.* Reason for the order of words? **17. hibernis**: provincial cities (with the exception of the *liberae civitates*) were required to furnish winter-quarters for the Roman forces; but they frequently purchased exemption from the intolerable burden with great sums of money.

18. Neque enim: 'And (with good reason), for — not.' **19. qui . . . continet**: perhaps a hint at the self-indulgence of the luxury-loving Lucullus. **21. Hic**: 'Under these conditions.' **23. non modo**: trans. as if *non modo non*; cf. p. 71, 21, and N. **manus, vestigium**: the former, as free from robbery and extortion; the latter, as doing no damage to fields and crops along the line of march. **24. cuiquam pacato**: freely, 'a single friendly native.' **26. sermones ac litterae**: we should say, 'verbal and written reports.' **27. militem**: collective, 'soldiery.' **28. Hiemis**: 'from the winter,' objective gen.; but *avaritiae*, 'for avarice,' is subjective.

XIV. 31. Age vero: 'But come,' like *Age nunc*, 'Come now,' a mark of vivid transition; used in the singular even when the following verb, as here, is a pl. imp. **temperantia**: one of the four cardinal virtues; see p. 87, 2, and N. **33. incredibilem cursum**: 'inconceivable (rapidity of) movement.' **inventum**: sc. *esse*, 'was acquired,' 'was made possible.'

Page 132. 5. amoenitas: i. e. *amoenitas locorum*, 'the charm of natural scenery.' **6. ad cognitionem**: = 'to make its acquaintance,' 'to visit it.' **7. signa et tabulas**: 'statues and paintings,' which Roman generals systematically appropriated and carried off, as Mummius at the sacking of Corinth.

13. delapsum: we should say, 'sent down,' as having a divinely appointed mission. **14. fuisse . . . quod**: i. e. 'that there really were men of Rome in the olden time who possessed such self-mastery as this (which we see in Pompey), a fact which.' **15. falso memoriae proditum**: we should say, 'based upon unfounded tradition.' **17. adferre**: cf. p. 129, 20. **19. ea**: for *tanta*.

21. aditus ad: in our idiom, 'audiences with.' The order in which the remaining *artes eximiae* are treated is somewhat different from that given at the beginning (p. 130, 26–27), and is as follows: *facilitas* (ll. 20–24); *ingenium* (25–28); *fides* (28-30); *humanitas* (30 et seq.). **liberae**: i. e. *non impeditae*. **23. par**: 'on a level with.'

25. quantum — valeat: 'how great power he possesses.' **consilio**: 'insight.' **26. in quo ipso**: '(a talent) in which of itself.' **27. imperatoria**: 'befitting a commander.' **hoc ipso ex loco**: put briefly for *cum hoc ipso ex loco* (i. e. the Rostra) *verba faceret*. For Cicero's estimate of Pompey's oratory, see Brut. LXVIII. 239. **33. Et**: 'then;' *Et quisquam* introduces the conclusion of the preceding line of argument. Notwithstanding the orator's high praise, Pompey's career as a whole shows that he was a cold-blooded and extremely selfish man, with whom his own advancement was ever the ruling motive. His humaneness is praised also by Dio Cassius (XXXVI. xx.); but the fact remains that he could be cruel, and even treacherous, when his own interests seemed to demand it. **34. transmittendum**: i. e. from the hands of Glabrio; hence not *deferendum*.

Page 133. 1. nostrae memoriae: i. e. *nostri temporis; eius temporis cuius meminimus.*

XV. 3. auctoritas: 'standing.' **4. multum, plurimum**: see IDIOMS. B. 176, 2, 3, *a*; A. 238, *b*; H. 378, 2. **5. ea re**: 'in this regard.' **6. Vehementer pertinere ad**: 'that it has a very important bearing on.' **8. quis**: cf. p. 61, 11, and N.

14. De: 'On.' **16. iudicia**: in the offices and commands conferred upon him by the people, as in the following instance. **17. illius diei**: when the bill of Gabinius (see p. 32) was passed. **19. templis**: i. e. the steps of the temples about the Forum.

23. ut plura non dicam neque: i. e. 'to leave more unsaid and not to;' stronger than *ne plura dicam.* **26. qui quo die**: = *nam eo die quo is*, 'for on the day on which he.' **27. vilitas annonae**: Plutarch says (Pomp. xxvi.) that 'the immediate fall in the prices of market goods (τῶν ὠνίων) caused the delighted people to remark that the very name of Pompey had ended the war.' **28. ex summa inopia**: temporal, while *ex summa ubertate* is causal. **29. hominis**: objective gen. with *spe* ('in such a man') and subjective with *nomine* (= 'his'). **31. potuisset**: why subj.?

33. invitus: trans. as if an adv. B. 239; A. 191; H. 443. **admonui**: p. 126, 1 et seq.

Page 134. 2. ad ipsum discrimen eius temporis: 'at the decisive moment of that crisis.' **3. ad**: not *in*, because Pompey did not enter the regions mentioned; trans. 'into the vicinity of.' **7. Et**: as p. 132, 33. **perfecturus sit**: 'he is going to accomplish;' stronger than *perficiat.* **10. rumore**: i. e. *eius adventus.*

XVI. 12. Age vero: cf. p. 131, 31, and N. **16. noster**

imperator: 'a commander of ours,' i. e. Quintus Metellus. The orator makes the most of a proceeding not at all creditable to Pompey; see N. to p. 130, 11. **17. esset**: B. 309, 3; A. 313, *d*; H. 515, III. **in ultimas prope terras**: rhetorical exaggeration; cf. p. 130, 11, and N.

19. Quid: cf. p. 64, 6, and N. **20. Mithridates**, etc.: Mithridates conducted negotiations with Sertorius in Spain (cf. p. 119, 12, and N.); but of this incident nothing is known beyond what is said — or intimated — here. The construction of *eum . . . iudicavit* is awkward and un-Ciceronian; Eberhard bracketed the words *eum — Pompeius legatum semper iudicavit* as spurious, so that the sentence would read *quem ei, quibus erat molestum*, etc. **22. quibus erat molestum**: 'who were vexed;' the reference is probably to Metellus Pius, the other commander in the war with Sertorius. **23. potissimum**: i. e. rather than to any one else. Cf. p. 126, 23, and N. **25. hanc auctoritatem**: why placed here rather than in the clause *quantum . . . valituram esse?* **27. iudiciis**: cf. p. 133, 16, and N.

30. Reliquum est, ut: 'It only remains to;' introduces a transition to the fourth and last consideration in the argument concerning Pompey's military character. Cf. p. 126, 19, and N. **praestare de**: 'guarantee for.' **31. meminisse**, etc.: asyndeton; in our idiom, '(but which) we,' etc. **32. sicut . . . deorum**: sc. *dicere;* 'as men ought to speak of (that which lies within) the power of the gods.' **33. timide et pauca**: = 'reverently and (with only) a few words.' **34. sic existimo**: = 'hold this opinion.'

Page 135. 3. Fuit enim profecto adiuncta: = 'For there has certainly been at the side of.' **4. ad . . . gloriam**: i. e. *ad amplitudinem augendam et ad gloriam adipiscendam.* **10. videamur**: trans. 'that we (I) may be seen.' Why? **invisa**: 'offensive' on account of arrogance and presumption, the manifestation of which on the part of mortal man was thought to call down the jealous vengeance and retribution of the gods. The story of Niobe illustrates this belief; see the editor's "Selections from Ovid," pp. 132–137. **11. ingrata**: 'thankless,' as not recognizing in past blessings the hope and promise of future gifts.

13. non sum praedicaturus: it would be difficult to present the good luck of Pompey more strongly than in this paragraph, where the orator professes to refrain from treating the topic, — a fine example of the rhetorical figure called by the ancient grammarians *praeteritio*. **17. venti tempestatesque**: in our phrase, 'wind and weather.' **18. hoc**: '(only) this.' **20. tacitus**: '(even) in silence,' — the unuttered prayers of the heart. **quot et quantas**: in our idiom simply 'as;' the Latin expression is more forcible than the English. **21. Quod . . . sit**: 'And that this (favor of fortune) may be his sure and lasting possession.' **24. facitis**: 'you are (actually) doing.'

25. Qua re: introduces a summary of all the preceding argument as a preparation for that which is to follow. Cf. N. to p. 66, 5. **29. dubitatis**: 'do you (still) hesitate;' followed by *quin* . . . *conferatis* ('to,' etc.) instead of *conferre*, because the interrogation gives the principal clause a negative force. B. 298, *b*; A. 319, *d*; H. 505, I. 1. **30. hoc tantum boni**: 'this so great blessing,' 'this so great advantage.'

XVII. 34. Quod si: B. 185, 2; A. 240, *b*; H. 453, 6. **privatus**: 'a private citizen.'

Page 136. 1. is erat deligendus: 'he would be the one to be chosen.' B. 304, 3, *b*; A. 308, *c*; H. 511, 2. **2. nunc**: cf. p. 68, 16, and N. **3. haec opportunitas**: explained by the following *ut*-clauses. **5. qui habent**: for *qui exercitus habent;* i. e. Lucullus, who with the remnants of his forces was on the upper Halys (see Map) near Pontus; Glabrio, who was lingering in the west of Asia; and Marcius Rex, who had three legions in Cilicia. **7. cetera summa cum salute**: 'other (trusts) — to the highest welfare' Cf. p. 74, 28, and N.

B. *Refutation*.

10. At enim: 'But (not so); for,' 'But indeed;' introduces an objection. Cf. p. 35. **11. adfectus**: 'honored;' he had been consul in 78 B. C. **12. honoris, fortunae, virtutis, ingeni**: i. e. as an ex-consul, as a man of wealth, as a man of character (though his methods of acquiring wealth were said not to be above reproach), and as a man of talent. Hortensius was Cicero's chief rival in oratory; cf. p. 14. **13. ratione**: 'view.' **14. Quorum**: 'Now of those men.' **auctoritatem**: here 'weight of opinion.' **15. multis locis**: 'on many occasions.' **plurimum valuisse**: see IDIOMS. **17. virorum**: the supporters of Manilius; see p. 143, 13 et seq. **18. omissis**

auctoribus: 'if we lay aside (the weight of) opinions.' **ipsa re ac ratione**: = 'the actual state of the case.' **21. isti**: the opponents of the bill. B. 246, 4; A. 102, *c*; H. p. 248, foot-note 4. **22. summa**, etc.: cf. p. 120, 26, and N.

25. ad . . . oportere: we should say, 'that all powers ought not to be vested in a single individual.' The concentration of power authorized by the bill of Gabinius and contemplated by that of Manilius was inconsistent with both the spirit and the letter of the Roman constitution. A balance of authority between the departments of government, so that, except in the emergencies provided for by the dictatorship, one person might not become supreme, had been the aim of the republican organization from the beginning. For this principle the aristocratic party had earnestly contended; and Cicero at heart was thoroughly in sympathy with it. He could not return any answer to the argument of Hortensius on constitutional grounds; and so he parried it skilfully by gliding off into a digression on the horrors and disgrace of the supremacy of the pirates, and Pompey's success in ridding the Mediterranean of this pest. His sole counter-argument is, if Pompey rescued the state then, why not now? In fact neither Hortensius nor Cicero nor any of their contemporaries, excepting possibly Caesar, understood that the tendencies of the Roman government were no longer within the channels of the constitution, or within the control of any political party. These had long since set toward imperialism, toward an absolute monarchy, which was sure to come sooner or later. The bill of Manilius was passed, not so much because it was supported by the eloquence of Cicero as for the reason that it was directly in the line of governmental tendencies at this time, another advance toward the permanent supremacy of an individual.

27. ista oratio: 'that argument of yours.' **28. Hortensi**: B. 25, 1; A. 40, *c*; H. 51, 5. **30. fortem**: as sustaining his position against the strenuous opposition of the aristocracy. Cf. p. 138, 26, and N. **32. promulgasset**: 'had given notice' in accordance with the rule which required that a bill be announced publicly at least seventeen days before it could be voted on. The interval afforded opportunity for the discussion of a measure in the Senate as well as among the people.

Page 137. **2. vera causa**: 'the true interest.' **4. An**:

B. 162, 4, *a*; A. 211, *b*; H. 353, N. 4. **5. legati**, etc.: see p. 129, 1 et seq. The quaestors were probably those in the retinue of the captured praetors. **6. commeatu**: see N. to p. 129, 7. **8. rem — obire**: 'to transact business.' See N. to p. 128, 13.

XVIII. 10. Quae civitas, etc.: for the argument see N. to p. 136, 25. **non dico Atheniensium**: = 'I do not mean that of Athens.' The sovereignty of Athens as a maritime power in the fourth century B. C. extended over the islands in the Aegean Sea, the coast of Asia Minor as far as Pamphylia, and the Thracian Bosporus as far north as the Euxine Sea. Cf. Map. **11. mare**: i. e. *imperium maris*. **12. permultum**: see IDIOMS. **13. Rhodiorum**: after the time of Alexander Rhodes became the most powerful among maritime states, and also a centre of art and culture. Its power had now declined, but even in Cicero's day men went to Rhodes to study oratory, as did Caesar and Cicero himself.

16. quae non: = *ut ea — non*. **19. legem Gabiniam**: see p. 32. **20. cuius nomen**: 'although its name.' B. 283, 3, *b*; A. 320, *e*; H. 515, III. **21. invictum**: true only in a rhetorical sense. **22. ac**: = 'and in fact.' **23. utilitatis**: because of inability to collect revenues and protect commerce. **dignitatis et imperi**: because unable to protect its allies or even its own officers.

24. Antiochum: after the battle at Thermopylae, in 191 B. C., the Romans opened a way to Asia across the Aegean Sea by defeating two fleets of Antiochus near the Ionian coast, and also an allied fleet, commanded by Hannibal, off Aspendus. **Persem**: after the battle of Pydna, B. C. 168, Perseus fled to Samothrace, but there gave himself up without a struggle to the Roman admiral Gnaeus Octavius. Octavius afterwards celebrated a triumph in honor of this event, a triumph, as Livy dryly remarks (XLV. XLII.), 'without captives and without spoils.'

25. omnibus navalibus pugnis: rhetorical overstatement; witness the crushing defeat of Marcus Claudius Pulcher off Drepanum, in Sicily, in 249 B. C. **27. ei**: saves the repetition of *nos*; = 'even we.' Cf. p. 129, 22, and N. **28. pares**: = 'a match for.' **30. salvos praestare**: = 'to guarantee the safety of.' **32. quo . . . commeabant**: Delos was a convenient stopping-place for the route between Greece and Asia, and was thought to be secure from all attack on account of the sacredness of its sanctuaries; cf. N. to p. 70, 1. After the destruction of Corinth, B. C. 146, it increased rapidly in importance as a centre of traffic. Already in the First Mithridatic War it had suffered at the hands of a general of Mithridates, Menophanes by name, who murdered the inhabitants, carried away the offerings and treasures of the temples, and razed the city Delos to the ground.

33. referta . . . muro: 'although filled,' etc. **34. eidem**: as *ei*, in l. 27.

Page 138. **2. Appia via,** etc.: i. e. even the Appian Way was unsafe; see N. to p. 128, 13. **4. hunc ipsum locum**: the Rostra, as adorned with the spoils of naval victories (*exuviis nauticis*); see N. on p. 227.

XIX. **7. Bono animo**: here 'with good intentions.' **10. in salute communi**: = 'in a matter affecting the public safety.' **dolori**: 'hurt.'

16. Quo, et seq.: 'Wherefore I think it all the more a shame that opposition has been raised,' etc. The rest of this chapter is devoted to a digression regarding the question whether Gabinius should be allowed to serve under Pompey as a lieutenant. Provincial lieutenants were nominated by the Senate, which ordinarily consulted the wishes of the governors. There was a law that if any one proposed a bill granting extraordinary powers to a magistracy, neither he nor his relatives should be eligible to the position; and this provision was construed to apply also to the subordinate officer under a magistrate with extraordinary authority. When Pompey undertook the command of the war with the pirates, Gabinius was a tribune, and could not leave the city. Though his term as tribune had expired, he was still ineligible to a lieutenancy so long as Pompey was holding the command proposed by him. Here again the orator does not argue the case on legal grounds, and touches very lightly on the point at issue.

20. idoneus . . . impetret: = 'is not fit to have his request granted.' Reason for the subjunctives? **26. periculo**: in the confusion and strife attending the passing of this bill Gabinius nearly lost his life. See Mommsen, Vol. IV. p. 135 et seq. **27. An,** et seq.: trans. the clause *C. Falcidius . . . potuerunt* with 'while,' commencing the interrogation with *in uno Gabinio*. The Latin often chooses the antithetical or co-ordinating form of statement where the English prefers the arrangement of principal and subordinate clauses.

28. honoris causa nomino: 'I mention with all due respect;' a kind of apology for bringing in the names of men still living. **29. anno proximo**: apparently there was a provision, or at least a custom, that tribunes of the people should not go out as lieutenants the next year after their term of office. **31. diligentes**: 'scrupulous.' **32. in**: trans. by 'under' with *hoc imperatore*, 'in' with *exercitu*. **33. praecipuo iure**: i. e. *praeter alios*; with *esse* [*legatus*] *deberet*, 'ought above all others to be (a lieutenant).' Some, however, think that *legatus* need not be supplied, and render 'ought to have the first claim.'

Page 139. **2. dubitabunt**: i. e. *rem ad senatum referre*. **ego . . . relaturum**: taking advantage of the right he had as praetor to bring business before the Senate. **4. inimicum edictum**: of a consul, who as presiding officer might endeavor to head off the threatened proposal by issuing a 'decree' confining the Senate to the order of the day. **vestrum ius beneficiumque**: as conferred upon Pompey and entitling him to have whom he might choose as lieutenants. **5. neque**, etc.: = 'and I shall heed nothing short of a veto,' pronounced by a consul or tribune. The orator could afford to threaten; for if the bill of Manilius failed to pass, there would be no opportunity for Gabinius to go as lieutenant; if it passed, so soon as Pompey undertook the commission established by it the main obstacle to Gabinius's lieutenancy ceased (see N. to p. 138, 16). In fact Gabinius did serve with Pompey under the new commission, and took advantage of his position to amass a fortune.

6. isti . . . considerabunt: i. e. it is very doubtful if they will dare to interpose a veto. **10. socius ascribitur**: 'is enrolled as an associate.'

XX. 13. Reliquum est: cf. p. 126, 19, and N. **auctoritate**: cf. p. 136, 14, and N. **15. quaereret**: i. e. in an address to the people on the bill of Gabinius. **omnia poneretis**: = 'you should vest all authority;' see N. to p. 136, 25. **si . . . factum esset**: 'if anything should happen to him,' euphemistic; cf. p. 104, 17, and N. B. 218, 6; A. 244, *d*; H. 415, III., N. I. **18. cum**: = *eo*, *quod*, 'in that.'

19. talis est vir, etc.: this high tribute to the character of Catulus is borne out by all that is known of him. **22. in hoc ipso**: 'on this very point,' the uncertainty of human life; the orator very neatly turns the point on Catulus. **vehementissime**: see IDIOMS. **23. quo minus — hoc magis**: 'the less — the more.' B. 223; A. 250, R.; H. 423. **25. viri vita atque virtute**: notice the alliteration.

27. At enim: cf. p. 136, 10, and N.; the ellipsis may be supplied thus, — *At imperium Cn. Pompeio deferendum non est; est enim cavendum ne quid,* etc. Our ancestors did not concentrate authority in the hands of one man; therefore we ought not to do so. Cf. N. to p. 136, 25. **28. Non dicam,** etc.: cf. p. 135, 13, and N. **30. ad . . . rationes**: freely, 'the considerations of new measures to the demands of new conditions.' **32. ab uno imperatore**: Scipio was consul in 147 B. C., and again in 134, in spite of the law that no one should be twice consul; and in both consulships he won glorious victories. Marius was seven times consul.

Page 140. 2. nuper: forty years previously. **7. summa Q. Catuli voluntate**: 'with the fullest approval of Quintus Catulus,' i. e. of the aristocratic party which Catulus represented; it is not necessary to suppose that Catulus himself actually voted for each measure mentioned.

XXI. 9. Quid: sc. *fuit.* **10. difficili,** etc.: see IDIOMS. **conficere**: 'raise.' For the incident referred to, see N. to p. 127, 4. **11. Huic praeesse**: sc. what? **Rem — gerere**: see IDIOMS.

14. a senatorio gradu: when Pompey was sent to Sicily (see N. to p. 127, 13) he was only twenty-four years old. In this period a man was not admitted to the Senate till he had held the office of quaestor, and one could not become quaestor before the end of his thirtieth year. **19. deportavit**: the term regularly used of bringing anything from the provinces to Rome. **20. equitem Romanum triumphare**: ordinarily only consuls and praetors were allowed to triumph; the triumph of Pompey, in celebration of his victory over Hiarbas (see N. to p. 127, 13; triumphs were not allowed for victories over Roman citizens in the civil wars), was the first exception to this rule. **22. vidit**: 'has witnessed,' 'has lived to see;' while *visere* means 'to go to see' out of curiosity, and *concelebrare* 'to join in celebrating' with festal attire and shouts of joy. **studio**: 'enthusiasm.'

24. inusitatum: in the sense of *contra morem.* **duo consules**: of the year 77 B. C., Mamercus Aemilius Lepidus and Decimus Junius Brutus, both of whom had declined to assume command of the war with Sertorius. **26. bellum**: see N. to *Hispaniense*, p. 127, 14. **pro consule**: i. e. with the rank and authority of a proconsul in a province. **28. non nemo**: we should say, 'more than one.' **29. L. Philippus**: famous for his sharp wit. **31. rei . . . gerendae**: 'of a successful handling of the state's interest.'

Page 141. 1. ex senatus consulto: well introduced here, as pointing out the favoring of Pompey by the Senate, the party which was opposing this bill. The Senate settled matters pertaining to triumphs; yet in setting aside the restrictions referred to, it assumed a prerogative belonging to the people. **2. legibus solutus**: 'released from the restrictions' which placed the earliest legal age for holding the consulship at forty-three, and made it necessary for a man to have been praetor before consul, and quaestor before praetor. Pompey became consul when he was thirty-five. **ullum alium magistratum**: Cicero is thinking only of the consular offices; for the quaestorship could have been held after the age of thirty. Mommsen, however, thinks that the legal age for the quaestorship was thirty-seven, though men were for various reasons admitted to it earlier.

4. iterum eques: i. e. not yet admitted to the Senate and into the senatorial order; cf. N. to p. 122, 23. This triumph was over the Spanish tribes in alliance with Sertorius (N. to p. 127, 14), and was celebrated Dec. 31, B. C. 71, the day before Pompey entered upon the duties of the consulship. **5. Quae in — nova, ea**: = 'And the innovations which in the case of.' **8. Atque**: 'And further;' the aristocracy through the Senate are responsible for all these innovations.

XXII. 12. non ferendum: = *intolerabile.* **16. cum**: 'now that.' **24. plus . . . vidistis**: 'have had a deeper insight in regard to public interests.' **26. aliquando**: for *tandem aliquando.* **isti principes**: Catulus and Hortensius as leaders of the aristocracy.

29. Atque, etc.: application of the more general statement in chapters XIII. and XIV. to the case in hand. **Asiatico et regio**: the epithets suggest the luxury of surroundings and wealth of plunder against the seductions of which few Roman officers were proof. **33. interiorum** : 'further inland.' **34. nostrum imperatorem** : 'a general of ours.' **nihil aliud**: i. e. *de alia re*. Kind of acc.?

Page 142. **2. pudore ac temperantia moderatiores**: = 'possessed of more than ordinary conscientiousness and self-mastery.' **3. cupidorum** : i. e. *pecuniae;* for *avarorum*. **7. libidines**: 'acts of lawlessness.' **11. quibus causa belli . . . inferatur**: 'against which a pretext for war can be devised.' **13. coram**: as we say, 'between ourselves,' where we can talk over men and deeds freely. **17. hostium simulatione**: = 'making the enemy a pretext (merely).' **19. non modo**: may be translated as if *non dicam*, 'I will not say'; the following *sed* is for *sed etiam*. **20. animos ac spiritus capere**: 'satisfy the arrogance and insolence.'

XXIII. **22. collatis signis**: see IDIOMS. How lit.? **24. erit idem**: 'shall also be (one).' **26. gaza**: Persian word, generally used of oriental treasure. **27. manus, oculos, animum**: rhetorical amplification of *se*. **29. Ecquam**: emphatic. **pacatam fuisse**: 'has been considered tranquillized,' i. e. 'has been left in peace.' **31. pacata esse**: 'to be in a state of tranquillity.' The only alleviating feature of the Roman provincial government of this period is, that it was in many cases no more harsh or rapacious than the government which preceded it.

Page 143. **1. pecunia publica**: see p. 131, 1–4, and N. **praeter paucos**: a saving phrase, to avoid giving offence by a sweeping statement. **2. neque . . . nomine**: 'and that they were gaining nothing else with their fleets existing only in name' (how lit?); i. e. the fleets being in so deplorable a state because the money appropriated for them had been embezzled. A notorious instance was that of Marcus Antonius, named Creticus, son of the orator, who in 74 B. C. held a command against the pirates which he turned to his own advantage, finally losing what fleet he had in a battle with the Cretans.

4. cupiditate: for money. Men ran heavily into debt with a view to recouping themselves from the governorship of a province. **5. iacturis**: 'outlays,' expenditures incurred in buying one's way to power. **6. condicionibus**: 'terms' with creditors and political supporters. **7. qui . . . arbitrantur**: cf.

p. 136, 25, and N. **10. nolite dubitare**: 'do not hesitate.' B. 276, *c*; A. 269, *a*, 2; H. 489, 1). For the constr. with *quin*, cf. p. 135, 29, and N. **11. unus**: 'the (only) one.'

14. est vobis auctor: 'you have as a supporter' of the bill. **15. P. Servilius**: see Vocab. under *Vatia*. **18. Curio**: see Vocab. under *Curio* (1). **20. ingenio**: here, as often, refers particularly to oratorical talent. **21. pro**: 'consistently with.' **22. gravitatem**: when censor in 70 B. C. with Lucius Gellius, this Lentulus (no. 4 in Vocab.) removed from the Senate no fewer than sixty-four members, not far from an eighth of the whole number. **24. ut**: here 'how,' 'whether.'

CONCLUSION. XXIV.

XXIV. 27. Quae . . . sint: here used to introduce the conclusion of the entire speech; cf. p. 36. **28. voluntatem et sententiam**: 'feeling and expressed opinion,' amplifying *legem*. **30. auctore populo Romano**: as we should say 'backed by the Roman people,' 'with the Roman people behind you.' **31. vim aut minas**: perhaps a hint at the unhappy experience of Gabinius the year before; cf. p. 138, 26, and N. **33. studio**: as p. 140, 22. **34. iterum nunc**: counting the passing of Gabinius's bill as the first time. **in**: 'in the case of.'

Page 144. 1. quid est, quod: 'what reason is there, that.' **de re**: i. e. *de praeficiendo Pompeio*.

4. quicquid: see IDIOMS. **hoc beneficio**: 'by reason of this preferment,' the honor of the praetorship, as explained and amplified by the following clause. **9. huic loco temploque**: 'this place and consecrated spot.' The original idea of *templum* was a place set aside for worship; after that either a place or a building that had been consecrated by certain religious acts. The Rostra belonged to the latter category. **12. quo**: = *quia*, 'because.' **13. quo**: = *ut eo*, 'in order that by this means.' **17. ab uno**: for *ab* ('at the hands of') *uno homine*, referring to Pompey. **18. ratione**: 'calling,' 'profession,' of advocate.

20. mihi: trans. as if *a me*; see N. to p. 159, 23. **22. tantum**, etc.: see Vocab. under *absum*. B. 284, 1; A. 332, *d*; H. 502, 3. **25. non inutiles**: litotes. B. 375, 1; A. 209, *c*; H. 637, VIII. **27. beneficiis**: praetorship, curule aedileship, quaestorship. **30. rationibus**: 'interests.'

THE ORATION FOR ARCHIAS.

Page 145. A. LICINIO ARCHIA: the name *Archias* (Ἀρχίας) was not an uncommon one, particularly among the Dorian Greeks. The Latin *nomen* and *praenomen* were assumed when the poet became a Roman citizen, *Licinius* being the gens name of his chief patrons, the Luculli; but why he chose the forename *Aulus* instead of one of those common in the family of the Luculli is not clear.

ORATIO: delivered before a court (*quaestio*), over which the orator's brother, Quintus Cicero, presided, being then praetor. Whether this was one of the regular courts (cf. p. 60), as the *quaestio de maiestate*, or a commission established by the statute under which the poet was brought to trial, is not known; it is more likely to have been the latter. For an outline of the thought, see p. 48.

INTRODUCTION.

Exordium — Partitio. I., II.

I. 1. Si quid, etc.: 'Whatever talent (i. e. for public speaking; see N. to p. 143, 20), . . . whatever readiness of speech, . . . whatever (acquaintance with the) theory of this art (of public speaking), . . . reside in me, jurors.' The orator mentions the first two essentials to success in oratory (natural ability and the readiness acquired by practice) as leading up to the third, in which lay the basis of his obligation to Archias. **ingeni**: why not *ingenii?* **quod**: subject of *sit;* trans. as if *et id.* Self-depreciatory beginnings were common in speeches of this kind, being intended to win the favorable attention of the jurors. **2. aut — aut**: for *et — et*, as more modest.

3. non infitior: litotes. B. 375, 1; A. 209, *c*; H. 637, VIII. Note the increase in positiveness, *sentio — non infitior — confiteor.* **4. optimarum . . . disciplina**: = 'the pursuit and training of the most liberal studies' (cf. p. 146, 29), i. e. philology, or grammar in the broad sense, rhetoric, music, and philosophy. Cicero was a firm believer in general culture as a foundation for oratory. **5. a qua . . . abhorruisse**: 'to which . . . has been inattentive,' or 'of which . . . has been neglectful;' the antecedent of *qua* is *ratio*. Cicero, as a practical lawyer, in a way apologizes to a jury of practical men for having given attention to the theory of oratory. **6. aetatis**: = *vitae*. **7. vel**: 'even.' **hic**: not necessarily spoken with a gesture; why? **A. Licinius**: the orator cleverly assumes the citizenship of Archias by using his Latin name.

8. suo iure: 'by an indefeasible right;' stronger than *iure* alone, as implying that the right is fully admitted by the speaker. Cf. B. 244, 4; H. 449, 2. **9. quoad longissime**: = 'just as far as.' **10. memoriam ultimam**: 'the earliest recollection.' **11. inde usque repetens**: = 'going back even to that time.' How lit.? **12. suscipiendam**: 'choosing.' **13. rationem**: 'course.'

14. Quod: 'Now.' B. 185, 2; A. 240, *b*; H. 453, 6. **praeceptis**: not *institutione*, 'instruction,' because Archias was only an intimate adviser, not a teacher, of Cicero. **15. non nullis aliquando**: modest expression. **a quo**: the apodosis begins here. **16. ceteris**: 'the rest' of my clients in general, who have availed themselves of my services. **alios**: '(many) others' than Archias, who have been brought to trial before a criminal court. Both *ceteris* and *alios* are proleptic, and should be introduced in trans. after *huic ipsi*. **17. quantum**, etc.: see IDIOMS.

19. ita: 'so (strongly).' **alia**, etc.: strange that an orator should confess obligation to a poet. **20. sit**: what different force would *est* have here? **neque**: 'and not.' **21. aut**: instead of *ac*, on account of the preceding negative. **huic uni studio**: of oratory. **22. penitus**: 'exclusively.' **dediti fuimus**: 'have been devoted;' *fuimus* is often preferred to *sumus* when the accompanying perfect pass. participle, as here, has more of an adjective than a participial force.

Page 146. **2. inter se continentur**: 'stand related to one another.' Cf. Cic. de Orat. III. VI. 21: *Est etiam illa Platonis vera . . . vox* ('saying') *omnem doctrinam harum ingenuarum et humanarum artium uno quodam societatis vinculo contineri.*

II. 4. in . . . publico: in our phrase, 'before a statute commission and state's court;' *quaestio legitima*, as established under a statute (*lex*) and not as a special commission (*quaestio extraordinaria*), such as were sometimes raised for criminal cases; *iudicium publicum*, as a court for cases affecting the state, not for the trial of contentions between individuals. **res agatur**: 'the case is being tried.' **5. praetorem**: see N. to *oratio*, on p. 298.

6. conventu hominum ac frequentia: in phrases like this Cicero usually puts the gen. after the first noun. Cf. A. 344, *g*; H. 564, II. **9. ut — detis veniam, ut patiamini**: forceful pleonasm. **11. huic reo**: 'to this (my) client.' **13. hoc**: 'such.' **14. hoc praetore**: the commentators interpret this as a complimentary reference to the taste and achievements of Quintus Cicero as a literary man and poet. His poems have all perished with the exception of a few verses, among which are a couple of cynical epigrams.

16. liberius: i. e. *liberius quam patitur consuetudo iudiciorum et fori*, as Cicero himself says elsewhere (Brut. XXXI. 120). **in eius modi persona**: 'in (the case of) a character such as this' of Archias. **17. otium ac studium**: 'retirement and devotion to study.' **in — tractata est**: we say 'has been drawn into.' **18. periculis**: = 'legal actions,' referring to criminal cases. **19. Quod si**: here = *et si id*. **20. tribui**: implies that a request is granted freely; *concedi*, not without opposition. **21. segregandum**: sc. *esse*. **23. asciscendum fuisse**: sc. *in numerum civium*; why not *esse*?

Narratio. III.–IV. (l. 8).

III. 24. ut primum: see IDIOMS. **a pueris**: concrete for abstract; = *a pueritia*. **25. ad**: 'with a view to.' **27. Antiochiae**: at this time second in importance only to Alexandria among the cities of the East, notwithstanding the fact that it had been greatly disturbed by the dynastic quarrels which had rent the kingdom of Syria, and by the inroads of the Parthians.

28. loco: 'station,' 'rank.' **urbe**: B. 169, 4; A. 184, *c*; H. 363, 4, 2). **29. studiis**: see N. to p. 145, 4. **adfluenti**: = *abundanti*. **30. contigit**: used with the infin. by Cicero only here. **31. cuncta Graecia**: cf. p. 120, 20, and N.

33. ipsius: subjective with *adventus*, objective with *admiratio*; 'his coming (in each case) and the admiration for him.' It was nothing uncommon for poets, particularly such as extemporized, to wander from place to place. Cf. p. 46.

Page 147. 1. Italia: contrasted with *Latio*, but referring particularly to Southern Italy, the region of the Greek cities. **2. Latio**: in a broad sense, meaning all that part of Italy where Latin was spoken; cf. p. 155, 2, and N. **3. tum**: before the Social War. **4. tranquillitatem**: between the death of Gaius Gracchus (121 B. C.) and the outbreak of the Social War (91) only the disturbance caused by Saturninus and Glaucia (100 B. C.) broke the 'calm' of the city. **5. et Tarentini**: the *et* is correlative with *et* before *omnes*, l. 7. A man might be a citizen of several of these Greek cities at the same time; but the citizenship of Rome was exclusive. **6. praemiis**: garlands, gifts, banquets, etc.

8. dignum: sc. *esse*. **9. absentibus**: from our point of view, *absens* might have been expected. **10. Mario consule et Catulo**: 102 B. C.; perhaps instead of the usual order, *Mario et Catulo consulibus*, because Marius was much the more prominent of the two. **11. res maximas, res gestas**: sc. *suppeditare* from *adhibere*, which governs them loosely by zeugma. **12. studium atque aures**: = 'literary interest and taste.' Catulus was a man of unusual culture.

14. praetextatus: = *adulescentulus*; see N. to p. 77, 30. The orator speaks of Archias as if he had always been a Roman. It is not easy to understand how the Greek cities could have granted their franchise so readily to a lad of sixteen or eighteen years; perhaps Cicero's words are not to be taken literally in regard to the age of the poet.

15. erat hoc: 'this was (an evidence).' **17. naturae atque virtutis**: 'of (his) disposition and character.' **19. temporibus illis**: following the year 102 B. C. **21. vivebat cum**: 'he was on intimate terms with.' **24. adficiebatur summo honore**: 'he was the recipient of the highest honor,' not only at the hands of those mentioned, but on the part of others also. **27. si qui**: 'whoever,' 'any who.' A taste for Greek was considered the proper thing; and many joined in lionizing Archias merely because it was the fashion. **simulabant**: sc. *se studere*, etc.

IV. **28. Interim**: Rome being still his place of residence. **satis**: 'tolerably.' **intervallo**: probably not far from ten years. Why abl.? **29. M. Lucullo**: he appears to have gone to Sicily on private business. **ex ea provincia decederet**: the ordinary expression used of a provincial officer leaving his province; employed here apparently to lend an air of dignity and formality to the journey of Archias. **30. Heracliam**: here probably the father of Marcus and Lucius Lucullus was living in exile.

31. iure: 'standing' in the eyes of Romans, coupled with *foedere*, 'treaty relations' with Rome. Since 278 B. C. Heraclea had been connected with Rome by a treaty, the terms of which were unusually favorable. **33. per se**: here 'for his own sake,' 'on his own account.' **34. auctoritate**: influence arising from high standing, as distinguished from *gratia*, influence due to private acquaintance.

Page 148. 1. civitas: *civitas Romana*. **Silvani lege et Carbonis**: known as the *lex Plautia Papiria*, passed 89 B. C.; see p. 46. **2. Si qui**: trans. as if *eis*, *qui*. **ascripti**: as citizens. **3. si — si**: introduce the conditions subordinate to the clause *si qui . . . fuissent*. **ferebatur**: B. 288, 1; A. 342, *a*; H. 529, II., N. 1, 2). **4. domicilium**: 'a (legal) residence.' **sexaginta diebus**: 'within sixty days.' Why abl.?

5. praetorem: in 89 B. C. there were six praetors (the number was raised to eight by Sulla; cf. p. 59), before any one of whom the acknowledgment contemplated by the law could be made; cf. l. 32. Three of the six are mentioned in this speech, Metellus Pius (no. 2 in Vocab.), Appius Claudius Pulcher (l. 34, below), and Lucius Lentulus. **essent professi**: sc. *nomina*. **6. haberet**: not *habuisset*, in order to emphasize the fact that Archias continued to reside at Rome. **7. familiarissimum**: used as subst., = *familiarissimum amicum*.

DISCUSSION.

A. *Proof that Archias is a Roman citizen.* IV. (l. 9)–X.

9. de civitate ac lege: i. e. *de civitate Romana lege Plautia Papiria data*. **10. causa dicta est**: 'our case is stated,' in that it has been shown that my client fulfilled the three conditions, enrolment as a citizen in an allied state, a legal residence in Italy, and proper acknowledgment before a praetor.

11. Grati: curtly addressed without his forename; cf. *Q. Hortensi* (p. 136, 28, and p. 138, 7); *C. Manili* (p. 143, 27); *C. Caesar* (p. 159, 21, et al.); and even in an invective we find *M. Antoni* (p. 173, 11). B. 25, 1; A. 40, *c*; H. 51, 5. **Heracliae**: B. 232, 1; A. 258, *c*, 2; H. 425, 2. **12. Adest**: as witness and supporter; sc. *nobis*. **auctoritate**: here 'weight,' 'reliability;' but *religione*, 'scrupulousness.' **14. opinari**: i. e. *hunc Heracliae adscriptum esse*. **15. egisse**: 'was instrumental' in bringing it about. **17. publico**: on behalf of the corporation of Heraclea.

19. Hic: 'At this point.' **tabulas**: 'registers,' 'records' containing the names of the citizens. **20. Italico bello**: probably some sacking of the city in the Social War caused the conflagration referred to. **21. ad**: 'in relation to,' 'in reply to.' **22. quaerere**: = *requirere*. **23. hominum memoria, litterarum memoriam**: repetition of *memoria* in order to heighten the contrast between the depositions of the witnesses and the missing documentary evidence. Cf. p. 118, 31, 32, and N. **tacere**: 'to remain silent;' like our phrase 'to keep still,' implying the suppression of that which might be spoken. **27. corrumpi**: see l. 34 et seq.

28. Romae: consistent with l. 6, above; stronger than *in Italia*, which might have been expected from the wording of the statute (l. 3). **29. ante civitatem datam**: i. e. to inhabitants of allied cities. See IDIOMS. B. 337, 5; A. 292, *a*; H. 549, 5, N. 2. **32. illa professione collegioque praetorum**: = *professione apud illud collegium praetorum facta*, covering the registration of the six praetors of 89 B. C.; cf. N. to l. 5.

V. 34. Appi: thought to have been the father of the dissolute Clodius, Cicero's enemy, for whom see pp. 7, 8.

Page 149. 1. Gabini: asyndeton; we should say 'and of Gabinius.' **2. calamitas**: mild expression for the loss of civil rights; Gabinius Capito had been condemned for provincial extortion in his governorship of Achaia. **omnem tabularum fidem resignasset**: 'had destroyed all confidence in his records.' For the force of *re-signare*, lit. 'to break open the seal of,' cf. p. 55. **3. sanctissimus modestissimusque**: 'the most conscientious and law-observing.' **4. diligentia**: 'painstaking.' **5. praetorem, iudices**: Metellus was probably giving testimony in a case concerning citizenship.

7. His in tabulis: of Metellus. **A. Licini**: not *A. Licini Archiae*, because the poet would be registered only by his Latin name. **8. quid est, quod**: 'what reason is there to.' **9. eius**: instead of *huius*, because referring to Archias as registered, as A. Licinius, rather than as present. **civitate**: at Heraclea. **10. fuerit**: not *sit*, because the registration of citizens in these places had ceased after 89 B. C., when the inhabitants became Roman citizens. **Etenim**, etc.: a *reductio ad absurdum*. **12. Graecia**: = *Magna Graecia*. **13. credo**: cf. p. 63, 4, and N. **Locrenses**: the people of *Locri Epizephyrii*, on the eastern side of the extreme southwestern part, the toe, of Italy. **14. scaenicis artificibus**: cf. N. to p. 79, 28.

17. Quid: cf. p. 64, 6, and N. **post**: cf. IDIOMS, and p. 148, 29. **18. legem Papiam**: passed in 65 B. C., enacting that all persons not possessing a legal residence in Italy must leave Rome. It was probably under this law that Archias was brought to trial. **20. illis** [tabulis]: the records of Regium, Locri, Naples, Tarentum. **21. Census**: including each census taken between 89 and 65 B. C.

22. Scilicet: 'Certainly;' sarcastic. **obscurum** [tibi]: = *tibi non notum*. **proximis censoribus**: = 'at the last taking of the census,' in 70 B. C., by Lucius Gellius Publicola and Gnaeus Lentulus Clodianus. Censors had been chosen for 65 and for 64 B. C., but they had resigned without taking the census. **24. apud exercitum**: not *in exercitu*, for Archias went merely as a companion, or *attaché*, of the commander. **superioribus** [censoribus]: 'at the next to the last census,' taken by Lucius Marcius Philippus and Marcus Perperna, in 86 B. C. **eodem quaestore**: 'the same' Lucullus, who was then 'quaestor' under Sulla. **25. primis** [censoribus]: 'the first' after Archias had become a citizen, in 89; Julius Caesar Strabo and Publicus Licinius Crassus, the censors for that year, resigned without undertaking the work.

29. pro: 'as.' **eis temporibus**: the apodosis begins here. **ne ipsius quidem iudicio**: because he did not have his name placed on the census registers. **30. in — esse versatum**: = 'had (any) share in.' **31. saepe**: perhaps in times of special danger, in his travels with Lucullus. The Roman law recognized only the wills of Roman citizens as valid. **32. heredi-**

tates civium Romanorum: in general only Roman citizens could inherit from Roman citizens. **33. delatus est**: 'he was reported,' instead of *nomen delatum est.* Proconsuls and propraetors were obliged to deliver their accounts to the Treasury within thirty days after they came back to Rome. In connection with these it was customary to hand in a list of those men on the staff or in the retinue of the provincial governor whose services were deemed worthy of compensation from the state.

Page 150. **1. hic . . . revincetur**: i. e. Archias and his friends have always acted on the assumption that he was a citizen. With this point the orator closes the technical side of his case. Cf. p. 48. **neque — neque**: 'either — or.' B. 347, 2; A. 209, *a*, 2; H. 553, 2.

B. *Proof that Archias ought to be a citizen.* VI.–XII. (l. 30).

VI. 3. Quaeres, etc.: introduces the remarks on literature anticipated in chap. II.; technically they are *extra causam.* Cf. p. 47. **4. ubi**: '(that) with which;' with the subj. of characteristic. **5. ex**: 'after.' **forensi**: cf. p. 117, 1, and N. **6. convicio**: i. e. *convicio litigantium*, 'din' of voices in the court. **7. suppetere**: = *suppeditari.* **nobis**: 'us' advocates and orators as a class. Quintilian (X. i. 27) recommends to orators the reading of poetry, and alludes to this passage.

11. his studiis: cf. p. 145, 4, and N. **esse deditum**: cf. p. 145, 22, and N. **12. litteris**: perhaps originally written *in litteris;* if not, must be construed as an instrumental abl. **13. neque — neque**: as in l. 1 above; *ad . . . fructum* (= *utilitatem*) refers to the public services of a man of literary culture, *in . . . proferre* to authorship. **14. aspectum lucemque**: = 'the light of publicity.' **quid**: as p. 71, 5. **pudeat**, etc.: another apology to the Roman jury of *practical* men; cf. N. to p. 145, 5. **16. tempore**: for *periculo* (cf. p. 146, 18, and N.); contrasted with *commodo*, referring to civil cases.

19. Qua re: cf. p. 66, 5, and N. **20. quantum — temporum**: why so far separated? **21. ludorum**: celebrated in connection with the religious festivals. **22. ipsam**: = 'simply,' 'merely.' **23. temporum**: pl. as referring to the portions of time given to each kind of recreation. **24. tempestivis**: 'early,' commencing before 3 P. M.; hence 'protracted.'

25. alveolo: cf. p. 80, 11, and N. **pilae**: why put after *conviviis* and *alveolo* is not clear; for ball-playing was considered an entirely respectable form of amusement.

28. oratio et facultas: hendiadys for *facultas oratoria*, 'oratorical power.' **29. quantacumque in me est**: 'so far as it resides in me,' 'so far as in me lies.' **amicorum periculis**: cf. p. 116, 11. **30. illa**: the moral principles set forth in the following paragraph.

33. praeceptis: the teachings of the philosophers. **multis litteris**: in our phrase, 'by wide reading.'

Page 151. **1. laudem atque honestatem**: i. e. 'glory gained by merit,' hendiadys; hence the sing. *eā* in l. 2. **3. mortis atque exsili**: by using *atque* the orator indicates that he considers exile worse than death. **parvi**: B. 203, 3; A. 252, *a*; H. 404. **5. profligatorum hominum**: sympathizers with the Catilinarian conspirators; they finally brought about the exile of Cicero.

6. pleni: i. e. *talium praeceptorum*. **7. sapientium voces**: the utterances of the philosophers. **8. quae omnia**: 'all of which,' 'and (yet) they all.' B. 201, 1, *b*; A. 216, *e*; H. 397, 2, N. **10. imagines — expressas**: 'forms,' 'ideals' — 'finely portrayed;' *exprimere* is used to denote the sharp, clear presentation of details by the art of the sculptor or painter. **14. hominum excellentium**: i. e. *de hominibus excellentibus*.

VII. **16. Quaeret quispiam**: introduces an objection, which the orator wishes to meet; cf. p. 48.

20. est certum: sc. *mihi*; 'I am decided what answer to give.' **25. naturam sine doctrina — sine natura doctrinam**: forceful chiasmus. **26. Atque idem ego contendo**: 'And I maintain (this) also.' **27. ratio quaedam conformatioque doctrinae**: *quidam* is often inserted by Cicero to indicate that he is using a word in an unusual sense, or is not altogether satisfied with it; 'what I may call the systematic training and culture afforded by learning.' **28. illud . . . singulare**: 'some noble and unique excellence.'

30. hunc — Africanum: the younger Scipio; *hic* is used to denote that which is nearer in time. **32. moderatissimos et continentissimos**: 'men of the greatest self-command and even temper.' **34. qui**: 'and these men.'

Page 152. **1. nihil**: as p. 61, 4. **2. adiuvarentur**: 'were (continually) aided,' so long as they lived; more forcible than the plup.

4. non — ostenderetur: 'were not shown (clearly),' i. e. 'were not assured.' **7. ceterae**: sc. *animi remissiones*. **8. omnium**: with *temporum*, *aetatum*, *locorum*. **9. alunt**: 'strengthen.' **10. adversis**: i. e. *eis qui in adversis rebus sunt*.

VIII. **15. etiam cum — videremus**: i. e. *etiam videntes*. **16. Rosci**: his chief characteristic as an actor was gracefulness. **17. commoveretur**: 'was deeply moved.' **20. Ergo**, etc.: argument from less to greater. **motu**: '(simply) by the movement.' **22. motus**: the Latin often uses the pl. where we prefer a sing. abstract noun; *motus animorum* = 'mental activity,' developed by training, as distinguished from *celeritatem ingenuorum*, 'natural quickness.'

23. utar: 'I shall take advantage of.' **26. nullam**: emphatic, 'not a.' **28. agerentur**: B. 324, 2; A. 342; H. 529, II. **29. revocatum**: for an encore. **eandem rem**: for *de eadem re*.

31. veterum scriptorum: i. e. *Graecorum*. All the writings of Archias have perished with the exception of eighteen epigrams (cf. Reinach, De Archia, p. 28, et seq.), which are assigned to him with a strong probability that they are genuine. To judge from these, his success as an extemporizer consisted chiefly in the ability to patch together, on the spur of the moment, phrases, lines, and passages from the older poets which had previously been committed to memory. The same explanation would account also for the resemblance of his more elaborate productions to the writings of the classic Greek writers. By having a memory stored with original and selected passages appropriate to many subjects and occasions, a good ear for metres, and constant practice, a professional extemporizer was able to perform feats that appeared little short of the marvellous, — and that, too, without being a great poet.

Page 153. **1. ex — constare**: 'are based on.' **2. natura ipsa valere**: 'derives his power from nature herself.' **3. mentis viribus excitari**: i. e. independently of outside influences, or of education. **4. suo iure**: see p. 145, 8, and N.; cf. the editor's "Selections from Ovid," pp. 62, 179. **noster**: 'of ours' as a Latin poet, in contrast with the Greek poets just referred to.

10. barbaria, etc.: there was never a people so sunk in savagery that it did not respect the poet. **Saxa . . . consistunt**: a reference to the mythical musicians, as Amphion, Arion, and Orpheus; cf. "Selections from Ovid," p. 278, N. to l. 40, and p. 52. **12. rebus**: for *artibus*. **13. Homerum**: according to the well-known Greek couplet, seven cities claimed to be the birthplace of Homer:—

> Ἑπτὰ πόλεις διερίζουσιν περὶ ῥίζαν Ὁμήρου,
> Σμύρνα, Ῥόδος, Κολοφών, Σαλαμίς, Χίος, Ἄργος, Ἀθῆναι.

In a Latin hexameter line,—

> Smyrna, Rhodos, Colophon, Salamis, Chios, Argos, Athenae.

14. Salaminii: the inhabitants of Salamis in Cyprus. **16. delubrum**: at Smyrna there was a square portico with a temple and statue of Homer (Strabo, XIV. 1. 37). **17. pugnant**: over the same thing. For the nativity of the Homeric poems, see Miss Clerke's "Familiar Studies in Homer," p. 10 et seq.

IX. 19. alienum: i. e. Homer was a 'foreigner' to all the cities excepting the one in which he was born. What would they have said to the assertion that Homer never lived? **12. praesertim cum olim**: 'and that although long ago.' **24. Cimbricas res**: = 'the war with the Cimbri,' of which Marius was naturally the hero. **25. attigit**: implies that the poem was not completed. **durior ad haec**: 'too rough for such.' **26. Neque enim quisquam est**: 'And (yet not strange), for there is no one.' **27. aversus a**: = 'unfriendly to;' difference between the Latin and the English point of view?' **28. aeternum — praeconium**: i. e. *praeconium quod aeternum sit*. **30. ex eo**: see IDIOMS. **31. cuius vocem**: i. e. *cuius cantantis vocem*. **34. ea, quae gesserat**: *res a se gestas*.

Page 154. 1. Mithridaticum bellum: no doubt chiefly that part of the war with Mithridates which reflected most credit on the name of Lucullus, whom the poet accompanied in the Asiatic campaigns. Reinach (De Archia, pp. 46–54) has made it appear at least probable that this poem consisted of four books, and that it was freely used by Plutarch in writing the life of Lucullus.

3. expressum est: 'has been treated.' **6. aperuit Pontum**: cf. p. 124, 5–7. **7. regiis opibus**: including strongholds, troops, financial resources, etc. **regione**: 'by its situation.'

9. innumerabilis Armeniorum copias: at the battle near Tigranocerta, in 69 B. C. (cf. p. 31 and Map). According to the figures given by Plutarch (Luc. XXVI., XXVII.), the Armenians outnumbered the Romans twenty to one, mustering more than 200,000 men, of whom 150,000 were infantry, against a Roman force of only 11,000. **10. urbem Cyzicenorum . . . servatam**: in 73 B. C.; cf. p. 123, 30–34, and N. In enumerating the victories of Lucullus Cicero does not confine himself to the chronological order. **12. ore ac faucibus**: we might say 'the open jaws.' Cf. p. 89, 7, and N.

14. interfectis ducibus: trans. as if *duces interfecti sunt et.* **15. apud Tenedum pugna illa navalis**: in 73 B. C. The Roman fleet sunk a part of the enemy's ships between the Trojan coast and Tenedos (see Map); but the main engagement took place near the island of Lemnos. The two victories are here spoken of as one. Cf. p. 124, 1–4.

19. noster: cf. p. 153, 4, and N. **20. in sepulcro Scipionum**: the disposition of the dead by burial was kept up in the Scipio family long after cremation became the prevalent method at Rome. The tomb of the Scipios was opened in 1780. It lies on the left side of the Appian Way, a short distance outside of the Servian wall. It consists of a number of narrow, winding passages excavated in the soft rock, in the sides of which places were cut out for the bodies of the dead as in the catacombs. At the entrance in Cicero's time (see Liv. XXXVIII. LVI. 4), there were three statues, of which one was thought to be that of Ennius.

21. eis laudibus: 'by such praises' as those which Ennius bestowed on Scipio. **23. huius**: *huius Catonis*, 'the present Cato,' i. e. Cato Uticensis; cf. *hunc Africanum*, p. 151, 30, and N. Cato the Censor found Ennius in Sardinia, serving in the Roman army, and brought him to Rome.

X. 28. haec fecerat: i. e. *haec carmina fecerat* ('had composed'); original meaning of "poet," *poeta*, ποιητής? **29. in civitatem receperunt**: the Roman franchise was bestowed on Ennius by the son of Marcus Fulvius Nobilior (cf. p. 156,

18–20), in 184 B. C. The poet says of himself (Cic. de Orat. III. XLII. 168): —,

Nos sumus Romani, qui fuvimus ante Rudini.

30. Heracliensem: sharply contrasted with *Rudinum*, because Heraclea was so much more important a place than Rudiae and possessed special treaty relations with Rome. Cf. p. 147, 31–33, and N.

33. Nam: introduces an answer to an assumed, or suppressed, objection; the ellipsis may be supplied thus, '(But Archias writes in Greek. That is no objection), for' . . . **34. vehementer:** see IDIOMS.

Page 155. **1. Graeca:** neut. pl.; we say 'Greek,' with a sing. verb. **2. suis finibus:** even in Cicero's time Latin was spoken very little outside of Latium and the Roman and Latin colonies. The Greek language had been carried by Greek commerce and settlements — in the East also by the conquests and colonies of Alexander — over the whole ancient world. Latin made little progress in superseding the native dialects of western Europe till the time of the Empire.

4. regionibus: = *terminis*. Cf. p. 101, 7, 8. **7. ampla:** = 'full of honor,' 'glorious.' It was an honor to any nation to be conquered by Rome! **8. de vita:** 'at the risk of life.' **9. periculorum:** i. e. *ad pericula subeunda*. Kind of gen.?

11. scriptores rerum suarum: among them are mentioned Anaximenes, Aristobulus, Callisthenes, the poet Choerilus, Onesicritus, and Ptolemaeus. **13. Achillis tumulum:** in the Troad, near the entrance of the Hellespont, there are several great prehistoric mounds, or tumuli, to which the names of heroes of the Trojan war were given at a very early date. At the mound said to mark the burial-place of Achilles there was a temple erected in his honor (Strabo, XIII. i. 32). See Illustration, p. 158. **15. Et vere:** sc. *dixit*.

18. noster hic Magnus: Pompey was no doubt pleased at this implied comparison of himself with Alexander. **20. civitate donavit:** magistrates sometimes received, by special enactment, the privilege of conferring the Roman franchise on those whom they might deem worthy of the distinction. **23. eiusdem laudis:** as that which Theophanes had bestowed on Pompey. **24. credo:** cf. p. 63, 4, and N.

27. petentem : = *si petisset.* **28. quem** : 'and (yet) we saw him,' Sulla. **in contione** : here *in contione civium* (cf. l. 20), in the Forum, where he was superintending the sale of the possessions of the proscribed at auction. **ei subiecisset** : 'had thrust up to him (from below)' as he sat on the tribunal. **29. libellum** : we should say 'a manuscript.' **de populo** : i. e. common, vulgar. **quod epigramma** : explains *libellum,* 'an epigram which.' B. 324, 1; A. 342; H. 529, II. **30. tantum . . . longiusculis** : i. e. it had no merit except that every other line was longer than its mate, being written apparently in elegiac stanzas, or distichs. Cf. B. 369, 1, 2; A. 363; H. 615. **33. sedulitatem** : 'persistency,' 'officiousness.'

Page 156. 3. donavit : when proconsul in Spain, engaged in the war with Sertorius. **4. per Lucullos** : Lucius and Marcus Lucullus were kinsmen of Metellus Pius, perhaps cousins. **impetravisset** : sc. *civitatem.* **qui** : 'since he,' Metellus Pius. **6. Cordubae** : a number of Roman veterans had been settled about Corduba, which was one of the first provincial cities to become Romanized. **pingue** : see IDIOMS.

XI. 10. optimus quisque : here 'all the best,' in a moral sense; the nobler a man, the more ardent his love of glory. **11. illi philosophi** : the Stoics and Epicureans especially claimed to be indifferent to fame. Cicero wrote a treatise *De Gloria,* which is now lost. **13. in eo ipso** : 'in regard to that very matter.' **14. nominari** : for *se nominari,* in the sense of *nobilitari.*

16. amicissimi sui : = 'of his most intimate friend.' Cf. p. 148, 7, and N. **templorum, monumentorum** : built with the proceeds from the sale of booty secured in the conquest of Further Spain. One of the temples was dedicated to Mars, and contained a colossal statue of the god by Scopas (Plin. Nat. Hist., XXXVI. v. 26).

19. Fulvius : see *Nobilior* in Vocab. He was severely censured by Cato the Censor for taking Ennius with him. **Musis** : Fulvius built a temple in honor of Hercules and the Muses, and adorned it richly with works of art taken from Ambracia in Epirus; cf. N. to p. 132, 7. **20. prope armati** : 'almost in military attire;' i. e. before they had assumed the garb suitable to the City and to civil life. **22. a — abhorrere** : 'be insensible to,' 'be inattentive to.'

28. vobis: i. e. *vobis iudicibus*, taken as representatives of your respective classes; for the jurors at this time were drawn from the ranks of the senators, knights, and tribunes of the treasury. These classes as a whole had supported Cicero heartily in the suppression of the Catilinarian conspiracy. Cf. p. 110, Chap. VII., and N. to p. 111, 3.

30. incohavit: a year later the poem was not yet finished, greatly to the disappointment of Cicero (cf. ad Att. I. XVI. 15); probably it was never completed. **Quibus auditis**: *De eis (versibus) cum audissem.* **31. res**: 'the theme.'

34. hanc: *hanc mercedem.* **laudis**: explanatory gen., 'which consists in praise.'

Page 157. 1. quid est, quod: cf. p. 149, 8, and N.

4. nihil — praesentiret: 'cherished no anticipation.' **5. regionibus**: as p. 155, 4. **8. angeretur**: 'would torment itself.' B. 256, 1; A. 111, *a*, N.; H. 465. **de ipsa vita**: = *etiam de vita.* **9. Nunc**: 'But as it is.' **quoque**: i. e. *quōque.* **virtus**: 'noble impulse,' 'noble instinct.' **11. non,** etc.: well expressed by Reid, 'that the story of our fame must not be given up to oblivion when the term of life ends, but that it must be made coextensive with all future time.'

XII. 14. videamur: 'are we to let ourselves appear.' **19. statuas**: 'statues;' *imagines*, 'portraits' moulded or carved in any material; *simulacra*, 'likenesses' whether carved, drawn, or painted; contrasted with *effigiem*, 'representation,' here used of the ideal. **animorum, corporum**: we say 'of the soul,' 'of the body,' preferring to use the generic sing. in many cases where the Latin has the pl. Cf. N. to p. 152, 22.

23. summis ingeniis: i. e. *a viris summo ingenio.* **expressam**: see N. to p. 151, 10. **27. sapientissimi homines**: philosophers who taught the immortality of the soul, as Pythagoras, Socrates. **28. ad . . . pertinebit**: 'it shall continue in relation to some part of my soul,' i. e. 'my soul shall remain conscious of it.' **30. spe**: i. e. of an immortality of fame.

CONCLUSION.

31. pudore eo: 'of so fine a sense of honor.'

Page 158. 1. eius modi: = *tali.* **2. testimonio municipi**: see p. 148, 15–18. **10. ex eo numero, qui**: = *ex illo-*

rum numero, qui. **11. sancti**: see p. 153, 5. **12. itaque**: = *et ita*.

15. de causa: 'in regard to the case,' referring to the earlier, technical portion of the speech. **20. qui iudicium exercet**: cf. p. 146, 14, and N.

THE SPEECH FOR MARCELLUS.

Page 159. PRO M. MARCELLO ORATIO: i. e. *oratio in qua Caesari gratias egit pro M. Marcelli restitutione* ('restoration' to standing as a citizen, 'pardon'); the title as it stands is inexact. The speech was delivered in the course of a meeting of the Senate, in the Senate-house (cf. p. 162, 10); but it was addressed to Caesar, who as consul presided. After Caesar, yielding to the urgent request of Gaius Marcellus and individual senators, declared that he would pardon Marcus Marcellus if the Senate so desired (see pp. 49, 50), the senators gave their votes in the usual order, nearly all expressing their thanks also (cf. N. to p. 64, 28); when it came to Cicero's turn to speak, he responded with this address (ad Fam. IV. IV. 4: *pluribus verbis egi Caesari*). The speeches for Ligarius and Deiotarus, likewise addressed to Caesar, were grouped with this by the early grammarians under the title *orationes Caesarianae.* In view of the circumstances of delivery, as well as the character of the subject-matter, the *pro Marcello* is seen to lie on the border line between the political speeches and those in criminal cases; but on the whole it may more appropriately be classed — as also the other *Caesarianae* — with the latter. Rhetorically it is an example of the demonstrative order (see p. 15).

INTRODUCTION. I.

I. 1. Diuturni silenti: lasting almost six years. In 51 B.C. Cicero was in Cilicia. He returned to Rome in 49 only to find the outbreak of hostilities between Caesar and Pompey inevitable: from that time to the present occasion he had had neither opportunity nor inclination to exercise his oratorical gifts, having firmly resolved never to let his voice be heard in public again (ad Fam. IV. IV. 4: *Statueram, non me hercule inertia, sed desiderio pristinae dignitatis, in perpetuum tacere*). **patres conscripti**: see N. to p. 62, 28. After the first paragraph, the address changes to Caesar, but returns to the Senate for a few sentences in Chap. v. **eram usus**: 'I had (have) maintained;' the Latin often uses the plup. of that which has just occurred, where our idiom prefers the perfect. **his temporibus**: of civil war.

2. dolore: explained by *Dolebam . . . fortuna*, ll. 13–15. **3. verecundia**: 'fear' of doing wrong, as indicated by *nec fas esse*, et seq., ll. 16–19. **hodiernus dies**: Cicero gives no clue by which the exact date can be determined; but he writes of 'this day' to Sulpicius (ad Fam. IV. iv. 3): *Ita mihi pulcher hic dies visus est, ut speciem aliquam viderer videre quasi reviviscentis rei publicae.* **4. initium**: notice the forceful order in *Diuturni silenti — finem, initium — dicendi.*

6. in summa potestate: Caesar had been made dictator for ten years, and censor under the title *praefectus morum* for three; he was now also consul for the third time (cf. N. to p. 139, 32). Thus under the forms of the republican constitution he was in reality an absolute monarch. Cf. N. to p. 136, 25. **7. rerum omnium modum**: = *in rebus omnibus moderationem* ('self-command').

10. vobis: Marcellus had been a member of the Senate. **11. illius**: i. e. *vocem et auctoritatem* ('influence'); hendiadys? **14. in eadem causa**: as having been a partisan of Pompey's. **in qua ego**: sc. what? **15. in eadem fortuna**: as having received pardon from Caesar. **17. aemulo**: here a subst. **18. quasi . . . distracto**: '(my) associate and travelling companion, as it were, torn away from me.'

20. mihi meae: the Latins liked to put words of kindred meaning, or different forms of the same word, in juxtaposition. B. 350, 5, *d*; H. 563. **21. interclusam aperuisti**: an expression appropriate to the implied comparison of life to a journey in the last sentence. **22. signum — sustulisti**: 'you have put up a flag, as it were,' in something the same way that a flag (*vexillum*) was raised over the general's tent in camp as a sign that the force must make ready for battle. Cf. Caes. de Bell. Gall. II. 20. **23. mihi**: may be translated as if *a me*; but the dat. in such cases is by no means equivalent to an expression of agency, indicating rather the person who is concerned in the action, on whom consequent results may rest **24. in multis**: 'in the case of many (others)' that Caesar had pardoned. **in me ipso**: 'in my own case.'

Page 160. **2. commemoratis praesertim offensionibus:** = 'that too although his acts of hostility have been brought to mind;' Caesar had just mentioned the 'bitter hatred' of Marcellus for him (*accusata acerbitate Marcelli*, ad Fam. IV. IV. 3). **3. auctoritatem . . . anteferre:** see p. 50, and N. on p. 314. **4. doloribus:** personal feelings. **suspicionibus:** Caesar had spoken to the effect that if his enemies were all allowed to come back his life would not be safe; cf. p. 165, 16, and N.

5. ante, etc.: see IDIOMS. **6. consensu:** shown by the unanimity with which the senators had urged the recall of Marcellus. **iudicio tuo:** which was a recognition of Marcellus's worth. **11. ventura sit:** as Marcellus was at Mytilene, it would take nearly a month for the news of his pardon to reach him. **12. optimo iure:** see IDIOMS. **13. optimarum artium studio:** cf. p. 145, 4, and N.; a reference to Marcellus's interest in philosophy and oratory. **14. innocentia:** as opposed to *avaritia;* cf. p. 130, 24, et seq.

DISCUSSION.

A. *The Deeds of Caesar.* II.–VI.

II. 15. Nullius: for the gen. of *nemo;* not with *ingeni.* **16. non dicam:** cf. p. 137, 10, and N. **17. sed:** 'but (even).' **18. Tamen:** we should have expected *Et tamen.* **pace tua:** see IDIOMS. **19. quam eam, quam:** it is surprising that the orator did not avoid the disagreeable assonance by saying *eā quam.*

25. numero proeliorum: Pliny the Elder (Nat. Hist., VII. XXV. § 92) says that Caesar fought in fifty pitched battles, being the only commander that surpassed the number of Marcus Marcellus (the conqueror of Syracuse), who fought in thirty-nine. **regionum:** in Gaul, Italy, Epirus, Thessaly, Asia Minor, Egypt, Africa.

26. celeritate conficiendi: cf. the editor's "Caesar's Gallic War," pp. 9, 10. **27. disiunctissimas terras citius:** in the campaigns of the Civil War, 49–46 B. C.

30. ea — capere: in our phrase, 'take them in.' **32. bellicas laudes:** introduced in contrast with the glory gained by showing mercy to the conquered (p. 161, 5 et seq.). **34. multis:** subordinate officers and soldiers.

Page 161. **1. in armis**: 'in the pursuit of arms,' = 'in war.' **3. suo iure**: cf. p. 145, 8, and N. **4. Fortuna**: for the important part good luck was supposed to play in the victories and reverses of war, see p. 134, 30 et seq. Caesar himself often attributed his successes to the kindness of fortune; cf. De Bell. Gall. VI. 42 et al. **6. es paulo ante adeptus**: by conquering all personal feeling and granting pardon to a political enemy; cf. p. 159, 23 et seq. Cicero's praise of Caesar's magnanimous treatment of the partisans of Pompey is hardly too great. See Mommsen's "History of Rome," Vol. IV., p. 550 et seq.

7. quantumcumque est: 'great as it is.' **9. ista laude**: i. e. *ista tua laude*. **12. tuam esse totam**: i. e. *istam gloriam totam esse tuam*. **13. temeritas, casus**: characteristic of Fortune.

III. 16. gentes, etc.: referring to the Gallic campaigns. **17. copiarum**: here 'of resources.' **19. condicionem**: 'environment.' **21. Animum**: asyndeton, where an English writer would use an adversative conj. **vincere,** etc.: the infinitives have a loose dependence on *iudico* (l. 26), but are gathered up by *haec*, the form of the sentence having been changed after it was started; anacoluthon. B. 374, 6; A. 385; H. 636, IV. 6. **iracundiam cohibere**: "He that is slow to anger is better than the mighty; and he that ruleth his spirit than he that taketh a city" (Prov. xvi. 32). **26. deo**: might *dei* have been used?

27. bellicae, etc.: has this prophecy been realized? **28. sed**: 'but (also).' **31. nescio**: see IDIOMS. **obstrepi**: as we say, 'to be drowned out.' **clamore militum — tubarum sono**: suggesting scenes of battle, siege, sacking, and carnage. Notice the chiastic order.

Page 162. **1. insolens**: especially in civil war. 'And in one respect particularly,' Cicero wrote to Sulpicius shortly after this speech was delivered (ad Fam. IV. IV. 2), 'your lot is better than mine, because you can freely write what gives you pain, but I cannot do even this with safety; and that too not the fault of our conqueror, — whose self-command is simply wonderful, — but because victory in a civil war is always arrogant.'

4. fictis [rebus]: in the drama and in epic poetry. Cicero wrote later (Lael. VIII. 28): 'There is nothing more attractive than a noble character, nothing which more draws out our affection; we even in a way conceive an affection for those whom we have never seen, on account of their lofty character and uprightness.'

5. Te . . . efferemus: B. 351, 5; A. 346; H. 573. **6. mentem sensusque et os**: i. e. 'thoughts and feelings expressed in his countenance;' cf. p. 61, 7, and N. **quicquid reliquum fecerit**: = *quicquid reliquerit*. **9. Parietes**, etc.: spirited hyperbole. **10. me dius Fidius**: see *Fidius* in Vocab. **11. futura sit**: not *futura est;* Cicero repeats the reason which the walls give. **illa auctoritas**: for *vir illa auctoritate*, or *vir tanta auctoritate*, i. e. Marcellus.

IV. 13. C. Marcelli: the brother of Marcus (cf. p. 169, 31, 32). There was another Gaius Marcellus, consul B. C. 50, who was probably a cousin of Gaius and Marcus; some have thought that he was the one mentioned here. **14. lacrimis . . . viderem**: as he cast himself at Caesar's feet; see p. 49, and cf. N. to p. 104, 21. **16. M. Marcello conservato**: trans. with 'by' and a participial phrase. **17. nobilissimam familiam**: sc. *quorum* from *quibus* (l. 16). **18. ad paucos**: only the three Marcelli mentioned in N. to l. 13 are spoken of as living at this time. **19. Hunc diem**: i. e. *huius diei gratulationem*.

23. multo magnoque: = 'a very large.' **comitatu**: why abl.? **24. quae quidem**: 'and (yet) in fact this.' **tanta est**: followed by a consecutive clause, *ut . . . sit aetas*, where a concessive clause ('although time,' etc.) might have been expected; after the parenthesis the sentence is resumed not with a parallel consecutive clause, but with a principal statement co-ordinate with *tanta est;* anacoluthon. Cf. p. 161, 21 et seq.

26. opere et manu: hendiadys; 'wrought by the work of (men's) hands.' **28. magis**: 'more (and more).' **33. perinde atque**: 'exactly as;' the orator cannot find words adequate to express his thought. **34. victoriam vicisse videris**: notice the alliteration; cf. p. 139, 25.

Page 163. 1. videris: 'you are seen.' **illa**: *illa victoria*. **victis**: used as subst.

2. ipsius victoriae condicione, etc.: the meaning is made clear by a passage in a letter to Marcellus (ad Fam. IV. IX. 3): 'All the conditions of civil war are wretched; . . . but nothing is more wretched than victory itself. Even if this has come into the hands of the better sort of men, yet it makes them savage and violent, that even though they may not be so by nature, they are forced to become so by necessity. You see, the conqueror is obliged, even against his will, to do many things at the beck of those with the help of whom he has conquered.'

V. 6. hoc . . . pateat: 'how wide a bearing this decision of Gaius Caesar has.' **7. Omnes, qui**: 'all (of us) who.' **8. illa arma**: the side of Pompey in the late war. **10. scelere**, etc.: in civil war each side considers the other an enemy of the state; Caesar's generous attitude relieves those who joined Pompey from the position of men charged with the 'crime' of taking up arms against their country.

12. me: sc. *reddidit;* for *me mihi* and *sibi ipsos* (for *ipsis*), see N. to p. 159, 20. **14. quorum et frequentiam et dignitatem**: abstract for concrete, = *quos et frequentes et summa dignitate* (*praeditos*). **15. ille induxit**: first principal clause; Caesar allowed his opponents to come back not as enemies, but as those against whom the charge of having been rebels, or traitors, would not be raised. After the battles of Pharsalus and Thapsus, he caused the correspondence discovered at the headquarters of the enemy to be burned.

16. ignoratione: i. e. of the facts or merits of the case. **17. metu**: as in the case of Metellus, who had done so much to offend Caesar that he feared Caesar's resentment.

19. Quo in bello, et seq.: Cicero improves this first opportunity to offer a public explanation of his reasons for having gone over to Pompey, and of his real attitude in the late war. He had previously made similar explanations to his friends, as indicated by a letter to Marius (ad Fam. VII. III. 6), in which he says: 'I would have preferred to talk this over with you by ourselves; but as it would be some time before I could see you, I wanted to lay the matter before you in a letter, in order that, if you should chance to fall in with any of my critics you might know what to say to them. For there are some people who, though my taking off would have brought no advantage to the state, yet think it a downright sin that I am alive;' i. e. not having laid down my life at Pharsalus or Thapsus. **de pace audiendum**: we say 'that the voice of peace should be heard.'

21. civium pacem flagitantium: among them Cicero himself, as the following sentence implies. **Neque enim**: 'And (with consistency) for I did not,' etc. **22. illa** [arma]: as in l. 8. **ulla**: 'any (other).' Cicero sympathized with the political affiliations of Sulla, but did not come forward as an active partisan. **23. civilia**: = 'in civil war.' Cicero did not take part in the battle of Pharsalus. **24. Hominem**: Pompey. **25. privato consilio**: i. e. as a matter of personal obligation. The statements here are borne out by Cicero's letters to Atticus, and to Pompey himself, in 49 B. C.

26. grati . . . memoria: 'the faithful recollection of a thankful heart,' remembering Pompey's kindnesses. **27. non modo**: see N. to p. 71, 21. **prudens et sciens**: a stereotyped phrase, borrowed originally from the law; like our expression, "with my eyes wide open." **30. integra re**: before the outbreak of hostilities between Caesar and Pompey. **31. eadem . . . sensi**: 'I retained the same opinions, even at the risk of my life.' After the battle of Pharsalus Cicero refused the command offered him by Cato and counselled peace, whereupon he was assailed by Pompey's son Gnaeus, and would have lost his life had not Cato interfered (Plut. Cic. XXXIX.).

Page 164. **1. ceteris fuerit iratior**: trans. as a subordinate clause with 'while.' Why? **id**: i. e. *Caesarem pacis auctores conservandos esse censere.*

VI. **5. huius rei,** etc.: Marcellus also was in favor of peace. **8. certorum hominum**: the language implies that their names were known to Caesar and the Senate. The leaders on the side of Pompey had indulged in the most extravagant plans of proscription and confiscation: *Tanta erat in illis crudelitas, tanta cum barbaris gentibus coniunctio, ut non nominatim, sed generatim* ('by classes') *proscriptio esset informata; ut iam omnium iudicio constitutum esset omnium vestrum* ('of you' who had not joined the party of Pompey, even though remaining neutral) *bona praedam esse illius victoriae* (ad Att. XI. VI. 2). Cf. ll. 21–23 below.

13. proeliorum exitu terminatam: i. e. scenes of bloodshed were not continued in proscriptions. **vagina vacuum**: for *e vagina eductum.* **17. ex eadem acie**: i. e. *in eodem exercitu.*

19. Alterius partis: the side of Pompey. **23. ubi fuisset**:

plup. because the war was now wholly in the past. Only those who had actually followed Pompey to Greece were to be spared. **25. poenas**: see IDIOMS. **26. qui**: = *eo, quod.* **28. omnem spem ad — contulisse**: 'to have rested all hope on,' 'to have placed all hope in.'

32. ex quo: = *et ex eo* (*bono*). **33. sapienti**: Caesar was a believer in the Epicurean philosophy. **Cetera tua**: 'your other (deeds).'

Page 165. **1. de nobis**: i. e. of your pardoning of us. **5. summa bona**: among the philosophers *summum bonum* was the term for 'the highest good.' **7. Virtute**: personified. **9. Noli**, etc.: the orator pleads for the others situated as Marcellus was. B. 276, *c*; A. 269, *a*, 2; H. 489, 1). **11. opinione stulta**: as we say, 'by a wrong idea,' 'by a mistaken notion.' **12. tua ulla culpa**: cf. p. 77, 10, and N. **13. -que**: 'but.'

B. *Caesar's Danger.* VII.–X.

VII. **16. suspicionem**: that there was danger of a plot against his life. **18. providenda**: milder word for *praecavenda.* **20. cautio**: 'safety.' As Drumann aptly remarks ("Geschichte Roms," Vol. VI., p. 264), "So far as human calculations can determine, if Caesar had not been murdered in 44 Cicero would not have been killed in 43."

22. tam demens: i. e. *tam demens ut tibi insidietur.* **23. quam quibus**: *quam* (*ei*), *quibus.* **24. ex hoc numero, qui**: = *ex horum numero, qui.* **26. summa**: 'in the highest degree,' 'to the fullest extent.' **28. nihil cogitant sceleris**: 'are plotting no crime.' **29. inimici**: sc. what? **fuerunt**: sc. *inimici.* **pertinacia**: as in the recent struggle in Africa. **31. de inimicis**: B. 201, 1, *a*; A. 216, *c*; H. 397, 3, N. 3. **qui fuerunt**: i. e. *qui fuerunt inimici et supersunt.*

33. in animis hominum: = 'in the heart of man;' cf. N. to p. 157, 19. **latebrae**: = 'depths.'

Page 166. **3. nihil — cogitans**: 'unreflecting,' 'thoughtless.' **nec — nec**: cf. p. 150, 1, and N. **5. ex**, etc.: (*vitam*) *omnium ex vita tui unius pendere.* Reason for the order? **7. dumtaxat humanos**: = 'yet only those common to humanity;' contrasted with *sceleris . . . consensio.* **9. debeat**: 'is bound to be;' cf. N. to p. 101, 4. **11. incertos motus**: = 'the variability,' 'the uncertainty;' with the same underlying idea as that of our colloquial expression, "Oh, he has his ups and downs." Cf. p. 152, 22, and N.

12. quem deum: owing to the association of each divinity with a particular sphere of activity, and the subordination of all to Fate, the gods of the ancient mythology were not looked upon as omnipotent. The expression here, however, is highly rhetorical. **si cupiat**: = *etiam si rei publicae opitulari cupiat.*

VIII. 14. sunt excitanda: 'must be lifted up,' 'raised up;' in contrast with *iacere*, etc. Measures looking toward all the reforms suggested — and many besides — had already been sanctioned, or were under consideration. See Mommsen's "History of Rome," Vol. IV., p. 586 et seq. **16. iudicia**: regulated by a *lex Iulia iudiciaria*, which took away from the tribunes of the treasury the privilege of sitting on juries; cf. N. to p. 111, 3 and 11.

17. fides: the *lex Iulia de fenore* (passed B. C. 49) ordered an assessment of mortgaged property at the valuation held before the depreciation caused by the civil wars, and obliged creditors to accept it at this valuation in satisfying their claims, without the payment of any arrears of interest that might be due. In this way burdensome debts were cancelled, with a loss to creditors of only about one fourth their original investment (Caes. de Bell. Civ. III. 1; Suet. Iul. Caes. XLII.). **libidines**: here refers particularly to extravagance in living. Caesar carried the enforcement of sumptuary laws so far as to place guards about the market to confiscate forbidden luxuries; in some cases even dishes were taken from the table in private houses (Suet. Iul. Caes. XLIII.). **18. suboles**: Caesar "proposed extraordinary rewards for the fathers of numerous families, while he at the same time as supreme judge of the nation treated divorce and adultery with a rigor according to Roman ideas unparalleled." Mommsen, Vol. IV., p. 623.

20. ardore: for the order cf. p. 146, 6, and N. **22. ornamenta dignitatis**: cf. p. 118, 12, and N. **praesidia stabilitatis**: cf. p. 122, 20, 21. **23. armatus, togatus**: cf. p. 156, 21–23.

28. vocem: 'utterance.' **Satis diu**: = 'long enough.' According to Suetonius (Iul. Caes. LXXXVI.) Caesar declared *neque voluisse se diutius vivere, neque curasse, quod valetudine minus prospera uteretur; . . . non tam sua quam rei publicae* *interesse, uti salvus esset; se iam pridem potentiae gloriaeque abunde adeptum (esse); rem publicam, si quid sibi eveniret, neque quietam fore et aliquanto deteriore condicione civilia bella subituram.*

29. naturae: i. e. for the space of life allotted by nature. How old was Caesar at this time? **31. parum**: = 'not long enough.' **32. doctorum hominum**: the philosophers; cf. p. 106, 22, et seq. **34. enim**: i. e. And I have reason for saying this; 'for' . . .

Page 167. **1. Credo**: i. e. *credo te ita sentire.* **tum — si**: = '(only) in case.' **id audirem**: 'I would listen to it,' in the sense of *id probarem*, 'I would approve of it.' **5. fundamenta, quae**: i. e. *fundamenta eorum (operum), quae;* reference not only to the great plans Caesar had formed for the reorganization of the state (see N. to p. 166, 14), but also to a series of magnificent public buildings on which work had already been commenced. **7. aequitate animi**: 'by the even balance of your mind,' the philosophic calm which even the thought of death cannot disturb.

11. Parum — magna: '(works) not great enough.' **12. satis**: i. e. *satis magna.* **15. futurus fuit**: 'was destined to be.' **17. vide**: 'see to it.' **18. virtus**: here 'character.' **19. magnorum . . . meritorum**: i. e. *fama magnorum meritorum vel in suos cives* ('towards one's fellow-citizens'), etc. Reason for the order? Cicero gives also a similar definition of *gloria* (Phil. I. xii. 29): *Est autem gloria laus recte factorum magnorumque in rem publicam meritorum, quae cum optimi cuiusque tum etiam multitudinis testimonio comprobatur.*

IX. **22. pars**: 'part;' implied comparison of life to a drama. **hic actus**: '(only) this act,' the last act. **24. in primis**: = 'above all others.' **26. solveris**: 'you shall have paid (the debt).' **satietate vivendi**: cf. Cic. Cato Mai. XX. 76: *Satietas vitae tempus maturum mortis adfert.* **28. hoc ipsum**: i. e. *vivere diu* or *vixisse diu.* **extremum**: in the sense of *finis;* 'And yet,' says Cicero (Cato Mai. XIX. 69), 'ye beneficent gods! what is there long in the life of man?' **29. pro nihilo**: 'as nothing' at all. **30. Quamquam**: as p. 70, 14. **31. his angustiis**: 'by these narrow bounds.' **32. fuit, semper**: asyndeton, where we should say 'but.' **immortalitatis**: cf. p. 156, 9–11, and N.

34. Nec . . . est: 'And in truth this ought not to be considered your (real) life.'

Page 168. 1. spiritu: 'breath,' as the necessary condition of the body's existence. **illa, illa**: cf. p. 62, 5, and N.; p. 98, 34 et seq. **4. inservias**: B. 295, 6, 8; A. 331, *i*, with N. 1; H. 502, 1. **te ostentes**: 'acquit yourself before;' *ostentare* is used in the sense of our phrase, "to place one's self in the right light" before another. **5. miretur**: for *admiretur*. **7. provincias**, etc.: i. e. the conquering of provinces, the crossing of the Rhine, the advance to the ocean, the victory by the Nile; condensed and vivid statement. **8. pugnas**: cf. p. 160, 25, and N. **9. triumphos**: Caesar had just celebrated a fourfold triumph for his victories in Gaul, Egypt, Asia Minor (*veni, vidi, vici*), and over the allies of the Pompeian leaders in Africa. **12. sedem . . . habebit**: the orator avoids saying outright that Rome will be destroyed; cf. p. 101, 4, and N.

14. magna dissensio: one has only to read the opinions passed on Caesar in recent times by Arnold and Mommsen, Froude and Trollope, to bear witness to the remarkable foresight revealed in this passage. **16. idque vel maximum**: = 'and this most of all.' **salute**: sc. *restituta*, 'by restoring the safety.' **17. illud**: the flames. **hoc**: the extinguishing of the flames.

18. Servi: 'look to.' **19. haud scio an**: 'probably.' **22. ad te**, etc.: cf. p. 157, 28–30, and N. **quidam**: the Epicureans; cf. p. 106, 22–24, and N. **falso**: as Cicero knew that Caesar was an Epicurean, and was not accustomed to express his own belief in the immortality of the soul so unreservedly, it seems hardly possible that he could have used the word *falso* as it stands here. Very likely it was inserted by some pious copyist of the Christian epoch. **23. nunc certe**: while you are still living.

X. 26. Diversae, etc.: referring again to the period of civil war through which they had just passed. **28. obscuritas**: = 'uncertainty,' 'wavering,' among those at Rome; explained by what follows. **30. quid optimum esset**: whether to remain neutral, or to join Caesar or Pompey. **32. quid liceret**: i. e. how far they would be allowed to take advantage of the undisturbed condition of affairs to their own interest. **34. neque omnes**, etc.: in implied contrast with the position assumed by Pompey, who had declared that he would treat as public enemies all who failed in their allegiance. Cf. N. to p. 164, 8.

Page 169. **2. posita** [sunt]: after the battle at Pharsalus. **erepta sunt**: as in the struggle in Africa. **5. ille**: antecedent to the following *qui;* he who gave up his life in battle rather than yield is a better man than he who submits to be pardoned and yet remains hostile. **6. Quae — eadem**: 'the same (trait) which.'

10. aliquid: 'any (measure).' **13. omnes**: 'all (of us).' **14. haec**: cf. p. 70, 11, and N. **17. subesse**: = *latēre*. **18. excubias**: 'watches' stationed outside of a camp or building, as distinguished from *custodiae*, 'guards' set to protect a given point or place, and *vigiliae*, 'patrol-men.' The following year the Senate voted Caesar a select body-guard, but he refused to accept it.

CONCLUSION. XI.

XI. **21. maximas gratias**: see IDIOMS. With *maximas — maiores* cf. *certissima — certiora*, p. 94, 15–18. **22. maiores** [gratias]: 'greater' than can be expressed. **idem sentiunt**: 'have the same feeling.' **24. stantibus — dicere**: trans. as if *stare et dicere*. **25. cui necesse est** [dicere]: i.e. as an ex-consul (cf. N. to p. 106, 10–12) and prominent member of the Senate, and as the most intimate friend of Marcellus.

30. Quod: refers as antecedent not only to *id*, l. 33, but also loosely to *id* understood as object of *praestare*, p. 170, 2; having performed the duty imposed by my affection in pleading for Marcellus, I ought now to perform the gracious duty of returning thanks. **mea**: 'on my part.' **34. tam diu — quam diu**: = 'so long as.'

Page 170. **3. omnibus rebus**: 'in all respects;' not in regard to life merely, but also as regards property, civil rights, and standing. **me — conservato**: trans. by a clause with 'although.' **6. maximus . . . accesserit**: trans. as if *hoc tuo facto maximum cumulum accessisse confitear*.

THE FOURTH SPEECH AGAINST ANTONY.

Page 171. ORATIO PHILIPPICA QUARTA: delivered from the Rostra (now in the new location; see N. on p. 227), Dec. 20, B. C. 44; for the occasion, and an outline of the matter, see pp. 51–53. Plutarch says (Cic. XXIV.) that the orator himself called the speeches against Antony 'Philippics;' whether that be true or not, the term was applied to them not long afterwards (cf. Juv. X. 123–126), and is found in the oldest MS.

INTRODUCTION. I. (ll. 1–19.)

I. 1. Frequentia vestrum: cf. p. 116, 1, and N. **incredibilis**: great or numerous beyond the belief of any one who had not actually seen it. **2. videor**: sc. *mihi.* **5. tempora**: immediately preceding the death of Caesar, but more particularly since. **quae simul ac**: = *et simul atque ea.* **6. princeps — fui**: 'I took the lead in.' **8. Hodierno enim die**: i. e. You will see that this is true; 'for to-day (first).' **9. rem actam**: sc. *esse* **10. reliquarum**: 'of all remaining;' with *actionum*, 'of all that remains to be done.' **14. tanto . . . approbavistis**: indicates that the statement *Nam . . . Antonius* had been vociferously applauded. **16. impii**: cf. p. 71, 2, and N. **17. ille hostis**: sc. *sit.*

DISCUSSION.

A. *Antony has been judged an enemy.* I. (l. 20) –IV.

20. C. Caesar: Octavianus; cf. p. 51. **23. Laudo**, etc.: the audience had again applauded, at the mention of Octavianus. **24. vel pueri potius**: he was in his twentieth year.

Page 172. 1. sunt . . . aetatis: = 'for his deeds are immortal; (only) his name (i. e. 'age') is that of youth.' **4. tale — qui**: 'like (the deed of him) who.' **6. a Brundisio . . . reditum**: Antony had, with the permission of the Senate, recalled four legions from Macedonia, the Second, Fourth, and

Thirty-fifth, and the Mars legion; on the 9th of October he had gone to Brundisium to assume command of them. The allegiance of the Fourth and Mars legions being doubtful (see N. to l. 16), he sent the other two north by detachments, with the design of concentrating a powerful force at Ariminum in Cisalpine Gaul. In the meantime, by the offer of a bounty of 500 denarii (= about $80) to each of the veterans who would enlist under him, Octavianus quickly raised an efficient corps, which after no long time comprised five legions.

8. exercitum invictum, etc.: cf. Phil. III. II. 3: *C. Caesar adulescens, paene potius puer, incredibili ac divina quadam mente atque virtute, cum maxime furor arderet Antoni cumque eius a Brundisio crudelis et pestifer reditus timeretur, nec postulantibus nec cogitantibus, ne optantibus quidem nobis, quia non posse fieri videbatur, firmissimum exercitum ex invicto genere veteranorum militum comparavit patrimoniumque suum effudit; quamquam non sum usus eo verbo, quo debui — non enim effudit; in rei publicae salute collocavit.*

II. 16. Suessae: i. e. Suessa Aurunca, in the southern part of Latium. On the way to or from Brundisium, probably on the journey thither, Antony had put to death some soldiers at Suessa (Phil. III. IV. 10, XIII. VIII. 18). **Brundisi**: here he had put to death chosen centurions of the Mars legion, and other citizens (about 300 in all), on account of their lack of allegiance to him personally. **17. nihil — cogitaret**: cf. p. 68, 17, and N. **18. erat**: why not *esset*, or *fuisset?* **19. militum**: '(composed) of soldiers.' **22. mihi adsensus**: in our parliamentary phrase, 'on my motion.' **23. ut — referretur**: i. e. *ad senatum*, for final action. **primo**, etc.: see IDIOMS.

25. Quem: we say 'what.' **26. contra . . . eis**: freely, 'for whose antagonists in war;' referring particularly to Octavianus. **29. a . . . generatum**: i. e. through Romulus. **30. suis decretis**: in deciding to desert the side of Antony; see p. 173, 1-3. **32. consulem**: Antony was still consul; see p. 51. **33. loco**: 'in place,' i. e. 'opportunely.' **reclamatione**: at the words *hos . . . hostes . . . iudicemus* the audience had shouted 'No! No!'

Page 173. 3. parricidam patriae: cf. *parricidio*, p. 68, 18, and N. **5. Albae**: *Alba* (2) in Vocab.

III. 11. M. Antoni: cf. N. to p. 148, 11. As Antony was not present, the direct address here is introduced simply to make the arraignment more vivid. **14. arcessitae sunt**: from Macedonia: see N. to p. 172, 6. **18. nisi forte**: used as *nisi vero;* cf. p. 109, 24, and N.

20. ut ostenditis: the irony of the preceding sentence had stirred the audience to another demonstration of feeling. The Roman populace were as wax in the hands of the orator. **23. haec**: as p. 70, 11. **25. hodierno eius edicto**: Decimus Brutus as governor of Cisalpine Gaul had issued a proclamation that he would hold this province 'in the power of the Senate and of the Roman people,' thus shutting Antony out and thwarting his plan of making Ariminum a centre of military operations. Cf. N. to p. 172, 6. **26. num . . . videtur**: followed by cries of 'No! No!' shown by *Recte . . . negatis.* **29. Brutorum genus**: i. e. in the expulsion of the last of the early Kings, Tarquin (*ad libertatem constituendam*), as well as in the overthrow of these later rulers, Caesar and Antony (*ad libertatem recipiendam*). **32. Galliam**: *Cisalpinam.*

Page 174. 1. Num . . . possumus: again shouts of 'No! No!' see l. 3, *una mente*, etc.

IV. 5. optime: see IDIOMS. **10. resistat**: why not *resistit?* **11. neque eum reciperet**: = 'and should not receive him as such.' **12. in consulis iure**: only in a general way, in showing the respect appropriate to the representative of the highest authority of the nation, unless, as sometimes happened, the consul received an extraordinary provincial commission; for each province had its own governor and staff of administration independent of the consular office (cf. p. 60). **14. rei publicae**: dat. **15. negat . . . vos**: climax and anaphora, heightened by the asyndeta.

17. latrones: i. e. Antony's followers. **putant**: why not *putat?* **22. quos**, etc.: veterans of Caesar, who had been rewarded with lands and other gifts, and had quickly wasted all they had received. Cf. p. 84, 24–34, and notes. **23. hasta**: i. e. auction sale of confiscated property. The place of auction, particularly of booty or of confiscated goods, was denoted by a spear placed upright in the ground. **28. hoc omen**: 'this prophetic word.'

29. Ita . . . precamini: the people had responded, with similar invocations, to the prayer just uttered (ll. 27, 28). **33. prodigiis, portentis**: referring perhaps to the unusual phenomena noticed about the time of Caesar's death, and afterwards. Cf. NN. to p. 97, 15 and 16.

B. *Remain in your judgment of Antony as an enemy.*
V., VI. (l. 15).

Page 175. V. 5. Reliquum est: cf. p. 126, 19, and N. **8. videant**: B. 324; A. 342; H. 529, II. **ut**: i. e. *solent* (*facere*) *ut.* B. 297, 1; A. 332, *e*; H. 498, II., N. 2.

17. cum . . . belua: cf. p. 77, 2–4, and N. **20. erit recusanda** [nobis]: i. e. we may expect to suffer everything. **tenetur**: = *deprehenditur.* **21. mox eis**: sc. what? **22. novi consules**: Gaius Vibius Pansa and Aulus Hirtius, who immediately upon their entry into office, eleven days after this time, were to take measures to head off Antony; so the Senate had decreed. **26. agitur**: 'the matter at issue is.'

29. crudelitatem mortis et dedecus: we should say, 'a cruel and shameful death.' Cf. N. to p. 146, 6. **33. virtus**: of *virtus* Cicero had written, early in this same year (Lael. XXVII. 100): *In ea est enim convenientia rerum, in ea stabilitas, in ea constantia.* **35. demoveri loco**: cf. p. 76, 13, and N.

Page 176. 3. reges: as Perseus and Antiochus; cf. p. 137, 24 et seq.

VI. 5. cum — res erat: = 'had to meet.' **7. rationem**: = 'basis.' **10. orbis terrae consilium**: cf. p. 64, 25. **13. qui**: 'how.'

CONCLUSION.

17. omne certamen: 'a contest throughout.' **18. Spartaco**: Cicero elsewhere intimates (Phil. III. VIII. 21) that Antony in his proclamations had alluded to Octavianus as 'a Spartacus.' **19. scelere, industria**: see p. 79. **20. Ille . . . conflavit**: cf. N. to p. 86, 24. **21. quem accepit**: *a senatu*, referring to the four legions from Macedonia, of which two had deserted him.

30. id: i. e. *ut quicquam praetermittam*, understood from the preceding sentence. **pro . . . beneficiis**: cf. p. 114,

26 et seq. **32. referente**: i. e. *ad senatum*. In the absence of the consuls the meeting of the Senate had been called by the tribunes, among whom Servilius took the lead. **33. hoc M. Servilio**: Servilius was probably on the Rostra, near the orator; cf. p. 108, 17, and N. **34. longo intervallo**: at the time of Caesar's death, more than nine months before, it seemed as if their liberties would be at once restored.

NOTES TO THE LETTERS.

Page 177. Epistolae: a letter was called *epistola* (= ἐπιστολή, from ἐπιστέλλω, 'send by a messenger'), as having the nature of a message, sent by one person to another; *litterae*, from the characters of the writing; or *tabellae*, from the surfaces on which the writing was placed; with us, "despatch," "line," "card," etc. For the form and address of Roman letters, see pp. 54–56.

I. TO ATTICUS, at Athens (ad Att. I. vii.).

Rome; b. c. 68.

Cicero Attico sal.: the usual heading of the letters to Atticus, *sal.* being put briefly for *salutem dicit.* This heading is probably not genuine, at least for the earlier letters; for in the letters themselves prior to 50 b. c. Atticus is addressed ordinarily as *mi Pomponi.* He owed his last name to a residence of twenty years at Athens; so Cicero playfully says to him (Cato Mai. i. 1): 'You brought back from Athens not only a surname, but also culture and practical wisdom.'

1. Apud . . . est: 'All's well at your mother's,' or 'Everything is all right at your mother's, and I am looking after her.' **2. HS.** xxcd.: '20,400 sesterces,' = about $840. This sum would ordinarily be written $\overline{\text{XX}}$CD; cf. A. 380; H. 180, ft. n. 1. But in familiar correspondence, or in speaking of a sum previously mentioned, the denomination might be omitted; by a similar ellipsis we say "I gave twenty-four hundred for a lot," meaning twenty-four hundred dollars. Atticus had probably expended this money in buying works of art in Athens for Cicero's villa at Tusculum; cf. ad Att. I. vi. 2. **curaturum** [esse]: 'that I would see to the payment of.' **Idibus**: see n. to p. 66, 34. What date? B. 371, 372; A. 376, *e*; H. 643.

3. Tu velim — des operam: 'I would like to have you see to it,' = 'Will you please to see to it;' *velim* is often used thus to soften a request. B. 280, 2, *a*; A. 267, *c*; H. 499, 2. **6. conficere**: either by purchase or by having copies made;

for among his slaves Atticus kept a number of copyists. **7. cum in otium venerimus**: = 'when I shall take a vacation.' How lit.? **8. positam habemus**: B. 337, 6; A. 292, *c*; H. 388, I, N.

II. TO GNAEUS POMPEY, IN ASIA (AD FAM. V. VII.).

Rome; B. C. 62.

M. Tullius, etc.: i. e. *Marcus Tullius Cicero, Marci filius, salutem dicit Gnaeo Pompeio, Gnaei filio, Magno, Imperatori.* In less formal correspondence forenames and titles were usually omitted.

10. S . . . E.: a stately greeting, appropriate to a commander with his army; not common. See Vocab. **litteris tuis**: despatches to the Senate announcing the finishing of the Mithridatic war. **12. oti**: for *pacis*. **13. pollicebar**: particularly in the speech 'On Pompey's Commission,' four years before. **14. veteres hostis, novos amicos**: a reference to certain persons who were then wishing to be on good terms with Pompey; perhaps Caesar and other members of the popular party are meant. **15. ex magna spe**, etc.: because Pompey's unparalleled successes would render him less disposed to effect a reconciliation with former enemies, and because the finishing of the war would make it possible for him to come back to Rome in the near future.

16. Ad me litteras: in answer to a letter of Cicero giving a full account of his consulship and of his services to the state in the suppression of the Catilinarian conspiracy. Pompey's letter in reply was cold and formal, containing slight evidence of any appreciation of the orator's achievements.

Page 178. 2. meorum officiorum: 'of my services' to others, particularly to you. **3. quibus . . . patior**: 'and if no adequate return is made to these, I am entirely satisfied to let the balance of service rendered remain on my side.' **5. mea . . . studia**: 'my most enthusiastic efforts on your behalf.' Cicero had not only urged the passing of the bill of Manilius, giving Pompey the command under which he was still exercising authority as *imperator*, but had also as consul in the latter part of 63 B. C. proposed a ten days' *supplicatio* (see N. to p. 95, 21; de Prov. cons. xi. 27) in recognition of his public services in the Mithridatic war. **6. inter nos**: here 'to each other.'

10. Res eas, etc.: i. e. the crushing of the Catilinarian conspiracy; Cicero had supposed that Pompey would make reference to this in his despatches to the Senate. **13. cuius**: some of Pompey's supporters, who happened to be ill-disposed toward Cicero at that time. **16. quae**: = *et ea*. **consilio**: 'discretion.' **18. Africanus**: the intimacy of the younger Scipio with Laelius was proverbial; Cicero afterwards made it the text of his treatise 'On Friendship.' It is not improbable that the ex-consul had looked forward to a kind of copartnership in public esteem and influence between himself and Pompey; cf. p. 101, 6–9.

III. TO ATTICUS, AT ROME (AD ATT. II. IV.).

Tusculan Villa; B. C. 59.

21. Fecisti . . . misisti: 'You did me a very great favor in sending,' etc. **24. praesentem**: 'at once.' **25. expensum**: sc. *eum* (i. e. *librum*); 'that you may (why not 'might'?) not have to carry it (in your accounts) as an expenditure under the head of gifts.' **26. amabo te, cura ut—transigas**: 'will you be so kind as to make a settlement;' *amabo te*, 'I shall be obliged to you,' = 'I request,' 'be so kind.' **28. mihi**, etc.: 'I should be most pleased to have those articles sent back.' **male**: = 'at too high a price,' 'too dear.'

Page 179. 1. Pomponiae: Quintus Cicero, or his wife, had been interested in the purchase referred to. **2. nummi**, etc.: pay an exorbitant price rather than have any trouble. **3. velim**: cf. N. to p. 177, 3.

5. Clodius ad Tigranem: as an ambassador. **Syrpiae**: from MS. readings *syrpie*, *Sirpiae*; unintelligible as it stands. The most probable explanation is that of Gronov, who reads the passage *velim Scepsii condicione*, 'I hope with the fate of the Scepsian;' for Metrodorus of Scepsis (see Map) went to Tigranes as ambassador for Mithridates, and was put to death by his king on account of his imprudent speech. Boot emends the passage to read thus: *Clodius ergo, ut ais, ad Tigranem vel in Cyprum: opimae condiciones; sed facile patior.*

6. facile patior: 'I am quite reconciled' to it, having no time for such a mission myself at present. **7. liberam legationem**: 'a free embassy;' sometimes a senator was allowed to travel with the rights and privileges of an ambassador, but 'free' from any responsibility as a government representative. **8. in otio**: 'in private life;' Quintus Cicero was now governor of Asia. **9. sacerdos Bonae Deae**: playful irony; see pp. 6, 7. **12. mihi . . . mentem**: see IDIOMS. **Crasso**: i. e. for his coalition with Pompey and Caesar in the so-called first triumvirate. **13. quod . . . desciverim**: 'that I have not proved false to myself.'

14. De geographia, etc.: Cicero evidently thought of writing a treatise on geography; Atticus was anxious to have him finish the work. **dabo operam, ut**: 'I 'll try to.' **16. peregrinationis**: in the southern part of Latium; the outing will do me so much good that I 'll get the book done all the sooner in consequence. **18. facito**, etc.: see IDIOMS. **20. nihil**: see IDIOMS.

21. saltum: no doubt a part of Terentia's dowry. **22. quercum Dodonaeam**: the famous oak at Dodona, at which oracles were received. **23. Epirum**: the appearance of Terentia's 'woodlands' was very like that of Epirus, where Atticus had extensive estates.

28. muro: Marcus and Quintus Cicero had adjoining residences on the Palatine hill. A wall between the orator's gymnasium and his brother's premises seemed to be unsafe; he does not wish to have it taken down, but refers the whole matter to Atticus, who naturally looked after the affairs of Pomponia in the absence of her husband.

30. adhibeas: 'consult.' **dubia vita**: B. 227, 1; A. 255, *a*; H. 431, 4. **31. optimi cuiusque**: cf. p. 116, 5, and N. **magni . . . fructum**: 'I consider a single summer's enjoyment — of great account.' **32. ita, ut**: '(only) on condition that.'

IV. TO ATTICUS, AT ROME (AD ATT. II. XIII.).

Formian Villa; B. C. 59.

Page 180. 1. Facinus indignum: 'Too bad!' **epistolam . . . reddidisse**: the infin. is sometimes used with the acc. in exclamations. B. 334; A. 274; H. 539, III. **αὐθωρεί**: 'the very hour' that yours was received. See p. 368. **2. ad**: 'in answer to.' **4. domum**: to Cicero's house on the Palatine. **6. tuam**: 'to you.' For *tibi tuam* cf. p. 159, 20, and N. **referri**: 'be carried back' to Rome again.

8. sileri: = 'that nothing is said,' i. e. about the course Caesar is taking. **9. regnum vestrum**: 'your lordship,' i. e. the lordship of the triumvirs, to which Atticus and men like him submitted without remonstrance. **10. Τηλέπυλον Λαιστρυγονίην**: 'Laestrygonian Telepylus,' a city of the fabulous Laestrygonians (Od. x. 81); applied to Formiae, which was said to have been founded by a colony of Laestrygonians. **11. dico**: 'I mean.' **13. cuius cognomen**, etc.: i. e. Pompey is no longer spoken of as 'Great,' nor Crassus Dives as 'Rich.' The Crassus mentioned is probably not the triumvir, but some wealthy member of the family who had become poor. **14. Credas mihi velim**: 'I hope you'll believe me.' **15. offendi**: 'I have come across.'

17. φιλοσοφῶμεν: 'let us be philosophers,' 'let us take refuge in philosophy.' **iuratus**: 'on my oath.' **18. nihil esse tanti**: 'nothing is of so great value,' 'there is nothing like (philosophy),' in these troubled times. **18. Sicyonios**: they were in debt to Atticus, who seems to have hoped to get a letter from the Senate or consuls advising them to pay him what they owed. **19. unde nos**: sc. what?

V. TO ATTICUS, AT ROME (AD ATT. II. X.).

Forum of Appius, B. C. 59; written before EP. IV.

21. Volo, etc.: 'I want you to admire my grit. I am resolved not to attend the games at Antium. For it would be in bad form (*ὑποσόλοικον*), when I wish to avoid all appearance of enjoying myself, suddenly to let myself be seen (*ἀναφαίνεσθαι*) travelling not merely for amusement but even for foolish amusement.' He had previously written that he was going with Tullia to see the games at Antium (ad Att. II. VIII. 2). Antium was a resort of pleasure-seekers; but attending the games there would be 'foolish amusement' for one accustomed to the games at Rome.

Page 181. 3. fac: see IDIOMS. **4. Dederam**: B. 265; A. 282;

H. 472, I. **5. aliam** [epistolam]: the letter which went wrong; see EP. IV.

VI. TO ATTICUS, IN EPIRUS (AD ATT. II. XXIII.).

Rome; B.C. 59.

6. meam: 'of mine.' **8. cum . . . haberem**: 'as I have no leisure.' B. 265; A. 282; H. 472, I. **9. recreandae voculae**: 'of strengthening my poor voice,' worn out with speaking in the courts (l. 22).

11. Sampsiceramum: 'the Emir,' i. e. Pompey. Sampsiceramus was an obscure Syrian prince, conquered by Pompey, whose boastful references to eastern victories led to the application of several sonorous oriental names to himself. Cicero calls him also *Arabarches*, 'the Sheikh' (ad Att. II. XVII. 3), and *Hierosolymarius*, 'the Jerusalemite,' (ad Att. II. IX. I).

12. sui status: his relation with Caesar and Crassus, and his loss of popularity. **16. illius partis**: the party of the triumvirate, which Cicero represents as losing all influence, with no one to come to the rescue. In this he did not read aright the signs of the times, and was sadly mistaken. **18. maiorem**: 'greater' against any party.

21. totos nos: 'myself wholly.' **22. forensem**: see N. to p. 117, I. **23. in . . . versamur**: freely, 'I live amid frequent recounting of my former deeds, and am aware of a sense of loss' which others feel. **25. βοώπιδος nostrae**: 'of our dear Cow-eyes;' ironical reference to Clodia, sister of Cicero's bitter enemy Clodius. See p. 368. **consanguineus**: Clodius. **26. terrores**: 'threats' against me. Cf. pp. 6, 7. **Sampsiceramo . . . ostentat**: 'he denies (all hostile intentions regarding me) to the Emir, (but) he makes open assertion of them and displays them to others.'

Page 182. **3. in — ponam**: 'I rely on.' **8. Permagni nostra**: see IDIOMS. B. 210; 211, I, *a*, 3, *a*; A. 222, *a*; H. 408, I, 2. **comitiis**: for the election of tribunes for 58. **9. potueris**: sc. *esse Romae*. **illo declarato**: 'when he (i. e. Clodius) is declared elected;' for Cicero looks upon the election of Clodius as settled. The tribunes were chosen in July, but did not qualify till the following December.

VII. TO ATTICUS, AT ROME (AD ATT. III. III.).

En route; B. C. 58.

11. Utinam — videam: 'May I live to see;' Cicero had fled from Rome, and was on his way into exile. He writes as if only the exhortation of Atticus had kept him from making away with himself. **14. multis de causis**: his friend Sicca would entertain him at Vibo, from which he thought of crossing over into Sicily.

VIII. TO HIS FAMILY, AT ROME (AD FAM. XIV. IV.).

Brindisi; B. C. 58.

18. Ego, etc.: Terentia had asked why he did not write oftener; he answers '(Yes), I send letters less often than I might.' **19. cum**: 'while.' **22. fuissemus**: 'that I had been;' he regrets not having committed suicide. **nihil**: *nihil mali.*

Page 183. **2. minus**: see IDIOMS. **3. fixa sunt**: 'are permanently fixed.' **5. di, quos tu,** etc.: the implication is, a woman may well busy herself with the worship of the gods; a man's business is with men. Cf. notes to p. 97, 15, and 107, 11.

9. periculum: he who harbored an exile ran the risk of losing his citizenship and one third of his property. **10. legis**: the enactment carried by Clodius, which forbade Cicero to live within four hundred miles of Rome (ad Att. III. IV.). **13. habebimus**: sc. *gratiam.* **14. profecti sumus, petebamus**: we say 'I am on the point of leaving,' 'I am setting out for.' B. 265; A. 282; H. 472, 1. **prid. K. Mai.**: B. 144, 2; A. 261, *a*; H. 437, 1.

19. sic agam: 'I shall put (it) this way.' **20. transactum est**: 'all is over (with me),' if there is no hope of a change. **21. venias**: sc. what? **23. Tulliola mea**: abl.; 'what will become of my dear Tullia?' B. 218, 6; A. 244, *d*; H. 415, III., N. 1. **vos**: Terentia and Piso. **25. res habebit**: cf. IDIOMS. **matrimonio . . . est**: 'we must look out for the poor child's married estate and good name;' seemingly her dowry had not been paid, though she had been married five years. **27. sit,** etc.: Tullia may remain with you and Piso, but my son should be with me. **29. aliquid teneas**: Cicero's property is to be confiscated; he fears that the private fortune of Terentia may share the same fate. **31. nostrum**: 'faithful to my interests.' Piso made most earnest efforts for the recall of Cicero; cf. p. 185, 32.

32. familia liberata: knowing that his property would be confiscated, Cicero had given his own slaves their freedom subject to two conditions: first, that in case they should be able to maintain their manumission as valid (i. e. against the claim that his giving them their freedom under the circumstances was not lawful), and his property should be permanently alienated, they should be his freedmen (p. 184, 1, 2); secondly, that if his property should again come into his hands, they should again be his slaves, 'excepting a very few,' to whom freedom had been given outright (p. 184, 2, 3). Terentia had heard that he had promised freedom to her slaves also, but he assures her that he had left their case entirely in her hands.

34. in officio: 'in (meritorious) service,' 'serviceable;' Orpheus was with Cicero. **35. magno opere**: 'especially (serviceable),' 'especially (deserving).'

Page 184. 1. ea causa est: 'the case stands thus.' **res**: *res familiaris*; 'my property.' **2. essent**: used after *est* as applied to an agreement made in the past and still valid. **obtinere**: 'to make (their manumission) good.' **3. pertineret**: i. e. *maneret nostra;* when his property should be put up at auction, he would have his friends bid it in for him, if possible, so that it should not go out of his hands. **oppido**: adv.

4. quod hortaris: B. 299, 2; A. 333, and N.; H. 540, IV., N. **ut . . . magno**: 'that I keep my courage up.' **9. tempestatem**: here 'favorable weather,' or 'favorable wind,' for sailing. **11. viximus**: 'I have lived.' **14. ornamentis**: '(my) dignities.' **17. ipse . . . possum**: i. e. *me ipsum confirmare* ('encourage') *non possum.*

20. officio: 'in kindness.' **27. Brundisio**: why abl.?

IX. TO HIS FAMILY, AT ROME (AD FAM. XIV. I.).

Dyrrachium; B. C. 58.

28. perfertur ad me: 'report is brought to me,' = 'I learn.' **29. virtutem et fortitudinem**: 'pluck and endurance.' Terentia possessed much force of character.

Page 185. **2. te . . . incidisse**: cf. N. to p. 180, 1. **4. ex quo patre — ex eo**: = *ex eo patre, ex quo.* B. 251, 4; A. 200, *b*; H. 445, 9. **6. cum . . . coepit**: 'ever since he began to think for himself;' Marcus was now seven years old. **7. acerbissimos . . . percepit**: 'has experienced (only) the bitterest pain and wretchedness.' For the pl. cf. N. to p. 152, 22. **11. nostris**, etc.: 'had followed my own judgment.' **14. Nunc**: N. to p. 68, 16. **15. ne . . . desit**; 'that the state of my health may not make your efforts of no avail;' I shall try to keep well. **16. quanta**: 'how important;' *res* refers to the matter of health. **18. habemus**: i. e. on our side, favoring my return from exile. **19. si vero**: 'particularly if;' sc. *habemus.*

21. De familia: see N. to p. 183, 32. **22. loco**: Thessalonica, where Cicero had been staying. The letter may have been written at Thessalonica, and brought on to Dyrrachium, whence it was sent with a postscript (p. 186, 20–22). **25. loco magis deserto**: 'a more out of the way place.' **26. Hispo**: perhaps sent to keep an eye on Cicero's movements. **28. Quem diem**: 'that day' when I may go back to Italy. **31. vestrae pietatis et meae**: 'of your loyalty (to me) and of mine (to my country).'

33. supra possit: sc. *esse.* **ei voluptati**: 'a source of gratification to him,' in having me back.

Page 186. **1. te accusavi**: 'I have made no complaint of you to my brother,' with whom Terentia seems not always to have been on the best of terms. **3. egi**: *egi gratias eis.* Terentia had asked Cicero to thank several persons for efforts in his behalf.

5. vicum: on one of her estates. **7. eadem fortuna**: i. e. of financial straits; as Cicero's property had been confiscated, it was all the more important that his wife's be kept in the family. **8. puero**: B. 218, 6; A. 244, *d*; H. 415, III., N. 1. **10. Tantum**: '(only) this much.' **erunt in officio**: 'shall do their duty.' **11. efficere**: 'to bring about' my return. **13. ne puerum perditum perdamus**: 'that we do not ruin the boy (by selling off property that ought to go to him), already ruined (by my misfortunes).' Notice the alliteration. **Cui . . . est**: = 'If he can but have enough to be above want, he needs (only),' etc.

16. Fac: see IDIOMS. **17. quid agatur**: 'what is going on.' **18. exspectatio est**: 'state of suspense must be.' **19. D. . . Decemb.**: *Data* (*est epistola*) *ante diem sextum Kalendas Decembris.*

20. libera civitas: 'free cities' possessed certain privileges which made them more desirable for residence than the ordinary provincial towns. **22. celebritas**: 'bustle.'

X. TO ATTICUS, AT ROME (AD ATT. III. XXVI.).

Dyrrachium; B. C. 57.

23. senatus consulto: of Jan. 1, B. C. 57; intended to prepare the way for the recall of Cicero. The Senate took the position that Cicero had been unlawfully banished, and it was proposed to request the people to unite in inviting him to return. No motion on the subject was passed, however, owing to the obstruction of a tribune who had been bought up by the orator's enemies; he did not actually interpose a veto, but was able to postpone action indefinitely by demanding time for deliberation; for particulars see Cic. pro Sest. XXXIII., XXXIV. Cicero supposes that the motion prevailed the day after the discussion mentioned in the letter of Quintus.

25. legum lationem: i. e. to the people, for the recall of Cicero: *legis lationem* might have been expected; but the pl. is used as referring to other matters besides the bill in his favor. **si obtrectabitur**: in the form of a tribune's veto. **26. utar**: 'I shall take advantage of.' **auctoritate senatus**: an expression often applied to a decree of the Senate which had been vetoed by a tribune; loosely used here, because the motion referred to had not been formally vetoed.

XI. TO ATTICUS (AD ATT. III. XXVII.).

Dyrrachium, B. C. 57.

Page 187. **1. tuis litteris**: containing the news that the bill for Cicero's recall was brought before the people Jan. 25, and failed to pass; a mob incited by Clodius broke up the assembly, and Quintus Cicero came near being killed (pro Sest. XXXV.). **2. mei**: 'my family;' he thinks of self-destruction. **4. cito videbo**: seems to imply that Atticus was already on the way, perhaps in Epirus; cf. N. to p. 179, 23.

XII. TO ATTICUS, AT ROME (AD ATT. IV. x.).

Cumaean Villa; B. C. 55.

5. Puteolis: Cumae was only six miles from Puteoli. **7. bibliotheca Fausti**: Sulla Faustus had collected a number of books in Athens and the eastern cities. **his rebus**: = 'the good things,' sc. *me pasci;* i. e. the oysters, of which the waters of this region yielded an exceptionally fine variety. **10. voluptatum**: '(consisting) of pleasures.' **12. sub imagine Aristotelis**: in Atticus's house, at Rome. **13. istorum**: Pompey and Crassus; Caesar was in Gaul. **sella curuli**: see N. to p. 103, 18. **apud te**: 'at your place.' **14. eo**: Pompey, who during Caesar's absence was all-powerful in Rome. **15. illa ambulatione**: 'that (political) path.' **si qui — deus**: 'the divinity, whichever it is.'

17. ambulationem: at his residence in Rome. **Laconicum**: like the Turkish baths of our day. **19. tibi . . . respondere**: 'to be in some degree a match for you in this department (of architecture).' **20. in Cumanum**: Pompey also had a villa near Cumae. **22. vadebam**: trans. 'I was intending to go.' Why?

XIII. TO TREBATIUS TESTA (AD FAM. VII. VII.).

Rome; B. C. 54.

Page 188. 1. commendare: to Caesar, under whom in Gaul Cicero's brother Quintus was serving as lieutenant. **4. Illud**: '(only) this.'

7. In Britannia: probably Trebatius was intending soon to go to Britain with Caesar's army; cf. Caes. de Bell. Gall. IV. 20–36. **auri**: both gold and silver were found in Britain later; cf. Tac. Agr. XII. **8. essedum**: as the only kind of plunder to be obtained from the island. **14. aetatem**: Trebatius was now thirty-five years old.

XIV. TO GAIUS CURIO (AD FAM. II. II.).

Rome; B. C. 53.

17. Gravi teste — patre tuo: written shortly after the death of the elder Curio. **18. laudibus**: 'honors.' **19. te**

filio: 'in having you as a son.' Why abl.? **23. aeque ac**: 'just as.'

XV. TO SILIUS (AD FAM. XIII. XLVII.).

Rome; date not known. To recommend Egnatius.

Page 189. **1. eum**: Egnatius. **2. scires**: why impf.? **diligi**: applied to an affection based upon respect, while *amari* indicates a warm personal regard arising from intimate acquaintance. **8. Illa nostra**: 'that scheme of ours has fallen through,' referring probably to some mutual business interest. **9. si hoc melius**: 'if it had been something better than this,' that turned out badly. **haec coram**: '(we'll talk) this over between ourselves.'

XVI. TO ATTICUS, AT ROME (AD ATT. V. XIII.).

Ephesus; B. C. 51. Cicero was on his way to his province, Cilicia; cf. p. 9.

13. post pugnam Bovillanam: half-humorous designation of the skirmish at Bovillae (Jan. 20, B. C. 52), which, as it caused the death of Clodius, the orator might well take as a starting-point for reckoning his dates. **17. mihi — praesto fuit**: 'waited upon me.' **18. aut**, etc.: *aut puto te dicturum esse "Quid ad me attinet?"* 'What is that to me?' **19. Verum tamen**: 'But (it is of interest to you) nevertheless;' taken by Tyrrell, however, in close connection with the following sentence, with a resumptive force.

20. imperio: as governor of the province Asia, to which Ephesus belonged. **venissem**: B. 307; A. 312; H. 513, II. **21. Ephesio praetori**: i. e. Thermus, propraetor of Asia; the term *praetor* was sometimes applied to provincial governors. **22. ostentationes**: probably 'boastings' that he would so conduct himself as to be just alike toward all and give offence to none, and that he would show no special favor to the tithe-collectors.

Page 190. **1. palaestra**: 'art' of keeping every one in good humor. **3. pactiones**: the 'agreements' between the tax-collectors and the provincials for the year 51; those for the next year were made during Cicero's term of office. **Sed**

haec hactenus: in our phrase, 'But enough on this point.' **5. se de nocte proficisci**: 'that he starts to-night.' The Romans dined late in the afternoon; and as Cestius was to carry the letter to Atticus, there was no time to write at length.

6. curae mihi fuerunt: 'I looked after.' **8. tuis**: 'your (representatives).' **9. tradidi**: = 'I introduced.' **10. rationem permutationis**, etc.: 'an account of that exchange which I got on your credit.'

15. ut simus annui: 'that I may be (here only) for a year;' brief for 'that my term of office may be limited to a year.' **ne intercaletur quidem**: 'that there be no intercalation even.' Before Julius Caesar reformed the calendar (B. C. 46), there was much confusion in the reckoning of the days of the month and of the year. Until the pontifices made their announcement on the first of February no one knew whether there would be an intercalation in that month or not.

16. de· 'in regard to.' **17. scrupulo**: 'difficulty,' 'misunderstanding,' perhaps about the betrothal of Tullia to Dolabella; she had now been left a widow for the second time. **18. te auctore**: 'on your advice.' Cicero had owed Caesar 20,800 sesterces (= $850; ad Att. V. v. 2), which he had now paid. **19. quam meum sit**: = 'how natural it is for me.' **20. fiat**, etc.: cf. p. 61. 14, and N. **22. iudiciorum**: 'of the trials.' **24. si**, etc.: see IDIOMS. **animadvertes**: B. 261, 3; A. 269, *f*; H. 487, 4.

XVII. TO TITIUS RUFUS (AD FAM. XIII. LVIII.).

From Cilicia; B. C. 50. To introduce Lucius Custidius.

M. Cicero, etc.: *Marcus Cicero Gaio Titio Rufo, Luci filio, Praetori Urbano, salutem dicit.*

25. tribulis, municeps: Custidius, like Cicero, was a member of the Cornelian tribe, and a native of Arpinum. **28. tantum**: 'to this extent.' **faciles aditus**: cf. p. 132, 21, and N.

Page 191. 1. quae aequa postulat: we should say, 'all reasonable requests.'

XVIII. TO MARCUS CAELIUS (AD FAM. II. XI.).

From Cilicia; B. C. 50.

M. Cicero, etc.: *Marcus Cicero Imperator salutem dicit Marco Caelio Aedili Curuli.* The governor of a province, possessing military authority (*imperium*), was permitted to use the title *imperator*; cf. p. 189, 20.

5. haec levia nostratia: = 'these humble (phrases) of our mother tongue;' he compliments the oratory of Caelius. **7. quidnam . . . decernatur**: he wishes to be relieved of his governorship at the expiration of his term of office: cf. p. 190, 13–15. **11. fortuna**: i. e. a change of fortune, ill-luck.

17. agitur: 'the matter is being attended to.' **19. cuiquam**: i. e. 'for any (other animal).' **22. Quicquid erit**: sc. *nobis*; 'All we get shall be yours,' 'You shall have all we can secure.' **23. esset, nesciebamus**: force of the impf.?

25. dies me admonebat: the festival of Cybele was in charge of the Curule Aediles. **26. velim**: cf. p. 177, 3, and N.

XIX. TO ATTICUS (AD ATT. VI. VIII.).

Ephesus; B. C. 50. Cicero is now on his way back from Cilicia. For the heading cf. N. to EP. I.

Page 192. 1. calamum: implies that this letter was written on paper; see p. 55.

4. opportunitate Piliae: i. e. 'your opportune meeting with Pilia,' who had somewhere joined her husband, bringing late news from Rome. **5. coniugio**: with Dolabella. **6. miros terrores Caesarianos**: 'astonishing (and) dreadful news about Caesar.' **9. cum illo . . . facere**: = 'are on his side.' **designatos**: with *Cassium* and *Lentulum* (no. 5 in Vocab.) as well as *praetores*. **12. illo, qui**: Marcus Calidius, who had been an unsuccessful competitor for the consulship for the year 49. **13. patruo sororis tuae fili**: humorous designation of himself; Pomponia and Quintus Cicero had a son named Quintus. Calidius had spoken slightingly of Cicero's oratory. **a quibus victus**: as we might say, 'just think who beat him!' Cicero had a poor opinion of the consuls for 49, Lentulus Crus and Claudius Marcellus.

15. xx. ipsos dies: = 'just twenty days;' the slowness of the Rhodian craft has caused a loss of twenty days beyond that due to the trade-winds. **19. tranquillitates**: 'calm spells,' or 'calm days;' these Rhodian vessels were without decks.

21. rauduseulo Puteolano: the payment of a debt to some one at Puteoli. **gratum**: = 'thanks.' **22. de triumpho**: see p. 10. **24. Bibulus**: Caesar's colleague in the consulship (B. C. 59), who had shut himself up in his house for eight months; Cicero hints that his governorship of Syria had been no more vigorous than his consulate, and yet he was bound to secure a triumph. **27. αἰσχρὸν σιωπᾶν**: = *turpe est tacere*; quoted from a fragment of Euripides. See p. 368.

Page 193. 1. Sat, etc.: '(I have written) quite enough, as I am in a hurry.' Reason for mood and tense? **2. ei**: see p. 192, 17.

4. Cicero: the orator's son, who was with him. For an interesting account of this young man, see the "New Englander and Yale Review" for 1891, pp. 236–248. **dices**: sc. *salutem*; 'please give the best regards of us both in my name' (*verbis* = *meis verbis*). B. 261, 3; A. 269, *f*; H. 487, 4.

XX. TO TIRO, AT PATRAE (AD FAM. XVI. VII.).

Corcyra; B. C. 50.

6. tenebamur: i. e. my son and I; they had left Tiro sick at Patrae (ad Fam. XVI. VI.). **7. filius**: the younger Quintus; cf. N. to p. 192, 13. **9. istim**: from Patrae; the same winds favor or retard one sailing from Patras to Corfu as from Corfu to Rome. See Map.

XXI. TO TERENTIA (AD FAM. XIV. XVII.).

End of B. C. 50, or early in 49.

17. S . . . v: see Vocab. **19. quo modo sim adfectus**: 'how I am affected' by the condition of affairs.' **21. fac, ut — cures**: a parallel to our familiar exhortation, 'Do take care of your health.'

XXII. TO TERENTIA AND TULLIA (AD FAM. XIV. XVIII.).

Formiae; B. C. 49. Young Marcus Cicero was with his father.

Page 194. 2. Romaene sitis, etc.: Cicero was becoming more and more fully committed to the side of Pompey. But he was not blind to the weakness of that leader, and was in the gravest quandary what course to recommend to his wife and daughter. If they remained at Rome, they would be under the protection of Dolabella, who had joined the party of Caesar.

5. Mihi . . . mentem: see IDIOMS. **9. bonos**: 'the patriotic' from Pompey's point of view. **10. Haec regio**: Campania, over which Pompey had placed him in command. **11. nostrorum oppidorum**: i. e. towns of which Cicero was the patron (cf. N. to p. 91, 9); *praediorum*, 'estates' of which he was the owner. **12. mecum**: in the towns.

15. isto loco: = 'in the same position as you.' **18. propugnacula, praesidium**: against robbers, who would take advantage of times of political disturbance to commit depredations. **20. certos**: 'special.' **22. viiii. Kal.**: probably *ix. Kalendas Ianuarias*, for Terentia and Tullia joined Cicero early in February; but the month is uncertain. There is much doubt about the month and even the year in which a number of Cicero's letters were written.

XXIII. TO TERENTIA (AD FAM. XIV. XXI.).

B. C. 48, or possibly 49; probably written from the camp of Pompey.

Page 195. 1. quod opus erit: i. e. *id, quod tibi opus erit*, 'whatever you may need.'

XXIV. TO TERENTIA (AD FAM. XIV. XI.).

Brundisium; B. C. 47. Cicero came back to Brundisium after the battle of Pharsalus (see p. 10), and received permission to remain in Italy from Antony, Caesar's representative.

8. alia in fortuna, etc.: a reference to her unhappy marriage with Dolabella. **9. erat**: trans. as if *est*. **10. Ciceronem**: the son; the orator wishes to make terms with Caesar.

XXV. TO TERENTIA (AD FAM. XIV. X.).

Brundisium; B. C. 47.

14. Quid fieri placeret: about the divorce of Tullia from Dolabella. **Pomponium**: Atticus had observed a strict neutrality in the war, and had even kept on good terms with both Pompey and Caesar; so he had been obliged neither to flee from Rome nor to stay in Italy.

XXVI. TO TERENTIA (AD FAM. XIV. XXIV.).

Brundisium; B. C. 47.

Page 196. **4. adventu**: Caesar did not return to Italy till September, after he had finished the Alexandrian war and the campaign against Pharnaces in Asia. **5. litteris**, etc.: he is specially anxious to hear from Caesar; Philotimus was at Ephesus. **7. fac, ut cures**: cf. p. 193, 21, and N.

XXVII. TO TERENTIA (AD FAM. XIV. XXIII.).

Brundisium; B. C. 47.

10. litterae satis liberales: the letter unfortunately is lost. Caesar treated those who had joined Pompey with unlooked-for clemency; cf. p. 163, 6 et seq. **11. cui obviam procedam**: 'I shall go to meet him;' Caesar landed at Tarentum.

XXVIII. TO TERENTIA (AD FAM. XIV. XXII.).

Brundisium; B. C. 47.

16. tabellarios nostros: those whom he had asked Terentia to send back at once (l. 13). It took more than two weeks to send from Brundisium to Rome and back; cf. p. 54.

XXIX. TO MARCUS MARIUS (AD FAM. VII. IV.).

Cumaean Villa; B. C. 46.

Page 197. **5. cogito**: sc. *me iturum esse*. **8. quod constitutum**: = 'any appointment.' **9. fac, ut differas**: 'do put it off,' 'please put it off.'

XXX. TO PAETUS (AD FAM. IX. XXIII.).

Cumaean villa; B. C. 46.

14. Etsi: '(And I shall come) although.' **15. quid ageres**: 'how you were.' **16. ex pedibus laborares**: 'you were having trouble with your feet,' i. e. had the gout.

XXXI. TO ATTICUS (AD ATT. XII. x.).

Villa at Antium; B. C. 46.

Page 198. **1. Male,** etc.: as we say, 'It is sad about Athamas;' *male factum*, or simply *male*, is a common expression of those mourning the death of any one. **4. impetret,** etc.: 'let reason gain what time is sure to bring;' how unsatisfactory Cicero himself found even this source of consolation may be seen from EP. XXXVI. (particularly p. 201, 1–4).

5. imaginem Tironis: Alexis was to Atticus what Tiro was to Cicero. **6. remisi**: Atticus had perhaps sent him to Cicero's place at Antium, thinking that the sea air might restore him to health. **collis**: i. e. *collis Quirinalis* at Rome, where the city residence of Atticus was. **ἐπιδήμιον**: with *quid*, lit. 'anything contagious,' = 'any contagious disease.' Cf. p. 368. **ad me**: 'to my house' on the Palatine. **7. Tisameno**: whom Cicero had detailed to take care of Alexis. **domus superior**: probably the part of the house nearer the top of the Palatine; for Cicero's house was built on the slope of the hill (cf. Plan, p. 76).

XXXII. TO SERVIUS (AD FAM. XIII. xx.).

Rome; B. C. 46. To recommend Dr. Asclapo.

9. utor familiariter: 'I am on intimate terms with.' **11. meorum**: Asclapo had probably taken care of Tiro at Patras; cf. N. to p. 193, 6.

XXXIII. TO GAIUS CASSIUS (AD FAM. XV. xviii.).

Rome; B. C. 45.

17. epistola: i. e. 'This letter.' **18. iretur**: sc. *a me*.

Page 199. **1. φλύαρον**: 'trifle,' 'foolery,' to write about. **σπουδάζειν**: = *de rebus seriis agere*; cf. p. 368. **2. periculo**: the supremacy of Caesar made it necessary for his former opponents to be careful about their expressions of opinion in regard to public matters. **3. facillime**: 'very readily.' **5. Ubi — philosophia**: cf. p. 180, 17, and N. **6. in culina**: Cicero rallies Cassius for his belief in Epicureanism, which laid much stress upon the enjoyment of the physical life. **in palaestra**: where I not only exercise the body, but also freshen and train the mind in oratorical practice. **6. servire**: 'to be a slave,' under the absolute government of Caesar. **7. facio**: 'I make out,' 'pretend.' **convicium Platonis**: in which the philosopher reproaches those who do not maintain their freedom.

9. Hispania: where Caesar was conducting a campaign against the sons of Pompey. **10. mea causa**: 'on my own account.'

XXXIV. TO ATTICUS (AD ATT. XII. XV.).

Astura; B. C. 45.

13. Apud Appuleium . . . ut excuser: = 'that excuse be made for me to Appuleius,' who had been chosen augur. It was customary to celebrate the admission of a new member into the college of augurs (cf. p. 59) by a splendid banquet, continued for several days, at which all the members were expected to be present unless suffering from illness. Cicero was stricken with grief at the death of Tullia (see pp. 10, 11); not wishing to seem ungracious by declining in advance to be present, he wished to have his absence excused 'each day' that the banquet lasted. **placet**: sc. *excusari*. **14. videbis**: for *velim* (*ut*) *videas*. **21. Cum . . . des**: = 'when you find a man to give it (the letter for Marcus Brutus) to.'

XXXV. TO ATTICUS (AD ATT. XII. XVI.).

Astura; B. C. 45.

23. tuis negotiis relictis venire: trans. as if *relinquere tua negotia et venire*. Why?

Page 200. 1. nihil: as p. 61, 4. **5. probabatur**: i. e. *mihi te convenire*. Cicero could not stay at Atticus's because of the bustle and publicity, which would be unendurable to him in the midst of his grief; nor at his own home, because of the number of those who would come to offer consolation which he could not accept. **9. Philippus**: he probably had a villa near Cicero, at Astura.

XXXVI. TO ATTICUS (AD ATT. XII. XVIII.).

Astura; B. C. 45.

12. recordationes fugio: Tullia was dead, after having been divorced from Dolabella; he himself had divorced Terentia, married Publilia, and now separated from her. He had had bitter quarrels with his brother Quintus, and was without hope for the future of the state.

16. quod, etc.: he proposes to build a chapel in honor of Tullia. **19. genere**: architectural 'style,' 'plan.' **21. Velim cogites**: 'will you kindly give the matter consideration.'

23. monumentorum: *monumentum* includes not only commemorative structures of every kind, but also memorial writings, whether poetry or prose; here the word has reference particularly to inscriptions and poems, the latter by both Greek and Roman poets. **28. ero**: = *exsistam*. **hoc exiguum** [tempus]: i. e. *vitae*.

Page 201. 2. nihil — in quo adquiescam: his philosophy breaks down in the presence of death; having no certain hope of reunion with his dear Tullia in a future life, he finds no consolation in anything. Cf. p. 157, 26–30, and N. **temptatis**: render 'having tried.' **3. illud**: a treatise on consolation, *De Consolatione*; cf. ad Att. XII. XIV. 3. **6. ut**: 'as soon as.'

9. curabis cum tua perferendum: 'Kindly have it sent (to him) along with your (letter).'

12. Domestica: 'my household affairs.' **quod**: B. 299, 2; A. 333, and N.; H. 540, IV., N. **scribes**: 'please write.' **13. quaedam enim exspecto**: i. e. *quaedam enim sunt, de quibus scire cupiam.* **Cocceius, Libo**: both seem to have owed Cicero money, Sulpicius and Egnatius perhaps being security for the latter, or for both.

16. quid . . . labores: 'what reason is there for you to give yourself uneasiness:' cf. p. 199, 13, and N.

18. vide . . . facile: = 'do not give yourself too much trouble.'

XXXVII. TO ATTICUS (AD ATT. XII. XXXVI.).

Astura, B. C. 45.

24. Fanum: see p. 200, 12–21, and N. **26. legis**: cf. p. 202, 7. **ἀποθέωσιν**: see p. 368. The deification of individuals — so foreign to our ideas — was familiar and acceptable to the Romans on account of their worship of ancestors (see Coulanges, "The Ancient City"). The deification of Julius Caesar was undoubtedly talked about at this time (cf. the editor's "Selections from Ovid," pp. 155-158); and later the Roman emperors were worshipped even before they were dead. What Cicero's exact idea was it is not easy to divine; probably he meant in some way to attach to the shrine an association of worship, so that it would always be kept in repair.

27. Quod poteram: 'And I could attain this end.' **in ipsa villa**: in one of the courts, which formed so attractive a feature of the Roman country houses.

Page 202. 1. dominorum: i. e. of the villa; future proprietors would alter or rebuild the villa, and the shrine would probably be neglected or destroyed. **3. habeat religionem**: i. e. treat the shrine with veneration; this the superstitious country folk were much more likely to do than the sceptical people of the upper classes. **4. non habeo — quicum**: = 'I have no one with whom.' **6. institutum**: i. e. *genus*; cf. p. 200, 19. **7. lege**: imp.; the law referred to (*legem*) was probably some enactment of the college of pontifices regarding rites in honor of the dead, and posted up where all could read it. **8. in mentem veniet**: sc. *tibi*.

11. Cumano: either Cicero's villa, or that of Marcus Brutus at Cumae. **13. facere rustice**: 'act rudely.'

XXXVIII. TO TREBATIUS TESTA (AD FAM. VII. XXII.).

18. Illuseras: 'You made fun (of me).' **20. furti recte agere**: 'could properly bring an action for theft,' for property filched or embezzled from an estate before the heir took possession. Testa had maintained that there was no division of opinion on the subject, and that the action would lie. B. 208, 1; A. 220; H. 409, II. **22. misi**: 'I send' with this. **23. sensisse**: used of the formal giving of a legal opinion.

XXXIX. TO ATTICUS (AD ATT. XII. XLVIII.).

Tusculan Villa; B. C. 45.

Page 203. **1. Domi,** etc.: see IDIOMS. **2. iamne confeceris**: 'whether you have quite finished' the business that took you away from home. **6. post discessum tuum**: he had apparently met Atticus for a brief interview at some point away from Tusculum. **7. totus**: 'wholly,' i. e. for a long and satisfactory visit; sc. *veniam*. **8. quod licebit**: = *quod facere poteris* (as Boot suggests); in our idiom, 'whatever shall best suit your convenience.'

XL. TO BASILUS (AD FAM. VI. XV.).

B. C. 44.

9. tibi gratulor: on the death of Caesar; see Vocab., *Basilus*.

XLI. TO ATTICUS (AD ATT. XV. XXIII.).

Tusculan Villa; B. C. 44.

13. nostro itinere: Antony had gained the upper hand at Rome; the conspirators against Caesar, and their friends, were fleeing. Cicero thought of going to Greece, having received a free embassy (see N. to p. 179, 7). His son was at this time studying at Athens. **in utramque partem**: whether to go or not. **14. Quo usque**: i. e. *Quo usque deliberabis, torqueris?* **erit** [integrum]: '(the question) shall remain open' until I am actually on shipboard. **17. Si quid novi**: i. e. *velim ad me scribas si quid novi sit.*

XLII. TO ATTICUS (AD ATT. XV. XXV.).

Tusculan villa; B. C. 44.

Page 204. **1. meo itinere**: cf. p. 203, 13, and N. **multi**: sc. *veniunt*. **3. cogitamus**: i. e. *ad urbem redire*. **meus animus**: I am content to go abroad or to return to Rome, provided by either course I can avoid giving offence. **5. piaculum, mysteria**: the 'mysteries' of Bona Dea, celebrated in December; called *piaculum*, because of the desecration by Clodius (see pp. 6, 7). **8. eo**: 'on that account;' he thinks of returning to Rome before bad weather (cf. N. to p. 128, 17), and would like to know what Atticus thinks about his being there by the time of the festival of Bona Dea.

XLIII. TO ATTICUS (AD ATT. XV. XXVIII.).

Villa at Arpinum; B.C. 44.

13. ludis: given by Marcus Brutus. **15. poteram, miseram**: trans. as if *possum, misi.* **17. in te**: Atticus had either neglected to give Caecilia the greeting sent by Cicero, or had not told her that he had come, so that she failed to meet him.

XLIV. TO ATTICUS (AD ATT. XVI. IX.).

Villa at Puteoli; B. C. 44.

Page 205. 1. Binae: B. 81, 4, *b*; A. 95, *b*; H. 174, 2, 3). **nunc quidem**: sc. *rogat.* **2. velle**: dep. on what? **3. Cui ego**: sc. *respondi.* **non posse**: 'could not take action.' **5. consilio tuo**: he declared that he would follow Cicero's advice. **Quid multa**: = 'Why (say) more?' **6. σκήπτομαι**: = *moras necto excusando;* see p. 368. **aetati**: cf. p. 171, 24, and N. **quo animo**: sc. *sit.*

10. pueri: Octavianus. **11. Brutum**: Decimus Brutus, who could hold Cisalpine Gaul against Antony. Cf. p. 173, 25, and N. **12. centuriat**: i. e. *veteranos milites centuriat.* See p. 172, 6–11, and N. **Iam iamque**: here = 'more and more clearly.'

XLV. TO PLANCUS (AD FAM. X. XIV.).

Rome; B. C. 43.

16. victoriam: over Antony, at Mutina, in April. Plancus had declared against Antony and raised a force, with which he afterwards joined Decimus Brutus.

22. exspectabam: 'I am looking for.' **23. Lepidum**: he soon afterwards united with Antony.

XLVI. TO DECIMUS BRUTUS (AD FAM. XI. XXV.).

Rome; B. C. 43.

Page 206. 8. quid vellem: sc. *scribere.* **10. acta**: 'proceedings' of the Senate, and also of the popular assemblies, which at this time were published at the close of each session or meeting.

13. collega: Plancus. **14. Bruto**: Marcus Brutus. **17. Intestinum urbis malum**: many were urging the choice of Octavianus for the consulship, though he was far from the legal age and had not held the earlier offices. **18. minus timeremus**: i. e. *si adesset.* **λακωνισμὸν tuum**: = 'your Spartan brevity.' **19. pagella**: the letter was written on a small tablet.

HELPS TO THE STUDY OF CICERO.

FOR references on the writings of Cicero, his public life, and the history of Rome in his time, see the editor's *Topical Outline of Latin Literature*, p. 15 (Boston, 1891).

For references on special topics, see HARRINGTON'S *Helps to the Intelligent Study of College Preparatory Latin* (Boston, 1888).

For a concise account of the manuscripts of the various works, with an enumeration of the more important editions, special treatises, dictionaries, and articles, see TEUFFEL and SCHWABE'S *History of Roman Literature*, English Translation of the Fifth German Edition, by WARR, Vol. I., §§ 177–189 (London, 1891).

For editions and literature prior to 1881, see Engelmann's *Bibliotheca scriptorum classicorum*, 8th ed., Part II. (Leipzig, 1882).

For ancient oratory, and Cicero as an orator, see JEBB'S *Attic Orators* (2 vols. London, 1876); BLASS, *Die attische Beredsamkeit* (3d ed., 4 vols. Leipzig, 1868–1880); CUCHEVAL and BERGER, *Histoire de l'éloquence latine depuis l'origine de Rome jusqu'à Cicéron* (2d ed., 2 vols. Paris, 1881); WESTERMANN, *Geschichte der römischen Beredsamkeit* (Leipzig, 1835), and the introductions to annotated editions of the *De Oratore*, *Brutus*, and *Orator*.

Lives of Cicero: ancient, by PLUTARCH; modern, among others, by MIDDLETON (2 vols. London, 1741. New ed. 1848); FORSYTH (2 vols. London, 1864); TROLLOPE (2 vols. London and New York, 1880); also, BOISSIER, *Cicéron et ses amis* (7th ed. Paris, 1884); ALY, *Cicero, sein Leben und seine Schriften* (Berlin, 1891); Collins, *Cicero*, in 'Ancient Classics for English Readers'; and Strachan Davidson.

EDITIONS.

TEXT OF COMPLETE WORKS.

BAITER and KAYSER: *M. Tullii Ciceronis opera quae supersunt omnia.* Leipzig, 1860–1869. *Memorabilia vitae Ciceronis* in Vol. I.; *Index nominum* in Vol. XI.

KLOTZ: *M. Tullii Ciceronis scripta quae manserunt omnia.* 5 parts, in 11 vols. Leipzig, 1863–1871. New revision in charge of C. F. W. Müller, of which 7 vols. have appeared.

ORELLI, BAITER, HALM: *M. Tullii Ciceronis opera quae supersunt omnia.* 8 vols. Zürich, 1833–1862. Vol. 5 contains a collection of the scholiasts on Cicero; Vols. 6-8, the valuable *Onomasticon Tullianum*, in which are included, — a chronological view of Cicero's life, the Roman calendar from 63 to 45 B. C., and a bibliography (Vol. 6); a full geographical and historical index (Vol. 7); a lexicon of Greek words, collections of the laws cited and of *formulae*, the *Fasti consulares*, and the Roman triumphs to the reign of Tiberius (Vol. 8).

ORATIONS.

The following are among the annotated editions: —

LONG: All the orations. 4 vols. London, 1855–1862.

HALM: *Die Reden gegen Catilina, und für Archias.* 13th ed., revised by LAUBMANN. Berlin, 1891. English version of Halm's 7th ed., with some additions, by A. S. WILKINS. London, 1870; latest reprint, 1891.

HALM: *Die Reden für Roscius aus Ameria und über das Imperium des Cn. Pompeius.* 10th ed., revised by LAUBMANN. Berlin, 1886. English version of the 8th ed., by WILKINS. London, 1879; latest reprint, 1889.

RICHTER and EBERHARD: *Catilinarische Reden.* 5th ed. Leipzig, 1888. *Rede über das Imperium des Cn. Pompeius.* 4th ed., 1890. *Rede für den Dichter Archias.* 3d ed., 1884. *Reden für Marcellus, Ligarius, Deiotarus.* 3d ed., 1886.

HACHTMANN: *Reden gegen Catilina.* 3d ed. Gotha, 1890.

UPCOTT: *Speeches against Catilina.* Oxford, 1887.

PASDERA: *Le orazioni Catilinarie.* Turin, 1885.

BENECKE: *Orationes in L. Catilinam.* Leipzig, 1828. *De inperio Cn. Pompei.* Leipzig, 1834.

DEUERLING: *Rede über das Imperium des Cn. Pompeius.* 2d ed. Gotha, 1889.

REID: *Pro Archia.* New ed. Cambridge, 1891.

STÜRENBURG: *Pro Archia.* Leipzig, 1839.

THOMAS: *Pro Archia*, with French notes. Mons, 1882.

WOLF: *M. Tulli Ciceronis quae vulgo fertur oratio pro M. Marcello.* Berlin, 1802. Cf. with this ed., *Orationem pro M. Marcello, quam Frid. Aug. Wolfius a M. Tullio Cicerone abiudicavit, denuo defendit* . . . FRANCISCUS HAHNE. Dis. inaug. Braunschweig, 1876.

KING: *The Philippic Orations.* 2d ed. Oxford, 1878.

GAST: *Erste, vierte, und vierzehnte Philippische Rede.* Leipzig, 1891.

Among special works bearing on the orations are: —

BEESLY: *Catiline, Clodius, and Tiberius.* London, 1878. Contains an erratic but brilliant apology for Catiline.

HAGEN: *Untersuchungen über römische Geschichte.* Erster Theil. *Catilina.* Königsberg, 1854.

STERN: *Catilina und die Parteikämpfe in Rom der Jahre* 66–63. Dorpat, 1883.

REINACH: *De Archia Poeta.* Paris, 1890.

LETTERS.

TYRRELL: *The Correspondence of M. Tullius Cicero, arranged according to its chronological order, with a revision of the text, a commentary, and introductory essays.* Dublin and London. Vol. I., 1879; Vol. II., 1886; Vol. III. (including letters of B.C. 50), 1890; Vol. IV., 1895.

SCHÜTZ: All the letters; Latin notes. 6 vols. Halle, 1809–12.

BOOT: *Epistolarum ad Atticum libri* XVI. Latin notes, critical and explanatory. 2 vols. Amsterdam, 1865–1866.

MENDELSSOHN: *Epistularum libri sedecim.* Leipzig, 1893.

There are numerous annotated collections of selected letters of Cicero. Among them may be mentioned those by TYRRELL (London and New York, 1891); SÜPFLE, 9th ed., revised by BOECKEL (Karlsruhe, 1885); WATSON (3d ed., Oxford, 1881);

PARRY (London, 1867); MUIRHEAD (London, 1885); PRITCHARD and BERNARD (2d ed., London, 1888).

Books useful in connection with the letters are: —

JEANS: *The Life and Letters of Cicero;* a translation of the Letters in Watson's ed. London, 1880.

MERIVALE: Abeken's *Cicero in his Letters.* London, 1854.

CHURCH: *Roman Life in the Days of Cicero.* London and New York, 1884.

Interesting estimates of Cicero by literary men will be found in the following works: —

DE QUINCEY: *Historical Essays and Researches.* Ed. by D. Masson. Edinburgh, 1890. Pp. 179–221.

J. Q. ADAMS: *Lectures on Rhetoric and Oratory.* Cambridge, 1810. Vol. I., pp. 117–138.

LAMARTINE: *Memoirs of Celebrated Characters.* New York, 1854. Vol. I., pp. 335–437.

J. H. NEWMAN: *Historical Sketches.* London, 1872. Vol. II., pp. 245–300.

The volume by Boissier (see p. 355) has been translated by A. D. Jones, and is published under the title, *Cicero and his Friends, a Study of Roman Society in the Time of Caesar.* New York, 1897.

IDIOMS AND PHRASES.

a me ipse non descivi, *I did not prove false to myself.*

ab eo vehementissime dissentio, *I disagree with him most emphatically.*

ab ineunte aetate, *from the beginning of (civil) life.*

ab inferis, *from the Underworld, from the dead.*

ab occidente, *in the west.*

abest non nemo, *more than one is away, some are away.*

abiectus metu, *prostrated with fear.*

accipere in vestram fidem, *to take into your confidence.*

ad caelum efferre laudibus, *to laud to the skies.*

ad expilandos socios diripiendasque provincias, *to rob allies and plunder provinces.*

ad Lepidum habitare, *to live at the house of Lepidus, to live at Lepidus's.*

ad rem publicam adire, *to engage in the administration of public affairs, to take office.*

adire hereditatem, *to enter upon an inheritance, take possession of an inheritance.*

adniti de triumpho, *to make every effort to secure a triumph.*

adversae res, *adversity, misfortune.*

aeque carus ac, *just as dear as.*

aequo animo, *calmly, without anxiety; with resignation.*

aequum est, *it is fair, it is right.*

aere alieno premi, *to be heavily in debt.*

aes alienum, *debt, indebtedness.*

in tantum **aes alienum,** *so deeply into debt.*

agere cum aliquo, *to treat with any one, plead with any one.*

agere gratias, *to thank.*

nihil agis, *you accomplish nothing.*

quid **agis?** *how do you do? how are you?* also, *what are you about? what do you mean?*

agitur populi Romani gloria, *the glory of the Roman people is at stake.*

agitur de vectigalibus, *the revenues are imperilled.*

alia omnia, *all things else, everything else.*

aliqua ex parte, *in some measure.*

aliquid amplum cogitare, *to entertain some noble sentiment.*

aliquid de ingeniis iudicare, *to form any judgment of (his) abilities.*

aliquid loci, *some place, some room.*

aliquid respondit, *he made some answer or other.*

aliquid sapientiae, *any degree of prudence, any prudence.*

amabo te, *will you kindly, please.*

amans rei publicae, *devoted to his country.*

amantissimus rei publicae, *very devoted to his country, of the loftiest patriotism.*

amplius negoti, *a larger measure of difficulty, more trouble.*

amplius negoti mihi contrahitur, *I am more deeply involved in difficulty.*

anceps contentio, *a contest on two sides.*

animo cernere, *to see in fancy, see in imagination.*

quo **animo esse debetis?** *what feeling ought you to have? how ought you to feel?*

quo **animo ferre debetis?** *with what spirit ought you to endure?*

animos ac spiritus capere, *to endure the arrogance and insolence.*

animose et fortiter facere aliquid, *to do something with spirit and bravery.*

animum armatum retinere, *to retain a spirit of hostility.*

animum inducere, *to make up* one's *mind.*

animum vincere, *to conquer* one's *spirit.*

ante acta vita, *past life.*

ante civitatem datam, *prior to the granting of citizenship.*

paucis **ante diebus,** *a few days ago.*

paulo **ante,** *a little while ago.*

ante me, *before me; before my time.*

apud inferos, *in the Underworld.*

apud Laecam, *at Laeca's house, at Laeca's.*

apud Tenedum, *off Tenedos.*

aspicere inter sese, *to look at one another.*

auctor gravior, *an adviser of greater weight.*

audita re, *having heard of the matter.*

aures dare, *to give attention.*

aversus a Musis, *unfriendly to the Muses.*

aversus a vero, *hostile to truth.*

bella legere, *to read about wars.*

bellum in multa varietate versatum, *a war waged with many vicissitudes.*

bellum apparare, *to get ready for war.*

bellum conficere, *to put an end to a war, bring a war to a successful termination.*

bellum coniungere, *to unite in waging war.*

bellum excitare, *to stir up war.*

bellum inferre, *to make war upon.*

bellum suscipere, *to commence war.*

bene barbatus, *with full beard.*

bene de re publica mereri, *to do good service for one's country, to be useful to the state.*

bene de re publica sperare, *to have great hope for the state.*

bene potus, *having drunk freely, being quite mellow.*

bono animo dicere, *to say with good intention.*

bono animo esse, *to be of good cheer; to be well disposed.*

mea **causa,** *on my account, for my sake.*

honoris **causa nomino,** *I mention in the way of honor; I mention with due respect.*

vitandae suspicionis **causa,** *in order to avoid suspicion.*

de **certa causa,** *for a certain reason.*

causam dicere, *to state a case, to plead a case.*

certior factus, *having been informed.*

certior fieri, *to be informed.*

certiorem facere, *to inform.*

civitatem alicui dare, *to grant citizenship to any one, bestow the franchise on any one.*

in civitatem ascribere, *to enroll as a citizen.*

eum civitate donare, *to bestow the franchise on him.*

cogere senatum, *to convene the Senate.*

collatis signis, *in the shock of battle, in regular engagements.*

colonias constituere, *to found colonies.*

concedi alicui necesse est, *it must inevitably be given up to some one.*

consilia inire, *to form plans.*

consulere alicui, *to look out for the interest of any one.*

consulere aliquem, *to consult any one, to ask advice of any one.*

consulere vobis, *to look out for your interest.*

contra atque, *opposite to what, contrary to what.*

dare operam, *to take pains, to make an effort.*

de caelo percelli, *to be struck by lightning.*

detrimentum accipere, *to suffer loss.*

difficili rei publicae tempore, *at a time of peril for the state, at a critical time for the state.*

diffidens rebus suis, *in a state of despair regarding his own resources.*

dilectum habere, *to raise a levy, to draft.*

domi libenter sum, *I am glad to be at home.*

domi meae, *at my house.*

e portu egredi, *to set sail.*

eadem fortuna quae illorum, *the same lot as that of those.*

eo magis, *all the more.*

eos hoc moneo, *I give them this warning.*

eos praemiis adfecit, *he bestowed gifts upon them.*

erit verendum mihi, *I shall have to be afraid, I shall have to fear.*

est mihi tanti, *it is well worth while for me, it is well worth my while.*

mihi est invidiosum, *I find it a source of unpopularity, it is a source of unpopularity to me.*

etiam atque etiam, *again and again.*

ex belli ore ac faucibus, *from the open jaws of war.*

ex eo quaeritur, *the question is put to him, inquiry is made of him.*

ex hac parte, *on this side.*

ex magna spe deturbari, *to be deprived of great hopes.*

ex marmore constitutus, *fashioned in marble.*

ex media morte, *from the midst of death.*

ex pedibus laborare, *to have trouble with one's feet, to have the gout.*

ex pueris, *from childhood.*

ex senatus consulto, *in accordance with a decree of the Senate, in accordance with the Senate's decree.*

ex tempore, *off-hand, on the spur of the moment, without preparation.*

ex vestro iudicio, *in consequence of your judgment.*

exercitum conficere, *to raise an army.*

extrema hieme, *at the end of winter.*

extrema pueritia, *at the end of boyhood.*

fac ut sciam, *let me know.*

fac ut valeas, *do keep well.*

fac ut tuam valetudinem cures, *do take care of your health.*

facere alicui pergratum, *to do any one a great favor.*

facere potestatem dicendi, *to offer an opportunity to speak, to give an opportunity for saying.*

faciam te certiorem, *I will inform you.*

facultas oblata est, *an opportunity was presented.*

falso memoriae proditum, *based upon unfounded tradition.*

familiarissime vivere, *to be on the most intimate terms.*

m e **fefellit dies,** *I was mistaken in the day.*

n u m m e **fefellit dies?** *I was not mistaken in the day, was I? was I mistaken in regard to the date?*

v i x **feram,** *I shall find it hard to endure, I shall hardly be able to bear.*

ferenda non fuerunt, *they ought not to have been endured.*

ferenda mihi non fuerunt, *I ought not to have put up with them.*

ferre moleste, *to be annoyed, to feel grieved.*

ferro flammaque, *with fire and sword.*

fidem facere, *to convince, to command confidence.*

m i n o r e m **fidem facere,** *to fail to convince, fail to command entire confidence.*

fidem publicam dare, *to give a pledge of safety in the name of the state.*

fingere sibi, *to imagine.*

fundamenta iacere, *to lay the foundations.*

gratiam alicuius conciliare, *to win the favor of some one.*

gratiam habere, *to feel thankful, to be grateful.*

b o n a m **gratiam quaerere,** *to court popularity.*

gratiam referre, *to return a favor, to requite, recompense.*

gratias agere, *to give thanks, to thank.*

m a x i m a s **gratias agere,** *to thank most heartily.*

gratum facere, *to do a favor.*

hieme summa, *in the dead of winter, in the depth of winter.*

hoc praecipiendum est, *this advice ought to be given.*

e i s **hoc praecipiendum est,** *they ought to be given this piece of advice.*

hodierno die mane, *this morning.*

i n **honore esse debebit is,** *h e will deserve to be in honor.*

honorum gradus, *the grades of public office, the avenues of official preferment.*

iam diu teneo, *I have long been holding.*

iam dudum hortor, *I have long been urging.*

iam pridem studes, *you have long been eagerly desiring, this long time you have been eager.*

iam tum, *even then, at that very time.*

id quod consequi conantur, *what they are trying to attain, their ends.*

id temporis, *at that particular time, at just that time.*

idem qui, *the same as.*

idem sentire, *to have the same feeling, the same opinion.*

imperare obsides, *to levy hostages, make a requisition for hostages.*

imperare omnibus gentibus, *to rule over all peoples.*

in agendo, *in action.*

in armis, *under arms, in arms; in the pursuit of arms, in war.*

in caelum, *to the skies.*

in custodiam dare, *to place in custody, to put under surveillance.*

in dato beneficio, *in the granting of a favor.*

in dies, *day by day, every day.*

in dies singulos, *each successive day.*

in eam partem, ut, *to the end that.*

in eandem fere sententiam, *to much the same effect, of about the same import.*

in malis, *in the midst of evils.*

in optimo quoque, *in all the best.*

in perditis rebus, *in profligacy.*

in perpetuum, *for all time, forever.*

in posteritatem, *for the future.*

in posterum, *for the future.*

in posterum tempus, *for future time, for the future.*

in praesens tempus, *for the present.*

in quaestu relinquere, *to leave on interest.*

incumbite in causam, *throw yourselves into the cause.*

ineunte adulescentia, *at the beginning of youth.*

ineunte vere, *at the opening of spring.*

inferre bellum, *to make war upon.*

inire consilium, *to form a plan.*

inspectante praetore, *under the eyes of the praetor.*

integris signis, *with the seals unbroken.*

inter se, *with each other, with one another.*

ira victoriae, *the fury of victory.*

isto pacto ut, *in such a way as, as.*

iudicium facere, *to pass an opinion, to pass judgment.*

ius civitatis, *the rights of citizenship, citizenship.*

latius opinione, *more widely than you think, than one would think.*

laudibus in caelum ferre, *to praise to the skies.*

loco motus est, *he was forced from his vantage-ground.*

locorum opportunitas, *advantages of position.*

magno in aere alieno, *deeply in debt.*

male emere, *to purchase at too high a price, to buy too dear.*

male gerere negotium, *to manage* one's *business badly.*

maximas gratias agere, *to return most hearty thanks.*

maxime elaborandum est, *very great effort must be made, all pains must be taken.*

me imperante, *at my bidding.*

me quid pudeat? *why should I be ashamed?*

mea interest, *it is for my interest, to my advantage; I am concerned.*

Medea illa, *the famous Medea.*

media aestate, *at midsummer.*

memoria tenere, *to remember, to keep in mind.*

mente captus, *beside himself.*

meo nomine, *in my name, on my account; in my honor.*

meorum factorum paenitebit, *I shall be sorry for what I did, I shall regret my action.*

mihi crede, credite, *believe me, upon my word.*

mihi in animo est, *it is my intention, I intend.*

mihi in mentem venit, *it occurs to me.*

mihi placet, *I think best, I resolve.*

mihi suadeo, *I am persuaded.*

minus est erratum, *no mistake has been made.*

moleste ferre, *to be annoyed, to feel grieved.*

multum valere, *to be very powerful; to have great influence, be very important.*

mutue respondere, *to make adequate return, make a fair return.*

ne longum sit, *not to be tedious, not to bore you.*

necesse est pervenire, *must inevitably come, must inevitably fall* (*to*).

nescio an, *perhaps I might better say, probably.*

nescio quid, *something, some.*

nescio quo modo, *somehow.*

nescio quo pacto, *somehow.*

nihil aliud nisi de hoste cogitare, *to think of nothing but the enemy, to have no thought for anything except the enemy.*

nihil de re publica cogitare, *to give no thought to political matters, give no thought to public affairs.*

nihil nisi de parricidio cogitare, *to think of nothing but murder.*

nihil decretum est, *no decree was passed, no motion was carried.*

nihil mihi noceri potest, *no harm can be done me.*

nobis consulibus, *in our consulship, in my consulship.*

noctes ac dies, *day and night.*

noli esse, *be not.*

noli defatigari, *be not wearied, do not allow yourself to become weary.*

nolite dubitare, *do not hesitate.*

m e o nomine, *in my name, in my honor.*

s u o nomine, *on his own account.*

novis rebus studere, *to be eager for a revolution, be desirous of a revolution.*

nudius tertius, *day before yesterday.*

nullo impediente, *with no one hindering, with none to hinder.*

nullo modo, *in no way, by no means.*

occasio oblata est, *an opportunity presented itself.*

omnes unum volunt, *all are of one opinion.*

omnium rerum desperatio, *utter despair.*

operae pretium est, *it is worth while.*

operam dare, *to take pains, to make an effort.*

opinione celerius, *sooner than was expected.*

t e oportet duci, *you ought to be led.*

t e iam pridem oportebat duci, *you ought long ago to have been led.*

optime de re publica mereri, *to render most important service to one's country.*

optimo iure, *with the fairest possible reason.*

optimus quisque, *all the best.*

opus est, *there is need, it is necessary.*

orbis terrae, orbis terrarum, *the world, the whole world.*

pace tua, *with your permission.*

parum comitatus, *with too small a retinue, with too small an escort.*

parvi refert, *it matters little.*

pauca dicere, *to say a few words.*

paulum mihi est morae, *I am suffering a little delay.*

pecunias collocatas habere, *to have sums of money invested.*

per causam, *under the pretext.*

per hanc causam, *under this pretext, with this as a pretext.*

per fortunas vide, *for heaven's sake see to it, take care.*

perinde atque, *just as, exactly as.*

permagni nostra interest, *it is of very great importance to us ;* or, *it is very important for me.*

permultum valere, *to be exceedingly powerful, to possess very great influence.*

pingue quiddam sonantes atque peregrinum, *offering some stupid and outlandish composition.*

eis placet, *they think best, they resolve.*

plurimum posse, *to have the greatest influence, to be most powerful, be pre-eminent.*

plurimum valere, *to have very great weight, exert very great influence.*

poenam sceleris sufferre, *to suffer punishment for crime.*

poenam suscipere, *to receive punishment, undergo punishment.*

poenas expetere ab aliquo, *to inflict punishment on any one, to visit any one with retribution.*

post civitatem datam, *after the granting of citizenship, after the franchise was granted.*

post hominum memoriam, *within the memory of man.*

post urbem conditam, *since the founding of the City, since the City was founded.*

post hanc urbem conditam, *since the founding of this City, since this City was founded.*

praeter opinionem omnium, *contrary to the expectation of all.*

praeter spem, *contrary to expectation, beyond one's expectation.*

primo quoque tempore, *at the earliest possible moment.*

priore nocte, *night before last.*

pro eo ac mereor, *in such measure as I deserve, in proportion to my deserts.*

proeliis secundis uti, *to have successful engagements, to come off victorious in battle.*

prope inspectantibus vobis, *almost under your eyes.*

proxima nocte, *last night.*

qua re, *wherefore.*

quae cum ita sint, *now since these things are so, and since this is so.*

quam ob rem, *on what account? wherefore.*

quam plurimi, *as many as possible.*

quam primum, *as soon as possible.*

quantum est situm in nobis, *so far as in us lies, so far as in me lies.*

quem ad finem? *to what limit? how far?*

quem ad modum, *in what way? how; as.*

quem venisse gaudent, *at the arrival of whom they rejoice.*

quicquid increpuerit, *at every sound.*

quicquid possum, *whatever influence I possess, whatever I can accomplish.*

quicquid studi, *whatever enthusiasm.*

quid consili? *what scheme? what plan?*

quid illo fieri placet? *what does he want to have done?*

quid interest? *what difference is there?*

quid mihi cum vobis est? *what business have I with you? what have I to do with you?*

quid novi? *what news?*

quid novi, *anything new, anything without precedent.*

quid telorum, *any weapons.*

si quid telorum, *whatever weapons.*

quid Tullia fiet? *what will become of Tullia?*

quieta re publica, *when the state is undisturbed, when the state is free from agitation.*

quoad erit integrum, *so long as it shall remain an open question.*

quod reliquum est, *for the rest, for the future.*

ratio totius belli, *the plan of the entire campaign*, or *of the entire war.*

referre ad senatum, *to lay before the Senate.*

referre gratiam, *to return a favor, to requite, recompense.*

reliquum est, *it remains.*

rem deferre ad patres conscriptos, *to report a matter to the Senate in session.*

rem gerere, *to manage business.*

rem optime gerere, *to manage business exceedingly well.*

remoto Catilina, *with Catiline out of the way.*

rerum potiri, *to get control of the government.*

res gestae, *achievements, exploits, deeds.*

res se habet, *the case stands.*

salutem dicere, *to send greeting.*

salutem nuntiare, *to carry one's regards.*

satis facere rei publicae, *to do one's duty by the state.*

satis laudis, *sufficient praise, praise enough.*

scriptor rerum, *writer of history, historian.*

scriptor rerum suarum, *chronicler of his achievements, biographer.*

se praetura abdicare, *to resign the office of praetor.*

se pro cive gerere, *to conduct one's self as a citizen.*

secundae res, *prosperity.*

a senatorio gradu longe abesse, *to be far too young for membership in the Senate.*

senatui placuit, *the Senate voted, the Senate passed a resolution.*

senatum consulere, *to ask the opinion of the Senate, to consult the Senate.*

senatum convocare, *to convoke the Senate, call a meeting of the Senate.*

sententiam ferre, *to cast a vote.*

sententiam rogare, *to put the question, to call for a vote.*

si curae tibi est, *if you care about it, if you take interest in it.*

si in eo stat, *if he persists in that, if he remains firm in that.*

si vestra voluntas feret, *if such be your pleasure.*

si vobis placet, *if you think best.*

simul ac, simul atque, *as soon as.*

sine controversia, *beyond question, indisputably.*

sine dubio, *beyond doubt.*

sine ulla mora, *at once.*

sua sponte, *of your own accord.*

sui conservandi causa, *in order to save themselves.*

summa res publica, *the highest interest of the state.*

summum supplicium, *the severest punishment.*

summus imperator, *a commander of the first rank.*

suo nomine, *on his own account.*

superiore nocte, *night before last.*

supplicium de aliquo sumere, *to inflict punishment upon any one.*

tandem aliquando, *now at length, then at length.*

tantum abest ut . . . videar, ut *so far am I from appearing, . . . that.*

te auctore, *on your advice.*

te oportet, see **oportet**.

terra marique, *on land and sea.*

tertia fere vigilia exacta, *at about the end of the third watch.*

si transactum est, *if all is over.*

tua sponte, *of your own accord.*

ubinam gentium sumus? *where in the world are we?*

ullo modo, *in any way, by any means.*

una significatione litterarum, *by a single written order.*

urbi satis praesidi est, *the city has a sufficient garrison, the city is amply garrisoned.*

ut arbitror, *in my judgment.*

ut levissime dicam, *to put the case very mildly, to speak with extreme moderation.*

ut primum, *as soon as.*

uti aliquo familiariter, *to be on intimate terms with any one.*

vacui temporis nihil, *no leisure time, no leisure.*

vadimonium deserere, *to forsake an obligation to appear in court, to forfeit one's recognizance.*

vehementer angi, *to be greatly troubled, be much disturbed.*

vehementer cum senatu consociari, *to be thoroughly in accord with the Senate.*

vehementer errare, *to be very much mistaken.*

velim dispicias res Romanas, *will you kindly think over matters at Rome.*

velim ei me excuses, *I should like to have you make excuse for me to him, excuse me to him.*

veniam dare, *to pardon.*

ventum est, *they* (or *he*) *came, have come.*

verba facere, *to speak.*

verbis amplissimis, *in most distinguished terms, in the handsomest terms.*

verendum erat mihi, *I ought to have feared.*

vereri ne, *to fear that.*

vereri ut, *to fear that . . . not.*

vestrum est providere, *it is your duty to make provision.*

vi et minis, *by threats of violence.*

vir optimus, *an exceedingly worthy gentleman, a most excellent man.*

vis et manus, *violent hands.*

vitae meae rationes, *my plan of life.*

vix feram, *I shall find it hard to bear, I shall hardly be able to endure.*

voculae recreandae causa, *in order to strengthen* (*my*) *poor voice.*

voluptatem capere, *to receive pleasure, take delight.*

GREEK WORDS.

αἰσχρός, -ά, -όν, adj., [αἶσχος, *shame*], comp. αἰσχίων, sup. αἴσχιστος, *shameful, base, contemptible, disgraceful.*

ἀναφαίνω, -φανῶ, -πέφαγκα, aor. ἀνέφηνα, [ἀνά + φαίνω], *show forth, display*; mid. ἀναφαίνομαι, *appear, be seen, be thought.*

ἀποθέωσις, -εως, ἡ, [ἀποθεόω, ἀπό + θεόω from θεός], *deification*, a form of consecration which caused the person receiving it to be considered as a divinity.

ἀριστεία, -ας, ἡ, [ἀριστεύω, *be best*, from ἄριστος], lit. *deed of him that is best; noble deed, heroic action.*

αὐθωρεί, adv., [αὔθωρος, adj., from αὐτός, ὥρα], *at the very hour, at the selfsame hour.*

βοῶπις, -ιδος, fem. adj. and subst. [βοῦς, ὤψ], *ox-eyed, cow-eyed*, i. e. having large, lustrous eyes; in Homer applied to Juno, suggesting her majestic beauty.

ἐπιδήμιος, -ον, adj., [ἐπί, δῆμος], *among the people, native; prevalent among the people*, as a disease, *epidemic.*

Λαιστρυγόνιος, -α, -ον, Homeric acc. sing. fem. Λαιστρυγονίην, adj., [Λαιστρυγόνες], *Laestrygonian, of the Laestrygonians*, a mythical folk of gigantic stature, said to have lived along the west coast of Italy below Formiae, or in Sicily.

λακωνισμός, -οῦ, ὁ, [λακωνίζω, from Λάκων, *Lacedaemonian*], *aping of that which is Lacedaemonian, imitation of Spartan custom* in anything.

σιωπάω, σιωπήσομαι, σεσιώπηκα, ἐσιώπησα, [σιωπή, *silence*], *be silent, keep silence, remain silent.*

σκήπτω, σκήψω, *prop*; mid. σκήπτομαι, *prop one's self, lean on, rely on*, hence *allege by way of excuse, make excuses, excuse one's self.*

σπουδάζω, -άσω, [σπουδή, *haste*], lit. *make haste*; hence *be eager, be earnest, speak seriously, be in earnest.*

Τηλέπυλος, -ου, ἡ, [τῆλε, *far*, πύλη, *gate*], lit. *City of the widely separated Gates, Telepylus*, mythical town of the Laestrygonians. Od. XXIII. 318.

ὑποσόλοικος, -ον, adj., [ὑπό + σόλοικος, *barbarous*], *of faulty speech; in bad taste, out of place.*

φιλοσοφέω or **φιλοσοφῶ**, -ήσω, [φιλόσοφος], *be a philosopher, love wisdom.*

φλύαρος, -ου, ὁ, [φλύω, *bubble over, talk foolishly*], *idle talk, foolery, trifle.*

ENGLISH PRONUNCIATION OF PROPER NAMES

The system used in the following list to indicate the English pronunciation is intended to be lucid and consistent, and at the same time to present as few points of divergence as possible from the systems found in the best dictionaries. The so-called long vowels have above them a macron or some mark indicative of quality; the short stressed vowels have no mark at all; the obscure unstressed vowels have a dot under them, thus: —

ā as in '*fa*te.'	ẹ as in 'hat*e*d.'*	ọ as in 'dem*o*crat.'*
a " " 'f*a*t.'	ė " " 'h*e*r.'	ū " " '*u*se.'
ạ " " 'ide*a*.'*	ī " " 'p*i*ne.'	u " " '*u*p.'
ä " " '*a*rm.'	i " " 'p*i*n.'	ụ̄ " " 'sing*u*lar.'*
â " " '*a*ll.'	ị " " 'un*i*ty.'*	ụ " " 'circ*u*s.'*
ē " " 'm*e*.'	ō " " 'n*o*.'	ᴜ̄ " " 'r*u*de.'
e " " 'm*e*t.'	o " " 'n*o*t.'	ᴜ " " 'f*u*ll.'

The chief stress or accent is indicated by ′, the secondary by ″; but the secondary stress is not marked when separated from another stress by a single intervening unstressed syllable, for in that case one naturally puts it in the proper place.

Accius, ak′sh(y)ụs.
Achaia, ạ-kā′(y)ạ.
Achilles, ạ-kil′ēz.
Aelius, ē′lị-ụs.
Aemilius, ẹ-mil′ị-ụs.
Africa, af′rị-kạ.
Ahala, ạ-hā′lạ.
Alba, al′bạ.
Alexander, al-ẹg-zan′dẹr.
Alexis, ạ-lek′sịs.
Allobroges, ạ-lob′rọ-jēz.
Amisus, ạ-mī′sụs.
Annius Chilo, an′ị-ụs kī′lō.
Antiochus, ạn-tī′ọ-kụs.
Antium, an′sh(y)ụm.
Antonius, ạn-tō′nị-ụs.
Apollonidenses, ap″ọ-lon-ị-den′sēz.
Appi Forum, ap′ī fō′rụm.
Appius, ap′ị-ụs.
Appuleius, ap-ụ̄-lē′(y)ụs.

* The obscure unstressed vowels are in effect very much alike, but they differ slightly according to the character of the adjoining consonants. They are most correctly sounded when one glides over them rapidly and naturally.

The editor is indebted to Professor George Hempl, of the chair of English Philology and General Linguistics, University of Michigan, for kindly revising this list.

Apulia, ạ-pū′lị-ạ.
Archias, är′kị-ạs.
Ariobarzanes, ā′rị-ọ-bạr-zā′nēz.
Asclapo, ạs-klā′pō.
Asia, ā′sh(y)ạ *or* ā′zh(y)ạ.
Astura, as′tụ̄-rạ.
Athamas, ath′ạ-mạs.
Athenae, ạ-thē′nē.
Attica, at′ị-kạ.
Atticus, at′ị-kụs.
Aulus, â′lụs.

Balbus, bal′bụs.
Basilus, bas′ị-lụs.
Batonius, bạ-tō′nị-ụs.
Bibulus, bib′ụ̄-lụs.
Bithynia, bị-thin′ị-ạ.
Bona Dea, bō′nạ dē′ạ.
Britannia, brị-tan′ị-ạ.
Brundisium, brụn-dizh′(y)ụm.
Brutus, brū′tụs.
Buthrotum, bụ̄-thrō′tụm.

Caelius, sē′lị-ụs.
Caeparius, sẹ-pā′rị-ụs.
Caesar, sē′zạr.
Caieta, kạ-yē′tạ.
Cappadocia, kap-ạ-dō′sh(y)ạ.
Capua, kap′ụ̄-ạ.
Carbo, kär′bō.
Caria, kā′rị-ạ.
Cassius, kash′(y)ụs.
Cato, kā′tō.
Catulus, kat′ụ̄-lụs *or* kat′chu-lụs.
Ceparius, sẹ-pā′rị-ụs.
Cestius, ses′tị-ụs.
Cethegus, sẹ-thē′gụs.
Cicero, sis′ẹ-rō.
Cilicia, sị-lish′(y)ạ.
Cimber, sim′bẹr.
Cimbri, sim′brī.
Cincius, sin′sh(y)ụs.
Cinna, sin′ạ.
Claudius, clâ′dị-ụs.
Clodius, clō′dị-ụs.
Cluatius, clu-ā′sh(y)ụs.

Cnidus, nī′dụs.
Cocceius, kọk-sē′(y)ụs.
Colophon, kol′ọ-phọn.
Corcyra, kọr-sī′rạ.
Corduba, kor′dụ̄-bạ.
Cornelius, kọr-nē′lyụs.
Cotta, kot′ạ.
Crassus, kras′ụs.
Curio, kū′rị-ō.
Custidius, kụs-tid′ị-ụs.
Cyziceni, siz-ị-sē′nī.
Cyzicus, siz′ị-kụs.

Decimus, des′ị-mụs.
Delos, dē′lọs *or* dē′los″.
Dives, dī′vēz.
Dolabella, dol-ạ-bel′ạ.
Drusus, drū′sụs.
Dyrrachium, dị-rak′ị-ụm.

Egnatius, ẹg-nā′sh(y)ụs.
Egnatuleius, eg′nạt-ụ̄-lē′(y)ụs *or* eg′nạ-chu-lē′(y)ụs.
Ennius, en′ị-ụs.
Ephesus, ef′ẹ-sụs.
Epirus, ẹ-pī′rụs.
Eros, ē′rọs *or* ē′ros″.
Etruria, ẹ-trū′rị-ạ.

Fabius, fā′bị-ụs.
Faesulae, fesh′ū-lē.
Falcidius, fạl-sid′ị-ụs.
Faustus, fâs′tụs.
Flaccus, flak′ụs.
Formiae, for′mị-ē.
Forum Aurelium, fō′rụm â-rē′-lị-ụm *or* ạ-rē′lị-ụm.
Fulvius, ful′vị-ụs.
Furius, fūr′ị-ụs.

Gabinius, gạ-bin′ị-ụs.
Gaius, gā′(y)ụs.
Galli, gal′ī.
Gallia Cisalpina, gal′ị-ạ sis-ạl-pī′nạ.
Gallia Transalpina, gal′ị-ạ trans″-ạl-pī′nạ *or* trạnz-ạl-pī′nạ.

Glabrio, glā′brị-ō.
Glaucia, glâ′sh(y)ạ.
Gnaeus, nē′(y)ụs.
Gracchus, grak′ụs.
Gratius, grā′sh(y)ụs.

Hannibal, han′ị-bạl.
Heraclia, her-ạ-klī′ạ.
Heraclienses, her″ạ-klị-en′sēz.
Hispo, his′pō.
Hortensius, họr-ten′sh(y)ụs.

Illyricum, ị-lir′ị-kụm.
Iugurtha, jụ̄-gėr′thạ *or* jū-gėr′thạ.
Iulius, jūl′yụs.
Iunius, jūn′yụs.
Iuppiter, jū′pị-tẹr.

Laeca, lē′kạ.
Laelius, lē′lị-ụs.
Laenius, lē′nị-ụs.
Latium, lā′sh(y)ụm.
Lentulus, len′tụ̄-lụs *or* len′chū-lụs.
Lepidus, lep′ị-dụs.
Lepta, lep′tạ.
Libo, lī′bō.
Licinius, lị-sin′ị-ụs.
Locrenses, lọ-kren′sēz.
Lucius, lū′sh(y)ụs.
Lucullus, lụ-kul′ụs.
Lupus, lū′pụs.

Macedonia, mas-ẹ-dō′nị-ạ.
Maelius, mē′lị-ụs.
Magna Graecia, mag′nạ grē′-sh(y)ạ.
Magnus, mag′nụs.
Manilius, mạ-nil′ị-ụs.
Manius, mā′nị-ụs.
Manlius, man′lị-ụs.
Marcellus, mạr-sel′ụs.
Marcus, mär′kụs.
Marius, mā′rị-ụs.
Mars, märz.
Massilia, mạ-sil′ị-ạ.
Maximus, mak′sị-mụs.

Medea, mẹ-dē′ạ.
Megalensia, meg-ạ-len′sh(y)ạ.
Memmius, mem′ị-ụs.
Metellus, mẹ-tel′ụs.
Minucius, mị-nū′sh(y)ụs.
Misenum, mị-sē′nụm.
Mithridates, mith-rị-dā′tēz.
Mulvius, mul′vị-ụs.
Murena, mụ̄rē′nạ.

Nobilior, nọ-bil′ị-ọr.
Numantia, nụ̄man′sh(y)ạ.

Octavianus, ok-tā-vị-ā′nụs.
Octavius, ok-tā′vị-ụs.
Opimius, ọ-pim′ị-ụs.
Orpheus, or′phẹ-ụs.

Paetus, pē′tụs.
Pamphylia, pạm-fil′ị-ạ.
Pansa, pan′sạ *or* pan′zạ.
Patiscus, pạ-tis′kụs.
Paulus, pâ′lụs.
Penates, pẹ-nā′tēz.
Perses, pėr-sēz.
Pescennius, pẹ-sen′ị-ụs.
Philhetaerus, fil-ẹ-tē′rụs.
Philippus, fị-lip′ụs.
Philogenes, fị-loj′ẹ-nēz.
Philotimus, fil-ọ-tī′mụs.
Picenum, pị-sē′nụm.
Pilia, pil′ị-ạ.
Piso, pī′sō.
Pius, pī′ụs.
Plancius, plan′sh(y)ụs.
Plancus, plang′kụs.
Plotius, plō′sh(y)ụs.
Poeni, pē′nī.
Pompeius, pọm-pē′(y)ụs.
Pomponia, pọm-pō′nị-ạ.
Pomponius, pọm-pō′nị-ụs.
Pomptinus, pọm(p)-tī′nụs.
Pontus, pon′tụs.
Praeneste, prẹ-nes′tẹ.
Ptolemaeus, tol-ẹ-mē′ụs.
Publicius, pụb-lish′(y)ụs.

Publius, pub′lị-ụs.
Pulcher, pul′kẹr.
Puteoli, pṳ̄-tē′ọ-lī.

Quintus, kwin′tụs.
Quirites, quị-rī′tēz.

Romulus, rom′ụ-lụs.
Roscius, rosh′(y)ụs.
Rufus, rū′fụs.

Samos, sā′mọs *or* sā′mos″.
Sampsiceramus, sam(p)-sị-ser′ạ-mụs.
Sardinia, sär-din′ị-ạ.
Saturnalia, sat-ụr-nā′lị-ạ.
Saturninus, sat-ụr-nī′nụs.
Scaevola, sev′ọ-lạ.
Scipio, sip′ị-ō.
Seius, sē′(y)ụs.
Sempronius, sẹm-prō′nị-ụs.
Serapio, sẹ-rā′pị-ō.
Servilius, sẹr-vil′ị-ụs.
Servius, sėr′vị-ụs.
Sestius, ses′tị-ụs.
Sextus, sex′tụs.
Sicca, sik′ạ.
Sicilia, sị-sil′ị-ạ.
Sigeum, sị-jē′ụm.
Silanus, sị-lā′nụs.
Silius, sil′ị-ụs.
Silvanus, sịl-vā′nụs.
Sinope, sị-nō′pẹ.
Spartacus, spär′tạ-kụs.
Spurius, spū′rị-ụs.
Statilius, stạ-til′ị-ụs.
Suessa, sṳ̄-es′ạ.
Sulla, sul′lạ.
Sulpicius, sụl-pish′(y)ụs.
Syria, sir′ị-ạ.

Tarquitius, tär-kwish′(y)ụs.
Tenedos, ten′ẹ-dọs.
Terentia, tẹ-ren′sh(y)ạ.
Testa, tes′tạ.
Teutoni, tū′tọ-nī.
Themistocles, thẹ-mis′tọ-klēz.
Theophanes, thẹ-of′ạ-nēz.
Thermus, thėr′mụs.
Tiberis, tib′ẹ-rịs.
Tiberius, tị-bē′rị-ụs.
Tigranes, tị-grā′nēz.
Tiro, tī′rō.
Tisamenus, tị-sam′ẹ-nụs.
Titinius, tị-tin′ị-ụs.
Titius, tish′(y)ụs.
Titus, tī′tụs.
Tongilius, ton-jil′ị-ụs.
Torquatus, tọr-kwā′tụs.
Trebatius, trẹ-bā′sh(y)ụs.
Tres Tabernae, trēz tạ-bėr′nē.
Tullia, tul′ị-ạ.
Tulliola, tụ-lī′ọ-lạ.
Tullius, tul′ị-ụs.
Tullus, tul′ụs.

Umbrenus, ụm-brē′nụs.

Valerius, vạ-lē′rị-ụs.
Varro, var′ō.
Vatia, vā′sh(y)ạ.
Vesta, ves′tạ.
Vettius, vet′ị-ụs.
Vibo, vī′bō.
Volturcius, vọl-tur′sh(y)ụs.

Xeno, zē′nō.

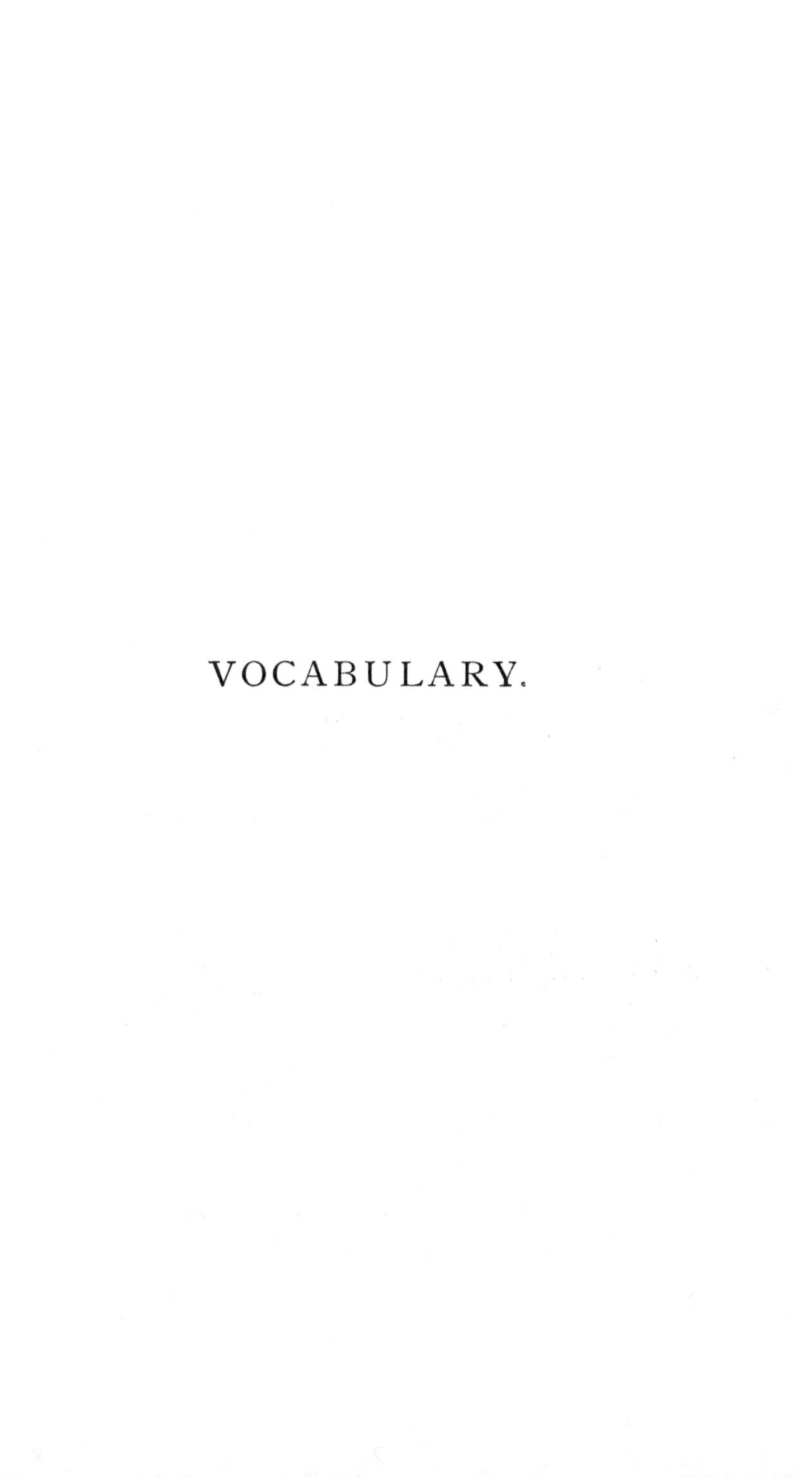

VOCABULARY.

ABBREVIATIONS.

a. = *active.*
abl. = *ablative.*
abs. = *absolute.*
acc. = *accusative.*
adj. = *adjective.*
adv. = *adverb, adverbial.*
causat. = *causative.*
chap. = *chapter.*
comp. = *comparative.*
conj. = *conjunction.*
dat. = *dative.*
decl. = *declension.*
def. = *defective.*
dem. = *demonstrative.*
dep. (in vocabulary) = *deponent.*
dim. = *diminutive.*
e. g. = *exemplī grātiā* = *for example.*
Eng. = *English.*
EP. = *Epistolae*, or *Epistola.*
et al. = *et alibī* = *and elsewhere.*
et seq. = *et sequentia* = *and what follows.*
etc. = *et cētera* = *and so forth.*
excl. = *exclamation.*
f. = *feminine.*
freq. = *frequentative.*
fut. = *future.*
gen. = *genitive.*
ibid. = *ibīdem* = *in the same place.*
id. = *īdem* = *the same.*
i. e. = *id est* = *that is.*
imp. = *imperative.*
impers. = *impersonal, impersonally.*
impf. = *imperfect.*
inch. = *inchoative.*
indecl. = *indeclinable.*
indef. = *indefinite.*
indic. = *indicative.*
inf. = *infinitive.*
inter. = *interrogative.*
interj. = *interjection.*
intr. = *intransitive.*
irr. = *irregular.*
lit. = *literally.*
m. = *masculine.*
MSS. = *manuscripts.*
n., neut. = *neuter.*
nom. = *nominative.*
num. = *numeral.*
Or. = *Ōrātiō.*
p., pp. = *page, pages.*
part. = *participle.*
pass. = *passive.*
patr. = *patronymic.*
pers. = *person, personal.*
pf. = *perfect.*
pl. = *plural.*
plup. = *pluperfect.*
pos. = *positive.*
pred. = *predicate.*
prep. = *preposition.*
pres. = *present.*
pron. = *pronoun, pronominal.*
reflex. = *reflexive.*
rel. = *relative.*
semi-dep. = *semi-deponent.*
sing. = *singular.*
subj. = *subjunctive.*
subst. = *substantive.*
sup. = *superlative.*
trans. = *transitive.*
v. = *verb.*
voc. = *vocative.*
1, 2, 3, 4 with verbs = 1st, 2d, 3d, or 4th conjugation.

ANT. IV. = *in M. Antōnium ōrātiō Philippica quārta.*
ARCH. = *prō A. Liciniō Archiā ōrātiō.*
CAT. I., II., III., IV. = *in L. Catilīnam ōrātiō prīma, secunda, tertia, quārta.*
IMP. P. = *dē Imperiō Gnaeī Pompēī ōrātiō.*
MAR. = *prō M. Mārcellō ōrātiō.*

VOCABULARY.

A., with proper names = **Aulus,** a Roman *praenōmen*, or forename.

a. **d.**, = **ante diem**; see **ante.**

a. u. c., = **annō urbis conditae,** 'in the year from the founding of the city,' or **ab urbe conditā,** 'after the founding of the city;' used with dates reckoned from the year in which Rome was said to have been founded, 753 B. C.

ā, ab, and **abs,** [cf. ἀπό, Eng. of, off], prep. with abl., originally implying separation, *from, away from, out of;* of place or direction, *from, out of, at,* especially with adverbs of distance, as **longē ā domō, procul ā nōbīs**; of time, *from, since, after,* as **ab ineunte aetāte, ab adulēscentiā, ab illō tempore, ā senātōriō gradū longē**; of agency, with passive verbs and gerundives, *by, on the part of;* of source, *from, through,* especially with verbs and adj. signifying fearing, hoping, expecting, defending, liquidating; the prep. **ā** with the person is used with **quaesō, postulō, poenās expetō,** and **dissentiō.**

abdicō, -āre, -āvī, -ātum, [**ab + dicō**], 1, a., *abdicate;* reflex., with abl., *resign, lay down, renounce,* used of withdrawal from an office before the expiration of the term of appointment, as **sē praetūrā abdicāvit,** *he resigned his office of praetor.*

abditus, -a, -um, [part. of **abdō**], adj., *concealed, hidden; secluded, secret.*

abdō, -dere, -didī, -ditum, [**ab + dō**], 3, a., *put away, remove, conceal;* reflex., **abdere sē,** *to betake one's self to, to devote one's self to, to hide one's self in.*

abeō, -īre, abīvī or **-iī, abitum,** fut. part. **abitūrus,** [**ab + eō**], irr., n., *go away, depart, leave; pass away, be gone, disappear, vanish.*

aberrātiō, -ōnis, [**aberrō,** from **ab + errō**], f., *relief, respite,* as from troubles.

abhorreō, -ēre, -uī, ——, [**ab + horreō**], 2, n. and a., *shrink back from, shudder at; be at variance with, be inconsistent with, be averse to; be not connected with;* often construed with **ā** and the abl.

abiciō, abicere, -iēcī, -iectum, [**ab + iaciō**], 3, a., *throw away, cast away, throw down; give up, abandon;* reflex., **abicere sē,** *throw one's self down, prostrate one's self, give up in despair.*

abiectus, -a, -um, [part. of abiciō], adj., *cast down, overwhelmed, despondent; low, mean, worthless.*

absconditus, -a, -um, [part. of abscondō], adj., *hidden, concealed, secret.*

abscondō, -dere, -dī, -ditum, [abs + condō], 3, a., *hide, conceal; make a secret of.*

absēns, -entis, [part. of absum], adj., *absent, away, not present.*

absolūtiō, -ōnis, [absolvō, *discharge*], f., as a legal term, *acquittal; completeness.*

abstrahō, -ere, abstrāxī, abstrāctum, [abs + trahō], 3, a., *draw away; withdraw, remove; divert, cut off.*

abstrūdō, -ere, abstrūsī, abstrūsum, [abs + trūdō], 3, a., *thrust away, hide, conceal.*

absum, abesse, āfuī, fut. part. āfutūrus, [ab + sum], irr., n., *be away from, be absent, be far, be from.* cūius aetās ā —— longē abesset, *whose age was far too young for* ——. tantum abest ut —— ut, *so far from* —— *that.*

abundāns, -antis, [part. of abundō], adj., *overflowing, rich, abounding.*

abundantia, -ae, [abundō], f., *plenty, abundance.*

abundō, -āre, -āvī, -ātum, [ab + undō, from unda, *wave*], 1, n., *overflow, abound in, be rich in.*

abūtor, -ūtī, -ūsus sum, [ab + ūtor], 3, dep., *use up; abuse, outrage.*

ac, see **atque.**

accēdō, -cēdere, -cessī, -cessum, [ad + cēdō], 3, n., *come to, draw near to, draw near, approach;* used often as synonymous with the passive of addō, *be added.*

accelerō, -āre, -āvī, -ātum, [ad + celerō, from celer], 1, a. and n., *hasten, quicken; hurry, make haste.*

accessiō, -ōnis, [accēdō], f., *a coming to, approach; increase, addition, enlargement.*

accidō, -cidere, -cidī, ——, [ad + cadō], 3, n., *fall upon, fall to; reach, come to; come to pass, happen, occur, take place.*

accipiō, -cipere, -cēpī, -ceptum, [ad + capiō], 3, a., *take to one's self, receive, accept; meet with, experience, suffer; take in, hear, learn, understand; undertake, assume.*

Accius, -ī, m., *L. Accius*, an early Roman tragic poet, born 170 B. C. He lived to a great age and wrote many tragedies; also an historical poem and three prose works. Only a few fragments of his writings are extant, but these indicate marked literary power.

accommodātus, -a, -um, [part. of accommodō], adj., *adapted, suited, fit, suitable, appropriate.*

accommodō, -āre, -āvī, -ātum, [ad + commodō, from commodus], 1, a., *fit, adjust, adapt, accommodate to.*

accubō, -āre, ——, ——, [ad + cubō], 1, n., *lie at, lie near;* especially *recline* at table, in accordance with the Roman custom, the body reclining on a couch, the left arm resting on a cushion, the right arm being left free to take food.

accūrātē, comp. accūrātius, sup. accūrātissimē, [accūrātus, *carefully wrought*], adv., *carefully, with pains, with painstaking; precisely, exactly.*

accūsō, -āre, -āvī, -ātum, [ad, causa], 1, a., *reproach, accuse, blame, find fault with; prosecute, indict.*

ācer, ācris, ācre, comp. **ācrior,** sup. **ācerrimus,** adj., *sharp, piercing; harsh, bitter; keen, zealous, spirited; passionate, violent; fierce, severe.*

acerbē, comp. **acerbius,** sup. **acerbissimē,** [**acerbus**], adv., *harshly, cruelly, bitterly; painfully, grievously, severely.*

acerbitās, -ātis, [**acerbus**], f., *bitterness; harshness, severity;* pl., *sorrows, anguish, affliction.*

acerbus, -a, -um, [**ācer**], adj., *sharp* to the taste, *bitter; harsh, severe, cruel; distressing, rigorous, burdensome.*

acervus, -ī, m., *heap, pile; great quantity, multitude, mass.*

Achāia, -ae, ['Αχαΐα], f., *Achāia,* a Roman province, comprising all of Greece except Thessaly. See N. to p. 130, 4.

Achillēs, -is, ['Αχιλλεύς], m., *Achillēs,* son of Peleus and Thetis, famous hero of the Greeks in the Trojan war. ARCH. X.

aciēs, -ēī, f., *sharp point, sharp edge;* of an army, *line of battle, battle-array; battle, engagement; force, efficiency.*

ācriter, comp. **ācrius,** sup. **ācerrimē,** [**ācer**], adv., *sharply, keenly, cruelly; earnestly, zealously, vigorously.*

acroāma, -atis, [ἀκρόāμα, from ἀκροάομαι, *listen*], n., lit. *entertainment for the ear; reader, story-teller, musician,* applied especially to those who furnished entertainment at table with stories, jests, or songs.

āctiō, -ōnis, [**agō**], f., *a driving* or *doing, action; action at law, lawsuit, prosecution, trial;* pl. often *public acts, measures.*

ācta, -ōrum, [**agō**], n., pl., *proceedings.*

āctus, -ūs, [**agō**], m., *a driving* or *doing; act, achievement.*

ad, prep. with acc. only, *to;* of motion and direction, *to, towards, up to;* of place, *in the vicinity of, at, near to, at the house of, in the presence of, among, according to;* of time, *till, to, up to, until;* of purpose, especially with the gerund, *for, in order to, for the purpose of, in;* of other relations, *with regard to, according to, in respect to, in consequence of, as to, in; about, almost, as many as.*

adaequō, -āre, -āvī, -ātum, [**ad + aequō**], 1, a. and n., *make equal to, make equal with, match; keep up with;* in Cicero usually followed by **cum** with an abl.

addō, -dere, -didī, -ditum, [**ad + dō**], 3, a., *put to, bring to; add, join to, increase, augment; consider also.*

addūcō, -dūcere, -dūxī, -ductum, [**ad + dūcō**], 3, a., *lead to, bring to, conduct, lead; prompt, induce, incite to, persuade, influence.*

adeō, -īre, -iī or **-īvī, -itum,** [**ad + eō**], irr., n. and a., *go to, come to, approach; enter upon, undertake; encounter, incur; undergo, submit to.* **ad rem pūblicam adīre,** *to engage in the administration of public affairs.* **hērēditātem adīre,** *to take possession of an inheritance.*

adeō [**ad + eō**], adv., *to this, thus far, so far, so much; so long, so.* **usque adeō,** *even to such a degree, even thus far, even so far.* **atque adeō,** *and even, yet more, still further.*

adeps, -ipis, m. or f., of animals, *fat, lard;* of men, *corpulence, fleshiness, obesity.*

adfectus, -a, -um, [part. of **adficiō**], adj., *provided, endowed, gifted; affected, disposed; weakened, impaired.*

adferō, -ferre, attulī, adlātum, [ad + ferō], irr., a., *bring to, carry to; convey, bring, introduce; report, announce; produce, contribute, offer.*

adficiō, -ficere, -fēcī, -fectum, [ad + faciō], 3, a., *do something to, treat, use; affect, influence; visit with, afflict; weaken, impair, break down.*

adfingō, -fingere, -fīnxī, -fīctum, [ad + fingō], 3, a., *attach; bestow, contribute.*

adfīnis, -e, [ad + fīnis], adj., *adjoining, neighboring; connected with, implicated in, accessory to.*

adfīrmō, -āre, -āvī, -ātum, [ad + fīrmō], 1, a., *strengthen; confirm by words, encourage; maintain, assert.*

adflīctō, -āre, -āvī, -ātum, [freq. of adflīgō], 1, a., *break to pieces; crush; distress, torment, harass.*

adflīctus, -a, -um, comp. adflīctior, [part. of adflīgō], adj., *cast down, prostrate; dejected, discouraged, wretched, distressed.*

adflīgō, -flīgere, -flīxī, -flīctum, [ad + flīgō], 3, a., *strike at, dash at; shatter; overthrow, ruin, damage, injure, distress.*

adfluēns, -entis, [pres. part. of adfluō], adj., *abounding, overflowing, abundant.*

adfluō, -fluere, -fluxī, -fluxum, [ad + fluō], 3, n., *flow to, flow by;* with abl., *abound in, be overflowing, be full.*

adhibeō, -ēre, -uī, -itum, [ad + habeō], 2, a., *hold to, bring, apply; furnish, offer, bestow; employ, use, exercise.*

adhortor, -ārī, -ātus sum, [ad + hortor], 1, dep., *encourage, arouse; urge, urge on, exhort.*

adhūc [ad + hūc], adv., *heretofore, hitherto, as yet, up to this time; still, yet.*

adimō, -ere, adēmī, adēmptum, [ad + emō], 3, a., *take away, remove; deprive of, free from.*

adipīscor, -ipīscī, -eptus sum, [ad + apīscor], 3, dep., *arrive at; obtain, attain, reach; get, gain, secure, win.*

aditus, -ūs, [adeō], m., *a going to, approach, access; way of approach, entrance, avenue, passage; arrival.*

adiūmentum, -ī, [for adiuvamentum, from adiuvō], n., *help, assistance, aid, support.*

adiungō, -ere, adiūnxī, adiūnctum, [ad + iungō], 3, a., *join to, attach to; join, add, annex, associate, unite to; win, secure; apply.*

adiuvō, -iuvāre, -iūvī, -iūtum, [ad + iuvō], 1, a., *help, assist; be of assistance to; aid, support, sustain.*

adliciō, -licere, -lexī, -lectum, [ad + laciō], 3, a., *entice to, allure; attract, persuade.*

administer, -trī, [ad + minister], m., *attendant, assistant, helper; tool, instrument.*

administra, -ae, [administer], f., *female assistant, (female) servant, handmaid.*

administrō, -āre, -āvī, -ātum, [ad + ministrō, from minister], 1, a., *manage, control, handle, administer, regulate; direct, guide, serve.*

admīrandus, -a, -um, [part. of admīror], adj., *worthy of admiration, to be admired, wonderful, admirable, strange.*

admīrātiō, -ōnis, [admīror], f., *admiration, wonder; surprise, astonishment.*

admīror, -ārī, -ātus sum, [ad + mīror], 1, dep., *admire, view with wondering approval, wonder at; wonder, be astonished.*

admittō, -ere, admīsī, admissum, [ad + mittō], 3, a., *send to, let go; admit, receive; give access, allow access, grant admittance; permit, allow to be done; become guilty of, commit, perpetrate.*

admoneō, -ēre, -uī, -itum, [ad + moneō], 2, a., *remind, suggest; advise, urge, warn; bid.*

admonitus, -ūs, used only in the abl., [admoneō], m., *reminding, request, suggestion, warning; remonstrance.*

admurmurātiō, -ōnis, [admurmurō], f., *murmuring, murmur* of a crowd, expressing approval or dissent.

adnītor, -nītī, -nīxus sum, [ad + nītor], 3, dep., *lean upon; exert one's self, strive, make an effort.*

adnuō, -nuere, -nuī, ——, [ad + nuō], 3, n., *nod to, nod; nod assent, give assent, signify approval, assent.*

adōrnō, -āre, -āvī, -ātum, [ad + ōrnō], 1, a., *provide, furnish, equip, prepare; decorate, embellish, adorn.*

adquiēscō, -quiēscere, -quiēvī, -quiētum, [ad + quiēscō], 3, n., *become quiet, be at rest, have peace, rest, repose; be content, be satisfied.*

adquīrō, -ere, adquīsīvī, adquīsītum, [ad + quaerō], 3, a., *get in addition, get besides, obtain besides; acquire, gain, add.*

adsēnsus, -ūs, [adsentiō], m., *agreement, approval.*

adsentiō, -īre, adsēnsī, adsēnsum, [ad + sentiō], 4, n., also dep., **adsentior**, -īrī, adsēnsus sum, *give assent, approve, agree with, agree to.*

adsequor, -sequī, -secūtus sum, [ad + sequor], 3, dep., *follow up, come up to; obtain, reach, gain; accomplish, effect.*

adservō, -āre, -āvī, -ātum, [ad + servō], 1, a., *watch over, keep, preserve; guard with care, keep under guard.*

adsīdō, -sīdere, -sēdī, ——, [ad + sīdō, *sit down*], 3, n., *sit down, take a seat.*

adsiduē [adsiduus, *continual*], adv., *constantly, continually, unceasingly.*

adsiduitās, -ātis, [adsiduus], f., *constant attendance; unremitting service, devotion; continuance, constancy.*

adsīgnātiō, -ōnis, [adsīgnō], f., *a marking out, allotting, assigning.*

adsuēfaciō, -facere, -fēcī, -factum, [adsuētus + faciō], 3, a., *accustom to, habituate;* pass., *become accustomed to, be used to.*

adsum, -esse, -fuī, [ad + sum], irr., n., *be near, be present, be at hand; stand by, assist, support, help;* of motion, *appear, attend;* of time, *have come, be at hand, impend.*

adulēscēns, -entis, [part. of adolēscō], adj., *young, youthful.* As subst., m. or f., *youth, young man, young woman.*

adulēscentia, -ae, [adulēscēns], f., *youth;* the period of life beyond pueritia, and reckoned ordinarily between the ages of 15 and 25 or 30 years; by metonymy, = adulēscentēs, *young people, youth.*

adulēscentulus, -ī, [adulēscēns], m., dim., *very young man, lad, young fellow.*

adulter, -tera, adj., *adulterous, unchaste.* As subst., **adulter**, -terī, m., *adulterer, seducer, paramour.*

adultus, -a, -um, [adolēscō], adj., *full grown, mature, fully developed, adult.*

adventīcius, -a, -um, [adveniō], adj., *foreign, imported; strange.*

adventus, -ūs, [adveniō], m., *a coming, approach; arrival; presence.*

adversārius, -a, -um, [adversor], adj., *opposed, opposite; antagonistic, hostile, contrary.* As subst., **adversārius**, -ī, m., *opponent, antagonist, enemy, adversary.*

adversiō, -ōnis, [advertō], f., *direction; occupation, employment.*

adversus, -a, -um, [advertō], adj., *turned towards, facing, in front; unfavorable, unsuccessful, adverse; opposed, hostile.* **adversae rēs**, *misfortune, calamity, adversity, trouble, troubles.*

advesperāscit, -āscere, -āvit, ——, [ad + vesperāscit], 3, n., impers., *evening approaches, it grows dusk, it is twilight.*

advolō, -āre, -āvī, -ātum, [ad + volō], 1, n., *fly to, hasten to.*

aedēs, see **aedis**.

aedificium, -ī, [aedificō], n., *building, edifice.*

aedificō, -āre, -āvī, -ātum, [aedis + faciō], 1, a., *erect a building, build, erect; construct.*

aedīlis, -is, [aedēs], m., *aedile, buildings commissioner,* designation of certain magistrates in Rome, who had charge of buildings and public works, had an oversight of public exhibitions and dramatic performances, and were entrusted with the keeping of the decrees of the Senate and other public documents.

aedīlitās, -ātis, [aedīlis], f., *office of aedile, aedileship.*

aedis or **aedēs**, -is, f., of the gods, *temple, sanctuary;* of men, in pl. only, *house, habitation, dwelling.*

Aegaeus, -a, -um, [Αἰγαῖος], adj., *Aegean.* **Aegaeum mare**, *the Aegean sea.*

aeger, -gra, -grum, adj., *sick, ill, suffering, feeble; afflicted, distressed, troubled.*

aegrē, comp. **aegrius**, sup. **aegerrimē**, [aeger], adv., *painfully, with distress; with difficulty, hardly, scarcely; unwillingly, reluctantly.*

Aelius, -ī, with **Sex.**, *Sextus Aelius Paetus,* an early Roman jurist. He was curule aedile B.C. 200, consul B.C. 198, and censor B.C. 193. He left an important work on Roman law, which has perished. EP. XXXVIII.

Aemilius, -ī, with M., *Mārcus Aemilius Scaurus,* a Roman statesman of the time of the Jugurthine war. He was born B.C. 163; consul B.C. 115, with M. Caecilius Metellus; censor B.C. 109. He was a warm supporter of the aristocratic party. He died B.C. 90. ARCH. III.

aemulus, -a, -um, adj., *emulating, vying with, emulous, rivalling; envious.* As subst., **aemulus**, -ī, m., *rival.*

aequē [aequus], adv., *equally; in like manner, just as, to the same extent.* **aequē ac**, *just as, as much as, as.*

aequitās, -ātis, [aequus], f., *evenness; fairness, equity; calmness, repose, equanimity, contentment, equability.*

aequus, -a, -um, adj., *even, plain, level; equal, equitable, reasonable, fair, just, honorable; calm, patient, resigned; favorable, kind.* **aequum est**, *it is fair, it is reasonable.*

aerārium, -ī, [aerārius], n., *treasury; the public treasure, finances.* The Roman treasury was a part of the temple of Saturn in the Forum, in which public funds were kept.

aerārius, -a, -um, [aes], adj., *of copper, of bronze; of the public treasury.* **tribūnī aerāriī**, *paymasters*, who disbursed funds among the soldiers.

aerumna, -ae, f., *hardship, trouble, tribulation.*

aes, aeris, n., *copper; bronze*, an alloy of copper and tin; by metonymy, applied to things made of copper or bronze, as *bronze tablet, money.* **aes aliēnum**, *debt.*

aestās, -ātis, f., *summer.* **mēdia aestās**, *midsummer.*

aestimō, -āre, -āvī, -ātum, 1, a., *value, estimate, appraise, rate.*

aestus, -ūs, m., lit. *violent agitation;* of fire or fever, *heat, glow;* also = **aestās**, *summer;* of water, *surge, swell, tide;* of human emotions and actions, *fire, warmth, ardor; doubt, indecision.*

aetās, -ātis, [for aevitās, from **aevum**], f., *period of life, age, lifetime; time, period, generation; old age; an age, epoch.* **ab ineunte aetāte**, *from youth up, from early manhood.*

aeternitās, -ātis, [aeternus], f., *eternity, immortality; undying fame, enduring renown.*

aeternus, -a, -um, [for aeviternus, from **aevum**], adj., *lasting, everlasting, eternal, endless; unbroken, perpetual, immortal, imperishable.*

Aetōlī, -ōrum, [Αἰτωλός], m., pl., *Aetolians*, inhabitants of Aetolia, a district in Greece north of the entrance of the Corinthian Gulf, and east of Acarnania.

Āfrica, -ae, f., *Africa*, referring at first only to that part of the continent under the dominion of the Carthaginians; then, the province *Africa*, comprising territory formerly held by Carthage, and organized after the destruction of the city, B.C. 146; **in the** broadest sense, *the African continent, Africa*, as the term is understood to-day.

Āfricānus, -a, -um, [**Āfrica**], adj., *of Africa, African.* Used as a surname for the two Scipios who were victorious in Africa, *P. Cornēlius Scīpiō Āfricānus*, who defeated Hannibal at Zama, B.C. 202; and *P. Cornēlius Scīpiō Aemiliānus Āfricānus*, adoptive grandson of the elder Scipio, who destroyed Carthage, B.C. 146.

ager, -grī, [cf. English acre], m., *land, field, estate*, referring to improved or productive land; *territory, district, domain;* pl. **agrī**, sometimes *country, the open country, plain*, as opposed to cities or mountains.

aggregō, -āre, -āvī, -ātum, [ad, grex], 1, a., lit. *add to a flock; attach, join; collect, bring together gather together.*

agitō, -āre, -āvī, -ātum, [freq. of **agō**], 1, a., *drive, set in motion; move to and fro, brandish, wave, agitate; stir up, vex, trouble, distress; consider, deliberate, discuss.*

agnōscō, -nōscere, -nōvī, -nitum, [ad + gnōscō], 3, a., *discern, recognize, identify; acknowledge; perceive, know by; perceive the meaning of, understand.*

agō, agere, ēgī, āctum, 3, a. and n., *set in motion, drive, lead; direct, conduct, guide; incite, urge; press forward, chase, pursue; drive off* as plunder, *rob; do, act, transact, perform; manage, carry on, accomplish;* of time, *spend, pass, live;* also, *treat, deal with, confer, plead with;* pass. sometimes, *be at stake, be in peril.* Imp. **age** as an interjection, *come now! come! well!* **grātiās agere**, *to give thanks.*

māximās grātiās agere, *to give heartiest thanks.* **Quid agis?** colloquially, *how are you?* also, *what are you about?*

agrārius, -a, -um, [ager], adj., *of land, belonging to land.* As subst., **agrāriī, -ōrum,** m., pl., *supporters of agrarian laws, the agrarians, the agrarian party.*

agrestis, -e, [ager], adj., *of fields, rural, rustic; rude, coarse, uncultivated, wild.* As subst., **agrestis, -is,** m., usually in pl., *countryman, peasant, boor.*

Ahāla, -ae, m., name of a patrician family of the Servilian gens. **C. Servīlius Ahāla,** cf. **Maelius,** and N. to p. 62, l. 4.

āiō (pres. ind. **āiō, aïs, aït, aïunt,** impf. **āiēbam**), 3, def., n., *say yes; assert, say, tell, affirm;* generally used parenthetically.

alacer, -cris, -cre, adj., *lively, quick, active; eager, excited; cheerful, happy.*

alacritās, -ātis, [alacer], f., *liveliness, eagerness, alacrity; cheerfulness, delight.*

Alba, -ae, [albus, *white*], f., name of two important towns in Italy:

(1) *Alba,* or *Alba Longa,* the mother-city of Rome, situated between Mons Albanus and the Alban Lake, 15 miles southeast of Rome; said to have been built by Ascanius, son of Aeneas, and destroyed at an early period.

(2) *Alba,* or *Alba Fūcentia,* a city and fortress situated on the borders of the Marsian country, about sixty miles northeast of Rome and a short distance northwest of the Fucine Lake.

ālea, -ae, f., *game of chance, gaming, gambling;* by metonymy, *chance, risk, hazard.*

āleātor, -ōris, [ālea], m., *player with dice, gambler.*

Alexander, -drī, ['Αλέξανδρος] m., *Alexander,* in this book referring only to Alexander III., surnamed the Great, king of Macedonia. He was born B. C. 356, the son of Philip II. of Macedonia and Olympias. He broke the power of Persia, and led an army beyond the Indus. He died at Babylon, 323 B. C.

Alexis ["Αλεξις], m., *Alexis,* a slave or freedman of Atticus, for whom he acted as amanuensis.

aliēnigena, -ae, [aliēnus + root GEN in **gīgnō**], adj., m., *foreign-born, foreign, strange.* As subst, **aliēnigena, -ae,** m., *foreigner, alien.*

aliēnus, -a, -um, [alius], adj., *of another, another's; strange, foreign; unsuitable, out of place, ill-adapted; unfriendly, hostile.* As subst., **aliēnus, -ī,** m., *stranger, foreigner.*

aliō [alius], adv., *to another place, elsewhere.*

aliquandō [alius + quandō], adv., *at some time or other, some time; at any time, ever; at some time in the past, once, formerly; at some time in the future, hereafter; at length, finally, at last.*

aliquantō [aliquantus], adv., *in a degree, considerably, somewhat, rather;* usually with comparatives. **post aliquantō,** *some time afterwards.*

aliquī, aliqua, aliquod, [alius, quī], indef. pron. adj., *some, any, some one or other, some other.* **in aliquās terrās,** *into some other countries.*

aliquis, aliqua, aliquid, nom. and acc. pl. n. **aliqua,** [alius, quis], indef. pron., *some one, any one, anybody;* pl., *some, any.* Neut. **aliquid** as subst., *something, anything.*

aliquō [aliquī], adv., *to some place, somewhere; to some other place, elsewhere.*

aliquot [**alius, quot**], num. adj., indecl., *some, several, a number.*

aliter [**alius**], adv., *otherwise, differently; in any other way, in another manner, in a contrary way.*

alius, -a, -ud, gen. **alīus,** dat. **aliī,** adj., *another, some other, other, different, else.* **alius —— alius,** *one —— another, the one —— the other;* pl., **aliī —— aliī,** *some —— others;* often as subst., **alius,** *another,* **aliī,** *others.*

Allobrogēs, -um, acc., **Allobrogas,** m., pl., *Allobrogēs,* a people of Transalpine Gaul, who lived on the east side of the Rhone, north of the Isara. Their chief city was Geneva. They were brought under the rule of Rome by Q. Fabius Maximus, B. C. 121, and in Cicero's time their territory formed a part of the Roman province in Gaul.

alō, alere, aluī, altum or **alitum,** 3, a., *nourish, sustain, maintain, support; cherish, promote, increase;* in pass., with abl., *be nourished by* (= **vescor**), *feed upon, live on.*

Alpēs, -ium, f., pl., *the Alps.*

altāria, -ium, [**altus**], n., pl., *high altar, altar.* See **āra.**

alter, -tera, -terum, gen. **alterīus** or **alterius,** dat. **alterī,** pron. adj., *one* of two, *the one, the other, another; second, next.* **alter —— alter,** *the one —— the other, the former —— the latter.*

alternus, -a, -um, [**alter**], adj., *one after the other, by turns, alternate, reciprocal;* of verses, *alternate hexameter and pentameter,* that is, *elegiac.*

alteruter, -utra, -utrum, [**alter + uter**], adj., *one or the other, one of two, either.* **in alterutrō,** *in either case, in the case of either.*

altus, -a, -um, comp. **altior,** sup. **altissimus,** [**alō**], adj., lit. *nourished, grown great; high, lofty, elevated; deep, profound.*

alveolus, -ī, [dim. of **alveus,** *hollow*], m., *tray, basin; dice-board,* a small board upon which dice were thrown; by metonymy, *gaming, gambling.*

amāns, -antis, comp. **amantior,** sup. **amantissimus,** [part. of **amō**], adj., *fond, affectionate towards, devoted to;* often followed by the gen.

amanter, comp. **amantius,** sup. **amantissimē,** [**amāns**], adv., *affectionately, amiably.*

ambulātiō, -ōnis, [**ambulō**], f., *walking about, walking; walk, promenade.*

ambulō, -āre, -āvī, -ātum, 1, n., *walk, walk about, take a walk.*

āmēns, -entis, [**ab + mēns**], adj., *out of one's senses, distracted, frantic, mad; foolish, stupid.*

āmentia, -ae, [**āmēns**], f., *madness; folly, stupidity.*

amiciō, -īre, amixī or **amicuī, amictum,** [**am-,** for **ambi-, + iaciō**], 4, a., *throw around, wrap about, wrap around,* used of outer garments; *clothe, cover, surround, enclose.*

amīcitia, -ae, [**amīcus**], f., *friendship; alliance.*

amīcus, -a, -um, comp. **amīcior,** sup. **amīcissimus,** [**amō**], adj., *loving, friendly, dear; kind, well disposed; pleasing, agreeable.*

amīcus, -ī, [adj. **amīcus**], m., *friend.*

Amīsus, -ī, ['Αμῖσός], f., *Amīsus,* an important city on the southern shore of the Pontus Euxinus southeast of Sinope; now Eski Samsun. IMP. P. v.

āmittō, -ere, āmīsī, āmissum, [**ab + mittō**], 3, a., *send away, dismiss, let go; lose, part with.*

amō, -āre, -āvī, -ātum, 1, a., *love, like; be fond of, take pleasure in;* in requests, *I pray, please.*

amoenitās, -ātis, [**amoenus,** *pleasant*], f., *pleasantness, charm.*

amor, -ōris, [**amō**], m., *love, affection, devotion; eager desire, passion.*

amplē, comp. **amplius,** sup. **amplissimē,** [**amplus**], adv., *largely, amply, abundantly; liberally, magnificently.* See **amplius.**

amplector, -ectī, -exus sum, [**ambi- + plectō**], 3, dep., *twine about, encircle, embrace; embrace with esteem, love, esteem, cling to.*

amplificō, -āre, -āvī, -ātum, [**amplificus,** from **amplus + faciō**], 1, a., *broaden, enlarge, extend; increase, amplify.*

amplitūdō, -inis, [**amplus**], f., *breadth, great extent, greatness, size; dignity, grandeur.*

amplius [comp. of **amplus** and **amplē**], indecl. adj. and adv., *further, besides, more.*

amplus, -a, -um, comp. **amplior,** sup. **amplissimus,** adj., *large, great, spacious, ample, considerable; magnificent, splendid, glorious; renowned, distinguished, honorable.*

an, conj., introducing the second member of a disjunctive question, direct or indirect, *or, or rather, or indeed.* The first member ordinarily has **utrum** or **-ne,** but it is sometimes omitted. In direct questions **an** is often not translated; in indirect questions, *whether.* **haud sciō an** = *I am inclined to think, perhaps, probably.*

anceps, -cipitis, [**ambi-, capiō**], adj, *two-headed, double, twofold; wavering, uncertain, doubtful, undecided.*

angō, angere, anxī, ——, 3, a., *draw tight, squeeze, choke; distress, torment, vex.*

angulus, -ī, m., *angle, corner;* by metonymy, *nook, lurking-place*

angustiae, -ārum, [**angustus,** *narrow*], f., *straitness, narrowness; narrow place, defile, strait;* of time, *shortness, brevity; scarcity, want; difficulty, distress.*

anhēlō, -āre, -āvī, -ātum, [**anhēlus**], 1, n. and a., *gasp, pant; breathe forth.*

anima, -ae, f., *current of air; air, breeze; breath, soul, life;* especially in pl., *souls* of the dead, *shades.* See **animus.**

animadversiō, -ōnis, [**animadvertō**], f., *observation, inquiry; reproach, censure; chastisement, punishment.*

animadvertō, -vertere, -vertī, -versum, [**animum + advertō**], 3, a., *direct attention to, regard; notice, observe, consider, perceive, see; censure, punish, inflict punishment.*

animōsē [**animōsus,** from **animus**], adv., *with spirit, courageously, boldly.*

animus, -ī, m., *soul, life; intellect, mind, reason; imagination; heart, feeling, desire, affection, passion; courage, spirit; temper, arrogance, haughtiness; design, resolution.* **animus** refers to the spiritual and emotional part of man's nature as distinguished on the one hand from the body (corpus) and on the other from the life-principle, the physical life (anima). **animō aequō,** *with resignation, calmly.* **animō bonō esse,** *to be of good cheer.*

Annius, **-ī**, with **Chīlō**, **-ōnis**, m., *Q. Annius Chīlō*, a Roman involved in the conspiracy of Catiline. No particulars about his life are known. CAT. III. VI.

annōna, **-ae**, [annus], f., *the year's produce, crop; grain, provisions;* by metonymy, *price of grain, market.*

annus, **-ī**, m., *year.*

annuus, **-a**, **-um**; [annus], adj., *for a year, lasting a year; annual, yearly.*

ante, adv. and prep., *before:*

(1) As adv., of space, *before, in front, ahead;* of time, *before, previously, earlier, ago.* **paulō ante**, *a little while ago.* **ante quam**, *sooner than, before.*

(2) As prep., with acc. only, of space and time, *before, before the time of, previous to, antedating;* in comparisons, *before, superior to, in comparison with.* **ante mē**, *before my time.* **ante cīvitātem datam**, *prior to the granting of citizenship.* **ante diem**, or (abbreviated) **a. d.**, used in expressing dates, see N. to p. 63, l. 24.

anteā [ante + eā], adv., *before, formerly, previously, hitherto.*

antecellō, **-ere**, ——, ——, [ante + unused cellō, *rise*], 3, n., *rise beyond, excel, surpass.*

anteferō, **-ferre**, **-tulī**, **-lātum**, [ante + ferō], irr., a., *carry before; place before, esteem more highly, prefer.*

antelūcānus, **-a**, **-um**, [ante + lūx], adj., *before light, before daybreak.* **antelūcānae cēnae**, *feasts continuing till morning, all-night dinners.*

antepōnō, **-pōnere**, **-posuī**, **-positum**, [ante + pōnō], 3, a., *set before; esteem above, prefer.*

ante quam, see **ante**.

Antiās, **-ātis**, adj., *of Antium.* In Cicero's letters **Antiātī** is used as a subst. in the abl. for **Antiātī praediō**, *estate at Antium*, a town on the sea-coast of Latium, about thirty miles south of Rome. Cicero had a country-place in the vicinity.

Antiochīa, **-ae**, ['Αντιόχεια], f., *Antioch*, name of several cities, of which the most important was that in Syria, on the Orontes river. ARCH. III.

Antiochus, **-ī**, ['Αντίοχος], m., *Antiochus*, name of several kings of Syria, of whom the most famous was Antiochus III., called the Great. He came to the throne of Syria B. C. 223; was defeated by the Romans at Thermopylae, in Greece, B. C. 191, and again the following year in a battle at the foot of Mt. Sipylus, in Asia Minor. Two years later he was forced to accept humiliating terms of peace, and was murdered B. C. 187.

antīquitās, **-ātis**, [antīquus], f., *antiquity, age; the past.*

antīquus, **-a**, **-um**, comp. **antīquior**, sup. **antīquissimus**, [ante], adj., *old, ancient, aged; primitive, former, old-fashioned; reverend, venerable.* As subst., **antīquī**, **-ōrum**, m., pl., *ancients, the ancients, the men of old.*

Antium, **-ī**, n., *Antium*, a city in Latium, on the sea-coast south of Rome, where there was a famous temple of Fortune.

Antōnius, **-a**, name of a Roman gens of which there were several distinguished members. The one most frequently mentioned is **M. Antōnius**, **-ī**, *Mārcus Antōnius, Mark Antony*, whom Cicero attacked in his Philippic orations.

aperiō, **-īre**, **-uī**, **-tum**, 4, a., *uncover, unclose, discover, reveal, open ; lay open, open up, render accessible, expose ; make known, unfold, explain.*

apertē [**apertus**], adv., *openly; plainly, clearly, without reserve.*

apertus, **-a**, **-um**, [part. of **aperiō**], adj., *uncovered ; unclosed, open ; unobstructed, plain, clear, manifest.*

aphractus, **-ī**, [ἄφρακτος, *uncovered,* sc. ναῦς], f., *uncovered ship, ship without a deck, open boat.*

Apollōnidēnsēs, **-ium**, [**Apollōnis**],m.,pl., *Apollonidensians, people of Apollōnis,* a city in Lydia. Sing. **Apollōnidēnsis**, **-is**, *a man of Apollōnis, an Apollonidensian.*

apparātus, **-a**, **-um**, [part. of **apparō**], adj., *made ready, ready, furnished ; sumptuous, magnificent.*

apparō, **-āre**, **-āvī**, **-ātum**, [**ad** + **parō**], 1, a., *prepare, make ready, provide ; make ready for.*

appellō, **-āre**, **-āvī**, **-ātum**, [**ad** + **pellō**], 1, a., *address, speak to, apply to ; name, term, entitle, call ; entreat, beg, call upon.*

Appennīnus, **-ī**, m., *the Appennine mountains, the Appennines,* the high mountain-range in Central Italy.

appetēns, **-entis**, [part. of **appetō**], adj , *eager for, desirous of ; greedy.*

appetō, **-petere**, **-petīvī** or **-petiī**, **-petītum**, [**ad** + **petō**], 3, a. and n., *strive for, reach after ; attack, assault ; long for, desire, seek.*

Appī Forum, **-ī**, n., *Appī Forum, Forum of Appius,* a small market town on the Appian Way, 43 miles southeast of Rome.

Appius, **-ī**, m., *Appius,* a Roman forename, common in the Claudian gens. See **Pulcher**.

Appius, **-a**, **-um**, adj., *Appian, of Appius.* **Via Appia**, *Appian Way,* the most famous of Roman roads, built by the censor Appius Claudius Caecus about 300 B. C., and extending from Rome to Capua.

approbō, **-āre**, **-āvī**, **-ātum**, [**ad** + **probō**], 1, a., *give assent to, approve, favor, sanction.*

appropinquō, **-āre**, **-āvī**, **-ātum**, [**ad** + **propinquō**, from **propinquus**], 1, n., *come near to, draw nigh to, approach.*

Appulēius, **-ī**, m., *M. Appulēius,* elected augur B. C. 45. EP. XXXIV., XXXVI.

Aprīlis, **-is**, [perhaps from **aperiō**], adj., *of April.* As subst., **Aprīlis**, **-is**, m., *April.*

aptus, **-a**, **-um**, [cf. **apīscor**], adj., *fitted, joined ; suited, suitable, proper, fit, appropriate, adapted.*

apud, prep. with acc. only, *with, near, at, by ;* of persons, *before, in the presence of, to, among, in the opinion of, in the power of, at the house of, with, in the time of ;* of place, *at, near to, in, in the vicinity of, off the coast of.* **apud Laecam**, *at the house of Laeca, at Laeca's.*

Āpūlia, **-ae**, f., *Āpūlia,* a region in the southeastern part of Italy, north of Calabria, east of Lucania and Samnium.

aqua, **-ae**, f., *water.*

aquila, **-ae**, f., *eagle ;* by metonymy, *eagle* of a standard, the metal eagle carried on a pole as the standard of a Roman legion.

āra, **-ae**, f., *altar.* **āra** is the general term for *altar,* while **altāria** refers primarily to an elevation on the altar to receive burnt-offerings ; though the later term by synecdoche is often used of the altar as a whole.

arbitror, -ārī, -ātus sum, [arbiter], 1, dep., *give one's judgment, declare a decision; be of the opinion, believe, think, consider, judge.*

arceō, -ēre, -cuī, ——, 2, a., *keep away, ward off; hinder, prevent.*

arcessō, -ere, arcessīvī, arcessītum, [intens. of accēdō, ar- for ad-], 3, a., *send for, summon, invite, fetch.*

Archiās, -ae, [Ἀρχίας], m., *A. Licinius Archiās,* a Greek poet, in whose defense Cicero delivered one of his most famous orations. See pp. 45–48.

ārdēns, -entis, [part. of ārdeō], adj., *glowing, hot; fiery, eager, ardent.*

ārdeō, -ēre, ārsī, ārsum, 2, n., *be on fire, burn, glow; flash, shine; be inflamed, be afire.*

ārdor, -ōris, [ārdeō], m., *flame, fire, heat; eagerness, zeal, animation.*

argenteus, -a, -um, [argentum], adj., *of silver, made of silver, silver.*

argentum, -ī, n., *silver;* by metonymy, *silverware, silver money, money.*

argūmentum, -ī, [arguō], n., *argument, evidence, proof; sign, mark, indication, token.*

Ariobarzānēs, -is, m., *Ariobarzānēs,* name of three kings of Cappadocia, in Asia Minor. The most important was *Ariobarzānēs Philorhōmaeus,* who came to the throne by election under Roman influence about B. C. 93. He gained his surname (= φίλος + Ῥωμαῖος) from his intimate relations with the Romans, by whom he was several times restored to his kingdom after having been driven out by Mithridates. He resigned the throne to his son, *Ariobarzānēs Philopatōr,* probably in B. C. 63.

Aristotelēs, -is, [Ἀριστοτέλης], m., *Aristotle,* a famous Greek philosopher, born at Stagīra, in Chalcidice, B. C. 384. He was a pupil of Plato, and the tutor of the Prince Alexander, afterwards called the Great. He was the founder of the so-called Peripatetic school of philosophy. He left numerous writings, some of the most important of which have been preserved. He died B. C. 322. EP. XII.

arma, -ōrum, n., pl., *armor, outfit,* as coat of mail, helmet, shield, greaves; *implements of war, arms, weapons;* by metonymy, *tools, implements.*

armātus, -a, -um, [armō], adj., *armed, equipped, furnished, under arms.* As subst., **armātī, -ōrum,** m., pl., *armed men, soldiers.*

Armenius, -a, -um, adj., *Armenian, of Armenia.* As subst., **Armeniī, -ōrum,** m., pl., *Armenians, inhabitants of Armenia,* a country in the northeastern part of Asia Minor, north of Mesopotamia.

Arpīnās, -ātis, adj., *of Arpīnum, near Arpīnum,* a town in Latium, about fifty miles southeast of Rome, celebrated as the birthplace of Gaius Marius and Cicero. As subst., **Arpīnās, -ātis,** n., *estate near Arpīnum,* Cicero's favorite country-place; his villa there was surrounded by the waters of the little river Fibrenus.

ars, artis, f., *skill, art; science, knowledge, learning; trait, practice, virtue, quality.*

arthrīticus, -a, -um, [ἀρθριτικός, from ἄρθρον, *joint*], adj., *gouty, having the gout.*

artifex, -**icis**, [**ars**, cf. **faciō**], m. and f., *master* of an art, *performer, actor, professional ; contriver, trickster.*

arx, **arcis**, f., *citadel, castle, stronghold ; bulwark, refuge, protection.*

ascendō, -**ere**, **ascendī**, **ascēnsum**, [**ad** + **scandō**], 3, n. and a., *mount, ascend, go up, rise.*

ascīscō, -**ere**, **ascīvī**, **ascītum**, [**ad** + **scīscō**], 3, a., *receive, accept, adopt ; associate with one's self, win over.*

Asclāpō, -**ōnis**, m., *Asclāpō*, a physician, native of Patrae in Achaia (modern Patras), and friend of Cicero. Ep. XXXII.

ascrībō, -**ere**, **ascrīpsī**, **ascrīptum**, [**ad** + **scrībō**], 3, a., *write in addition, write in a list, enroll, enter, add ; appoint, assign ; ascribe, impute.*

Asia, -**ae**, ['Ασία], f., *Asia*, usually referring to Asia Minor.

Asiāticus, -**a**, -**um**, [**Asia**], adj., *of Asia, Asiatic.*

aspectus, -**ūs**, [**aspiciō**], m., *sight, look, glance ; view, appearance, aspect, countenance.*

asper, -**era**, -**erum**, adj., *adverse, cruel, perilous ; harsh, rough, wild, fierce.*

aspiciō, -**icere**, -**exī**, -**ectum**, [**ad** + **speciō**], 3, a. and n., *look upon, behold, look, glance ; observe, see, consider.* **inter sēsē aspiciēbant**, *they glanced at one another.*

astō, -**stāre**, -**stitī**, ——, [**ad** + **stō**], 1, n., *stand by, stand near, stand at ; stand up, stand.*

astringō, -**ere**, **astrinxī**, **astrictum**, [**ad** + **stringō**], 3, a., *bind to ; bind together, fasten, attach ; put under obligation, bind.*

Astura, -**ae**, f., *Astura*, a small island on the coast of Latium, about forty miles south of Rome, at the mouth of a small river also called **Astura** (m.) There were several fine country-places on the island, among which was one belonging to Cicero. Ep. XXXV. *et al.*

at, conj., introducing

(1) A contrast, *but, but on the other hand, but yet.*

(2) A qualification after a negative and **sī**, **etsī**, etc., *but yet, nevertheless, however, at least.*

(3) A direct opposition, *but, but on the contrary.*

Athamās, -**antis**, ['Αθάμας], m., *Athamās*, a favorite slave of Cicero's friend Atticus. Ep. XXXI.

Athēnae, -**ārum**, ['Αθῆναι], f., pl., *Athens.*

Athēniēnsis, -**e**, [**Athēnae**], adj., *of Athens, Athenian.* As subst., **Athēniēnsis**, -**is**, m., *man of Athens, Athenian.*

atque, before consonants **ac**, [**ad** + **que**], conj., copulative and comparative :

(1) Copulative, *and also, and even, as well as, and, and especially, and so, and too, and yet.* **etiam atque etiam**, *again and again, repeatedly.*

(2) Comparative, *as, than, than as.* **contrā atque**, *contrary to what.* **perinde atque**, *just as.* **prō eō ac**, *according as.*

atquī [**at** + **quī**], conj., *and yet, but yet, and nevertheless, however, but somehow, but in any case.*

atrōcitās, -**ātis**, [**atrōx**], f., *fierceness, cruelty ; severity, harshness, barbarity.*

atrōx, -**ōcis**, [**āter**], adj., *fierce, cruel, savage ; severe, harsh ; horrible, terrible, violent.*

attendō, -**ere**, **attendī**, **attentum**, [**ad** + **tendō**], 3, a., *direct to*, used either with or without **animum** ; *consider, give heed ; listen, pay attention to, listen to.*

attenuō, **-āre**, **-āvī**, **-ātum**, [**ad** + **tenuō**], 1, a., *make thin; lessen, diminish, reduce, weaken; make less formidable.*

Attica, **-ae**, [**Atticus**], f., *Attica,* a pet name given by Cicero to Caecilia, the little daughter of his friend Atticus.

Atticus, **-ī**, ['Αττικός], m., *Atticus, Titus Pompōnius Atticus,* an intimate friend of Cicero, to whom he dedicated several of his works and addressed many letters.

attineō, **-ēre**, **attinuī**, **attentum**, [**ad** + **teneō**], 2, a. and n., *hold fast, detain; belong to, concern, relate to, pertain to.*

attingō, **-ere**, **attigī**, **attāctum**, [**ad** + **tangō**], 3, a. and n., *touch, touch upon; lay hands on, seize, attack; approach, reach, attain to; relate to, concern; mention, refer to.*

attribuō, **-buere**, **-buī**, **-būtum**, [**ad** + **tribuō**], 3, a., *assign, allot, bestow; intrust, give in charge; attribute, ascribe.*

auctiōnārius, **-a**, **-um**, [**auctiō**], adj., *of auction, for auction.*

auctor, **-ōris**, [**augeō**], m., *producer; father, progenitor; founder; writer, authority; counsellor, adviser, promoter.*

auctōritās, **-ātis**, [**auctor**], f., *authority, supremacy; decision, resolve, will, opinion; decree, warrant, assurance; influence, dignity, reputation, weight, importance, consequence.*

aucupor, **-ārī**, **-ātus sum**, [**auceps**, *fowler*], 1, dep., *chase, hunt; lie in wait for, strive after, catch.*

audācia, **-ae**, [**audāx**], f., *daring, boldness, courage, bravery; audacity, impudence, insolence, presumption; deed of boldness, daring deed, effrontery.*

audācter, comp. **audācius**, sup **audācissimē**, [**audāx**], adv., *boldly, bravely, with courage; rashly, audaciously, with desperation.*

audāx, **-ācis**, comp. **audācior**, sup. **audācissimus**, [**audeō**], adj., *daring, bold, courageous; audacious, rash, foolhardy, desperate.*

audeō, **audēre**, **ausus sum**, 2, semi-dep., a. and n., *dare, be bold, venture, risk.*

audiō, **-īre**, **-īvī** or **-iī**, **-ītum**, 4, a., *hear, hear of; listen to, learn from; assent to, agree to, approve, grant.*

auferō, **auferre**, **abstulī**, **ablātum**, [**ab** + **ferō**], irr., a., *take away, remove, withdraw; carry off, snatch away, rob, steal; sweep away, destroy.*

augeō, **augēre**, **auxī**, **auctum**, 2, a. and n., *increase, enlarge, augment; extend, add to, enrich; praise, extol.*

Aulus, **-ī**, m., *Aulus,* a common Roman forename.

Aurēlium, **-ī**, see **Forum Aurēlium**.

Aurēlius, **-a**, **-um**, adj., *of an Aurelius, Aurelian,* name of a Roman gens. **Aurēlia via**, *Aurelian Way,* the great north coast-road, leading from Rome to Pisa.

auris, **-is**, [cf. **audiō**], f., *ear.* **aurēs adhibēre**, **aurēs dare**, *to give attention, to listen.*

aurum, **-ī**, n., *gold.*

auspicium, **-ī**, [**auspex**, *diviner*], n., *augury from birds, auspices, divination; sign, omen; guidance, authority.*

aut, conj., marking an important difference, *or;* corrective or emphatic, *or at least, or surely, or rather, or else.* **aut —— aut**, *either —— or.*

autem, conj., always postpositive and generally in weak antitheses, sometimes in contrasted conditions, *however, but, on the contrary, and now.*

auxilium, **-ī**, [cf. **augeō**], n., *help, aid, assistance, support;* in pl., often *auxiliary troops, auxiliaries.*

avāritia, **-ae**, [**avārus**], f., *greed, avarice, covetousness.*

āversus, **-a**, **-um**, [part. of **āvertō**], adj., *turned away, turned back; withdrawn; unfavorable, averse, hostile, opposed.*

āvertō, **-ere**, **āvertī**, **āversum**, [**ā** + **vertō**], 3, a., *turn away, turn aside; remove, carry off, withdraw; ward off, avert, estrange.*

avidus, **-a**, **-um**, [**aveō**], adj., *eager, desirous, coveting; covetous, greedy, avaricious.*

avītus, **-a**, **-um**, [**avus**], adj., *of a grandfather; ancestral, hereditary.*

āvocō, **-āre**, **-āvī**, **-ātum**, [**ā** + **vocō**], 1, a., *call away, withdraw; call off, divert, turn aside, turn.*

avus, **-ī**, m., *grandfather.*

B.

bacchor, **-ārī**, **-ātus sum**, [**Bacchus**], 1, dep., *celebrate the festival of Bacchus; revel, hold revelry, rave, exult.*

Balbus, **-ī**, **m.**, name of several men mentioned in Roman history, of whom the most important is *Lūcius Cornēlius Balbus*, a native of Gades, in Spain. He served under several Roman generals in the war with Sertorius, and was rewarded by Pompey with the Roman citizenship. He afterwards moved to Rome, where he came to possess great influence, through his wealth and his friendship with Caesar, Pompey, and other prominent men. His citizenship was called in question, and defended by Cicero in the oration *Prō Balbō*, which is extant. He was consul B. C. 40, but the time of his death is not known. EP. XIII.

barbaria, **-ae**, [**barbarus**], f., *foreign country;* = barbarī, *uncivilized people; savagery, barbarism.*

barbarus, **-a**, **-um**, [*βάρβαρος*], adj., *unintelligible; strange, foreign; of foreigners, barbarian; barbarous, cruel, savage, rude, uncivilized.*

barbātus, **-a**, **-um**, [**barba**], adj., *bearded, with a beard.*

Basilus, **-ī**, m., name of a family of the Minucian gens. Prominent among those bearing the name was *L. Minucius Basilus*, who won distinction while serving under Caesar in Gaul. Afterwards, however, he was one of the assassins of Caesar, and his share in the killing of the Dictator drew from Cicero a celebrated letter of congratulation (EP. XL. p. 203). The year after Caesar's death Basilus was himself murdered by his slaves, on account of his inhuman treatment of them.

Batōnius, **-ī**, m., *Batōnius*, a friend of Cicero and Atticus. EP. XIX.

beātus, **-a**, **-um**, [**beō**, *make happy*], adj., *happy, fortunate, prosperous; wealthy, rich, opulent.*

bellicōsus, **-a**, **-um**, [**bellicus**], adj., *warlike, martial.*

bellicus, **-a**, **-um**, [**bellum**], adj., *of war, military; warlike.*

bellō, **-āre**, **-āvī**, **-ātum**, [**bellum**], 1, n., *wage war, carry on war, war; fight, contend.*

bellum, **-ī**, [for **duellum**, from **duo**], n., *war*.

bēlua, **-ae**, f., *great beast, beast, wild beast, monster*.

bene, comp. **melius**, sup. **optimē**, [**bonus**], adv., *well, successfully, prosperously; very, quite*. Comp., *better*. Sup., *best*.

beneficium, **-ī**, [**beneficus**], n., *kindness, favor, service, benefit; honor, promotion*.

benevolentia, **-ae**, [**benevolēns**], f., *good-will, kindness, friendship*.

benīgnitās, **-ātis**, [**benīgnus**], f., *kindness, courtesy; favor, liberality, bounty*.

bēstia, **-ae**, f., *beast, animal, brute*.

bibliothēca, **-ae**, [βιβλιοθήκη], f., *library, room for books; collection of books*.

bibō, **bibere**, **bibī**, **bibitum**, 3, a. and n., *drink*.

Bibulus, **-ī**, m., name of a family of the Calpurnian gens. The best known member is *L. Calpurnius Bibulus*, who was consul with Caesar in the year 59 B. C. Being in sympathy with the aristocratic party, he opposed Caesar whenever possible, both during the consulship and afterwards. He had a commission under Pompey in the Civil War, but died B. C. 48, just before the battle of Dyrrhachium. EP. XIX.

bīduum, **-ī**, [**bis**, cf. **diēs**], n., *period of two days, two days*.

bīnī, **-ae**, **-a**, [cf. **bis**], dist. num. adj., *two each, two by two, two at a time; double*.

bipertītō [**bipartītus**, from **bi** for **bis**, **partior**], adv., *in two divisions, in two parts, in two parties*.

Bīthȳnia, **-ae**, [Βιθυνία], f., *Bithynia*, a province in Asia Minor, bounded on the west by the Propontis and on the north by the **Pontus Euxinus**.

Bona Dea, **-ae**, f., *Bona Dea, the Good Goddess*, an Italian divinity, also called *Fauna* and *Māia*. She was supposed to preside over the fructifying powers of the earth, as well as over the chastity and faithfulness of women. She was worshipped at Rome as an austere virgin, men being forbidden to enter her temple. Her rites were celebrated by the Vestal Virgins and by matrons. EP. III.

bonitās, **-ātis**, [**bonus**], f., *goodness, kindness, friendliness; excellence*.

bonus, **-a**, **-um**, comp. **melior**, sup. **optimus**, adj., *good, worthy, excellent, kind*. As subst., **bonus**, **-ī**, m., *good man*; pl. **bonī**, **-ōrum**, *the good*. **bonum**, **-ī**, n., *good thing, advantage*; pl. **bona**, **-ōrum**, *goods, property, possessions, blessings*.

Bosporānī, **-ōrum**, [**Bosporus**], m., pl., *people along the Bosporus, dwellers by the Bosporus*.

Bovīllānus, **-a**, **-um**, [**Bovīllae**], adj., *of Bovillae, at Bovillae*, an ancient town in Latium on the Appian Way, about 12 miles southeast of Rome.

brevis, **-e**, adj., *short, brief, little*.

brevitās, **-ātis**, [**brevis**], f., *shortness, brevity; conciseness*.

breviter [**brevis**], adv., *shortly, briefly, concisely, in a few words*.

Britannia, **-ae**, f., *Britain*, including England and Scotland.

Brundisium, **-ī**, n., *Brundisium*, an important seaport on the Adriatic, in Calabria. It was the usual port of departure for Greece and the East; now Brindisi.

Brūtus, **-ī**, m., cognomen of several well-known Romans, of whom four are mentioned in this book:

(1) *Decimus Iūnius Brūtus*, consul B. C. 138. As proconsul of Further Spain he gained important victories, for which he celebrated a splendid triumph, B. C. 136. ARCH. XI.

(2) *Decimus Iūnius Brūtus Albīnus*, who served under Caesar in Gaul, later in the Civil War. Afterwards he joined the conspiracy against Caesar's life, and conducted the Dictator to the Senate-house on the day of the assassination. After Caesar's death he obtained Cisalpine Gaul as a province, and refused to give it up to Antonius. When Octavianus prepared to wreak vengeance on the murderers of Caesar, Brutus attempted to escape into Macedonia, but was betrayed by a Gallic chief and put to death by order of Antonius, B. C. 43. ANT. IV. III., IV., EP. XLVI.

(3) *Mārcus Iūnius Brūtus*, the friend of Cassius and Cicero, born B. C. 85. In the Civil War he joined the side of Pompey, but was pardoned by Caesar, and was one of the assassins that took Caesar's life. He joined with Cassius in gathering an army against Antonius and Octavianus. In the first engagement at Philippi, B. C. 42, Brutus came off victorious. But three weeks later he suffered a complete defeat and put an end to his life by falling on his sword. EP. XXXIV., XXXVI., XXXVII.

(4) *Mārcus Iūnius Brūtus*, a celebrated jurist, who lived in the second century B. C. EP. XXXVIII.

Būthrōtum, -ī, [Βουθρωτόν], n., *Būthrōtum*, a town on the coast of Epirus, opposite Corcyra.

C.

C, in expressions of number, = 100.

C., see **Gāius.**

cadō, cadere, cecidī, cāsum, 3, n., *fall, fall down; fall away, fall dead, die, be slain, perish; fall under, be subject to; fall to the lot of, befall, happen.*

cadūcus, -a, -um, [cadō], adj., *inclined to fall, falling; perishable, transitory, frail, fleeting.*

caedēs, -is, [cf. caedō], f., *slaughter, massacre, carnage, murder.*

caelestis, -e, [caelum], adj., *of heaven, heavenly, celestial.* As subst., **caelestēs, -ium,** m., pl., *heaven-dwellers, the gods.*

Caelius, -ī, m., name of a Roman gens, of which two members are mentioned in this book:

(1) *Q. Caelius Latīniēnsis*, tribune of the people and the next year legatus, contrary to the usual practice. IMP. P. XIX.

(2) *M. Caelius Rūfus*, aedile B. C. 50. In the Civil War he supported the cause of Caesar for a time, but prepared to join a movement against the Dictator and soon met a violent death. EP. XVIII.

caelum, -ī, n., *sky, heaven, heavens; the skies; air, atmosphere, climate, weather.*

Caepārius, -ī, [caepe, *onion***],** m., *M. Caepārius*, an acquaintance of Cicero; nothing further is known about him. EP. XXX.

Caesar, -aris, m., name of a prominent family in the Julian gens, of which four members are mentioned in this book:

(1) *Gāius Iūlius Caesar*, the Dictator, born B. C. 100, assassinated March 15, B. C. 44.

(2) *L. Iūlius Caesar*, consul B. C. 64, uncle of Mark Antony,

whose course after the death of the Dictator he opposed. CAT. IV. VI.

(3) *Gāius Iūlius Caesar Octāviānus*, see **Octāviānus**.

(4) *L. Iūlius Caesar Strabō*, consul with P. Rutilius B.C. 90, censor with P. Crassus the following year; killed by Cinna. ARCH. V.

Caesariānus, -a, -um, [Caesar], adj., *of Caesar, Caesar's.*

Cāiēta, -ae, [Καιήτη], f., *Cāiēta*, a sea-coast town, with a harbor, in the southwestern part of Latium.

calamitās, -ātis, f., *loss, damage, hurt; calamity, misfortune, ruin, disaster, adversity.*

calamus, -ī, [κάλαμος], m., *reed;* by metonymy, *pen* made of reed, *reed pen; reed pipe.*

callidus, -a, -um, [calleō], adj., *skilful, shrewd; crafty, cunning, artful.*

campus, -ī, m., *plain, level field, open field;* often = **Campus Mārtius**, *the Campus Mārtius*, a grassy open space in the northwestern part of Rome, along the Tiber and outside the Servian Wall, where the people met for reviews and elections by centuries.

canō, **canere**, **cecinī**, **cantum**, [for c a s n ō, from root CAS, *sing*], 3, n. and a., *sing, make music, play; sing of, celebrate;* as prophecies were given in verse, *foretell, predict.*

cantō, -āre, -āvī, -ātum [freq. of canō], 1, n. and a., *sing, play.*

cantus, -ūs, [canō], m., *singing, playing; song, music.*

capillus, -ī, [cf. caput], m., *hair* of the head, *the hair.*

capiō, **capere**, **cēpī**, **captum**, 3, a., *take, lay hold of, seize, grasp; get possession of, master, control; capture, storm, reduce; captivate, win; deceive, betray, catch; harm, deprive of; suffer, experience; receive, entertain; enter upon, undertake; accept, gain, enjoy, reap; take in, comprehend, grasp; hold, be large enough for.*

capitālis, -e, [caput], adj., *of the head, foremost; involving life, capital; deadly, dangerous, baneful.*

Capitōlium, ī, [caput], n., (1) in a narrower sense, *the Capitol*, a temple on Mons Saturnius dedicated by the Tarquinii to Jupiter, Juno, and Minerva, afterwards made the most splendid temple at Rome; very often, (2) *the Capitoline Hill, the Capitoline*, the hill on which the Capitol stood, which contained also the citadel of Rome. See Map, p. 76.

Cappadocia, -ae, [Καππαδοκία], f., *Cappadocia*, an extensive country of Asia Minor lying south of the Euxine sea, north of Cilicia, and west of the upper course of the Euphrates.

Capua, -ae, f., *Capua*, an ancient and luxurious city of Campania, 136 miles southeast of Rome.

caput, -itis, n., *head;* by metonymy, *person, being, life, soul;* of elevation, *top, summit;* of streams, *source, fountain-head;* of plants, *tops, heads;* of civil rights, *citizenship;* of writings, *chapter, passage, point;* of things in general, *chief thing, principal thing.*

Carbō, -ōnis, m., *Carbō*, name of a plebeian family of the Papirian gens; in this book, = *C. Papīrius Carbō Arvīna*, tribune B.C. 90 or 89. He joined with his colleague M. Plautius Silvanus in proposing a law on citizenship, which was afterwards known as the *Lēx Plautia Papīria.* ARCH. IV.

carcer, -eris, m., *prison, dungeon, place of confinement;* by metonymy, of a race-course, usually pl., **carcerēs, -um,** *starting-places, barriers.*

careō, -ēre, -uī, fut. part. **caritūrus,** 2, n., *be without, not have; do without, abstain from, keep from, hold aloof from; want, lack, be deprived of;* usually with abl.

Cāria, -ae, [Καρία], f., *Cāria,* a province in the southwestern part of Asia Minor, south of Lydia.

cāritās, -ātis, [cārus], f., *dearness, high price; love, affection.*

carmen, -inis, [for casmen, from root CAS, *sing,* found in ca(s)nō], n., *song, strain of music; poem, verse, hymn;* as oracular responses and incantations were in verse, *response* of an oracle, *prophecy, incantation, charm;* also *metrical inscription, inscription in verse.*

cārus, -a, -um, adj., *dear, precious, valued; esteemed, beloved; affectionate; costly.*

Cassius, -a, name of a prominent Roman gens. Four Cassiī are mentioned in this book:

(1) *L. Cassius Longīnus,* a competitor of Cicero for the consulship for 63 B. C.; afterwards prominent in the conspiracy of Catiline, in which he asked to be assigned the burning of Rome as his part. He also conducted negotiations with the Allobroges, but escaped arrest. His fate is unknown. CAT. III. IV. *et seq.*

(2) *C. Cassius Longīnus,* originator of the conspiracy against the life of Caesar; defeated by Antony in the first engagement at Philippi, B. C. 42, and killed by one of his freedmen at his own request. EP. XXXIII.

(3) *Q. Cassius Longīnus,* tribune of the people B. C. 49. He commenced public life as a quaestor of Pompey in Spain, but in the Civil War he held a command under Caesar in the same country. EP. XIX.

(4) *C. Cassius Longīnus Vārus,* consul B. C. 73, proconsul in Cisalpine Gaul the following year. IMP. P. XXIII.

castē [castus], adv., *without spot, purely, virtuously; piously, religiously.*

castrēnsis, -e, [castra], adj., *of camp, in camp;* of a military movement, *with a camp,* i. e. *open,* as opposed to treacherous or secret operations.

castrum, -ī, n., *fortress, castle.* Pl. **castra, -ōrum,** *camp, encampment.*

cāsus, -ūs, [cadō], m., lit. *a falling, fall; a happening, accident, event, occurrence; chance, emergency; destruction; mishap, misfortune, calamity.*

Catilīna, -ae, m., *L. Sergius Catilīna, Catiline,* originator of a dangerous conspiracy suppressed by Cicero, who pronounced against him the famous Catilinarian orations.

Catō, -ōnis, [catus, *shrewd*], m., *Cato,* name of a noted family of the Porcian gens. Three Catos are mentioned in this book:

(1) *M. Porcius Catō,* known as *Cato the Elder,* or *Cato the Censor;* born 234 B. C. at Tusculum, 14 miles southeast of Rome; died B. C. 149. He was eminent as a general, statesman, orator, and writer. He was considered by Romans of later times, as the ideal of Roman character. His treatise "On Farming" is extant; only fragments of his other writ-

ings are preserved. ARCH. VII., IX.

(2) *Porcius Catō*, a friend of Archias. It is uncertain what Cato this was; but probably it was *M. Porcius Catō*, father of Cato Uticensis. ARCH. III.

(3) *M. Porcius Catō Uticēnsis*, so named from Utica in Africa, the place of his death; born B. C. 95. In the midst of an active public life he was a consistent adherent of the stoic philosophy. Accepting a commission from Pompey in the war with Caesar, he proved a failure as an officer. Finding himself in straits he preferred suicide to surrender and fell on his sword, B. C. 46. ARCH. IX.

Catulus, **-ī**, m., name of a family of the Lutatian gens, of which two members are mentioned in this book:

(1) *Q. Lutătius Catulus*, consul with C. Marius 102 B. C., when the poet Archias came to Rome. ARCH. III.

(2) *Q. Lutătius Catulus*, son of the preceding, consul 78 B. C. He was prominent as a leader of the aristocratic party, and was a man of fine character. He opposed the Gabinian and Manilian laws, but supported Cicero warmly against the Catilinarian conspirators. He died B. C. 60. CAT. III. X., IMP. P. XVII., XX., ARCH. III.

causa, **-ae**, f., *cause, reason; pretext, excuse, motive; condition, case, situation; lawsuit, judicial process; side, faction.* **causā** with preceding gen., *for the sake of, on account of.*

cautiō, **-ōnis**, **[caveō]**, f., *watchfulness, precaution; safety, security.*

caveō, **cavēre**, **cāvī**, **cautum**, 2, n. and a., *be on one's guard, beware of; take precautions against, guard against, take heed;* as a legal term, *provide, order, decree;* with dat. of person, *protect, take care of.*

cēdō, **cēdere**, **cessī**, **cessum**, 3, n. and a., *go away, retire, retreat; yield, give place to; submit, comply; be inferior to; conform to, concede.*

celeber, **-ĕbris**, **-ĕbre**, adj., *frequented, crowded, thronged with;* hence *honored* by the presence of many, *renowned, famous, celebrated, distinguished.*

celebritās, **-ātis**, **[celeber]**, f., *crowd, throng, multitude; publicity, fame, renown, celebrity.*

celebrō, **-āre**, **-āvī**, **-ātum**, **[celeber]**, 1, a., *crowd, fill, throng, frequent; practice, engage in, repeat; celebrate, solemnize; praise; honor.*

celeritās, **-ātis**, **[celer]**, f., *swiftness, speed, quickness.*

celeriter, comp. **celerius**, sup. **celerrimē**, **[celer]**, adv., *swiftly, quickly, speedily; in haste, immediately.*

cēna, **-ae**, f., *dinner*, the principal meal of the Romans, in early times taken at noon, afterwards later in the day.

cēnō, **-āre**, **-āvī**, **-ātum**, **[cēna]**, 1, n. and a., *dine, eat dinner.*

cēnseō, **cēnsēre**, **cēnsuī**, **cēnsum**, 2, a., *assess, rate, estimate; be of the opinion, propose, vote, urge; suppose, imagine, think, believe; decide, determine.*

cēnsor, **-ōris**, **[cēnseō]**, m., *censor*, title of a Roman magistrate. At Rome there were two censors, who had charge of the registration lists, the valuation and assessment of property, the farming of certain revenues and the letting of contracts for public works. They were chosen every five years, and served eighteen months.

cēnsus, -ūs, [cēnseō], m., *registration* of citizens and of property, *enrolment, appraisement, census;* by metonymy, *register of the census, registration list.*

centuria, -ae, [centum], f., *division of one hundred, century,* a division recognized in the civil as well as in the military organization of the Romans. The assembly of the people by centuries was called comitia centuriāta.

centuriātus, -ūs, [centuriō], m., *office of centurion, centurionship.*

centuriō, -āre, -āvī, -ātum, [centuria], 1, a., *divide into centuries, organize in companies, organize;* used of the organization of infantry.

centuriō, -ōnis, [centuria], m., *commander of a century, centurion, captain,* an officer ranking next to the legionary tribune.

Cēpārius, -ī, m., *M. Cēpārius,* one of the Catilinarian conspirators, from Tarracina. He had just left Rome in order to stir up an insurrection among the shepherds of Apulia when he was arrested and placed in custody. He was executed with the other conspirators, B.C. 63. CAT. III. VI.

cernō, **cernere**, **crēvī**, **crētum**, 3, a., *separate* in observation, *distinguish, discern, make out; perceive, see, behold; comprehend, understand;* of judicial or legislative acts, *decide, decree, resolve.*

certāmen, -inis, [certō], n., *contest* to decide a matter, *conflict, struggle, battle, combat, strife; dispute, dissension; match, trial* of strength or skill; *rivalry, ambition* to excel, *competition.*

certē, comp. **certius**, [**certus**], adv., *surely, certainly, really; at least, yet surely, yet certainly.*

certō [**certus**], adv., *with certainty, certainly, surely, really, in fact, positively.*

certō, -āre, -āvī, -ātum, [certus], 1, n., *vie with,* either as an enemy or as a friend; *fight, contend, struggle, combat; strive; rival, compete, emulate.*

certus, -a, -um, [old part. of **cernō**], adj., *certain, fixed, decided, settled; definite, special, particular; confident, trustworthy, reliable, sure; unerring, conclusive.* **illum certiōrem facere**, *to inform him.* **certior esse**, *to be informed.*

cervīx, -īcis, f., *neck, throat.*

Cestius, -ī, m., *Cestius,* a friend of Cicero. Nothing further is known about him. EP. XVI.

cēterus, -a, -um, nom. sing. m. not in use, adj., *other, the other, rest, remainder;* pl., *the rest, all other, the other.* As subst., pl., m., **cēterī**, **-ōrum**, *the others, all the rest, every one else;* n., **cētera**, **-ōrum**, *the rest, all else, everything else.*

Cethēgus, -ī, m., name of a patrician family of the Cornelian gens; in this book *C. Cornēlius Cethēgus,* one of the boldest and most dangerous of the Catilinarian conspirators. He joined the conspiracy on account of debts contracted in profligate living, and was assigned the task of murdering the principal senators. He was arrested, convicted on the evidence of weapons found at his house and of his letter to the Allobroges, and condemned along with the other conspirators.

Chīlō, -ōnis, [Χίλων], m., see **Annius**.

Chīus, -**a**, -**um**, [Χῖος], adj., *Chian, of Chios*, an island off the west coast of Asia Minor. As subst., **Chiī**, -**ōrum**, m., pl., *the people of Chios, the Chians.* ARCH. VIII.

cibus, -**ī**, m., *food, victuals, nutriment; sustenance.*

Cicerō, -**ōnis**, [**cicer**, *chickpea*], m., name of a family in the Tullian gens. Three Ciceros are mentioned in this book:

(1) *M. Tullius Cicerō*, the orator and writer. See Introduction.

(2) *Q. Tullius Cicerō*, brother of the orator; born about 102 B. C. He served with distinction under Caesar in Gaul, and held several offices. In the Civil War he went over to the side of Pompey, but after the battle of Pharsalia he quarreled with his brother and came to terms with Caesar. A reconciliation was soon effected, however, and Quintus was put to death in the proscription of the triumvirs, 43 B. C. EP. XIII.

(3) *M. Tullius Cicerō*, son of the orator and Terentia; born B. C. 65. He was not a strong character, but had an eventful life, being finally admitted by Octavianus as a colleague in the consulship, B. C. 30. EP. VIII., IX.

Cilicia, -**ae**, [Κιλικία], f., *Cilicia*, a Roman province in the southern part of Asia Minor.

Cimber, -**brī**, m., see **Gabinius**.

Cimbrī, -**ōrum**, [= Κίμβροι], m., pl., *Cimbrī, Cimbrians*, a barbaric people, apparently of Germanic origin, which passed over the Alps and invaded Cisalpine Gaul B. C. 102. They were finally defeated near Vercellae (west of Milan) by Gaius Marius, 101 B. C.

Cimbricus, -**a**, -**um**, [**Cimbrī**], adj., *of the Cimbri, Cimbrian.*

Cīncius, -**ī**, m., *L. Cīncius*, a steward of Cicero's friend Atticus. EP. I.

cingō, -**ere**, **cīnxī**, **cīnctum**, 3, a., *surround, enclose; gird, wreathe, gird on;* of places, *surround, encircle, invest, beset, besiege.*

cinis, -**eris**, [cf. κόνις, *dust, ashes*] m., *ashes, embers;* of the dead, *ashes*, the remains left after cremation.

Cinna, -**ae**, m., in this book *L. Cornēlius Cinna*, an unprincipled demagogue who became a leader of the popular party during Sulla's absence in the east, B. C. 87–84, and joined with Marius in the massacre of the aristocracy. He was slain in a mutiny of the forces which he had collected in order to meet Sulla, B. C. 84.

circiter [**circus**], adv., and prep. with acc., *about, not far from, near.*

circum [acc. of **circus**, *circle*], adv. and prep.:

(1) As adv., *about, around, round about.*

(2) As prep., with acc., *around, about, all around; among, through; in the neighborhood of, near, near by.*

circumclūdō, -**clūdere**, -**clūsī**, -**clūsum**, [**circum** + **claudō**], 3, a., *shut in, enclose; hem in, surround.*

circumdō, -**dare**, -**dedī**, -**datum**, [**circum** + **dō**], 1, a., *put around, place about; surround, encircle, besiege.*

circumscrībō, -**scrībere**, -**scrīpsī**, -**scrīptum**, [**circum** + **scrībō**], 3, a., *encircle, limit, bound, circumscribe; cheat; cancel, set aside.*

circumscrīptor, -**ōris**, [**circumscrībō**], m., *defrauder, cheat.*

circumsedeō, -sedēre, -sēdī, -sessum, [circum + sedeō], 2, a., *sit around; surround, besiege, beset.*

circumspiciō, -spicere, -spexī, -spectum, [circum + speciō], 3, n. and a., *look about; survey, observe; be cautious, exercise caution; ponder, consider.*

circumstō, -stāre, -stetī, ——, [circum + stō], 1, n. and a., *stand around; surround; be at hand, threaten;* as a military term, *surround, besiege, beset.*

cito, comp. **citius**, sup. **citissimē**, [citus], adv., *quickly, speedily, soon.*

cīvīlis, -e, [cīvis], adj., *of a citizen, of citizens, civil, civic; political, public.*

cīvis, -is, m. or f., *citizen, fellow-citizen.*

cīvitās, -ātis, [cīvis], f., *citizenship; community of citizens, state, commonwealth.*

clam, adv. and prep., *secretly, in secret.*

clāmō, -āre, -āvī, -ātum, 1, n. and a., *cry out, shout, exclaim; call upon, invoke; proclaim, declare.*

clāmor, -ōris, [clāmō], m., *loud cry, outcry, shout; din, uproar; acclamation, applause; war-shout; sound, noise.*

clārus, -a, -um, adj., *clear, bright, shining; distinct, manifest, plain; renowned, noble, illustrious, honored, famous.*

classis, -is, f., *fleet.*

Claudius, -a, name of a Roman gens with both patrician and plebeian branches. See **Mārcellus, Pulcher.**

claudō, claudere, clausī, clausum, 3, a., *shut, shut up, close; bring to a close, finish, end; shut in, invest, besiege.*

clēmēns, -entis, adj., *mild, calm; gentle, kind, forbearing.*

clēmenter [clēmēns], adv., *calmly, mildly; gently, kindly, with forbearance.*

clēmentia, -ae, [clēmēns], f., *mildness, forbearance, clemency.*

clientēla, -ae, [cliēns], f., *relation of client to patron, clientship;* pl. often = **clientēs**, *clients, retainers, dependants.*

Clōdius, a form of the name **Claudius**; in this book = *P. Clōdius Pulcher*, a bitter enemy of Cicero. He was killed in a skirmish between his followers and those of Milo near Bovillae, Jan. 20, B. C. 52. EP. III. See also **Philhetaerus.**

Cluātius, -ī, m., *Cluātius*, an architect employed by Cicero. EP. XXXVI., XXXVII.

Cn., see **Gnaeus.**

Cnidus or **Cnidos**, -ī, [Κνίδος], f., *Cnidus*, a city in Caria, in the extreme southwestern part of Asia Minor.

coāctus, see **cōgō.**

Coccēius, -a, name of a Roman gens. Cicero in his letters mentions a *Coccēius* about whom nothing is known. EP. XXXVI.

coepiō, -ere, coepī, coeptum, pres. not found in classical Latin, def., a. and n., *begin, commence.* Part. **coeptus, -a, -um,** *commenced, begun, undertaken.*

coërceō, -cēre, -cuī, -citum, [com- + arceō], 2, a., *confine* on all sides, *hold together, shut in, encompass; restrain, repress, hold, control, curb.*

coetus, -ūs, [coëō], m., *assembly, company; crowd, meeting.*

cōgitātē [cōgitātus, from cōgitō], adv., *with reflection, thoughtfully.*

cōgitātiō, -ōnis, [cōgitō], f., *reflection, meditation; thought, reasoning, imagination.*

cōgitō, -āre, -āvī, -ātum, [com- + agitō], 1, a., *consider thoroughly, think over, ponder, reflect upon; meditate, design, plan, purpose, plot.*

cognātiō, -ōnis, [cognātus], f., *kinship, relationship; connection, affinity.*

cognitiō, -ōnis, [cognōscō], f., *a becoming acquainted with, knowledge, acquaintance;* as a legal term, *investigation, inquiry.*

cognitor, -ōris, [cognōscō], m., *attorney, advocate; defender, protector, supporter.*

cognitus, -a, -um, [part. of cognōscō], adj., *known, acknowledged, approved.*

cognōmen, -inis, [cf. cognōscō], n., *family name, surname; name.*

cognōscō, -ere, cognōvī, cognitum, [com- + (g)nōscō], 3, a., *become acquainted with; learn, ascertain, know thoroughly; know; examine, inquire into, investigate; recognize, identify, acknowledge; appreciate.*

cōgō, cōgere, coēgī, coāctum, [com- + agō], 3, a., *drive together; collect, gather together, assemble; urge, oblige, constrain, compel, force.*

cohaereō, -ēre, cohaesī, cohaesum, [com- + haereō], 2, n., *cling together, be united; be closely connected with.*

cohibeō, -ēre, -uī, -itum, [com- + habeō], 2, a., *hold together, confine, contain; hold in check, restrain, repress, subdue.*

cohors, -hortis, f., *enclosure, yard; crowd, company, throng, multitude;* as a military term, *cohort, battalion,* the tenth part of a legion; also, *staff* of a general, *body-guard, retinue.* **cohors praetōria,** *general's body-guard.*

cohortor, -ārī, -ātus sum, [com- + hortor], 1, dep., *encourage, admonish, exhort, urge on, address.*

collēctiō, -ōnis, [collēctus, from colligō], f., *bringing together, collecting, gathering.*

collēga, -ae, [cf. colligō, *unite*], m., *associate in office, colleague.*

collēgium, -ī, [cf. collēga], n., *association in office, colleagueship; association, corporation, society, college.*

colligō, -ere, collēgī, collēctum, [com- + legō], 3, a., *gather, bring together, collect, assemble; acquire, incur; deduce, infer.*

collis, -is, m., *hill, height, elevation.*

collocō, -āre, -āvī, -ātum, [com- + locō], 1, a., *set right, place, set, put, arrange; set up, erect; locate, station;* of money, *invest, lay out.*

colloquium, -ī, [colloquor], n., *conversation, discourse, conference.*

colō, colere, coluī, cultum, 3, a. and n., *till, cultivate; stay at, abide in, dwell in, inhabit; care for, cherish, esteem, love, favor;* of the gods, and the services of religion, *honor, worship, revere, reverence;* of pursuits or virtues, *follow, seek, practice, devote one's self to, adhere to, cherish.*

colōnia, -ae, [colōnus], f., *colony, settlement.*

colōnus, -ī, [colō], m., *husbandman, tiller of the soil;* by metonymy, *colonist, settler.*

Colophōn, -ōnis, [Κολοφών], m., *Colophōn,* a city in the western part of Asia Minor, north of Ephesus.

Colophōnius, -a, -um, [Colophōn], adj., *of Colophon.* As subst., **Colophōniī**, -ōrum, m., pl., *the people of Colophon, the Colophonians.*

color, -ōris, m., *color, tint, hue; complexion; appearance, coloring*

com-, prep., old form of **cum**; found only in composition. See cum.

comes, -itis, [com-, eō], m. or f., *companion, associate, comrade, mate; intimate; attendant, retainer, dependant.*

cōmissātiō, -ōnis, [cōmissor, *revel*], f., *carousal, Bacchanalian revel, revelry.*

comitātus, -a, -um, [part. of comitor], adj., *attended, accompanied, escorted.*

comitātus, -ūs, [comitor], m., *escort, train, retinue; company, band, crowd.*

comitia, -ōrum, [pl. of comitium], n., pl., *assembly of the people, assembly, election* by the people in assembly. **comitia cōnsulāria**, *assembly for electing consuls, consular election.*

comitium, -ī, [com-, eō], n., *place of meeting;* at Rome, *the Comitium,* an open place north of the Forum, where assemblies were held. See Map, p. 76.

commeātus, -ūs, [commeō], m., *a passing to and fro; furlough; provisions, supplies.*

commemorābilis, -e, [commemorō], adj., *memorable, remarkable.*

commemorātiō, -ōnis, [commemorō], f., *a calling to mind, reminding; remembrance, reminder.*

commemorō, -āre, -āvī, -ātum, [com- + memorō], 1, a., *call to mind, keep in mind, remember; bring to mind, recall; relate, recount, mention.*

commendātiō, -ōnis, [commendō], f., *a commending, recommendation;* that which recommends, *excellence, worth.*

commendō, -āre, -āvī, -ātum, [com- + mandō], 1, a., *commit* for safe keeping, *intrust, confide; commend, recommend, ask favor for.*

commeō, -āre, -āvī, -ātum, [com- + meō], 1, n., *pass to and fro, go and come; make frequent visits.*

commisceō, -miscēre, -miscuī, -mixtum or -mistum, [com- + misceō], 2, a., *mingle together, mingle; unite, join.*

committō, committere, -mīsī, -missum, [com- + mittō], 3, a., *bring together, combine, put together, unite;* of military engagements, *set together, engage in, fight, carry on, wage; intrust, commit; expose; commit* a crime, *perpetrate, be guilty of, do, practice.*

commodē [commodus], adv., *properly, skilfully; conveniently, suitably, comfortably.*

commodō, -āre, -āvī, -ātum, [commodus], 1, a. and n., *supply, furnish, grant, lend.*

commodum, -ī, [commodus], n., *convenience, opportune moment; advantage, interest, gain; emolument.*

commoror, -ārī, -ātus sum, [com- + moror], 1, dep., *linger, stay, tarry, remain.*

commoveō, -movēre, -mōvī, -mōtum, [com- + moveō], 2, a., *stir, shake, move,* used especially of violent motion; *trouble, disturb, disquiet; affect, influence.*

commūnicō, -āre, -āvī, -ātum, [commūnis], 1, a., *divide with, share; join, add.*

commūnis, -e, [com-, mūnus], adj., *common, in common; general, public;* of manners, *affable, courteous.*

commūniter [commūnis], adv., *in common, generally, together.*

commūtātiō, -ōnis, [commūtō], f., *change, alteration.*

commūtō, -āre, -āvī, -ātum, [com- + mūtō], 1, a., *change throughout, change entirely; exchange, substitute, change.*

comparātiō, -ōnis, [comparō], f., *preparing, preparation.*

comparō, -āre, -āvī, -ātum, [com- + parō], 1, a., *make ready, provide, prepare; get together, get, collect, obtain.*

comparō, -āre, -āvī, -ātum, [compār, *equal to*], 1, a., *match, join; count as equal; compare.*

compellō, -ere, compulī, compulsum, [com- + pellō], 3, a., *drive together; drive, impel, force; incite, urge, constrain.*

comperiō, -īre, comperī, compertum, 4, a., *find out, learn, ascertain.*

competītor, -ōris, [competō], m., *competitor, rival, opponent.*

complector, -plectī, -plexus sum, [com- + plectō, *braid*], 3, dep., *embrace, clasp; encircle, enclose, seize; comprehend, understand; explain, describe, sum up.*

compleō, -ēre, -ēvī, -ētum, [com- + pleō, *fill*], 2, a., *fill up, fill; complete, fulfil, accomplish, finish; live through, pass.*

complexus, -ūs, [complector], m., *embracing, embrace.*

complūrēs, -a or -ia, gen. complūrium, [com- + plūrēs], adj., pl., *several, a number, many.*

compōnō, -ere, composuī, compositum, [com- + pōnō], 3, a., *put together, collect, unite; compare, contrast; compose, write; construct, build; set in order, arrange, prepare; lay at rest, bury.*

comprehendō, -hendere, -hendī, -hēnsum, [com- + prehendō], 3, a., *take hold of, seize, catch; lay hold of, arrest, capture; grasp, comprehend; recount, set forth.*

comprimō, -primere, -pressī, -pressum, [com- + premō], 3, a., *press together, compress; check, repress, restrain; subdue, suppress, keep under.*

comprobō, -āre, -āvī, -ātum, [com- + probō], 1, a., *approve, sanction, assent to; attest, establish, prove.*

cōnātus, -ūs, [cōnor], m., *attempt, endeavor, effort, undertaking.*

concēdō, -ere, concessī, concessum, [com- + cēdō], 3, n. and a., *withdraw, depart; yield, give place to, submit; grant, concede, allow; admit, acknowledge; give up, forgive, pardon.*

concelebrō, -āre, -āvī, -ātum, [com- + celebrō], 1, a., *attend in crowds, frequent; solemnize, celebrate.*

concertō, -āre, -āvī, -ātum, [com- + certō], 1, n., *contend with, strive with; dispute, debate with.*

concido, -cidere, -cidī, ——, [com- + cadō], 3, n., *fall down, collapse; fall dead, fall; decline, fail, be destroyed.*

conciliō, -āre, -āvī, -ātum, [concilium], 1, a., *obtain, procure, win, gain; win over, win the favor of, conciliate.*

concipiō, -cipere, -cēpī, -ceptum, [com- + capiō], 3, a., *take up, receive; imagine, conceive of; understand; harbor, entertain, plan.*

concitō, -āre, -āvī, -ātum, [freq. of conciō], 1, a., *stir up, arouse, excite; urge, move, instigate.*

concordia, -ae, [concors], f., *harmony, union, concord.* Personified, **Concordia, -ae**, f., *goddess of Union, Concord,* in whose honor several temples were erected at Rome.

concupīscō, -īscere, -īvī, -ītum, [com-, cupiō], 3, inch., *greatly desire, long for, eagerly desire, covet.*

concursō, -āre, ——, ——, [freq. of concurrō], 1, n. and a., *run to and fro, rush about, run about.*

concursus, -ūs, [concurrō], m., *running together; concourse, throng, assembly; assault, attack; meeting, collision.*

condemnō, -āre, -āvī, -ātum, [com- + damnō], 1, a., *sentence, find guilty, convict, condemn.*

condiciō, -ōnis, [condīcō], f., *agreement, condition, compact, terms; position, rank, lot, circumstances.*

condiscō, -discere, -didicī, ——, [com- + discō], 3, a., *learn carefully, learn well.*

conditus, -a, -um, see condō.

condō, condere, condidī, conditum, [com- + dō], 3, a., *put together, found, build; compose, write; lay aside, store up; preserve; lay* in the tomb, *bury; hide, conceal.*

cōnferō, -ferre, -tulī, collātum, [com- + ferō], irr., a., *bring together, collect, gather, join; match against, oppose; compare, contrast; consult, confer, consider; carry, bring; employ, devote, apply; bestow, lend, grant; refer, assign; put off, postpone.* sē cōnferre, *to betake himself, to turn, to go; to devote himself.*

cōnfertus, -a, -um, [part. of cōnferciō], adj., *crowded, dense; compact, close; crammed, filled, gorged.*

cōnfessiō, -ōnis, [cōnfiteor], f., *confession, acknowledgment.*

cōnfestim [com-, cf. festīnus], adv., *immediately, speedily, forthwith, suddenly.*

cōnficiō, -ficere, -fēcī, -fectum, [com- + faciō], 3, a., *accomplish, execute, complete; do, make, bring about, draw up; bring together, procure, provide, prepare; wear out, consume, subdue, overcome, exhaust; kill, destroy, despatch.*

cōnfīdō, -fīdere, -fīsus sum, [com- + fīdō], 3, semi-dep., n., *trust, rely on, confide, believe, be confident, be assured.*

cōnfīrmō, -āre, -āvī, -ātum, [com- + fīrmō], 1, a., *make firm, make strong, strengthen, reinforce; encourage, cheer; confirm, establish; assert, affirm, assure, prove.*

cōnfiteor, -fitērī, -fessus sum, [com- + fateor], 2, dep., *confess, acknowledge, admit; allow, grant, concede; disclose, show.*

cōnflagrō, -āre, -āvī, -ātum, [com- + flagrō], 1, n. and a., *burn, be on fire, be consumed, burn up; be destroyed* by fire.

cōnflīgō, -ere, cōnflīxī, cōnflīctum, [com- + flīgō], 3, a. and n., *dash together; be in conflict, contend, fight; be at war, be at variance.*

cōnflō, -āre, -āvī, -ātum, [com- + flō], 1, a., *blow up, kindle, inflame; get together, bring together, raise, compose; cause, produce, bring about.*

cōnfōrmātiō, -ōnis, [cōnfōrmō], f., *shaping, moulding, form, fashion; training, culture.*

cōnfōrmō, -āre, -āvī, -ātum, [com- + fōrmō], 1, a., *shape, mould, form, fashion; train, educate, cultivate.*

cōnfringō, -ere, cōnfrēgī, cōnfrāctum, [com- + frangō], 3, a., *break in pieces, break up, shatter; crush, destroy.*

congerō, -ere, congessī, congestum, [com- + gerō], 3, a., *bring together, collect, heap up, accumulate; build, construct.*

congredior, -gredī, -gressus sum, [com- + gradior], 3, dep., *come together, meet; meet in strife, contend, fight.*

congregō, -āre, -āvī, -ātum, [com-, grex], 1, a., lit. *gather into a flock; assemble, gather together, collect; associate, unite.*

congruō, -gruere, -gruī, ——, 3, n., *agree, coincide; harmonize, correspond, accord.*

coniciō, -icere, -iēcī, -iectum, [com- + iaciō], 3, a., *cast together, unite; drive, throw, cast, hurl, direct, aim; urge, force; place, put; conjecture, guess; forecast, foretell.*

coniectūra, -ae, [coniciō], f., *conjecture, inference, guess.*

coniugium, -ī, [coniungō], n., *marriage, wedlock.*

coniūnctiō, -ōnis, [coniungō], f., *union, agreement; intimacy, close friendship.*

coniūnctus, -a, -um, comp. **coniūnctior**, sup. **coniūnctissimus**, [part. of **coniungō**], adj., *united, allied, connected; intimate, accordant.*

coniungō, -ere, **coniūnxī**, **coniūnctum**, [com- + iungō], 3, a., *unite, connect, join; associate, combine in, wage in common.*

coniūnx, -ugis, [cf. **coniungō**], m. and f., *married person, consort, spouse,* whether *husband* or *wife.*

coniūrātī, -ōrum, [coniūrātus, from **coniūrō**], m., pl., *conspirators.*

coniūrātiō, -ōnis, [coniūrō], f., *association under oath, conspiracy, confederacy.*

coniūrō, -āre, -āvī, -ātum, [com- + iūrō, *swear*], 1, n. and a., *swear together; plot together, form a conspiracy.*

cōnīveō, -ēre, **cōnīvī** or **cōnixī**, ——, [com- + nīveō], 2, n., *shut the eyes; overlook, connive, wink at.*

cōnor, -ārī, -ātus sum, 1, dep., *undertake, endeavor, attempt, try; make an effort, seek, aim.*

conquiēscō, -iēscere, -iēvī, **conquiētum**, [com- + quiēscō], 3, n., *rest, repose; stop, cease; find rest, be at rest, enjoy peace.*

cōnsanguineus, -a, -um, [com- + sanguineus], adj., *related by blood, kindred.* As subst., **cōnsanguineus**, -ī, m., *kinsman, relative.*

cōnsceleratus, -a, -um, [cōnscelerō], adj., *stained with guilt, wicked, criminal, depraved, villanous.*

cōnscendō, -scendere, -scendī, -scēnsum, [com- + scandō], 3, a. and n., *ascend, climb, mount;* of a ship, *go on board, embark.*

cōnscientia, -ae, [cōnsciō], f., *knowledge shared by others, common knowledge;* of the individual, *feeling, sense, consciousness, knowledge; sense of right, conscience; sense of guilt.*

cōnscrīptus, -ī, [part. of **cōnscrībō**], m., *one enrolled;* used especially in addressing the Roman Senate in the designation **patrēs cōnscrīptī**, *fathers elect, chosen fathers,* for patrēs et cōnscrīptī, *fathers and elect.*

cōnsecrō, -āre, -āvī, -ātum, [com- + sacrō], 1, a., *offer as sacred, dedicate, consecrate; devote, deify, immortalize.*

cōnsenēscō, -nēscere, -nuī, ——, [com- + senēscō, *grow old*], 3, inch., *grow old together, become old, grow gray.*

cōnsēnsiō, -ōnis, [cōnsentiō], f., *agreeing together, agreement, unanimity.*

cōnsēnsus, -ūs, [cōnsentiō], m., *agreement, unanimity, concord.*

cōnsentiō, -īre, **cōnsēnsī**, **cōnsēnsum**, [com- + sentiō], 4, n., *agree together, agree, be in accord; determine in common, resolve together, decree; conspire, plot.*

cōnsequor, **-sequī**, **-secūtus sum**, [**com-** + **sequor**], 3, dep., *follow after, follow up, press upon, pursue; overtake, reach; arrive at, get, attain, secure; copy after, imitate, adopt; result, ensue.*

cōnservātor, **-ōris**, [**cōnservō**], m., *preserver, defender.*

cōnservō, **-āre**, **-āvī**, **-ātum**, [**com-** + **servō**], 1, a., *preserve, keep safe, keep, maintain, save; keep intact, observe, guard.*

cōnsessus, **-ūs**, [**cōnsīdō**], m., *assembly, convention.*

cōnsīderātē [**cōnsīderātus**, from **cōnsīderō**], adv., *considerately, thoughtfully.*

cōnsīderō, **-āre**, **-āvī**, **-ātum**, 1, a., *look at closely, examine; reflect upon, consider, contemplate.*

cōnsīdō, **-sīdere**, **-sēdī**, **-sessum**, [**com-** + **sīdō**], 3, n., *sit down, seat one's self, be seated, sit; settle, sink down.*

cōnsilium, **-ī**, [cf. **cōnsulō**], n., *body of counsellors, deliberative body, council; deliberation, consultation; plan, design, measure, purpose, determination, resolution; advice, counsel; understanding, judgment, prudence.*

cōnsistō, **-ere**, **cōnstitī**, ——, [**com-** + **sistō**, *place*], 3, n., *stand still, stop; stay, remain; stand, be firm; exist, stand forth; consist of, consist in, depend on.*

cōnsociō, **-āre**, **-āvī**, **-ātum**, [**com-** + **sociō**], 1, a., *associate, ally one's self, join, unite; agree upon.*

cōnsōlātiō, **-ōnis**, [**cōnsōlor**], f., *comforting, comfort, consolation.*

cōnsōlor, **-ārī**, **-ātus sum**, [**com-** + **sōlor**, *comfort*], 1, dep., *encourage, comfort, cheer, console.*

cōnspectus, **-ūs**, [**cōnspiciō**], m., *sight, look, view; presence.*

cōnspiciō, **-spicere**, **-spexī**, **cōnspectum**, [**com-** + **speciō**], 3, a. and n., *observe, see, catch sight of, perceive, gaze upon; face towards;* pass., *be conspicuous, be distinguished.*

cōnspīrātiō, **-ōnis**, [**cōnspīrō**], f., *unanimity, harmony, agreement; plot, conspiracy.*

cōnstanter [**cōnstāns**], adv., *with firmness, firmly, resolutely; with consistency, consistently, evenly.*

cōnstantia, **-ae**, [**cōnstāns**], f., *firmness, steadiness, steadfastness; consistency, harmony; constancy, self-possession.*

cōnstituō, **-ere**, **cōnstituī**, **cōnstitūtum**, [**com-** + **statuō**], 3, a., *put, place, set, set up; draw up, station, cause to halt; establish, constitute, prepare, construct, erect, found; designate, appoint; set in order, regulate, administer; arrange, decide, determine, decree, resolve.*

cōnstō, **-āre**, **cōnstitī**, **cōnstātum**, [**com-** + **stō**], 1, n., *be consistent, agree, be correct; be established, be settled, remain firm, stand firm; be certain, be known, be clear; consist of; be dependent, depend.* Impers., **cōnstat**, **cōnstāre**, *it is clear, it is agreed, it is proved.*

cōnstringō, **-ere**, **cōnstrinxī**, **cōnstrictum**, [**com-** + **stringō**], 3, a., *bind, fetter; curb, restrain, hold firmly.*

cōnsuētūdō, **-inis**, [**cōnsuētus**], f., *custom, habit, usage, practice; intimacy, companionship, close friendship.*

cōnsul, **-ulis**, [cf. **cōnsulō**], m., *consul,* title of the two chief magistrates of Rome, who were chosen annually. **cōnsul dēsīgnātus**, *consul elect,* one who has been elected consul, but has not yet entered upon the discharge of official duties. **prō**

cōnsule, pl. prō cōnsulibus, used as an indecl. noun, *deputy consul, proconsul.*

cōnsulāris, -e, [cōnsul], adj., *of a consul, consular; of consular rank, who has been consul.* As subst., **cōnsulāris**, -is, m., *ex-consul, man of consular rank.*

cōnsulātus, -ūs, [cōnsul], m., *office of consul, consulship, consulate.*

cōnsulō, -ere, cōnsuluī, cōnsultum, 3, n. and a., *deliberate, take counsel; decide, resolve;* with acc., *consult, refer to, ask advice of, counsel with;* with dat., *consult for, look out for the interests of, take thought for.*

cōnsultō [cōnsultum], adv., *on purpose, designedly, intentionally.*

cōnsultum, -ī, [cōnsultus, from cōnsulō], n., *deliberation; decree, resolution, decision.*

cōnsūmō, -ere, cōnsūmpsī, cōnsūmptum, [com- + sūmō], 3, a., *use up, devour; destroy, consume; waste, exhaust, weaken, waste away, wear away;* of time or divisions of time, *spend, pass, consume.*

contāminō, -āre, -āvī, -ātum, 1, a., *mingle, blend; pollute, stain, defile.*

contegō, -tegere, -tēxī, -tēctum, [com- + tegō], 3, a., *cover up, cover; bury; conceal, hide.*

contemnō, -ere, contempsī, contemptum, [com- + temnō], 3, a., *esteem lightly, despise, disdain, contemn; disparage, speak of with contempt; disregard, defy.*

contendō, -ere, contendī, contentum, [com- + tendō], 3, a. and n., *stretch tight, strain; aim, hurl; press, hasten; contend, vie, strive, fight; dispute; compare, contrast; maintain, assert, affirm, protest.*

contentiō, -ōnis, [contendō], f., *straining, strain, struggle, effort, exertion; strife, contention, contest; dispute, controversy; comparison, contrast.*

contentus, -a, -um, [contineō], adj., *satisfied, pleased, happy, contented, content.*

conticēscō, -ere, conticuī, ——, [cōm- + taceō], 3, inch., *become silent, be still, cease speaking; be hushed, cease, stop.*

continēns, -entis, [contineō], adj., *bordering, adjacent; connected, consecutive, continual;* of character, *self-restrained, of self-control, temperate.*

continentia, -ae, [continēns], f., *restraint, self-restraint, self-control; self-mastery, temperance.*

contineō, -ēre, continuī, contentum, [com- + teneō], 2, a. and n., *hold together, enclose, bound, comprise, contain; shut in, restrain, repress, hold, check, curb; include, comprehend, involve.*

contingō, -tingere, -tigī, -tāctum, [com- + tangō], 3, a. and n., *touch, take hold of; extend to, reach to; affect; reach, arrive at, come to; happen, turn out, come to pass, occur.*

continuus, -a, -um, [cf. contineō], adj., *continuous, unbroken, without interruption.*

cōntiō, -ōnis, [for conventiō, from conveniō], f., *gathering, assembly, convocation; address, discourse, harangue.*

cōntiōnātor, -ōris, [cōntiōnor, *harangue*], m., *haranguer, agitator, demagogue.*

contrā, adv. and prep.:

(1) As adv., *opposite, in front of; face to face, in opposition, on the other side; on the contrary; in answer, in reply.* **contrā atque, contrā ac,** *otherwise than,*

different from what, contrary to.

(2) As prep., with acc. only, *against, before, opposite to, facing, over against, contrary to; in reply to; in hostility to, to the disadvantage of, in spite of.* **quod contrā,** *whereas on the contrary, while on the contrary.*

contrahō, -ere, contrāxī, contrāctum, [com- + trahō], 3, a., *draw together, collect, assemble; draw in, contract, shorten, diminish, lessen; accomplish, bring about, execute;* of a debt, *contract.*

contrārius, -a, -um, [contrā], adj., *opposite, lying over against; contrary, opposed, conflicting.*

contrōversia, -ae, [contrōversus], f., *quarrel, dispute, controversy, contention.*

contumēlia, -ae, [com-, cf. **tumeō],** f., *reproach, insult, invective, abuse.*

convalēscō, -ere, convaluī, ——, [com- + valeō], 3, inch., *grow strong, gain strength; recover, regain health.*

conveniō, -īre, convēnī, conventum, [com- + veniō], 4, n. and a., *come together, meet together, meet, assemble; be agreed upon, be settled; be fit, be suitable to, be appropriate to.* Impers. **convenit, -īre, convēnit,** *it is agreed, it is settled, it is fit, it is suitable, it is appropriate, it is consistent.*

conventus, -ūs, [conveniō], m., *assembly, meeting, throng; corporation; court.*

convertō, -ere, convertī, conversum, [com- + vertō], 3, a. and n., *turn around, turn about, reverse, invert, throw back; turn, direct; change, alter, transform; undergo change, be changed.*

convīcium, -ī, [com-, cf. **vōx],** n., *outcry, cry, utterance; din, noise; wrangling, altercation, reproach, insult, abuse.*

convincō, -ere, convīcī, convictum, [com- + vincō], 3, a., *overcome, convict, refute; prove beyond question, show clearly.*

convīvium, -ī, [com- + vīvō], n., *banquet, feasting together, social meal, feast.*

convocō, -āre, -āvī, -ātum, [com- + vocō], 1, a., *call together, summon together, convoke, summon.*

cōpia, -ae, [co-opia, from **com- + ops],** f., *abundance, ample supply, plenty; multitude, number, throng; fulness, copiousness; ability, power, facility, fluency;* mostly in pl., *wealth, resources, riches, prosperity; forces, troops.*

cōpiōsus, -a, -um, [cōpia], adj., *well supplied, rich, abounding in; copious, eloquent.*

coquus, -ī, [coquō], m., *cook.*

cōram [com-, cf. **ōs],** adv. and prep., *before:*

(1) As adv., *before the eyes, face to face; present, in person.*

(2) As prep., with abl. only, *before, in the face of, in the presence of.*

Corcȳra, -ae, [Κέρκῡρα], f., *Corcȳra,* an island in the Adriatic Sea, off Epirus; now Corfu.

Corduba, -ae, [Κορδύβη], f., *Corduba,* a city on the Baetis river, in the southern part of Spain; now Cordova.

Corinthus, -ī, [Κόρινθος], f., *Corinth,* a city on the Isthmus of Corinth. The name survives in the village Corinto, which stands near the ancient site.

Cornēlius, -a, name of a Roman gens which included a number of prominent families, both patrician and plebeian. The *Cornēliī* mentioned in this book are described under their family names; see **Balbus, Cethēgus, Cinna, Dolābella, Lentulus, Scīpiō, Sulla.**

corpus, -oris, n., *body; living body, flesh; dead body, trunk, corpse; substance, reality; person, individual; frame, structure, system, mass.*

corrigō, -rigere, -rēxī, -rēctum, [**com-** + **regō**], 3, a., *straighten out, make straight; amend, correct, change* for the better; *improve, reform, make good.*

corrōborō, -āre, -āvī, -ātum, [**com-** + **rōborō,** from **rōbur**], 1, a., *strengthen, encourage; fortify, confirm.*

corrumpō, -ere, corrūpī, corruptum, [**com-** + **rumpō**], 3, a., *destroy, spoil, ruin, waste; bribe, corrupt, buy over; falsify, pervert, tamper with.*

corruō, -ere, corruī, ——, [**com-** + **ruō**], 3, n. and a., *fall together, fall down, sink down.*

corruptēla, -ae, [**corruptus**], f., *seduction, corruption.*

corruptor, -ōris, [**corruptus**], m., *seducer, corruptor, briber.*

corruptus, -a, -um, [part. of **corrumpō**], adj., *spoiled; bad, profligate, corrupt.* As subst., **quis corruptus,** *what reprobate, what profligate.*

cotīdiānus, -a, -um, [**cotīdiē**], adj., *of every day, of each day, daily.*

cotīdiē [**quot** + **diēs**], adv., *every day, daily.*

Cotta, -ae, m., in this book *L. Aurēlius Cotta,* praetor B. C. 70 and consul, with L. Manlius Torquatus, B. C. 65. After the Catilinarian conspiracy was crushed Cotta proposed a public thanksgiving for Cicero, whose firm friend he remained in the troubled times that followed. CAT. III. VIII.

crās, adv., *to-morrow.*

Crassus, -ī, m., name of a prominent family in the Licinian gens. Three of the family are mentioned in this book:

(1) *L. Licinius Crassus,* born 140 B. C., consul B. C. 95. He was the most distinguished orator of his time. He died B. C. 91. ARCH. III.

(2) *P. Licinius Crassus Dīves,* who was consul B. C. 97. Afterwards for several years he commanded in Spain, and was awarded a triumph in B. C. 93. He was censor with L. Julius Caesar in 89 B. C. Being a partisan of the aristocracy, he killed himself to escape proscription when Cinna and Marius gained possession of Rome. ARCH. V.

(3) *M. Licinius Crassus Dīves,* born about 105 B. C. He had an inordinate desire for wealth, and amassed a large fortune. He conquered Spartacus in the Servile War, B. C. 71, and was consul with Pompey in the following year. He united with Pompey and Caesar in the first triumvirate. He set out upon an expedition against the Parthians, in which he was defeated with great loss and slain, B. C. 53. Cf. N. to p. 180, l. 13.

crēber, -bra, -brum, adj., *thick, close, frequent, numerous; crowded, abundant, abounding.*

crēbrō, comp. **crēbrius,** sup. **crēberrimē,** [**crēber**], adv., *in quick succession, frequently, repeatedly, often.*

crēdibilis, -e, [**crēdō**], adj., *to be believed, worthy of belief, likely, credible.*

crēdō, crēdere, crēdidī, crēditum, 3, a. and n., *lend; intrust, commit, consign; trust, confide in,* *believe in; believe, think, suppose, imagine*; often used parenthetically, = *I dare say, likely enough, perhaps, of course.* **mihi crēde,** *believe me, upon my word.*

crēscō, crēscere, crēvī, crētum, 3, inch., *spring up; grow, increase, swell, enlarge; grow strong, be strengthened.*

Crētēnsis, -e, [**Crēta**], adj., *of Crete, Cretan.* As subst., **Crētēnsēs, -ium,** m., pl., *the inhabitants of Crete, the Cretans.*

crīminor, -ārī, -ātus sum, [**crīmen**], 1, dep., *accuse of crime; charge with, denounce, charge.*

cruciātus, -ūs, [**cruciō,** *torture*], m., *torture, torment; anguish, agony.*

crūdēlis, -e, [**crūdus,** *unfeeling*], adj., *unfeeling, cruel, merciless, hard-hearted*; of things, *pitiless, harsh, bitter.*

crūdēlitās, -ātis, [**crūdēlis**], f., *harshness, cruelty, severity.*

crūdēliter, comp. **crūdēlius,** sup. **crūdēlissimē,** [**crūdēlis**], adv., *harshly, cruelly, with cruelty.*

cruentus, -a, -um, [cf. **cruor**], adj., *blood-stained, bloody, smeared with blood, gory; delighting in blood, bloodthirsty.*

cruor, -ōris, m., *blood, stream of blood, gore; bloodshed, murder.*

cubīle, -is, [cf. **cubō,** *lie down*], n., *couch, bed.*

cuicuimodī [for **cūiuscūius modī,** gen. of **quisquis** + **modus**], adv., *of whatever kind, of whatsoever sort.*

culīna, -ae, f., *kitchen.*

culpa, -ae, f., *fault, error, ground of reproach, blame; crime, offence, reproach.*

cultūra, -ae, [**colō**], f., *tillage, cultivation, care; training, education, culture; refinement, style; reverence, adoration.*

cum, prep. with ablative only, *with*; of association, *with, along with, in the company of, together with*; of comparison, *with, as over against, compared with*; of time, *at, at the time of, together with, at the same time with*; of manner and circumstance, *with, under, amid, to, at.* With the personal pronouns and with **quī cum** is enclitic; as, **mēcum, nōbīscum, quōcum.**

In composition the earlier form **com-** is used, which remains unchanged before **b, p, m,** but is changed to **col-** or **con-** before **l, cor-** or **con-** before **r, con-** before other consonants, and **co-** before vowels and **h.**

cum, conj., *when*; of definite time, *at the time when, when, while, as long as, after*; of indefinite time or repeated action, *whenever, as often as, at times when*; of relative time, descriptive or circumstantial, *when, while, after, on the occasion that, under the circumstances that, at the moment when*; of cause or concession, with subj., *since, inasmuch as, although, notwithstanding.* **tum — cum,** *then — when* or *while.* **cum — tum,** *both — and, not only — but also, while — especially.* **cum prīmum,** *as soon as.* **cum praesertim,** *especially since.* **cum quippe,** *since of course.*

Cūmānus, -a, -um, [**Cūmae**], adj., *Cumaean, of Cumae,* an ancient city on the coast of Campania, west of Naples. As subst., **Cūmānum, -ī,** (properly sc. **praedium**), n., *estate near Cumae, Cumaean estate,* where Cicero had a villa. Ep. XII, XXIX, XXX.

cumulō, -āre, āvī, -ātum, [**cumulus**], 1, a., *heap up; pile up;*

increase, augment, accumulate; overload, overwhelm, crown.

cumulus, **-ī**, m., *heap, pile, mass; increase, accession, addition.*

cūnctus, **-a**, **-um**, [for co-iūnctus, **com-** + **iūnctus**], adj., *all together, all, whole, entire.*

cupiditās, **-ātis**, [**cupidus**], f., *desire, eagerness, passion; greed, covetousness, cupidity, lust.*

cupidus, **-a**, **-um**, [**cupiō**], adj., *eagerly desirous, desirous, eager; fond, loving; passionate, lustful; greedy, avaricious.*

cupiō, **cupere**, **cupīvī** or **-iī**, **cupītum**, 3, a., *long for, wish, desire; be well disposed, wish well, favor; be devoted to, be zealous for.*

cur., see **curūlis**.

cūr [older **quōr**, from early dat. **quoi** + **reī**], adv., *why? for what purpose? wherefore? for what reason?* rel., *why, wherefore.*

cūra, **-ae**, f., *care, attention, pains; pursuit, business, office;* arising from love, *love, affection;* arising from mental disturbances, *anxiety, solicitude, concern, trouble, sorrow, grief.*

cūria, **-ae**, f., *cūria, association,* one of the ten divisions into which each of the three primitive Roman tribes were divided; by metonymy, *Senate-house,* the place where the Roman Senate sat; *the Senate.* In Cicero's time there were at Rome two Senate-houses:

(1) *The Senate-house* proper, known as the Cūria Hostīlia, named from Tullus Hostilius, situated north of the Forum. See Map, p. 76. It was enlarged, destroyed by fire in 52 B. C., rebuilt by Faustus Sulla, son of the Dictator, and called Cūria Cornēlia; but Sulla's structure was soon afterwards torn down by Julius Caesar. Caesar commenced a new Senate-house, which was finished in magnificent style after his death by Augustus, and called Cūria Iūlia.

(2) *The Senate-house of Pompey, Pompey's Senate-house,* Cūria Pompēia, in the same edifice with the Portico erected by Pompey in the Campus Martius. Here Cæsar was assassinated; after that the Senate house of Pompey was closed.

Cūriō, **-ōnis**, [**cūriō**, *priest of a cūria*], m., name of a family in the Scribonian gens. Two of the name are mentioned in this book:

(1) *C. Scrībōnius Cūriō,* who was consul B. C. 76, and celebrated a triumph over the Dardanians in 71 B. C. He was an intimate friend of Cicero, whom he supported in the defence of the Manilian bill and in the execution of the Catilinarian conspirators. He died B. C. 53. EP. XIV.

(2) *C. Scrībōnius Cūriō,* son of the former, a man of fine talents, but of profligate habits, which Cicero tried in vain to reform. He rendered important services to Caesar in the Civil War, and was killed in Africa B. C. 49. EP. XIV.

cūriōsus, **-a**, **-um**, [**cūra**], adj., *painstaking, careful, thoughtful, attentive; inquisitive, curious.*

cūrō, **-āre**, **-āvī**, **-ātum**, [**cūra**], 1, a., *care for, look after, see to, attend to; preside over, govern; pay, settle.*

curriculum, **-ī**, [dim. of **currus**], n., *small chariot; race, race-course; course, career.*

currō, **currere**, **cucurrī**, **cursum**, 3, n., *run, hasten;* of motion over water or through the air, *move quickly, sail, fly* ; of water, *run, flow, roll, spread.*

currus, -ūs, [cf. **currō**], m., *chariot, car, wagon ; triumphal chariot.*

cursus, -ūs, [**currō**], m., *a running ; course, passage, way, march, journey, voyage ; speed, race ; career, progress.*

curūlis, -e, abbreviated **cur.**, [**currus**], adj., *of a chariot ; curule.* **sella curūlis**, *curule chair, official chair*, in which consuls, praetors, and curule aediles were permitted to sit when discharging their official duties. See p. 254.

Custidius, -ī, m., *L. Custidius*, a fellow-townsman and friend of Cicero's. Ep. xvii.

cūstōdia, -ae, [**cūstōs**], f., *a guarding ; guard, watch, care, protection ; confinement, custody ; guard-house, prison.*

cūstōdiō, -īre, -īvī, -ītum, [**cūstōs**], 4, a., *guard, watch, protect, keep ; hold back, restrain ; keep in custody, hold captive.*

cūstōs, -ōdis, m. and f., *guard, watch, keeper, overseer ; guardian, protector.*

Cyrēa, ōrum, [= Κύρεια], adj., n., pl., *of Cyrus, in the province of Cyrus*, designed by the architect Cyrus, employed by Cicero. Ep. xii.

Cyzicēnī, -ōrum, m., pl., *inhabitants of Cyzicus.*

Cyzicus, or **Cyzicum**, -ī, [Κύζικος], n., *Cyzicus, Cyzicum*, an important city of Asia Minor on the south shore of the Propontis.

D.

D, as a sign of number, = 500.

D., see **Decimus**.

damnātiō, -ōnis, [**damnō**], f., *conviction, condemnation.*

damnō, -āre, -āvī, -ātum, [**damnum**], 1, a., lit. *inflict loss upon ; find guilty, convict, condemn.*

dē, prep. with abl., denoting separation, *from ;* of place and motion, *from, away from, out of ;* of time, *away from, after, during, in the course of, in ;* of source, *of, from, out of, proceeding from, sprung from ;* of the whole, partitively, *of, out of, from among ;* of material, *made of, out of, from ;* of cause, *on account of, for, through, by ;* of relation, *concerning, about, in respect to, of, in the matter of.* **dē imprōvīsō**, *unexpectedly.* **dē industriā**, *intentionally.*

dea, -ae, [**deus**], f., *goddess.*

dēbeō, **dēbēre**, **dēbuī**, **dēbitum**, [for **dēhibeō**, **dē** + **habeō**], 2, a., *withhold, keep back ; owe, be indebted, be in debt to, be under obligations ; ought, must, should.*

dēbilis, -e, [**dē** + **habilis**, *easily handled*], adj., *weak, frail, feeble ; crippled, disabled, helpless.*

dēbilitō, -āre, -āvī, -ātum, [**dēbilis**], 1, a., *make weak, weaken, cripple, disable ; dishearten, crush.*

dēbitus, -a, -um, [part. of **dēbeō**], adj., *due, appropriate, fitting, becoming, meet ; doomed, fated.*

dēcēdō, -ere, **dēcessī**, **dēcessum**, [**dē** + **cēdō**], 3, n., *go away, withdraw, depart ; retreat, retire, leave.*

December, -bris, -bre, [**decem**], adj., *of the tenth ; of the tenth month, of December*, so named because the tenth month counting from March, which was reckoned by the early Romans the beginning of the year.

decet, **decēre**, **decuit**, 2, impers., n. and a., *be becoming, be meet, be fitting, be proper ;* with acc. as obj., *befit, be seemly for, be becoming to, be appropriate to.*

dēcernō, **-ere**, **dēcrēvī**, **dēcrētum**, [**dē** + **cernō**], 3, a. and n., *decide, determine, resolve, vote, decree; decide by combat, fight, contend.*

dēcerpō, **-ere**, **dēcerpsī**, **dēcerptum**, [**dē** + **carpō**], 3, a., *pluck off, break off, pluck, gather; take away, tear away.*

dēcidō, **-ere**, **dēcidī**, ——, [**dē** + **cadō**], 3, n., *fall down, fall away; fall, perish.*

decimus, **-a**, **-um**, [**decem**], adj., *tenth.*

Decimus, **-ī**, abbreviated **D.**, [**decimus**], m., *Decimus,* a common Roman forename.

dēclārō, **-āre**, **-āvī**, **-ātum**, [**dē** + **clārō**], 1, a., *make clear, disclose; show, prove; declare, proclaim, announce.*

dēclīnātiō, **-ōnis**, [**dēclīnō**], f., *a bending aside, movement to one side; slight deviation, avoidance.*

dēcoctor, **-ōris**, [**dēcoquō**, *boil away, ruin one's self*], m., *spendthrift, prodigal, bankrupt.*

decorō, **-āre**, **-āvī**, **-ātum**, [**decus**], 1, a., *adorn, embellish, beautify; honor, distinguish.*

dēcrētum, **-ī**, [**dēcernō**], n., *decree, decision, resolution, vote.*

decuma, **-ae**, [i. e. **decima pars**], f., *tenth part; tithe, land-tax.*

decumānus, **-a**, **-um**, [**decimus**], adj., *of the tenth part, of tithes.* As subst., **decumānus**, **-ī**, m., *tithe-gatherer, tax-farmer, tax-collector.*

dēdecus, **-oris**, [**dē** + **decus**], n., *disgrace, shame, infamy, dishonor; cause of shame, reproach.*

dēdicō, **-āre**, **-āvī**, **-ātum**, [**dē** + **dicō**], 1, a., *dedicate, consecrate, set apart* as sacred.

dēditiō, **-ōnis**, [**dēdō**], f., *giving up, surrendering; surrender, capitulation.*

dēditus, **-a**, **-um**, [part. of **dēdō**], adj., *given up, devoted to, addicted to.*

dēdō, **-dere**, **-didī**, **-ditum**, [**dē** + **dō**], 3, a., *give up, surrender, yield, deliver up; devote, consign, submit, abandon.*

dēdūcō, **-dūcere**, **-dūxī**, **-ductum**, [**dē** + **dūcō**], 3, a., *lead down, bring down, draw out; draw off, take off, remove; bring out, withdraw, lead off* or *away; derive, deduce;* of colonists, *lead forth, conduct;* of a ship, *draw out* from the dock, *draw down, launch.*

dēfatīgō, **-āre**, **-āvī**, **-ātum**, [**dē** + **fatīgō**, *tire*], 1, a., *tire out, exhaust; wear out, make weary.*

dēfendō, **-ere**, **dēfendī**, **dēfēnsum**, [**dē** + obsolete **fendō**], 3, a., *ward off, repel, keep off; defend, guard, protect; maintain* in defence, *allege.*

dēfēnsiō, **-ōnis**, [**dēfendō**], f., *defence.*

dēferō, **-ferre**, **-tulī**, **-lātum**, [**dē** + **ferō**], irr., a., *bear away, bring down; carry off, bear, carry; grant, allot, give; take, transfer, deliver; report, give account of, announce, state; bring before, lay before, refer to; enter for registration, register, return.*

dēfessus, **-a**, **-um**, [part. of **dēfetīscor**, *become weary*], adj., *tired out, weary, worn out, exhausted.*

dēficiō, **-ficere**, **-fēcī**, **-fectum**, [**dē** + **faciō**], 3, n. and a., *withdraw, fall off, revolt; fail, cease, be wanting, run out; faint, sink, become exhausted; forsake, abandon, desert, leave.*

dēfīgō, **-fīgere**, **-fīxī**, **-fīxum**, [**dē** + **fīgō**], 3, a., *fasten, fix; drive, thrust; set up, plant; direct, turn.*

dēfīniō, -īre, -īvī, -ītum, [dē + fīniō], 4, a., *bound, limit; fix, determine, establish.*

dēflagrō, -āre, -āvī, -ātum, [dē + flagrō], 1, n. and a., *burn down, be destroyed by fire, be consumed by fire.*

dēiciō, -icere, -iēcī, -iectum, [dē + iaciō], 3, a., *throw down, hurl down; strike down, kill, slay, destroy; turn aside, avert; deprive of, rob;* of the eyes or face, *cast down.*

deinceps [dein, for deinde, + capiō], adv., *one after another, in order; next, next in order.*

deinde [dē + inde], adv., *from that time, thereafter, thence; afterwards, then, next; besides, still.*

dēlābor, -lābī, -lāpsus sum, [dē + lābor], 3, dep., *glide down, slip down, descend; come down, sink, fall.*

dēlectātiō, -ōnis, [dēlectō], f., *delight, pleasure, gratification, enjoyment.*

dēlectō, -āre, -āvī, -ātum, [freq., dē, root LAC in obsolete laciō, *entice*], 1, a., *delight, please, charm, entertain.*

dēlēctus, -a, -um, [part. of dēligō], adj., *chosen, elect, choice, select, picked.*

dēleō, -ēre, -ēvī, -ētum, 2, a., *erase, efface, obliterate; blot out, destroy utterly, overthrow, extinguish.*

dēlīberātiō, -ōnis, [dēlīberō], f., *deliberation, consideration; ground of deliberation.*

dēlīberō, -āre, -āvī, -ātum, [dē + lībrō, from lībra, *balance*], 1, a. and n., *weigh well, consider, deliberate, take counsel; consult; resolve.*

dēlicātē [dēlicātus], adv., *delicately, luxuriously.*

dēlicātus, -a, -um, [cf. dēliciae], adj., *delightful, charming; given to pleasure, voluptuous, effeminate.*

dēliciae, -ārum, [dēlectō], f., *pleasure, delight, charm; luxury.*

dēlīctum, -ī, [dēlinquō], n., *fault, misdoing, offence; crime, wrong.*

dēligō, -ligere, -lēgī, -lēctum, [dē + legō], 3, a., *choose, select, pick out, designate.*

Dēlos, -ī, [Δῆλος], f., *Dēlos,* one of the Cyclades; see Map.

dēlūbrum, ī, [dē, luō, *cleanse*], n., lit. *place of cleansing* or *expiation; shrine, sanctuary, temple.*

dēmēns, -entis, [dē + mēns], adj., *out of one's mind, distracted, mad, insane; foolish, rash, blind.*

dēmenter [dēmēns], adv., *recklessly, foolishly, blindly.*

dēmentia, -ae, [dēmēns], f., *insanity, madness, folly.*

dēmigrō, -āre, -āvi, -ātum, [dē + migrō], 1, n., *migrate, remove; go off, go away, depart.*

deminuō, -uere, -uī, -ūtum, [dē + minuō], 3, a., *make smaller, diminish; take away, reduce, impair; curtail*

dēminūtiō, -ōnis, [dēminuō], f, *lessening, diminution, decrease, loss*

dēmōnstrō, -āre, -āvi, -ātum, [dē + mōnstrō], 1, a., *point out, show, indicate; prove, establish.*

dēmoveō, -ēre, dēmōvī, dēmōtum, [dē + moveō], 2, a, *move away, stir from, remove, drive forth from.*

dēmum [dē], adv., *at length, at last, then, just, only.* **tum dēmum,** *then at length, then indeed, not till then.*

dēnique, adv., *at last, at length, finally; besides, and thereafter; in a word, in short, briefly.* **nunc dēnique,** *now at length, only now, not till now.* **tum dēnique,** *then at last, not until then, then only.*

dēnotō, -āre, -āvī, -ātum, [dē + notō], 1, a., *mark out, point out, specify, designate.*

dēnsus, -a, -um, adj., *compact, dense, crowded; thick, close, full.*

dēnūntiō, -āre, -āvī, -ātum, [dē + nūntiō], 1, a., *announce, declare, proclaim; intimate, warn, threaten, denounce; order.*

dēpellō, -pellere, -pulī, -pulsum, [dē + pellō], 3, a., *drive out, drive away, expel; turn aside, ward off, avert, thwart; dissuade, drive, force.*

dēpendō, -ere, dēpendī, dēpēnsum, [dē + pendō], 3, a. and n., *pay, render.*

dēplōrō, -āre, -āvī, -ātum, [dē + plōrō], 1, n. and a., *weep bitterly, wail, lament; bewail, deplore; abandon, give up for lost.*

dēpōnō, -ere, dēposuī, dēpositum, [dē + pōnō], 3, a., *lay down, set down, set, place; lay aside, put off, put away; commit, intrust; give up, resign.*

dēportō, -āre, -āvī, -ātum, [dē + portō], 1, a., *carry down, take away, carry off;* of movement from the provinces to Rome, *bring home, bring back, bring away.*

dēposcō, -poscere, -poposcī, ——, [dē + poscō], 3, a., *demand, request earnestly, call for; request, claim.*

dēprāvō, -āre, -āvī, -ātum, [dē, prāvus], 1, a., *distort, pervert; corrupt, seduce, spoil, deprave.*

dēprecātor, -ōris, [dēprecor], m., *averter; advocate, intercessor.*

dēprecor, -ārī, -ātus sum, [dē + precor], 1, dep., *pray to avert, seek to avert by prayer, plead against; plead for, intercede for.*

dēprehendō, -hendere, -hendī, -hēnsum, [dē + prehendō], 3, a., *take away; seize upon, seize, catch, capture; overtake, surprise; discover, detect, find out; comprehend, understand.*

dēprimō, -ere, dēpressī, dēpressum, [dē + premō], 3, a., *press down; sink; overwhelm.*

dēprōmō, -prōmere, -prōmpsī, -prōmptum, [dē + prōmō], 3, a., *draw out, bring forth, fetch; derive, obtain.*

dērelinquō, -linquere, -līquī, -līctum, [dē + relinquō], 3, a., *forsake entirely, leave altogether, abandon.*

dēscīscō, -ere, dēscīvī, dēscītum, [dē + scīscō], 3, n., *withdraw, leave, desert; be untrue, be unfaithful.*

dēscrībō, -scrībere, -scrīpsī, -scrīptum, [dē + scrībō], 3, a., *copy off, transcribe, write off; draw, describe; define, fix, assign, designate.*

dēserō, -serere, -seruī, -sertum, [dē + serō, *join*], 3, a., *leave, forsake, desert, abandon; leave in the lurch; forfeit.*

dēsertus, -a, -um, [dēserō], adj., *deserted, solitary; lonely, waste.*

dēsīderium, -ī, [dēsīderō], n., *longing for, ardent desire, want, wish; regret, grief.*

dēsīderō, -āre, -āvī, -ātum, [cf. cōnsīderō], 1, a., *long for, desire ardently, want, wish for; call for, demand, desire, expect; miss, lack, feel the want of.*

dēsīgnātus, -a, -um, [part. of dēsīgnō], adj., *elect, chosen,* applied to public officers elected but not yet installed.

dēsīgnō, -āre, -āvī, -ātum, [dē + sīgnō], 1, a., *mark out, point out, designate; choose, elect.*

dēsinō, -sinere, dēsiī, dēsitum, [dē + sinō], 3, a. and n., *leave off, cease, quit, desist; come to an end, stop, close.*

dēsistō, -sistere, -stitī, -stitum, [dē + sistō], 3, n., *leave off, cease, desist from.*

dēspērātiō, -ōnis, [dēspērō], f., *losing of hope, hopelessness, despair.*

dēspērātus, -a, -um, [part. of dēspērō], adj., *beyond hope, desperate, abandoned.*

dēspērō, -āre, -āvī, -ātum, [dē + spērō], 1, a. and n., *lose all hope of, despair of; be hopeless, give up hope, give up.*

dēspiciō, -spicere, -spexī, -spectum, [dē + speciō], 3, n. and a., *look down upon; despise, disdain.*

dēstringō, -stringere, -strinxī, -strictum, [dē + stringō], 3, a., *strip off;* of a sword, *unsheathe, draw.*

dēsum, -esse, -fuī, [dē + sum], irr., n., *be away, be absent; be wanting, be lacking, be missing, fail; be neglectful, be not at hand, be at fault; be inadequate.*

dētestor, -ārī, -ātus sum, [dē + testor], 1, dep., *curse; call down upon, denounce; ward off, avert.*

dētrahō, -ere, dētrāxī, dētrāctum, [dē + trahō], 3, a., *draw off, pull down, pull off; take from, take away; remove, withdraw, deprive, rob; disparage.*

dētrīmentum, -ī, [dēterō, *rub away*], n., *loss, damage, hurt, harm.*

dēturbō, -āre, -āvī, -ātum, [dē + turbō], 1, a., *thrust down, strike down, expel; dispossess, deprive of.*

deus, -ī, m., *god, deity, divinity.* For declension see A. 40, *f;* G. 29, 5; H. 51, 6.

dēvinciō, -īre, dēvinxī, dēvinctum, [dē + vinciō], 4, a., *bind fast, fetter; attach closely, lay under obligation, oblige.*

dēvincō, -ere, dēvīcī, dēvictum, [dē + vincō], 3, a., *conquer completely, subdue; overpower, supersede.*

dēvius, -a, -um, [dē + via], adj., *off the road, out of the way; retired; inconsistent.*

dēvocō, -āre, -āvī, -ātum, [dē + vocō], 1, a., *call away, recall; call off, draw away from.*

dēvoveō, -vovēre, -vōvī, -vōtum, [dē + voveō], 2, a., *vow, offer, devote, consecrate.*

dextera, or **dextra**, -ae, [properly **dextera manus**], f., *right hand.*

dī-, see **dis-**.

diciō, -ōnis, nom. sing. and pl. not used, [dīcō], f., *dominion, rule, sway, authority, jurisdiction.*

dīcō, dīcere, dīxī, dictum, 3, a. and n., *say, tell, utter, speak; relate, declare, affirm, assert, maintain; name, call; appoint, fix upon, settle, fix.*

dictātor, -ōris, [dictō], m., *dictator,* a Roman magistrate of unlimited power, at first appointed only in great emergencies.

dictātūra, -ae, [dictātor], f., *dictatorship, office of dictator.*

dictitō, -āre, -āvī, -ātum, [intens. of dictō], 1, a., *say frequently, keep saying; declare, maintain, assert; allege, pretend.*

dictō, -āre, -āvī, -ātum, [freq. of dīcō], 1, a., *say for another, suggest;* of dictation to an amanuensis, *dictate.*

diēs, -ēī, m. and f., f. usually of a period of time, *day; daylight; set day, appointed time; time, space of time, interval, period.* **in diēs**, *day by day.*

differō, -ferre, distulī, dīlātum, [dis + ferō], irr., a. and n., *bear apart, disperse; put off, defer, postpone; be different from, differ, vary.*

difficilis, **-e**, comp. **difficilior**, sup. **difficillimus**, [**dis-** + **facilis**], adj., *not easy, hard, difficult; troublesome, perilous; hard to manage, obstinate.*

difficultās, **-ātis**, [**difficilis**], f., *trouble, difficulty, embarrassment, distress.*

diffīdō, **-fīdere**, **-fīsus sum**, [**dis-** + **fīdō**], 3, semi-dep., *distrust, lack confidence in, be distrustful of, despair of.*

diffluō, **-fluere**, **-fluxī**, ——, [**dis-** + **fluō**], 3, n., *flow* in different directions, *flow away; be dissolved, become lax, go to ruin.*

dīgnitās, **-ātis**, [**dīgnus**], f., *worth, desert, merit; distinction, eminence, reputation; greatness, majesty, dignity; self-respect, honor.*

dīgnus, **-a**, **-um**, adj., *worthy, deserving, suitable; fit, becoming, proper.*

dīiūdicō, **-āre**, **-āvī**, **-ātum**, [**dī-** + **iūdicō**], 1, a. and n., *distinguish, discern; decide, determine, settle, adjust.*

dīlābor, **-lābī**, **-lāpsus sum**, [**dī-** + **lābor**], 3, dep., *fall apart, fall to pieces; scatter, disperse, go to ruin, perish.*

dīlātiō, **-ōnis**, [**dī-** + **lātiō**, *bearing*], f., *putting off, postponement, adjournment, delay.*

dīlēctus, **-ūs**, [**dīligō**], m., *a choosing, selection, choice;* especially as a military term, *levy, recruiting, draft, conscription.*

dīligēns, **-entis**, comp. **dīligentior**, sup. **dīligentissimus**, [part. of **dīligō**], adj., *painstaking, careful, attentive, diligent; scrupulous, faithful, watchful.*

dīligenter, comp. **dīligentius**, sup. **dīligentissimē**, [**dīligēns**], adv., *with painstaking, carefully, diligently, attentively; faithfully.*

dīligentia, **-ae**, [**dīligēns**], f., *carefulness, attentiveness, watchfulness, diligence, care; faithfulness.*

dīligō, **-ere**, **dīlēxī**, **dīlēctum**, [**dī-** + **legō**], 3, a., *select out, single out; choose* above all others, *esteem, prize, love, cherish; be content with, appreciate.*

dīlūcēscō, **-ere**, **dīlūxī**, ——, [**dīlūceō**, *be clear*], 3, inch., *grow light, dawn.*

dīmicātiō, **-ōnis**, [**dīmicō**], f., *combat, fight, struggle; contest, rivalry.*

dīmicō, **-āre**, **-āvī**, **-ātum**, [**dī-** + **micō**, *flash*], 1, n., *contend, fight, struggle; be in conflict, be in peril, be in danger, run risk.*

dīmittō, **-ere**, **dīmīsī**, **dīmissum**, [**dī-** + **mittō**], 3, a., *send in different directions, send out, send away, send forth; dismiss, break up; let go, discharge, release; forsake, leave, renounce, abandon.*

dīnumerō, **-āre**, **-āvī**, **-ātum**, [**dī-** + **numerō**], 1, a., *count, number, reckon, compute.*

dīreptiō, **-ōnis**, [**dīripiō**], f., *a plundering, pillaging.*

dīreptor, **-ōris**, [**dīripiō**], m., *plunderer, pillager, marauder.*

dīripiō, **-ere**, **dīripuī**, **dīreptum**, [**dī-** + **rapiō**], 3, a., *tear asunder, tear in pieces; lay waste, pillage, plunder, rob, ravage.*

dis- or **dī-**, inseparable prep., used only as a prefix with other words, adding the force of *apart, asunder, in different directions; between, among; not, un-; utterly, entirely.* **dis-** is found before **c**, **p**, **q**, **s**, and **t**, but becomes **dif-** before **f**, and **dir-** before vowels. **dī-** is found before **d**, **g**, **l**, **m**, **n**, **r**, and **v**.

discēdō, **-ere**, **discessī**, **discessum**, [**dis-** + **cēdō**], 3, n., *go apart, withdraw; go away, de-*

part, leave, retire; come off, be left, remain, as the result of a battle or struggle.

discessus, -ūs, [**discēdō**], m., *a parting, separation; a going away, departure, removal.*

disciplīna, -ae, [for **discipulīna**, from **discipulus**], f., *training, instruction, education; learning, science, discipline; study, culture.*

discō, discere, didicī, ——, 3, a. and n., *learn, learn to know; become acquainted with; learn how.*

discrībō, -ere, **dīscrīpsī**, **dīscrīptum**, [**dis-** + **scrībō**], 3, a., *assign* by parts, *apportion, divide off.*

discrīmen, -inis, [**discernō**], n., *intervening space, interval; separation, division; distinction, difference; turning point, decisive moment, crisis; peril, danger, hazard.*

disiūnctus, -a, -um, [part. of **disiungō**], adj., *separated, parted, apart; remote, distant.*

dispergō, -ere, **dīspersī**, **dīspersum**, [**dis-** + **spargō**], 3, a., *scatter, strew here and there, disperse.*

dispersus, -a, -um, [part. of **dispergō**], adj., *scattered, dispersed.*

dispertiō, -īre, -īvī, -ītum, [**dis-** + **partiō**, from **pars**], 4, a., *distribute, divide, apportion.*

dīspiciō, -ere, **dīspexī**, **dīspectum**, [**dis-** + **speciō**], 3, n. and a., *discern, make out, perceive; reflect upon, think about, regard, consider.*

displiceō, -ēre, -uī, -itum, [**dis-** + **placeō**], 2, n., *displease.* **mihi displicet**, *I dislike.*

disputō, -āre, -āvī, -ātum, [**dis-** + **putō**], 1, a. and n., *investigate, discuss, treat; argue, maintain; dispute, controvert.*

dissēminō, -āre, -āvī, -ātum, [**dis-** + **sēminō**, *sow seed*], 1, a., *spread abroad, scatter abroad, disseminate.*

dissēnsiō, -ōnis, [**dissentiō**], f., *difference of opinion, disagreement; strife, discord.*

dissentiō, -īre, **dissēnsī**, **dissēnsum**, [**dis-** + **sentiō**], 4, n., *differ in opinion, disagree, dissent.*

dissideō, -ēre, **dissēdī**, **dissessum**, [**dis-** + **sedeō**], 2, n., *sit apart, be at variance, disagree; differ, be unlike.*

dissimilis, -e, [**dis-** + **similis**], adj., *unlike, different, dissimilar.*

dissimilitūdō, -inis, [**dissimilis**], f., *unlikeness, difference, dissimilarity.*

dissimulō, -āre, -āvī, -ātum, [**dis-** + **simulō**], 1, a. and n., *keep secret, conceal; dissemble, disguise.*

dissipō, -āre, -āvī, -ātum, [**dis-** + unused **supō**, *throw*], 1, a., *scatter, strew, disperse, spread abroad.*

dissolūtus, -a, -um, [part. of **dissolvō**], adj., *loose; negligent, remiss, careless; abandoned, dissolute.*

dissolvō, -ere, **dissolvī**, **dissolūtum**, [**dis-** + **solvō**], 3, a., *take apart, unloose, separate; dissolve, destroy; free from debt.*

distineō, -ēre, **distinuī**, **distentum**, [**dis-** + **teneō**], 2, a., *hold apart; keep back, detain, occupy, engage.*

distrahō, -ere, **distrāxī**, **distrāctum**, [**dis-** + **trahō**], 3, a., *pull asunder, pull to pieces; part, separate; divide, distract.*

distribuō, -ere, **distribuī**, **distribūtum**, [**dis-** + **tribuō**], 3, a., *apportion, distribute, divide off.*

districtus, -a, -um, [part. of **distringō**], adj., *hesitating, wavering; distracted, harassed.*

diū, comp. **diūtius**, sup. **diūtissimē**, [cf. **diēs**], adv., *for a long time, a long time, long, too long.* **quam diū**, *how long; as long as.* **satis diū**, *long enough.* **tam diū**, *so long.*

dīus, **-a**, **-um**, [for **dīvus**], adj., *divine, godlike.* As subst., **dīus**, **-ī**, m., *god, divinity.* **mē dīus Fidius**, see **Fidius**.

diūturnitās, **-ātis**, [**diūturnus**], f., *length of time, long duration, continuance.*

diūturnus, **-a**, **-um**, [**diū**], adj., *of long duration, long, lasting, protracted, prolonged.*

dīvello, **-ere**, **dīvellī**, **dīvulsum** or **-volsum**, [**dī-** + **vellō**], 3, a., *rend asunder, tear apart, tear in pieces; separate, remove, destroy.*

dīversus, **-a**, **-um**, [part. of **dīvertō**], adj., lit. *turned different ways; opposite, contrary, conflicting; separate, apart, remote, far distant; different, unlike, diverse.*

dīves, **-itis**, adj., *rich, opulent, wealthy; costly, sumptuous.*

Dīves, **-itis**, [**dīves**], m., a name in the Crassus family; see **Crassus**.

dīvidō, **-ere**, **dīvīsī**, **dīvīsum**, 3, a., *divide, part, separate; divide up, distribute, apportion, share; scatter, spread, extend; separate.*

dīvīnitus [**dīvīnus**], adv., *divinely, by inspiration; marvelously, admirably.*

dīvīnus, **-a**, **-um**, [**dīvus**], adj., *of a god, of a divinity, divine; godlike, superhuman; religious, sacred; inspired* by divine influence, *prophetic.*

dīvīsus, **-a**, **-um**, [part. of **dīvidō**], adj., *divided, separated, spread.*

dīvitiae, **-ārum**, [**dīves**], f., pl., *riches, wealth, treasures.*

dō, **dare**, **dedī**, **datum**, 1, a., *give, deliver; grant, present, confer, bestow, offer; afford, furnish; surrender, give up, yield, concede; resign, abandon; spare, forgive; place, put, cause, produce, inflict; excite, awaken; announce, report.* **operam dare**, *to give heed, to make an effort, to take pains, take care.*

doceō, **docēre**, **docuī**, **doctum**, 2, a., *teach, instruct, inform, train; explain, show, set forth, tell.*

doctrīna, **-ae**, [**doceō**], f., *teaching, instruction; learning, science.*

doctus, **-a**, **-um**, [part. of **doceō**], adj., *trained, learned, taught, experienced; skilled, cultured.*

Dōdōnaeus, **-a**, **-um**, [**Dōdōna**], adj., *of Dōdōna*, a city in Epirus, famous as the seat of a very ancient oracle.

Dolābella, **-ae**, m., in this book *P. Cornēlius Dolābella*, a profligate man, who nevertheless gained the hand of Cicero's daughter Tullia. They were married B. C. 50, and divorced four years later. Dolabella joined the party of Caesar, after whose death he secured the consulship by unfair means. He obtained Syria as a province, where he conducted himself with so great injustice and brutality that he was declared a public enemy. To escape capture he ordered a soldier to kill him, B. C. 43. Ep. XXII.

doleō, **dolēre**, **doluī**, ——, 2, n. and a., *suffer, be in pain; feel pain, grieve, lament; feel pained, feel hurt, be sorry; cause pain, hurt.*

dolor, **-ōris**, [**doleō**], m., *pain, suffering, pang; grief, sorrow, affliction, trouble, woe, anguish; anger, resentment.*

domesticus, -a, -um, [domus], adj., *of the house; domestic, private, personal;* as opposed to that which is foreign, *internal, intestine, civil.*

domicilium, -ī, [domus], n., *habitation, dwelling, abode; dwelling-place, home.*

domina, -ae, [dominus], f., *mistress, lady; she that rules, ruler.*

dominātiō, -ōnis, [dominor, from dominus], f., *mastery, rule, dominion, supremacy.*

dominus, -ī, m., *master, lord, possessor, owner; ruler, chief.*

domō, -āre, -uī, -itum, 1, a., *tame, break in, train; master, subdue, vanquish, conquer, reduce.*

domus, -ūs, loc. **domī**, f., *house, dwelling, abode, home; household, family.* **domī**, *at home.*

dōnātiō, -ōnis, [dōnō], f., *a giving, presenting, donation.*

dōnō, -āre, -āvī, -ātum, [dōnum], 1, a., *give, present, grant* as a gift; *forgive, pardon.*

dōnum, -ī, [dō], n., *gift, present;* of an offering to a deity, *offering, sacrifice.*

dormiō, -īre, -īvī, -ītum, 4, n., *sleep; be at ease.*

Drūsus, -ī, m., in this book *M. Līvius Drūsus*, a Roman prominent as a political leader at the beginning of the first century B.C. He at first sided with the aristocracy, but afterwards won over the people by carrying measures in their interest. Having finally organized a conspiracy, he was murdered in his own house, B.C. 91. ARCH. III.

dubitātiō, -ōnis, [dubitō], f., *doubt, hesitation; uncertainty, perplexity.*

dubitō, -āre, -āvī, -ātum, [dubius], 1, n. and a., *doubt, call in question, question; be uncertain, waver; deliberate, consider; hesitate, delay, be irresolute.*

dubius, -a, -um, adj., *doubtful, wavering, uncertain, undecided, dubious; precarious, critical.* **nōn dubium est quīn**, *there is no doubt that.* **sine dubiō**, *beyond doubt, undoubtedly, certainly.*

dūcō, dūcere, dūxī, ductum, 3, a., *lead, guide, conduct, direct; lead forth, draw forth; derive, deduce; take in, inhale; calculate, consider, esteem, reckon.* **in mātrimōnium dūcere**, *to marry.*

ductus, -ūs, [dūcō], m., *a leading, conducting;* as military term, *generalship, command.*

dūdum [diū + dum], adv., *a little while ago, but now; before, formerly.* See **iam**.

dulcēdō, -inis, [dulcis], f., *sweetness; agreeableness, pleasantness, charm.*

dulcis, -e, adj., *sweet; agreeable, pleasant, charming; dear.*

dum, conj., *while, whilst, all the time that, as long as, until, till, to the time when; provided that, if only.* **dum modo**, *if so be that, provided that, if only.*

dumtaxat [dum + taxō, *examine*], adv., lit. *while one examines; to this extent, so far; simply, merely, only.*

duo, -ae, -o, num. adj., *two, the two.*

duodecim, or **XII**, [duo + decem], num. adj., *twelve.*

duodecimus, -a, -um, [duodecim], num. adj., *twelfth.*

dūrus, -a, -um, adj., *hard; rough, rude, uncultivated; unfeeling, pitiless, stern, cruel, inexorable; hard to bear, burdensome.*

dux, ducis, [cf. dūcō], m. and f., *leader, guide; master, counsellor; commander, general; ruler, head, chief, leading man.*

Dyrrachium, -ī, [Δυρράχιον], n., *Dyrrachium*, formerly called *Epidamnus*, a city on the seacoast of Illyria, nearly opposite Brundisium. EP. IX.

E.

ē, see **ex**.

ēbriōsus, -a, -um, [ēbrius, *drunk*], adj., *given to drink, intoxicated, drunk, drunken.*

ecquī, **ecquae** or **ecqua**, **ecquod**, gen. wanting, [**ec** + **quī**], inter. adj., in direct questions, *is there any? any?* in indirect questions, *whether any.*

ecquid [**ecquis**], inter. adv., in direct questions, *at all?* giving merely an emphatic turn to the question, and often not translated in words; in indirect questions, *if at all, whether.*

edāx, -ācis, [**edō**], adj., *greedy, voracious, gluttonous.*

ēdictum, -ī, [**ēdīcō**], n., *proclamation, edict, order.*

ēdō, **ēdere**, **ēdidī**, **ēditum**, [**ē** + **dō**], 3, a., *give out, put forth; bring forth, beget, produce; relate, tell, utter; publish, declare, disclose, give account of.*

ēdoceō, -ēre, **ēdocuī**, **ēdoctum**, [**ē** + **doceō**], 2, a., *teach thoroughly, show in detail; instruct, inform, show.*

ēdūcō, -ere, **ēdūxī**, **ēductum**, [**ē** + **dūcō**], 3, a., *lead forth, lead out; draw out, draw forth; bring up, rear;* of a sword, *draw.*

efferō, **efferre**, **extulī**, **ēlātum**, [**ex** + **ferō**], irr., a., *carry forth, bring out, remove; carry out* for burial, *bear* to the grave; *bring forth, bear, produce; lift up, raise, elevate, extol; set forth, spread abroad, publish, proclaim;* pass., of emotions, *be carried away, be puffed up, be inspired.*

efficiō, -ere, **effēcī**, **effectum**, [**ex** + **faciō**], 3, a., *bring about, bring to pass, cause, accomplish, make; produce, yield, bear; make out, show, prove.*

effigiēs, -eī, [cf. **effingō**], f., *copy, representation, image, likeness; ideal, symbol.*

effrēnātus, -a, -um, [**ex** + **frēnātus**, *bridled*], adj., *unbridled, unrestrained, uncontrolled.*

effugiō, -ere, **effūgī**, ——, [**ex** + **fugiō**], 3, n. and a., *flee away, slip out of; flee from, avoid, shun; escape, get away.*

egēns, -entis, [part. of **egeō**], adj., *needy, lacking; in want, destitute.*

egeō, **egēre**, **eguī**, ——, 2, n., *be in want of, be lacking; need, lack, want, be without, be destitute of.*

egestās, -ātis, [**egēns**], f., *want, need, poverty, indigence.*

Egnātius, -ī, m., name of two persons mentioned in this book:

(1) *L. Egnātius*, a debtor of Cicero's. EP. XXXVI.

(2) *L. Egnātius Rūfus*, a Roman knight and friend of Cicero, who appears to have had extensive investments in the provinces. Cicero recommends him by letters to several provincial governors. EP. XV.

Egnātulēius, -ī, m., *L. Egnātulēius*, quaestor 44 B.C. He was in command of the fourth legion, which deserted from Antony to Octavianus. ANT. IV. II.

ego, **meī**, pl. **nōs**, gen. **nostrum** and **nostrī**, [cf. ἐγώ], pers. pron., *I, we.*

egomet [**ego** + **-met**, *self*], strengthened form of **ego**, *I myself.*

ēgredior, ēgredī, ēgressus sum, [**ē + gradior**], 3, dep., *go out, go forth, come forth; depart, go out; go up, ascend;* of an army, *march out;* from a ship, *disembark, land.*

ēgregius, -a, -um, [**ē, grex**], adj., *extraordinary, remarkable, distinguished; excellent, fine, noble.*

ēiciō, ēicere, ēiēcī, ēiectum, [**ē + iaciō**], 3, a., *cast out, cast forth, hurl forth; thrust out, drive away, expel; banish, drive into exile; wreck.* **sē ēicere,** *to rush out, to break forth.*

ēlābor, ēlābī, ēlāpsus sum, [**ē + lābor**], 3, dep., *slip away, slip off, escape, drop.*

ēlabōrō, -āre, -āvī, -ātum, [**ē + labōrō**], 1, n. and a., *labor, struggle, make an effort; take pains, work out, elaborate.*

ēlūdō, ēlūdere, ēlūsī, ēlūsum, [**ē + lūdō**], 3, n. and a., *quit playing; parry, avoid, evade, elude, escape; delude, deceive; trifle with, make sport of, mock.*

ēmergō, -ere, ēmersī, ēmersum, [**ē + mergō**], 3, a. and n., *bring to light, raise up; come forth, come up out of, emerge, rise up,* as from water; *free one's self, get clear, escape.*

ēmissus, see **ēmittō.**

ēmittō, -ere, ēmīsī, ēmissum, [**ē + mittō**], 3, a., *send forth, send out, drive out, expel; hurl, discharge; send out, publish; set free, let go, let slip; utter, give utterance to.*

emō, emere, ēmī, ēmptum, 3, a., *buy, purchase.*

ēmorior, ēmorī, ——, [**ē + morior**], 3, dep., *die off, die.*

ēnārrō, -āre, -āvī, -ātum, [**ē + nārrō**], 1, a., *set forth in detail, recount, describe.*

enim, conj., postpositive, *for, because; for instance, now really, in fact; indeed, of course, really, certainly; no doubt, to be sure.*

ēnītor, ēnītī, ēnīxus or **ēnīsus sum,** [**ē + nītor**], 3, dep., *struggle upwards; bring forth, bear; exert one's self, strive, make an effort.*

Ennius, -ī, m., *Quīntus Ennius,* the most eminent among the early Roman poets; born at Rudiae, in Calabria, B.C. 239, died at Rome, 169 B.C. He wrote epic, dramatic, and miscellaneous poetry, none of which is now extant except in fragments. His *Annālēs,* treating of the history of Rome from the beginning to his own times, was the first Latin poem in hexameter verse. ARCH. IX., XI.

eō, īre, īvī or **iī, itum,** irr., n., *go, come; go forth, depart; move on, sail, fly, march, advance, enter; concur in; pass, prosper, turn out.*

eō [cf. **is**], adv., *there, in that place; for that reason, on that account; to that place, thither; to that degree, so far.*

eōdem [**idem**], adv., *in the same place; to the same place, thither; to the same point, to the same purpose; thereto, besides.*

Ephesius, -a, -um, [**Ephesus**], adj., *of Ephesus, Ephesian.*

Ephesus, -ī, [Ἔφεσος], f., *Ephesus,* a celebrated Greek city on the west coast of Asia Minor.

epigramma, -atis, [ἐπίγραμμα], n., *inscription; epigram.*

Ēpīrus, -ī, [Ἤπειρος], f., *Ēpīrus,* a country east of the Adriatic Sea, north of Greece and west of Thessaly.

epistola, -ae, [ἐπιστολή], f., *letter, epistle.*

eques, -itis, [equus], m., *horseman, rider; cavalryman, trooper; knight, member of the equestrian order.* In the early days of Rome the poorer citizens served in the army as infantry, the wealthier as cavalry. As the state grew the class of cavalrymen increased in importance and influence, and gained special privileges. In Cicero's time the Roman knights (equitēs Rōmānī) formed a distinct and powerful order, between the Senate and the plebs. They were engaged especially in farming the revenues.

equidem [interj. **e** + **quidem**], adv., *indeed, truly, certainly, at all events, at least, surely; for my part, in my case; by all means, of course, to be sure.*

equitātus, -ūs, [equitō, from equus], m., *cavalry; equestrian order.*

ērēctus, **-a**, **-um**, comp. **ērēctior**, [part. of **ērigō**], adj., *directed upwards, upright, high; lofty, noble; arrogant, haughty; intent, eager, on the alert.*

ergā, prep. with acc., *towards, to, in respect to.*

ergō, adv., *therefore, then, accordingly;* often used, like causā and grātiā, with preceding gen., *on account of, because of, for the sake of.*

ērigō, **ērigere**, **ērēxī**, **ērēctum**, [ē + **regō**], 3, a., *raise up, set up, erect, elevate; stir up, arouse, animate, cheer, encourage.*

ēripiō, **ēripere**, **ēripuī**, **ēreptum**, [ē + **rapiō**], 3, a., *snatch away, tear away, take away; rescue, save, deliver, set free, free.*

Erōs, **-ōtis**, [Ἔρως], m., *Erōs*, a steward of Cicero's friend Atticus. Ep. xxxvi.

errō, **-āre**, **-āvī**, **-ātum**, 1, n. and a., *wander, go astray, roam about, stray; be in error, err, go wrong; go astray, mistake.*

error, **-ōris**, [errō], m., *a wandering, straying, missing the way; doubt, uncertainty, ambiguity; a going wrong, mistake, error, delusion.*

ērūctō, **-āre**, ——, ——, [ē + **rūctō**, *belch*], 1, a., *belch forth, throw up, vomit.*

ērudiō, **-īre**, **-īvī**, **-ītum**, [ē, **rudis**], 4, a., *teach, instruct; educate, polish.*

ērudītus, **-a**, **-um**, [part. of **ērudiō**], adj., *learned, educated; skilled, accomplished, cultured.*

ērumpō, **-ere**, **ērūpī**, **ēruptum**, [ē + **rumpō**], 3, n. and a., *break out, burst forth, sally forth; cause to burst forth, hurl forth.*

ēscendō, **-ere**, **ēscendī**, **ēscēnsum**, [ē + **scāndō**], 3, n. and a., *climb up, ascend; come up, go up, mount.*

essedum, **-ī**, n., two-wheeled *war-chariot, car,* of the early Britons.

et, adv. and conj.:

(1) As adv., *also, too, besides, moreover, even.*

(2) As conj., *and;* introducing a contrasted thought or *question, and yet, but still, but.* **et — et**, *both — and, as well — as, on the one hand — on the other.* **et — neque**, *both — and not.* **neque — et**, *both not — and.*

etenim [**et** + **enim**], conj., *for truly, and really, and indeed, because, since.*

etēsiae, **-ārum**, [ἐτησίαι], m., pl., *Etesian winds, trade-winds;* used especially of the northwest winds which blow regularly in summer in the eastern parts of the Mediterranean Sea.

etiam [**et** + **iam**], adv. and conj., *and also, and furthermore, now too, even yet, also, even, likewise; certainly, by all means.* **etiam atque etiam,** *again and again, repeatedly, persistently.* **etiam nunc,** *yet still, even now, even till now.* **etiam sī,** *even if, although.*

Etrūria, -ae, f., *Etrūria,* a country in Italy, west of the Tiber and south of the valley of the Po.

etsī [**et** + **sī**], conj., *although, though, even if, and yet.*

ēvādō, ēvādere, ēvāsī, ēvāsum, [**ē** + **vādō**], 3, n. and a., *go forth, come forth, come out; get away, escape; turn out, prove to be, result.*

ēveniō, -īre, **ēvēnī, ēventum,** [**ē** + **veniō**], 4, n., *come out; come to pass, happen, turn out.*

ēventus, -ūs, [**ēveniō**], m., *outcome, issue, result; occurrence, event.*

ēvertō, -ere, **ēvertī, ēversum,** [**ē** + **vertō**], 3, a., *overturn, overthrow, upturn; throw down, hurl down, ruin, destroy.*

ēvocātor, -ōris, [**ēvocō**], m., lit. *one who calls forth* to arms; *recruiter, summoner.*

ēvomō, -ere, **ēvomuī, ēvomitum,** [**ē** + **vomō**], 3, a., *vomit forth; cast out, expel.*

ex, often before consonants **ē**, prep. with abl. only, *out of, out from;* of place, *from, out of, down from;* of time, *from, since, after;* of source and material, *from, of;* of partition, *of, out of, from among;* of transition, *from, out of;* of cause, *from, by reason of, by, in consequence of;* of measure and correspondence, *according to, with, in, by, on.* **aliquā ex parte,** *in some measure.*

exacuō, -ere, **exacuī, exacūtum,** [**ex** + **acuō,** *sharpen*], 3, a., *sharpen; stimulate, stir up, inflame.*

exaggerō, -āre, -āvī, -ātum, [**ex** + **aggerō,** from **agger**], 1, a., *heap up, pile up, accumulate; magnify, exaggerate.*

exanimis, -e, [**ex, anima**], adj., *breathless; lifeless, dead; dismayed, terrified.*

exanimō, -āre, -āvī, -ātum, [**exanimus**], 1, a., *put out of breath, fatigue; deprive of life, kill; wear out, prostrate, unnerve.*

exārdēscō, -ere, **exārsī, exārsum,** [**ex** + **ārdēscō**], 3, inch., *blaze out, blaze up; take fire, be inflamed, kindle, glow; become aroused.*

exaudiō, -īre, -īvī, -ītum, [**ex** + **audiō**], 4, a., *hear from without; hear clearly; perceive; listen to, obey.*

excēdō, -ere, **excessī, excessum,** [**ex** + **cēdō**], 3, n. and a., *go forth, depart, withdraw, leave; go beyond, exceed, pass beyond; pass, tower above.*

excellēns, -entis, [part. of **excellō**], adj., *eminent, pre-eminent; superior, surpassing, distinguished.*

excellō, -ere, **excelluī, excelsum,** 3, a. and n., *be eminent; be superior, excel, surpass.*

excelsus, -a, -um, [part. of **excellō**], adj., *elevated, high, lofty.* As subst., **excelsum,** -ī, n., *elevation, height.*

excidō, -ere, **excidī,** ——, [**ex** + **cadō**], 3, n., *fall from, fall away; slip away, escape; pass away, perish.*

excīdō, -ere, **excīdī, excīsum,** [**ex** + **caedō**], 3, a., *cut out, cut down, hew down; raze, demolish, destroy utterly.*

excipiō, -ere, excēpī, exceptum, [ex + capiō], 3, a., *take out, withdraw; except, make an exception of; take up, receive, welcome; catch, capture; intercept; follow, succeed.*

excitō, -āre, -āvī, -ātum, [freq. of exciō], 1, a., *call out, rouse, summon; call up, raise; build, construct; stimulate, inspire, awaken; stir up, kindle, excite.*

exclūdō, -ere, exclūsī, exclūsum, [ex + claudō], 3, a., *shut out, exclude, cut off; prevent, hinder.*

excolō, -ere, excoluī, excultum, [ex + colō], 3, a., *cultivate, improve, refine.*

excruciō, -āre, -āvī, -ātum, [ex + cruciō], 1, a., *torture, torment, rack; harass, afflict, trouble.*

excubiae, -ārum, [cf. excubō, *watch*], f., pl., *a watching; watchmen, sentinels, guards.*

excursiō, -ōnis, [excurrō], f., *a running forth; sally, dash, attack; inroad, invasion, expedition.*

excūsātiō, -ōnis, [excūsō], f., *excusing, excuse.*

excūsō, -āre, -āvī, -ātum, [ex, causa], 1, a., *excuse, make an excuse for, apologize for; plead as excuse, allege as an excuse.*

exemplum, -ī, [eximō, lit. *that which is taken out*], n., *specimen, sample; pattern, model; precedent, warning, example, lesson; penalty; way, manner;* of writing, *transcript, copy.*

exeō, -īre, -iī, -itum, [ex + eō], irr., n., *go out, come forth; go away, depart, withdraw; turn out, result;* of time, *run out, end, expire.*

exerceō, -cēre, -cuī, -citum, [ex + arceō], 2, a., *keep busy, keep active, keep at work; train, discipline; employ, exercise, practice, administer; disturb, plague, vex.*

exercitātiō, -ōnis, [exercitō, freq. of exerceō], f., *exercise, practice; training, experience.*

exercitātus, -a, -um, [part. of exercitō, freq. of exerceō], adj., *practiced, trained, experienced, versed.*

exercitus, -ūs, [exerceō], m., *army.*

exhauriō, -īre, exhausī, exhaustum, [ex + hauriō], 4, a., *draw off,* as liquid from a vessel; *draw out, take out; take away, remove; empty, exhaust, bring to an end; fulfil.*

exigō, -ere, exēgī, exāctum, [ex + agō], 3, a., *drive out, thrust out; thrust, drive; exact, demand, require, collect; pass, spend; examine, consider.*

exiguus, -a, -um, [cf. exigō], adj., *small, little, scanty; poor, mean, paltry.*

eximiē [eximius], adv., *exceedingly, very much.*

eximius, -a, -um, [eximō, *take out*], adj., *choice, fine, excellent; uncommon, extraordinary, remarkable.*

exīstimātor, -ōris, [exīstimō], m., *appraiser, judge.*

exīstimō, -āre, -āvī, -ātum, [ex + aestimō], 1, a. and n., *reckon, estimate; esteem, consider; think, suppose.*

exitiōsus, -a, -um, [exitium], adj., *destructive, deadly, pernicious.*

exitium, -ī, [exeō], n., *destruction, ruin, mischief, death.*

exitus, -ūs, [exeō], m., *a going forth, departure, exit; outlet, passage; way out, end, conclusion; end of life, death; outcome, result, issue.*

exōrnō, -āre, -āvī, -ātum, [ex + ōrnō], 1, a., *equip, furnish, supply, provide; deck out, embellish, adorn.*

exōrsus, -ūs, [exōrdior], m., *a beginning, commencement.*

expediō, -īre, -īvī, -ītum, [ex, pēs], 4, a., lit. *make the foot free; set free, let loose, liberate, extricate; bring out, make ready; arrange, settle; be of advantage, be expedient, be profitable.*

expedītē, comp. **expedītius**, sup. **expedītissimē**, [expedītus], adv., *readily, quickly, without hindrance.*

expellō, -ere, expulī, expulsum, [ex + pellō], 3, a., *drive out, thrust forth, cast forth, expel.*

expēnsum, -ī, [expēnsus], n., *payment, disbursement, expense.*

expergīscor, -gīscī, experrēctus sum, [expergō, *arouse*], 3, dep., *wake up, awake; be alert.*

experior, -īrī, expertus sum, 4, dep., *try, prove, test, find out* by a test; *make trial of, undertake; undergo, experience.*

expers, -tis, [ex + pars], adj., lit. *having no part in; destitute of, devoid of, without.*

expetō, -ere, expetīvī, expetītum, [ex + petō], 3, a., *seek after, strive for, aim at; ask, demand, request; desire, wish.*

expīlō, -āre, -āvī, -ātum, [ex + pīlō], 1, a., *pillage, rob.*

expleō, -ēre, -ēvī, -ētum, [ex + -pleō], 2, a., *fill up, fill full; complete, finish; satisfy, appease; discharge, perform, do.*

explicō, -āre, -āvī and -uī, -ātum and -itum, [ex + plicō], 1, a., *unfold, unroll; spread out, display; set free, release; set in order, adjust, set forth, explain.*

explōrō, -āre, -āvī, -ātum, [ex + plōrō], 1, a., *search out, investigate; spy out, examine.*

expōnō, -ere, exposuī, expositum, [ex + pōnō], 3, a., *put forth, exhibit; put on shore, disembark; set forth, relate, explain.*

exportō, -āre, -āvī, -ātum, [ex + portō], 1, a., *carry away, send away, export.*

exprimō, -ere, expressī, expressum, [ex + premō], 3, a., *press out, squeeze forth; extort, wrest from; represent, copy, imitate; portray, express, describe.*

exprōmō, -ere, exprōmpsī, exprōmptum, [ex + prōmō], 3, a., *show forth, exhibit, display; utter, state.*

expūgnātiō, -ōnis, [expūgnō], f., *taking by storm, a storming.*

exquīrō, -ere, exquīsīvī, exquīsītum, [ex + quaerō], 3, a., *search out, inquire into, inquire, ask; seek out, devise.*

exquīsītus, -a, -um, [part. of exquīrō], adj., *choice, select, exquisite.*

exsilium, -ī, [exsul], n., *exile, banishment; place of exile, retreat.*

exsistō, -ere, exstitī, exstitum, [ex + sistō], 3, n., *come forth, come out, appear; spring up, arise, become; be manifest, be, exist.*

exsolvō, -ere, exsolvī, exsolūtum, [ex + solvō], 3, a., *unloose, free, release, deliver; discharge, pay.*

exspectātiō, -ōnis, [exspectō], f., *awaiting for, expecting, expectation; longing for.*

expectātus, -a, -um, [part. of exspectō], adj., *longed for, welcome.*

exspectō, -āre, -āvī, -ātum, [ex + spectō], 1, a. and n., *look out for, wait for, await; long for, desire, expect; apprehend, dread.*

exstinguō, -ere, exstīnxī, exstīnctum, [ex+stinguō, *quench*], 3, a., *quench, put out, extinguish; deprive of life, kill; blot out, destroy utterly, annihilate.*

exstō, -āre, ——, ——, [ex + stō], 1, n., *stand out, stand forth, project; appear, exist, be found.*

exsul, -ulis, m. and f., *exile, outlaw, wanderer.*

exsultō, -āre, -āvī, -ātum, [freq. of **exsiliō**], 1, n., *leap up, bound up; revel, exult, delight in.*

extenuō, -āre, -āvī, -ātum, [ex + tenuō], 1, a., *make thin; lessen, diminish, detract from.*

exter or **exterus**, -a, -um, adj., *outward, outer; foreign, strange.* Comp. **exterior**, -us, *outer, exterior.* Sup. **extrēmus**, -a, -um, *outermost, utmost; last, remotest, extreme.* As subst., **extrēmum**, -ī, n., *end.*

exterminō, -āre, -āvī, -ātum, [ex, terminus], 1, a., *drive out, expel, banish, remove.*

externus, -a, -um, [exter], adj., *outward, external; foreign, strange.*

extimēscō, -ere, extimuī, ——, [ex + timēscō, from timeō], 3, inch., *fear greatly, dread.*

extollō, -ere, ——, ——, [ex + tollō], 3, a., *lift up, raise, elevate; extol, praise highly.*

extorqueō, -ēre, extorsī, extortum, [ex + torqueō], 2, a., *wrench from, wrest away; obtain by force, extort.*

extrā [exter; for exterā, sc. parte], adv. and prep.:

(1) As adv., *on the outside, without.*

(2) As prep., *outside of, beyond, aside from, except.*

extrēmus, -a, -um, see **exter**.

exūro, -ere, exussī, exūstum, [ex + ūrō], 3, a., *burn up, consume.*

exuviae, -ārum, [exuō], f., pl., *equipments, arms,* especially those taken from an enemy; *spoils.*

F.

F., see **fīlius**.

faber, -brī, m., *workman, artisan, smith.*

Fabius, -a, name of an ancient and distinguished patrician gens. See **Māximus**.

facile, comp. **facilius**, sup. **facillimē**, [facilis], adv., *easily, without trouble; readily, willingly, promptly.*

facilis, -e, comp. **facilior**, sup. **facillimus**, [faciō], adj., *easy, not difficult; accessible, approachable, affable, courteous, kindly.*

facilitās, -ātis, [facilis], f., *ease, readiness, facility; affability, courtesy.*

facinerōsus, -a, -um, [facinus], adj., *criminal, vicious.* As subst., **facinerōsus**, -ī, m., *criminal, felon, malefactor.*

facinus, -oris, [cf. faciō], n., *deed, act, action; evil deed, misdeed; outrage, crime, villainy.*

faciō, facere, fēcī, factum, 3, a. and n., *make, fashion, construct; compose; do, perform, execute; bring about, cause, produce; conduct, represent; choose, appoint; render, grant; value, esteem.* **satis facere**, *to give satisfaction, to satisfy; to make amends, to excuse.* See **fīō**.

factum, -ī, [factus, faciō], n., *deed, act, exploit, achievement; event.*

facultās, -ātis, [facilis], f., *capability, ability, power; possibility, opportunity, means; supply, stock, property;* especially in pl., *resources, goods, riches.*

Faesulae, -ārum, f., pl., *Faesulae,* an ancient city in the northern part of Etruria; now Fiesole, near Florence.

Faesulānus, -a, -um, adj., *of Faesulae, Faesulan.*

falcārius, -ī, [falx], m., *scythe-maker, sickle-maker.*

Falcidius, -ī, m., *C. Falcidius*, a Roman citizen who was tribune of the people and in the following year legatus. IMP. P. XIX.

fallō, fallere, fefellī, falsum, 3, a. and n., *deceive, cheat, betray; disappoint; escape the notice of, escape notice, be unobserved;* pass. often *be mistaken, deceive one's self, be wrong, be deceived.*

falsō [falsus], adv., *falsely, untruly, erroneously.*

falsus, -a, -um, [part. of **fallō**], adj., *deceptive, false, delusive; groundless, unfounded, misleading.*

fāma, -ae, [for, *speak*], f., *report, rumor, saying, tradition; public opinion, repute, renown, fame, reputation.*

famēs, -is, f., *hunger, starvation; want, famine.*

familia, -ae, [famulus, *servant*], f., *body of servants, household, domestics; family, kindred; estate.* **pater familiās**, *master of a house, head of a family.* **māter familiās**, *mistress of a house, matron.*

familiāris, -e, [familia], adj., *belonging to a household, private; intimate, friendly, familiar.* As subst., **familiāris**, -is, m., *intimate friend, friend, companion.*

familiāriter, comp. **familiārius**, sup. **familiārissimē**, [familiāris], adv., *intimately, on intimate terms.*

fānum, -ī, [for], n., *shrine, sanctuary.*

fās, only nom. and acc. in use, [for, *speak*], n., *right* according to divine law; *divine law, justice.* **fās est**, *it is right, it is allowable, it is proper, it is permitted.*

fasciculus, -ī, [dim. of **fascis**], m., *little packet, small package.*

fascis, -is, m., *bundle, packet;* in pl., *the fasces,* the bundle of rods tied about an axe, carried before the highest magistrates of Rome as a symbol of authority.

fātālis, -e, [fātum], adj., *of fate, ordained by fate, destined; fateful, destructive, dangerous.*

fateor, fatērī, fassus sum, [for], 2, dep., *confess, admit, own, acknowledge; show, indicate.*

fātum, -ī, [for], n., *prophetic utterance, prediction, oracle; destiny, fate; ill fate, calamity, ruin, destruction; death.*

faucēs, -ium, f., pl., *pharynx, throat, jaws; entrance, defile, pass.*

Faustus, -ī, [faustus, *lucky*], m., *Faustus,* surname of L. Cornelius Sulla, son of the dictator. See Sulla (2).

faveō, favēre, fāvī, fautum, 2, n., *be kind to, be well disposed toward, favor; befriend, protect, promote.*

fax, facis, [cf. **faciō**], f., *torch, firebrand;* by metonymy, *fire-ball, meteor, comet; fire, flame.*

febris, -is, f., *fever.*

Februārius, -a, -um, [februa, *expiatory rites*], adj., *of February,* originally the last month of the Roman year, later the second.

fēlīcitās, -ātis, [fēlīx], f., *good fortune, good luck, success.*

fēmina, -ae, f., *female, woman.*

ferē, adv., *almost, nearly, about; usually, generally, for the most part.*

ferō, ferre, tulī, lātum, irr., a. and n., *bear, carry, bring; lead, conduct, drive; bring forth, produce; yield; endure, put up with, suffer, tolerate; report, tell, celebrate; allow, permit, require.* **prae sē ferre**, *to profess, to show, to manifest.* **sententiam ferre**, *to cast a vote.*

ferōcitās, -ātis, [ferōx], f., *wildness, fierceness; savageness, fury.*

ferrāmentum, -ī, [ferrum], n., *iron tool, tool; axe, hatchet.*

ferreus, -a, -um, [ferrum], adj., *of iron, iron; hard-hearted, unfeeling, cruel.*

ferrum, -ī, n., *iron;* by metonymy, *iron tool, sword.* **flamma atque ferrum**, *fire and sword.*

fertilis, -e, [ferō], adj., *fertile, fruitful, productive.*

festīnō, -āre, -āvī, -ātum, [festīnus, *hasty*], 1, n. and a., *hasten, hurry; do quickly, quicken.*

fēstus, -a, -um, adj., *festal.*

fīctum, -ī, [fingō], n., *falsehood, fiction.*

fidēlis, -e, [fidēs], adj., *faithful, trustworthy, trusty; safe, reliable.*

fidēlitās, -ātis, [fidēlis], f., *faithfulness, trustworthiness, fidelity.*

fidēs, -ē or -eī, [fīdō], f., *confidence, trust, reliance, faith, credence; good-faith, trustworthiness, fidelity, honor; credibility; assurance, promise, pledge of safety;* in business relations, *credit.*

Fidius, -ī, [fidēs], m., *All-faithful,* an epithet of Jupiter as protector of oaths and defender of good faith. **mē dīus Fidius**, = ita mē dīus Fidius iuvet, *so help me the All-faithful! by the god of Truth! most certainly!* MAR. III.

fīdus, -a, -um, [fīdō], adj., *trusty, faithful; trustworthy, credible.*

fīgō, fīgere, fīxī, fīxum, 3, a., *fix, set, place, fasten, attach; set up, post up.*

fīlia, -ae, [fīlius], f., *daughter.*

fīliola, -ae, [dim. of fīlia], f., *little daughter.*

fīlius, -ī, sometimes abbreviated, F., f., m., *son.*

fingō, fingere, fīnxī, fīctum, 3, a., *touch gently; mould, fashion; compose; instruct, teach; imagine, think; invent, contrive, feign.*

fīnis, -is, [cf. findō], m., *limit, border, boundary, end;* in pl., *borders,* hence *territory, land, country.*

fīnitimus, -a, -um, [fīnis], adj., *bordering on, neighboring, adjoining.*

fīō, fierī, factus sum, irr., n., used as pass. of faciō, *be made, be done; become, happen, come to pass.* **fierī potest**, *it may happen.*

fīrmāmentum, -ī, [fīrmō], n., *means of strengthening; support, stay, prop.*

fīrmō, -āre, -āvī, -ātum, [fīrmus, *steadfast*], 1, a., *make firm, strengthen, fortify, secure; encourage, animate; confirm, establish, declare.*

fīrmus, -a, -um, adj., *steadfast, strong, powerful; firm, fast, trusty, faithful.*

fīxus, -a, -um, [part. of fīgō], adj., *fixed, fast; established, settled.*

Flaccus, -ī, [flaccus, *flabby, flap-eared*], m., a Roman surname especially common in the Fulvian and Valerian gentes. Four of the name are mentioned in this book:

(1) *M. Fulvius Flaccus,* a friend of the Gracchi, and consul 125 B.C. In the disturbances attending the attempt of C. Gracchus to carry out reforms, Flaccus organized an armed band. He came into conflict with the forces of the senatorial party, and was routed and slain, B.C. 121. CAT. I. II. XII.

(2) *L. Valerius Flaccus,* consul with Marius, B.C. 100. In this year the reckless measures and violent deeds of Saturninus and Glaucia led to a decree of the Senate that the consuls should

maintain the dignity of the state. As Marius was in sympathy with the revolutionary party, Valerius Flaccus was instrumental in putting Saturninus and Glaucia to death. He was Master of the Horse under Sulla, B. C. 82. He is often confused with another Flaccus of the same name; Mommsen, Vol. III., N. on p. 394. CAT. I. 11

(3) *L. Valerius Flaccus,* son of the preceding. He was praetor B. C. 63, and assisted Cicero in obtaining evidence of the Catilinarian conspiracy. The following year he had Asia as his province. In 59 B. C. he was accused of extortion in his administration of the province, and defended by Cicero in an oration which is still extant. Though no doubt guilty, he was acquitted. CAT. III. II., III., VI.

(4) *M. Laenius Flaccus,* a friend of Atticus. When Cicero was driven into exile by the edict of Clodius, B. C. 58, Flaccus provided him with a place of refuge at a country-seat near Brundisium until he could take ship for the East. EP. VIII.

flāgitiōsē, sup. **flāgitiōsissimē,** [**flāgitiōsus**], adv., *shamefully, basely.*

flāgitiōsus, -a, -um, [**flāgitium**], adj., *shameful, base, disgraceful; profligate, dissolute.*

flāgitium, -ī, [cf. **flāgitō**], n., lit. *importunity; shameful act, outrage; burning shame, shame, disgrace.*

flāgitō, -āre, -āvī, -ātum, 1, a., *ask urgently, demand, require; press earnestly, importune.*

flagrō, -āre, -āvī, -ātum, 1, n., *burn, blaze, flame, glow; burn* with desire for anything, *be on fire, be stirred.*

flamma, -ae, f., *blaze, flame, fire; warmth, passion; glow, rage, wrath.*

flectō, flectere, flexī, flexum, 3, a. and n., *bend, turn, direct; sway, change; move, persuade, influence; prevail upon, soften, appease.*

flētus, -ūs, [**fleō**], m., *weeping, crying.*

flōrēns, -entis, [**flōreō**], adj., *in bloom, flowering, blooming; flourishing, prosperous.*

flōreō, -ēre, -uī, ——, [**flōs**], 2, n., *bloom, blossom; flourish, prosper; be eminent.*

flōrēscō, -ere, ——, ——, [**flōreō**], 3, inch., *begin to blossom; begin to flourish, bloom.*

flōs, flōris, m., *flower, blossom, bloom; period of bloom, prime, promise; ornament, best part.*

flūmen, -inis, [**fluō**], n., *stream, flood, river; flow, fluency.*

focus, -ī, m., *fire-place, hearth; home.*

foederātus, -a, -um, [part. of **foederō**], adj., *leagued, allied, confederate.*

foedus, -a, -um, adj., *foul, filthy, ugly; vile, base, shameful.*

foedus, -eris, [cf. **fīdō**], n., *treaty, compact, league, alliance; covenant, agreement, contract.*

fōns, fontis, m., *spring, fountain, well; source, origin, cause.*

forās [cf. **foris,** *door*], adv., of direction, *out of doors, out, forth.*

fore, see **sum.**

forēnsis, -e, [**forum**], adj., *of the market, of the forum; public, forensic.*

forīs [**foris**], adv., of place, *out of doors, without, abroad.*

Formiae, -ārum, f., pl., *Formiae,* a coast city in the southern part of Latium, on the Appian Way. Cicero had an estate and a favorite villa in the vicinity.

Formiānus, -a, -um, [Formiae], adj., *of Formiae, Formian.* As subst., **Formiānum**, -ī, (properly sc. **praedium**), n., *estate at Formiae, Formian country-seat.*

formīdō, -inis, f., *dread, fear, terror ;* of religious emotions, *awe, reverence.*

formīdolōsus, -a, -um, [formīdō], adj., *dreadful, fearful, terrible.*

fors, fortis, [cf. ferō], f., *chance, luck, accident.*

forsitan [= fors sit an], adv., *perhaps, perchance, it may be.*

fortasse [for fortassis, = forte an sī vīs], adv., *perhaps, possibly, perchance.*

forte [abl. of fors], adv., *by chance, by accident, accidentally ; perhaps, perchance.*

fortis, -e, adj., *strong, mighty ; sturdy, brave, manly, bold, fearless ; spirited, impetuous.*

fortiter, comp. fortius, sup. fortissimē, [fortis], adv., *strongly, steadily ; boldly, bravely, manfully.*

fortitūdō, -inis, [fortis], f., *strength ; firmness, courage, bravery, fortitude.*

fortūna, -ae, [fors], f., *chance, luck, fate, fortune ; condition, lot, circumstances ; prosperity, success ; misfortune, adversity ;* by metonymy, *possessions, property ;* personified, *Goddess of Fortune, Fortune.* **per fortūnās**, *for heaven's sake !*

fortūnātus, -a, -um, [part. of fortūnō], adj., *prosperous, fortunate, lucky, happy.*

fortūnō, -āre, -āvī, -ātum, [fortūna], 1, a., *make prosperous, prosper, bless.*

Forum Appī, see **Appī Forum**.

Forum Aurēlium, -ī, n., *Forum Aurēlium,* or *Forum Aurēlī,* a town on the coast of Etruria and the Via Aurelia, about 75 miles north of Rome.

forum, -ī, n., *public square, public place ; market-place, exchange, forum ;* at Rome, often for **Forum Rōmānum**, *the Roman Forum, the Forum,* an open space between the Palatine and Capitoline hills, surrounded by public buildings and shops, where the political and commercial life of the Roman world centred. See Map, p. 76.

fovea, -ae, f., *pit ;* especially a pit dug as a trap for wild beasts, *pitfall.*

foveō, fovēre, fōvī, fōtum, 2, a., *warm, keep warm ; cherish, foster ; encourage.*

fragilitās, -ātis, [fragilis], f., *weakness, frailty.*

frangō, frangere, frēgī, frāctum, 3, a., *break, shatter, dash to pieces, crush ; break down, weaken, subdue, overcome.*

frāter, -tris, m., *brother.*

fraudātiō, -ōnis, [fraudō], f., *cheating, deceiving, deception.*

fremitus, -ūs, [fremō], m., *loud noise, rushing, roaring, murmuring.*

frequēns, -entis, adj., *regular, repeated ; frequent, common, usual ; in great numbers, crowded ; thronged, in crowds.*

frequentia, -ae, [frequēns], f., *assembling in great numbers, thronging together, concourse ; multitude, great numbers, crowd, throng.*

frequentō, -āre, -āvī, -ātum, [frequēns], 1, a., *visit often ; visit in great numbers, throng, frequent ; gather in throngs, crowd together.*

frētus, -a, -um, adj., *sustained by, relying on ; depending, trusting, confident ;* usually followed by an abl.

frīgus, -oris, n., *cold, chilliness*

frōns, frontis, f., *brow, forehead, countenance, face; front, forepart.*

frūctus, -ūs, [fruor], m., *enjoyment, delight, pleasure; fruit, produce; income, yield, profit; reward, return, recompense.*

frūmentārius, -a, -um, [frūmentum], adj., *of grain, of provisions, grain-.*

fruor, fruī, frūctus sum, 3, dep., *enjoy, delight in, take pleasure in, rejoice in.*

frūstror, -ārī, -ātus sum, [frūstrā, *in error, in vain*], 1, dep., *deceive, elude, disappoint.*

fuga, -ae, [cf. fugiō], f., *flight, escape; exile, banishment; avoidance, shunning.*

fugiō, -ere, fūgī, fugitum, 3, n. and a., *flee, fly, run away; become a fugitive, go into exile; vanish, disappear; avoid, shun; escape the notice of, escape; omit, forbear.*

fugitīvus, -a, -um, [fugiō], adj., *that has run away, fugitive.* As subst., **fugitīvus**, -ī, m., *runaway, deserter.*

fulgeō, fulgēre, fulsī, ——, 2, n., *flash, lighten; gleam, glisten, shine, glitter.*

fulmen, -inis, [fulgeō], n., *flash of lightning, stroke of lightning, thunderbolt; destructive power.*

Fulvius, -a, name of a prominent plebeian gens, which removed to Rome at an early date from Tusculum; pl. **Fulviī**, -ōrum, m., *the Fulvii*, meaning the eminent men of the gens who had done good service for the state. For the Fulviī mentioned in this book see the family names, **Flaccus**, **Nōbilior**.

fundāmentum, -ī, [fundō], n., *foundation, basis, support.*

funditus [fundus], adv., *from the bottom; utterly, entirely.*

fundō, -ere, fūdī, fūsum, 3, a., *pour, pour out, shed; scatter, diffuse; bring forth, bear; overthrow, vanquish, rout.*

fundō, -āre, -āvī, -ātum, [fundus], 1, a., *found, establish.*

fūnestus, -a, -um, [fūnus], adj., *deadly, fatal, destructive; associated with death, mournful, sad.*

fungor, fungī, fūnctus sum, 3, dep., *be engaged in, perform; fulfil, discharge, execute, do.*

furēns, -entis, [part. of furō], adj., *raving, raging, mad, furious.*

furiōsus, -a, -um, [furia], adj., *full of raging, mad, furious.*

Furius, -a, name of an ancient patrician gens. Two of the name are mentioned in this book:

(1) *P. Furius*, one of the Catilinarian conspirators, from Faesulae. CAT. III. VI.

(2) *L. Furius Philus*, consul B.C. 136. Receiving Spain as his province he took thither two of his bitterest enemies as quaestors, that they might be forced to attest to the uprightness of his administration. He was a man of unusual culture for the times. ARCH. VII.

furō, -ere, furuī, ——, 3, n., *rave, rage, be mad, be furious.*

furor, -ōris, [furō], m., *frenzy, rage, fury, madness; prophetic frenzy, inspiration.*

fūrtim [fūrtum], adv., *by stealth, secretly, furtively.*

fūrtum, -ī, n., *theft, robbery; thing stolen; artifice, craft.*

futūrus, -a, -um, see **sum**. As subst., **futūrum**, -ī, n., *the future.*

G.

Gabīnius, -a, name of a plebeian gens. In this book three of the name are mentioned:

(1) *A. Gabīnius*, tribune of the people, B. C. 66. He proposed a bill the result of which was to put the entire command of the war against the pirates into the hands of Pompey, with almost unlimited power. He was praetor B. C. 61. In 58 B. C. he was consul with Clodius, whom he assisted in procuring the exile of Cicero. As proconsul he governed the province of Syria so unlawfully that on his return to Rome he was sent into exile, his property being confiscated. He died B. C. 48. IMP. P. XVII., XIX.

(2) *P. Gabīnius Capitō*, praetor B. C. 89. ARCH. V.

(3) *P. Gabīnius Cimber*, one of the worst of the Catilinarian conspirators. CAT. III. III. *et al.*

Gabīnius, -a, -um, adj., *of a Gabinius, Gabinian.* **lēx Gabīnia,** *bill of Gabinius*; see p. 32.

Gāius, -ī, abbreviated **C.**, m., *Gāius*, a Roman forename.

Gallī, **-ōrum**, m., pl., *natives of Gaul, Gauls.*

Gallia, -ae, f., *Gaul*, including

(1) Gallia Cisalpīna, or Gallia citerior, *Cisalpine Gaul*, south of the Alps and north of the Apennines.

(2) Gallia Trānsalpīna, or Gallia ulterior, *Transalpine Gaul, Gaul*, covering the regions now included in France, Belgium, Holland, the western parts of Germany and Switzerland.

Gallicānus, -a, -um, adj., *of Cisalpine Gaul, Gallican.*

Gallicus, -a, -um, adj., *of the Gauls, of Gaul, Gallic.*

gallīnārius, -a, -um, [gallīna], adj., *of hens, of poultry.* **silva Gallīnāria,** *Gallinarian Wood, Hen Forest*, an extensive forest on the coast of Campania, north of Cumae. It was on the road to Cumae, and a favorite resort of bandits. EP. XXX.

gāneō, -ōnis, [gānea, *eating house*], m., *glutton, debauchee.*

gaudēns, -entis, [part. of **gaudeō**], adj., *joyful, joyous, glad, cheerful.*

gaudeō, -ēre, gāvīsus sum, 2, semi-dep., n., *rejoice, be glad, delight in.*

gaudium, -ī, [gaudeō], n., *joy, gladness, delight, enjoyment.*

gaza, -ae, f., *treasure, wealth, riches.*

gelidus, -a, -um, [gelū], adj., *very cold, ice-cold, cold.*

gener, -erī, m., *daughter's husband, son-in-law.*

generō, -āre, -āvī, -ātum, [genus], 1, a., *beget, produce*; pass., *be begotten, spring.*

gēns, gentis, [cf. **genō,** *bear*], f., *clan, house*, used of a group of families tracing descent from a common ancestor, having a common name, and participating in the same religious rites; hence, *species, breed, brood; people, nation, race.*

genus, -eris, [cf. **genō,** *bear*], n., *birth, descent, family; sort, kind; race, breed, stock; class, order, description.*

geōgraphia, -ae, [γεωγραφία], f., *geography.*

gerō, -ere, gessī, gestum, 3, a., *bear, carry, have; cherish, entertain; perform, do; manage, conduct, transact, accomplish*; of war, *carry on, wage.* **sē gerere,** *to conduct one's self, to behave, to act.* **rēs gestae,** *exploits, deeds, achievements.*

gestiō, **-īre**, **-īvī**, **-ītum**, **[gestus**, *bearing*], 4, n., *leap with joy*, *skip*, *desire eagerly*, *earnestly desire*, *long*.

Glabriō, **-ōnis**, m., *M' Acīlius Glabriō*, consul with C. Calpurnius Piso, B. C. 67. The following year he was proconsul of Cilicia, and succeeded Lucullus in the direction of the war against Mithridates. He proved a failure as a general and was succeeded by Pompey. At the trial of the Catilinarian conspirators he spoke in favor of the death penalty. IMP. P. IX.

gladiātor, **-ōris**, **[gladius]**, m., *swordsman*, *fighter* in the public games, *gladiator*.

gladiātōrius, **-a**, **-um**, **[gladiātor]**, adj., *of gladiators*, *gladiatorial*.

gladius, **-ī**, m., *sword*.

Glaucia, **-ae**, m., *C. Servīlius Glaucia*, praetor B. C. 100. He united with Saturninus in opposition to the Senatorial party, was declared an outlaw, and perished with Saturninus at the hands of a mob. CAT. I. II., III. VI.

glōria, **-ae**, f., *glory*, *fame*, *praise*; *pride*, *vanity*, *ambition*.

glōrior, **-ārī**, **-ātus sum**, **[glōria]**, 1, dep., *boast*, *brag*, *vaunt*, *pride one's self*.

Gnaeus, **-ī**, abbreviated **Cn.**, m., *Gnaeus*, a Roman forename.

gnāvus, **-a**, **-um**, adj., *busy*, *active*, *diligent*.

Gracchus, **-ī**, m., name of a family of the Sempronian gens. The two most distinguished members, often together called **Gracchī**, gen. **-ōrum**, *the Gracchi*, were:

(1) *Tiberius Semprōnius Gracchus*, quaestor in Spain B. C. 137, where he distinguished himself. He was tribune of the people B. C. 133, and inaugurated salutary reforms looking toward an equable distribution of the public lands. Standing for re-election for the next year, he was slain in a tumult stirred up by the aristocracy. CAT. I. I., IV. II.

(2) *C. Semprōnius Gracchus*, brother of Tiberius. He entered upon the tribuneship B. C. 123, followed in the footsteps of his brother as a reformer, and met a violent death B C. 121. CAT. I. II., IV. II.

gradus, **-ūs**, m., *step*, *pace*, *walk*; *position*, *base*; *stairs*; *approach*, *advance*; *degree*, *grade*, *rank*, *interval*.

Graecia, **-ae**, f., *Greece*; sometimes = Māgna Graecia, *Magna Graecia*, a name applied to Lower Italy on account of the number of Greek cities there.

Graecus, **-a**, **-um**, **[Γραϊκός]**, adj., *of the Greeks*, *Grecian*, *Greek*. As subst., **Graecī**, **-ōrum**, m., pl., *the Greeks*. **Graeca**, **-ōrum**, n., pl., *Greek writing*, *Greek*.

grātia, **-ae**, **[grātus]**, f., *favor*, *esteem*, *regard*, *love*; *kindness*, *courtesy*; *gratitude*; *grace*; *return of courtesy*, *thanks*, *return*, *recompense*. **grātiā**, with gen., *for the sake of*, *on account of*. **grātiās habēre**, *to be grateful*, *to feel grateful*. **grātiam referre**, *to make grateful return*, *to recompense*.

Grātius, **-ī**, m., *Grātius*, the opponent of the poet Archias ARCH. IV., VI.

grātuītō **[grātuītus**, *without pay*], adv., *without pay*, *without recompense*, *for nothing*, *gratuitously*.

grātulātiō, **-ōnis**, **[grātulor]**, f., *showing joy*, *rejoicing*, *congratulation*; *joyful festival*, *public thanksgiving*.

grātulor, **-ārī**, **-ātus sum**, [**grātus**], 1, dep., *show joy, rejoice; congratulate.*

grātus, **-a**, **-um**, adj., *pleasing, agreeable, acceptable, dear; thankful, grateful, deserving.*

gravis, **-e**, adj., *heavy, of weight; loaded, laden; oppressive, offensive, severe, difficult; hard to bear, burdensome; weighty, important; eminent, venerable; great, of authority.*

gravitās, **-ātis**, [**gravis**], f., *weight, heaviness; oppressiveness, severity; importance, dignity, gravity, influence.*

graviter, comp. **gravius**, sup. **gravissimē**, [**gravis**], adv., *weightily; vehemently, violently, severely, strongly; deeply, sadly.*

gravor, **-ārī**, **-ātus sum**, [pass. of **gravō**, from **gravis**], 1, dep., *be burdened; be reluctant, hesitate.*

grex, **gregis**, m., *flock, herd; band, company, clique, gang.*

gubernātiō, **-ōnis**, [**gubernō**], f., *piloting, guidance; direction, management.*

gubernō, **-āre**, **-āvī**, **-ātum**, [cf. κυβερνάω], 1, a., *steer, act as pilot; direct, guide, control.*

gustō, **-āre**, **-āvī**, **-ātum**, [**gustus**], 1, a., *taste, partake of; enjoy.*

H.

habeō, **-ēre**, **-uī**, **-itum**, 2, a., *have, hold, possess; carry, wear; retain, keep, detain, contain; occupy, inhabit; be master of, own, rule; treat, use; pronounce, utter; have in mind, entertain; purpose, intend; think, believe, esteem; exercise, practice; receive, accept: reserve, conceal.*

habitō, **-āre**, **-āvī**, **-ātum**, [freq. of **habeō**], 1, a. and n., *occupy continually, inhabit; dwell, reside, live.*

habitus, **-ūs**, [**habeō**], m., *condition, appearance; attire, dress; nature, character, quality.*

hāctenus [**hāc** + **tenus**], adv., *so far, thus far, no farther.*

haereō, **-ēre**, **haesī**, **haesum**, 2, n., *stick, hang, cleave, cling; hold fast, be fixed; be perplexed, hesitate, be at a loss.*

haesitō, **-āre**, **-āvī**, **-ātum**, [freq. of **haereō**], 1, n., *stick fast; be at a loss, hesitate.*

Hannibal, **-alis**, m., *Hannibal*, the famous general of the Carthaginians in the second Punic War. When only twenty-nine years of age he led an army from Spain and over the Alps into Italy, where he sustained himself for fifteen years. His campaigns cost the Romans not less than 300,000 men. He was finally forced to withdraw to Africa, where he was defeated at Zama, B. C. 202. He led the life of a fugitive for twenty years afterwards, and perished, it is said by poison, in Bithynia. CAT. IV. X.

haruspex, **-icis**, m., *soothsayer, diviner.*

hasta, **-ae**, f., *staff, pole; spear, lance.*

haud, adv., *not at all, by no means*

hauriō, **-īre**, **hausī**, **haustum**, 4, a., *draw off, drain, empty; pierce, penetrate; drink in, imbibe, take in, receive.*

hebēscō, **-ere**, ——, ——, [**hebeō**, *be dull*], 3, inch., *grow blunt, become dull.*

Hēraclīa, **-ae**, [Ἡράκλεια], f., *Hēraclēa*, a Greek city in Lucania, near the shore of the Gulf of Tarentum, below Metapontum.

Hēracliēnsēs, -ium, [**Hēraclīa**], m., pl., *people of Heraclea, Heracleans;* sing. **Hēracliēnsis**, -is, m., *man of Heraclea, Heraclean.*

hercule [voc. of **Herculēs**], interj., *by Hercules! assuredly!* **mē hercule**, *in Hercules' name! most assuredly!*

hērēditās, -ātis, [**hērēs**], f., *heirship, inheritance.*

hērēs, -ēdis, m. and f., *heir, heiress; successor.*

herī, adv., *yesterday.*

hesternus, -a, -um, [**herī**], adj., *of yesterday, yesterday's.*

heus! interj., *ho! holloa! ho there!*

hībernō, -āre, -āvī, -ātum, [**hībernus**], I, n., *pass the winter, winter, be in winter quarters, have winter quarters.*

hībernus, -a, -um, [**hiems**], adj., *of winter, in the winter, winter-.* As subst., **hīberna**, -ōrum, (properly sc. **castra**), n., pl., *winter quarters.*

hīc, **haec**, **hōc**, gen. **hūius**, dem. pron., *this, this — here,* used with reference to the speaker; *the present, the actual; the following, the one,* referring to that which follows; *he, she, it.* **ille — hīc**, *the former — the latter.*

hīc [**hīc**], adv., *here, in this place; herein, in this, on this point; now, at this time, then.*

hīce, **haece**, **hōce**, gen. **hūiusce**, emphatic form of **hīc**, *this.*

hiems, -emis, f., *winter, winter time; wintry weather, storm, tempest.*

hinc [**hīc**], adv., *hence, from this place, from this.* **hinc — illinc**, *on the one side — on the other, on this side — on that, here — there.*

Hispānī, -ōrum, m., pl., *Spaniards.*

Hispānia, -ae, f., *Spain.*

Hispāniēnsis, -e, adj., *of Spain, Spanish, in Spain.*

Hīspō, -ōnis, m., *Hīspō,* apparently a centurion, whom Cicero at the time of his exile was anxious to avoid. EP. IX.

hodiē [**hōc**, **diē**], adv., *to-day; at this time, now; to this day.*

hodiernus, -a, -um, [**hodiē**], adj., *of to-day, to-day's.* **hodiernus diēs**, *this day, to-day.*

Homērus, -ī, [Ὅμηρος], m., *Homer.* ARCH. VIII.

homō, -inis, m. and f., *human being, man; race of man, mankind, human race.*

honestās, -ātis, [**honōs**], f., *honor* bestowed by others, *reputation; uprightness, integrity.*

honestē [**honestus**], adv., *honorably, creditably, virtuously.*

honestō, -āre, -āvī, -ātum, [**honestus**], I, a., *cover with honor, dignify, honor, adorn.*

honestus, -a, -um, [**honōs**], adj., *honored, respected; worthy of respect, honorable; noble, worthy.*

honōs, or **honor**, -ōris, m., *honor, esteem, repute; praise, glory, renown; public honor, dignity, office.*

hōra, -ae, [cf. ὥρα], f., *hour,* which among the Romans was properly a twelfth part of the time from sunrise to sunset.

horribilis, -e, [**horreō**], adj., *fearful, dreadful, terrible, horrible.*

hortātus, -ūs, found only in the abl., [**hortor**], m., *encouragement, incitement.*

Hortēnsius, -a, name of a plebeian gens. Three of the name, the orator, his father, and his brother, are spoken of by Cicero together as **Hortensiī**, gen. -**ōrum**. *Q. Hortēnsius,* the orator, was born B.C. 114. He became eminent as an advocate at an early age. He was consul B. C. 69. In 66 B. C. he spoke in opposition to the Manilian bill, which Cicero defended. Afterwards he was viewed by Cicero with jealousy as a rival, though sometimes they were both retained upon the same side of a case. He died B. C. 50. IMP. P. XVII., XIX.

hortor, **-ārī**, **-ātus sum**, 1, dep., *urge, encourage, exhort, incite.*

hospes, -itis, m., *entertainer, host; one entertained, guest, visitor.*

hospitium, **-ī**, [**hospes**], n., *entertainment, reception* as a guest; *tie of hospitality, hospitality, friendship; guest-chamber, inn.*

hostīlis, **-e**, [**hostis**], adj., *of an enemy, enemy's; hostile, inimical.*

hostis, -is, m. and f., *stranger, foreigner; public enemy, enemy, foe.*

HS., see **sēstertius.**

hūc [**hīc**], adv., *hither, to this place, to this point, so far.*

hūmānitās, -ātis, [**hūmānus**], f., *human nature, humanity; kindness, good nature, politeness; culture, refinement.*

hūmānus, -a, -um, [**homō**], adj., *of man, human; humane, kind, courteous, polite; cultured, refined.*

humilis, -e, [**humus**], adj., *low; slight, small, base, mean, obscure, insignificant.*

humus, **-ī**, f., *ground, soil, earth; land, country;* locative **humī**, *on the ground, to the ground.*

hypomnēma, -atis, [ὑπόμνημα], n., *written remark, memorandum, note.*

I.

iaceō, -ēre, -uī, ——, [cf. **iaciō**], 2, n., *lie, lie prostrate, be prostrate; lie dead, have fallen; be level; be cast down, be dejected; be despised.*

iaciō, **iacere**, **iēcī**, **iactum**, 3, a., *throw, cast, hurl; lay, establish; build, construct; throw up, charge; throw out, mention, declare, utter.*

iactō, **-āre**, **-āvī**, **-ātum**, [freq. of **iaciō**], 1, a., *throw, fling, hurl; toss, toss about; shake, brandish; emit, utter, say.* **sē iactāre**, *to boast, show off, make a display.*

iactūra, **-ae**, [**iaciō**], f., *throwing away; loss, damage; outlay, expense, sacrifice.*

iactus, **-ūs**, [**iaciō**], m., *throwing, casting, throw, cast, stroke.*

iam, adv., *now, at this time, just now; already, ere now, so soon; forthwith, straightway, immediately, presently; then, then surely, no doubt, precisely, indeed, even; besides, again, moreover;* with comp., *from time to time, gradually.* **iam dūdum**, *long before, for a long time, this long time.* **iam prīdem**, *long since, long ago.* **iam tum**, *even then, at that very time.*

Iānuārius, **-a**, **-um**, [**Iānus**], adj., *of January.* As subst., **Iānuārius**, **-ī**, m., *January.*

ibī or **ibi**, adv., *there, in that place; then, thereupon; in that case, on that occasion.*

Īd., see **Īdūs.**

idcircō [**id**, **circus**], adv., *therefore, on that account, for this reason.*

īdem, eadem, idem, gen. ēiusdem, [is], dem. pron., *the same;* often with the force of an adv., *also, besides, too, likewise, furthermore,* followed by **et**, **-que**, or **atque**, *the same as, identical with.*

ideō [**id** + **eō**], adv., *for that reason, on this account, therefore.*

idōneē [**idōneus**], adv., *fitly, suitably.*

idōneus, **-a**, **-um**, adj., *fit, suitable, proper; capable, sufficient.*

Īdūs, Īduum, abbreviated **Īd.**, f., pl., *the Ides, the middle of the month*, one of the three days to which dates were reckoned in the Roman Calendar. In March, May, July, and October the Ides came on the 15th; in other months, on the 13th.

igitur, conj., *then, therefore, accordingly;* in summing up, *I say then, you see, in short.*

ignārus, -a, -um, [in- + gnārus], adj., *unfamiliar with, not knowing, unacquainted with, ignorant; unskilled in, inexperienced.*

ignāvia, -ae, [ignāvus], f., *laziness, idleness, listlessness, cowardice.*

īgnis, -is, m., *fire.*

ignōminia, -ae, [in-, nōmen], f., *disgrace, dishonor, infamy, ignominy; degradation.*

ignōrātiō, -ōnis, [ignōrō], f., *lack of knowledge, ignorance.*

ignōrō, -āre, -āvī, -ātum, [cf. ignārus], 1, a. and n., *not know, be unacquainted with, be ignorant.*

ignōscō, -ere, ignōvī, ignōtum, [in- + (g)nōscō], 3, a., *pardon, forgive, excuse, overlook.*

ignōtus, -a, -um, [in- + (g)nōtus], adj., *unknown, unrecognized, unfamiliar, strange; without repute, obscure, mean.*

Īlias, -ados, [Ἰλιάς], f., *the Iliad.*

ille, illa, illud, gen. illīus or illius, dem. pron., *that*, referring to that which is remote; *he, she, it;* referring to that which is familiar, *the well-known, the famous.* **ille — hīc**, *the former — the latter.*

illecebra, -ae, [in, laciō, *entice*], f., *enticement, allurement, charm, seduction.*

illim [ille], adv., *thence, from that place.*

illinc [illim], adv., *from that place, thence; on that side.* See **hinc**.

illūdō, -ere, illūsī, illūsum, [in + lūdō], 3, n. and a., *play at; make sport; ridicule, jeer at, mock.*

illūstris, -e, [in, cf. lūstrō, *make bright*], adj., *bright, shining, brilliant; clear, manifest, plain; famous, distinguished, noble.*

illūstrō, -āre, -āvī, -ātum, [in + lūstrō, *make bright*], 1, a., *make light; make clear, clear up, disclose, explain; make famous, make renowned.*

Īllyricum, -ī, n., *Illyria*, a country on the east side of the Adriatic sea, north of Epirus.

Īllyricus, -a, -um, adj., *of the Illyrians, of Illyria, Illyrian.*

imāgō, -inis, [cf. imitor], f., *copy, likeness, form, image; statue, bust; phantom, ghost; conception, thought; semblance, shadow.*

imbēcillitās, -ātis, [imbēcillus, *feeble*], f., *feebleness, weakness; helplessness, powerlessness.*

imberbis, -e, [in- + barba], adj., *beardless, without a beard.*

imitātor, -ōris, [imitor], m., *imitator, copyist.*

imitor, -ārī, -ātus sum, 1, dep., *imitate, copy after; copy, portray.*

immānis, -e, adj., *monstrous, huge; fierce, cruel, wild, inhuman.*

immānitās, -ātis, [immānis], f., *hugeness, enormity; monstrosity, heinousness, savageness, cruelty.*

immātūrus, -a, -um, [in- + mātūrus], adj., *unripe; untimely, premature.*

immineō, -ēre, ——, ——, [in, cf. minor], 2, n., *overhang; be near, be at hand, impend; threaten, menace; be eager for, long for.*

imminuō, -ere, -uī, -ūtum, [in + minuō], 3, a., *lessen, diminish; encroach upon, infringe upon, reduce.*

immittō, -ere, immīsī, immissum, [in + mittō], 3, a., *send in, let in, admit, introduce ; send against, set on ; discharge, hurl.*

immō, adv., *nay indeed, nay, on the contrary, no indeed.* **immō vērō**, *nay rather, nay more.*

immortālis, -e, [in- + mortālis], adj., *undying, immortal ; endless, eternal, imperishable.*

immortālitās, -ātis, [immortālis], f., *immortality, endless life ; undying renown, imperishable fame.*

impediō, -īre, -īvī, -ītum, [in, cf. pēs, ped-is], 4, a., *entangle ; hinder, embarrass ; obstruct, impede, check, prevent.*

impellō, -ere, impulī, impulsum, [in + pellō], 3, a., *strike against, strike ; move, impel ; urge, incite, persuade.*

impendeō, -ēre, ——, ——, [in + pendeō], 2, n. and a., *overhang ; be near, be at hand, be imminent ; impend, threaten.*

imperātor, -ōris, [imperō], m., *commander-in-chief, general ; commander, leader, director.*

imperātōrius, -a, -um, [imperātor], adj., *of a commander, of a general.*

imperītus, -a, -um, [in- + perītus], adj., *inexperienced, unskilled, unacquainted with.*

imperium, -ī, [imperō], n., *command, order ; authority, control ; sovereignty, dominion, empire, supremacy, sway.*

imperō, -āre, -āvī, -ātum, [in + parō], 1, a. and n., *command, order ; control, be master of ; rule, govern ; make requisition for, require, levy.*

impertiō, -īre, -īvī, -ītum, [in + partiō, from pars], 4, a., *share with, bestow upon, bestow, impart ; assign, give.*

impetrō, -āre, -āvī, -ātum, [in + patrō, *perform*], 1, a., *gain one's end, accomplish, get, obtain, procure,* by request or by means of influence.

impetus, -ūs, [impetō], m., *onset, attack, assault ; impulse, rapid motion, rush ; violence, fury.*

impius, -a, -um, [in- + pius], adj., *undutiful, irreverent, ungodly ; wicked, impious, shameless.* As subst., **impiī**, -ōrum, m., pl., *the wicked.*

implicō, -āre, -āvī or -uī, -ātum or -itum, [in + plicō], 1, a., *entangle, involve, encircle, clasp ; connect intimately, unite, join.*

implōrō, -āre, -āvī, -ātum, [in + plōrō], 1, a. and n., *beseech, entreat, implore.*

importūnus, -a, -um, adj., *unsuitable ; harsh, rude, hard, cruel, savage.*

improbitās, -ātis, [improbus], f., *wickedness, badness, depravity.*

improbō, -āre, -āvī, -ātum, [in- + probō], 1, a., *disapprove of, censure, condemn, blame.*

improbus, -a, -um, [in- + probus], adj., *wicked, bad, depraved, base ; shameless, outrageous.*

impūbēs, -eris, [in- + pūbēs], adj., *under age, youthful, beardless.*

impudēns, -entis, [in- + pudēns], adj., *without sense of shame, shameless, indecent, impudent.*

impudenter [impudēns], adv., *shamelessly, indecently, impudently.*

impudentia, -ae, [impudēns], f., *shamelessness, impudence.*

impudīcus, -a, -um, [in- + pudīcus], adj., *shameless, immodest, unchaste.* As subst., **impudīcī**, -ōrum, m., pl., *the unchaste.*

impulsus, -ūs, [impellō], m., *striking against, shock ; impulse, influence.*

impūnītus, -a, -um, [in- + pūnītus], adj., *unpunished, without restraint, unrestrained, secure.*

impūrus, -a, -um, [in- + pūrus], adj., *unclean, filthy; defiled, abandoned, vile.* As subst., **impūrī**, **-ōrum**, m., pl., *the filthy.*

in, prep. with acc. and abl.:

(1) With the acc.: of place, after verbs implying motion, *into, to, up to, towards, against;* of time, *into, till, to, unto, for;* of purpose, *for, with a view to;* of result, *to, unto;* of other relations, *to, in, respecting, concerning, according to, after.*

(2) With the abl.: of place, *in, within, on, upon, among, over, under;* of time, *in, in the course of, within, during, while;* of other relations, *involved in, under the influence of, in case of, in relation to, on the condition, respecting.*

In composition **in** retains its form before the vowels and most of the consonants; is often changed to **il-** before **l**, **ir-** before **r**; usually becomes **im-** before **m**, **b**, **p**.

in-, inseparable prefix, = un-, *not,* as in **inaudītus**, *unheard;* **incertus**, *uncertain.*

inānis, -e, adj., *empty, vacant, unoccupied; useless, profitless, worthless, vain.*

inaudītus, -a, -um, [in- + audītus], adj., *unheard-of, unusual, strange.*

inaurātus, -a, -um, [part. of **inaurō**, *gild*], adj., *gilded, golden.*

incendium, -ī, [incendō], n., *fire, conflagration;* of the feelings, *heat, flame, vehemence, passion.*

incendō, -ere, incendī, incēnsum, 3, a., *set fire to, kindle, burn;* of the feelings, *inflame, arouse, incite, irritate, enrage.*

incēnsiō, -ōnis, [incendō], f., *burning.*

inceptum, -ī, [incipiō], n., *beginning, undertaking; attempt.*

incertus, -a, -um, [in- + certus], adj., *unsettled, not determined, uncertain, unascertained, doubtful;* of persons or character, *wavering, irresolute, at a loss.*

incidō, -ere, incidī, incāsum, [in + cadō], 3, n., *fall in, strike; light upon, fall in with; fall into, become involved; fall out, happen, occur.*

incīdō, -ere, incīdī, incīsum, [in + caedō], 3, a., *cut into, cut open, cut through; carve, engrave; break off, interrupt.*

incipiō, -cipere, -cēpī, -ceptum, [in + capiō], 3, a. and n., *take hold of; begin, commence, begin to speak; begin to be* or *to appear.*

incitāmentum, -ī, [incitō], n., *incentive, inducement.*

incitō, -āre, -āvī, -ātum, [in + citō, *hasten*], 1, a., *hasten, quicken; urge on, spur on, rouse, stir.*

inclīnō, -āre, -āvī, -ātum, 1, a. and n., *bend, turn; incline; be inclined, be favorably disposed.*

inclūdō, -ere, inclūsī, inclūsum, [in + claudō], 3, a., *shut in, enclose, confine, shut up in; obstruct, hinder; include, comprehend.*

incognitus, -a, -um, [in- + cognitus], adj., *not examined, untried, unknown.*

incohō, -āre, -āvī, -ātum, 1, a. and n., *begin, commence;* of a subject, *take in hand, begin to discuss, undertake to treat.*

incolumis, -e, [in- + columis], adj., *unharmed, uninjured, safe, sound, whole.*

incommodum, -ī, [incommodus], n., *inconvenience, disadvantage, trouble; misfortune, loss, defeat.*

incorruptē, comp. **incorruptius**, [incorruptus], adv., *uncorruptly, fairly, justly.*

incrēdibilis, -e, [in- + crēdibilis], adj., *beyond belief, incredible, extraordinary, unparalleled.*

increpō, -āre, -uī, -itum, [in + crepō], 1, n. and a., *make a noise, resound, crash; occur, be noised abroad; cause to resound; upbraid, scold.*

incumbō, -ere, incubuī, incubitum, [in + obsolete cumbō, *lie*], 3, n., *lie upon, lean, rest, recline; press upon, oppress; exert one's self, make an effort, apply one's self; be inclined, lean towards.*

indagō, -āre, -āvī, -ātum, [indu, old form of **in**, + **agō**], 1, a., *seek out, investigate, trace, explore.*

inde, adv., *from that place, thence, from that point; therefrom, from that; from that time, thereafter, after that; in consequence, therefore.*

indemnātus, -a, -um, [in- + damnātus], adj., *uncondemned, without being sentenced.*

index, -icis, [cf. indicō], m. and f., *discloser, informer, witness; sign, mark; inscription, title; forefinger.*

indicium, -ī, [indicō], n., *disclosure, information; mark, sign, proof; testimony, evidence.*

indicō, -āre, -āvī, -ātum, [index], 1, a., *point out, make known, disclose, reveal, designate; accuse, charge.*

indīcō, -ere, indīxī, indictum, [in + dīcō], 3, a., *announce, declare publicly, declare, proclaim; convoke, order; impose, enjoin.*

indigeō, -ēre, -uī, ——, [indu, old form of in, + egeō], 2, n., *need, want, lack; stand in need of, require.*

indīgnē [indīgnus], adv., *unworthily, undeservedly, shamefully.*

indīgnus, -a, -um, [in- + dīgnus], adj., *unworthy, undeserving, unbecoming, not fit; shameful, outrageous.* As subst., **indīgnum**, -ī, n., *outrage, shame.*

indūcō, -ere, indūxī, inductum, [in + dūcō], 3, a., *lead in, introduce, bring forward, conduct; spread over, overspread, overlay; move, persuade, induce.* **animum indūcere**, *to make up one's mind, to bring one's self to, to resolve.*

industria, -ae, [industrius], f., *activity, diligence, zeal, industry.*

industrius, -a, -um, adj., *active, diligent, zealous, industrious.*

ineō, -īre, -īvī or -iī, -itum, [in + eō], irr., a. and n., *go into, enter; come in, come on, begin; undertake, engage in, adopt.*

ineptē [ineptus], adv., *improperly, unbecomingly, absurdly.*

ineptia, -ae, [ineptus], f., *folly, absurdity, foolishness;* pl., *trifles, notions, absurdities.*

iners, -ertis, [in- + ars], adj., *unskilful, awkward; idle, indolent, inactive, sluggish, worthless.*

inertia, -ae, [iners], f., *unskilfulness, want of skill; idleness, indolence, inactivity.*

īnfāmis, -e, [in- + fāma], adj., *disreputable, notorious, infamous.*

īnferior, -ius, [comp. of īnferus], adj., *lower, inferior.*

īnferō, -ferre, intulī, illātum, [in + ferō], irr., a., *carry in, bring in, introduce; bring to, carry into, convey, bring; bring against, wage, direct; bring forward, produce; excite, cause, inflict.* **sē īnferre**, *to present one's self, to repair, to enter.*

īnferus, **-a**, **-um**, comp. **īnferior**, sup. **īnfimus** or **īmus**, [cf. **īnfrā**], adj., *below, underneath, lower, underground; of the Underworld.* As subst., **īnferī**, **-ōrum**, m., pl., *folk of the Underworld, inhabitants of the Lower World; the dead, the shades.*

īnfēstus, **-a**, **-um**, adj., *unsafe, disturbed, molested; hostile, troublesome, dangerous.*

īnfimus, **-a**, **-um**, [sup. of **īnferus**], adj., *lowest, last; meanest, most degraded, basest.*

īnfīnītus, **-a**, **-um**, [**in-** + **fīnītus**], adj., *boundless, unlimited; endless, infinite.*

īnfīrmō, **-āre**, **-āvī**, **-ātum**, [**īnfīrmus**], 1, a. and n., *weaken; refute, disprove.*

īnfīrmus, **-a**, **-um**, [**in-** + **fīrmus**], adj., *not strong, weak, infirm, feeble, unhealthy; inconstant, superstitious; of no account, trivial, invalid.*

īnfitiātor, **-ōris**, [**īnfitior**], m., *denier, repudiator.* **lentus īnfitiātor**, *bad debtor.*

īnfitior, **-ārī**, **-ātus sum**, [**in-** + **fateor**], 1, dep., *not acknowledge, deny, disown; repudiate.*

īnflammō, **-āre**, **-āvī**, **-ātum**, [**in** + **flammō**], 1, a., *set on fire, light up, kindle; inflame, excite, arouse, stir.*

īnflō, **-āre**, **-āvī**, **-ātum**, [**in** + **flō**], 1, a., *blow into, breathe upon; inspire; puff up, elate.*

īnfōrmō, **-āre**, **-āvī**, **-ātum**, [**in** + **fōrmō**], 1, a., *shape, mould; instruct, educate; describe.*

ingenium, **-ī**, [**in**, cf. **gīgnō**], n., *innate quality, nature; disposition, character, temper; ability, capacity, talent, genius.*

ingēns, **-entis**, adj., *beyond natural size, huge, enormous; great, remarkable.*

ingenuus, **-a**, **-um**, [**in**, cf. **gīgnō**], adj., *native; free-born, of free parents; noble, upright, ingenuous.* As subst., **ingenuī**, **-ōrum**, m., pl., *the free-born,* meaning the better classes of Roman citizens.

ingrātus, **-a**, **-um**, [**in-** + **grātus**], adj., *unacceptable, unpleasant; ungrateful, thankless.*

ingravēscō, **-ere**, **——**, **——**, [**ingravō**], 3, inch., *grow burdensome; grow worse, be aggravated, increase.*

ingredior, **-gredī**, **-gressus sum**, [**in** + **gradior**], 3, dep., *advance, go forward, proceed; go into, enter; enter upon, engage in, undertake, begin.*

inhiō, **-āre**, **-āvī**, **-ātum**, [**in** + **hiō**], 1, n. and a., *gape, open the mouth to; gape with amazement, be amazed; gaze eagerly.*

inhūmānus, **-a**, **-um**, [**in-** + **hūmānus**], adj., *rude, brutal, inhuman; ill-bred, coarse, uncultivated.*

iniciō, **-icere**, **-iēcī**, **-iectum**, [**in** + **iaciō**], 3, a., *cast into, throw in; hurl upon, cast upon; heap up, build; put on, throw around; lay hands upon, take possession of; inspire in, cause.*

inimīcitia, **-ae**, [**inimīcus**], f., *hostility, enmity.*

inimīcus, **-a**, **-um**, [**in-** + **amīcus**], adj., *unfriendly, hostile, inimical; hurtful, injurious.* As subst., **inimīcus**, **-ī**, *personal enemy, enemy.*

inīquitās, **-ātis**, [**inīquus**], f., *inequality; unfavorableness, difficulty; unfairness, injustice.*

inīquus, **-a**, **-um**, [**in-** + **aequus**], adj., *uneven, sloping, steep; ill-matched, unequal; unfavorable, disadvantageous; unfair, unjust; adverse, hostile.*

initiō, **-āre**, **-āvī**, **-ātum**, [initium], 1, a., *initiate*, *consecrate*; used especially of initiation into the sacred mysteries.

initium, **-ī**, [ineō], n., *entrance*; *beginning*, *commencement*.

iniūcundus, **-a**, **-um**, [in- + iūcundus], adj., *unpleasant*, *displeasing*, *disagreeable*.

iniūria, **-ae**, [iniūrius, from in- + iūs], f., *outrage*, *wrong*, *injury*, *injustice*; *insult*; abl. **iniūriā**, often with the force of an adv., *unjustly*, *undeservedly*, *wrongfully*.

iniūriōsē, comp. **iniūriōsius**, [iniūriōsus], adv., *unfairly*, *unjustly*, *unlawfully*.

iniussus, **-ūs**, found only in abl., [in + iussus], m., *without command*, *without bidding* or *orders*.

iniūstus, **-a**, **-um**, [in- + iūstus], adj., *unfair*, *unjust*, *unreasonable*; *wrongful*; *excessive*, *burdensome*.

innocēns, **-entis**, [in- + nocēns], adj., *harmless*, *inoffensive*; *blameless*, *innocent*, *upright*.

innocentia, **-ae**, [innocēns], f., *blamelessness*, *innocence*; *uprightness*, *integrity*.

innumerābilis, **-e**, [in- + numerābilis], adj., *countless*, *innumerable*.

inopia, **-ae**, [inops], f., *want*, *lack*; *need*, *scarcity*, *poverty*.

in prīmīs, see **prior**.

inquam, **inquis**, **inquit**, def., n., postpositive, *say*.

inrēpō, **-ere**, **inrēpsī**, **inrēptum**, [in + rēpō], 3, n., *creep in*, *steal in*; *be stealthily inserted*.

inrētiō, **-īre**, **-īvī**, **-ītum**, [in, rēte, *net*], 4, a., *catch in a net*, *ensnare*; *entangle*, *entrap*, *involve*.

inrītō, **-āre**, **-āvī**, **-ātum**, 1, a., *incite*, *instigate*; *irritate*, *exasperate*, *provoke*.

inruptiō, **-ōnis**, [inrumpō], f., *breaking in*; *inroad*, *incursion*, *invasion*.

īnscrībō, **-ere**, **īnscrīpsī**, **īnscrīptum**, [in + scrībō], 3, a., *write upon*, *inscribe*; *assign*, *appropriate*; *mark*.

īnsepultus, **-a**, **-um**, [in- + sepultus], adj., *unburied*, *without burial*.

īnserviō, **-īre**, ——, **-ītum**, [in + serviō], 4, n. and a, *devote one's self to*, *be devoted to*; *be submissive to*, *serve*.

īnsideō, **-ēre**, **īnsēdī**, **īnsessum**, [in + sedeō], 2, n. and a., *sit upon*; *settle*, *be inherent in*, *inhere*; *take possession of*, *hold*.

īnsidiae, **-ārum**, [cf. **īnsideō**], f., pl., *ambush*, *ambuscade*; *snare*, *trap*, *plot*, *artifice*, *device*.

īnsidiātor, **-ōris**, [īnsidior], m., *lurker*, *waylayer*, *highwayman*.

īnsidior, **-ārī**, **-ātus sum**, [īnsidiae], 1, dep., *lie in wait for*, *watch for*, *plot against*.

īnsidiōsus, **-a**, **-um**, [īnsidiae], adj., *deceitful*, *treacherous*, *dangerous*.

īnsīdō, **-ere**, **īnsēdī**, **īnsessum**, [in + sīdō], 3, n. and a., *settle on*, *occupy*; *be fixed in*, *remain*, *adhere to*.

īnsīgne, **-is**, [īnsīgnis], n., *mark*, *sign*, *token*; *indication*, *proof*; *badge*, *decoration*, *distinction*.

īnsimulō, **-āre**, **-āvī**, **-ātum**, [in + simulō], 1, a., *charge*, *bring as a charge*; *accuse*, *blame*.

īnsolēns, **-entis**, [in- + solēns], adj., *unusual*; *immoderate*, *arrogant*, *haughty*, *insolent*.

īnsolenter, comp. **īnsolentius**, [īnsolēns], adv., *unusually*; *immoderately*, *haughtily*, *insolently*.

īnsolentia, **-ae**, [īnsolēns], f., *novelty*, *strangeness*; *haughtiness*, *arrogance*, *insolence*.

īnsolitus, -a, -um, [in- + solitus], adj., *unaccustomed, unwonted, unusual; uncommon, strange.*

īnspectō, -āre, -āvī, -ātum, only pres. part. found in classical Latin, [freq. of **īnspiciō**], 1, a. and n., *look at, observe, view.* **īnspectante praetōre,** *under the eyes of the praetor.*

īnspērāns, -antis, [in- + **spērāns**, **spērō**], adj., *not hoping, beyond hope, not expecting.*

īnspērātus, -a, -um, [in- + **spērātus**, **spērō**], adj., *unhoped for, unexpected, unforeseen.*

īnstituō, -ere, **īnstituī**, **īnstitūtum**, [in + **statuō**], 3, a. and n., *put in place, plant; found, establish; arrange, draw up; build, construct; provide, prepare; undertake, begin; appoint, designate; purpose, resolve, decide, propose; teach, instruct, train up.*

īnstitūtum, -ī, [**īnstituō**], n., *purpose, design, plan; custom, usage, practice, precedent; institution, regulation.*

īnstō, -stāre, -stitī, -stātum, [in + **stō**], 1, n., *stand upon, be near at hand, approach, draw nigh; press upon, pursue, harass; menace, threaten; insist upon, urge.*

īnstrūctus, -a, -um, [part. of **īnstruō**], adj., *furnished, provided, equipped; arranged; versed.*

īnstrūmentum, -ī, [**īnstruō**], n., *implement, tool, appliance; set of tools, stock, furniture; supply, store, means, furtherance.*

īnstruō, -ere, **īnstrūxī**, **īnstrūctum**, [in + **struō**], 3, a., *build in; make ready, furnish, provide, prepare, equip;* of troops, *draw up, set in array, array.*

īnsula, -ae, f., *island, isle.*

īnsum, inesse, **īnfuī**, [in + **sum**], irr., n., *be in, be on; exist in, belong to.*

integer, -gra, -grum, comp. **integrior**, sup. **integerrimus**, [in, cf. **tangō**], adj., *untouched, whole, entire; unimpaired, unhurt; sound, fresh, vigorous; undecided, undetermined; impartial; blameless, spotless, pure;* of a seal, *unbroken.*

integrē [**integer**], adv., *faultlessly; blamelessly, irreproachably, without prejudice.*

integritās, -ātis, [**integer**], f., *completeness, soundness; blamelessness, integrity, uprightness.*

intellegō, -ere, **intellēxī**, **intellēctum**, [**inter** + **lēgo**], 3, a., *see into, perceive, gather; understand, discern, comprehend.*

intendō, -ere, **intendī**, **intentum** or **-sum**, [in + **tendō**], 3, a. and n., *stretch out, extend; stretch, fasten; direct, aim; bend, strain, turn; urge; purpose, intend.*

inter, prep. with acc. only, *among;* of position and relation, *between, among, amid, surrounded by, into the midst of;* of time, *between, during, in the course of, through, while, in, within.*

intercalō, -āre, -āvī, -ātum, [**inter** + **calō**], 1, a., *insert in the calendar, intercalate; put off, postpone.*

intercēdō, -ere, **intercessī**, **intercessum**, [**inter** + **cēdō**], 3, n., *come between, intervene, pass; come to pass, occur; interpose; oppose, withstand.*

intercessiō, -ōnis, [**intercēdō**], f., *intervention, protest, veto.*

interclūdō, -ere, **interclūsī**, **interclūsum**, [**inter** + **claudō**], 3, a., *shut out, cut off, intercept; hinder; divide.*

interdum [**inter** + **dum**], adv., *now and then, sometimes, at times.*

intereā [**inter** + **eā**], adv., *meanwhile, in the meantime.*

intereō, -īre, -iī, -itum, [inter + eō], irr., n., *go among; be lost among*, hence *go to ruin, decay, perish, die.*

interficiō, -ficere, -fēcī, -fectum, [inter + faciō], 3, a., *destroy; slay, kill, murder.*

interim, adv., *meanwhile, in the meantime; nevertheless.*

interimō, -ere, interēmī, interēmptum, [inter + emō], 3, a., *do away with, destroy; slay, kill.*

interior, -ius, gen. -ōris, sup. intimus, adj., *inner, interior; nearer, deeper;* sup., *inmost, innermost, deepest; intimate, close.*

interitus, -ūs, [intereō], m., *overthrow, ruin; destruction, death.*

interneciō, -ōnis, [inter, cf. nex], f., *massacre, slaughter; utter destruction, destruction.*

interpellō, -āre, -āvī, -ātum, [inter + unused pellō], 1, a., *interrupt; hinder, obstruct, prevent.*

interpretor, -ārī, -ātus sum, [interpres], 1, dep., *explain, interpret; understand, comprehend, make out; conclude, decide.*

interrogō, -āre, -āvī, -ātum, [inter + rogō], 1, a., *ask, inquire of, question.*

intersum, -esse, -fuī, [inter + sum], irr., n., *be between, lie between; intervene, elapse; be different, differ; be present, take part in.* Impers., **interest**, *it concerns, it is important, it makes a difference.*

intervāllum, -ī, [inter + vāllum], n., lit. *room between* (*two*) *palisades;* hence, *intermediate distance, distance, interval; intermission.*

interventus, -ūs, [interveniō], m., *coming between, coming in; intervention, appearance.*

intestīnus, -a, -um, [intus], adj., *internal, intestine.*

intimus, -a, -um, see **interior**.

intrā [cf. interior], prep. with acc. only, *within, inside of; into; during, in the course of.*

intrōdūcō, -ere, intrōdūxī, intrōductum, [intrō + dūcō], 3, a., *lead in, bring in, introduce.*

intueor, -ērī, intuitus sum, [in + tueor], 2, dep., *look upon, gaze at; contemplate, consider; admire, wonder at.*

intus [in], adv., *within, on the inside.*

inultus, -a, -um, [in- + ultus], adj., *unavenged; unpunished, unchastised; safe, with impunity.*

inūrō, -ere, inussī, inūstum, [in + ūrō], 3, a., *burn in; brand upon, brand, imprint.*

inūsitātus, -a, -um, [in- + ūsitātus], adj., *unusual, uncommon, rare.*

inūtilis, -e, [in- + ūtilis], adj., *useless, unprofitable, unserviceable; inexpedient, unavailing, hurtful.*

inveniō, -īre, invēnī, inventum, [in + veniō], 4, a., *come upon, find, meet; discover, invent, contrive, devise; find out, learn.*

investīgō, -āre, -āvī, -ātum, [in + vestīgō], 1, a., *track; trace out, search into, investigate, find out.*

inveterāscō, -ere, inveterāvī, ——, [in + veterāscō], 3, inch., *grow old; become fixed, be established, become rooted.*

invictus, -a, -um, sup. invictissimus, [in- + victus], adj., *unconquered; unconquerable, invincible.*

invideō, -ēre, invīdī, invīsum, [in + videō], 2, n. and a., *look askance at, be prejudiced, be jealous; envy, grudge.*

invidia, -ae, [invidus], f., *envy, jealousy; dislike, hatred, grudge; odium, unpopularity.*

invidiōsus, -a, -um, [invidia], adj., *full of envy, invidious; exciting envy, enviable, envied; causing hatred, hateful, hated, odious.*

invidus, -a, -um, [invideō], adj., *envious, jealous.* As subst., **invidus, -ī**, m., *envious person*, pl., *the envious.*

invīsō, -ere, **invīsī, invīsum**, [in + **vīsō**], 3, a., *go to see, look after, visit.*

invīsus, -a, -um, [part. of **invideō**], adj., *hated, detested, odious, hostile.*

invītō, -āre, -āvī, -ātum, 1, a., *invite, ask, urge; attract, allure; entertain, feast.*

invītus, -a, -um, adj., *unwilling, reluctant, against the will.*

ipse, -a, -um, gen. **ipsīus**, dem. pron., *self; himself, herself, itself;* often emphatic, *he;* often best rendered freely, as *very, precisely, likewise, in person.*

īra, -ae, f., *anger, wrath; rage, passion, indignation, fury.*

īrācundia, -ae, [**īrācundus**], f., *proneness to anger; anger, rage, passion, violence.*

īrācundus, -a, -um, [**īra**], adj., *prone to anger, irritable; passionate, wrathful, angry.*

īrāscor, -āscī, -ātus sum, [**īra**], 3, dep., *be in anger, get angry; fly into a passion, rave, be furious.*

īrātus, -a, -um, [part. of **īrāscor**], adj., *angered, angry, furious, violent.*

is, ea, id, gen. **ēius**, dem. pron., *he, she, it, that, this, the, the one;* before **ut**, = tālis, *such;* with comparatives abl. **eō** = *the, all the*, as **eō magis**, *all the more;* after **et, -que, atque**, *and that too, and in fact.* **id temporis**, see IDIOMS.

iste, ista, istud, gen. **istīus**, dem. pron., referring to the person addressed, sometimes ironically, *that, that of yours; he, she, it; this; such.*

istim, adv., *thence, from thence.*

ita, adv., *thus, so, in this way, as follows; such, of this kind; to such a degree, so far.* **quae cum ita sint**, *and since this is so, and accordingly.*

Italia, -ae, [ἰταλός], f., *Italy.*

Italicus, -a, -um, adj., *of Italy, Italic, Italian.*

itaque [**ita** + **-que**], conj., *and so, and thus, accordingly; consequently, therefore.*

item, adv., *likewise, also, besides, moreover, too.*

iter, itineris, [cf. **eō**], n., *a going; way, journey, march; road, path, passage, course.*

iterum, adv., *a second time, again; once more, in turn.* **iterum et saepius**, *again and again.*

iubeō, -ēre, **iussī, iussum**, 2, a., *order, bid, give orders, command, direct; exhort, entreat; decree, ratify, approve.*

iūcunditās, -ātis, [**iūcundus**], f., *pleasantness; delight, enjoyment.*

iūcundus, -a, -um, adj., *pleasant, agreeable, pleasing, delightful.*

iūdex, -icis, [**iūs**, cf. **dīcō**], m. and f., *judge; juror; decider, umpire.*

iūdiciālis, -e, [**iūdicium**], adj., *of a court, of the courts, judicial.*

iūdicium, -ī, [**iūdex**], n., *trial, court; judgment, sentence; decision, opinion, conviction.*

iūdicō, -āre, -āvī, -ātum, [**iūdex**], 1, a., *judge, pass judgment, decide; pronounce judgment upon, judge of; declare, proclaim.*

iugulum, -ī, [dim. of **iugum**], n., *collar-bone; throat, neck.*

Iugurtha, -ae, m., *Jugurtha*, king of Numidia, who came to the throne on the death of Micipsa, B.C. 118. Through his treatment of the sons of Micipsa he became involved in a war with Rome, and was captured by Marius, B C. 106. After adorning the triumph of Marius, B. C. 104, he was thrown into the lower chamber of the Mamertine prison, and there starved to death. IMP. P. XX.

Iūlius, **-a**, name of a celebrated patrician gens, of which the Caesar family formed a part. See **Caesar**.

iungō, **iungere**, **iūnxī**, **iūnctum**, [cf. **iugum**], 3, a., *join, unite, connect; yoke, attach; bring together, associate, ally*.

Iūnius, **-a**, **-um**, adj., *of June*. As subst., **Iūnius**, **-ī**, m., *June*.

Iūnius, **-a**, name of prominent plebeian gens, to which the Brutus family belonged. See **Brūtus**.

Iuppiter, **Iovis**, m., *Jupiter*, son of Saturn, chief of the gods; by metonymy, *heaven, sky, air*.

iūrātus, **-a**, **-um**, [**iūrō**], adj., *sworn, oath-bound, under oath*.

iūs, **iūris**, n., *right, law, duty; justice, equity; prerogative, authority, power; court* of justice; abl. **iūre** often with adverbial force, *by right, rightfully, justly*.

iūs iūrandum, **iūris iūrandī**, n., *oath*.

iussum, **-ī**, [**iubeō**], n., *order, command, prescription, direction*.

iussus, **-ūs**, only abl. in use, [**iubeō**], m., *order, command, decree*.

iūstē [**iūstus**], adv., *rightly, justly; fairly, uprightly*.

iūstitia, **-ae**, [**iūstus**], f., *justice, equity, uprightness; clemency, compassion*.

iūstus, **-a**, **-um**, [**iūs**], adj., *just, upright; fair, lawful, proper, equitable; right, suitable, sufficient, complete*.

iuventūs, **-ūtis**, [**iuvenis**], f., *age of youth, youth*, reckoned ordinarily from the twentieth to the fortieth year; by metonymy, *young people, young folk, youth*.

iuvō, **-āre**, **iūvī**, **iūtum**, 1, a. and n., *help, aid, assist, support; gratify, please, delight*.

K.

Kal., = **Kalendae**.

Kalendae, **-ārum**, abbreviated **Kal.**, [cf. **calō**, *convoke*], f., pl., *the Calends*, the first day of the month. **Kalendae Māiae**, *the first of May*.

Karthāginiēnsis, **-e**, [**Karthāgō**], adj., *of Carthage, Carthaginian*. As subst., **Karthāginiēnsēs**, **-ium**, m., pl., *people of Carthage, Carthaginians*.

Karthāgō, **-inis**, f., *Carthage*.

L.

L., = **Lūcius**.

labefactō, **-āre**, **-āvī**, **-ātum**, [freq. of **labefaciō**], 1, a., *cause to totter, shake, disturb; weaken, undermine; overthrow, ruin, destroy*.

lābēs, **-is**, [**lābor**], f., *sinking in, settling; spot, blemish, stain, disgrace*.

lābor, **lābī**, **lāpsus sum**, 3, dep., *glide, slip, sink, fall; go to ruin, perish; fall into error, err, go astray*.

labor, **-ōris**, m., *labor, toil, effort, exertion, care; hardship, trouble*.

labōriōsus, **-a**, **-um**, [**labor**], adj., *laborious, toilsome, wearisome; troubled*.

labōrō, **-āre**, **-āvī**, **-ātum**, [**labor**], 1, n. and a., *toil, labor; be in distress, be in trouble, suffer pain, suffer; totter, threaten to give way*.

lăcessō, -ere, **lacessīvī**, **lacessītum**, [laciō, *entice*], 3, a., *excite, provoke ; irritate, harass, defy.*

Lacōnicus, -a, -um, [Λακωνικός], adj., *of Laconia, Laconian.* As subst., **Lacōnicum**, -ī, n., *sweating-room, sweating-bath*, of the sort first used by the Lacedaemonians.

lacrima, -ae, f., *tear.*

lacrimō, -āre, -āvī, -ātum, [lacrima], 1, n. and a., *shed tears, weep ; bewail, lament.*

lactēns, -entis, [part. of unused lacteō, from **lac**], adj., *taking milk, suckling.*

Laeca, -ae, m., *M. Porcius Laeca*, a senator who took a prominent part in the conspiracy of Catiline. CAT. I. IV., II. VI.

laedō, -ere, **laesī**, **laesum**, 3, a., *hurt, wound, injure ; offend, grieve, pain, vex ; betray, violate.*

Laelius, -ī, m., *Gāius Laelius Sapiēns*, whose friendship with the younger Scipio Africanus was proverbial, and is celebrated in Cicero's *Dē Amīcitiā.* He was born about 186 B. C., performed heroic exploits in the third Punic War, and was consul B. C. 140. He is Cicero's typical example of the best results of cultivation acting on a character which exhibited in their fullest extent the ideal Roman virtues. ARCH. VII.

Laenius, -ī, m., see **Flaccus**, (4).

laetitia, -ae, [laetus], f., *joy, rejoicing ; delight, gladness, pleasure.*

laetor, -ārī, -ātus sum, [cf. laetus], 1, dep., *rejoice, be joyful, be glad.*

lāmentātiō, -ōnis, [lāmentor], f., *wailing, moaning, weeping ; lamenting, lamentation.*

lāmentor, -ārī, -ātus sum, [lāmentum, *wailing*], 1, dep., *wail, moan ; lament, bewail, bemoan.*

languidus, -a, -um, adj., *weak, sluggish, languid ; feeble, inactive, listless.*

largior, -īrī, -ītus sum, [largus], 4, dep., *lavish, dispense, distribute, bestow ; give largesses, bribe.*

largītiō, -ōnis, [largior], f., *lavish giving, dispensing, bestowing, distribution ; bribery.*

largītor, -ōris, [largior], m., *lavish giver, dispenser, spendthrift, prodigal ; giver of bribes, briber.*

lātē [lātus], adv., *broadly, widely ; extensively, far and wide.*

latebra, -ae, [lateō], f., *hiding-place, lurking-place, recess, retreat ; pretence, excuse.*

lateō, -ēre, -uī, ——, 2, n., *lie hid, be hidden, lurk ; be concealed, escape notice.*

Latīniēnsis, -is, m., see **Caelius**, (1).

Latīnus, -a, -um, adj., *of Latium, Latin ; Roman.*

lātiō, -ōnis, [cf. **lātus**, **tollō**], f., *bringing forward ;* of a law, *proposal.*

Latium, -ī, n., *Latium*, the country in which Rome was situated, on the west side of Italy, between Etruria and Campania.

lātor, -ōris, [cf. **lātus**, **tollō**], m., *bringer ;* of a law, *proposer, mover.*

lātrō, -ōnis, m., originally *mercenary soldier;* hence, *highwayman, bandit, brigand.*

lātrōcinium, -ī, [lātrōcinor], n., *highway-robbery, brigandage, robbery ; band of robbers.*

lātrōcinor, -ārī, -ātus sum, [lātrō], 1, dep., originally *be a hired soldier ;* hence *practice highway robbery, plunder, rob along the highways.*

latus, **-eris**, n., *side, flank;* by metonymy, *body, person, life.*

laudō, **-āre**, **-āvī**, **-ātum**, [laus], 1, a., *praise, commend, extol, eulogize.*

laus, **laudis**, f., *praise, commendation; glory, fame, renown; credit, merit.*

lēctitō, **-āre**, **-āvī**, **-ātum**, [freq. of **legō**], 1, a., *read often, read again and again, peruse.*

lectulus, **-ī**, [dim. of **lectus**], m., *small couch, (little) bed.*

lēctus, **-a**, **-um**, [part. of **legō**], adj., *chosen, picked, selected; choice, excellent.*

lectus, **-ī**, m., *couch, bed, lounge.*

lēgātiō, **-ōnis**, [**lēgō**], f., *embassy, legation.*

lēgātus, **-ī**, [**lēgō**], m., *embassador, envoy, legate; lieutenant.*

legiō, **-ōnis**, [cf. **legō**], f., *legion*, a body of soldiers containing ten cohorts of infantry, and accompanied ordinarily by three hundred cavalrymen.

lēgitimus, **-a**, **-um**, [**lēx**], adj., *legal, lawful, legitimate; just, proper.*

lēgō, **-āre**, **-āvī**, **-ātum**, [**lēx**], 1, a., lit. *appoint legally;* hence, *commission, send as embassador; send as deputy, commission as lieutenant; leave by will, will.*

legō, **-ere**, **lēgī**, **lēctum**, 3, a., *bring together, collect; select, choose; coast along; elect, appoint; read, peruse.*

lēniō, **-īre**, **-īvī**, **-ītum**, [**lēnis**], 4, a., *soften, mollify, calm, soothe; appease, mitigate, pacify.*

lēnis, **-e**, adj., *soft, gentle, mild, smooth, calm; kind, moderate.*

lēnitās, **-ātis**, [**lēnis**], f., *softness, gentleness, mildness, tenderness.*

lēnō, **-ōnis**, m., *panderer, procurer, seducer.*

lentē [**lentus**], adv., *slowly, leisurely; calmly, indifferently.*

Lentulus, **-ī**, [**lēns**, *lentil*], m., name of one of the proudest families of the Cornelian gens. Of the eighteen Lentuli mentioned by Cicero the following are referred to in this book:

(1) *P. Cornēlius Lentulus*, consul 162 B. C., afterwards princeps senatus. He was wounded in the riot in which C. Gracchus was slain, B. C. 121, and died soon afterwards. He was grandfather of the Lentulus associated with Catiline. CAT. IV. VI.

(2) *L. Cornēlius Lentulus*, praetor B. C. 89. ARCH. V.

(3) *Cn. Cornēlius Lentulus*, tribune of the people and the following year legatus. IMP. P. XIX.

(4) *Cn. Cornēlius Lentulus Clōdiānus*, consul in 72, censor 70 B. C., and one of the lieutenants of Pompey in the campaign against the pirates. IMP. P. XXIII.

(5) *L. Cornēlius Lentulus Crūs*, consul B. C. 49. In the strife between Caesar and Pompey he took sides with the latter. After the battle of Pharsalia he followed Pompey to Egypt, and was there imprisoned and put to death. EP. XIX.

(6) *P. Cornēlius Lentulus Spinther*, consul B. C. 57. On the day of his entering upon the duties of his office he brought forward a proposal for the recall of Cicero from exile. In the Civil War he joined the party of Pompey. EP. IX.

(7) *P. Cornēlius Lentulus Sūra*, an important member of the Catilinarian conspiracy. He was consul B. C. 71, but was expelled

from the senate the following year on account of his infamous morals. He expected, from his high rank, to become a leader in the conspiracy, but he lacked the resolution requisite for success. He was executed along with the other conspirators, Dec. 5, B.C. 63. CAT. III. II. *et seq.*

lentus, -a, -um, [cf. **lēnis**], adj., *pliant, yielding, tough; slow, backward; easy, unconcerned.*

lepidus, -a, -um, [cf. **lepōs**], adj., *pleasant, agreeable, fine; nice, pretty.*

Lepidus, -ī, [**lepidus**], m., name of a distinguished family of the Aemilian gens. The following members are mentioned in this book:

(1) *M. Aemilius Lepidus,* consul B.C. 78. He attempted to overthrow the constitution established by Sulla, was opposed by Catulus, his colleague in the consulship, and unsuccessful. The following year he took up arms against his opponents, was defeated in a battle in the Campus Martius, fled from Italy, and died shortly after. CAT. III. X.

(2) *M'. Aemilius Lepidus,* consul B.C. 66. He was a member of the aristocratic party, but when the war broke out between Caesar and Pompey he went into retirement. CAT. I. VI., VIII.

(3) *M. Aemilius Lepidus,* consul with Julius Caesar, B.C. 46. He rendered valuable assistance to Caesar in the war with Pompey, and afterwards was united with Antony and Octavianus in the second triumvirate. He died B.C. 13. EP. XLV.

Lepta, -ae, m., *Q. Lepta,* a native of Cales, in Campania, and commander of the engineering corps (*praefectus fabrūm*) under Cicero in Cilicia, B.C. 51. He was a debtor of Cicero, with whom he remained on intimate terms. EP. XIX., XXI.

levāmen, -inis, [**levō**], n., *consolation, solace.*

levis, -e, adj., *light; airy, flitting, swift, nimble; slight, trifling, trivial, easy; capricious, inconstant, fickle.*

levitās, -ātis, [**levis**], f., *lightness; light-mindedness, fickleness, inconstancy.*

leviter, comp. **levius,** sup. **levissimē,** [**levis**], adv., *lightly; slightly, somewhat; easily.*

levō, -āre, -āvī, -ātum, [**levis**], I, a., *lift up, raise; lighten, make lighter, relieve; remove; take away, take down; console, refresh; mitigate, alleviate, lessen; release, discharge, free.*

lēx, lēgis, f., *law, enactment, statute; rule, regulation; manner; agreement; condition, stipulation, terms.*

libellus, -ī, [dim. of **liber**], m., *little book, pamphlet; memorial, notice, indictment.*

libēns, -entis, [**libet**], adj., *willing, with good will; glad, with pleasure.*

libenter [**libēns**], adv., *willingly, cheerfully; gladly, with pleasure.*

līber, -era, -erum, [cf. **libet**], adj., *free; unrestrained, unrestricted; unimpeded, loose.*

liber, -brī, m., *book.*

līberālis, -e, [**līber**], adj., *of freedom; worthy of a freeman, noble, honorable, dignified, ingenuous; kind, gracious; generous, liberal.*

līberālitās, -ātis, [**līberālis**], f., *nobility, kindness, courtesy; generosity, liberality.*

līberāliter [**līberālis**], adv., *nobly, kindly; generously, liberally.*

līberē, comp. **līberius**, [**līber**], adv., *freely ; frankly, openly, boldly.*

līberī, -**ōrum** or **līberūm**, [**līber**], m., properly *free persons ;* hence, *children of a family, children.*

līberō, -**āre**, -**āvī**, -**ātum**, [**līber**], 1, a., *set free, make free, free, liberate ; release, extricate, deliver ; acquit, absolve.*

lībertās, -**ātis**, [**līber**], f., *freedom, liberty, independence.*

lībertīnus, -**a**, -**um**, [**lībērtus**], adj., *of a freedman.* **lībērtīnus homō**, *freedman.* As subst., **lībērtīnus**, -**ī**, m., *freedman.*

lībertus, -**ī**, [**līber**], m., *one made free, freedman.*

libet, -**ēre**, **libuit** and **libitum est**, 2, n., impers., *it pleases, it is pleasing, it is agreeable.*

libīdō, -**inis**, [**libet**], f., *desire, longing, inclination ; passion, sensuality, wantonness, lust.*

Lībō, -**ōnis**, m., *L. Scribōnius Lībō*, consul B. C. 34. His daughter married one of the sons of Pompey, to whom he rendered valuable assistance in the Civil War. Ep. XXIX., XXXVI.

licet, -**ēre**, **licuit** and **licitum est**, 2, n., impers., *it is allowed, it is lawful, it is permitted ;* used to introduce a concessive subj., passing over into a conjunction, *granted that, even if, conceding that, notwithstanding.*

Licinius, -**a**, name of a plebeian gens, to which belonged several prominent families and many distinguished members. See **Archiās**, **Crassus**, **Lūcullus**, **Mūrēna.**

lingua, -**ae**, f., *tongue ;* by metonymy, *language, utterance ; speech, dialect ; garrulity, boastful speech.*

līnum, -**ī**, [λίνον], n., *flax ;* by metonymy, *flaxen thread, thread, cord ; rope, cable ; linen cloth ; net.*

liquefaciō, -**facere**, -**fēcī**, -**factum**, pass. **liquefīō**, -**fierī**, -**factus sum**, [**liqueō** + **faciō**], 3, a., *make liquid, dissolve, melt.*

littera, -**ae**, f., *letter, written character ; writing, document, inscription ; letter, epistle ; literature, letters.*

litterātus, -**a**, -**um**, [**littera**], adj., *of letters ; learned, liberally educated.*

litūra, -**ae**, [**linō**, *smear*], f., *smearing, erasure,* especially of wax on a writing-tablet in order to make an erasure ; hence, *blotting out, correction.*

locō, -**āre**, -**āvī**, -**ātum**, [**locus**], 1, a., *put, place ; arrange, dispose ; place by contract, let a contract.*

Locrēnsēs, -**ium**, m., pl., *Locrians,* inhabitants of Locri Epizephyrii, in the southwestern part of Italy.

locuplēs, -**ētis**, [**locus**, cf. -**pleō**], adj., *rich in lands, opulent, wealthy ; richly stored, well supplied ; trustworthy.*

locuplētō, -**āre**, -**āvī**, -**ātum**, [**locuplēs**], 1, a., *enrich, make rich.*

locus, -**ī**, m., pl. **locī**, -**ōrum**, when referring to single places, **loca**, -**ōrum**, when referring to places connected, as a region, *place, spot ; post, station, position ; location, region, country ; topic, subject* under discussion or cited ; *opportunity ; room.*

longē, comp. **longius**, sup. **longissimē**, [**longus**], adv., *far, far off, at a distance ; for a long time, long ; greatly, much, by far.*

longīnquitās, -**ātis**, [**longīnquus**], f., *distance, remoteness ;* of time, *length, duration.*

longinquus, -a, -um, [longus], adj., *far removed, remote, distant; prolonged, lasting.* As subst., **longinqua, -ōrum**, n., pl., *far-off events, remote events.* IMP. P. XII.

longiusculus, -a, -um, [longior], adj., *rather long, quite long.*

longus, -a, -um, adj., *long, extended, far-reaching, expanded; of long duration, prolonged, tedious; distant, remote.* **nē longum sit**, *not to be tedious, to speak briefly.*

loquor, loquī, locūtus sum, 3, dep., *speak, say, talk; tell, mention, declare; show, indicate, testify.*

Lūcius, -ī, abbreviated **L.**, m., *Lūcius*, a Roman forename.

Lucrīnēnsis, -is, [Lucrīnus], adj., *Lucrine, of the Lucrine Lake*, near Baiae, west of Naples. EP. XII.

lūctuōsus, -a, -um, [lūctus], adj., *full of sorrow, lamentable, sorrowful, mournful.*

lūctus, -ūs, [lūgeō, *mourn*], m., *mourning, grief, sorrow, lamentation; distress, affliction.*

Lūcullus, -ī, m., name of a family in the Licinian gens. Three members of it, L. Licinius Lucullus and his sons Lucius and Marcus, are mentioned together by Cicero as **Lūcullī**, gen. **-ōrum**, (ARCH. III. *et al.*):

(1) *L. Licinius Lūcullus*, praetor B. C. 103. He was sent the following year to quell an insurrection of slaves in Sicily. Though at first successful, he soon lost ground to the enemy and was recalled. On his return to Rome he was convicted of maladministration and exiled.

(2) *L. Licinius Lūcullus*, son of the preceding, consul B. C. 74. He distinguished himself as quaestor of Sulla in Greece and Asia, and afterwards by his successes in the war with Mithridates. As he failed to bring this to a successful termination, he was recalled, and afterwards resigned himself to a life of luxury. IMP. P. II. *et al.*

(3) *M. Licinius Lūcullus*, brother of (2), consul B. C. 73. Having obtained Macedonia as his province, he defeated the barbarous tribes along the northern frontier in numerous engagements and captured several seditious Greek cities on the Euxine sea. He was honored with a triumph, B. C. 71. ARCH. IV.

lūdus, -ī, [cf. lūdō], m., *play, game, sport, pastime; joke, fun;* pl. often *public games, spectacles.*

lūgeō, -ēre, lūxī, lūctum, 2, a. and n., *mourn, lament, bewail, deplore.*

lūmen, -inis, [cf. lūceō], n., *light;* by metonymy, *source of light*, as *lamp, torch; light of the eye, eye; brightness, glory.*

lupīnus, -a, -um, [lupus], adj., *of a wolf, wolf's.*

Lupus, -ī, m., *Lupus*, a friend of Cicero and of D. Brutus. EP. XLVI.

lūstrō, -āre, -āvī, -ātum, [lūstrum], 1, a., *make light, light up; wander over, traverse;* of religious services, *make pure by expiatory offerings, purify, lustrate.*

lūx, lūcis, [cf. lūceō], f., *light, brightness;* by metonymy, *daylight, day; light of life, life; eyesight, eye; public view, the public; help, succor.*

lūxuria, -ae, [lūxus], f., *extravagance, riotous living, excess, luxury.*

M.

M., = *Mārcus*, a common Roman forename.

M'., = *Mānius*, a Roman forename.

Macedonia, **-ae**, [Μακεδονία], f., *Macedonia*, *Macedon*. EP. VIII.

māchinātor, **-ōris**, [**māchinor**], m., *contriver*, *designer*, *deviser*, *inventor*.

māchinor, **-ārī**, **-ātus sum**, [**māchina**], I, dep., *contrive*, *design*, *devise*, *invent*; *scheme*, *plot*.

mactō, **-āre**, **-āvī**, **-ātum**, [**mactus**, *glorified*], I, a., *glorify*, *extol*; *sacrifice*, *devote* in honor of the gods; *kill*, *put to death*; *afflict*, *visit* with punishment, *punish*.

macula, **-ae**, f., *spot*, *stain*; *blemish*, *fault*, *disgrace*.

Maelius, **-ī**, m., with **Sp.**, *Spurius Maelius*, a wealthy plebeian who, in a time of great famine at Rome, 440 B. C., bought up grain in Etruria and either distributed it among the poor gratuitously or sold it at a very low price. In the following year he was accused of aiming at the supreme power and slain by Servilius Ahala, the master of the horse, while attempting to escape arrest. CAT. I. I.

maeror, **-ōris**, [**maereō**], m., *mourning*, *sadness*, *grief*, *sorrow*.

magis [root MAG in **māgnus**], adv., *more*, *in a greater measure*; *in a higher degree*, *far more*, *rather*, *in preference*.

magister, **-trī**, [cf. **māgnus**], m., *master*, *leader*, *director*; *instructor*, *teacher*; *guide*, *guardian*.

magistrātus, **-ūs**, [**magister**], m., *office of magistrate*, *civil office*, *magistracy*; by metonymy, *magistrate*, *public officer*.

māgnificē, comp. **māgnificentius**, sup. **māgnificentissimē**, [**māgnificus**], adv., *nobly*, *grandly*, *gloriously*; *splendidly*, *magnificently*.

māgnitūdō, **-inis**, [**māgnus**], f., *greatness*, *size*, *magnitude*; *quantity*, *abundance*, *extent*.

māgnus, **-a**, **-um**, comp. **māior**, sup. **māximus**, adj., *great*, *vast*, *wide*, *large*, *tall*; *abundant*, *considerable*; *grand*, *noble*, *mighty*; *stately*, *lofty*; *eminent*, *powerful*; *old*, *aged*; *proud*, *boastful*. As subst., comp. **māiōrēs**, **-um**, m., pl., *fathers*, *ancestors*.

Māgnus, **-ī**, m., surname of Pompey. See **Pompēius**.

māior, see **māgnus**.

Māius, **-a**, **-um**, adj., *of May*. As subst., **Māius**, **-ī**, m., *May*.

male [**malus**], comp. **pēius**, sup. **pessimē**, adv., *ill*, *badly*, *wretchedly*, *awkwardly*; *maliciously*, *evilly*, *wickedly*; *unfortunately*; *unsuccessfully*; *excessively*, *greatly*; sometimes with adj., *scarcely*, *not at all*.

maleficium, **-ī**, [**maleficus**], n., *evil deed*, *offense*, *wickedness*; *mischief*, *hurt*, *wrong*.

malleolus, **-ī**, [dim. of **malleus**, *hammer*], m., *small hammer*; by metonymy, *fire-dart*, *fire-brand*.

mālō, **mālle**, **māluī**, [**magis** + **volō**], irr., a., *wish rather*, *choose rather*, *prefer*.

malum, **-ī**, [**malus**], n., *evil*, *misfortune*, *calamity*; *hurt*, *punishment*; *wrong-doing*, *crime*.

malus, **-a**, **-um**, comp. **pēior**, sup. **pessimus**, adj., *bad*; *wicked*, *depraved*, *evil*, *impious*; *pernicious*, *hostile*, *injurious*, *destructive*.

mandātum, **-ī**, [**mandō**], n., *charge*, *commission*; *command*, *order*, *instruction*.

mandātus, **-ūs**, used only in the abl., [**mandō**], m., *order*, *command*.

mandō, **-āre**, **-āvī**, **-ātum**, **[manus + dō]**, I, a., *put in hand, commit; deliver over, confide, intrust; enjoin, order, command.*

māne, adv., *in the morning, early in the morning.*

maneō, **-ēre**, **mānsī**, **mānsum**, 2, n. and a., *stay, remain, tarry; continue, last, persist, endure; await, wait for, expect; fall to one's lot, be destined to.*

manicātus, **-a**, **-um**, **[manica,** *sleeve*], adj., *with long sleeves, long-sleeved.*

manifēstō **[manifēstus]**, adv., *clearly, plainly, manifestly.*

manifēstus, **-a**, **-um**, **[manus**, cf. unused **fendō]**, adj., *clear, plain; evident, manifest, exposed; convicted* from direct evidence, *caught in the act.*

Mānīlius, **-a**, name of a plebeian gens. Two Manilii are mentioned in this book:

(1) *C. Mānīlius*, tribune of the people B. C. 66. He brought forward the bill placing Pompey in command of the war with Mithridates. After the expiration of his term of office he was brought to trial and condemned. The nature of his offence is not understood. IMP. P. XXIV.

(2) *M'. Mānīlius*, a celebrated jurist, consul B. C. 149. Cicero introduces him as one of the speakers in his dialogue *Dē Rē pūblicā*, 'On the State.' EP. XXXVIII.

Mānius, **-ī**, abbreviated **M'.**, **[māne]**, m., *Mānius*, a Roman forename.

Mānliānus, **-a**, **-um**, adj., *of Manlius, Manlian.*

Mānlius, **-a**, name of a patrician gens. Two of the name are mentioned in this book:

(1) *C. Mānlius*, an important member of the Catilinarian conspiracy. Having served with distinction as a centurion under Sulla, he was placed by Catiline in charge of the troops at Faesulae. In the final battle with Antony, Manlius commanded the right wing and was killed. CAT. I. III. *et al.*

(2) *L. Mānlius Torquātus*, consul with L. Aurelius Cotta, B. C. 65. He was active in helping to suppress the Catilinarian conspiracy. CAT. III. VIII.

mānō, **-āre**, **-āvī**, **-ātum**, I, n. and a., *drip, trickle, flow; spread abroad, be diffused.*

mānsuētē **[mānsuētus]**, adv., *gently, mildly, calmly.*

mānsuētūdō, **-inis**, **[mānsuētus]**, f., *gentleness, mildness, clemency.*

manubiae, **-ārum**, **[manus]**, f., pl., *booty* taken in war, *spoils;* proceeds from the sale of booty, *booty-money, prize-money.*

manus, **-ūs**, f., *hand; handwriting, style; band, force, company, forces, troops.*

Mārcellus, **-ī**, **[Mārcus]**, m., name of a plebeian family in the Claudian gens. Prominent members are together referred to as **Mārcellī**, gen. **-ōrum** (ARCH. IX., MAR. IV.). Three are mentioned in this book:

(1) *M. Claudius Mārcellus*, the most illustrious of the family, five times consul. When consul the third time, B. C. 214, he went to Sicily, and after a siege of two years' duration took Syracuse, though it was defended by the engines of Archimedes. He also rendered other important services to the state. IMP. P. XVI.

(2) *M. Claudius Mārcellus*, consul B. C. 51 and subject of

the oration *Prō Mārcellō;* see pp. 159–170 and notes. CAT. I. VIII.

(3) *C. Claudius Mārcellus,* brother of the preceding, consul B. C. 49. He was an opponent of Caesar, but did not follow Pompey to Greece, and easily obtained pardon from the dictator, with whom he interceded for the restoration of his brother to civil rights. MAR. IV., XI.

Mārcus, -ī, abbreviated **M.**, m., *Mārcus,* a common Roman forename; our *Mark.*

mare, -is, abl. **marī,** sometimes **mare,** n., *sea.*

maritimus, -a, -um, [mare], adj., *of the sea, marine, maritime.*

marītus, -ī, [cf. **mās,** *male*], m., *married man, husband.*

Marius, -a, name of a plebeian gens. Two of the name are mentioned in this book:

(1) *C. Marius,* famous as the conqueror of the Teutones and Cimbri, and as a leader of the popular party; born 157 B. C., near Arpinum. He served with distinction under Scipio in Spain, being present at the siege of Numantia. He put an end to the war with Jugurtha, B. C. 106. He annihilated the Teutones near Aix, in France, B. C. 102, and the Cimbri the following year near Vercelli, in Italy. His opposition to the aristocratic party led to a merciless Civil War. He was seven times consul, and died B. C. 86. CAT. I. II. *et al.*

(2) *M. Marius,* a congenial friend of Cicero's. EP. XXIX.

marmor, -oris, [= μάρμαρος], n., *marble, block of marble;* by metonymy, *marble monument, statue.*

Mārs, Mārtis, m., *Mārs,* the Roman god of war, identified with the Greek Ares; by metonymy, *war, battle; conflict, contest.*

Mārtiālis, -e, adj., *of Mars, Martial.* As subst., **Mārtiālēs, -ium,** m., pl., *men of the Mars legion, soldiers of the Mars legion.*

Mārtius, -a, -um, [Mārs], adj., *of Mars, sacred to Mars; of the month of March, of March.* **Mārtia legiō,** *the Mars legion.*

Massilia, -ae, [= Μασσιλία], f., *Massilia,* an important city of Greek origin on the south coast of Gaul; now Marseilles.

Massiliēnsēs, -ium, [Massilia], m., *people of Massilia, Massilians.*

māter, -tris, f., *mother; parent, nurse; origin, source.*

mātrimōnium, -ī, [māter], n., *marriage, wedlock, matrimony.*

mātūrē, comp. **mātūrius,** sup. **mātūrissimē, [mātūrus],** adv., *seasonably, opportunely; early, soon, speedily.*

mātūritās, -ātis, [mātūrus], f., *ripeness, maturity.*

mātūrō, -āre, -āvī, -ātum, [mātūrus], 1, a. and n., *make ripe, bring to maturity, ripen; hasten, accelerate.*

mātūrus, -a, -um, adj., *ripe, mature; fit, proper; of mature years; early, speedy.*

māximē [māximus], adv., *in the highest degree, especially, particularly; exceedingly, very.*

Māximī, -ōrum, pl. of **Māximus,** m., *men like Maximus* (referring to Q. Fabius Maximus), *Māximī.* ARCH. IX.

māximus, see **māgnus.**

Māximus, -ī, *Māximus,* m., name of a family of the Fabian gens. The most famous was *Q. Fabius Māximus,* whose policy of avoiding open battle wore out Hannibal, and won for him the epithet *Cūnctātor.* IMP. P. XVI.

Mēdēa, **-ae**, [Μήδεια], f., *Mēdēa*, a mythical sorceress, said to have been a daughter of Aeëtes, king of Colchis, and to have been married to Jason, leader of the Argonauts, by whom she was afterwards deserted. IMP. P. IX.

medeor, **-ērī**, **——**, 2, dep., *heal, cure; relieve, remedy, correct, restore.*

medicīna, **-ae**, [**medicus**], f., *the healing art, medicine; remedy, antidote.*

medicus, **-ī**, m., *physician, doctor.*

mediocris, **-e**, [**medius**], adj., *middling, moderate, ordinary; mean, poor, inferior, indifferent.*

mediocriter [**mediocris**], adv., *moderately, ordinarily; somewhat, slightly.*

meditor, **-ārī**, **-ātus sum**, I, dep., *reflect upon, think of, consider; meditate, plan, devise; study, exercise, practice, prepare.*

medius, **-a**, **-um**, adj., *middle, in the middle, in the midst; midway, intervening, between, among.* **mediā aestāte**, *at midsummer.* **ex mediā morte**, *from the midst of death.*

Megalēnsia, **-ium**, [Μεγάλη μήτηρ, i. e. Māgna Māter, a name for Cybele], n., pl., *festival of Cybele*, whose worship was introduced at Rome from Pessinus, in Asia Minor, B. C. 204. The festival began on April 4th, and the games, at least in later times, lasted till the 10th. EP. XVIII.

melior, see **bonus**.

membrum, **-ī**, n., *limb, member; part, branch, portion, division.*

meminī, **-isse**, **——**, def., n. and a., *remember, recollect; be mindful, bear in mind.*

Memmius, **-ī**, m., *C. Memmius*, tribune of the people, B. C. III. He exposed the bribery of influential nobles by Jugurtha, thus arousing bitter hatred. When a candidate for the consulship, B. C. 100, he was slain by a mob acting under the direction of Saturninus and Glaucia. CAT. IV. II.

memor, **-oris**, [cf. **meminī**], adj., *mindful, remembering, heedful.*

memoria, **-ae**, [**memor**], f., *memory, remembrance, recollection; narration, tradition.*

mendīcitās, **-ātis**, [**mendīcus**, *beggarly*], f., *beggary, indigence, extreme poverty.*

mēns, **mentis**, f., *mind, intellect, soul; feeling, disposition, heart, spirit; plan, purpose, design, intent; boldness, courage.* **captus mente**, *beside himself.*

mēnsis, **-is**, m., *month.*

mentiō, **-ōnis**, f., *mention.*

mercātor, **-ōris**, [**mercor**, *trade*], m., *trader, merchant, dealer.*

mercēs, **-ēdis**, f., *price, pay, wages; reward, recompense.*

mereor, **-ērī**, **-itus sum**, 2, dep., *deserve, be entitled to, merit; merit recompense, behave.*

meritō [**meritum**], adv., *deservedly, justly.*

meritum, **-ī**, [**meritus**], n., *merit, service, kindness, favor.*

meritus, **-a**, **-um**, [part of **mereō**], adj., *deserving; deserved, just, due, proper.*

merx, **mercis**, f., *goods, merchandise, commodities, wares.*

-met, enclitic suffix used with most of the personal pronouns, adding an intensive force.

Metellus, **-ī**, m., name of a prominent plebeian family of the Caecilian gens. The Metelli mentioned in this book are:

(1) *Q. Caecilius Metellus Numidicus*, consul B. C. 109. For two years, first as consul, then

as proconsul, he conducted the war against Jugurtha, with such success that, although superseded in command by Marius, he was honored with a triumph on his return to Rome B. C. 107, and received the honorary surname *Numidicus*. Having incurred the enmity of the leaders of the popular party, he was driven into exile, B. C. 100, but was recalled the following year. ARCH. III.

(2) *Q. Caecilius Metellus Pius*, son of the preceding, praetor B. C. 89, consul B. C. 80. He received the surname *Pius* (='Devoted') because of his activity in procuring the recall of his father from exile. He was a successful general under Sulla in the war against the Marian party. Like his father he was a patron of literature and the arts. ARCH. III. *et al.*

(3) *Q. Caecilius Metellus Crēticus*, tribune of the people B. C. 75; legatus the following year, and consul B. C. 69. He gained his honorary surname from his conquest of Crete, which he completed in two years, returning to Rome B. C. 66. IMP. P. XIX.

(4) *Q. Caecilius Metellus Celer*, praetor B. C. 63, consul B. C. 60. He rendered valuable assistance to Cicero in suppressing the conspiracy of Catiline, and was an ardent supporter of the aristocratic party. He died B. C. 59. CAT. I. VIII., II. III., XII.

(5) *M. Metellus*, an associate of Catiline, about whom nothing further is known. CAT. I. VIII.

metuō, **-ere**, **-uī**, **-ūtum**, **[metus]**, 3, a. and n., *fear, be afraid, dread; be apprehensive of, avoid.*

metus, **-ūs**, m., *fear, dread, apprehension, anxiety.*

meus, **-a**, **-um**, **[mē]**, poss. pron., adj., *of me, mine, my, my own.* As subst., **meī**, **-ōrum**, m., *my kindred, my friends.*

mī, voc. of **meus**.

mīles, mīlitis, m. and f., *soldier, common soldier; foot-soldier, infantry;* by metonymy, *soldiery, army.*

mīlitāris, **-e**, **[mīles]**, adj., *of a soldier, of war, warlike, military.* **rēs mīlitāris**, *art of war.* **sīgna mīlitāria**, *military standards.*

mīlitia, **-ae**, **[mīles]**, f., *military service, warfare, service, war;* by metonymy, *soldiery.*

mīllēsimus, **-a**, **-um**, **[mīlle]**, adj., *the thousandth.*

minae, **-ārum**, f., pl., of a wall, *projecting points, pinnacles; threats, menaces.*

minimē, see **parum**.

minimus, **-a**, **-um**, see **parvus**.

minitor, **-ārī**, **-ātus sum**, [freq. of **minor**], 1, dep., *keep threatening, threaten, menace.*

minor, **-ārī**, **-ātus sum**, **[minae]**, 1, dep., *project; threaten, menace.*

minor, see **parvus**.

Minucius, **-a**, name of a Roman gens, with both patrician and plebeian branches. **Minucius**, **-ī**, *Minucius*, an associate of Catiline. CAT. II. II. See also **Basilus**, **Thermus**.

minuō, **-ere**, **minuī**, **minūtum**, [cf. **minor**], 3, a. and n., *make small, lessen, diminish; reduce, lower, weaken.*

minus, see **parvus** and **parum**.

mīrābilis, **-e**, **[mīror]**, adj., *marvellous, wonderful, admirable; extraordinary, strange, singular.*

mīrificē **[mīrificus]**, adv., *wonderfully, exceedingly.*

mīror, **-ārī**, **-ātus sum**, [**mīrus**], 1, dep., *wonder at, marvel; be astonished, be amazed; admire, esteem, regard.*

mīrus, **-a**, **-um**, adj., *wonderful, marvellous, strange, amazing, extraordinary.* **Nec mīrum**, *and no wonder, and it is not strange.*

misceō, **-ēre**, **miscuī**, **mixtum**, 2, a., *mix, mingle, blend; unite, join, associate, assemble; stir up, disturb, embroil.*

misellus, **-a**, **-um**, [**miser**], adj., *poor, wretched.* As subst., **misella**, **-ae**, f., *unhappy one, poor thing.* EP. VIII.

Mīsēnum, **-ī**, [= Μισηνόν], n., *Mīsēnum*, a promontory and town on the coast of Campania, west of Neapolis (= Naples); now Capo Miseno, Miseno.

miser, **-era**, **-erum**, adj., *wretched, miserable, unhappy, pitiable; sad, distressing; poor, worthless, vile.* **Mē miserum!** *ah, unhappy me! wo me!*

miserandus, **-a**, **-um**, [part. of **miseror**], adj., *to be pitied, pitiable, deplorable; wretched, touching.*

miseria, **-ae**, [**miser**], f., *wretchedness, affliction, misery, distress.*

misericordia, **-ae**, [**misericors**], f., *tender-heartedness, compassion, mercy, pity.*

misericors, **-cordis**, [**misereor** + **cor**], adj., *tender-hearted, compassionate; merciful, pitiful.*

Mithridātēs, **-is**, [= Μιθριδάτης, name of Persian origin, = *given to Mithras, gift to the Sun*], m., *Mithridātēs*, name of several kings of Pontus, of whom the best known is *Mithridātēs Eupatōr*, also called *the Great.* He waged war with Rome for many years. He committed suicide, B. C. 63. IMP. P. VIII. *et al.*

Mithridāticus, **-a**, **-um**, [**Mithridātēs**], adj., *of Mithridates.* **Mithridāticum bellum**, *the war with Mithridates.* ARCH. IX.

mītis, **-e**, adj., *mild, mellow, ripe; soft, gentle, kind.*

mittō, **-ere**, **mīsī**, **missum**, 3, a., *send, despatch; announce, report, suggest; furnish, produce; dismiss, let go; forget, cease; release; put forth, send forth; hurl, cast, throw.*

mixtus, **-a**, **-um**, [part. of **misceō**], adj., *mixed, confused.*

mōbilis, **-e**, [**moveō**], adj., *easy to be moved, movable; pliant, flexible; nimble, quick; inconstant, fickle, changeable.*

moderātē [**moderātus**], adv., *with moderation, with self-control, moderately.*

moderātiō, **-ōnis**, [**moderor**], f., *keeping within bounds, regulation; self-restraint, self-control, moderation, temperance.*

moderātus, **-a**, **-um**, [part. of **moderor**], adj., *kept within bounds, restrained; self-restrained, moderate.*

moderor, **-ārī**, **-ātus sum**, [**modus**], 1, dep., *to keep within bounds, limit, regulate; control, restrain, govern.*

modestus, **-a**, **-um**, [**modus**], adj., *keeping within bounds; gentle, forbearing, modest, discreet.*

modo [**modus**], adv. and conj.:

(1) As adv., *only, merely, simply, but; just now, lately, a little while ago, recently.* **nōn modo . . . sed**, *not only . . . but.* See **dum**.

(2) As conj., *if only, on condition that, provided that.*

modus, **-ī**, m., *measure, extent; rhythm, melody; proper measure, moderation; limit, bound; way, manner, fashion, method.* **hū-**

iusce modī, *of this sort, of such a kind.*

moenia, -ium, n., pl., *walls* for defence, *city walls, fortifications;* by metonymy, *walled town, city.*

mōlēs, -is, f., *mass, bulk; massive structure, dam, dyke, foundation; weight, greatness, strength, quantity; difficulty, labor.*

molestē [molestus], adv., *with difficulty, with vexation.* **molestē ferre**, *to bear with vexation, to be annoyed.*

molestia, -ae, [molestus], f., *trouble, annoyance, vexation, distress.*

molestus, -a, -um, [mōlēs], adj., *troublesome, annoying, irksome, grievous.* **quibus erat molestum**, *who were annoyed.*

mōlior, -īrī, -ītus sum, [mōlēs], 4, dep., *endeavor, strive, toil; set in motion, labor upon; direct, continue; undertake, attempt; build, construct.*

mollis, -e, adj., *supple, pliant; tender, delicate, soft; mild, easy, agreeable; effeminate, weak.*

moneō, -ēre, -uī, -itum, 2, a., *remind, admonish, warn; instruct, teach; foretell, announce.*

mōnstrum, -ī, [moneō], n., *omen, portent, miracle; prodigy, monster, monstrosity, abomination.*

monumentum, -ī, [moneō], n., lit. *means of reminding; memorial, monument; chronicle, record.*

mora, -ae, f., *delay, pause; cause of delay, hindrance, obstacle.*

morbus, -ī, [morior], m., *sickness, disease, ailment, disorder.*

morior, morī and morīrī, mortuus sum, 3 and 4, dep., *die, expire; wither, decay, pass away.*

mors, mortis, f., *death;* by metonymy, *dead body, corpse.*

morsus, -ūs, [mordeō], m., *biting, bite; pain, sting.*

mortālis, -e, [mors], adj., *subject to death, mortal; of a mortal, human, transitory.* As subst., **mortālēs, -ium**, m., pl., *mortals, mortal men, men, mankind.*

mortuus, -a, -um, [part. of **morior**], adj., *dead; decayed.* As subst., **mortuī, -ōrum**, m., pl., *the dead.*

mōs, mōris, m., *manner, habit, custom, way, humor; usage, practice, fashion;* pl., **mōrēs, -um**, *manners, morals,* often *character.*

mōtus, -ūs, [moveō], m., *motion, movement; graceful movement, gesticulation; emotion, affection, impulse, agitation; disturbance, tumult, commotion.* **terrae mōtus**, *earthquake.*

moveō, -ēre, mōvī, mōtum, 2, a. and n., *move, set in motion, disturb, remove; excite, affect, stir up; produce, promote; change, transform.*

mox, adv., *soon, presently; afterwards; thereupon, then, in the next place.*

mūcrō, -ōnis, m., *point, edge,* especially of a sword; by metonymy, *sword; sharpness, edge.*

mulier, -eris, f., *woman, female; wife.*

muliercula, -ae, [dim. of **mulier**], f., *little woman, girl.*

multitūdō, -inis, [multus], f., *great number, multitude, crowd, throng.*

multō, -āre, -āvī, -ātum, [multa, *fine*], 1, a., *punish.*

multō [abl. n. of **multus**], adv., *by much, much; far, by far, very, greatly.*

multum [multus], adv., *much, greatly, far; often, frequently.*

multus, -a, -um, comp. **plūs**, sup. **plūrimus**, adj., *much,* pl. *many, in large numbers; abundant,* *considerable;* often used as subst. in m. and n., pos., comp., and sup.

Mulvius, adj., *Mulvian.* **Mulvius pōns**, *the Mulvian bridge*, which crossed the Tiber two miles north of Rome; now Ponte Molle. It was built by M. Aemilius Scaurus, the censor, B. C. 109. CAT. III. II.

mūniceps, **-ipis**, [**mūnia**, *official duties*, **capiō**], m. and f., *inhabitant of a free town, citizen, burgher; fellow citizen.*

mūnicipium, **-ī**, [**mūniceps**], n., *free city, free town, municipality*, a city which had lost its independence and submitted to Rome, but which was permitted to retain self-government in local affairs, its citizens becoming Roman plebeians.

mūniō, **-īre**, **-īvī**, **-ītum**, [**moenia**], 4, a., *defend with a wall, wall; fortify, defend, protect; secure, guard, strengthen.*

mūnītus, **-a**, **-um**, [part. of **mūniō**], adj., *fortified, defended; secure, safe.*

mūnus, **-eris**, **n.**, *service, office, employment, function, duty; favor, kindness; present, gift.*

Mūrēna, -ae, m., *L. Licinius Mūrēna.* He went with Sulla to Asia Minor B. C. 84, and remained there as propraetor two years. He provoked Mithridates, who had made a treaty with the Romans, to hostilities, and after some successes suffered defeat. He returned to Rome in 81 B. C. and celebrated an ill-deserved triumph. IMP. P. III.

mūrus, **-ī**, m., *wall*, especially of a city, *city wall.*

Mūsa, -ae, [Μοῦσα], f., *Muse, one of the nine Muses*, goddesses of music, poetry, and the sciences.

Mutinēnsis, -e, [**Mutina**], adj., *of Mutina*, an important city of Cisalpine Gaul, now Modena. **proelium Mutinēnse**, *the battle at Mutina*, April 27, B. C. 43, in which Antony was defeated and forced to leave the city.

mūtō, **-āre**, **-āvī**, **-ātum**, [freq. of **moveō**], 1, a. and n., *move, remove; change, alter, transform; interchange, exchange.*

mūtuē [**mūtuus**], adv., *in return, mutually.*

mūtus, **-a**, **-um**, adj., *dumb, without speech, speechless, voiceless; silent, mute, still.*

mystērium, **-ī**, [μυστήριον], n., *secret rite, divine mystery*, a secret service in honor of some divinity which only the initiated were permitted to witness.

Mytilēnaeus, **-a**, **-um**, [**Mytilēnē**], adj., *of Mytilene*, a city on the island of Lesbos; now Mytilini.

N.

nam, conj., explanatory and causal, *for, for instance; for, seeing that, because, inasmuch as.*

nancīscor, **-ī**, **nactus** and **nanctus sum**, 3, dep., *obtain, secure, get, receive; meet with, fall in with, find, reach; incur.*

nāscēns, **-entis**, [part. of **nāscor**], adj., *rising, young, newly fledged.*

nāscor, **nāscī**, **nātus sum**, 3, dep., *be born, be produced; spring up, grow, start; arise, begin.*

nātiō, **-ōnis**, [**nāscor**, **nātus**], f., *birth; breed, stock, kind; nation, people.*

nātūra, **-ae**, [**nāscor**], f., *birth; innate quality, disposition; inclination, temper, character; law of nature, course of things, nature, world.*

nātus, -a, -um, [part. of **nāscor**], adj., *born, produced, sprung from; designed by nature, constituted by nature.* As subst., **nātus, -ī**, m., *son.*

naufragus, -a, -um, [**nāvis + frangō**], adj., *shipwrecked, wrecked; ruined.* As subst., **naufragī, -ōrum**, m., pl., *castaways; ruined men, bankrupts.*

nausea, -ae, [ναυσία, ναῦς], f., *sea-sickness.*

nauta, -ae, [for **nāvita**, from **nāvis**], m., *sailor, seaman.*

nauticus, -a, -um, [= ναυτικός], adj., *of ships, of sailors, naval, nautical.*

nāvālis, -e, [**nāvis**], adj., *of ships, ship-, naval, nautical.*

nāviculārius, -a, -um, [**nāvicula**], adj., *of a boat.* As subst., **nāviculārius, -ī**, m., *ship-master, boat-owner.*

nāvigātiō, -ōnis, [**nāvigō**], f., *sailing, navigation.*

nāvigō, -āre, -āvī, -ātum, [**nāvis + agō**], I, n. and a., *sail, set sail, cruise; sail over, navigate.*

nāvis, -is, f., *ship.* **nāvis longa**, *ship of war, war-ship.*

nē, adverb and conj.:

(1) As adv., *not.* **nē — quidem**, *not — even.*

(2) As conj., *in order that not, that not, lest, for fear that.*

nē, [= ναί, νή], interj., *truly, indeed, verily.* CAT. II. III.

-ne, enclitic adv. and conj.:

(1) As adv., purely interrogative and marking a direct question, untranslatable except in the inflection of the voice.

(2) As conj., introducing an indirect question, *whether.* **-ne — an, -ne — -ne**, *whether — or.*

Neāpolitānī, -ōrum, m., pl., *Neapolitans, inhabitants of Neapolis*, now Napoli, Naples.

nec, neque, [**nē + -que**], adv. and conj., *and not, also not, nor, nor yet, nor however.* **nec — nec**, *neither — nor.* **nec — et, nec — -que**, *on the one hand not — on the other, not only not — but also.* **nec nōn**, *and certainly, and indeed.* **neque enim**, *for — not, and yet — not.*

necessāriō, [**necessārius**], adv., *unavoidably, inevitably.*

necessārius, -a, -um, [**necesse**], adj., *unavoidable, inevitable, pressing, needful.* As subst., **necessārius, -ī**, m., *kinsman, relative, friend, client.*

necesse, adj., n., indecl., *unavoidable, inevitable, necessary.* **necesse est**, *it is inevitable, it is necessary, one must.*

necessitās, -ātis, [**necesse**], f., *unavoidableness, necessity, exigency; need, want; connection, relationship, friendship.*

necessitūdō, -inis, [**necesse**], f., *inevitableness, necessity; intimate relation, relationship, intimacy, friendship.*

necne [**nec + -ne**], conj., found in the second part of a double question, direct or indirect, *or not.*

necō, -āre, -āvī, -ātum, [**nex**], I, a., *kill, slay, put to death, destroy.*

nefandus, -a, -um, [**nē + fandus**, from **for**], adj., *not to be mentioned, unutterable; wicked, impious, heinous, abominable.*

nefāriē [**nefārius**], adv., *impiously, heinously, abominably.*

nefārius, -a, -um, [**nefās**], adj., *impious, heinous, abominable, nefarious; wicked, dastardly.*

neglegenter, comp. **neglegentius**, [**neglegēns**], adv., *carelessly, negligently, heedlessly.*

neglegentia, -ae, [**neglegēns**], f., *carelessness, negligence, heedlessness, neglect.*

neglegō, **-ere**, **neglēxī**, **neglēctum**, [**nec** + **legō**], 3, a., *disregard, neglect, not attend to, not heed, slight ; despise, contemn, treat with indifference.*

negō, **-āre**, **-āvī**, **-ātum**, 1, n. and a., *say no ; deny, refuse, decline.*

negōtiolum, **-ī**, [dim. of **negōtium**], n., *small matter of business, small affair.*

negōtior, **-ārī**, **-ātus sum**, [**negōtium**], 1, dep., *do business, carry on business, trade, traffic.*

negōtium, **-ī**, [**nec** + **ōtium**], n., *business, employment, occupation ; difficulty, trouble ; matter, affair.*

nēmō, pl. and gen. and abl. sing. not in use, being replaced by forms from **nūllus**, [**nē** + **homō**], m. and f., *no one, no body.* **nōn nēmō**, *many a one, somebody.*

nempe [**nam** + **-pe**], conj., *certainly, without doubt, obviously, indeed ; of course, forsooth, to be sure.*

nepōs, **-ōtis**, m., *grandson ; spendthrift, prodigal.*

nēquam, pos. indecl., comp. **nēquior**, sup. **nēquissimus**, adj., *worthless, vile, bad.*

neque, see **nec**.

nēquior, see **nēquam**.

nēquitia, **-ae**, [**nēquam**], f., *worthlessness, inefficiency ; wickedness, vileness.*

nervus, **-ī**, m., *sinew, muscle, tendon ;* by metonymy, *string of a bow, bow-string ;* of a musical instrument, *string, chord.*

nesciō, **-īre**, **-īvī** or **-iī**, **-ītum**, [**nē** + **sciō**], 4, a., *not know, be ignorant ;* often used in parenthetical phrases expressing uncertainty. **nēsciō an**, *I know not whether = perhaps, probably.* **nēsciō quid**, **nēsciō quod**, *I know not what = something, some, certain.* **nēsciō quō modō**, *I know not how = somehow.*

neu, see **nēve**.

nēve, or **neu**, [**nē** + **-ve**], conj., *and not, nor ; and that not, and lest, and in order that not.*

nex, **necis**, f., *death* by violence, *murder, slaughter.*

nihil, or **nīl**, [**nē** + **hilum**, *trifle*], n., indecl., *nothing ;* acc. often with adverbial force, *not at all, in no respect, by no means.*

Nīlus, **-ī**, [Νεῖλος], m., *Nile,* the great river of Egypt. MAR. IX.

nīmīrum [**nī** + **mīrum**], adv., *doubtless, without doubt, certainly ; to be sure, truly.*

nimis, adv., *too, too much, beyond measure, excessively.*

nimium [**nimius**], adv., *too much, too ; very, greatly, exceedingly.*

nimius, **-a**, **-um**, [**nimis**], adj., *excessive, beyond measure, too great, too much.* As subst., **nimium**, **-ī**, n., *too much, excess.*

nisi [**nē** + **sī**], conj., *if not, unless, except, save only.* **nisi vērō**, ironical, *unless perchance, unless perhaps.* **nisi quod**, *except that.*

niteō, **-ēre**, **-uī**, ——, 2, n., *shine, glisten ; be sleek, look spruce ; thrive.*

nitidus, **-a**, **-um**, [cf. **niteō**], adj., *shining, bright, glittering ; sleek, spruce, trim, blooming.*

nix, **nivis**, f., *snow.*

Nōbilior, **-ōris**, [**nōbilis**], m., name of a family of the Fulvian gens. The most distinguished member was *M. Fulvius Nōbilior,* who was curule aedile B. C. 195, and praetor two years later. When consul, B. C. 189, he set out against the Aetolians, taking the poet Ennius with him. Having been successful in his expedition, he returned to Rome B. C. 187, and celebrated the most magnificent triumph and games witnessed up to that time. He was a patron of the liberal arts, and left many public works. ARCH. XI.

nōbilis, -e, [cf. nōscō], adj., *well-known, famous, renowned, illustrious; high-born, of noble descent; noble, excellent, fine.*

nōbilitās, -ātis, [nōbilis], f., *celebrity, fame; high birth, noble origin; aristocracy, nobles; nobility, excellence, superiority.*

nocēns, -entis, [noceō], adj., *harmful, hurtful; guilty, criminal.* As subst., **nocēns, -entis**, m., *culprit, criminal.*

noceō, -ēre, -uī, -itum, 2, n. and a., *harm, hurt, injure; inflict injury, do mischief.*

nocturnus, -a, -um, [nox], adj., *of night, by night, nocturnal.*

nōlō, nōlle, nōluī, ——, [nē + volō], irr., n., *wish not, will not, not wish, not will, be unwilling.* **nōlī esse**, *be not.*

nōmen, -inis, [cf. nōscō], n., *name, appellation, designation; fame, renown, repute.*

nōminātim [nōminō], adv., *by name; expressly, in particular, especially.*

nōminō, -āre, -āvī, -ātum, [nōmen], 1, a., *call by name, name; render famous, make renowned: nominate, designate; mention, report; accuse, charge.*

nōn, [old noenum, from ne + oenum, = ūnum], adv., *not, not at all, by no means.* **nōn modo — sed**, *not only — but.* **nōn nisi**, *only.* **nōn tam**, *not particularly, not so very.*

Nōnae, -ārum, abbreviated **Nōn.**, [nōnus], f., *the Nones*, one of the days of the month to which dates were reckoned in the Roman calendar. It was the ninth day before the Ides, and hence came on the fifth day of the month, except in March, May, July, and October, when it fell on the seventh. See **Īdūs, Kalendae.**

nōndum [nōn + dum], adv., *not yet.*

nōnne [nōn + -ne], inter. adv. expecting an affirmative answer, in a dir. question, *not;* in an indir. question, *if not, whether not.*

nōnus, -a, -um, [novem], num. adj., *ninth.*

nōs, **nostrum**, see **ego.**

nōscō, -ere, nōvī, nōtum, 3, a., *become acquainted with, get knowledge of, learn;* in tenses from pf. stem, *have learned,* hence *know, be familiar with, understand.*

noster, -tra, -trum, [nōs], poss. pron. adj., *our, ours, our own, of us.* **dē nostrō omnium interitū**, *about the destruction of us all.* CAT. I. IV.

nostrās, -ātis, [noster], adj., *of our country, native.* EP. XVIII.

nota, -ae, [cf. nōscō], f., *mark, sign; stamp, spot; letter; nod, token; mark* of ignominy, *disgrace.*

notō, -āre, -āvī, -ātum, [nota], 1, a., *mark, stamp; note, observe; single out, designate; censure, reprimand.*

nōtus, -a, -um, [part. of nōscō], adj., *known, familiar; well-known, famous, notorious; of ill repute, ill-reputed.*

novem or **VIIII., IX.**, num. adj., *nine.*

November, -bris, -bre, [novem], adj., lit. *of the ninth; of November*, the ninth month reckoning from March, which the early Romans considered the first month of the year.

novus, -a, -um, adj., *new, recent, fresh, young; unfamiliar,* *strange; last, latest, extreme.* **rēs novae,** *new things;* in a political sense, *innovations, revolution.* **tabulae novae,** *new accounts, a new account,* meaning the cancelling or abolition of debts.

nox, **noctis,** f., *night;* by metonymy, *darkness, obscurity.*

nūdius [for **nunc diēs,** sc. **est**], adv., used only with an ordinal number in phrases expressing time, *it is now the . . . day since.* **nūdius tertius,** *it is now the third day, day before yesterday.*

nūdus, **-a, -um,** adj., *naked, bare, uncovered;* often, *without an outer garment* or *without a shield, lightly clad, exposed; vacant, destitute, without; mere, only.*

nūllus, **-a, -um,** gen. **nūllīus,** [**nē** + **ūllus**], adj., *not any, none, no.* As subst., **nūllus, -īus,** m., *nobody, no one, no man.* **nōn nūllus,** *some one,* pl. *some.* **nūllus nōn,** *every, all.*

num, inter. adv., usually expecting a negative answer, in a direct question, *now, then,* or, following a negative translation of the question, . . . *not so, . . . is it?* in an indirect question, *whether, if.*

Numantia, **-ae,** f., *Numantia,* an important city in Spain near the upper course of the river Durius. It was besieged and destroyed by Scipio Africanus B.C. 134.

nūmen, **-inis,** [**nuō**], n., *nod; will, command; divine will, divine power, divinity, deity; divine favor, favor of the gods.*

numerus, **-ī,** m., *number; large number, multitude, quantity, body; rank, position, place; measure* of music or poetry, *rhythm, time, numbers.*

Numidicus, **-a, -um,** [**Numidia**], adj., *Numidian, of Numidia,* a country in northern Africa between Mauritania and the territory of Carthage; modern Algiers. See **Metellus** (1).

nummus, **-ī,** m., *coin, money;* referring to the Roman silver coin of account, *sestertius, sesterce; penny, farthing, trifle.*

numquam [**nē** + **umquam**], adv., *never, at no time; by no means.*

nunc [**num** + **-ce**], adv., *now, at this time, at present, at the present time; under these circumstances, as it is, as matters are.*

nūntiō, **-āre, -āvī, -ātum,** [**nūntius**], 1, a., *announce, declare; report, communicate.*

nūntius, **-a, -um,** adj., *that brings tidings, announcing, informing.* As subst., **nūntius, -ī,** m., *news-carrier, messenger, reporter; news, message, tidings.*

nūper, sup. **nūperrimē,** [**novus** + **per**], adv., *lately, recently, not long since.*

nūptiae, **-ārum,** [**nūpta,** *bride*], f., pl., *marriage, wedding, nuptials.*

nūtus, abl. **-ū,** found only in nom., acc., and abl. sing., acc. and abl. pl., [**nuō**], m., *nod; compliance, assent; will, command.*

O.

Ō, interj., *O! oh!*

ob, prep. with acc., *to, towards, for, on account of, by reason of.* **quam ob rem,** *wherefore, hence.*

In composition **ob** is usually assimilated before **c, f, g, p,** but remains unchanged before other letters. It adds the meaning *towards, at, before, against.*

obeō, **-īre, -īvī, -itum,** [**ob** + **eō**], irr., n. and a., *go to meet; come* *up to, reach; go over, traverse, visit; engage in, undertake, enter upon; perform, discharge, execute, accomplish;* of a crime, *commit.*

obiciō, -icere, -iēcī, -iectum, [ob + iaciō], 3, a., *throw before; offer, present, expose; upbraid, reproach with, taint.*

obiūrgō, -āre, -āvī, -ātum, [ob + iūrgō], 1, a., *chide, rebuke, reprove; urge, adjure.*

oblectātiō, -ōnis, [oblectō], f., *delight, charm.*

oblectō, -āre, -āvī, -ātum, [ob + lactō, *allure*], 1, a., *delight, amuse, entertain, divert, interest.*

obligō, -āre, -āvī, -ātum, [ob + ligō], 1, a., *bind up; bind, oblige, put under obligation; pledge, mortgage.*

oblinō, -ere, oblēvī, oblitum, [ob + linō], 3, a., *besmear, smear, stain, daub; cover with, defile.*

oblitus, see oblinō.

oblītus, -a, -um, [part. of oblīvīscor], adj., *forgetful, unmindful, regardless.*

oblīviō, -ōnis, [oblīvīscor], f., *forgetfulness, oblivion.*

oblīvīscor, -vīscī, oblītus sum, 3, dep., *forget, be forgetful; disregard, neglect, omit.*

oboediō, -īre, -īvī, -ītum, [ob + audiō], 4, n., *hearken, listen; give heed to, obey, yield obedience, be subject.*

obruō, -ere, obruī, obrutum, [ob + ruō], 3, a., *overwhelm, cover, bury; overthrow, destroy.*

obscūrē [obscūrus], adv., *darkly, indistinctly, obscurely, covertly.*

obscūritās, -ātis, [obscūrus], f., *obscurity, indistinctness, uncertainty.*

obscūrō, -āre, -āvī, -ātum, [obscūrus], 1, a., *make dark, darken, obscure; hide, conceal; keep hidden, suppress.*

obscūrus, -a, -um, adj., *dark, dusky, dim, obscure; not known, unfamiliar; indistinct, unintelligible, hard to understand; ignoble, mean, low.*

obsecrō, -āre, -āvī, -ātum, [ob + sacrō], 1, a., *beseech, implore, entreat.*

obsecundō, -āre, -āvī, -ātum, [ob + secundō], 1, n., *be favorable, comply with, humor, accommodate.*

observāns, -antis, [part. of observō], adj., *watchful, attentive, respectful.*

observō, -āre, -āvī, -ātum, [ob + servō], 1, a., *watch, heed, observe, take notice of; guard, keep; treat with respect, pay attention to, regard, honor.*

obses, -idis, [ob, cf. sedeō], m. and f., *hostage; security, pledge, surety, assurance.*

obsideō, -ēre, obsēdī, obsessum, [ob + sedeō], 2, n. and a., *stay, remain; beset, invest, besiege; lie in wait for, look out for.*

obsidiō, -ōnis, [obsideō], f., *siege, blockade.*

obsistō, -ere, obstitī, obstitum, [ob + sistō], 3, n., *take one's stand before, stand in the way; withstand, oppose, resist.*

obsolēscō, -lēscere, -lēvī, -lētum, [obs, old form of ob, + unused olēscō, *grow*], 3, inch., *grow old, become antiquated; lose force, become obsolete.*

obstipēscō, -ere, obstipuī, ——, 3, inch., *be astounded, stand amazed, be amazed; become senseless, be stupefied.*

obstō, -āre, obstitī, obstātum, [ob + stō], 1, n., *stand before; be in the way; withstand, oppose, hinder, thwart, restrain.*

obstrepō, **-ere**, **-uī**, **-itum**, [**ob** + **strepō**], 3, n. and a., *roar at, resound, make a noise; outbawl, drown out* by cries.

obstupefaciō, **-facere**, **-fēcī**, **-factum**, pass. **obstupefīō**, **-fierī**, **-factus sum**, [**ob** + **stupefaciō**], 3, a., *astonish, amaze, astound, benumb.*

obsum, **-esse**, **-fuī**, [**ob** + **sum**], irr., n., *be against; injure, hurt, be prejudicial to.*

obtemperō, **-āre**, **-āvī**, **-ātum**, [**ob** + **temperō**], 1, n., *comply, conform, submit, obey.*

obtineō, **-ēre**, **obtinuī**, **obtentum**, [**ob** + **teneō**], 2, a. and n., *hold fast, keep, maintain; assert, prove, show.*

obtingō, **-ere**, **obtigī**, ——, [**ob** + **tangō**], 3, a. and n., *fall to one's lot, befall; happen, occur.*

obtrectō, **-āre**, **-āvī**, **-ātum**, [**ob** + **tractō**], 1, a. and n., *disparage, underrate, decry; raise objections to, be opposed to, thwart.*

obturbō, **-āre**, **-āvī**, **-ātum**, [**ob** + **turbō**], 1, a., *stir up, trouble; confuse, disturb, distract.*

obviam [**ob** + **viam**], adv., *in the way, against, in face of, to meet.* **mihi obviam vēnit**, *he came to meet me.*

occaecō, **-āre**, **-āvī**, **-ātum**, [**ob** + **caecō**, from **caecus**], 1, a., *make blind, blind, darken; delude.*

occāsiō, **-ōnis**, [**ob**, cf. **cāsus**, **cadō**], f., *opportunity, suitable time, favorable moment, occasion; pretext, excuse.*

occāsus, **-ūs**, [**ob** + **cāsus**, from **cadō**], m., of the heavenly bodies, *going down, setting;* by metonymy, *sunset, west; downfall, destruction, ruin, death.*

occidēns, **-entis**, pl. wanting, [part. of **occidō**], m., *sunset, west.* **ab occidente**, *in the west.*

occīdō, **-ere**, **occīdī**, **occīsum**, [**ob** + **caedō**], 3, a., *strike down; cut down, kill, slay, murder.*

occidō, **-ere**, **occidī**, **occāsum**, [**ob** + **cadō**], 3, n., *fall down, fall; die, perish, be slain;* of heavenly bodies, *go down, set.*

occlūdō, **-ere**, **occlūsī**, **occlūsum**, [**ob** + **claudō**], 3, a., *shut up, close.*

occultē [**occultus**], adv., *secretly, privately; in concealment, in secret.*

occultō, **-āre**, **-āvī**, **-ātum**, [freq. of **occulō**, *cover*], 1, a., *conceal, hide, secrete.*

occultus, **-a**, **-um**, [part. of **occulō**, *cover*], adj., *concealed, covered up; hidden, secret.*

occupātiō, **-ōnis**, [**occupō**], f., *taking possession, seizure; business, employment.*

occupātus, **-a**, **-um**, [part. of **occupō**], adj., *absorbed, busy, engaged, employed.*

occupō, **-āre**, **-āvī**, **-ātum**, [**ob**, cf. **capiō**], 1, a., *take possession of, seize, gain; fall upon, surprise, attack; anticipate, outstrip; take up, employ.*

occurrō, **-ere**, **occurrī**, **occursum**, [**ob** + **currō**], 3, n., *run to, run to meet, meet, fall in with; rush upon, attack; oppose, resist; present* itself or one's self, *occur, suggest itself, be thought of.*

Ōceanus, **-ī**, [Ὠκεανός], m., *the great sea* that encompasses the land, *outer sea, ocean.*

Octāviānus, **-ī**, [**Octāvius**], m., *Octavian,* usually called *Augustus;* born B.C. 63, son of C. Octavius and Atia, daughter of Julia, sister of Julius Caesar. His name was at first the same as that of his father, *C. Octāvius.* He was adopted by Julius Caesar, and his name became, according to the rule in such cases, *C. Iūlius Caesar Octāviānus.* The title *Augustus* was added B.C. 27, when the supremacy of Octavian as emperor was formally recognized. His reign lasted till his death, A.D. 14. ANT. IV. I. et seq., EP. XLIV.

Octāvius, -a, [octāvus], name of a plebeian gens, raised to patrician standing by Julius Caesar. *Cn. Octāvius*, consul B.C. 76, *L. Octāvius*, consul 75, and perhaps other members of the family are mentioned together by Cicero as **Octāviī**, gen. -ōrum (ARCH. III.).

The father of L. Octavius was *Cn. Octāvius*, a partisan of Sulla, consul with Cinna B.C. 87. As Cinna endeavored to bring back the party of Marius to power, Octavius opposed him with force. In the violent conflict that ensued he was murdered. CAT. III. X.

octāvus, -a, -um, or **VIII.**, [octō], num. adj., *eighth.*

Octōber, -bris, -bre, [octō], adj., lit. *of the eighth ; of October.*

oculus, -ī, m., *eye.*

ōdī, **ōdisse**, fut. part. **ōsūrus**, def., a., *hate ; dislike, be displeased with.*

odiōsus, -a, -um, [odium], adj., *hateful, offensive ; unpleasant, disagreeable.*

odium, -ī, [cf. ōdī], n., *hatred, grudge, ill-will, enmity ; offence, aversion, abomination, nuisance ; disgust, dissatisfaction.*

offendō, **-ere**, **offendī**, **offēnsum**, [ob + unused fendō], 3, a. and n., *strike against, stumble ; hit upon, find ; commit a fault, offend, be offensive ; vex, displease.*

offēnsiō, -ōnis, [offendō], f., *stumbling ; aversion, dislike, disgust, hatred ; mishap, misfortune, defeat.*

offēnsus, **-a**, **-um**, [part. of offendō], adj., *offended, vexed, imbittered ; offensive, odious.*

offerō, **-ferre**, **obtulī**, **oblātum**, [ob + ferō], irr., a., *present, offer, exhibit ; bring forward, adduce ; bestow, confer.*

officiōsus, **-a**, **-um**, **[officium]**, adj., *courteous, obliging, serviceable.*

officium, **-ī**, [for **opificium**, **opus** + **faciō**], n., *service, kindness, favor, courtesy ; duty, obligation ; office, function, employment.*

offundō, **-ere**, **offūdī**, **offūsum**, [ob + fundō], 3, a., *pour out, pour down ; fill to overflowing, flood, fill.*

ōlim [cf. **ollus**, old form of **ille**], adv., *at that time, formerly, once, long since ; ever ; some time, some day, hereafter.*

ōmen, -inis, n., *omen, sign, token, harbinger.*

omittō, **-ere**, **omīsī**, **omissum**, [ob + mittō], 3, a., *let go, let loose ; lay aside, give up, dismiss, neglect ; pass by, pass over, omit.*

omnīnō [omnis], adv., *altogether, wholly, at all, by all means, certainly ;* with numerals, *in all, just.*

omnis, -e, adj., *all, every, entire ; all sorts of.* As subst., pl., **omnēs**, **-ium**, m. and f., *all men, all ;* **omnia**, **-ium**, n., *everything, all things.*

onus, -eris, n., *load, burden, freight, cargo ; weight, trouble, difficulty.*

opera, -ae, [opus], f., *effort, exertion, work, labor ; service.*

Opīmius, -ī, m., *L. Opīmius*, consul B.C. 121. He was an ardent and unscrupulous adherent of the aristocratic party, and was responsible for the death of C. Gracchus. CAT. I. II.

opīmus, -a, -um, adj., *fat; fertile, fruitful, rich; abundant, sumptuous, noble.*

opīniō, -ōnis, [opīnor], f., *opinion, supposition, conjecture, expectation.* **praeter opīniōnem,** *contrary to expectation.* **opīniōne celerius,** *sooner than was expected.*

opīnor, **-ārī, -ātus sum,** 1, dep., *be of the opinion, suppose; conjecture, imagine, think, judge.*

opitulor, **-ārī, -ātus sum,** [ops, cf. **tulī**], 1, dep., *bear aid, aid, help, assist, succor.*

oportet, -ēre, **oportuit**, 2, impers., *it is necessary, it behooves.* mē oportet, *I ought, I must.*

oppetō, **-ere, -īvī, -ītum,** [ob + **petō**], 3, a., *go to meet, encounter.*

oppidō [abl. of **oppidum**], adv., *very, exceedingly, very much.*

oppidum, **-ī**, n., *town, city.*

oppōnō, -ere, **opposuī, oppositum,** [ob + **pōnō**], 3, a., *place opposite, set before, oppose; bring forward, present, adduce.*

opportūnitās, -ātis, [opportūnus], f., *suitableness, fitness, advantage.*

opportūnus, -a, -um, [ob, **portō**], adj., *suitable, fit, convenient; meet, advantageous, useful.*

oppositus, -ūs, used only in abl. sing. and acc. pl., [oppōnō], m., *placing against, opposition, interposition.*

oppressus, see **opprimō**.

opprimō, -ere, **oppressī, oppressum,** [ob + **premō**], 3, a., *press against, press upon; oppress, weigh down, overwhelm, cover; put down, suppress; overthrow, crush, subdue;* of a fleet, *sink.*

oppūgnō, -āre, -āvī, -ātum, [ob + **pūgnō**], 1, a., *attack, assail; assault, storm, besiege.*

ops, **opis**, nom. and dat. sing. not in use, f., *aid, assistance, help, support; power, ability;* often in pl., *property, riches, means, resources, treasure, wealth.*

optimās, **-ātis,** [**optimus**], adj., *of the best, aristocratic.* As subst., **optimās, -ātis,** m., *adherent of the nobility, aristocrat.*

optimē, see **bene**.

optimus, see **bonus**.

optō, **-āre, -āvī, -ātum,** 1, a., *choose, select, prefer; wish, desire, wish for, long for.*

opus, **-eris,** n., *work, task, labor, toil; structure, building; work of art, book; deed, action, effect;* in phrases with esse, *necessity;* as **opus est,** *it is necessary, there is need of,* often followed by the abl. **māgnō opere,** *very much, exceedingly, greatly; earnestly, vehemently, urgently.* **tantō opere,** *so much, so very, in so great a measure.*

ōra, -ae, f., *edge, border; boundary, limit; coast, sea-coast;* by metonymy, *territory, region, country.*

ōrātiō, -ōnis, [**ōrō**], f., *speaking, speech, discourse; diction, style; set speech, harangue, oration; subject, theme; oratorical power, eloquence.*

ōrātōrius, -a, -um, [**ōrātor**], adj., *of an orator, of oratory, oratorical.*

orbis, **-is,** m., *ring, circle; orb, disk;* by metonymy, *wheel; region, country, territory; round, circuit.* **orbis terrae** or **terrārum,** *earth, world, universe.*

ōrdior, **-īre, ōrsus sum,** 4, dep., *begin, commence; set about, undertake.*

ōrdō, -inis, m., *row, line; order, rank; series, array.*

oriēns, **-ientis,** [part. of **orior**], m., *rising sun, morning sun;* by metonymy, *east, Orient.*

orior, orīrī, ortus sum, 4, dep., *arise, rise, become visible ; spring, descend, begin, originate ; be born, be descended.*

ōrnāmentum, -ī, [ōrnō], n., *outfit, equipment, apparatus ; mark of honor, decoration ; distinction, ornament.*

ōrnātē [ōrnātus], adv., *elegantly, ornately.*

ōrnātus, -a, -um, [part. of **ōrnō**], adj., *fitted out, equipped, provided ; furnished, decorated, adorned ; eminent, illustrious.*

ōrnō, -āre, -āvī, -ātum, 1, a., *fit out, equip, prepare ; adorn, embellish, decorate ; honor, distinguish.*

ōrō, -āre, -āvī, -ātum, [ōs, *mouth*], 1, n. and a., *speak ; argue, plead, entreat, implore, beseech.*

Orpheus, -eī or **-eos,** acc. **-eum, -ea** or **-ēā,** [Ὀρφεύς], m., *Orpheus:*

(1) A mythical singer of Thrace, son of Apollo and Calliope.

(2) A slave or freedman of Cicero. Ep. VIII.

ortus, -ūs, [orior], m., *a rising, rise ; beginning, origin, source.* **ortus sōlis,** *sunrise ;* by metonymy, *east.*

ōs, ōris, n., *mouth ;* by metonymy, *face, look, countenance, features ; orifice, aperture.*

ostendō, -ere, ostendī, ostentum, [obs, old form of **ob,** + **tendō**], 3, a., *stretch out, spread before ; show, disclose, manifest, point out ; make known, tell, declare.*

ostentātiō, -ōnis, [ostentō], f., *exhibition, display ; vain display, pomp, ostentation, boasting.*

ostentō, -āre, -āvī, -ātum, [freq. of **ostendō**], 1, a., *show, exhibit ; show off, display, parade, boast.*

Ōstiēnsis, -e, [ōstium], adj., *of Ostia,* the seaport of Rome at the mouth of the Tiber. **Ōstiēnse incommodum,** *the disaster at Ostia.* Imp. P. XII.

ōstium, -ī, [ōs], n., *door ;* by metonymy, *mouth, entrance.* **Ōceanī ōstium,** *the mouth of the Ocean,* i. e. the Straits of Gibraltar.

ōtiōsus, -a, -um, [ōtium], adj., *at leisure, unoccupied, disengaged ; indifferent, neutral ; calm, quiet, peaceful.* As subst., **ōtiōsī, -ōrum,** m., pl , *the idle, the neutral, the peaceable.*

ōtium, -ī, n., *leisure, ease, idleness ; repose, rest ; quiet, peace.*

P.

P., see **Pūblius.**

pacīscor, pacīscī, pactus sum, 3, dep., *agree, agree upon ; contract, covenant, stipulate.*

pācō, -āre, -āvī, -ātum, [pāx], 1, a., *make peaceful, pacify, subdue.*

pactiō, -ōnis, [pacīscor], f., *agreement, covenant, contract, stipulation.*

pactum, -ī, [pactus], n., *agreement, compact, manner, way, means.* **nūllō pactō,** *by no means.*

pactus, -a, -um, [part. of **pacīscor**], adj., *agreed, settled, stipulated.*

paene, adv., *almost, nearly.*

paeniteō, -ēre, -uī, ——, 2, a., *make sorry ; be sorry, repent.* Impers., **paenitet, -ēre, paenituit,** *it makes sorry, it repents, it grieves, it displeases, it offends.* **mē numquam paenitēbit,** *I shall never regret.* Cat. IV. x.

Paetus, -ī, m., *L. Papīrius Paetus,* a friend of Cicero, who had a residence near Naples. Ep. XXX. See also **Aelius.**

pāgella, -ae, [dim., cf. pāgina], f., *small page, little page, sheet* of writing-material.

palaestra, -ae, [παλαίστρα], f., *wrestling-place, wrestling-school, gymnasium ;* by metonymy, *wrestling, wrestling-match ; school of rhetoric, school ; practice, skill, art.*

palam, adv., *openly, plainly, publicly.*

Palātīnus, -a, -um, [Palātium], adj., *of the Palatine hill, Palatine.* **Palātīna palaestra**, Cicero's *gymnasium on the Palatine.* EP. III.

Palātium, -ī, [Palēs, an ancient divinity of shepherds], n., *Palatine,* one of the seven hills of Rome, southeast of the Forum. See Map, p. 76.

Pamphȳlia, -ae, [Παμφυλία], f., *Pamphȳlia,* a narrow country on the south coast of Asia Minor, bounded on the east by Cilicia, on the north by Pisidia, and on the west by Lycia.

Pānsa, -ae, m., *C. Vibius Pānsa,* consul with A. Hirtius B.C. 43. He was a partisan of Caesar. Both Pansa and Hirtius set out against Antony, and fell before Mutina. EP. XLI., XLIV.

panthēra, -ae, [πάνθηρ], f., *panther.*

Pāpius, -a, -um, adj., *of a Papius.* **lēx Pāpia**, *the law of Papius,* a law proposed by C. Papius concerning the expulsion of foreigners from Rome. ARCH. V.

pār, paris, adj., *equal ; as large as, like ; well-matched ; suitable.*

parātus, -a, -um, [part. of parō], adj., *prepared, ready ; furnished, provided ; versed, skilled.*

parcō, -ere, **pepercī** and **parsī**, **parsum**, 3, n., *spare ; treat with forbearance, use carefully, be indulgent ; abstain, cease, refrain, stop ; let alone, omit.*

parēns, -entis, [pariō], m. and f., *parent, father, mother ; ancestor, progenitor.*

pāreō, -ēre, -uī, -itum, 2, n., *appear, be visible ; obey, submit, comply ; gratify, yield.*

pariēs, -etis, m., *wall, house wall.*

Parīlis, -e, [Palēs], adj., *of Pales,* an ancient Italian divinity of flocks and shepherds. As subst., **Parīlia**, -ium, n., pl., *Parīlia, festival of Pales,* celebrated annually on April 21.

pariō, **parere**, **peperī**, **partum**, fut. part. **paritūrus**, 3, a., *bring forth, give birth to, produce ; acquire, obtain, secure ; procure, get, gain.*

parō, -āre, -āvī, -ātum, 1, a. and n., *make ready, prepare, provide, furnish, arrange ; intend, purpose, design ; procure, acquire, get.*

parricīda, -ae, [pater, caedō], m., *murderer of a parent, parricide ; murderer, assassin ; murderous criminal, outlaw.*

parricīdium, -ī, [parricīda], n., *murder of a parent, parricide ; murder, assassination ; horrible crime, treason.*

pars, **partis**, f., *part, portion, share, division ; several, some ; party, side ; office, function ; rôle, character ; region, country ; direction, end.*

particeps, -cipis, [pars + capiō], adj., *sharing, partaking.* As subst., **particeps**, -cipis, m., *sharer, partner, comrade, colleague.*

partim [pars], adv., *partly, in part.*

parum, comp. **minus**, sup. **minimē**, [cf. **parvus**], adv., *too little, not enough, insufficiently ;* comp., *less, too little;* sup., *least, in the smallest degree, very little, not at all, not in the least.*

parvulus, -a, -um, [dim. of **parvus**], adj., *very small, little; young.*

parvus, -a, -um, comp. **minor,** sup. **minimus,** adj., *little, small; inconsiderable, insignificant.* As subst., **parvum, -ī,** n., *a little.* **parvī,** *of little value, of slight moment, of small account.* **parvī rēfert,** *it matters little, it makes little difference.*

pāscō, -ere, pāvī, pāstum, 3, a. and n., *feed, nourish, support, sustain; pasture, attend; feed upon, feast;* pass., **pāscor, -ī, pāstus sum,** often with reflex. sense, *be fed, feed, feast upon.*

passus, -ūs, [cf. **pandō**], m., *step, pace, footstep; track, trace.*

pāstiō, -ōnis, [**pāscō**], f., *grazing, pasturage, pasture.*

pāstor, -ōris, [**pāscō**], m., *shepherd, herdsman.*

patefaciō, -facere, -fēcī, patefactum, [**pateō + faciō**], 3, a., *open up, lay open, throw open; disclose, bring to light.*

pateō, -ēre, -uī, ——, 2, n., *lie open, be open, stand open; be accessible, be exposed; extend; be evident, be clear, be well known.*

pater, -tris, m., *father;* pl., *fathers, forefathers, ancestors; elders, senators.* See **cōnscrīptus.**

paternus, -a, -um, [**pater**], adj., *of a father, father's, paternal; of* one's *native country, of the fatherland.*

patientia, -ae, [**patiēns**], f., *long-suffering, endurance, submission, patience; forbearance, indulgence, lenity.*

patior, patī, passus sum, 3, dep., *suffer, bear, endure, undergo, meet with; allow, permit, let.*

Patiscus, -ī, m., *Patiscus,* an acquaintance of Cicero, who, while Cicero was proconsul of Cilicia, obtained panthers for the shows of the aediles at Rome. In B. C. 43 he was pro-quaestor in Asia. EP. XVIII.

Patrēnsis, -e, [**Patrae**], adj., *of Patrae,* a city on the south shore of the entrance of the Gulf of Corinth; now Patras. EP. XXXII.

patria, -ae, [**patrius**], f., *fatherland, native country, native place; dwelling-place, home.*

patricius, -a, -um, [**pater**], adj., *of fatherly dignity; patrician, noble.* As subst., **patriciī, -ōrum,** m., pl., *patricians, nobility.*

patrimōnium, -ī, [**pater**], n., *inheritance from a father, inheritance, patrimony.*

patrius, -a, -um, [**pater**], adj., *of a father, father's, fatherly; of one's fathers, ancestral.*

patruus, -ī, [**pater**], m., *father's brother, uncle on the father's side.*

paucitās, -ātis, [**paucus**], f., *fewness, scarcity.*

paucus, -a, -um, adj., *few, small, little.* As subst., pl., **paucī, -ōrum,** m., *few, a few;* **pauca, -ōrum,** n., *a few things, little, a few words, few words.*

paulisper [**paulum + per**], adv., *for a little while, for a short time.*

paulō [abl. of **paulum**], adv., *by a little, a little, somewhat.* **paulō ante,** *a little while ago, shortly before.*

paulus, -a, -um, adj., *little, small, slight.* As subst., **paulum, -ī,** n., *a little, trifle.*

Paulus, -ī, [**paulus**], m., *L. Aemilius Paulus,* named also *Macedonicus* after his victory over Perseus, born B. C. 230 or 229; consul 182 and 168 B. C. When consul the first time he subdued the Ingauni, a piratic people of Liguria, and was honored with a triumph. In 168 B.C. he took command of the war with Perseus, king of Macedonia, whom he completely defeated at the battle of Pydna. He celebrated a splendid triumph the following year, and died B.C. 160. CAT. IV. x.

pāx, **pācis**, f., *peace; treaty, agreement, reconciliation; concord, harmony; tranquillity, rest, quiet.* **pāce tuā**, *by your leave, with your permission.* MAR. II.

peccātum, **-ī**, [**peccō**], n., *fault, transgression, sin.*

peccō, **-āre**, **-āvī**, **-ātum**, I, n. and a., *make a mistake, transgress, offend; commit a fault, sin, do wrong.*

pectō, **-ere**, **pexī**, **pexum**, 3, a., *comb, comb out.*

pectus, **-oris**, n., *breast, breastbone;* by metonymy, *heart, soul, feeling; mind, understanding.*

pecuārius, **-a**, **-um**, [**pecū**, *cattle*], adj., *of cattle.* As subst., **pecuāria**, **-ae**, (properly sc. **rēs**), f., *stock-raising, cattle-breeding.*

pecūnia, **-ae**, [**pecus**], f., lit. *wealth in cattle;* hence *property, wealth; money.*

pecus, **-udis**, f., *a head of cattle,* meaning one of a number; *brute, animal, beast;* especially, *a sheep.*

pedester, **-tris**, **-tre**, [**pēs**], adj., *on foot, pedestrian; on land.* **pedestrēs cōpiae**, *forces of infantry.*

pēior, see **malus**.

pellō, **-ere**, **pepulī**, **pulsum**, 3, a., *strike, push; drive away, force back, banish, rout; remove, dispel;* of a musical instrument, *strike, touch, play.*

Penātēs, **-ium**, [**penus**, *provision*], m., pl., *household gods, guardian deities of the house, Penātēs;* by metonymy, *hearth, home.*

pendeō, **-ēre**, **pependī**, ——, [**pendō**], 2, n., *hang, hang down; be suspended, overhang, float; rest, be dependent; be in suspense, be undecided, hesitate.*

penetrō, **-āre**, **-āvī**, **-ātum**, I, a. and n., *enter, penetrate; make way to, reach.*

penitus, adv., *inwardly, deeply, far within; thoroughly, utterly, through and through.*

pēnsitō, **-āre**, **-āvī**, **-ātum**, [freq. of **pēnsō**], I, a., *weigh out, pay.*

per, prep. with acc. only, *through;* of space, *through, across, along, over, among;* of time, *through, during, in the course of, at the time of;* of agency, means, and manner, *through, by, by the hands of, by means of, under pretence of, for the sake of;* in oaths, *in the name of, by.*

In composition **per** adds the force of *through, thoroughly, perfectly, completely, very much, very.*

peradulēscēns, **-entis**, [**per** + **adulēscēns**], adj., *very young.*

peragrō, **-āre**, **-āvī**, **-ātum**, [**per**, **ager**], I, a., *wander through, pass over, traverse.*

perbenevolus, **-a**, **-um**, [**per** + **benevolus**], adj., *very friendly, exceedingly kind.*

perbrevis, **-e**, [**per** + **brevis**], adj., *very short, very brief.*

percellō, **-ere**, **perculī**, **perculsum**, 3, a., *beat down, strike down, smite; overthrow, destroy; deject, dishearten.*

percipiō, **-cipere**, **-cēpī**, **-ceptum**, [**per** + **capiō**], 3, a., *take wholly, seize; perceive, observe; learn, know, understand.*

perculsus, see **percellō**.

percussor, -ōris, [percutiō], m., *striker, smiter; murderer, assassin.*

percutiō, -cutere, **percussī**, **percussum**, [**per** + **quatiō**, *shake*], 3, a., *strike through, thrust through, pierce, transfix; strike hard, smite, hit, kill, slay.* **dē caelō percussus**, *struck by lightning.*

perditus, -a, -um, [part. of **perdō**], adj., *lost, hopeless, ruined, desperate; corrupt, profligate, incorrigible.*

perdō, -ere, **perdidī**, **perditum**, [**per** + **dō**], 3, a., *make way with, waste, destroy, ruin; squander, dissipate, lose utterly.*

perdūcō, -ere, **perdūxī**, **perductum**, [**per** + **dūcō**], 3, a., *lead through, conduct, guide; lengthen, prolong; win over, gain over, induce.*

peregrīnātiō, -ōnis, [**peregrīnor**], f., *sojourning abroad, travelling, wandering, travel.*

peregrīnor, -ārī, -ātus sum, [**peregrīnus**], 1, dep., *sojourn abroad, travel, wander, roam.*

peregrīnus, -a, -um, [**per** + **ager**], adj., *strange, foreign, alien.* As subst., **peregrīnus**, -ī, m., *foreigner, stranger.*

pereō, -īre, -iī or -īvī, -itum, [**per** + **eō**], irr., n., *pass away, vanish, disappear; perish, be destroyed, die; be wasted, fail, be lost.*

perfectiō, -ōnis, [**perficiō**], f., *finishing, completion, perfecting, accomplishment.*

perfectus, -a, -um, [part. of **perficiō**], adj., *finished, complete, perfect, excellent.*

perferō, -ferre, -tulī, -lātum, [**per** + **ferō**], irr., a., *bear through; bring, convey; carry news, announce, report; carry through, accomplish, bring about; put up with, bear, suffer, endure.*

perficiō, -ficere, -fēcī, -fectum, fut. part. **perfectūrus**, [**per** + **faciō**], 3, a., *carry through, complete, accomplish; bring about, cause, effect.*

perfringō, -ere, **perfrēgī**, **perfrāctum**, [**per** + **frangō**], 3, a., *break through, break in pieces, shatter, fracture;* of laws, *violate, break.*

perfruor, -fruī, -frūctus sum, [**per** + **fruor**], 3, dep., *enjoy fully, be greatly delighted.*

perfugium, -ī, [**perfugiō**], n., *refuge, shelter, asylum.*

perfungor, -fungī, -fūnctus sum, [**per** + **fungor**], 3, dep., *perform, discharge; go through with, undergo, get rid of, pass through.*

pergō, -ere, **perrēxī**, **perrēctum**, [**per** + **regō**], 3, a. and n., *go on, proceed, advance, march; hasten, make haste.*

pergrātus, -a, -um, [**per** + **grātus**], adj., *very agreeable, exceedingly pleasant.* As subst., **pergrātum**, -ī, n., *a great favor,* as **fēcistī mihi pergrātum**, *you have done me a great favor.*

perhorrēscō, -ere, **perhorruī**, ——, [**per** + **horrēscō**], 3, inch., *become rough, bristle up; quake with terror, tremble greatly; shudder at, shudder to think of, have a great horror of.*

perīclitor, -ārī, -ātus sum, [**perīculum**], 1, dep., *try, test, make trial of; imperil, risk, endanger.*

perīculōsus, -a, -um, [**perīculum**], adj., *full of danger, dangerous, perilous.*

perīculum, -ī, n., *trial, attempt; risk, hazard, danger, peril; legal action, lawsuit, suit.*

perinde [**per** + **inde**], adv., *in the same manner, just so, equally, in like manner.* **perinde ac**, or **atque**, *just as.*

perinīquus, -a, -um, [per + inīquus], adj., *very unfair, exceedingly unjust.*

perītus, -a, -um, adj., *experienced, practised, trained; skilled, skilful, expert.*

periūcundus, -a, -um, [per + iūcundus], adj., *very agreeable, very acceptable.*

permāgnus, -a, -um, [per + māgnus], adj., *very great, very extensive, exceedingly important.* As subst., **permāgnum**, -ī, n., *a very great thing.* **permāgnī interest**, *it is of very great importance.*

permaneō, -ēre, **permānsī**, **permānsum**, [per + maneō], 2, n., *remain, stay; hold out, continue, persist.*

permittō, -ere, **permīsī**, **permissum**, [per + mittō], 3, a., *let go; commit, surrender, intrust, put in charge of; allow, suffer, permit, grant.*

permodestus, -a, -um, [per + modestus], adj., *exceedingly modest, very shy.*

permoveō, -ēre, **permōvī**, **permōtum**, [per + moveō], 2, a., *move deeply; arouse, agitate, influence, prevail upon.*

permultum [permultus], adv., *very much, very far.*

permultus, -a, -um, [per + multus], adj., *very much; pl., very many, in great numbers.* As subst., **permultum**, -ī, n., *a great deal, very much.*

permūtātiō, -ōnis, [permūtō], f., *complete change, revolution; exchange, interchange, barter.*

perniciēs, -ēī, [per + nex], f., *destruction, ruin, overthrow, disaster.*

perniciōsus, -a, -um, [perniciēs], adj., *destructive, ruinous, baleful, pernicious.*

pernoctō, -āre, -āvī, fut. part. **pernoctātūrus**, [per + noctō], 1, n. *remain all night, stay all night, pass the night.*

perpetuus, -a, -um, [per, cf. petō], adj., *continuous, uninterrupted, constant, perpetual; whole, entire.* As subst., n., in the phrase **in perpetuum**, *for all time, forever.*

persaepe [per + saepe], adv., *very often, very frequently.*

perscrībō, -ere, **perscrīpsī**, **perscrīptum**, [per + scrībō], 3, a., *write in full, write out; describe fully* in writing, *recount, detail;* of public documents, *put on record, record.*

persequor, -sequī, -secūtus sum, [per + sequor], 3, dep., *follow persistently, follow after, pursue; prosecute, avenge; perform, accomplish; set forth, relate.*

Persēs, -ae, [Πέρσης], m., *Persēs* or *Perseus*, last king of Macedonia. He came to the throne B. C. 179. He entered into a war with Rome B. C. 171, and was totally defeated by L. Aemilius Paulus at Pydna, B. C. 168. He adorned the triumph of Paulus, B. C. 167, and passed the remainder of his life in captivity. CAT. IV. X., IMP. P. XVIII.

persevērantia, -ae, [persevērō], f., *steadfastness, persistency, perseverance.*

persevērō, -āre, -āvī, -ātum, [per, sevērus], 1, n. and a., *continue steadfastly, persist, persevere.*

persōna, -ae, [per, cf. sonus], f., *mask, part, character, role; personage, person.*

perspiciō, -spicere, -spexī, **perspectum**, [per + speciō], 3, a., *look through, look into; inspect, examine; perceive clearly, see plainly, observe, discern, note.*

persuādeō, -ēre, persuāsī, persuāsum, [per + suādeō], 2, n. and a., *convince, persuade; induce, prevail upon.*

perterreō, -ēre, perterruī, perterritum, [per + terreō], 2, a., *frighten greatly, terrify.*

pertimēscō, -ere, pertimuī, ——, [per + timēscō], 3, inch., *be greatly alarmed, be much frightened; fear greatly, be much afraid of.*

pertināċia, -ae, [pertināx], f., *persistency, obstinacy, stubbornness.*

pertineō, -ēre, -uī, ——, [per + teneō], 2, n., *reach, extend; belong, pertain, concern, refer; tend, lead, be conducive, conduce.*

perturbātus, -a, -um, [part. of perturbō], adj., *disturbed, agitated, embarrassed, unsettled.*

perturbō, -āre, -āvī, -ātum, [per + turbō], 1, a., *greatly disturb, throw into disorder; disturb, confuse, unsettle.*

pervādō, -ere, pervāsī, pervāsum, [per + vādō], 3, n. and a., *go through, spread through, prevail; penetrate, pervade, extend, reach.*

pervagātus, -a, -um, [part. of pervagor], adj., *wide-spread, well-known.*

perveniō, -īre, pervēnī, perventum, [per + veniō], 4, n., *come through, come up, arrive, reach; attain, come to; come, fall.*

Pescennius, -ī, m., *Pescennius*, a friend of Cicero who befriended him during his exile, especially during his stay at Brundisium. Ep. VIII.

pestifer, -era, -erum, [pestis, ferō], adj., *destructive, pernicious, noxious, baleful.*

pestilentia, -ae, [pestilēns], f., *infectious disease, epidemic, pestilence; unhealthful climate, unwholesome atmosphere.*

pestis, -is, f., *plague, pest, pestilence; bane, curse; ruin, destruction, death.*

petītiō, -ōnis, [petō], f., in fencing or fighting, *thrust, blow, aim, attack; canvass for votes, candidacy; claim, suit.*

petō, -ere, petīvī and -iī, petītum, 3, a., *strive for, aim at, seek; rush at, attack, assail; demand, require; beg, beseech, entreat; woo, court; pursue; wrest, draw from.*

petulantia, -ae, [petulāns, *pert*], f., *pertness, sauciness, impudence.*

pexus, -a, -um, see **pectō**.

Philhetaerus, -ī, [φιλέταιρος, *true to comrades*], m., *Clōdius Philhetaerus*, a freedman of Cicero's. Ep. VIII.

Philippus, -ī, [Φίλιππος], m., *Philip*, name of three persons mentioned in this book:

(1) *Philippus V., Philip V.*, king of Macedonia B. C. 220–179. He was an active and able ruler, and for a time greatly increased the power of his state. He entered into an alliance with Hannibal, but rendered little assistance against the Romans, who, after the close of the second Punic War, engaged in active hostilities against him. He was conquered in B. C. 196 and obliged to submit to humiliating terms. Imp. P. VI.

(2) *L. Mārcius Philippus*, consul B. C. 91. He was prominent as an orator and as a political leader. Imp. P. XXI.

(3) *L. Mārcius Philippus*, propraetor in Syria B. C. 59, consul B. C. 56. He was the stepfather of C. Octavius. During the civil wars, however, he remained neu-

tral, and lived to see his stepson the emperor Augustus. Ep. XVI., XXXV.

Philogenēs, -is, [φίλος, cf. γένος], m., *Philogenēs*, a freedman of Atticus. Ep. XVI.

philosophia, -ae, [φιλοσοφία], f., *philosophy.*

philosophus, -a, -um, [φιλόσοφος], adj., *philosophical.* As subst., **philosophus**, -ī, m., *philosopher.*

Philotīmus, -ī, [Φιλότῑμος], m., *Philotimus*, a freedman of Cicero or of Terentia. Ep. III. *et al.*

piāculum, -ī, [piō], n., *propitiatory sacrifice, expiatory offering; victim offered in sacrifice, offering; atonement, sacrifice.*

Pīcēnum, -ī, n., *Pīcēnum*, a district on the east coast of Italy, lying northeast from Rome and east of Umbria.

Pīcēnus, -a, -um, adj., *of Picenum, Picene.*

pietās, -ātis, [pius], f., *dutiful conduct, dutifulness, sense of duty; religiousness; faithfulness* in discharge of duty, particularly toward kindred; *duty, fealty, affection, gratitude, loyalty, devotion;* towards one's country, *patriotism.*

piget, -ēre, **piguit** and **pigitum est**, 2, a., impers., *it annoys, it troubles, it disgusts; it causes to repent, it makes sorry.* **nec mē piget**, *and I am not sorry.*

pila, -ae, f., *ball;* by metonymy, *ball-playing, game of ball.*

Pilia, -ae, f., *Pilia*, wife of Cicero's friend Atticus, to whom she was married B. C. 56. Ep. XIX.

pīnguis, -e, adj., *fat, rich, fertile; dull, stupid.*

Pīsō, -ōnis, m., *C. Calpurnius Pīsō Frūgī*, son-in-law of Cicero. He was betrothed to Cicero's daughter Tullia B. C. 67, married B. C. 63. He was quaestor, B. C. 58, and made every effort to secure the recall of Cicero from banishment. He died the following year. Ep. VIII., IX.

pius, -a, -um, adj., *dutiful, conscientious, devout, religious; devoted,* especially to kindred; *faithful, loving, filial.*

Pius, -ī, [pius], m., *Pius*, honorary surname of *Q. Caecilius Metellus.* See **Metellus**, (2).

pl., see **plēbs.**

placeō, -ēre, -uī or -itus sum, 2, n., *please, be pleasing; give pleasure, meet with approval, suit, satisfy;* often impers., **placet**, -ēre, -itum est, *it pleases, it is agreed, it seems right, it is resolved, it is decided.*

plācō, -āre, -āvī, -ātum, [cf. placeō], 1, a., *quiet, soothe, calm; appease, conciliate, reconcile.*

Plancius, -ī, m., *Cn. Plancius*, quaestor in Macedonia B. C. 58, where he showed great kindness to Cicero, then in exile. Some years later Plancius was charged with bribery at an election and defended by Cicero, who secured his acquittal. Ep. IX.

Plancus, -ī, m., *L. Munātius Plancus*, consul B. C. 42. He was a lieutenant of Caesar in Gaul (Caes. Bel. Gal. v. 24, 25), and afterwards a partisan of the Dictator. After the death of Caesar he was active in political affairs until the establishment of the Empire. Ep. XLV.

plānē [plānus], adv., *plainly, clearly, distinctly; wholly, quite.*

Platō, -ōnis, [Πλάτων], m., *Plato*, a Greek philosopher.

plēbs, plēbis, and **plēbēs**, -ēī or -ī, often abbreviated **pl.**, plural wanting, f., *common people, commons, common folk, populace; mass, throng, multitude.*

plēnus, **-a**, **-um**, [cf. -**pleō**], adj., *full, filled; complete, whole; abounding, rich.*

plērumque [**plērusque**], adv., *for the most part, generally, commonly, very often.*

plērusque, **-raque**, **-rumque**, [**plērus**], adj., *a very great part, the majority, most.* As subst., **plērīque**, **-ōrumque**, m., pl., *the greater part, the majority, about all.*

Plōtius, **-ī**, m., *L. Plōtius Gallus*, a native of Cisalpine Gaul, and a rhetorician. He opened a school for the study of Latin and rhetoric at Rome about 88 B. C. ARCH. IX.

plūrimum [**plūrimus**], adv., *very much, very greatly; for the most part, commonly.*

plūrimus, **-a**, **-um**, see **multus**.

plūs, **plūris**, see **multus**.

podagra, **-ae**, [ποδάγρα], f., *gout.* EP. XXIX.

poena, **-ae**, [ποινή], f., *compensation, recompense; penalty, punishment, retribution, vengeance.*

Poenī, **-ōrum**, m., pl., *Phoenicians; Carthaginians.*

poēta, **-ae**, [ποιητής], m., *poet.*

poliō, **-īre**, **-īvī**, **-ītum**, 4, a., *smooth, polish; adorn, decorate, embellish.*

polliceor, **-ērī**, **-itus sum**, [**por**, for **prō**, + **liceor**], 2, dep., *offer, promise.*

Pompēiānus, **-a**, **-um**, [**Pompēiī**], adj., *Pompeian, of Pompēiī*, a city in the southern part of Campania, near Neapolis (Naples), buried by an eruption of Vesuvius, A. D. 79. As subst., **Pompēiānum**, **-ī**, n., *estate near Pompēiī, Pompeian villa*, belonging to Cicero. EP. III., XXIX.

Pompēius, **-a**, name of a plebeian gens. The most distinguished person bearing the name was *Cn. Pompēius Măgnus*, born Sept. 30, B. C. 106. He was victorious over the pirates and over Mithridates, was a member of the first triumvirate, and was killed in Egypt, whither he had fled for refuge, after the battle of Pharsalia, Sept. 29, B. C. 48.

Pompōnia, **-ae**, f., *Pompōnia*, sister of Cicero's friend Atticus, and wife of Q. Cicero, the orator's brother. EP. III.

Pompōnius, **-a**, name of a plebeian gens. The best known member is *T. Pompōnius Atticus.* See **Atticus.**

Pomptīnus, **-ī**, m., *C. Pomptīnus*, praetor when Cicero was consul, B. C. 63. He rendered important service in crushing the Catilinarian conspiracy. In B. C. 51 he was legatus to Cicero in Cilicia. CAT. III. II., III., VI.

pōnō, **-ere**, **posuī**, **positum**, 3, a., *set down, place, set, put; lay, fix, station; lay aside, take off; allay, quiet; spend, employ; count, reckon, consider; assert, allege, maintain; propose, offer; put away, dismiss;* of arms, *lay down.*

pōns, **pontis**, m., *bridge.*

pontifex, **-icis**, [**pōns**, cf. **faciō**], m., *high-priest, pontiff, pontifex.* **Pontifex Māximus**, *suprem pontiff, chief of the priests*, the chief of the guild of *pontificēs*, or pontiffs, who had the supervision of all sacred observances at Rome.

Pontus, **-ī**, [Πόντος], m., *Pontus*, a large country in the northeastern part of Asia Minor, south of the Pontus Euxinus, from which it received its name.

popīna, **-ae**, f., *eating-house, cookshop.*

populāris, -e, [populus], adj., *of the people; devoted to the people, democratic; acceptable to the people, popular.*

populus, -ī, m., *people, nation; multitude; host, throng.* **populus Rōmānus**, *the Roman people*, meaning *the whole body of citizens* taken together, as distinguished from foreign peoples or from the classes and factions at Rome.

porta, -ae, f., *gate of a city, city-gate, gate; passage, outlet.*

portentum, -ī, [portendō], n., *omen, sign, portent; monster, monstrosity.*

portuōsus, -a, -um, [portus], adj., *rich in harbors, supplied with harbors.*

portus, -ūs, m., *harbor, port; haven, refuge.* **ex portū vectīgal**, *revenue from customs.*

positus, -a, -um, [part. of pōnō], adj., *placed, situated, lying.*

possessiō, -ōnis, [por, for prō, + sedeō], f., *taking possession, seizure; occupation, possession;* especially in pl., *property, estates, possessions.*

possideō, -sidēre, -sēdī, -sessum, [por, for prō, + sedeō], 2, a., *possess, be master of, own; hold possession of, occupy.*

possīdō, -sīdere, -sēdī, -sessum, [por, for prō, + sīdō], 3, a., *take possession of, possess one's self of, occupy, seize.*

possum, posse, potuī, [potis + sum], irr., n., *be able, can, have power; have influence, avail.*

post, adv., of place, *behind, back, backwards;* of time, *afterwards, after, later, next.*

post, prep. with acc., *after;* of place, *behind;* of time, *after, since;* of other relations, *after, inferior to, beneath, next to.*

posteā [post + eā], adv., *after that, thereafter, later; then, afterwards.* **posteā quam**, followed by a clause, *after, after that.*

posteritās, -ātis, [posterus], f., *future time, the future; future generations, posterity.* **in posteritātem**, *for the future.*

posterus, -a, -um, nom. sing. m. not found, comp. **posterior**, sup. **postrēmus**, [post], adj., *following, coming after, subsequent, future.* Comp., **posterior, -us**, *later, inferior, less important.* Sup., **postrēmus, -a, -um**, *last, hindmost; lowest, worst.* As subst., **posterī, -ōrum**, m., pl., *men of the future, descendants, posterity;* also, n. sing. in the phrase **in posterum**, = **in posterum tempus**, *for the future.*

posthāc [post + hāc], adv., *after this, henceforth, hereafter, in the future.*

postrēmō [postrēmus], adv., *at last, finally, lastly.*

postrēmus, see **posterus**.

postrīdiē [posterī + diē], adv., *the next day, the day after.*

postulō, -āre, -āvī, -ātum, 1, a., *ask, request; demand, require, claim, desire.*

potēns, -entis, [part. of possum], adj., *able, strong, powerful, mighty; potent, influential.*

potestās, -ātis, [potis], f., *ability, power, capacity; authority, sovereignty; magistracy, office; opportunity, privilege.*

potior, -īrī, -ītus sum, [potis], 4, dep., *become master of, take possession of, obtain, acquire; be master of, hold, possess.*

potis or **pote**, comp. **potior**, sup. **potissimus**, pos. indecl., adj., *able, capable.* Comp., *better, preferable, superior, more impor-*

tant. Sup., *chief, principal, most prominent.*

potissimum [potissimus], adv., *chiefly, principally; especially, above all, most of all.*

potius [potis], adv., comp., *rather, more.*

pōtus, -a, -um, adj., *that has drunk, drunken.* **bene pōtus**, *having drunk freely.* Ep. xxxviii.

pr., see prīdiē.

P R., see praetor.

prae, prep. with abl., *before, in front of; in comparison with, compared with, in view of; by reason of, on account of, because of.* In composition, *before, very.*

praebeō, -ēre, -uī, -itum, [prae + habeō], 2, a., *hold forth, offer; give, furnish, supply, grant; present, show.*

praeceps, -cipitis, [prae + caput], adj., *headlong, head foremost, in haste; steep, precipitous, abrupt; rash, hasty, inconsiderate.*

praeceptum, -ī, [praecipiō], n., *maxim, precept, teaching; injunction, direction, order.*

praecipiō, -cipere, -cēpī, praeceptum, [prae + capiō], 3, a. *take beforehand, anticipate; advise, admonish, instruct, enjoin, bid.*

praecipuē [praecipuus], adv., *especially, chiefly, eminently.*

praecipuus, -a, -um, [prae, cf. capiō], adj., lit. *taken before others;* hence, *special, particular, peculiar; eminent; distinguished; extraordinary.*

praeclārē [praeclārus], adv., *very clearly, very plainly; excellently, admirably.*

praeclārus, -a, -um, [prae + clārus], adj., *very bright; splendid, admirable, excellent; distinguished, famous, illustrious, renowned.*

praecō, -ōnis, [prae + vocō], m., *crier, herald; auctioneer; eulogist.*

praecōnium, -ī, [praecōnius, from praecō], n., *proclaiming, heralding; commendation, eulogy.*

praecurrō, -ere, praecucurrī, ——, [prae + currō], 1, n. and a., *run before, hasten on before; outstrip, surpass, excel.*

praeda, -ae, f., *booty, plunder, spoil;* by metonymy, *gain, profit.*

praedātor, -ōris, [praedor], m., *plunderer, pillager.*

praedicātiō, -ōnis, [praedicō], f., *proclaiming, proclamation; commendation, praise.*

praedicō, -āre, -āvī, -ātum, [prae + dicō], 1, a. and n., *proclaim, announce; relate, declare openly, assert; praise, boast.* **ut praedicās**, *as you assert.*

praedīcō, -dīcere, -dīxī, -dictum, [prae + dīcō], 3, a., *tell beforehand, foretell, predict; advise, warn, admonish.*

praeditus, -a, -um, [prae + datus], adj., *gifted, endowed, provided.*

praedium, -ī, n., *farm, estate.*

praedō, -ōnis, [praeda], m., *plunderer, robber.*

praedor, -ārī, -ātus sum, [praeda], 1, dep., *take booty, plunder, rob, spoil.*

praefectūra, -ae, [praefectus], f., *overseership, office of prefect, prefectship; prefecture,* a subject community governed by a prefect sent from Rome.

praefectus, -ī, [praeficiō], m., *overseer, director, prefect; governor, commander; cavalry captain.*

praeferō, -ferre, -tulī, -lātum, [prae + ferō], irr., a., *carry in front of; bear before, bear forward; place before, set before, prefer; manifest, reveal.*

praeficiō, -**ficere**, -**fēcī**, **praefectum**, [**prae** + **faciō**], 3, a., *set over, put in charge; appoint to command, place at the head.*

praefulciō, -**īre**, **praefulsī**, **praefultum**, [**prae** + **fulciō**], 4, a., *prop up, support; make sure.*

praemittō, -**ere**, **praemīsī**, **praemissum**, [**prae** + **mittō**], 3, a., *send forward, despatch in advance.*

praemium, -**ī**, [**prae**, cf. **emō**], n., *advantage, favor; reward, recompense, prize, booty.*

praemūniō, -**īre**, -**īvī**, -**ītum**, [**prae** + **mūniō**], 4, a., *fortify in front, protect; set forth as a defence; secure beforehand.*

Praeneste, -**is**, n., *Praeneste*, an ancient city of Latium, 23 miles east of Rome; now Palestrina. CAT. I. III.

praepōnō, -**ere**, **praeposuī**, **praepositum**, [**prae** + **pōnō**], 3, a., *place before; set over, put in charge, place in command, appoint; set before, prefer.*

praescrībō, -**ere**, **praescrīpsī**, **praescrīptum**, [**prae** + **scrībō**], 3, a., *write before; determine beforehand, order, prescribe, give directions.*

praesēns, -**entis**, [part. of **praesum**], adj., *at hand, present, in person; prompt, instant, impending; powerful, influential; favoring, propitious.*

praesentia, -**ae**, [**praesēns**], f., *presence; present time.*

praesentiō, -**īre**, **praesēnsī**, **praesēnsum**, [**prae** + **sentiō**], 4, a., *perceive in advance, presage, divine.*

praesertim [**prae**, cf. **serō**], adv., *especially, chiefly; particularly, principally.*

praesideō, -**ēre**, **praesēdī**, ——, [**prae** + **sedeō**], 2, n and a., lit. *sit before;* hence *watch over, guard, protect; preside over, direct, manage.*

praesidium, -**ī**, [**praeses**], n., *defence, protection; guard, garrison; post, intrenchment, fortification; aid, help, assistance.*

praestāns, -**antis**, [part. of **praestō**], adj., *pre-eminent, excellent, superior, distinguished.*

praestō, adv., *at hand, present, here.*

praestō, -**āre**, -**stitī**, -**stātum** or -**stitum**, [**prae** + **stō**], 1, n. and a., *stand before; stand out, excel, be pre-eminent, be excellent; vouch for, be responsible for, answer for; fulfil, perform, discharge; maintain, keep, preserve.*

praestōlor, -**ārī**, -**ātus sum**, 1, dep., *stand ready for, wait for.*

praesum, -**esse**, -**fuī**, [**prae** + **sum**], irr., n., *be set over, have charge of, rule, command.*

praeter [**prae**], prep. with acc., *past, by, before, in front of, along; contrary to, against; except, besides, apart from.* In composition, *past, by, beyond, besides.*

praetereā [**praeter** + **eā**], adv., *besides, moreover, further.*

praetereō, -**īre**, -**īvī** or -**iī**, -**itum**, [**praeter** + **eō**], irr., a. and n., *go by, go past, pass by; pass over, disregard, omit.*

praeteritus, -**a**, -**um**, [part. of **praetereō**], adj., *gone by, past.* As subst., **praeterita**, -**ōrum**, n., pl., *the past, bygones.*

praetermittō, -**mittere**, -**mīsī**, -**missum**, [**praeter** + **mittō**], 3, a., *let pass; omit, leave undone, neglect; pass over, overlook.*

praeterquam [**praeter** + **quam**], adv., *except, besides, save.*

praetextātus, -**a**, -**um**, [**praetexta**], adj., *wearing the toga praetexta; juvenile.*

praetextus, **-a**, **-um**, [part. of **praetexō**, *border*], adj , *bordered, edged.* **toga praetexta**, or, as subst., **praetexta**, **-ae**, f., *bordered toga, toga praetexta, the praetexta*, a toga having a purple border, worn as the official robe of the higher magistrates, and by the children of Roman citizens until they became of age.

praetor, **-ōris**, sometimes abbreviated **PR.**, [for unused prae-itor, from **praeeō**], m., *chief magistrate, commander ;* as an officer of Rome, *praetor*, a magistrate intrusted with the administration of justice.

praetōrius, **-a**, **-um**, [**praetor**], adj., *of a praetor, of praetors, praetorian ; of a general, of a commander.*

praetūra, **-ae**, [**praeeō**], f., *office of praetor, praetorship.*

prāvitās, **-ātis**, [**prāvus**], f., *crookedness, irregularity ; perverseness, viciousness.*

precor, **-ārī**, **-ātus sum**, [cf. **prex**], 1, dep., *entreat, pray, supplicate, beg, beseech ; call upon, invoke.*

premō, **-ere**, **pressī**, **pressum**, 3, a., *press ; press hard, pursue closely, crowd ; cover, crown, adorn ; press down, cause to sink ; load, burden, oppress ; overwhelm, crush, restrain, check ; urge.*

pretium, **-ī**, n., *price, value, worth ; reward, recompense, return.* **operae pretium est**, *it is worth the effort, it is worth while.*

prex, **precis**, nom. and gen. sing. not found, [cf. **precor**], f., *prayer, petition, entreaty ; imprecation, curse.*

prīd., see **prīdiē**.

prīdem, adv., *long ago, long since.* **iam prīdem**, *this long time.*

prīdiē, in dates often abbreviated **pr.**, **prīd.**, [root pri in **prior**, + **diē**], adv., *on the day before, the previous day.*

prīmō [**prīmus**], adv., *at first, first, in the first place.*

prīmum [**prīmus**], adv., *at first, in the first place, first ; for the first time.* **ut prīmum**, *as soon as.* **quam prīmum**, *as soon as possible.*

prīmus, see **prior**.

prīnceps, **-ipis**, [**prīmus**, cf. **capiō**], adj., *first, foremost, chief.* As subst., **prīnceps**, **-ipis**, m., *chief, leader, head ; founder, originator, contriver.*

prīncipium, **-ī**, [**prīnceps**], n., *beginning, commencement, origin, principle.* **prīncipiō**, abl., *in the beginning, at first, in the first place.*

prior, **-us**, gen. **-ōris**, adj. in the comp. degree, sup. **prīmus**, *former, previous, prior, first.* Sup. **prīmus**, **-a**, **-um**, *first, foremost ; chief ; first* in excellence, *noble, eminent, distinguished.* As subst., n., pl., in the phrase **in prīmīs**, *among the first, especially, chiefly, principally.*

prīstinus, **-a**, **-um**, [**prius**], adj., *former, early, original.*

prius [**prior**], adv., in the comp. degree, *sooner, before ; previously.* **prius quam**, *sooner than, earlier than, before, before that.*

prīvātus, **-a**, **-um**, [part. of **prīvō**], adj., *personal, individual, private, retired.* As subst., **prīvātus**, **-ī**, m., *private citizen, private person*, as opposed to one holding office.

prīvō, **-āre**, **-āvī**, **-ātum**, [**prīvus**, *one's own*], 1, a., *deprive, strip, rob ; free, release, deliver.*

prō, prep. with abl., *before, in front of, in the presence of ; for, in behalf of; instead of, in place of, in return for, for ; in comparison* *with, according to, because of, on account of.* **prō eō atque,** *just the same as, just as, even as.* In composition, *before, forwards, for.*

prō, interj., *O! ah! alas!*

proavus, -ī, [**prō + avus**], m., *great-grandfather; forefather, ancestor.*

probitās, -ātis, [**probus,** *good*], f., *goodness, uprightness, worth.*

probō, -āre, -āvī, -ātum, [**probus,** *good*], 1, a., *approve, commend, esteem, recommend; make credible, show, prove, demonstrate.*

prōcēdō, -ere, prōcessī, prōcessum, [**prō + cēdō**], 3, n., *go before, go forward, proceed, advance; appear, arise.*

procella, -ae, f., *violent wind, storm, tempest;* by metonymy, *violence, commotion.*

prōcessiō, -ōnis, [**prōcēdō**], f., *a marching forward, advance.*

procul, adv., *afar off, at a distance, far away; from afar.*

prōcūrātiō, -ōnis, [**prōcūrō**], f., *charge, management, administration.*

prōdigium, -ī, n., *omen, sign, portent; prodigy, monster.*

prōdigus, -a, -um, adj., *lavish, wasteful, prodigal.* As subst., **prōdigus, -ī,** m., *spendthrift, prodigal.*

prōdō, -ere, prōdidī, prōditum, [**prō + dō**], 3, a., *put forth, exhibit; relate, report, hand down, transmit; make known, disclose, betray.*

proelior, -ārī, -ātus sum, [**proelium**], 1, dep., *join battle, engage in battle, fight.*

proelium, -ī, n., *battle, strife, contest, combat.*

profectiō, -ōnis, [**profectus,** *from* **proficīscor**], f., *setting out, departure.*

profectō [**prō + factō**], adv., *actually, indeed, in fact, really, by all means.*

prōferō, -ferre, -tulī, -lātum, [**prō + ferō**], irr., a., *carry out, bring out, bring forth, produce; put forth, stretch out, extend; make known, reveal, show.*

professiō, -ōnis, [**profiteor**], f., *acknowledgment, declaration, profession, promise.*

prōficiō, -ficere, -fēcī, -fectum, [**prō + faciō**], 3, n. and a., *make progress, advance, succeed; accomplish, effect, bring about, gain; help, avail, be serviceable.*

proficīscor, -ficīscī, -fectus sum, [**prōficiō**], 3, dep., *set out, go forward, start, go, depart, proceed; begin, commence.*

profiteor, -fitērī, -fessus sum, [**prō + fateor**], 2, dep., *declare publicly, make a declaration; acknowledge, own, profess; avow one's self, profess to be; promise.*

prōflīgātus, -a, -um, [part. of **prōflīgō**], adj., *abandoned, vile, dissolute, profligate.*

prōflīgō, -āre, -āvī, -ātum, 1, a., *strike to the ground, overthrow, overcome; destroy, crush, ruin.*

profugiō, -fugere, -fūgī, ——, [**prō + fugiō**], 3, n. and a., *flee, run away, escape; flee for refuge, take refuge.*

profundō, -ere, profūdī, profūsum, [**prō + fundō**], 3, a., *pour out, pour forth; spend freely, lavish; squander, dissipate, waste.*

prōgredior, -gredī, -gressus sum, [**prō + gradior**], 3, dep., *go forth, go forward, proceed, advance.*

prohibeō, -ēre, -uī, -itum, [**prō + habeō**], 2, a., *hold before; hold back, hold, restrain, check, repress; hinder, prevent; keep, protect, defend, preserve.*

prōiciō, -icere, -iēcī, -iectum, [prō + iaciō], 3, a., *throw forth, cast out, expel, banish; hold forth, extend; throw away, give up, resign.*

proinde [prō + inde], adv., *hence, accordingly, then; just so, in like manner, equally, even.*

prōlātō, -āre, -āvī, -ātum, [prōlātus, from prōferō], 1, a., *extend, enlarge; put off, postpone, defer, delay.*

prōmissum, -ī, [prōmittō], n., *thing promised, promise.*

prōmittō, -ere, prōmīsī, prōmissum, [prō + mittō], 3, a., *put forth; foretell; promise, assure; hold out, give hope of, cause to expect.*

prōmulgō, -āre, -āvī, -ātum, 1, a., *propose openly, bring forward, publish.*

prōnūntiō, -āre, -āvī, -ātum, [prō + nūntiō], 1, n. and a., *proclaim, announce, publish; decide, pronounce; promise, offer.*

prōpāgō, -āre, -āvī, -ātum, 1, a., *extend, enlarge, increase; generate, propagate; prolong, continue, preserve.*

prope, comp. **propius**, sup. **proximē**, adv., *near, near by, nigh; nearly, almost;* often having the force of a preposition and followed by the acc., *near, near to, almost to, in the vicinity of.* Comp., **propius**, *nearer.* Sup., **proximē**, *next, most nearly, very near, nearest.*

properō, -āre, -āvī, -ātum, [properus, *quick*], 1, n. and a., *make haste, hasten, hurry; quicken, accelerate, do quickly.*

propinquus, -a, -um, [prope], adj., *near, neighboring, near at hand; kindred, related.* As subst., **propīnquus**, -ī, m., *relative, kinsman.*

propior, -us, gen. -ōris, adj. in comp. degree, sup. **proximus**, *nearer, closer, nigher; later, more recent; of more concern, of greater importance.* Sup. **proximus**, -a, -um, *nearest, next, closest; latest, last, most recent; most important.*

propius, see **prope**.

prōpōnō, -ere, prōposuī, prōpositum, [prō + pōnō], 3, a., *put forth, set before, display; propose, resolve, intend; point out, declare; determine upon, settle, determine.*

proprius, -a, -um, adj., *own, individual, peculiar; personal, characteristic; exact, appropriate; lasting, enduring.*

propter [prope], adv. and prep., *near:*

(1) As adv., *near, at hand, hard by, near by.*

(2) As prep., with acc., *near, next to, close to; on account of, by reason of, for, because of, for the sake of.*

propterea [propter + eā], adv., *therefore, for this reason, on that account.* **propterea quod**, *because.*

prōpūgnāculum, -ī, [prōpūgnō], n., *bulwark, rampart, place of defence; defence, protection.*

prōpulsō, -āre, -āvī, -ātum, [freq. of prōpellō], 1, a., *ward off, repel, repulse, avert.*

prōscrīptiō, -ōnis, [prōscrībō], f., *public notice of sale; confiscation, proscription.*

prōsequor, -sequī, -secūtus sum, [prō + sequor], 3, dep., *follow, attend, accompany, escort; follow up, pursue; honor, distinguish.*

prōsperē [prōsperus], adv., *favorably, fortunately, luckily, prosperously.*

prōspiciō, -spicere, -spexī, prōspectum, [prō + speciō], 3, n. and a., *look forward, look out,* *behold; look out for, provide for, take care of.*

prōsternō, **-ere**, **prōstrāvī**, **prōstrātum**, [**prō** + **sternō**], 3, a., *spread out; cast down, overthrow, prostrate; throw to the ground, ruin, destroy.*

prōstrātus, see **prōsternō**.

prōsum, **prōdesse**, **prōfuī**, [**prō** + **sum**], irr., n., *be of use, profit, serve, help.*

prōvidentia, **-ae**, [**prōvidēns**], f., *foresight; forethought, precaution.*

prōvideō, **-ēre**, **prōvīdī**, **prōvīsum**, [**prō** + **videō**], 2, a. and n., *see beforehand, see in advance, foresee, discern; see to, take care, look after, provide, be careful.*

prōvincia, **-ae**, f., *office, duty; public office, command; province,* territory governed by a magistrate sent out from Rome; *administration of a province, provincial government.*

prōvinciālis, **-e**, [**prōvincia**], adj., *of a province, provincial.*

prōvocō, **-āre**, **-āvī**, **-ātum**, [**prō** + **vocō**], 1, a. and n., *call out, summon, challenge; arouse, provoke, exasperate.*

proximē, see **prope**.

proximus, **-a**, **-um**, see **propior**.

prūdēns, **-entis**, [for **prōvidēns**], adj., *foreseeing; knowing, experienced, versed; with knowledge, deliberate; discreet, wise, prudent, circumspect.*

prūdentia, **-ae**, [**prūdēns**], f., *foresight; knowledge, acquaintance, skill; sagacity, discretion, practical wisdom, good sense.*

pruīna, **-ae**, f., *hoar-frost, frost, rime.*

Ptolemaeus, **-ī**, m., *Ptolemy*, name of a line of Egyptian kings; in this book *Ptolemy XI.*, surnamed *Aulētēs.* He came to the throne of Egypt B. C. 80, was driven out of the country on account of his vices and extortionate government B. C. 58, but was restored with the help of Gabinius three years later. He died B. C. 51. EP. XII.

pūblicānus, **-a**, **-um**, [**pūblicus**], adj., *of the public revenue.* As subst., **pūblicānus**, **-ī**, m., *farmer of the public revenue, revenue farmer, publican.*

pūblicātiō, **-ōnis**, [**pūblicō**], f., *seizure for the state, confiscation.*

pūblicē [**pūblicus**], adv., *for the state, in the name of the state, publicly, officially.*

Pūblicius, **-ī**, m., *Pūblicius*, an intimate of Catiline's. CAT. II. 11.

pūblicō, **-āre**, **-āvī**, **-ātum**, [**pūblicus**], 1, a., *seize for the state, confiscate.*

pūblicus, **-a**, **-um**, [for populicus, from **populus**], adj., *of the people, public; common, general; usual, ordinary.* **rēs pūblica**, *commonwealth, state, republic.*

Pūblius, **-ī**, abbreviated **P.**, m., *Pūblius*, a Roman forename.

pudeō, **-ēre**, **-uī**, and **puditum est**, 2, n. and a., *be ashamed, make ashamed, put to shame.* Commonly impers., **pudet**, **-ēre**, **puditum est**, *it makes ashamed.* **mē pudet**, *I am ashamed.*

pudīcitia, **-ae**, [**pudīcus**], f., *modesty, virtue, chastity.*

pudor, **-ōris**, [**pudeō**], m., *shame, sense of shame; sense of right, conscientiousness; feeling of decency, modesty, propriety; cause for shame, ignominy, disgrace.*

puer, **-erī**, m., *boy, lad, youth,* properly used of boys and young men till they reached the seventeenth year.

puerīlis, **-e**, [**puer**], adj., *boyish, childish, youthful; puerile, triv-*

ial. **aetās puerīlis,** *the age of childhood.*

pueritia, -ae, [puer], f., *boyhood, childhood, youth.*

pūgna, -ae, f., *fight, battle, engagement, contest.*

pūgnō, -āre, -āvī, -ātum, [pūgna], 1, n. and a., *fight, give battle; contend, engage in strife, dispute; struggle, strive, endeavor.*

pulcher, -chra, -chrum, comp. **pulchrior,** sup. **pulcherrimus,** adj., *beautiful, handsome, lovely, fair; fine, excellent; noble, honorable; illustrious, glorious.*

Pulcher, -chrī, m., a surname in the Claudian gens. **Appius Claudius Pulcher,** praetor B. C. 89. ARCH. V.

pulvīnar, -āris, [pulvīnus, *bolster*], n., *couch of the gods,* placed before a statue of a deity at the time of a religious festival; by metonymy, *shrine, temple.*

pūnctum, -ī, [pungō], n., *puncture; point.* **pūnctum temporis,** *moment, instant.*

Pūnicus, -a, -um, [Poenī], adj., *Punic, Carthaginian.*

pūniō, -īre, -īvī, -ītum, [poena], 4, a., *punish, chastise.*

pūrgō, -āre, -āvī, -ātum, [for pūrigō, **pūrus** + **agō**], 1, a., *make clean, cleanse, purify; justify, vindicate.*

purpura, -ae, [πορφύρα, *purple-fish, purple*], f., *purple color, purple; purple cloth, purple garment.* The color meant is not our purple, but more like our crimson or scarlet.

purpurātus, -a, -um, [purpura], adj., *clad in purple.* As subst., **purpurātus,** -ī, m., *purple-clad attendant,* as those about a king, *courtier.*

Puteolānus, -a, -um, [Puteolī], adj., *of Puteoli, Puteolan.* As subst., **Puteolānum,** -ī, n., *estate at Puteoli, Puteolan villa,* belonging to Cicero.

Puteolī, -ōrum, m., pl., *Puteolī,* a city of Campania, situated on the coast seven miles west of Neapolis (Naples); now Pozzuoli.

putō, -āre, -āvī, -ātum, 1, a., *cleanse; reckon, estimate, esteem, value, deem, regard; think, judge, consider, suspect, believe, suppose.*

Q.

Q., see **Quīntus.**

quā [abl. fem. of **quī**], adv., *on which side, at what place, by what way, where.*

quaerō, -ere, **quaesīvī, quaesītum,** 3, a., *seek, look for, strive to obtain; save, acquire, get, gain; miss, lack; demand, require; make inquiry, investigate; aim at, plan.*

quaesītor, -ōris, [quaerō], m., *investigator, prosecuting officer.*

quaesō, -ere, ——, ——, [cf. quaerō], def., a. and n., *beg, pray, beseech, entreat;* often parenthetical, **quaesō,** *I pray, please.*

quaestiō, -ōnis, [quaerō], f., *examination, inquiry, investigation; judicial investigation, trial, court; subject of investigation, question, case.*

quaestor, -ōris, [for quaesitor, from **quaerō**], m., *quaestor,* an officer charged with public duties which varied according to the period and circumstances. At first there were but two quaestors, but the number was increased from time to time until it reached forty under Caesar's administration, B. C. 45. At that time the quaestors were engaged in the care of public moneys and of military stores, partly at Rome and partly in the provinces, which were assigned by lot. They were chosen annually, at the comitia tribūta.

quaestus, -ūs, [**quaerō**], m., *gain, acquisition; profit, advantage, interest; business, employment, occupation.*

quālis, -e, [cf. **quī**], pron. adj., inter. and rel., *of what sort? what kind of? of such a kind, such.* **tālis — quālis**, *such — as.*

quam [**quī**], adv., *in what manner? how, how much, as, just as, even as;* after comparatives, *than.* **quam diū**, *as long as, how long?* **quam prīmum**, *as soon as possible.* **tam — quam**, *so — as.*

quam ob rem, see **ob**.

quamquam [**quam + quam**], conj., *though, although, notwithstanding that; and yet, however.*

quamvīs [**quam + vīs**, from **volō**], adv. and conj.:

(1) As adv., *as you will, as much as you will, however much.*

(2) As conj., *however much, although, albeit, no matter how much* or *many.*

quandō [**quam**], adv. and conj., *when:*

(1) As adv., *when, at what time;* inter., *when? at what time?* after **nē, nisi, num**, or **sī**, *some time, at any time, ever.*

(2) As conj., *when, at the time that; since, because, seeing that, inasmuch as.*

quantum [**quantus**], adv., relat., *so much as, so far as, as far as;* inter., *how much? how far?*

quantumcumque [**quantuscumque**], adv., *as much soever, however much.*

quantus, -a, -um, adj., inter., *how great? how much?* rel., *as great as, as much as.* **tantus — quantus**, *as great as, as much as.*

quantuscumque, **-tacumque**, **-tumcumque**, [**quantus + -cumque**], rel. adj., *of whatsoever size, however great, no matter how great; however small, however trifling.*

quāpropter [**quā + propter**], adv., inter., *wherefore? for what reason? why?* rel., *wherefore, and on this account.*

quā rē, adverbial phrase, inter., *by what means? whereby? how? on what account? wherefore? why?* rel., *wherefore, and for that reason, therefore; by reason of which, so that.*

quārtus, -a, -um, or **IV.**, [**quattuor**], num. adj., *fourth.*

quasi [**qua + sī**], adv. and conj., *as if, just as if, as though, as it were, as one might say.*

quassō, -āre, -āvī, -ātum, [freq. of **quatiō**], 1, a. and n., *shake violently, brandish; dash to pieces, shatter; shake, impair, weaken.*

quattuor, or **IIII.**, **IV.**, num. adj., indecl., *four.*

quattuordecim, **XIIII.**, or **XIV.**, [**quattuor + decem**], num. adj., indecl., *fourteen.*

-que, enclitic conj., *and, and so;* adversatively, usually after a negative, *but.* **-que — -que, -que — et** or **atque**, *both — and, as well — as.*

quem ad modum, adverbial phrase, inter., *in what way? how?* rel., *in what way, how, just as, as.*

queō, **quīre**, **quīvī** or **quiī**, **quitum**, irr., n., *be able, can.*

quercus, -ūs, f., *oak-tree, oak.*

querella, -ae, [**queror**], f., *complaining, complaint, lament, lamentation, plaint.*

querimōnia, -ae, [queror], f., *complaining, lamentation ; complaint, accusation, charge, reproach.*

queror, **querī**, **questus sum**, 3, dep., *complain, lament ; bewail, bemoan ; make complaint.*

quī, quae, quod, gen. **cūius**, inter. adj. pron., *which? what? what sort of a?*

quī, quae, quod, gen. **cūius**, rel. pron., *who, which, what, that ;* at the beginning of a clause often best rendered by a personal or demonstrative pron., with or without *and* or *but.*

quī, quae, quod, gen. **cūius**, indef. adj. pron., used after **sī**, **nisi**, **nē**, and **num**, *any.*

quī [old abl. of rel. **quī**], adv., inter., *how? in what way? by what means?* rel., *whereby, wherewith.*

quia, conj., *because, since.*

quīcum [old abl. of rel. and inter. **quī** + **cum**], = **cum quō** or **cum quā**, *with whom, together with whom.*

quīcumque, quaecumque, quodcumque, [**quī**+-**cumque**], indef. rel. pron., *whoever, whatever, whichever ; whosoever, whatsoever; any whatever, every, all that.*

quid, see **quis**.

quīdam, quaedam, quiddam, and, as adj., **quoddam**, [**quī**], indef. pron., *a certain one, a certain ; a certain man, one, somebody, something ;* pl., *some, certain, certain ones.*

quidem [**quī**], adv., *indeed, in fact, certainly ; at least, yet.* **nē — quidem**, setting off an emphatic word, *not — even.*

quiēs, -ētis, f., *rest, repose, quiet ; sleep.*

quiēscō, -ere, **quiēvī**, **quiētum**, [**quiēs**], 3, n., *rest, repose, be at rest, keep quiet ; sleep, be silent.*

quiētus, -a, -um, [part. of **quiēscō**], adj., *at rest, undisturbed, quiet, at peace.*

quīn [**quī** + -**ne**], adv. and conj., *why not? wherefore not? but indeed, in fact, nay indeed ;* in dependent clauses, *so that not, but that, but, without ;* after words of doubting, *that ;* after words of hindering translate by *from* with a participle. **quīn etiam**, *moreover, nay more.*

quīnam, quaenam, quodnam, [**quī** + **nam**], inter. adj. pron., *which then? what, pray?*

Quīnctīlis, -e, [**quīntus**], adj., *of the fifth month,* i. e. *of July.* The name of the month was changed to *Iūlius* (July) in honor of Julius Caesar.

quīndecim, or **XV**., [**quīnque** + **decem**], num. adj., indecl., *fifteen.*

quīngentēsimus, -a, -um, [**quīngentī**], num. adj., *five hundredth.*

quīnque, or **V**., num. adj., indecl., *five.*

quīntus, -a, -um, or **V**., [**quīnque**], num. adj., *fifth.*

Quīntus, -ī, abbreviated **Q.**, [**quīntus**], m., *Quīntus,* a common Roman forename. See especially **Cicerō** (2).

Quirītēs, -ium, [**Curēs**, an ancient town of the Sabines], m., pl., originally *people of Cures ;* after the union of the Sabines with the Romans, *Roman citizens, Quirītēs ;* sometimes in sing., **Quirīs**, -**ītis**, *a Roman citizen, Quirite.*

quis, quae, quid, inter. pron., *who? which? what?* acc. n. **quid**, often with an adverbial force, *why?*

quis, qua, quid, indef. pron., often found after **sī**, **nisi**, **nē**, and **num**, *any one, any, anything.*

quisnam, **quaenam**, **quidnam**, [**quis** + **nam**], inter. pron., *who then? which, what, pray? who in the world?*

quispiam, **quaepiam**, **quidpiam**, and, as adj., **quodpiam**, indef. pron., *any one, anybody, anything; some one, something, some, any.*

quisquam, **quaequam**, **quicquam**, indef. adj. pron., *any;* often as subst., *any one, anybody, anything.* **neque quisquam**, *and no one, and none.*

quisque, **quaeque**, **quidque**, and, as adj., **quodque**, indef. pron., *each, every, every one, everything, all.*

quisquis, ——, **quicquid**, and, as adj., **quodquod**, indef. rel. pron., *whoever, whatever, whatsoever, every one who, everything which.*

quīvīs, **quaevīs**, **quidvīs**, and, as adj., **quodvīs**, [**quī** + **vīs**, from **volō**], indef. pron., *whom you please, what you please, any you please; any at all, any one, anything.*

quō [old dat. and abl. of **quī**], adv. and conj.:

(1) As adv., inter., *whither? to what place? to what end? wherefore? why?* rel., *whither, where, at what time, when;* of degree of difference, *by what, by as much as;* of result, *by reason of which, wherefore, whereby, and so.*

(2) As conj., *that, in order that, that thereby.* **quō minus**, *that not,* usually best translated by *from* with a participle.

quoad [**quō** + **ad**], adv., *as far as, till, until; as long as, while.*

quōcumque [**quō** + **-cumque**], adv., *whithersoever, to whatever place.*

quod [acc. neut. of **quī**], conj., *that, in that, the fact that; because, since, inasmuch as; in view of the fact that, as regards the fact that, wherein; so far as, to the extent that.*

quondam [**quom**, old form of **cum**, + **-dam**], adv., *once on a time, at one time, once, formerly; at times, sometimes, once in a while.*

quoniam [**quom**, old form of **cum**, + **iam**], conj., *since, seeing that, whereas, because.*

quoque, conj., placed after the emphatic word, *also, too, even.*

quot, indecl. adj., *how many?*

quotannīs [**quot** + **annīs**, from **annus**], adv., *annually, every year, year by year.*

quotiēns [**quot**], adv., *how often? as often as, as many as, as.*

quotiēnscumque [**quotiēns** + **-cumque**], adv., *just as often as, as often as.*

quō ūsque, adverbial phrase, *till what time? how long?*

R.

rādīx, **-īcis**, f., *root;* by metonymy, *foot, foundation, base, source.*

rapīna, **-ae**, [**rapiō**], f., *robbery, plundering; pillage, plunder.*

rapiō, **rapere**, **rapuī**, **raptum**, 3, a., *seize, snatch, tear away, carry off; snatch away, hurry along, impel; rob, ravage, plunder, lay waste.*

ratiō, **-ōnis**, [**reor**], f., *reckoning, calculation, account; transaction, business, matter, affair; respect, regard, consideration; relation, condition; manner, way, mode, plan, kind, style; judgment, reason, understanding; propriety, order, rule; theory, doctrine, science, knowledge.*

raudusculum, -ī, [raudus, *bit of bronze*], n., *small bronze coin;* by metonymy, *small debt, trifling debt.*

re- or **red-**, inseparable prefix, *again, back, anew, against.*

Reātīnus, -a, -um, [**Reāte**], adj., *of Reate*, an important town in the Sabine country, 48 miles northeast of Rome. In Cicero's time it was governed as a prefecture. Cf. **praefectūra**.

recēns, -entis, adj., *fresh, young, recent, new; vigorous.*

receptus, see **recipiō**.

recessus, -ūs, [recēdō], m., *retreat, withdrawal, departure;* by metonymy, *retired spot, recess, nook, corner, retired place.*

recidō, -ere, reccidī, recāsum, [re- + cadō], 3, n., *fall back; fall, sink, be reduced; fall to, be handed over;* of evil, *recoil, return, be visited.*

recipiō, -ere, recēpī, receptum, [re- + capiō], 3, a., *take back, receive back, regain, recover; admit, receive, welcome; acquire, gain; promise.* **sē recipere**, *to withdraw, to retire.*

recitō, -āre, -āvī, -ātum, [re- + citō], 1, a., *read aloud, declaim, rehearse.*

reclāmātiō, -ōnis, [reclāmō], f., *shout of disapproval.*

reclāmō, -āre, -āvī, -ātum, [re- + clāmō], 1, n. and a., *cry out against, exclaim against, protest.*

recognōscō, -gnōscere, -gnōvī, -gnitum, [re- + cognōscō], 3, a., *recall to mind, recollect, recall; review, examine, look over.*

recolō, -ere, recoluī, recultum, [re- + colō], 3, a., *cultivate again; practice again, resume, renew.*

reconciliātiō, -ōnis, [reconciliō], f., *restoration, renewal.*

recondō, -ere, recondidī, reconditum, [re- + condō], 3, a., *put back; put away, shut up, hide, conceal, cover.*

recordātiō, -ōnis, [recordor], f., *recollection, remembrance.*

recordor, -ārī, -ātus sum, [re-, cor], 1, dep., *call to mind, recall, remember, recollect.*

recreō, -āre, -āvī, -ātum, [re- + creō], 1, a., *recreate; renew, restore, revive, invigorate.*

rēctā [abl. of **rēctus**, sc. **viā**], adv., *straightway, directly, straight.*

rēctē [rēctus], adv., *in a straight line; rightly, correctly, properly; suitably, well, duly, appropriately.*

rēctus, -a, -um, [part. of **regō**], adj., *straight; upright; correct, proper, befitting; just, virtuous.*

recuperō, -āre, -āvī, -ātum, 1, a., *get back, regain, recover.*

recurrō, -ere, recurrī, ——, [re- + currō], 3, n., *run back, hasten back; return, revert, recur.*

recūsātiō, -ōnis, [recūsō], f., *declining, refusal, protest.*

recūsō, -āre, -āvī, -ātum, [re-, causa], 1, a. and n., *raise objections to, decline, refuse, reject; protest.*

red-, see **re-**.

redāctus, see **redigō**.

reddō, -ere, reddidī, redditum, [red- + dō], 3, a., *give back, return, restore; pay back, requite; render, make; give, grant; surrender, resign; report, declare.*

redeō, -īre, -iī, -itum, [red- + eō], irr., n., *go back, return, come back; be brought back, be restored.*

redigō, -ere, redēgī, redāctum, [red- + agō], 3, a., *drive back, lead back, bring back; bring under, reduce, subdue.*

redimiō, -īre, -iī, -ītum, 4, a., *wreathe around, encircle, crown, deck.*

redimō, -ere, redēmī, redēmptum, [red- + emō], 3, a., *buy back, redeem, ransom ; buy up, take by contract, farm ; gain, acquire, secure.*

reditus, -ūs, [redeō], m., *going back, returning, return ; income, revenue.*

redundō, -āre, -āvī, -ātum, [red- + undō, from unda], 1, n., *run over, overflow ; swim, reek ; remain, be left, be in excess, abound.*

referō, -ferre, rettulī, relātum, [re- + ferō], irr., a., *bring back, lead back, carry back ; give back, restore, repay ; reply, answer ; repeat ; report, announce, relate ; consider, refer.* **ad senātum referre,** *lay before the senate, submit to the senate for consideration.* **sē referre,** *to go back, to return.* Cf. grātia.

rēfert, rēferre, rētulit, [rē, from rēs, + ferō], impers., *it is of advantage, it profits ; it is of importance, it matters.*

refertus, -a, -um, [part. of referciō], adj., *crowded full, stuffed, filled ; thronged, replete.*

reficiō, -ficere, refēcī, refectum, [re- + faciō], 3, a., *make over, reconstruct, restore ; renew, refresh, reinvigorate, recruit.*

reformīdō, -āre, ——, -ātum, [re- + formīdō], 1, a., *dread greatly, shrink from, shudder at, be afraid of.*

refricō, -āre, -uī, -ātum, [re- + fricō], 1, a. and n., *rub again, irritate ;* of a wound, *reopen.*

refugiō, -fugere, refūgī, ——, [re- + fugiō], 3, n. and a., *flee back, take refuge, flee ; turn away, avoid, shun.*

refūtō, -āre, -āvī, -ātum, 1, a., *repel, resist, oppose ; disprove, rebut, refute.*

rēgālis, -e, [rēx], adj., *kingly, royal.* **nōmen rēgāle,** *the name of king.*

rēgiē [rēgius], adv., *after the manner of a king, despotically.*

Rēgīnus, -a, -um, [Rēgium], adj., *of Regium,* a city in the southwestern part of Italy, now Reggio. As subst., **Rēgīnī, -ōrum,** m., pl., *people of Regium.*

regiō, -ōnis, [regō], f., *direction, line ;* by metonymy, *boundary line, limit ; region, territory, country ; tract, quarter.*

rēgius, -a, -um, [rēx], adj., *of a king, like a king, kingly, royal, regal.* **bellum rēgium,** *war with the king.*

rēgnō, -āre, -āvī, -ātum, [rēgnum], 1, n. and a., *be king, rule, reign ; hold sway, prevail.*

rēgnum, -ī, [regō], n., *kingship ; dominion, rule, government, power, authority ; realm, kingdom.*

regō, regere, rēxī, rēctum, 3, a., *keep straight, lead straight ; direct, lead, guide ; control, regulate ; rule, govern, be master of.*

reiciō, -icere, reiēcī, reiectum, [re- + iaciō], 3, a., *throw back, force back ; cast off, repel, reject ; refuse, disdain.*

relaxō, -āre, -āvī, -ātum, [re- + laxō], 1, a., *make wide, loosen, open ; relieve, ease, cheer, lighten.*

relevō, -āre, -āvī, -ātum, [re- + levō, *lift up*], 1, a., *lift up ; make light, lighten ; relieve, free, ease ; soothe, alleviate, mitigate, console.*

religiō, -ōnis, f., *conscientiousness, sense of right ; devoutness, piety, reverence, devotion ; religious scruple, fear of the gods, religious obligation ; worship of the gods, religion, faith, cult ; sacredness, holiness.*

religiōsus, -a, -um, [religiō], adj., *conscientious, scrupulous, devout,* *pious; sacred, consecrated, holy, venerable.*

relinquō, **-ere**, **relīquī**, **relīctum**, [re- + linquō], 3, a., *leave behind, leave, abandon; forsake, desert; relinquish, dismiss, give up; bequeath, transmit.*

reliquus, **-a**, **-um**, [cf. **relinquō**], adj., *left, remaining; future, subsequent; other, rest.* As subst., **reliquum**, **-ī**, n., *the rest, the future;* also, **reliqua**, **-ōrum**, n., pl., *the balance, the future.* **reliquum est ut**, *it remains that, it only remains to.*

remaneō, **-ēre**, **remānsī**, ——, [re- + maneō], 2, n., *stay behind, remain, be left; continue, last, abide, endure.*

rēmex, **-igis**, [rēmus + agō], m., *rower, oarsman.*

remissiō, **-ōnis**, [remittō], f., *sending back; easing, relaxing, abatement; relaxation, recreation.*

remissus, **-a**, **-um**, [part. of **remittō**], adj., *relaxed; mild, gentle, indulgent; negligent, slack, remiss; light, merry.*

remittō, **-ere**, **remīsī**, **remissum**, [re- + mittō], 3, a. and n., *send back, cause to return; loosen, slacken, relax; give back, return, restore; give up, grant, pardon.*

remoror, **-ārī**, **-ātus sum**, [re- + moror], 1, dep., *hold back, delay, detain, hinder.*

removeō, **-ēre**, **remōvī**, **remōtum**, [re- + moveō], 2, a., *move back; remove, take away; withdraw, set aside; abolish, deprive of.* **remōtō Catilīnā**, *with Catiline out of the way.*

renovō, **-āre**, **-āvī**, **-ātum**, [re- + novō], 1, a., *renew, restore, revive.*

renūntiō, **-āre**, **-āvī**, **-ātum**, [re- + nūntiō], 1, a., *bring back word, report; give notice, announce, declare, proclaim;* with two acc., *declare elected, proclaim as chosen.*

repellō, **-ere**, **reppulī**, **repulsum**, [re- + pellō], 3, a., *drive back, thrust back, repel; keep back, ward off, repulse, reject.*

repente [repēns], adv., *suddenly, unexpectedly.*

repentīnus, **-a**, **-um**, [repēns], adj., *sudden, unexpected, unlooked for, hasty.*

reperiō, **-īre**, **repperī**, **repertum**, 4, a., *find again, find, meet with; find out, discover, learn; invent, devise.*

repetō, **-ere**, **repetīvī**, **repetītum**, [re- + petō], 3, a., *seek again; attack anew, fall upon again; demand anew, demand back, claim; repeat, undertake again, renew; recall, recollect.*

reportō, **-āre**, **-āvī**, **-ātum**, [re- + portō], 1, a., *carry back; carry off, obtain, get, gain.*

reprehendō, **-ere**, **reprehendī**, **reprehēnsum**, [re- + prehendō], 3, a., *hold back, hold fast, seize; restrain, check; blame, censure, rebuke, reprove.*

reprimō, **-ere**, **repressī**, **repressum**, [re- + premō], 3, a., *press back; check, restrain, confine, curb, repress.*

repudiō, **-āre**, **-āvī**, **-ātum**, [repudium, *casting off*], 1, a., *cast off, put away; reject, refuse, repudiate, scorn, disdain.*

repūgnāns, **-antis**, [part. of **repūgnō**], adj., *inconsistent, contradictory.*

repūgnō, **-āre**, **-āvī**, **-ātum**, [re- + pūgnō], 1, n., *oppose, resist, struggle, contend against.*

requiēs, **-ētis**, acc. **requiētem** or **requiem**, [re- + quiēs], f., *rest, pause; repose, recreation; respite, relief.*

requīrō, -ere, requīsīvī or -iī, requīsītum, [re- + quaerō], 3, a., *seek again, search for; ask, inquire, demand; miss, lack, feel the want of.*

rēs, reī, f., *thing, object, matter, affair; occurrence, event, case; condition, circumstance; reality, fact; effects, property, possessions, estate; profit, advantage, interest; cause, reason, ground, account; business, suit, action; battle, campaign; state, commonwealth, government.* **rēs gestae**, *exploits.* **rēs secundae**, *prosperity.* **rērum potīrī**, *to obtain the sovereignty.*

rescrībō, -ere, rescrīpsī, rescrīptum, [re- + scrībō], 3, a., *write back, reply in writing.*

resecō, -āre, resecuī, resectum, [re- + secō], 1, a., *cut off, cut loose; check, restrain, stop.*

reservō, -āre, -āvī, -ātum, [re- + servō], 1, a., *keep back, save up, reserve, retain.*

resideō, -ēre, resēdī, ——, [re- + sedeō], 2, n. and a., *remain sitting; remain, stay, reside; remain behind, be left, stay.*

resīgnō, -āre, -āvī, -ātum, [re- + sīgnō], 1, a., *unseal, open; annul, cancel, destroy.*

resistō, -ere, restitī, ——, [re- + sistō], 3, n., *stand back; remain behind, stay, be left; withstand, oppose, resist.*

respiciō, -ere, respexī, respectum, [re- + speciō, *look*], 3, n. and a., *look back, look behind; look back upon, gaze upon; look out for, have a care for, be mindful of, consider.*

respondeō, -ēre, respondī, respōnsum, [re- + spondeō], 2, a. and n., *answer, reply; give answer, respond; be a match for; accord, agree.*

respōnsum, -ī, [respondeo], n., *answer, reply, response.*

rēs pūblica, reī pūblicae, f., see **pūblicus**.

respuō, -ere, respuī, ——, [re- + spuō], 3, a., *spit back, spit out; reject, repel, spurn.*

restinguō, -ere, restīnxī, restīnctum, [re- + stinguō], 3, a., *put out, extinguish, quench; annihilate, destroy.*

restituō, -ere, restituī, restitūtum, [re- + statuō], 3, a., *replace, restore; revive, renew, reinstate.*

restō, restāre, restitī, ——, [re- + stō], 1, n., *withstand, resist, oppose; be left, remain.* Impers., restat, *it remains.*

retardō, -āre, -āvī, -ātum, [re- + tardō, *impede*], 1, a. and n., *keep back, hinder, impede; delay, tarry.*

reticeō, -ēre, reticuī, ——, [re- + taceō], 2, n. and a., *be silent, keep silent; keep secret, conceal.*

retineō, -ēre, retinuī, retentum, [re- + teneō], 2, a., *hold back, hold fast; detain, restrain, check, repress; keep, preserve, maintain.*

retorqueō, -ēre, retorsī, retortum, [re- + torqueō], 2, a., *turn back, throw back.*

retundō, -ere, rettudī, retūsum or retūnsum, [re- + tundō], 3, a., *beat back, blunt, dull; check, restrain.*

reus, -ī, [rēs], m., *defendant in a legal action, the accused, prisoner.*

revertor, revertī, reversus sum, [re- + vertor], 3, dep., *turn back, return, go back.*

revincō, -ere, revīcī, revictum, [re- + vincō], 3, a., *conquer; convict, refute.*

revocō, -āre, -āvī, -ātum, [re- + vocō], 1, a., *call back, call again, recall, bring back; withdraw, turn aside, divert.*

rēx, **rēgis**, [cf. **regō**], m., *king, chief, ruler, monarch, despot.*

Rhēnus, -ī, m., *the Rhine.* MAR. IX.

Rhodius, -a, -um, [**Rhodus**, Ῥόδος], adj., *Rhodian, of Rhodes,* an important island near the southwestern coast of Asia Minor. As subst., **Rhodiī**, -ōrum, m., pl., *people of Rhodes, Rhodians.*

rīdeō, -ēre, **rīsī**, **rīsum**, 2, n. and a., *laugh; laugh at, ridicule, deride.*

rīdiculus, -a, -um, [**rīdeō**], adj., *laughable, amusing; absurd, ridiculous, contemptible.*

rōbur, -oris, n., *hard wood; oak-tree, oak; strength, power, vigor, force; best part, pith, kernel.*

rōbustus, -a, -um, [**rōbur**], adj., *of oak-wood; strong, hardy, firm, robust.*

rogātus, -ūs, found only in the abl., [**rogō**], m., *request, entreaty.*

rogō, -āre, -āvī, -ātum, 1, a., *ask, question, inquire; request, implore, beg for;* of a bill or resolution, *bring forward for approval, propose, introduce.* **sententiam rogō**, *ask an opinion, call upon to vote.*

Rōma, -ae, f., *Rome.*

Rōmānus, -a, -um, [**Rōma**], adj., *of Rome, Roman, Latin.* As subst., **Rōmānus**, -ī, m., *Roman.*

Rōmulus, -ī, m., *Rōmulus,* mythical founder and first king of Rome; said to have been the son of Mars and Rhea Silvia.

Rōscius, -ī, m., *Q. Rōscius,* the most famous comic actor at Rome. He was an intimate friend of Cicero. He died B. C. 62. ARCH. VIII.

Rudīnus, -a, -um, [**Rudiae**], adj., *of Rudiae,* a town in Calabria, celebrated as the birth-place of Ennius. ARCH. X.

rudis, -e, adj., *unwrought, wild, coarse; rude, uncultivated, rough, unpolished; unskilled, ignorant.*

Rūfus, -ī, [**rūfus**, *red, red-haired*], m., a family name common to several gentes. See **Caelius**, **Sulpicius**, **Titius**.

ruīna, -ae, [**ruō**], f., *a tumbling down, falling down; downfall, fall, ruin, destruction, overthrow, calamity;* pl., *ruins.*

rūmor, -ōris, m., *report, rumor, common talk; current opinion, reputation.*

rumpō, -ere, **rūpī**, **ruptum**, 3, a., *break, tear, split; break open, burst, break through; interrupt, cut short; violate, annul.*

ruō, -ere, **ruī**, **rutum**, 3, n. and a., *fall with violence, tumble down, fall in ruins, go to ruin; hasten, hurry, dash along, run.*

rūrsus or **rūrsum**, [for **reversus**, **reversum**, from **revertō**], adv., *on the contrary, on the other hand, in turn; again, once more, anew.*

rūsticē [**rūsticus**], adv., *like a rustic; boorishly, awkwardly, rudely.*

rūsticor, -ārī, -ātus sum, [**rūsticus**], 1, dep., *sojourn in the country, stay in the country, rusticate.*

rūsticus, -a, -um, [**rūs**, *country*], adj., *of the country, rural, rustic; rough, coarse, plain, simple.* As subst., **rūsticus**, -ī, m., *rustic, peasant, countryman.*

S.

S. D. = **salūtem dīcit**, *sends greeting.*

S. D. PLUR. = **salūtem dīcit plūrimam**, *sends heartiest greeting.*

S. T. E. Q. V. B. E. = **sī tū exercitusque valētis, bene est.**

S. V. B. E. V. = **sī valēs, bene est; valeō.**

sacerdōs, -ōtis, [sacer, cf. dō], m. and f., *priest, priestess.*

sacrārium, -ī, [sacrum], n., *shrine, sanctuary, chapel.*

sacrōsānctus, -a, -um, [sacer + sānctus], adj., *revered as sacred, inviolable.*

sacrum, -ī, [sacer], n., *sacred thing, sacred place, sanctuary; act of worship, sacred rite, rite, sacrifice, worship.*

saeculum, or, by syncope, **saeclum**, -ī, n., *race, breed; generation, lifetime, age; century, hundred years.*

saepe, comp. **saepius**, sup. **saepissimē**, adv., *often, frequently, many times.* **iterum et saepius**, *over and over again.*

saepiō, -īre, **saepsī**, **saeptum**, [saepēs, *hedge*], 4, a., *hedge in, enclose, surround; fortify, protect, guard.*

sagāx, -ācis, adj., *of acute senses, keen-scented; sagacious, keen, quick, shrewd.*

SAL., see **salūs**.

Salamīnius, -a, -um, [Salamīs], adj., *of Salamis*, an island southwest of Attica; also, *of* the city *Salamis* on the island of Cyprus. As subst., **Salamīniī**, -ōrum, m., pl., *people of Salamis.*

Sallustius, -ī, m., *Cn. Sallustius*, a client or friend of Cicero's, and a man of some literary taste. Ep. viii., xxiv.

saltō, -āre, -āvī, -ātum, [freq. of saliō], 1, n. and a., *dance.*

saltus, -ūs, m., *woodland, forest; wooded mountain land, forest pasture; mountain valley, glen, thicket; pass, defile.*

salūs, -ūtis, in addresses of letters abbreviated **Sal.**, **S.**, f., *health, vigor; welfare, prosperity, safety, deliverance; greeting, salutation.*

salūtō, -āre, -āvī, -ātum, [salūs], 1, a., *greet, salute, hail; wish health to, visit, call upon.*

salvus, -a, -um, adj., *well, sound, safe; unharmed, uninjured, in good condition, in good health.*

Samos or **Samus**, -ī, [Σάμος], f., *Samos*, an island in the Aegean sea, near Ephesus.

Sampsiceramus, -ī, m., *Sampsiceramus*, a nickname of Pompey. See N. to p. 181, l. 11.

senciō, -īre, **sānxī**, **sānctum**, 4, a., *make sacred, consecrate; establish, decree, ordain, enact; approve, ratify.*

sānctus, -a, -um, [part. of **sanciō**], adj., *consecrated, inviolable, sacred; venerable, holy, divine; pure, upright, conscientious, just.*

sānē [sānus], adv., *sensibly, reasonably, discreetly; indeed, by all means, truly, very.*

sanguis, -inis, m., *blood;* by metonymy, *bloodshed, slaughter; stock, family; vigor, force.*

sānitās, -ātis, [sānus], f., *soundness, health; right reason, discretion, sanity.*

sānō, -āre, -āvī, -ātum, [sānus], 1, a., *make sound, heal, cure; restore, repair, allay.*

sānus, -a, -um, adj., *sound, whole, healthy, well; sensible, discreet, sober, sane.*

sapiēns, -entis, [part. of **sapiō**], adj., *wise, discreet, sensible, prudent.*

sapienter [sapiēns], adv., *wisely, discreetly, prudently.*

sapientia, -ae, [sapiēns], f., *good sense, discernment, discretion, prudence; wisdom, philosophy; science.*

sapiō, **sapere**, **sapīvī**, ——, 3, n. and a., *taste; have taste, have discernment, discern; be wise, be discreet.*

Sardinia, **-ae**, f., *Sardinia*, an island west of Italy.

sat, see **satis**.

satelles, **-itis**, m. and f., *attendant, follower; assistant in crime, accomplice, abettor, tool.*

satietās, **-ātis**, [**satis**], f., *sufficiency, fulness, satiety; weariness, loathing, disgust.*

satiō, **-āre**, **-āvī**, **-ātum**, [**satis**], 1, a., *satisfy, sate, satiate; appease, glut, fill; cloy, disgust.*

satis, or **sat**, adj., indecl. subst., and adv.:

(1) As adj., *enough, sufficient, ample.*

(2) As subst., *enough, sufficiency, plenty.*

(3) As adv., *sufficiently, enough, adequately, amply.*

satis faciō, **facere**, **fēcī**, **factum**, 3, n., *satisfy, give satisfaction; do enough for, do one's duty by.*

Sāturnālia, **-ōrum**, abl. **-ibus**, [**Sāturnus**,] n., *festival of Saturn, the Saturnalia*, which commenced on the 17th of December, and at different periods lasted three, four, five, or seven days.

Sāturnīnus, **-ī**, m., *L. Appulēius Sāturnīnus*, a leader of the democratic party, tribune for the second time B. C. 100. Resorting to violent measures in order to carry out his plans, he was declared a public enemy by the Senate, and was slain by a mob in the Curia Hostilia. CAT. I. II., XII.; IV. II.

saucius, **-a**, **-um**, adj., *wounded, hurt; injured, weakened, smitten.*

saxum, **-ī**, n., *large stone, rock.*

scaena, **-ae**, [σκηνή], f., *stage, scene.* **in scaenā**, *on the stage.*

scaenicus, **-a**, **-um**, [**scaena**], adj., *scenic, dramatic, theatrical.* **scaenicī artificēs**, *actors.*

Scaevola, **-ae**, [**scaeva**, *left-handed*], m., *P. Mūcius Scaevola*, one of the most eminent of the early Roman jurists, consul B. C. 133. EP. XXXVIII.

scelerātē [**scelerātus**], adv., *impiously, wickedly, scandalously.*

scelerātus, **-a**, **-um**, [part. of **scelerō**, *pollute*], adj., *polluted, defiled, profaned; wicked, impious, accursed; sacrilegious, infamous, scandalous.* As subst., **scelerātus**, **-ī**, m., *scoundrel, rogue.*

scelus, **-eris**, n., *wicked deed, crime; sin, wickedness.*

sciēns, **-entis**, [part. of **sciō**], adj., *knowing, intelligent, skilled, expert, versed;* often used where the English idiom prefers an adv., *knowingly, intentionally.*

scientia, **-ae**, [**sciēns**], f., *knowledge, acquaintance, science, skill, art.*

scīlicet [= **scīre licet**], adv., *you may know, certainly, obviously, of course; no doubt, forsooth, likely.*

scintilla, **-ae**, f., *spark; glimmer, trace.*

sciō, **scīre**, **scīvī**, **scītum**, 4, a., *know, understand; perceive, have knowledge of, be assured.*

Scīpiō, **-ōnis**, [**scīpiō**, *staff*], m., *Scīpiō*, name of a celebrated family of the Cornelian gens; pl., **Scīpiōnēs**, **-um**, *the Scipios, the Scipio family.* Three Scipios are mentioned in this book:

(1) *P. Cornēlius Scīpiō Āfricānus*, also called *Māior* to distinguish him from (2), born about B. C. 234. After several years of successful generalship in Spain, he was consul B. C. 205. In the following year he conveyed an

army to Africa, where he was uniformly successful against the Carthaginians, finally defeating Hannibal near Zama, B. C. 202. He was honored with a triumph, B. C. 201. The year of his death is uncertain. CAT. IV. X., ARCH. IX.

(2) *P. Cornēlius Scīpiō Aemiliānus Āfricānus*, often called *Minor* to distinguish him from (1), born about B. C. 185. He was the son of L. Aemilius Paulus, the conqueror of Macedonia (see **Paulus**), and was adopted by Scipio Africanus Maior. He was elected consul for B. C. 147, and took charge of the war against Carthage then in progress, capturing and destroying the city the following year. In 134 B. C. he was again made consul, and took command of the war in Spain. He captured and razed Numantia in 133 B. C. Returning to Rome, he violently opposed the measures of Ti. Gracchus. He died B. C. 129. CAT. IV. X., ARCH. VII., IMP. P. XX.

(3) *P. Cornēlius Scīpiō Nasīca Serāpiō*, consul B. C. 138, and pontifex maximus. He also opposed Ti. Gracchus, and was the leader of the mob which slew Gracchus. CAT. I. I.

scortum, -ī, n., *hide ; harlot, prostitute.*

scr. = **scrīpta**, i. e. **scrīpta est epistola.**

scrība, -ae, [scrībō], m., *scribe, clerk, secretary.*

scrībō, -ere, scrīpsī, scrīptum, 3, a., *scratch, engrave ; write, write out ; compose.*

scrīptiō, -ōnis, [scrībō], f., *a writing ; composing in writing, composition.*

scrīptor, -ōris, [scrībō], m., *writer, scribe ; author, composer, reporter, narrator.* **rērum scrīptor**, *writer of history, historian.*

scrīptūra, -ae, [scrībō], f., *writing ; composing, composition ; tax on public pastures, pasture tax.*

scrūpulus, -ī, [dim. of scrūpus, *sharp stone*], m., *difficulty, trouble ; doubt, scruple.*

scyphus, -ī, [σκύφος], m., *cup, goblet, wine-cup.* **inter scyphōs**, *over the wine.*

sē, see **suī**.

sē or **sēd**, old prep. with abl., *apart from, without ;* used especially in composition.

sēcēdō, -ere, sēcessī, sēcessum, [sē + cēdō], 3, n., *go apart, separate ; withdraw, go away.*

sēcernō, -ere, sēcrēvī, sēcrētum, [sē + cernō], 3, a., *separate, part, sever, divide ; set apart.*

secundum [secundus], prep. with acc., *following, after, next to ; according to, in accordance with.*

secundus, -a, -um, [sequor], adj., *following, next, second ; secondary, inferior ; favorable, fair, prosperous ; fortunate, propitious.*

secūris, -is, abl., secūrī, [secō], f., *axe, battle-axe.*

sēd, see **sē**.

sed, conj., *but, but also, on the contrary ; however, yet.* **nōn sōlum — sed etiam**, *not only — but also.* **sed iam**, *now however.* **sed vērō**, *but actually.*

sēdēcula, -ae, [dim. of sēdēs], f., *little seat, low seat.*

sedeō, -ēre, sēdī, sessum, 2, n., *sit ; sit idle, be inactive ; be settled, remain fast.*

sēdēs, -is, [cf. sedeō], f., *seat, chair ; abode, dwelling-place, habitation ; place, site, foundation.*

sēditiō, -ōnis, [sēd + itiō, from eō], f., *dissension, discord; insurrection, mutiny, sedition.*

sēdō, -āre, -āvī, -ātum, [cf. sedeō], 1, a. and n., *bring to rest; calm, quiet, check, stop; allay, appease.*

sēdulitās, -ātis, [sēdulus], f., *assiduity, persistency, earnestness.*

sēdulō [sēdulus], adv., *busily, diligently; eagerly, zealously, assiduously.*

sēgregō, -āre, -āvī, -ātum, [sē, grex], 1, a., lit. *separate from the flock; separate, set apart, remove.*

sēiungō, -ere, sēiūnxī, sēiūnctum, [sē + iungō], 3, a., *disjoin, disunite, part, separate; keep apart, disconnect.*

Sēius, -ī, m., *M. Sēius*, a friend of Atticus and of Cicero. He was aedile B. C. 74, died B. C. 45. EP. XVI.

sēlēctus, -a, -um, [part. of sēligō], adj., *chosen, selected, select.*

sella, -ae, f., *seat, chair; work-stool; official chair.*

semel, adv., *once, a single time; once for all, but once; finally.*

sēmen, -inis, [cf. serō, *sow*], n., *seed;* by metonymy, *race; source, origin, essence, principle.*

sēminārium, -ī, [sēmen], n., *nursery, school; hot-bed.*

semper, adv., *always, ever; at all times, perpetually, forever.*

sempiternus, -a, -um, [semper], adj., *everlasting, eternal, perpetual, imperishable.*

Semprōnius, -a, name of a Roman gens with both patrician and plebeian branches. See **Gracchus**. As adj., *of a Sempronius, Sempronian.*

senātor, -ōris, [cf. senex], m., *senator, member of the Senate.*

senātōrius, -a, -um, [senātor], adj., *of a senator, senatorial.*

senātus, -ūs, [senex], m., *council of elders, Senate.* **senātūs cōnsultum**, *decree of the senate.*

senectūs, -ūtis, [senex], f., *old age, advanced years.*

senex, senis, comp. **senior**, adj., *old, aged.* As subst., **senex**, **-is**, m., *old man;* **senior**, **-ōris**, m., *elder, older person.*

senior, **-ōris**, see **senex**.

sēnsus, -ūs, [sentiō], m., *perception, sense, consciousness; sensation, emotion, feeling, sentiment.*

sententia, -ae, [sentiō], f., *opinion, judgment, notion; decision, will; resolution, determination, sentence.*

sentīna, -ae, f., *bilge-water; off-scourings, dregs, refuse.*

sentiō, -īre, sēnsī, sēnsum, 4, a., *feel, hear, see, perceive; experience, discern, observe; think, believe, suppose, judge; decide, declare.*

sepeliō, -īre, sepelīvī or -iī, sepultum, 4, a., *bury, inter; overwhelm, ruin, destroy.*

septem or **VII.**, num. adj., indecl., *seven.*

September, -bris, [septem], adj., *of the seventh; of the seventh month,* reckoning March as the first month of the year, *of September.*

septemdecim, or **XVII.**, [septem + decem], num. adj., indecl., *seventeen.*

septimus, -a, -um, or **VII.**, [septem], adj., *seventh.*

sepulchrum, -ī, [cf. sepeliō], n., *grave, tomb, sepulchre.*

sepultus, see **sepeliō**.

sequor, sequī, secūtus sum, 3, dep., *follow, attend, accompany; come after, come next; seek, be destined for; chase, pursue; result, ensue; conform to, comply with; strive after, aim at.*

Serāpiō, -ōnis, m., *Serāpiō*, a native of Antioch and writer on geography. Cicero found his work unintelligible. Ep. III.

sērius, see **sērō**.

sermō, -ōnis, [**serō**, *weave, compose*], m., *conversation, talk, discourse, speech; report, rumor, common talk.*

sērō, comp. **sērius**, sup. **sērissimē**, [**sērus**], adv., *late, at a late hour, at a late period.* Comp., **sērius**, *later*, often *too late.*

serpō, -ere, **serpsī**, **serptum**, 3, n., *creep, crawl, glide; come imperceptibly, extend gradually, spread abroad stealthily, increase.*

serta, -ōrum, [**serō**, *entwine*], n., pl., *garlands, wreaths.*

Sertōriānus, -a, -um, adj., *of Sertorius, Sertorian, from Sertorius,* referring to Q. Sertorius, a Roman general of the party of Marius. He carried on war in Spain for ten years against the party of Sulla until he was murdered, B. C. 72.

servīlis, -e, [**servus**], adj., *slavish, servile, of a slave.*

Servīlius, -a, name of a Roman gens, at first patrician, afterwards including plebeian families also. The following *Servīliī* are mentioned in this book:

(1) *M. Servīlius*, tribune of the people B. C. 43. Ant. IV. vi.

(2) *C. Servīlius Ahāla*, cf. **Maelius**, and N. to p. 62, l. 4.

(3) *C. Servīlius Glaucia*, see **Glaucia**.

(4) *P. Servīlius Vatia*, see **Vatia**.

serviō, -īre, -īvī, -ītum, [**servus**], 4, n., *be a servant, serve; be devoted to, aim at, labor for, have regard to; gratify, court.*

servitium, -ī, [**servus**], n., *servitude, slavery; body of slaves.*

servitūs, -ūtis, [**servus**], f., *slavery, service, serfdom.*

Servius, -ī, m., *Servius*, a friend of Cicero's, to whom he wrote a letter introducing the physician Asclapo. Ep. XXXII.

servō, -āre, -āvī, -ātum, 1, a., *save, preserve, keep, protect, guard; store away, maintain; give heed, watch, observe.*

servus, -ī, m., *slave, servant.*

sēsē, see **suī**.

sēstertius, -a, -um, [for **semis tertius**, *three less one half*], or **H S** [for **I I** + **semis**], num. adj., *two and a half.* As subst., **sēstertius**, -ī, gen. pl. **sēstertiūm**, (originally sc. **nummus**), m., *sesterce*, a small silver coin, originally $2\frac{1}{2}$ *asses*, = about $4\frac{1}{10}$ cents.

Sēstius, -ī, m., *P. Sēstius*, quaestor of C. Antonius, Cicero's colleague in the consulship B. C. 63. He was tribune B. C. 57, and was active in procuring Cicero's recall from banishment. The following year he was brought to trial for the use of violence, and was defended by Cicero in an oration which is still extant. In the Civil War he at first joined the side of Pompey, but afterwards went over to Caesar. Cat. I. viii.

seu, see **sive**.

sevērē [**sevērus**], adv., *gravely, seriously; with severity, severely.*

sevēritās, -ātis, [**sevērus**], f., *gravity, seriousness; sternness, severity.*

sevērus, -a, -um, adj., *grave, serious; stern, strict, severe, rigid.*

Sex., see **Sextus**.

sex, or **VI.**, num. adj., indecl., *six.*

sexāgēsimus, -a, -um, [**sexāgintā**], num., adj., *sixtieth.*

sexāgintā, or **LX.**, num. adj., indecl., *sixty.*

Sext., see **Sextīlis.**

Sextīlis, -e, in dates often abbreviated **Sext.**, [**sextus**], adj., *sixth ; of the sixth month*, reckoning from March, *of August.* The name of the month *Sextīlis* was changed to *Augustus* in honor of the emperor, B. C. 8.

sextus, -a, -um, or **VI.**, [**sex**], num. adj., *sixth.*

Sextus, -ī, abbreviated **Sex.**, [**sextus**], m., *Sextus,* a Roman forename. See **Aelius.**

sī, conj., *if; if indeed, inasmuch as, since ; when ; even if, though, although ;* in indir. questions, *whether ;* in purpose clauses, *to see if, to try whether.* **sī quidem,** *if only, if indeed.*

Sibyllīnus, -a, -um, [**Sibylla**], adj., *of a Sibyl, Sibylline.* Cf. N. to p. 92, l. 24.

sīc [**sī** + **-ce**], adv., *thus, in this way ; so, in such a manner ; just so, in the same way.* **sīc — ut,** *thus — so, just as — so.* **ut — sīc,** *while — yet, though — still.*

sīca, -ae, f., *dagger, poniard.*

sīcārius, -ī, [**sīca**], m., *assassin, murderer.*

Sicca, -ae, m., *Sicca,* an intimate friend of Cicero. He had an estate at Vibo, in the southwestern part of Italy, where Cicero took refuge from his enemies for a time in B. C. 58, and again in 44 B. C. EP. VIII.

Sicilia, -ae, [Σικελία], f., *Sicily.*

sīcut, or **sīcutī**, [**sīc** + **ut**], adv., *just as, so as, as ; as indeed, as it were, as if.*

Sicyōnius, -a, -um, [**Sicyōn**], adj., *Sicyonian, of Sicyon,* a city on the Asopus river near the south shore of the Corinthian Gulf, northwest of Corinth. As subst., **Sicyōniī**, -ōrum, m., pl., *people of Sicyon, Sicyonians.* EP. IV.

Sīgēum, -ī, [Σιγειον], n., *Sīgēum,* a promontory of Troas, at the entrance of the Hellespont. Near it there was a town of the same name.

sīgnificātiō, -ōnis, [**sīgnificō**], f., *expression, indication, sign, token.*

sīgnum, -ī, n., *sign, mark, token, indication ; ensign, standard ; omen, prognostication ; image, figure, statue ;* of a letter, *seal, signet.*

Sīlānus, -ī, m., *D. Iūnius Sīlānus.* He distinguished himself by the magnificent games which he gave in his aedileship, about 70 B. C. He was consul B. C. 62. CAT. IV. IV., VI.

silentium, -ī, [**silēns**], n., *silence, quiet, stillness.*

sileō, -ēre, -uī, ——, 2, n. and a., *be silent, keep silence, be still ; pass over in silence, suppress.*

Sīlius, -ī, m., *P. Sīlius Nerva,* a friend of Atticus, propraetor of Bithynia and Pontus B. C. 51. EP. XV., XLI.

silva, -ae, f., *forest, wood, grove.*

Silvānus, -ī, [**silva**], m., *M. Plautius Silvānus,* tribune of the people B. C. 89, at the same time with C. Papirius Carbo. ARCH. IV.

silvestris, -e, [**silva**], adj., *of a forest, wooded, woody.*

similis, -e, comp. **similior**, sup. **simillimus**, adj., *like, similar, resembling.* Sup., *very like, closely resembling.*

similiter, comp. **similius**, sup. simillimē, [**similis**], adv., *in like manner, likewise, similarly.*

similitūdō, -inis, [**similis**], f., *likeness, similarity, resemblance.*

simpliciter [**simplex**], adv., *simply, plainly ; frankly, artlessly.*

simul, adv., *at the same time, at once, simultaneously, together; and also.* **simul — simul**, *partly — partly, not only — but at the same time.* **simul ac**, or **simul atque**, *as soon as.*

simulācrum, -ī, [simulō], n., *likeness, image, form, figure; appearance, semblance, pretence.*

simulātiō, -ōnis, [simulō], f., *feigning, pretence, simulation, deceit.*

simulō, -āre, -āvī, -ātum, [similis], 1, a., *make like, imitate, copy, reproduce, represent; feign, simulate, pretend.*

simultās, -ātis, [simul], f., *hostile encounter; grudge, jealousy, enmity, hatred, animosity.*

sīn [sī + nē], conj., *if however, but if.*

sine, prep. with abl., *without.*

singulāris, -e, [singulī], adj., *one by one, alone, single, solitary; singular, matchless, extraordinary, unique, remarkable.*

singulī, -ae, -a, adj., pl., *one at a time, single, individual; one to each, separate.* **in diēs singulōs**, *each successive day, day by day.*

sinō, -ere, sīvī, situm, 3, a., *let down, place, situate, give leave, permit, allow, suffer, let.*

Sinōpē, -ēs, [Σινώπη], f., *Sinōpē*, a prosperous commercial Greek city on the southern shore of the Pontus Euxinus, about half way between Trapezus and Heraclea; originally a colony from Miletus.

sinus, -ūs, m., *fold, curve, hollow, coil; fold of a garment;* by metonymy, *bosom, lap; bay, gulf; hollow, valley.*

sitis, -is, acc. -im, pl. wanting, f., *thirst; eager desire, eagerness.*

situs, -a, -um, [part. of sinō], adj., *placed, situated, lying; buried, laid at rest.*

sīve, or **seu**, [sī + -ve], conj., *or if, or.* **sīve — sīve**, *whether — or, be it that — or that, either — or.*

Smyrnaeī, -ōrum, [Smyrna], m., pl., *people of Smyrna.*

sōbrius, -a, -um, [sē + ēbrius], adj., *not intoxicated, sober; temperate, self-possessed, moderate.*

societās, -ātis, [socius], f., *fellowship, association, union, society; league, alliance.*

socius, -a, -um, [cf. sequor], adj., *sharing, partaking, associated, allied.* As subst., **socius**, -ī, m., *fellow, partner, sharer; companion, associate, friend; ally, helper.*

sodālis, -is, adj., *companionable, sociable, friendly.* As subst., m. and f., *companion, associate, intimate friend, comrade.*

sōl, sōlis, m., *sun;* by metonymy, *sunshine, sun's heat.*

sōlācium, -ī, n., *comfort, solace, consolation.*

soleō, -ēre, solitus sum, 2, semi-dep., *be accustomed, be wont, be used.*

sōlitūdō, -inis, [sōlus], f., *being alone, loneliness; lonely place, solitude, wilderness.*

sollicitātiō, -ōnis, [sollicitō], f., *vexing, harassing, vexation; inciting, instigation, solicitation.*

sollicitō, -āre, -āvī, -ātum, [sollicitus], 1, a., *stir, agitate, move; trouble, harass; urge, incite, instigate, tempt, solicit.*

sollicitūdō, -inis, [sollicitus], f., *apprehension, anxiety, solicitude.*

sollicitus, -a, -um, [unused sollus, = tōtus, + citus], adj., *agitated, disturbed; troubled, worried, anxious, alarmed; causing anxiety, alarming, distressing; uneasy, restless.*

solum, **-ī**, n., *bottom, base, foundation; ground, soil, floor;* by metonymy, *country, region, place.*

sōlum [**sōlus**], adv., *only, merely.* **nōn sōlum**, *not only, not merely.*

sōlus, **-a**, **-um**, gen. **sōlīus**, dat. **sōlī**, adj., *alone, only, single; lonely, solitary, deserted, unfrequented.*

solūtiō, **-ōnis**, [**solvō**], f., *loosing, relaxation; payment.*

solūtus, **-a**, **-um**, [part. of **solvō**], adj., *unbound, free, loose; lax, negligent, careless, remiss.*

solvō, **-ere**, **solvī**, **solūtum**, [**sē** + **luō**], 3, a., *loose, unbind, release, disengage, free; break up, dismiss; relax, overcome; annul, make void, end; perform, keep, fulfil; pay, pay off.*

somnus, **-ī**, m., *sleep, slumber.*

sonō, **-āre**, **-uī**, **-itum**, [**sonus**], 1, n. and a., *sound, resound; sing, celebrate; speak, utter, express.*

sonus, **-ī**, m., *sound, noise.*

soror, **-ōris**, f., *sister.*

sors, **sortis**, f., *lot; casting of lots, drawing of lots; destiny, fortune, condition; oracular response, prophetic utterance, prophecy.*

spargō, **-ere**, **sparsī**, **sparsum**, 3, a., *strew, scatter; cast, hurl; spread abroad, disperse, disseminate.*

Spartacus, **-ī**, m., *Spartacus.* He was a Thracian by birth, but taken prisoner and trained as a gladiator in the school at Capua. Making his escape with about 70 followers in 73 B. C., he became the leader of the Servile War, which taxed the energies of Rome for two years. He fell bravely fighting B. C. 71. Mark Antony is called *a Spartacus*, ANT. IV. VI.

spatium, **-ī**, n., *space, distance, interval; room, extent; path, track; period, time.*

speciēs, **-ēī**, [**speciō**], f., *aspect, sight, appearance; vision, apparition; beauty, splendor, show.*

spectō, **-āre**, **-āvī**, **-ātum**, [freq. of **speciō**, *look*], 1, a., *look on, behold, observe; gaze at, inspect; face, lie, be situated; try, test, prove;* of games, *attend.*

speculātor, **-ōris**, [**speculor**], m., *spy, scout, explorer.*

speculor, **-ārī**, **-ātus sum**, [**specula**, *watch-tower*], 1, dep., *spy out, watch, examine, explore.*

spērō, **-āre**, **-āvī**, **-ātum**, [**spēs**], 1, a., *hope, hope for, look for, expect; believe, trust.*

spēs, **speī**, f., *hope, expectation; trust, promise; anticipation, prospect.*

spīritus, **-ūs**, [**spīrō**, *breathe*], m., *breath, breathing;* by metonymy, *breeze, air; breath of a god, inspiration; breath of life, life, spirit; courage, haughtiness, pride.*

splendor, **-ōris**, [cf. **splendeō**], m., *brightness, brilliancy; splendor, dignity, eminence, honor.*

spoliō, **-āre**, **-āvī**, **-ātum**, [**spolium**], 1, a., *strip, uncover; rob, plunder, despoil, deprive.*

spolium, **-ī**, n., *skin, hide;* by metonymy, *arms* stripped from an enemy, *spoils, booty, prey.*

spōns, found only in the abl. **sponte**, [cf. **spondeō**], f., *free will, accord.* **suā sponte**, *of one's own accord, of their own accord, freely, voluntarily.*

Sp., see **Spurius**.

Spurius, **-ī**, abbreviated **Sp.**, [**spurius**, *illegitimate*], m., *Spurius*, a Roman forename.

stabiliō, **-īre**, **-īvī**, **-ītum**, [**stabilis**], 4, a., *make firm, stay, support; fix, establish, secure.*

stabilis, **-e**, [**stō**], adj., *firm, steadfast, stable, fixed; lasting, enduring, secure.*

stabilitās, **-ātis**, [**stabilis**], f., *steadfastness, stability, durability, security.*

Statilius, **-ī**, m., *L. Statilius*, a man of equestrian rank who joined the conspiracy of Catiline. He was arrested and executed along with the other conspirators in December, B.C. 63. CAT. III. III. *et seq.*

statim [**stō**], adv., *steadily, regularly; forthwith, straightway, instantly, immediately, at once.*

stator, **-ōris**, [cf. **sistō**, **stō**], m., *stay, supporter, protector;* used as an epithet of Jupiter, *Iuppiter Stator.* Cf. N. to p. 74, 32.

statua, **-ae**, [**stō**], f., *image, statue.*

statuō, **-ere**, **statuī**, **statūtum**, [**status**], 3, a., *set up, erect, construct, make; establish, fix; resolve, determine, decide, settle.*

status, **-ūs**, [**stō**], m., *standing, posture; position, attitude; state, situation, condition, constitution.*

stimulus, **-ī**, m., *goad, prick; spur, incentive, encouragement; torment, pain.*

stīpendium, **-ī**, [**stips**, *gift*, cf. **pendō**], n., *tax, tribute; income, pay, bounty; military service, campaigning.*

stirps, **stirpis**, f., *trunk, stem, stalk; race, family; offspring, descendant; source, origin, beginning.*

stō, **stāre**, **stetī**, **statum**, 1, n., *stand; stand up, be upright; stand firm, abide, endure, continue; stand still, delay, linger; remain, be fixed, be determined.*

strepitus, **-ūs**, [**strepō**], m., *noise, din, clash, crash, murmur.*

studeō, **-ēre**, **-uī**, ——, 2, a. and n., *be eager, be zealous, be devoted; strive after, desire, wish.*

studiōsē [**studiōsus**], adv., *eagerly, zealously, devotedly, studiously, carefully.*

studiōsus, **-a**, **-um**, [**studium**], adj., *eager, zealous, assiduous, devoted, studious; friendly, favorable.*

studium, **-ī**, [**studeō**], n., *zeal, desire, inclination, enthusiasm, endeavor; pursuit, inquiry, study, research; good-will, devotion, attachment.*

stultus, **-a**, **-um**, adj., *foolish, simple; stupid, dull, silly.*

stuprum, **-ī**, n., *defilement, disgrace, outrage; debauchery, lewdness.*

suādeō, **-ēre**, **suāsī**, **suāsum**, 2, n. and a., *advise, recommend; exhort, urge, impel, persuade.*

suāvis, **-e**, adj., *sweet, agreeable, grateful, pleasant.*

sub, prep. with acc. and abl., *under:*

(1) With acc., after verbs of motion, *under, below, near to, to, up to, towards, down into; until, about, just before; following, after, just after.*

(2) With abl., of place, *under, beneath, below, behind, at the foot of, by, near;* of time, *during, in, within, at, by, in the time of;* of other relations, *under, in the power of, subject to; by reason of, in consequence of.*

In composition, **sub** is often assimilated before **m**, **r**, and usually before **c**, **f**, **g**, **p**. It adds the force of *under, beneath; somewhat, a little; secretly, by stealth.*

subeō, **-īre**, **-īvī** or **-iī**, **-itum**, [**sub** + **eō**], irr., n. and a., *go under, enter; advance, draw near; come after, succeed; come up, occur, suggest itself; undergo, submit to, be subject to, endure, suffer.*

subiciō, -icere, -iēcī, -iectum, [sub + iaciō], 3, a., *throw under, place under; submit, present, give; subordinate; subjoin, append; forge, counterfeit.*

subiector, -ōris, [subiciō], m., *forger.*

subigō, -ere, subēgī, subāctum, [sub + agō], 3, a., *bring under; subdue, conquer, subjugate, reduce.*

subitō [subitus], adv., *suddenly, unexpectedly.*

subolēs, -is, f., *sprout, shoot; offspring, posterity, stock, race.*

subsellium, -ī, [sub, sella], n., *low bench, seat, form; court, tribunal.*

subsidium, -ī, [sub, sedeō], n., *reserve force; aid, help, assistance, support, protection.*

subsum, -esse, ——, ——, [sub + sum], irr., n., *be under; be near at hand, be near; impend, approach; be concealed, lurk in, be in reserve.*

succēdō, -ere, successī, successum, [sub + cēdō], 3, n. and a., *come under, enter; approach, draw near, come to; follow, succeed, take the place of; be successful, prosper.*

Suessa, -ae, f., *Suessa*, a town in the southern part of Latium, near the border of Campania; sometimes reckoned a city of Campania. ANT. IV. II.

sufferō, -ferre, sustulī, sublātum, [sub + ferō], irr., a., *undergo, endure, suffer.*

suffrāgium, -ī, [sub, cf. frangō], n., lit. *fragment; voting-tablet, vote, ballot, suffrage; right of suffrage, elective franchise.*

suī, sibī, sē or sēsē, nom. wanting, reflex. pron., *himself, herself, itself, themselves; him, her, it,* etc. **inter sē**, *mutually, reciprocally, one another, each other.*

Sulla, -ae, m., *Sulla*, name of a patrician family of the Cornelian gens. Two members of it are mentioned in this book:

(1) *L. Cornēlius Sulla*, the dictator, born B. C. 138. He served with distinction under Marius, first in the Jugurthine War, afterwards, B. C. 104–101, in the campaigns against the Teutones and Cimbri. He became a leader of the aristocratic party, defeated his enemies, and in B. C. 82 was made dictator. After two years of absolute government, in which he introduced many reforms, he retired from the dictatorship, and died the following year, B. C. 78. CAT. II. IX. *et al.*

(2) *L. Cornēlius Sulla Faustus*, son of the dictator, born about B. C. 89. In the war between Caesar and Pompey he took sides with the latter, but was captured by Caesar B. C. 46, and lost his life at the hands of Caesar's soldiers in a tumult. EP. XII.

Sulpicius, -a, name of a Roman gens, at first patrician, afterwards including plebeian families also. Three of the name are mentioned in this book:

(1) *Sulpicius*, with whom Cicero had some financial transaction. EP. XXXVI.

(2) *C. Sulpicius*, praetor B. C. 63. CAT. III. III.

(3) *P. Sulpicius Rūfus*, born 124 B. C., tribune of the people B. C. 88. At first he supported the aristocratic party. Afterwards he joined Marius, with whom he fled on the approach of Sulla, but was captured and murdered. CAT. III. X.

sum, esse, fuī, fut. part. futūrus, irr., n., *be, exist; stay; fall;* with gen., *belong to, be the part* or *duty of, be possessed of, be valued at, cost;* with dative, *be for, serve for, belong to, possess, have.*

summa, **-ae**, [properly f. of **summus**, sc. **rēs**], f., *chief place, highest rank, leadership; sum, aggregate, whole; main thing, chief reason.*

summus, **-a**, **-um**, see **superus**.

sūmō, **-ere**, **sūmpsī**, **sūmptum**, [**sub** + **emō**], 3, a., *take, lay hold of; assume, take on; consume, spend; enter upon, begin; exact; obtain, acquire; select, choose.*

sūmptuōsē [**sūmptuōsus**], adv., *expensively, sumptuously.*

sūmptuōsus, **-a**, **-um**, [**sūmptus**], adj., *expensive, costly, sumptuous; wasteful, extravagant.*

sūmptus, **-ūs**, [**sūmō**], m., *expenditure, expense, cost, outlay* **sūmptum facere**, *to be at an expense, to make an expenditure.*

superbē [**superbus**], adv., *haughtily, proudly.*

superbus, **-a**, **-um**, [**super**], adj., *haughty, proud, arrogant, domineering.*

superior, see **superus**.

superō, **-āre**, **-āvī**, **-ātum**, [**superus**], I, n. and a., *rise above, overtop, surmount, transcend; exceed, be abundant; surpass, outstrip; overcome, subdue, defeat, suppress, conquer.*

supersum, **-esse**, **fuī**, [**super** + **sum**], irr., n., *be left, remain over* or *from, remain; live after, survive, outlive, be still alive.*

superus, **-a**, **-um**, comp. **superior**, sup. **suprēmus** or **summus**, [**super**], adj., *above, upper, higher.* Sup **suprēmus**, **-a**, **-um**, *highest, loftiest, topmost; last, final; extreme, utmost, outermost;* sup. **summus**, *highest, topmost; greatest, best, utmost, extreme;* often used of a part, as **summus mōns**, *the top of the mountain.* Comp. as subst., **superiōrēs**, **-um**, m., pl., *men of the older time, elders.*

suppeditō, **-āre**, **-āvī**, **-ātum**, [**sub**, **pēs**], I, a. and n., *furnish, provide, supply freely; abound, be in store, be at hand.*

suppetō, **-ere**, **-īvī** or **-iī**, **-ītum**, [**sub** + **petō**], 3, n., *be at hand, be in store, be available; be sufficient for, be equal to.*

supplex, **-icis**, [**sub**, cf. **plicō**], adj., *bending the knee, begging, entreating; submissive, suppliant.* As subst., m., *suppliant, petitioner.*

supplicātiō, **-ōnis**, [**supplicō**], f., *public supplication, public thanksgiving, day of prayer.*

supplicium, **-ī**, [**supplex**], n., *entreaty, supplication; kneeling* for punishment, *punishment, penalty, torture, torment.*

suprā [for **superā**, abl. f of **superus**, properly sc. **parte**], adv. and prep.

(1) As adv., *above, on top, over.*

(2) As prep., with acc., *over, above, beyond, more than.*

suprēmus, see **superus**.

surgō, **-ere**, **surrēxī**, **surrēctum**, [**sub** + **regō**], 3, a. and n., *rise, get up, stand up.*

suscēnseō, **-ēre**, **-uī**, ——, [**succēnsus**, from **succendō**], 2, n., *be angry, be provoked.*

suscipiō, **-cipere**, **-cēpī**, **susceptum**, [**subs**, old form of **sub**, + **capiō**], 3, a., *take up; undertake, begin, enter upon; incur, undergo, submit to, suffer, bear.*

suspectus, **-a**, **-um**, [part. of **suspiciō**], adj., *mistrusted, suspected, subject to suspicion.*

suspīciō, **-ōnis**, [**suspiciō**], f., *mistrust, suspicion, distrust.*

suspicor, **-ārī**, **-ātus sum**, [**sub**, cf. **speciō**], 1, dep., *mistrust, distrust, suspect; surmise, suppose.*

sustentō, **-āre**, **-āvī**, **-ātum**, [freq. of **sustineō**], 1, a., *hold up, sustain; hold out, endure, suffer, bear; put off, defer, delay.*

sustineō, **-ēre**, **sustinuī**, **sustentum**, [**subs**, old form of **sub**, + **teneō**], 2, a., *hold up, bear up, support, sustain; hold in, control, check; bear, undergo, endure, hold out.*

suus, **-a**, **-um**, [cf. **suī**], poss. pron. adj., *his, her, its, their, his own, their own; own, peculiar, just, suitable, favorable; dear, beloved; self-possessed, composed.* As subst., **suī**, **-ōrum**, m., pl., *one's people, friends, relatives, party.* **sua**, **-ōrum**, n., pl., *one's possessions, one's property.*

Syria, **-ae**, [Συρία], f., *Syria*, a country lying east of the Mediterranean Sea, between Cilicia and Palestine; organized into a Roman province B. C. 64. EP. XIX.

Syrpiae, see n. to p. 179, l. 5.

T.

T., see **Titus**.

tabella, **-ae**, [dim. of **tabula**], f., *tablet; writing-tablet, juror's tablet, vote;* pl. often *writing, letter, despatch.*

tabellārius, **-a**, **-um**, [**tabella**], adj., *of a tablet.* As subst., **tabellārius**, **-ī**, m., *letter-carrier, messenger, courier.*

Tabernae, see **Trēs**.

taberna, **-ae**, f., *hut, cabin; booth, stall, shop, office; inn, tavern.*

tābēscō, **-ere**, **tābuī**, ——, [**tābeō**, *waste away*], 3, inch., *melt, decay, decompose; pine away, languish, waste away.*

tabula, **-ae**, f., *board, plank; tablet, writing-tablet; writing, record, memorandum, account; picture, painting.* **tabulae pūblicae**, *public records.*

tabulārium, **-ī**, [**tabula**], n., *depository of records, archives.*

taceō, **-ēre**, **-uī**, **-itum**, 2, n. and a., *be silent, keep silence; pass over in silence, leave unsaid.*

tacitē [**tacitus**], adv., *silently, in silence.*

taciturnitās, **-ātis**, [**taciturnus**], f., *keeping silent, silence.*

tacitus, **-a**, **-um**, [part. of **taceō**], adj., *silent, passed in silence; concealed, hidden, secret; still, mute, noiseless.*

taeter, **-tra**, **-trum**, comp. **taetrior**, sup. **taeterrimus**, adj., *offensive, loathsome, foul; repulsive, shameful, abominable, base.*

tālāris, **-e**, [**tālus**, *ankle*], adj., *of the ankles, reaching to the ankles.*

tālis, **-e**, pron. adj., *such, of such a kind; such as this, as follows; of so especial a kind, so distinguished.* **tālis — quālis**, *such — as.*

tam, adv., *so much, to such a degree, so, so very.* **tam — quam**, *so — as, as much — as.*

tamen, adv., *notwithstanding, nevertheless, for all that; however, yet, still.* **quī tamen**, *although he.*

tametsī [for **tamen etsī**], conj., *although, though, notwithstanding that; and yet.*

tamquam [**tam** + **quam**], adv., *just as, as if; as it were, just as if, as much as.*

tandem [**tam** + **-dem**], adv., *at length, at last, finally;* in questions, *pray now, now, I pray.*

tangō, **-ere**, **tetigī**, **tāctum**, 3, a., *touch; border on, adjoin; arrive* *at, come to; move, affect, impress;* of lightning, *strike.*

tantō opere, see **opus**.

tantum [**tantus**], adv., *so much, so greatly, to such a degree; only so much, only, merely.*

tantum modo, adv., *only, merely.*

tantus, -a, -um, adj., *of such size, so great, such; so very great, so important; only so much, so trivial, so small.* As subst., **tantum, -ī**, n., *so much.* **tantī**, gen. of price, *of such a price, of so great value; of so little account, of so slight importance.* **tantō**, abl. of degree of difference, *by so much, so much.* **tantus — quantus**, *so much — as, so great — as.*

tardē, comp. **tardius**, sup. **tardissimē**, [**tardus**], adv., *slowly, late.* Sup., *latest, very late.*

tarditās, -ātis, [**tardus**], f., *slowness, tardiness.*

tardō, -āre, -āvī, -ātum, [**tardus**], 1, a. and n., *make slow, hinder, delay, retard; linger, tarry.*

Tarentīnus, -a, -um, [**Tarentum**], adj., *Tarentine, of Tarentum*, an important Greek city on the Gulf of Tarentum. As subst., **Tarentīnī, -ōrum**, m., pl., *people of Tarentum.*

Tarquitius, -ī, m., *L. Tarquitius*, an acquaintance of Cicero's. EP. XIX.

tēctum, -ī, [**tegō**], n., *covered place, shelter; house, dwelling; covering, roof.*

tegō, -ere, tēxī, tēctum, 3, a., *cover; hide, conceal, shelter; cloak, veil; protect, guard.*

tēlum, -ī, n., *missile, spear, dart, javelin, arrow;* by metonymy, *sword, axe, dagger, weapon.*

temere, adv., *by chance, at random, without design; rashly, heedlessly, thoughtlessly, recklessly.*

temeritās, -ātis, [**temere**], f., *chance, accident; rashness, recklessness, indiscretion, foolhardiness.*

temperantia, -ae, [**temperāns**], f., *moderation, discretion, self-control, temperance.*

temperō, -āre, -āvī, -ātum, [**tempus**], 1, n. and a., *be moderate, control one's self, forbear, be temperate; control, rule, govern, regulate, restrain.*

tempestās, -ātis, [**tempus**], f., *period, time, season; weather, bad weather, storm, tempest; calamity, misfortune.*

tempestīvus, -a, -um, [**tempestās**], adj., *seasonable, opportune, timely; appropriate, fitting, suitable; in good season, early.*

templum, -ī, n., *consecrated place, sacred enclosure, sanctuary; temple, shrine, fane.*

temptō, -āre, -āvī, -ātum, [intensive of **tendō**], 1, a., *handle, touch, feel; try, attempt, essay; attack, assail.*

tempus, -oris, n., *period of time, time, season, point of time; right time, opportunity, occasion; condition, times, circumstances; time of need, exigency, emergency.* **id temporis**, *at that time.* **ex tempore**, *off hand, without preparation.*

tendō, -ere, tetendī, tentum and **tēnsum**, 3, a. and n., *stretch out, stretch, extend; hold a course, direct* one's *course, go, proceed; aim at, strive, endeavor.*

tenebrae, -ārum, f., pl., *darkness, gloom; darkness of night, night.*

Tenedos or **Tenedus, -ī**, [Τένεδος], f., *Tenedos*, an island in the Aegean Sea, near the coast of Troas. ARCH. IX.

teneō, -ēre, -uī, tentum, 2, a. and n., *hold, have, keep; possess,* *be master of, occupy; grasp firmly, hold fast, fetter, bind; restrain, check, guard, preserve, defend.*

tenuis, -e, adj., *thin, fine; narrow, slight, insignificant; mean, poor, weak.*

ter [cf. **trēs**], num. adv., *thrice, three times.*

Terentia, -ae, f., *Terentia*, wife of Cicero, to whom she was married about B. C. 80. She was a woman of strong character, and had a large property. Cicero divorced her B. C. 46. She is said to have married again and to have lived to be over a hundred years old. EP. VIII., IX., XXI.–XXVIII.

terminō, -āre, -āvī, -ātum, [**terminus**], 1, a., *bound, limit; set limits to, circumscribe; close, end, finish, terminate.*

terminus, -ī, m., *boundary, limit, end.*

terra, -ae, f., *land*, as opposed to the water; *soil, ground, region, country; earth.* **orbis terrae** or **terrārum**, *the world, the whole world.* **terrā marīque**, *by land and sea.*

terror, -ōris, [cf. **terreō**], m., *fright, alarm, terror, overwhelming fear;* by metonymy, *cause of fright, dread; terrible news.*

tertius, -a, -um, or **III.**, [**ter**], num. adj., *third.*

Testa, -ae, m., *C. Trebātius Testa*, an eminent jurist, a friend of Cicero and of Caesar. He wrote on legal subjects, but his writings have perished. EP. XIII., XXI., XXXVIII.

testāmentum, -ī, [**testor**], n., *will, testament.*

testimōnium, -ī, [**testis**], n., *evidence, attestation, testimony, proof.*

testis, -is, m. and f., *witness.*

testor, -ārī, -ātus sum, [**testis**], 1, *cause to serve as a witness, call to witness, appeal to, invoke.*

Teutonī, -ōrum, or **Teutones**, -um, m., pl., *Teutones, Teutons*, a people of Germanic origin, that appeared in Gaul about 113 B. C., and were well-nigh annihilated by Gaius Marius at Aquae Sextiae (Aix), B. C. 102. IMP. P. XX.

Themistoclēs, -ī or -is, [Θεμιστοκλῆς], m., *Themistoclēs*, the great leader of the Athenians and of Greece in the wars with Persia. ARCH. IX.

Theophanēs, -is, [Θεοφάνης], m., *Cn. Pompēius Theophanēs*, a learned Greek, native of Mytilene. He became an intimate friend of Pompey, whose name he took. He accompanied Pompey, who considered his advice of much weight, in a number of campaigns. After the battle of Pharsalia he returned to Italy, and was pardoned by Caesar. He appears to have outlived both Caesar and Cicero. ARCH. X.

Thermus, -ī, m., *Q. Minucius Thermus*, propraetor of the province of Asia 51–50 B. C. His administration was praised by Cicero. In the Civil War he joined the party of Pompey. EP. XVI.

Ti., see **Tiberius**.

Tiberīnus, -a, -um, [**Tiberis**], adj., *of the Tiber.*

Tiberis, -is, m., *Tiber*, the great river of western Italy, on which Rome is situated; now Tevere.

Tiberius, -ī, abbreviated **Ti.**, m., *Tiberius*, a Roman forename.

Tigrānēs, -is, [Τιγράνης], m., *Tigrānēs*, king of Armenia and neighboring regions, and son-in-law of Mithridates, whom he assisted in the wars with Rome. He surrendered to Pompey B. C. 66, who left him the government of Armenia proper and the title of king. IMP. P. II. *et al.*

timeō, -ēre, -uī, ——, 2, a. and n., *be afraid, be fearful; be apprehensive, be anxious; dread, fear.*

timidē [timidus], adv., *fearfully, timidly.*

timidus, -a, -um, [timeō], adj., *afraid, fearful, timid, cowardly.*

timor, -ōris, [cf. timeō], m., *fear, dread, apprehension, alarm, timidity; awe, reverence.*

Tīrō, -ōnis, [tīrō, *recruit*], m., *Tīrō*, at first a slave of Cicero, then set free and given the name *M. Tullius Tīrō.* Being a man of ability and culture, he became the confidential secretary and literary assistant of the orator. He also wrote works of his own. He is said to have collected and published Cicero's letters. A system of short-hand was credited to him as inventor. EP. XX. *et al.*

Tīsamenus, -ī, [*τῑσάμενος*, from *τίνω, requite*], m., *Tīsamenus*, a slave of Cicero's. EP. XXXI.

Titinius, -ī, m., *Q. Titinius*, a money-lender. EP. III.

Titius, -ī, m., *C. Titius Rūfus*, city praetor B. C. 50. EP. XVII.

Titus, -ī, abbreviated **T.**, m., *Titus*, a Roman forename, said to be of Sabine origin.

toga, -ae, [tegō], f., *toga, gown*, an outer robe of white woolen stuff, worn by Roman citizens when not engaged in military pursuits; hence, *peace.*

togātus, -a, -um, [toga], adj., *wearing the toga, clad in the toga; in the garb of peace, in civil life, as a civilian.*

tolerābilis, -e, [tolerō], adj., *bearable, endurable, tolerable.*

tolerō, -āre, -āvī, -ātum, [cf. tollō], 1, a., *bear, endure, sustain, suffer.*

tollō, -ere, sustulī, sublātum, 3, a., *lift, lift up, raise, elevate; bring up, educate; make away with, remove, dispose of; ruin, destroy.*

Tongilius, -ī, m., *Tongilius*, a disreputable youth, a favorite of Catiline. CAT. II. II.

Torquātus, -ī, [torquātus, from torquis, *necklace*], m., *T. Mānlius Torquātus*; see **Mānlius** (2).

torqueō, -ēre, torsī, tortum, 2, a., *turn, turn about, bend, wind, twist; rack, torture, torment.*

tot, num. adj., indecl., *so many, in such numbers.*

totiēns [tot], num. adv., *so often, as often, so many times.*

tōtus, -a, -um, gen. tōtīus, adj., *all, the whole, total, entire, all*; used where the English idiom prefers an adv., *altogether, wholly, entirely, fully.*

tractō, -āre, -āvī, -ātum, [freq. of trahō], 1, a., *draw, pull; touch, handle; manage, practice, conduct, control; treat.*

trādō, -ere, trādidī, trāditum, [trāns + dō], 3, a., *deliver, surrender, hand over; commit, intrust, confide; give over, betray; transmit, relate.*

trahō, -ere, trāxī, tractum, 3, a., *draw, drag; draw in, take on, assume; lead on, attract, influence; get, obtain, derive; protract, extend.*

tranquillitās, -ātis, [tranquillus], f., *quietness, stillness, calmness; tranquillity, serenity.*

tranquillus, -a, -um, adj., *quiet, still, calm, tranquil; peaceful, undisturbed, serene.*

trāns, prep. with acc., *across, over, beyond.* In composition **trāns**

stands as trān-, rarely **trāns-**, before **s**; **trāns-**, or **trā-**, before **i, d, l, m, n**; **trāns-**, rarely **trā-**, before **f, v**; and remains unchanged before the other letters.

Trānsalpīnus, **-a, -um**, [**trāns + Alpīnus**], adj., *beyond the Alps, Transalpine*. Cf. **Gallia**.

trānscendō, **-ere**, **trānscendī**, **trānscēnsum**, [**trāns + scandō**], 3, a. and n., *climb over, pass over, surmount; overstep, transgress.*

trānsferō, **-ferre**, **-tulī**, **-lātum**, [**trāns + ferō**], irr., a., *bear across, convey over, transport, transfer, turn.*

trānsigō, **-ere**, **trānsēgī**, **trānsāctum**, [**trāns + agō**], 3, a., *pierce through; carry through, bring to an end, conclude, perform, accomplish, transact; settle, agree, make a settlement.*

trānsmarīnus, **-a, -um**, [**trāns + marīnus**], adj., *beyond the sea, transmarine.*

trānsmittō, **-ere**, **trānsmīsī**, **trānsmissum**, [**trāns + mittō**], 3, a. and n., *send across, carry over, bring across, transmit; pass over, cross over, traverse; hand over, intrust, commit, devote.*

Trebātius, **-ī**, see **Testa**.

tredecim, or **XIII.**, [**trēs + decem**], num. adj., indecl., *thirteen.*

trēs, **tria**, gen. **trium**, num. adj., *three.*

Trēs Tabernae, abl. **Tribus Tabernīs**, f., pl., *the Three Taverns*, a station on the Appian Way, 31 miles from Rome. EP. IV., V.

tribūlis, **-is**, [**tribus**], m., *man of the same tribe, fellow tribesman.*

tribūnal, **-ālis**, [**tribūnus**], n., *judgment-seat, tribunal*, a raised platform on which were the seats of magistrates.

tribūnus, **-ī**, [**tribus**], m., *representative of a tribe, tribune.* **tribūnus plēbis** or **plēbēī**, or simply **tribūnus**, *tribune of the people*, i. e. of the common people or commons, a magistrate whose duty it was to protect the plebeians against the patricians.

tribuō, **-ere**, **tribuī**, **tribūtum**, [**tribus**], 3, a., *assign, bestow, confer, grant, give; concede, allow; spend, devote.*

trīduum, **-ī**, [**trēs + diēs**], n., *three days' time, space of three days, three days.*

triumphō, **-āre**, **-āvī**, **-ātum**, [**triumphus**], 1, n. and a., *celebrate a triumph, triumph; exult, greatly rejoice.*

triumphus, **-ī**, m., *triumphal procession, triumph*, the ceremonial entrance of a commander into Rome in celebration of an important victory; *celebration of victory.*

tropaeum, **-ī**, [τρόπαιον], n., *memorial of victory, trophy.*

trucīdātiō, **-ōnis**, [**trucīdō**], f., *slaughter, massacre, butchery.*

trucīdō, **-āre**, **-āvī**, **-ātum**, [**trux, caedō**], 1, a., *slaughter, massacre, butcher.*

tū, **tuī**, pl., **vōs**, pers. pron., *thou, you.*

tuba, **-ae**, f., *trumpet, war-trumpet.*

tueor, **-ērī**, **tuitus sum**, 2, dep., *look at, gaze upon, consider; care for, preserve, guard, uphold, defend, keep, maintain.*

Tullia, **-ae**, f., *Tullia*, daughter of Cicero and Terentia, born probably 79 or 78 B. C. She was married in 63 B. C. to C. Calpurnius Piso, but was left a widow B. C. 57. The following year she became the wife of Furius Crassipes, a young man of wealth and high position, but was soon divorced. In B. C. 50 she was married to P. Cornelius Dolabella. She died 45 B. C. Though her life was far from fortunate, she appears to have possessed a lofty nature, and was the idol of her father, who was broken-hearted over her death. See **Dolābella, Pīsō.** EP. VIII., XIX., XXI., XXIV.

Tulliola, -ae, [dim. of **Tullia**], f., *Tulliola,* Cicero's pet name for his daughter Tullia. EP. VIII., IX.

Tullius, -a, name of a Roman gens, to which the Cicero family belonged. See **Cicerō.**

Tullus, -ī, m., *L. Volcātius Tullus,* consul B. C. 66 with M'. Aemilius Lepidus. CAT. I. VI.

tum, adv., *then, at that time; thereupon, moreover.* **cum — tum,** often *both — and, not only — but also.* **tum vērō,** *then indeed, just then.*

tumultus, -ūs, [**tumeō**], m., *commotion, disturbance, tumult, uproar; insurrection, mutiny.*

tumulus, -ī, [**tumeō**], m., *mound, hillock, hill; grave, sepulchral mound.*

tunc, adv., *then, at that time, just then, thereupon.*

tunica, -ae, f., *under-garment, tunic, shirt.*

turbulentus, -a, -um, [**turba**], adj., *disturbed, boisterous, stormy; restless, disordered, troublesome.*

turma, -ae, f., *throng, crowd, band, body;* of calvary, *squadron, company, troop.*

turpis, -e, adj., *ugly, unsightly, repulsive; shameful, base, disgraceful, dishonorable.*

turpiter, comp. **turpius,** sup. **turpissimē,** [**turpis**], adv., *in an unsightly manner, repulsively; shamefully, basely, disgracefully, dishonorably.*

turpitūdō, -inis, [**turpis**], f., *unsightliness, repulsiveness; shamefulness, baseness, disgrace, dishonor.*

Tusculānus, -a, -um, [**Tūsculum**], adj., *Tusculan, of Tusculum,* a town on a spur of the Alban mountains, 15 miles southeast of Rome. As subst., **Tūsculānum, -ī,** n., *estate at Tusculum, Tusculan villa,* a favorite villa of Cicero's.

tūtō, sup. **tūtissimō,** [**tūtus**], adv., *safely, securely, in safety.* Sup., *in the greatest safety, most safe.*

tūtor, -ārī, -ātus sum, [**tueor**], I, dep., *watch, guard, defend, protect.*

tūtus, -a, -um, [part. of **tueor**], adj., *guarded, safe, secure, out of danger; watchful, cautious.*

tuus, -a, -um, [**tū**], poss. pron. adj., *thy, thine, your, yours; your own.* As subst., pl., **tuī, -ōrum,** m., *your kinsmen, your friends;* **tua, -ōrum,** n., *your property, your possessions.*

tyrannus, -ī, [τύραννος], m., *ruler, monarch, sovereign, king; despot, tyrant.*

U.

ūber, -eris, n., *udder, breast.*

ūbertās, -ātis, [**ūber**], f., *richness, fertility, fruitfulness, productiveness.*

ubi or **ubī,** adv., of place, *where, wheresoever, in what place;* of time, *when, whenever, as soon as;* used in place of a relative pron., *wherewith, by which, with whom, by whom.*

ubicumque or **ubīcumque,** [**ubi** + **-cumque**], adv., *wherever, wheresoever.*

ubinam, [**ubi** + **nam**], adv., inter., *where? where on earth?*

ubīque [**ubī** + **-que**], adv., *anywhere, in any place; in every place, everywhere.*

ulcīscor, ulcīscī, ultus sum, 3, dep., *take vengeance on, punish; avenge, requite.*

ūllus, -a, -um, gen. **ūllīus,** adj., *any.* As subst., **ūllus, ūllīus,** m., *any one, anybody.*

ūlterior, -ius, gen. **-ōris,** sup. **ūltimus,** [cf. **ūltrā**], adj. in the comp. degree, *farther, beyond, more distant, more remote.* Neut. **ūlterius,** often as adv., *beyond, farther on, further, more, longer, to a greater degree.* Sup. **ūltimus, -a, -um,** *farthest, most distant, uttermost, extreme, last.*

ūltimus, -a, -um, see **ūlterior.**

ūltrō [cf. **ūltrā**], adv., *beyond, on the other side; besides, moreover, of one's own accord, voluntarily.*

Umbrēnus, -ī, m., *P. Umbrēnus,* a freedman, one of the Catilinarian conspirators. Having been engaged in the business of money-lending in Gaul, he was employed to try to win the support of the Allobroges to the conspiracy. CAT. III. VI.

umquam, adv., *at any time, ever.*

ūnā [**ūnus**], adv., *together, at once, at the same time.*

unde, adv., *whence, from which place; from which, from whom.*

ūndecim, or **XI.**, [**ūnus** + **decem**], num. adj., indecl., *eleven.*

ūndecimus, -a, -um, or **XI.**, [**ūndecim**], num. adj., *eleventh.*

ūndēquīnquāgēsimus, -a, -um, [**ūndēquīnquāgintā**], num. adj., *forty-ninth.*

undique [**unde** + **-que**], adv., *from all sides, on all sides, all around, everywhere.*

unguentum, -ī, [**unguō**], n., *ointment, perfume.*

ūnicē [**ūnicus**], adv., *singularly, uniquely, above all others.*

ūniversus, -a, -um, [**ūnus** + **versus**], adj., *all together, whole, entire; general, universal.* As subst., **ūniversī, -ōrum,** m., pl., *the whole body of men, all men.*

ūnus, -a, -um, gen. **ūnīus,** sometimes in poetry, **ūnius,** num. adj., *one, one only, a single one; alone, sole, single; one and the same.*

URB., see **urbānus.**

urbānus, -a, -um, in titles sometimes abbreviated **urb.**, [**urbs**], adj., *of the city; in city fashion, polite, refined, courteous.* As subst., **urbāna, -ōrum,** n., pl., *the affairs of the city.*

urbs, urbis, f., *city;* especially *the city, Rome.*

urgueō, -ēre, ursī, ——, 2, a. and n., *press, press on, push, impel, urge; press hard, weigh down, oppress; urge on, drive.*

ūspiam, adv., *at any place, anywhere, somewhere.*

ūsquam, adv., *anywhere, at any place, in any place, to any place.*

ūsque, adv., *even to, even, as far as; all the way, continuously, as long as.*

ūsūra, -ae, [**ūtor**], f., *use, enjoyment; interest on money, usury.*

ūsūrpō, -āre, -āvī, -ātum, [**ūsus,** cf. **rapiō**], 1, a., lit. *seize for use; make use of, use, employ; practice, adopt; speak of, talk of; resort to.*

ūsus, -ūs, [**ūtor**], m., *use, employment, enjoyment; practice, experience, skill; intercourse, familiarity; benefit, profit, advantage, service, need.*

ut or **utī**, adv., of place, *where;* of time, *as, as soon as, just as;* of manner, interrogative, *how?*

in what way? in what manner? relative, *as, as for instance, seeing that, as if, on the supposition that.* **ut prīmum,** *as soon as.* **ut — ita,** *so — as, while — still.*

ut or **utī,** conj. with subj., of result, *that, so that;* of purpose, *in order that, that;* of concession, *though, although.*

uter, -tra, -trum, gen. **utrīus,** pron. adj., *which* of two, *whichever, either* of two.

uterque, utraque, utrumque, gen. **utrīusque, [uter + -que],** adj., *each, either; one and the other, both;* pl. as subst., *each party, each side, both.*

ūtilis, -e, [ūtor], adj., *useful, serviceable; profitable, expedient, advantageous; fit, suitable.*

ūtilitās, -ātis, [ūtilis], f., *utility, use; profit, benefit, advantage, expediency.*

utinam [utī + nam], adv., *oh that! if only! would that!*

ūtor, ūtī, ūsus sum, 3, dep., *use, employ, make use of; exercise, practice, perform; serve one's self with, enjoy, indulge in; find to be, find.*

utrum [uter], adv., in direct questions indicated only by the inflection of the voice in translating; in indirect questions, *whether.* **utrum — an,** *whether — or.*

utut, adv., *however, in whatever manner.*

uxor, -ōris, f., *wife.*

V.

vacillō, -āre, -āvī, -ātum, 1, n., *sway to and fro, stagger, totter; waver, hesitate, vacillate.*

vacō, -āre, -āvī, -ātum, 1, n., *be empty, be vacant; be without; be idle, be at leisure, have time.*

vacuēfaciō, -facere, -fēcī, -factum, [vacuus + faciō], 3, a., *make empty, make vacant, clear, free.*

vacuus, -a, -um, [vacō], adj., *empty, void, vacant, free, without; idle, unemployed, unengaged, at leisure.*

vadimōnium, -ī, [vas, *bail***],** n., *guarantee* of an appearance before a tribunal at a given time *by bail; bail-bond, bail, security.* **vadimōnium dēserere,** *to forfeit one's bail.*

vādō, -ere, ——, ——, 3, n., *go,* especially *go in haste, rush, proceed rapidly.*

vāgīna, -ae, f., *scabbard, sheath.*

vagor, -ārī, -ātus sum, [vagus], 1, dep., *stroll about, wander, roam, rove; be spread, extend, spread abroad, diffuse itself.*

valdē, comp. **valdius, [for validē from validus],** adv., *strongly, exceedingly; very much, very.*

valēns, -entis, [part. of **valeō**], adj., *strong, vigorous, powerful, mighty.*

valeō, -ēre, -uī, -itum, 2, n., *be strong, be vigorous, be healthy; have power, avail, prevail, succeed; be able, be capable.* Imp. **valē,** as a greeting, *farewell, good-bye.*

Valerius, see **Flaccus,** (2), (3).

valētūdō, -inis, [valeō], f., *health, state of health; ill health, sickness, feebleness, weakness.*

vāllō, -āre, -āvī, -ātum, [vāllum], 1, a., *fortify with a rampart; fortify, protect, defend.*

varietās, -ātis, [varius], f., *diversity, variety; difference, disagreement, dissension; change, vicissitude.*

varius, -a, -um, adj., *diversified, varying, changeable, various, manifold; diverse, different.*

Varrō, -ōnis, m., *M. Terentius Varrō*, "the most learned of the Romans," born 116 B.C. In the Civil War he held a command under Pompey, but was pardoned by Caesar, and afterwards devoted himself exclusively to literary pursuits. He wrote voluminously, on a great variety of subjects. He was an intimate friend of Cicero. He died B.C. 28. EP. XLIV.

vāstātiō, -ōnis, [vāstō], f., *laying waste, devastating, devastation.*

vāstitās, -ātis, [vāstus], f., *waste, desert; desolation, ruin, destruction.*

vāstō, -āre, -āvī, -ātum, [vāstus], 1, a., *make desert, lay waste, make desolate, devastate, destroy.*

vātēs, -is, m. and f., *seer, prophet, diviner, soothsayer.*

Vatia, -ae, m., [vatius, *bow-legged*], m., name of a family of the Servilian gens. The most prominent member was *P. Servīlius Vatia*, grandson of Q. Metellus Macedonicus, consul B.C. 79. In B.C. 78 he was proconsul of Cilicia, and went against the pirates that infested the southern coast of Asia Minor. He was successful, receiving the honorary surname *Isauricus* for the reduction of the Isauri. He was honored with a triumph, B.C. 74. He died B.C. 44. IMP. P. XXIII.

-ve, enclitic conj., [vel], *or, or if you please, or also;* after a negative, *and.*

vectīgal, -ālis, [vehō], n., *revenue* of the state, *tax, impost, duty, tribute.*

vectīgālis, -is, [vectīgal], m., *payer of tribute, tributary.*

vehemēns, -entis, adj., *eager, ardent, impetuous, vehement; strong, forcible, vigorous, effective.*

vehementer, comp. **vehementius**, sup. **vehementissimē**, [vehemēns], adv., *eagerly, impetuously, vehemently; strongly, exceedingly, very much, extremely.*

vel [old imp. of **volō**], conj., *or, or if you will, or even.* **vel — vel**, *either — or, whether — or.*

vel [volō], adv., *or even, or indeed, assuredly, certainly; perhaps, it may be; very, utmost.* **vel māximē**, *in the very highest degree, most of all.*

vēlum, -ī, n., *sail;* by metonymy, *awning, curtain, veil.*

vēna, -ae, f., *blood-vessel, vein, artery;* pl. *veins, heart.*

vēndō, -ere, vēndidī, vēnditum, [vēnum, *sale*, dō], 3, a., *sell; sell for a bribe, give for pay, betray.*

venēficus, -ī, [venēnum, cf. faciō], m., *poisoner.*

venēnum, -ī, n., *poison, venom;* by metonymy, *magical potion, charm.*

vēneō, -īre, -īvī or -iī, -ĭtum, [vēnum, *sale*, + eō], irr., n., *go to sale, be sold.*

veneror, -ārī, -ātus sum, 1, dep., *reverence, worship, adore; venerate, do homage to; beseech.*

venia, -ae, f., *indulgence, favor, kindness; permission; pardon, forgiveness.*

veniō, -īre, vēnī, ventum, 4, n., *come; come into, enter; approach; spring; result, occur.*

vēnor, -ārī, -ātus sum, 1, dep., *hunt, chase.*

ventus, -ī, m., *wind.*

venustās, -ātis, [venus, *charm*], f., *comeliness, attractiveness, beauty; artistic grace, taste, art.*

vēr, vēris, n., *spring, spring-time.*

verber, -eris, n., *lash, whip, scourge;* by metonymy, *blow, stroke, scourging, flogging.*

verbum, **-ī**, n., *word.* **verba facere**, *to speak.*

vērē [**vērus**], adv., *really, truly, in fact; properly, rightly.*

verēcundia, **-ae**, [**verēcundus**], f., *coyness, shyness, modesty, sense of shame, bashfulness.*

vereor, **-ērī**, **-itus sum**, 2, dep., *reverence, stand in awe of, revere; fear, be afraid, dread, apprehend.*

vēritās, **-ātis**, [**vērus**], f., *truth, truthfulness; sincerity, straightforwardness; reality, fact.*

vērō [**vērus**], adv., *truly, certainly, in truth; but in fact, however, but.* **immō vērō**, *no indeed, nay rather.*

versō, **-āre**, **-āvī**, **-ātum**, [freq. of **vertō**], 1, a., *turn often, keep turning, turn over, turn; manage, direct; revolve, consider.* Pass., **versor**, **-ārī**, **-ātus sum**, *move about, dwell, remain, stay; be situated, be associated, be; be engaged in, be busy, be employed.*

versus, **-ūs**, [**vertō**], m., *line, verse.*

vērum, **-ī**, [**vērus**], n., *truth, fact, reality.*

vērum [**vērus**], adv., *truly; but in truth, but notwithstanding, but, however, still.* **nōn modo — vērum**, *not only — but.* **nōn modo — vērum etiam**, *not only — but also.*

vērus, **-a**, **-um**, adj., *true, real, genuine, well founded; proper, reasonable, just; truthful, veracious.*

vesper, **-erī** or **-eris**, m., *evening-star;* by metonymy, *evening, eve.* Loc. **vesperī**, *in the evening.*

vespera, **-ae**, f., *evening.*

Vesta, **-ae**, [cf. Ἑστία], f., *Vesta,* a Roman divinity, daughter of Saturn and Ops; in her service were the Vestal Virgins, who kept a fire always burning on her altar.

Vestālis, **-e**, [**Vesta**], adj., *of Vesta, Vestal.* **virgō Vestālis**, *Vestal virgin.*

vester, **-tra**, **-trum**, [**vōs**], poss. pron. adj., *your, yours.*

vēstīgium, **-ī**, n., *sole of the foot;* by metonymy, *foot, step, foot-print, track; trace, sign, vestige.*

Vettius, **-ī**, m., *Vettius Chrysippus,* an architect, freedman of the architect Cyrus. This is probably the *Vettius* referred to in Ep. III.

vetus, **-eris**, sup. **veterrimus**, adj., *old, aged; of long standing; of a former time, former, earlier, ancient.*

vetustās, **-ātis**, [**vetus**], f., *old age, age; long duration, long standing; great age, antiquity, ancient times.*

vēxātiō, **-ōnis**, [**vēxō**], f., *disturbing, troubling, harassing; distress, hardship, trouble.*

vēxō, **-āre**, **-āvī**, **-ātum**, [freq. of **vehō**], 1, a., *shake, jolt; disturb, harass, trouble, waste.*

via, **-ae**, f., *way, road, street;* by metonymy, *passage, march, journey; mode, manner.*

Vibō, **-ōnis**, f., *Vibō,* a city in the southwestern part of Italy, on the west coast of Bruttium. It was originally a Greek settlement with the name *Hippōnium* (Ἱππώνιον), but it received a Roman colony B.C. 192. In Cicero's time it was a flourishing municipal town. Ep. VII.

vibrō, **-āre**, **-āvī**, **-ātum**, 1, a. and n., *brandish, shake, hurl, throw; quiver, gleam, flash.*

vīcēsimus, **-a**, **-um**, [**vīgintī**], num. adj., *twentieth.*

vīcīnus, **-a**, **-um**, [**vīcus**, *street, quarter*], adj., *of the neighborhood, neighboring, near, adjacent.* As subst., **vīcīnus**, **-ī**, m., *neighbor.*

victor, **-ōris**, [vincō], m., *conqueror, victor;* often in apposition with the force of an adj., *victorious, conquering.*

victōria, **-ae**, [victor], f., *victory; success, triumph.*

vīcus, **-ī**, m., properly *abode;* hence, *street, quarter,* of a city; *village, hamlet; country-seat, villa.*

vidēlicet [for **vidēre licet**], adv., *it is evident, clearly, plainly, obviously, evidently; of course, you see, forsooth, to wit, namely;* often used ironically.

videō, **-ēre**, **vīdī**, **vīsum**, 2, a., *see, discern, perceive; look at, observe; understand, comprehend; see to, care for, provide.* Pass. **videor**, **vidērī**, **vīsus sum**, *be seen, appear, seem, be regarded;* impers., **vidētur**, *it seems right, it seems best.*

vigeō, **-ēre**, **-uī**, ——, 2, n., *be vigorous, be strong, thrive, flourish, bloom.*

vigilāns, **-antis**, [part. of **vigilō**], adj., *watchful, vigilant, anxious, careful.*

vigilia, **-ae**, [**vigil**], f., *watching, wakefulness; watch, guard; watchfulness, vigilance;* pl., *watchmen, sentinels.*

vigilō, **-āre**, **-āvī**, **-ātum**, [**vigil**], 1, n. and a., *keep awake, be wakeful; be watchful, keep watch, be vigilant, watch.*

vīgintī, or **XX**., num. adj., indecl., *twenty.*

vīlis, **-e**, adj., *of small price, of little value, cheap; poor, mean, worthless, base, vile.*

vīlitās, **-ātis**, [**vīlis**], f., *cheapness.*

vīlla, **-ae**, f., *country-seat, farm-dwelling, villa, farm.*

vinciō, **-īre**, **vinxī**, **vinctum**, 4, a., *bind, fetter, tie; fasten, restrain, confine.*

vincō, **-ere**, **vīcī**, **victum**, 3, a. and n., *conquer, overcome, defeat, subdue; be superior, excel, surpass; convince, get the better of; demonstrate.*

vinculum, or in shorter form **vinclum**, **-ī**, [**vinciō**], n., *band, fetter, rope, cord; bond, tie, relation.*

vindex, **-icis**, m. and f., *defender, protector; avenger, punisher.*

vindicō, **-āre**, **-āvī**, **-ātum**, [**vindex**], 1, a., *lay claim to, claim, assume; protect, defend, liberate, deliver; avenge, punish, take vengeance.*

vīnum, **-ī**, n., *wine.*

violō, **-āre**, **-āvī**, **-ātum**, [cf. **vīs**], 1, a., *treat with violence, injure, outrage; profane, desecrate.*

vir, **virī**, m., *man; husband; man of courage, hero.*

virgō, **-inis**, [cf. **vireō**], f., *maid, maiden, girl, virgin.*

virtūs, **-ūtis**, [**vir**], f., *manliness; courage, fortitude, bravery; moral worth, goodness, virtue, merit.* Personified, **Virtūs**, **-ūtis**, *goddess of Valor, Virtūs.*

vīs, acc. **vim**, abl. **vī**, pl. **vīrēs**, **-ium**, f., *force, strength, energy, power; violence, compulsion; quantity, number;* pl. often *military forces, forces, troops.*

vīscus, **-eris**, often in pl., **vīscera**, **-um**, n., *internal organs, vitals, inwards, viscera; inmost part, bowels, centre, heart.*

vīsō, **vīsere**, **vīsī**, **vīsum**, [freq. of **videō**], 3, a., *look at attentively, view, behold; go to see, visit.*

vīta, **-ae**, [**vīvō**], f., *life, existence; mode of life, course of life; career.*

vitium, **-ī**, n., *fault, blemish, defect; failing, offence, vice, crime.*

vītō, **-āre**, **-āvī**, **-ātum**, 1, a. and n., *shun, avoid, evade.*

vituperātiō, -ōnis, [vituperō], f., *blaming, blame, censure, reproach, charge.*

vīvō, vīvere, vīxī, vīctum, 3, n., *live, be alive; pass the time, reside, dwell; support life, sustain life; live at ease; last, endure.*

vīvus, -a, -um, [cf. **vīvō**], adj., *alive, living, having life; green, vigorous.* As subst., **vīvī, -ōrum**, m., pl., *the living, those who are alive.*

vix, adv., *hardly, with difficulty, scarcely, barely.*

vixdum [**vix** + **dum**], adv., *scarcely yet, hardly, but just.*

vocō, -āre, -āvī, -ātum, [**vōx**], 1, a. and n., *call, summon, invoke; call together, convoke; call by name, name, designate.*

vōcula, -ae, [dim. of **vōx**], f., *weak voice, small voice.*

volitō, -āre, -āvī, -ātum, [freq. of **volō**], 1, n., *flit about, fly about, flutter; hover about, wander.*

volō, velle, voluī, irr., a., *will, wish, desire; intend, purpose, mean; claim, assume, assert.*

Volturcius, -ī, m., *T. Volturcius*, a native of Croton, one of the Catilinarian conspirators. After his arrest at the Mulvian Bridge he turned state's evidence, was pardoned, and was rewarded for the information he gave. CAT. III. II. *et seq.*

voluntārius, -a, -um, [**voluntās**], adj., *of one's free will, willing; wilful, intentional, voluntary.*

voluntās, -ātis, [**volō**, *wish*], f., *will, wish, inclination, desire; purpose, aim; good-will, favor.*

voluptās, -ātis, [cf. **volō**], f., *pleasure, delight, enjoyment; gratification, satisfaction.*

vōs, see **tū**.

vōsmet [**vōs** + **-met**], strengthened form of **vōs**.

vōtum, -ī, [**voveō**], n., *vow, pledge; wish, desire, prayer.*

vōx, vōcis, [cf. **vocō**], f., *voice, sound; call, cry, speech, word, utterance, saying.*

vulgāris, -e, [**vulgus**], adj., *of the multitude, common; commonplace, low, mean, vulgar.*

vulgō [**vulgus**], adv., *generally, commonly, publicly, everywhere.*

vulnerō, -āre, -āvī, -ātum, [**vulnus**], 1, a., *wound, hurt, injure, harm, pain.*

vulnus, -eris, n., *wound, injury; blow, stroke; disaster, misfortune, calamity.*

vultus, -ūs, m., *look, expression; features, face, countenance, visage.*

X.

Xenō, -ōnis, m., *Xenō*, a native of Apollonis, in Lydia. EP. XVI.

www.ingramcontent.com/pod-product-compliance
Lightning Source LLC
LaVergne TN
LVHW010223110826
845148LV00022B/1245

* 9 7 8 1 5 5 6 3 5 4 2 2 9 *